THE CAMBRIDGE HISTORY OF
LITERARY CRITICISM

VOLUME 1: CLASSICAL CRITICISM

THE CAMBRIDGE HISTORY OF
LITERARY CRITICISM

THE CAMBRIDGE HISTORY OF LITERARY CRITICISM

VOLUME 1

Classical Criticism

EDITED BY

GEORGE A. KENNEDY

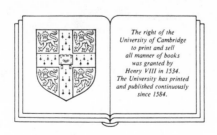

The right of the
University of Cambridge
to print and sell
all manner of books
was granted by
Henry VIII in 1534.
The University has printed
and published continuously
since 1584.

CAMBRIDGE UNIVERSITY PRESS

CAMBRIDGE

NEW YORK   PORT CHESTER

MELBOURNE   SYDNEY

Published by the Press Syndicate of the University of Cambridge
The Pitt Building, Trumpington Street, Cambridge CB2 1RP
40 West 20th Street, New York, NY 10011, USA
10 Stamford Road, Oakleigh, Melbourne 3166, Australia

First published 1989

Printed in Great Britain at the University Press, Cambridge

British Library cataloguing in publication data

The Cambridge history of literary criticism
Vol. 1, Classical criticism
1. Literature. Criticism, to 1988
I. Kennedy, George A. (George Alexander), *1928–*
801'.95'09

Library of Congress cataloguing in publication data

The Cambridge history of literary criticism.
Bibliography.
Includes index.
Contents: v. 1. Classical criticism.
I. Criticism–History. I. Kennedy, George Alexander, 1928–
PN86.C27 1989 801'.95'09 89-901
V.1
ISBN 0 521 30006 1

WG

CONTENTS

PREFACE

But where's the man who counsel can bestow,
Still pleas'd to teach, and yet not proud to know?
Unbiass'd or by favour or by spite;
Not dully prepossess'd nor blindly right;
Tho' learn'd, well bred, and tho' well bred sincere;
Modestly bold, and humanly severe;
Who to a friend his faults can freely show,
And gladly praise the merit of a foe;
Bless'd with a taste exact, yet unconfin'd,
A knowledge both of books and humankind;
Gen'rous converse; a soul exempt from pride;
And love to praise, with reason on his side?
Such once were critics; such the happy few
Athens and Rome in better ages knew.

Alexander Pope, 'An Essay on Criticism', 631–44.

Criticism as an instinctive audience reaction to the performance of poetry is as old as song. Literary theory begins to emerge in Archaic Greece in the self-reference of oral bards and early literate poets and as part of the conceptualisation of ideas which marked the birth of Greek philosophy. A sense of literary history developed in observation of the changing functions of poetry in the Greek states, in the realisation that the composition of heroic epic was becoming a thing of the past, and later in the perception that tragedy too had passed its acme. Aristophanes' *Frogs* in the fifth century and Plato's dialogues in the fourth show historical awareness of literary change, and in the *Poetics* Aristotle ventured a theory of the origins of tragedy and comedy. Some awareness that literary criticism too has had a history existed in later times: Horace, for example, in the first century BC looked back to his predecessors, including Aristophanes and Aristotle; but only in the case of grammar and rhetoric do we find systematic critical surveys of an historical sort in, for example, introductory chapters to separate books of Quintilian's *Institutio*. Suetonius' *Lives of the Grammarians* is perhaps the earliest work directly devoted to what might be called the history of criticism.

Italian critics of the Renaissance thought of criticism in historical terms, sharpened by the rediscovery of Greek texts and by the reawakened dispute between Platonists and Aristotelians. No systematic history of criticism seems to have appeared, but the ground was laid with increased knowledge of major critical texts in the sixteenth century. A new stage can be said to begin with Pope's 'Essay on Criticism' (published 1711), where Aristotle, Horace, Dionysius, Petronius, Quintilian, and Longinus are memorably characterised in chronological order. There followed, according to Pope, an age of superstition and dullness, until the appearance of Erasmus. Boswell reports[1] that Dr Johnson once projected 'A History of Criticism, as it Relates to Judging Authors', but it was never completed. Perhaps the earliest scholarly work on the subject was *L'histoire des opinions littéraires chez les anciens et chez les moderns* by A. F. Théry, of which the first edition appeared about 1844 and the second in 1848. Classical criticism was apparently first given a systematic treatment by Emile Egger in his *Essai sur l'histoire de la critique chez les grecs* of 1849. Other surveys followed with the growth of nineteenth-century philology, leading to *An Introduction to the Methods and Materials of Literary Criticism* by C. M. Gayley and F. N. Scott (1899), which includes an historical survey, and then *A History of Criticism and Literary Taste in Europe* in three volumes (1900–1904) by George Saintsbury, Professor of Rhetoric and English Literature in the University of Edinburgh. This elegant, if largely non-theoretical, work confirmed the subject as an established part of philological and literary studies for the twentieth century.

Study of the history of criticism is thus a product of modern philological research. In the case of the great Classical critics its primary thrust has been classicising: to emphasise the timelessness and the continuing influence, though often with much misunderstanding or distortion, of the major texts – especially works of Plato, Aristotle, Cicero, Horace, Quintilian, and Longinus. This emphasis has, however, regularly been accompanied by historicism, the assumption that the ancient critics provide, or should provide, the best basis for the interpretation of the literature of their own time. Such a view led to a number of problems and in the twentieth century has been partially abandoned or at least practised with restraint. Aristotle's *Poetics* does indeed provide some insights into Greek epic and tragedy that we would otherwise lack, but a simplistic use of conceptions of a 'tragic flaw' or of 'catharsis' prevents an understanding of the Homeric poems or Attic tragedy in their own terms, for Aristotle was constructing a philosophical theory, not engaging in practical criticism, and he lived late in the history of Greek poetry. Similarly, the use of Horace's *Ars poetica* as the basis of criticism of his other poetry leaves much unaccounted for, though Horace's *Odes* and *Satires* can shed some light on the *Ars poetica*. The principal values of the study of the history

---

[1] *Life of Samuel Johnson* (Oxford, 1934–50), IV, p. 381.

of ancient criticism as a whole perhaps lie in parallels between its developments and the intellectual history of antiquity, seen for example in changing assumptions about the roles of poetry and rhetoric in society, and in a succession of reactions to critical stances, such as the reactions of Aristotle or the neo-Platonists to Plato, or of Augustan and imperial critics to Hellenistic criticism. For the general reader, the great value of ancient criticism will doubtless continue to be found in its major texts, but the student of Medieval or Renaissance criticism will also discover in lesser texts the beginnings of interpretative methods, as well as assumptions about genre and language, which long continued powerful in the West and which are a continuing part of its epistemic field.

Several sound histories of ancient literary criticism have been published. Two especially deserving mention as complementing this volume are *The Greek and Roman Critics* by G. M. A. Grube (1965), historical in orientation and providing summaries of the major critical works, and *Criticism in Antiquity* by D. A. Russell (1981), more thematic in organisation. Also noteworthy is *Ancient Literary Criticism: The Principal Texts in New Translations*, edited by D. A. Russell and Michael Winterbottom (1972). In attempting a new history we have sought to draw on the scholarship published since the appearance of these works, we have provided a more extended introduction to the formative stage of Greek literary genres, we have somewhat expanded the consideration of language theory and of later antiquity, and sought to provide a background for the history of criticism in later periods, not only the Middle Ages and the Renaissance, but from time to time for critical interests of the twentieth century. It was our original hope to include a chapter on Byzantine criticism, but this has proved impractical and reference to that subject is thus left to contributors to later volumes in the series.

Readers who come to this volume from study of modern theory may be interested in the extent to which Classical criticism anticipated features of such twentieth-century developments as semiotics, hermeneutics, deconstruction, psychoanalysis, and reader-response criticism. Some analogies to all these can be found, though expressed in different terms and often implicit rather than explicit. Two phenomena are especially striking. The first is the extent to which the earlier criticism, at least until Aristotle's *Poetics*, de-emphasises authorial intent and tends to interpret poetry as contained solely within the text. This is thought of as resulting from inspiration by a god or, in Aristotle's case, from a working out of the inherent logical structure of a *muthos*. In modern terminology, derived ultimately from Immanuel Kant, Greek criticism of the Classical period thus interests itself primarily in 'purposive' intent: that is, meaning as inherent in the text rather than as given it by a human author. The development of rhetoric, however, changed the emphasis to put priority on the 'purposeful' intent of the author as accomplished through control of the text and encouraged critics to identify their own interpretations, however unhistorically, with the author's purpose. This humanistic bias is reflected in biographical criticism in the Hellenistic period and in the allegorical interpretation of the Empire, and is seen throughout antiquity in the common metonymy of substituting the name of the author for the text: 'Homer says', rather than 'in the *Iliad* it is written'. Though the Classical and later Greeks had no real awareness of the oral origins of their poetry, the metaphor of speaking, encouraged by the goals of the rhetorical schools, is often preferred to that of writing.

A second connection between ancient and modern criticism is the interest in signs and symbols, and thus in what has come to be known as semiotics, seen in Aristotle and the Stoic and sceptical philosophers, with which may be associated an interest in interpretation and thus in hermeneutics. Though often unsystematic, this is consistently present in writings of the imperial period, where it is applied to literature, to dreams, to religious and mystical texts, and even to Being as a whole. Study of the subject is not yet fully developed, but some introduction to it will be offered in later chapters.

With occasional exceptions, we have thought it best to expound the ancient critics in their own terms rather than to recast their thought in alien concepts. Modern critical writing, however, is replete with references to the Classical critics, and their ideas are often the starting point for new theories. Among the better known are *A Rhetoric of Motives* (1950) and other works by Kenneth Burke, 'Plato's Pharmacy' (1968) by Jacques Derrida, *Figures I–III* (1966–72) by Gérard Genette, *Theories of the Symbol* (1982) by Tzvetan Todorov, *Muses of One Mind* (1983) by Wesley Trimpi, and *Time and Narrative* (1984) by Paul Ricoeur. Modern literary theorests often come to ancient criticism with an interest in the novel and have explored the understanding of fiction in Classical times; for others, the Classical material is used to understand the nature of language.

An article by the Dutch scholar W. J. Verdenius (see bibliography under General Works) suggested in 1983 that rather than approach Greek criticism historically, it would be more illuminating to examine it in terms of five principles which he called those of Form, Skill, Authority, Inspiration, and Contemplation. Some of these concepts are perceptively scrutinised over the whole range of criticism by K. K. Ruthven in *Critical Assumptions*. In a volume of this scale such an approach would have led to much repetition and would have been inconvenient for readers who wish to learn more about specific major works. All five of the principles Verdenius identified are, however, touched upon in their appropriate contexts, especially in chapter 1, where the reader will find a background for them and for such related matters as the origins of the term 'critic', the phenomenon of 'mimesis', and the view of poetry as oral production rather than written composition.

A special word of explanation should be said about chapter 1, which differs significantly from accounts of the early period in other histories and as a result may prove difficult for some readers. No area of Greek studies is undergoing more radical change as a result of modern, comparative linguistic and anthropological investigations. We have thought it valuable to give an account of the ways in which oral and written literature may have developed in Archaic Greece. Criticism of poetry by poets and philosophers is a part of this process, but there are other features of the history which now seem important as creating the conditions under which criticism as we now know it emerged in the Classical period.

Although Verdenius' topics provide an interesting grouping of ideas about poetry and poets in Archaic and Classical Greece, there are other topics which emerge subsequently. One is Visualisation, which is connected with the analogy between literature and the arts, but also with the developing interest in epistemology from the fourth century BC onward. The most famous *dicta* are those of Simonides, 'Painting is silent poetry', and Horace, 'ut pictura poesis'. Early Greek writers certainly achieve vividness and realism, and there continues to be a strong realistic impulse in Greek and Latin literature, with the development of naturalistic detail. The critics take some account of this. Although Plato generally distrusted mimesis and image-making, the theory of memory in the *Philebus* (38e–40a) assumes that it imprints words on the mind which are then, in recollection, illustrated by images (*eikones*). Aristotle in the *Poetics* (17.1455a22–6) urges the poet, in constructing plots, to keep the scene before his eyes; only the clearest (*enargestata*) visualisation will discover what is fitting (*to prepon*) and avoid contradictions or implausibilities, and in the *Rhetoric* (3.11) there is a discussion of expressions which 'set things before the eyes' and achieve actuality (*energeia*). In *De Anima* (3.427b29ff.) there is a discussion of imagination (*phantasia*) which provides a conceptual basis for this in a theory of perception. The Stoics were later much interested in *phantasia* and its validity, as we shall see in chapters 6 and 11 below, and their theories influenced both writers and critics. *Enargeia* and *energeia* are useful concepts in neoclassical and modern criticism. The former 'implies the achievement in verbal discourse of a natural quality or of a pictorial quality that is highly natural', the latter 'refers to the actualisation of potency, the realisation of capacity or capability, the achievement in art or rhetoric of the dynamic and purposive life of nature'.[2] It has been claimed that modern writers have 'exchanged the notion of *enargeia* for *energeia* in determining how art could be like reality'.[3] The ancient critics are the starting point both for the history of mimesis and for exploration of analogies and differences among the arts.

The Decline of Eloquence, and of literature generally, becomes another

[2] Jean H. Hagstrum, *The Sister Arts: The Tradition of Literary Pictorialism and English Poetry from Dryden to Gray* (Chicago, 1958), p. 12.
[3] Wendy Steiner, *The Colors of Rhetoric: Problems in the Relations between Literature and Painting* (Chicago, 1982), pp. 10–11.

recurring topic in ancient criticism. Although the antecedents of it go back to a general sense of decline in society, voiced by Hesiod and other early poets, and to the perception by the fourth century that not only epic, but also tragedy had passed its peak, the gulf between the Classical past and present realities was first keenly felt in the Hellenistic period. Discussions of possible causes for decline are found in writers of the Augustan period and in the following centuries, especially in the writings of Philo, the two Senecas, Velleius Paterculus, Petronius, Quintilian, Tacitus, and Longinus. We will have occasion to examine their explanations in later chapters.

In the modern world criticism is found chiefly in three contexts: in schools and universities, where literature is taught and where at the more advanced levels critical theory is developed or tested; in literature itself, where creative writers comment on their own work or on that of others; and in journalism, especially in the writing of book reviews, addressed either to the general public or to specialised scholars. In antiquity this third medium did not exist, but both of the others are found. Schools of philosophers and sophists emerged in the Classical period and were the primary setting for the conceptualisation of criticism with a theoretical basis. The teaching of literature in schools of grammar and rhetoric beginning in the Hellenistic period extended some critical consciousness to the entire literate public. Criticism within literature itself is found in all periods from the earliest to the latest, from references to bards in the Homeric poems to the satire of Aristophanes, the self-conscious reflections of Hellenistic and Roman poets, and the theories of late Greek sophists; but the general decline of poetry under the Roman Empire brought with it a decline in the quality of criticism by poets. A new critical impulse was added, however, by the developing need of neo-Platonist and Christian theologians to interpret their sacred texts.

There is much that is interesting in Classical criticism, especially perhaps to a modern critic; there is much that is frustrating about it as well, especially perhaps to a Classical scholar. Taken as a whole, it provided the terminology and defined many of the critical issues of the Western tradition, but it is an inadequate critical response to the great achievements of Greek and Latin literature. It is at its best on such questions as the function of poetry in society and on details of grammar and rhetoric, such as the naming and defining of figures. It is at its weakest in describing the over-all structure of a specific work of literature, except in the case of an oration, and in dealing with imagery. Although Plato and others speak in general terms of a need for measure, organic unity, and proportion, no Classical critic articulates in detail features of Classical literary composition which have been stressed by twentieth-century scholars. One is the tendency, existing already in the Homeric poems and found in virtually every literary form throughout antiquity, to organise incidents, scenes, or speeches into antithetical or chiastic patterns much like the arrangement of figures in pedimental sculpture. To us, symmetry and proportion, in extreme cases perhaps even mathematical proportion in the number of lines used, seems central to Classical composition, and there is a corresponding tendency for the climax, or at least the most significant thought, to come near the centre of a work, with some fall-off of intensity thereafter. The *Odyssey*, Plato's *Phaedrus*, many Greek tragedies, Demosthenes' *On the Crown*, and Horatian odes all illustrate the principle. For centuries students have ended their reading of the *Aeneid* with the sixth of twelve books. In the case of imagery, Classical critics were well aware of the use of metaphor, simile, and other tropes and figures, and of instances of irony seen in the use of individual words. What they do not seem to have observed, although again everywhere present in the greatest works, are over-all patterns of the use of imagery, for example, the pervasive irony of blindness and insight in the *Oedipus Tyrannus*, or the symbolic use of wounding, snakes, and fire in the *Aeneid*. All of this remained a secret of composition, surely perceived by poets, but unspoken by critics, who read their texts column by column or line by line.

In preparing this work the editor is deeply indebted to the patience and learning of authors of individual chapters. Among them, Professor Russell has also been a source of wise counsel in a more general way. In addition, the editor wishes to acknowledge the assistance, admonitions, or suggestions, in varied ways, of Dr Malcolm Schofield, Professor Peter Smith, Mr Andrew Becker, Ms Laurette DeVeau, Ms Susan Foutz, and Mr Mark Falcon. Mr Terence Moore of Cambridge University Press has had a major role in planning the series and in bringing this volume to the public. It has been a pleasure to work with him. For copy-editing we are indebted to the patient work of Dr Con Coroneos.

George A. Kennedy

ABBREVIATIONS

Works in series

AJP	*American Journal of Philology* (Baltimore)
ANRW	*Aufstieg und Niedergang der römischen Welt. Geschichte und Kultur Roms in Spiegel der neueren Forschung* (Berlin)
CP	*Classical Philology* (Chicago)
CQ	*Classical Quarterly* (Oxford)
GRBS	*Greek, Roman, and Byzantine Studies* (Durham, North Carolina)
HSCP	*Harvard Studies in Classical Philology* (Cambridge, Mass.)
JHS	*Journal of Hellenic Studies* (London)
JRS	*Journal of Roman Studies* (London)
LCL	*The Loeb Classical Library* (Co-published by William Heinemann in London and the Harvard University Press in Cambridge, Mass.)
REG	*Revue des études grecques* (Paris)
TAPA	*Transactions and Proceedings of the American Philological Association* (Currently, Scholars Press, Atlanta, Georgia)

Other abbreviations

ad loc.	*ad locum*. Refer to commentary on passage indicated
Aen.	*The Aeneid* of Virgil
AP	*The Art of Poetry* (*Ars poetica*; *Epistles* 2.3) of Horace
Cic.	Cicero
Comp.	*De compositione verborum* (*On Composition*) of Dionysius
Contr.	*Controversiae* of Seneca the Elder
De or.	*De oratore* (*On the Orator*) of Cicero
Diog. Laert.	Diogenes Laertius
Dion. Hal.	Dionysius of Halicarnassus
Ecl.	*Eclogues* of Virgil
Ep.	*Epistles* (of Horace or other authors)
fl.	*floruit*. Date of mature activity
fr.	fragment(s)

Il.	*Iliad* of Homer
Met.	*Metamorphoses* of Ovid
Od.	*Odyssey* of Homer
Or. vet.	*De veteribus oratoribus* (*On the Ancient Orators*) of Dionysius
Ph.	*Phaedrus* of Plato
pr.	preface
Po.	*Poetics* of Aristotle
Quint.	Quintilian
Rep.	*Republic* of Plato
Rh.	*Rhetoric* of Aristotle
Sat.	*Satires* of Horace
Suas.	*Suasoriae* of Seneca the Elder

1

EARLY GREEK VIEWS OF POETS AND POETRY

Histories of criticism in early Greece are usually based on surveys of those relatively few passages where the Greek poets speak about themselves and their poetry. Although this chapter will comment on many of these passages, the publication of a new history offers an opportunity to go beyond this fragmentary evidence by considering it in the wider framework of the society or societies for which this poetry existed. In what follows, the primary evidence is not restricted to whatever the poets say about themselves and their world: rather, it embraces the context in which they say what they say. The task will be to describe the social function of early Greek poetry and to present a picture of the traditional thought-patterns that shape the very concept of poet and poetry. It is through these thought-patterns that early Greek poetry defines itself and the poet as well, making it ultimately possible for critics of later times to talk about poetry.

The very notion of 'critics' and 'criticism' can best be seen in the post-Classical context of a great period of scholarship, in Hellenistic Alexandria. The Alexandrian concept of *krisis*, in the sense of 'separating', 'discriminating', 'judging' those works and those authors that are to be preserved and those that are not, is crucial to the concept of 'canon' in the Classical world. Literally, *kanōn* means 'rod', 'straight-edge rule', then by synecdoche a 'standard', 'model'. The Alexandrian scholars who were in charge of this process of separation, discrimination, judgement, were the *kritikoi*, while the Classical authors who were 'judged worthy of inclusion' within the canon were called the *enkrithentes*, a term that corresponds to the Roman concept of the *classici*, who are authors of the 'first class', *primae classis*.[1] The *krisis* of the *enkrithentes*, however, starts not with the Alexandrian scholars, nor even with Aristotle. It is already under way in the Archaic period of Greece, the point of departure for this inquiry. As we shall see in more detail at a later point, songs and poetry were traditionally performed in a context of competition. A striking example is the tradition of dramatic festivals at Athens, with the *krisis*, 'judgement', of winners by *kritai*, 'judges' (cf. Plato, *Laws* 659a–b).

---

[1] Pfeiffer, *Classical Scholarship*, pp. 206–7.

1

But the criteria of the *krisis*, as we shall see, are different at different times. In the earlier periods of Greek literary development, what is at stake is the survival or non-survival not merely of specific works or specific authors but of tradition itself.

Of particular concern, then, for an understanding of early Greek views about poets and poetry, is the ongoing crisis in the formation of canons. In time, this crisis leads to an impulse that we know as classicism. Another area of major concern is the development of genres, a phenomenon that shapes much of subsequent Greek trends in literary criticism. Still another is the differentiation and individualisation of authorship. These concerns will be addressed in the context of early Greek views about myth, truth, and inspiration. Also pertinent are the Greek notions about *mimēsis*, 'imitation, representation', and about how poetry was taught, especially in the watershed of the fifth century BC.

1 Poetry, myth, and ritual

It is important to begin with an examination of the very concept of 'poetry'. A fundamental question is: how is the language of poetry distinct from everyday language?

The distinction can best be comprehended in terms of the qualifications 'marked' and 'unmarked' as formulated by Roman Jakobson.[2] These terms have been defined as follows: 'The general meaning of a marked category states the presence of a certain (whether positive or negative) property A; the general meaning of the corresponding unmarked category states nothing about the presence of A, and is used chiefly, but not exclusively, to indicate the absence of A'.[3] The unmarked category is the general category, which can include the marked category, whereas the reverse situation cannot hold. For example, in an opposition of the English words 'long' and 'short', the unmarked member of the opposition is 'long' because the word can be used not only as the opposite of 'short' when we say 'This is long, not short', but also as a general category, when we say 'How long is this?' Such a question does not judge whether something is long or short, whereas 'How short is this?' does.

From a cross-cultural survey of a broad range of societies, we find a general pattern of opposition between marked and unmarked speech.[4] The function of marked speech is to convey meaning in the context of ritual and myth. Before we may proceed, it is important to stress that the words 'ritual' and 'myth' are used here not in terms of our own cultural preconceptions but in

[2] Discussion and bibliography in Waugh, 'Marked and unmarked'.

[3] Jakobson, 'Signe zéro', p. 136.

[4] Ben-Amos, 'Analytical categories', p. 228.

terms of the broadest possible anthropological perspective. For 'ritual' we may use the working definition of Walter Burkert: 'Ritual, in its outward aspect, is a programme of demonstrative acts to be performed in set sequence and often at a set place and time – sacred insofar as every omission or deviation arouses deep anxiety and calls forth sanctions. As communication and social imprinting, ritual establishes and secures the solidarity of the closed group.'[5] As for 'myth', it can be defined as 'a traditional narrative that is used as a designation of reality. Myth is applied narrative. Myth describes a meaningful and important reality that applies to the aggregate, going beyond the individual.'[6]

It is in small-scale rather than complex societies that we can observe most clearly the symbiosis of ritual and myth, how neither is to be derived from the other, and how the language of ritual and myth is 'marked', while everyday language is 'unmarked'. The perception of plain or everyday speech is a variable abstraction that depends on the concrete realisation of whatever special speech is set apart for a special context. In small-scale societies, the setting apart would normally happen in ritual and myth, and the ritual may include such diverse activities as hunting, gathering, farming, building, travelling, meeting, eating and drinking, courtship, and the like. Internal criteria for marked acts and speech-acts can be expected to vary from society to society: what may be marked in one may be unmarked or 'everyday' in another. In complex societies, and the situation in Archaic Greece can already be described as such, the pervasiveness of myth and ritual, as well as their interconnections with each other, may be considerably weakened. Still, the marking of speech, that is, the turning of unmarked speech into marked, may persist as the basic way to convey meaning in the context of ritual and myth.

There is a reflex of this pattern in the usage of the Greek verb *muō*, which means 'I have my mouth closed' or 'I have my eyes closed' from the standpoint of everyday situations, but 'I say in a special way' or 'I see in a special way' from the standpoint of marked situations in ritual. The latter meaning is evident in the derivatives *mustēs*, 'one who is initiated', and *mustērion*, 'that in which one is initiated, mystery (Latin *mysterium*)'. So also in *muthos*, 'myth', which is a derivative of the same root from which *muō* is derived and the special meaning of which seems to be 'special speech' as opposed to everyday speech.[7] For an illustration of the semantics underlying the usage of these Greek words, let us consider Sophocles, *Oedipus at Colonus* 1641–4: the visualisation and the verbalisation of whatever it was that finally happened to Oedipus in the precinct of the Eumenides at Colonus is restricted, in that the precise location of his corpse is a sacred secret (1545–6; 1761–3).

[5] Burkert, *Greek Religion*, p. 8.
[6] Modified translation of Burkert, 'Mythisches Denken', p. 29.
[7] Chantraine, *Dictionnaire*, pp. 718, 728.

Only Theseus, by virtue of being the proto-priest for the Athenians of the here-and-now, is to witness what happened, which is called the *drōmena* (1644). Thus the visualisation and the verbalisation of the myth, what happened to Oedipus, is restricted to the sacred context of ritual, controlled by the heritage of priestly authority from Theseus.

From an anthropological standpoint, to repeat, 'myth' is indeed 'special speech' in that it is a given society's way of affirming its own reality through narrative. Let us for the moment take it as a given, then, that the function of marked speech is to convey meaning in the context of ritual and myth. In most societies the pattern of opposition between marked and unmarked speech takes the form of an opposition between singing and speaking respectively, with 'singing' being marked by a wide variety of constraints on available features of the given language. From the standpoint of our own cultural preconceptions, 'singing' is a combination of melody (stylised tone or intonation) and rhythm (stylised stress, duration, intensity, or any combination of the three).[8] From a cross-cultural survey of a variety of societies, however, we find that 'singing' may be a matter of melody alone or rhythm alone, or of even less, such as isosyllabism or other types of stylised formal parallelism.[9] In Plato's *Laws* (653e – 4a; 665a) the combination of rhythmic and melodic idiom is synthetically visualised as *khoreia*, 'choral song and dance'. But the essential characteristic of song is the actual markedness from everyday speech, and the markedness may be reinforced by not only dance but also instrumental accompaniment. It appears that patterns of convergence and reinforcement between language and dance or musical accompaniment are primary, while patterns of divergence and contrast are secondary. Moreover, instrumental accompaniment tends to be primary, while instrumental solo is secondary. There is a tendency, in both dance and instrumental accompaniment, for transition from marking speech as special to imitating special speech.

2 Poetry and song

In the case of Greek traditions, as in many others, there is a further complication: singing as distinct from speaking is further differentiated into what we know as song as distinct from poetry. This differentiation is most evident in the attested fifth-century institution of Athenian tragedy, where the numerous metres of song are distinct from the one metre that represents everyday speech, iambic trimeter, in that the metres of song are marked by

---

[8] For cross-cultural linguistic and ethnographical criteria, see Nettl, *Music*, p. 136, and *Theory*, pp. 281–92; Merriam, *Anthropology*, p. 285.

[9] Guillén, *Introducción*, pp. 93–121; Jakobson, 'Linguistics and poetics', p. 358; Tambiah, 'Performative approach', pp. 164–5.

vocal melody, instrumental accompaniment, or dance, whereas iambic trimeter is recited and not sung, not accompanied, not danced. Thus the opposition between what we may call song and poetry is a mimesis or 'imitation' of the fundamental opposition between singing and speaking. Even the uniqueness of the iambic trimeter as the medium of recitative presentation reinforces this imitation, since the experience of ethnographic fieldwork suggests that unmarked speech tends to be perceived as unique in any given social context, whereas marked speech is clearly perceived as multiple or potentially multiple.[10]

The major formal categories of ancient Greek poetry are traditionally classified according to the following metrical types: (1) dactylic hexameter (Homeric epic and hymns, Hesiodic wisdom and catalogue poetry); (2) elegiac distich = dactylic hexameter + 'pentameter' (as in Archilochus, Callinus, Mimnermus, Tyrtaeus, Theognis, Solon, Xenophanes); (3) iambic trimeter (as in Archilochus, Hipponax, Semonides, Solon, or in fifth-century Attic tragedy and comedy). Paradoxically, what we call poetry, namely the compositions framed by these three metrical forms, is historically further removed from everyday speech than what we call song, in that all three of these metres are apparently derived from the rhythms of song.[11] That is, these three metrical forms are derived from earlier forms of song with built-in melody as well as built-in rhythm. Such forms, in gradually losing the melodic component of song, could compensate for that loss with a tightening up of prosodic features. Yet Aristotle can say that the iambic trimeter of tragedy is closest to every-day speech (*Po.* 1449a22; cf. *Rh.* 1408b33) because it is the medium of mimesis for everyday speech. The paradox is extended, in that poetry becomes finally differentiated into verse as opposed to prose. Along the present lines of thought, as we shall see later, the development of the art of prose would represent a stage even further removed from everyday speech.

That the major types of ancient Greek poetry were recited and not sung may at first seem startling in view of such internal testimony as Homer's bidding his muse to *sing* the anger of Achilles (*Il.* 1.1) or Archilochus' boasting that he knows how to lead off a choral performance of a dithyramb (fr. 120 West). Such evidence, however, may be misleading. To begin, the internal evidence of Homeric and Hesiodic diction tells us that the word *aeidō*, 'sing', (as in *Il.* 1.1) is a functional synonym, in contexts where the medium refers to its own performance, of the word *e(n)nepō*, 'narrate, recite' (as in *Od.* 1.1), which does not explicitly designate singing.[12] The equating of a word that

[10] Ben-Amos, 'Analytical categories', p. 228.

[11] Nagy, 'Origins of the hexameter'.

[12] Thus the *aoidē* of the muses at Hesiod, *Theogony* 104, is in the context of the poet's bidding them to 'narrate' (*espete*, 114) and to 'say' (*eipate*, 115).

refers to recitation with a word that refers to the format of singing accompanied by a lyre proves only that such poetry had the latter format in some phase of its evolution. Self-references in Archaic Greek poetry may be diachronically valid without being synchronically 'true'. For example, the epic poetry of Homer refers to epic poetry as a medium that was performed in the context of an evening's feast. And yet, we know that the two epic poems of Homer, by virtue of their sheer length alone, defy this context. If we look for the earliest historical evidence, we see that the actually attested context for performing the *Iliad* and *Odyssey* was already in the sixth century not the informal occasion of an evening's feast but rather the formal occasion of a festival such as the Panathenaia.[13] The performers at such festivals were *rhapsōidoi*, 'rhapsodes'. In Plato the rhapsode Ion is dramatised as just having arrived at Athens in order to compete in the rhapsodic contest of the Panathenaia (*Ion* 530a–b).

In the case of Homeric poetry, the earliest phases of rhapsodic transmission are associated with the *Homēridai*, a corporation of rhapsodes who traced themselves back to an ancestor called 'Homēros'.[14] The sources make it explicit that the rhapsodes, in performing Homeric poetry at the Panathenaia, were legally constrained to take turns in narrating the poetry in its proper sequence.[15] In other words, even if the size of either the *Iliad* or the *Odyssey* ultimately defied performance by any one person at any one sitting, the monumental proportions of these compositions could evolve in a social context where the sequence of performance, and thereby the sequence of narrative, could be regulated, as in the case of the Panathenaia. Thus the simultaneous composition and performance of the oral poet at a feast can be viewed as organically evolving into the continuity of composed narrative achieved through a continuum of performance by rhapsodes who take turns at occasions like the Panathenaia.

The point that is being made here about the context of performance applies also to the medium of performance. Just as the Homeric testimony about the performance of epic by singers at feasts belies the synchronic reality of the performance of epic by rhapsodes at festivals, so also the Homeric testimony about the singer's singing to the accompaniment of the lyre belies the synchronic reality of the rhapsode's reciting without any accompaniment at all. On the basis of available evidence, it appears that rhapsodes did not sing the compositions that they performed but rather recited them without the accompaniment of the lyre.[16] So also with Hesiodic poetry: the internal

---

[13] Lycurgus, *Against Leokrates* 102; Isocrates, *Panegyricus* 159; Plato (?), *Hipparchus* 228b; Diog. Laert. 1.57.

[14] Scholia to Pindar, *Nemean* 2.1c (III, p. 29 Drachmann).

[15] Plato (?), *Hipparchus* 228b; Diog. Laert. 1.57.

[16] West, *Theogony*, p. 163. The iconographic testimony of vase paintings showing rhapsodes either with a lyre or with a staff can be viewed as a parallel phenomenon of diachronic perspective on an evolving institution.

testimony of the composition represents a theogony that is simultaneously sung and danced by the local muses of Helikon (*Theogony* 3 – 4, 8), and yet we know that the *Theogony* itself, as also the other Hesiodic compositions, was in fact recited by rhapsodes.[17] This is not to say that hexameter could not be sung in the Archaic period,[18] only that hexameter evolved into *poetry* as distinct from *song*, and that its fundamental form of rendition, as poetry, was recitation.[19]

Similarly with old iambic and elegiac poetry. We see that the internal testimony refers to choral singing and dancing to the accompaniment of the lyre (as in Theognis 791; cf. 776 – 9), or singing to both the lyre and *aulos*, 'reed' (531 – 4, 759 – 64), or singing to the reed alone (825 – 30, 943 – 4, 1055 – 8, 1065 – 8). But in point of fact, the external evidence of historical testimony establishes that the attested traditional format of performing the iambic trimeter and the elegiac distich was simply recitative.[20] Also, the professional performers of such poetry were not singers but rhapsodes.[21] This is not to say that the references made in Archaic iambic or elegiac poetry to choral performance or instrumental accompaniment are diachronically wrong: as we already had occasion to see, they are in fact diachronically correct, and it is not without reason that even the performance of a rhapsode is from a traditional point of view an act of 'singing' (Plato, *Ion* 535b). Still, such references are synchronically misleading.

We can be satisfied with the diachronic correctness of ancient Greek poetry's references to itself as song by noting that these self-references are traditional, not innovative. The formulas in Homeric poetry and elsewhere about the subject of singing and song have an ancestry going back to an Indo-European heritage.[22] Even the word 'rhapsode', designating the professional reciter of poetry, is built on a concept of artistic self-reference ('he who stitches together the song'; cf. Pindar, *Nemean* 2.1 – 3) that is likewise of Indo-European provenience.[23] The institutional reality of formal competition among rhapsodes, immortalised for us in Plato's dialogue *Ion* (530a), seems to be a direct heritage of formal competition among singers, as reflected directly in passages like *Homeric Hymn* 6.19 – 20 and indirectly in the numerous myths about such competitions. Most famous is the *Contest of Homer and Hesiod*.[24] The word for such competition is *agōn* (*Hymn* 6.19), the semantics of which are best

[17] Plato, *Ion* 531a, 532a; *Laws* 658d. Conversely, the concept of rhapsode can be retrojected to Homer and Hesiod, *Rep.* 600d.

[18] E.g., the hexameters of Terpander; pseudo-Plutarch, *On Music* 1132c; Barker, *Greek Music*, p. 208, n. 18.

[19] Aristotle, *Po.* 1447a29 – b8, 1448a11, 1449b29; Plato, *Laws* 2.669d – 70a.

[20] Aristotle, *Po.* 1447b9 – 23; Else, *Aristotle's Poetics*, pp. 56 – 7.

[21] Plato, *Ion* 531a, 532a; Athenaeus 620c – d, 632d.

[22] Nagy, *Comparative Studies*, p. 10, n. 29, and pp. 244 – 61.

[23] Schmitt, *Dichtung*, pp. 300 – 1.

[24] Tr. by E. G. Evelyn-White in Loeb Classical Library Hesiod, pp. 567 – 97.

reflected in two English borrowings: 'antagonism' and 'agony'. The ritual dimensions of this concept will be explored further below.

There is enough evidence, then, to conclude that what the rhapsodes recited was directly descended from what earlier singers had sung.[25] It is important to add that there is no compelling reason to believe that the medium of writing had anything to do with the traditions of the rhapsodes. This is not to say that in historical times they could not have owned texts of what they recited (cf. Xenophon, *Memorabilia* 4.2.10); in any case, it is clear that the rhapsodes recited from memory (Xenophon, *Symposium* 3.6).

3 Occasion and authority

In light of the preceding sketch of poetry as differentiated from song, let us now consider the references to these categories in Greek song and poetry. It is easiest to start with a further differentiation, that of prose as distinct from poetry, and then to work backward to poetry as distinct from song.

From the earliest evidence, it is clear that prose assumes the prior existence of poetry. A prime illustration is the first sentence of Herodotus' *Histories*, where the diction and the conventions can be analysed as a set of reactions to corresponding poetic norms.[26]

This is the public display [*apodeixis*] of the inquiry [*historia*] of Herodotus of Halicarnassus, with the purpose of bringing it about that whatever results from men may not, with the passage of time, become evanescent, and that great and wondrous deeds – some of them publicly performed [*apodeiknumai*] by Hellenes, others by barbarians – may not become *aklea* [without *kleos*].

The prose of Herodotus is here presenting itself as an extension of the poetry of Homer. In Homeric poetry, we find that *kleos* means not only 'fame' or 'glory' but also, more specifically, 'the fame or glory that is conferred by the medium of poetry' (as in *Il.* 2.486, 11.227). In the prooemium of Herodotus, it is implied that *kleos* is 'the fame or glory that is conferred by the medium of poetry or prose'. Thus the prose of Herodotus does not differentiate itself, in self-reference, from the poetry of Homer. The language of early Greek prose may look more like everyday speech, but it imitates the most highly developed special language, poetry. In this sense, the prose of Herodotus is even further removed from everyday speech than poetry itself.

The medium of Herodotus, in calling itself *apodeixis* in the proemion, is public. By contrast, Thucydides presents his writings as a private possession, a *ktēma*, of permanent value, something that is not the product of a 'competitive public performance meant to be heard and intended merely for the

---

[25] For further arguments, see Nagy, 'Hesiod', pp. 43–9.

[26] Krischer, 'Herodots Prooimion', pp. 159–67.

here-and-now' (1.22.4). The word here for 'competitive public performance' is *agōnisma*, derived from *agōn*, 'assembly, contest'. This concept of *agōn*, throughout what follows, is crucial for understanding the Archaic Greek performance-traditions of prose, poetry, and song.

Having seen that both early prose and poetry refer to themselves as *kleos*, 'fame', we come to the medium of song as distinct from poetry. Here again, self-reference is in terms of *kleos*, as when the voice of Pindar declares: 'keeping away dark blame and bringing genuine *kleos*, like streams of water, to a man who is near and dear [*philos*], I will praise him' (*Nemean* 7.61 – 3). Thus song, like poetry, can call itself *kleos*. All Greek literature – song, poetry, prose – originates in *kleos*, the act of praising famous deeds, and never entirely loses that focus. It reasserts itself in the dominance of epideictic rhetoric in later antiquity. The traditional concern with praise, together with the phenomenon of mimesis, to be discussed below, goes far toward explaining Plato's criticism of poetry and its dangers. Moreover, song, like prose, can refer to its own medium as *apodeixis*. In the diction of song, the three distinct media of song, poetry, and prose are all a matter of *apodeixis*, but there is an explicit distinction between song and poetry on one hand and prose on the other: there are references to two kinds of masters of *kleos*, the *aoidoi*, 'those who sing', and the *logioi*, 'those who speak' (Pindar, *Nemean* 6.45 – 7). From the language of Herodotus in the sentence that immediately follows the prooemium and from related passages, it is clear that Herodotus considers himself a *logios*, or, at least, as someone who supersedes the *logioi*. The dichotomy of *aoidos*, 'he who sings', and *logios*, 'he who speaks', is paralleled, again in the language of Herodotus, by the dichotomy of *mousopoios*, 'artisan of singing' (e.g., Sappho: Herodotus 2.135.1), and *logopoios*, 'artisan of speaking' (e.g., Hecataeus: Herodotus 2.143.1). In sum, the language of both prose and song indicates that prose is to be performed by *logioi*, 'those who speak', while poetry and song are both performed by *aoidoi*, 'those who sing'.

The strategy of Herodotus' first sentence assumes the existence of traditions of singing or reciting or speaking before a public, not of writing for readers. That in itself is enough to justify calling such traditions 'oral'. For many, however, this same word, 'oral', has a much more narrow meaning, restricted by our own cultural preconceptions about writing and reading. If something is 'oral', we tend to assume a conflict with the notion of 'written'. From the standpoint of cultural anthropology, however, it is 'written' that has to be defined in terms of 'oral'. 'Written' is not something that is not 'oral', rather, it is something *in addition* to being oral, and that additional something will vary from society to society. It is dangerous to universalise the phenomenon of literacy.

In the case of Archaic Greece, as is evident from the heritage of words like *apodeixis*, the traditions of song, poetry, and prose, all three, are fundamentally a matter of performance. As such, they are oral traditions. Such a description is compatible with the cumulative experience of cultural anthropologists, who have found that various forms of song, poetry, and prose have functioned and continue to function in various ways in various societies without the aid of – in most cases without the existence of – writing.[27] From this vantage point, to repeat, we should not even be talking about oral poetry, for example, as distinct from poetry but rather about written poetry as possibly distinct from poetry: in other words, written poetry is the marked member of the opposition, and the poetry that we call 'oral' is the unmarked.

It can be argued in general that the traditions of Archaic Greek song, poetry, and prose required the medium of writing neither for composition nor for performance or reperformance. The reasons for this argument are founded on the central observation of Albert Lord, based primarily on ethnographic fieldwork in South Slavic traditions, that composition and performance in oral poetry are aspects of the same process, in that each performance is an act of recomposition.[28] So long as the traditions of oral poetry are alive in a given society, a written record cannot by itself affect a composition or a performance, and it does not necessarily stop the process of recomposition-in-performance.

In order to grasp the essence of oral tradition in composition and perform-ance, we must understand the social context, specifically, the requirements of the actual occasions for composing and performing. The occasionality of any given medium of poetry and song is reflected in a word used in Pindar's diction to designate his own medium: the word is *ainos* or *epainos*, which may be translated primarily as 'praise', indicative of Pindar's overarching purpose.[29] We have seen that another word used in Pindar's diction to designate his medium is *kleos*, which can be interpreted to mean 'glory' or 'fame' – as conferred by song or poetry. From the epic poetry of Homer, we have also seen that this medium too refers to itself as *kleos*. But it does not refer to itself as *ainos*.

By contrast with *kleos*, the word *ainos* is more exclusive in its applications. It is concerned more with the *function* of poetry and song, rather than the *form*. Or, to put it another way, it stresses the *occasion* for which a given form is used. As we see from Pindar's traditional diction, the *ainos* as a medium is osten-sibly restricted to those who have specific qualifications: (1) the *sophoi*, that is, those who are 'skilled' in decoding the message encoded by the poet in his poetry;[30] (2) the *agathoi*, that is, those who are intrinsically 'noble' by virtue of having been raised on proper ethical standards, which are the message

---

[27] Zumthor, *Introduction*, p. 34.

[28] Lord, *Singer of Tales*, pp. 3–29, 99–123. The intellectual and emotional resistance to the findings of Milman Parry (*Collected Papers*) and Lord stems for the most part from cultural preconceptions of our own times concerning 'folk poetry'; Bausinger, *Formen*, pp. 41–55.

[29] Bundy, *Studia*, pp. 1–5.

[30] E.g., Pindar, *Isthmian* 2.12–13; see discussion in Nagy, *Best of the Achaeans*, pp. 236–8.

encoded in the poetry;[31] (3) the *philoi*, that is, those who are 'near and dear' and who are thereby interconnected to the poet and to each other, so that the message that is encoded in the poetry may be transmitted to them and through them: communication through community.[32] In the terminology of the Prague School of Linguistics,[33] the *ainos* is a 'code' that carries the right 'message' for those who are qualified and the wrong message or messages for those who are unqualified. By way of its self-definition, the *ainos* assumes the ideology of the ideal audience, listening to an ideal performance of an ideal composition. But at the same time it also assumes the reality of uncertainties in interaction between performer and audience in the context of the actual performance of a composition: as we shall see, the *ainos* of Pindar is by its very character ambiguous, both difficult in its form and enigmatic in its content. As a difficult code that bears a difficult but correct message for the qualified and a wrong message or messages for the unqualified, the *ainos* communicates like an 'enigma' – to use an English word that was borrowed from and serves as a translation for the Greek *ainigma* (as in Sophocles, *Oedipus Tyrannus* 393, 1525), which in turn is an actual derivative of *ainos*. An important example of this usage occurs in the poetry of Theognis (667 – 82), where the poet finishes an extended metaphor, the image of the Ship of State caught in storm, with the following declaration about the meaning of the symbol:

Let these things be allusive utterances [*ainigma*] hidden by me for the noble [*agathoi*]. One can be aware of even [future] misfortune, if one is skilled [*sophos*].

(Theognis 681 – 2)[34]

By contrast with the praise poetry of Pindar, the epic poetry of the Homeric *Iliad* and *Odyssey* makes no claims to exclusiveness and does not qualify as a form of *ainos*. Whereas both the epic poetry of Homer and the praise poetry of Pindar qualify as *kleos*, only praise poetry, to repeat, qualifies as *ainos*. On the other hand, whereas all praise poetry may qualify as *ainos*, not all examples of *ainos* are praise poetry. For example, the word *ainos* can also refer to a speech of admonition, or *par-ain-esis*.[35] Or again, it can designate animal fables, such as those used by Archilochus to admonish his friends or blame his enemies (e.g., fr. 174 West). As a double-edged mode of discourse, the *ainos* can admonish or blame as well as praise. Moreover, the *ainos* can assume a variety of poetic forms. While it is sung and danced by choral groups in the Aeolic and the 'dactylo-epitrite' metres of Pindar, it is also recited by rhapsodes in such formats as the iambic metres of Archilochus and the elegiac distichs of Theognis (e.g., 681 – 2, quoted above). In other words, it is better to think

---

[31] E.g., Pindar, *Pythian* 2.81–8, 2.94–6, 10.71–2.
[32] E.g., again, *Pythian* 2.81–8; Nagy, *Best of the Achaeans*, pp. 238–42.
[33] Cf., e.g., Jakobson, 'Linguistics and poetics', pp. 350–77.
[34] For a defence of the ms. reading *kakon* and commentary, see Nagy, 'Theognis', pp. 22–6.
[35] Maehler, *Auffassung des Dichterberufs*, p. 47; Nagy, *Best of the Achaeans*, pp. 238–9.

of the *ainos* as a mode of discourse, not as a genre. Still, the point is that the genre of Homer's epic and the genre of Pindar's praise poetry are differentiated by the absence and presence respectively of self-definition in terms of *ainos*.

How, then, does the fact that the *kleos* of epic fails to define itself as *ainos* make this *kleos* different from the *kleos* of praise poetry? In order to comprehend the difference, we must first consider the implications of the word *kleos* itself. In the epic poetry of Homer just as in the praise poetry of Pindar, *kleos* denotes the act of praising, but in epic the praise takes place by the very process of narrating the deeds of heroes, predominantly in the third person. In praise poetry, the praise is more direct: here too *kleos* denotes that act of praising, but the praise in this case applies to the here-and-now, narrated generally in the second person. In the epinicians or victory odes of Pindar, for example, the praise applies to the victories of athletes who competed in the great pan-Hellenic games. The victory would be celebrated on the occasion of the victor's return from the games to his native city. The praise poetry of Pindar, then, is occasional. Occasionality is the essence of *ainos*. The epic poetry of the Homeric *Iliad* and *Odyssey*, on the other hand, is distinctly not occasional: unlike the praise poem, it does not praise anyone in the here-and-now of its own performance. The praise of Homeric poetry is restricted to the heroes of the distant past.

By contrast, the praise of Pindaric poetry is not restricted to the victorious athletes of the poet's here-and-now. The word *kleos* in Pindar's praise poetry applies equally to the athlete of the present and the hero of the past, as we can see most clearly from the following example: 'It is said that *kleos* bloomed for Hector near the streams of Scamander. And near the steep cliffs that rise above Heloros ... this light shone upon the coming of age of the son of Hagesidamos' (*Nemean* 9.39 – 42). The parallelism of the two settings, the native rivers of the hero from the past and the athlete from the here-and-now, reinforces the participation of both figures in the same radiant *kleos*. Moreover, what is being praised about the athlete is ideologically parallel to what is being praised about the hero. In the inherited diction of praise poetry, what an athlete undergoes in his pursuit of victory is denoted by *ponos*, 'ordeal',[36] also called *kamatos*,[37] and these very same words apply also to the life-and-death struggle of heroes with their enemies, man and beast alike.[38] There is a parallel situation with the partial synonym *aethlos* (*āthlos*), from which *āthlētēs*, 'athlete', is derived: besides meaning 'contest', *aethlos* also means 'ordeal' and is applicable both to the athletic event of the athlete in the present and to the life-and-death struggle of the hero in the past.[39]

---

[36] E.g., Pindar, *Olympian* 5.15, 11.4; *Nemean* 4.1; *Isthmian* 5.25.
[37] E.g., Pindar, *Pythian* 5.47; *Nemean* 3.17.
[38] E.g., Pindar, *Pythian* 4.178, 4.236, 4.243; *Nemean* 1.70.
[39] *Athlos* of an athlete, e.g., *Isthmian* 5.7; of a hero, e.g., *Pythian* 4.220; *Isthmian* 6.48.

In decidedly not making a distinction between the *kleos* due to an athlete of the present for his athletic event and the *kleos* due to a hero for his heroic deed, the ideology of Pindar's praise poetry is parallel to the ideology of the athletic games in which the athletes earned their *kleos*. This ideology of the games is fundamentally a religious one: each athletic festival, held on a seasonally recurring basis into perpetuity, is predicated on the death of a hero, on an eternally important proto-ordeal, as it were, for which the seasonally recurring ordeals of athletes serve as eternal compensation. The religious ideology of the games, clearly attested in Pindar's poetry, is matched by the religious ideology of the poetry itself: each ordeal of each victorious athlete, compensating for the proto-ordeal of the hero who struggled and died, demands compensation of its own in the form of song offered as praise for the athlete.[40] And the song in turn demands compensation from the victorious athlete and his family, to be offered to the composer of the song (e.g., *Pythian* 9.93). This concluding link in the chain of compensation is clearly articulated throughout the poetry of Pindar whenever the voice of the poet says that he owes it to his patrons to create a song (e.g., *Olympian* 10.3, 10.8), but has been misunderstood by latter-day experts on Pindar as if it were a blatant illustration of Pindar's 'mercenary muse': when Pindar says that he owes the song to his patrons, critics misunderstand him as referring merely to a contract between patron and poet, entailing services to be performed and to be paid for. This is to ignore the premonetary and in some respects sacral heritage of the very concept of value in Archaic Greek society.

There were of course other contemporary deeds besides those in athletics that could have demanded requital in song and praise. The most obvious category is victorious deeds in war, which are in fact denoted by the same terms that are used for victorious deeds in athletics: in the diction of Pindar and elsewhere as well, a man who fights in a war undergoes an ordeal as denoted by the words *ponos, kamatos, aethlos* (e.g., *Isthmian* 8.1 – 16). So once again we see a collapsing of distinctions between the *kleos* due a hero and the *kleos* due a man. Only, in this case, both hero and man are potentially getting *kleos* in return for the same activity, martial struggle. The internal evidence of poetic diction can be reinforced by external evidence: fighting in wars was indeed a ritual activity, parallel to the ritual activity of engaging in athletic games.[41] Accordingly, the compensation for deeds of war through songs of praise, like the compensation for deeds of athletes, can be considered a vital link of a ritual chain.

But the picture is drastically affected by other developments in the history of Archaic Greek civilisation. With the evolution of the polis or city-state and

---

[40] The occasion of a victory ode is a *lutron*, 'compensation', for the *kamatoi*, 'ordeals', of the athlete, *Isthmian* 8.2; the ordeal of the athlete is a formal *lutron* for a primordial death, *Olympian* 7.77.

[41] Brelich, *Guerre, passim*.

the concurrent evolution of the phalanx, an army of citizen soldiers, the factor of communal effort in warfare tends to counteract the factor of individual aristocratic enterprise. Thus the opportunity for individual feats of war, let alone the opportunity for celebrating them, is considerably reduced. The archaic polis discourages, often by way of actual legislation, the glorification of the individual in the context of funerary practices in general and funerary praise poetry in particular. The very art-form of the poetic epigram, where the factor of performance is replaced by the factor of the written record, is in fact a reflex of the strictures imposed by the polis against songs of praise in the context of funerals.[42]

In the so-called age of tyrants, we witness the emergence of personalities who 'represent a force for innovation in Greek political history and step upon its stage as Greece's first true individuals'.[43] To overreach the polis is to become an individual, at least in recorded history. Towards the end of this Archaic phase of Greek civilisation, the age of tyrants, where important families were generating public personalities that could and did overreach the institutions of the polis, enters the figure of Pindar (518–438 BC), master of choral lyric poetry. Pindar and his contemporaries or near-contemporaries, figures such as Simonides and Bacchylides, made their own breakthroughs as individuals, as historically verifiable persons whom we may call 'authors', by virtue of being protégés of powerful families of tyrants or quasi-tyrants. Such a line of interpretation concerning Pindar's patronage may at first seem unsettling, in light of the commonly-held and comforting assumption that poets like Pindar were simply protégés of aristocrats in general, and that their association with tyrants like Hieron in *Olympian* 1 developed out of their already-established prestige in smaller aristocratic circles. Though many of Pindar's most famous compositions were commissioned by tyrants or tyrant-like personalities, still, many other compositions were commissioned by aristocratic figures about whom we have no explicit historical evidence pointing to anything as specific as the power of tyrants. As we shall now see, however, first impressions may deceive.

In the case of the aristocratic families of victors from Aegina as celebrated in the victory odes of Pindar there seems at first little evidence for anything that would even suggest the presence of tyrants or tyrant-like personalities. And there is no denying that it is difficult indeed to find direct evidence that would help us weigh their relative power. Even in the case of Aegina, however, there are indirect indications that the patrons of Pindar tend to be a closed and specially privileged group within their own aristocratic communities. Among these indications is the special use of *patrā*, 'patriliny', in all attestations of the word as applied to the lineages of Aegina in the Aeginetan odes

---

[42] Alexiou, *Ritual Lament*, pp. 104–6.
[43] Most, 'Greek lyric poets', p. 83.

of Pindar. In each case there is a pointed mention of the Aiakidai, 'descendants of Aiakos', or of Aiakos himself, elsewhere in the same composition: the word *patrā* designates the Theandridai at *Nemean* 4.77 (Aiakidai at 11), the Bassidai at *Nemean* 6.35 (Aiakidai at 17), the Euxenidai at *Nemean* 7.70 (Aiakidai at 10), the Psalukhiadai at *Isthmian* 6.63 (Aiakidai at 19, 35), and the Meidulidai in *Pythian* 8.38 (Aiakos at 99). In non-Aeginetan contexts, by contrast, *patrā* seems to mean simply 'homeland' (e.g., *Pythian* 11.23). This consistency in the pattern of referring to Aeginetan lineages, and in associating them with the Aiakidai, suggests a closed and specially privileged group. The very name Aiakidai may serve as implicit evidence in this regard. Such a patronymic formation suggests a group that is linked by ties of common ancestry leading back to the cult of a given hero (cf. Herodotus 8.64.2).

In pursuing the argument that poets such as Pindar achieved their definitive identities as authors ultimately through the authority and patronage of powerful families of tyrants or quasi-tyrants, we may also observe the internal evidence of the traditional themes inherent in the medium of Pindar's self-expression, the *ainos*. This medium of ethical discourse, as an inherited instrument of social criticism, consistently warns against the emergence of tyranny from an aristocracy that it can blame for losing its ethical foundations. Since the *ainos*, as we have seen, presupposes an idealised community of aristocrats with whom it can communicate, it is important to add that the *historical* reasons for the emergence of tyrants and quasi-tyrants are indeed to be found in the social context of aristocratic circles. In other words, the social context of aristocracy in the polis is the breeding-ground of would-be tyrants both from the external standpoint of history and from the internal standpoint of the *ainos* as an instrument of social criticism that warns against tyranny.

What, then, gives Pindar the opportunity to warn against tyranny, if indeed the social circles of his patronage are the very breeding-ground of tyranny? It can be argued that the epinician or victory odes of Pindar are an ideal occasion, in that there was a pervasive thematic parallelism between the reality of an athlete's victory and the potential of a tyrant's power, as dramatised by the Olympic victor Kylon when he chose the season of the Olympics for his attempt at a *coup d'état* in Athens. To repeat, the *ainos* of Pindaric poetry even has the built-in ideology of warning about this potential. And if the potential has already become a reality, the poetry can even shift to a stance of praising the 'tyrant' as a *basileus*, 'king' (e.g., *Olympian* 1.23), while all along maintaining a condemnation of tyranny.

The poetry that celebrated the figures who commissioned the likes of Pindar was occasional poetry, potentially exempt from the process of ongoing recomposition-in-performance that would have characterised any poetry that was transmitted solely through the ever-evolving polis. While such poets owe their fame as historical individuals to their patrons, the tyrants owe their corresponding fame at least partly to these same poets, who enhance the breakthrough of their patrons into the remote past of the heroes. The poet Ibycus says this explicitly, as he tells the tyrant Polykrates of the everlasting *kleos* that is to be conferred on him by the poet's song, which is also called *kleos*. 'You too [i.e., you as well as the heroes just mentioned in the song], Polykrates, will have *kleos* that is unwilting, in accordance with my song, my *kleos*' (Ibycus, fr. 282a, 47–8 Page). The double use of *kleos* here re-enacts the notion of reciprocity built into the word: the patron gets fame from the praise of the poet, whose own fame depends on the fame of his patron in the here-and-now.

But the poet effects the fame of his patron not merely by recording the subject's accomplishments or qualities in the here-and-now but also by linking him with the heroes of the past. This linking can even be directly genealogical. Thus for example the praise poetry of Pindar confirms the political claim of the tyrant Theron of Akragas, to the effect that Theron is descended from Polyneikes, a hero of the Seven-against-Thebes epic tradition (*Olympian* 2.41–7).

The situation is altogether different with the poetry of epic. By the time of the age of tyrants, the epic traditions of the Greeks, as represented by the *Iliad* and *Odyssey*, had reached a stage of evolution where they had already become pan-Hellenic and thereby canonical, exempt from the political exigencies of tyrants. The universality of the Homeric poems is the consequence not of a single event, such as the writing down of the poems, but rather of an evolutionary process whereby the pan-Hellenic diffusion of the Homeric traditions, concomitant with ongoing recomposition-in-performance at international festivals, led gradually to one convergent pan-Hellenic version at the expense of many divergent local versions. While the divergence of localised versions might be to the occasional advantage of the localised concerns of tyrants, the convergent pan-Hellenism of the Homeric performances could in the end become an obstacle to the tyrants' current political ideologies: we recall the testimony of Herodotus (5.67.1) to the effect that Kleisthenes, tyrant of Sikyon, banished the public performances of 'Homer' in his city on the grounds that the contents were partial to Argos, a city that was at that point an enemy of Sikyon. With its pan-Hellenic stature, then, the poetry of 'Homer' would not accommodate the occasional and localised needs of the audience, and we cannot expect it to be responsive to such considerations as the genealogies of powerful patrons. In the epic poetry of Homer, the gap that separates the heroes of the past and the men of the present could not and would not be bridged. Little wonder, then, that heroes could lift stones that not even two of us 'today' could even manage to budge (*Il.* 12.445–9).

As for the praise poetry of Pindar, it does more than just confirm the extension of the genealogies of powerful families into the heroic past: as we have already seen, the *kleos* of victorious athletes who come from such families is pointedly equated with the *kleos* of heroes as they are known from epic. But the praise poetry of Pindar does not claim to be descended from the epic of Homer – which would have matched the way in which his patrons may claim to be descended from heroes praised by the narration of epic poetry. In the praise poetry of Pindar, Homer figures as but one in a long line of poets who are masters of *kleos*. In other words, the *kleos* of Homer is treated as an offshoot of the *kleos* that survives as the praise poetry of Pindar. Unlike the *kleos* of Homer, however, the *kleos* of Pindar extends into the here-and-now, linking the heroes of the past with the men of the present. In the diction of Pindar, the very concept of *nea* or *neara*, 'new things', applies not to poetic innovations but to poetic applications of the past glories of heroes to the present glories of men who are being praised in the here-and-now.[44]

The built-in conceit of Pindaric poetry, that its praise collapses the distinction between heroes of the past and men of the here-and-now, accentuates the occasionality of his medium. Which brings us back to the self-definition of this medium as *ainos* – a self-definition not shared by Homeric poetry. Contemporary feats of war would have been equally appropriate for celebration by praise poetry, had it not been for the evolution of the polis. Moreover, even if we discount for the moment the emphasis that the polis placed on the communal effort as opposed to individual aristocratic enterprise, any celebration of martial feats still raises the problem of inter-polis politics: what is a success for one polis will be a failure for another, so that it becomes difficult for any military victory to achieve pan-Hellenic recognition in poetry. By contrast, the victories of athletes at the four great pan-Hellenic games are by definition recognised by all Hellenic city-states. It should come as no surprise, then, that in the case of military victories, the one notable exception meriting pan-Hellenic recognition in poetry was in fact a supposedly pan-Hellenic victory: the Greek victory over the Persians in 479 BC, as for example celebrated by Pindar in *Isthmian* 8 alongside the supposedly central topic of that composition, an athletic victory by an Aeginetan in the Isthmian Games of 478 BC. The special appropriateness of athletics to praise poetry is best illustrated by Pindar's claim that epinician praise poetry had existed even before epic (*Nemean* 8.50–1). We may add that the Seven against Thebes, in the same Pindaric context, are represented as having engaged in an athletic contest specifically before they embarked on their famous war. This athletic contest, serving as prototype for the Nemean Games, would have been celebrated by the prototype of Pindar's current Nemean Ode in honour of the current victor at the Nemean Games.

In the poetry of Pindar, to repeat, the link of the victorious athlete to his ancestors is celebrated through the *kleos* of heroes. In this case, as we have seen, the *kleos* of heroes is not epic but *ainos*. Alternatively, however, the *kleos*

[44] Miller, '*Nemean* 8', p. 114.

of heroes can even be *ainos* as represented by epic. For example, in *Iliad* 9, when old Phoenix gives his admonition to Achilles in the format of an *ainos*, he refers here to his own discourse as *tōn prosthen … klea andrōn hērōōn*, 'glories of men of the past, heroes' (9.524–5). In the story of Phoenix, a prime example of 'men of the past' is Meleager, a hero. And the story is aimed at a man of the present, Achilles, whom the *Iliad* presents as a hero in the making. The actual message of the story told by Phoenix to Achilles turns out to be – from the standpoint of Achilles and the *Iliad* itself – the very name of Patroklos, *Patro-kleēs*, 'he who has the glories of the ancestors'. In the Homeric theme of Patroklos, the differentiation between heroes and ancestors has not yet happened. In this theme, the praise of ancestors and the praise of heroes are as yet one. So too in the poetry of Pindar in praise of athletes: the praise of their ancestors is realised in the praise of heroes.

The Iliadic theme of Patroklos, as conveyed by the *ainos* told by Phoenix to Achilles, is an instance where epic refers to the format of the *ainos* without actually identifying itself with it. We can find other instances as well, especially in the *Odyssey* (e.g., 14.508), and each time we may observe the same pattern: whereas epic can refer to the format of the *ainos*, it is not an *ainos* itself.

Which brings us back to the self-references of *ainos* as praise poetry. As we have seen, praise poetry both calls itself *kleos* and explicitly identifies itself with the *kleos* of epic. It is as if praise poetry were the primordial form of epic. This is in fact what Aristotle says, that epic is descended from poetry praising gods and men (*humnoi* and *enkōmia*, *Po.* 1449b27, 1449b32–4). It is also what epic itself seems to be saying in situations where one character, in praising another, predicts that this praise will become the *kleos* heard by future audiences (e.g., *Il.* 24.192–202). Even the sporadic instances in Homeric poetry where a hero is addressed in the second person give the impression that the third-person narrative of epic is but a transformation of the second-person direct address of praise poetry (e.g., *Il.* 16.787). Still, however much we may want to formulate the transformation of epic poetry as a derivative form from praise poetry as a parent form, we must keep in mind that, while the derivative form was evolving into the generalised and universally accessible medium of Homeric poetry, the parent form was in the meantime evolving into the specialised and restrictively difficult medium attested later in the epinician poetry of Pindar.

4 *The poet as artisan*

In complex societies, which are characterised by the division of labour, we can expect references to singer or poet in terms of profession. This is not to say, of course, that all types of song or poetry within the competence of singers or poets would be restricted to these professionals. Nor is it to say that other types of song or poetry may not stay outside the realm of professionals.

Examples that readily come to mind are lullabies and laments, resulting from a division of tasks among the sexes.

Let us examine, then, some explicit references to both professionals and non-professionals in the performance of song and poetry. To begin, the professional *aoidos*, 'singer', belongs to the category of the *dēmiourgoi*, 'artisans in the district (*dēmos*)' (*Od.* 17.381–5). Other professions that belong to this category are the *mantis*, 'seer', the *iatēr*, 'physician', the *tektōn*, 'carpenter', and the *kērux*, 'herald' (*Od.* 17.381–5, 19.135). In Hesiod (*Works and Days* 25–6) the *aoidos* is juxtaposed with the *tektōn* and the *kerameus*, 'potter'. The *dēmiourgoi* are socially mobile, being juridically immune as they travel from one district to another. For an example of a cognate institution, we may compare the Old Irish 'people of the craft' (*cerd*), the designation for artisans, including poets, who were, again, juridically immune as they travelled from one tribe to another. In fact, two of the most basic metaphors for the art of poetry in Greece are the crafts of carpentry (Pindar, *Pythian* 3.113; cf. Pausanias 10.5.8) and weaving (Bacchylides 5.9–10, 19.8). Old Irish *cerd*, 'craft', is cognate with Greek *kerdos*, 'craft, craftiness, profit'; in the diction of poets like Pindar, *kerdos* refers positively to the craft and negatively to the potential craftiness of poetry (*Isthmian* 1.51; *Pythian* 1.92).

Homeric narrative occasionally makes further distinctions between professional *aoidoi* and what we would call 'amateur' singers. For example, at the funeral of Hector, the *aoidoi* are those who sing a more stylised kind of lament, called the *thrēnos*, while non-professional singers, next-of-kin to the deceased, sing a more fundamental kind of lament, called the *goos* (*Il.* 24.723, 24.747, 24.761). Correspondingly, at the funeral of Achilles, the next-of-kin, the Nereids, sing undifferentiated laments (*Od.* 24.58–9), while the muses sing a differentiated *thrēnos* (24.60–1). Or again, Phemios and Demodokos in the *Odyssey* are poets by profession, whereas Achilles in the *Iliad*, as he sings the *klea andrōn*, 'glories of heroes', in his tent (9.189), is an 'amateur'.

Such distinctions between 'amateur' and 'professional' have to be viewed, however, in light of Archaic concepts of value. Clearly the *dēmiourgos* gets material compensation for the services that he renders. Still, this compensation has to be honorific as well as material, parallel to the honorific compensation owed to any member of society in return for services rendered. In the Archaic Greek model, the system of compensation is simultaneously reciprocal and hierarchical.

With the transition from premonetary to monetary economies, however, there arises a crisis concerning the services rendered by artisans, with a progressive overvaluing of the material aspect of compensation on the part of the provider of services and a corresponding undervaluing of the honorific aspect of compensation on the part of the receiver of services. This crisis is evident in the semantic shift of the Greek word *misthos*, with the inherited

meaning of 'honorific compensation for services performed'.[45] The word's
heritage of agonistic reciprocity is evident in the meaning of its cognate in
Sanskrit *mīḍha-*, 'competition' or 'prize won in competition'. Even in the early
attestations of Greek *misthos*, however, we can detect a process of adjustment:
the sense of compensation in *misthos* is already becoming limited to the work
of artisans, becoming ever less appropriate for designating the contribution
of the citizen to the polis. This emerging split leads to the notion of 'wages
for an artisan' and tends to put *misthos* into a negative light from an artistic
standpoint.[46]

A crisis in the semantics of value is articulated by poetry itself. For example,
although the notion of material compensation for the composition of a Pindaric
poem is treated as a positive value by the poetry, as in *Isthmian* 2.1 – 13 and
elsewhere, it is clear that the picture of a muse who is *philokerdēs*, 'lover of
profit', and *ergatis*, 'working for wages', at *Isthmian* 2.6 is a foil for the even
more positive value of the honorific reciprocity between the poet and his
subject.[47] For Pindaric poetry, the 'wages' of compensation for song are
equated with *kharis*, the beauty and pleasure of reciprocity between the poet
and the subject of his praise: 'I will earn, as my wages [*misthos*], the *kharis* of
the Athenians concerning Salamis, and of Sparta, concerning the fighting at
the foot of Mount Kithairon (= Plataia)' (Pindar, *Pythian* 1.75 – 7). This more
positive value of compensation is simultaneously materialistic and transcendent, because it is sacred: inside the framework of Pindaric poetry, the notion
of compensation for composition is sacred so long as it stays within the sacred
context of such occasions as an epinician celebration.

Outside the framework of Pindaric poetry, of course, in the real world of
Pindar, compensation for the artisan, including the poet, is becoming a purely
economic value.[48] It is this outside reality that makes it possible for Pindar's
poetry to set up the 'mercenary Muse' as a foil for its own transcendence.
In this real world, the sytem of reciprocity within the community at large,
as represented by the polis, is breaking down. It is an era when individuals
can achieve the economic power to overreach the polis itself, and the pattern
of overreaching extends to the realm of song. In this real world, the craft of
song is in danger of shifting from an expression of community to an expression
of the individual whose power threatens the community. This shift has been
aptly described as a diverting of the poetic art:

Before the end of the [fifth] century choral poetry was divested of its traditional
connections with the festivals of cult, probably by Ibycus, certainly by Simonides, and
diverted to the praise of the great. The change meant that the expense of the poet's

---

[45] Benveniste, *Vocabulaire*, I, pp. 163–9.
[46] Will, '*Misthos*', p. 437.
[47] Kurke, *Pindar's Oikonomia*.
[48] Descat, 'Idéologie', pp. 26–7.

fee and the choral production was assumed by a wealthy patron, with whom lay the power of decision in regard to all questions relating to the performance of the ode. The Muse, in Pindar's phrase, had grown fond of money and gone to work for a living.[49]

In the real world the great men who are being praised are the potential tyrants and quasi-tyrants that are being generated by the aristocracy. In the ideological world of Pindar, by contrast, the aristocracy remains an ideal that must resist the degeneration that breeds tyrants. And it is the real world, to repeat, that makes it possible for Pindar's poetry to set up the 'mercenary Muse' as a foil for its own transcendence. In Pindar (*Isthmian* 1.47 – 51), and in Homeric and Hesiodic poetry, the hungry stomach serves as a symbol for the dependence of the poet, as itinerant artisan, on the patronage of a localised audience (*Theogony* 26 – 8, in the context of *Od.* 14.124 – 5 and 7.215 – 21). The juxtaposed ideal, as we shall see presently, is the ostensibly absolute truth of pan-Hellenic poetry.

Since the praise of poetry, as represented by Archaic poetry, is held to be a transcendent value, it follows that a deed worthy of praise by poetry is incompatible with wages suitable for artisans. Thus we read (Apollodorus 2.5.5) that the taskmaster Eurystheus tried to invalidate one of the Labours of Heracles, the cleaning of the Stables of Augeias, on the grounds that the hero had performed it for a 'wage'; conversely, Augeias refuses to pay Heracles when he learns that the hero's labour was at the behest of Eurystheus, in other words, that this labour was one of *the* Labours. The idealised vision of compensation for poetry is preserved in the medium of the epinician or victory ode, where the athlete's deed literally demands to be requited in song, and the realisation of the song in turn demands to be requited by way of a *kharis*, a pleasurable and beautiful reciprocity that is simultaneously material and transcendent in nature. Such a vision is also preserved in epic with reference to its evolution from occasional poetry. The idealised description in *Odyssey* 9.3 – 11 of the singer's performance at an evening's feast, with its programmatic reference to the spirit of *euphrosunē*, 'mirth', that holds sway on such an occasion, serves as a 'signature' for the evolution of poetic performance from the occasionality of the *ainos* to the universality of the epic Homeric poetry. In the medium of Pindar, which as we have seen calls itself *ainos*, the word *euphrosunē* (as in *Nemean* 4.1) refers programmatically to the actual occasion of performing poetry and song.[50] In the *Odyssey* (9.5), in reference to *euphrosunē* generated by the singer's performance at the feast, it is said that there is no *telos*, that is, no social function to be fulfilled, that has more beauty and pleasure in its reciprocity than does such an occasion, and the concept of beauty and pleasure in reciprocity is expressed as a matter of *kharis*.

[49] Woodbury, 'Mercenary muse', p. 535.
[50] Bundy, *Studia Pindarica*, p. 2.

The dependence of the professional *aoidos*, along with the other *dēmiourgoi*, on the reciprocity of *kharis* is crucial for understanding early Greek patterns of thought about the relationship of poetry to reality and truth. As noted earlier, myth is a given society's way of affirming its own reality through narrative. From the standpoint of our own usage in everyday English, however, the word 'myth' stands for the opposite, that is, it denies reality. Much the same was also already true from the standpoint of fifth-century Greece: *muthos* is multiple and multidirectional ('crooked'), and thus opposed to *alētheia*, conventionally translated as 'truth', which is singular and uni-directional ('straight'). As we shall see, poetry can be either *muthos* or *alētheia*, and this split can be connected with the social mobility of the *aoidos*, 'singer' and his need to maintain reciprocal relationships with a variety of communities holding a variety of world-views through myth. It is, fundamentally, the need of an itinerant *aoidos* to be aware and therefore critical of variations in myth that develops ultimately into the impulse of classicism.

In order to understand poetry in terms of a struggle between *muthos* and *alētheia*, let us begin with a celebrated reference in the poetry of Pindar:

Indeed there are many wondrous things. And yet, the words that men tell, *myths* [*muthoi*] embellished by varying falsehoods, beyond wording that is *true* [*alēthēs*], are deceptive.

(*Olympian* 1.27–9)

The eventual specialisation of *muthos* as 'myth' in this ambiguous sense of the word is caused by an eventual restriction of symbiosis between myth and ritual in the Archaic period of Greece. Such a restriction can be explained in terms of two fundamental social processes that give Archaic and Classical Greece its distinctive shape: the development of the polis or 'city-state' and a corresponding development of intensive intercommunication among the élite of the city-states, that is, the impetus of pan-Hellenism.

In the case of the distinctively Greek institution of the polis, its importance for defining the concepts of Hellenism and even civilisation can be most simply illustrated with Aristotle's dictum 'man is by nature an organism of the polis' (*Politics* 1253a2–3). As for the general phenomenon of pan-Hellenism, it can be readily observed on the basis of archaeological and historical evidence, which reveals a pattern of intensified intercommunication among the city-states of Hellas, starting in the eighth century BC, as evidenced in particular by the Olympic Games, Delphic Oracle, and Homeric poetry.[51] This general pattern can be linked with the very nature of Homeric poetry, in that one can envisage as aspects of a single process the ongoing recomposition and diffusion of the *Iliad* and *Odyssey*. This concept can be extended to apply to Hesiodic poetry, to Theognidean poetry, and, still further, to lyric poetry in general, that is, to song.

[51] Snodgrass, *Dark Age*, pp. 421, 435.

The hermeneutic model of pan-Hellenism should be viewed as an evolutionary trend extending into the Classical period, not some *fait accompli* that can be accounted for solely in terms of, say, the eighth century. In other words, the concept of pan-Hellenism as used here is a relative one. Thus, various types of Archaic Greek poetry, such as the elegiac tradition preserved by Theognis, make their bid for pan-Hellenic status considerably later than Homeric and Hesiodic poetry. Still, such poetry as the *Theognidea* is representative of a pattern of ongoing recomposition, concomitant with pan-Hellenic diffusion. The most obvious reflex of this ongoing recomposition in diffusion is the ultimate crystallisation of the *Theognidea* not in the native Doric dialect of Megara but in an accretive Ionic dialect that is for all practical purposes the same as we see in the poetry of Archilochus, Callinus, Mimnermus, Tyrtaeus, Solon, Xenophanes, and others.

The Archaic Greek 'city-state' and the tendency of pan-Hellenism are the context for a distinction that is regularly being made, already in the earliest evidence, between poetry and prophecy, as reflected by the word *aoidos*, 'singer', on one side, and by the words *mantis*, 'seer', and *kērux*, 'herald', on the other. We have already seen that the *mantis* and *kērux* are *dēmiourgoi*, 'artisans in the district', like the *aoidos*. While the notion of *aoidos*, as we have also seen, corresponds to our notion of 'poet', the notions of *mantis* and *kērux*, taken together, correspond roughly to our notion of 'prophet'. Such a pattern of distinction, however, was preceded by an earlier stage when poet and prophet were as yet undifferentiated. This stage is evident in the self-references of Hesiod's *Theogony*, where the muses of Mount Helicon are represented as endowing Hesiod with a sacral voice that enables him not only to sing a theogony (33–4) but also to tell the future as well as the past (32); in addition, the muses give Hesiod a *skēptron*, 'staff, sceptre', as a symbol of his sacral authority to proclaim the absolute truth (30, in the context of 26–9). In effect, then, the figure of Hesiod presents himself as *mantis* and *kērux* as well as *aoidos*, whereas a figure like Homer is strictly an *aoidos*, a poet.

The words *mantis* and *kērux*, as we shall see presently, could once have been appropriate designations for an undifferentiated poet/prophet; after differentiation set in, the word *aoidos* filled the need for designating a general category, as distinct from *mantis* and *kērux*, which became specialised sub-categories. By the time of the Classical period, another round of differentiation had led to a new general category, *poiētēs*, the ancestor of our word 'poet' (as used, e.g., in Herodotus 2.53). Unlike *mantis* and *kērux*, however, which had become specialised sub-categories of *aoidos*, *aoidos* in its own turn did not become a specialized sub-category of the word that replaced it as a general category, *poiētēs*. Whereas the *aoidos* had remained in the sacral realm of prophecy, as evidenced by the institutional dependence of the *aoidos* on the divine inspiration of the muse, the *poiētēs* entered the desacralised realm of poetry as we are used to it, where the very notion of inspiration is but a literary convention.[52] The *poiētēs* was a professional; he was a master of *tekhnē*, the work of an artisan. In the *Frogs* of Aristophanes, the very art of tragedy is consistently called *tekhnē* (93, 766, 770, etc.).

5 Poetry and inspiration

In the sacral realm of prophecy, there survived such specialised sub-categories as the designations *prophētēs* and *theōros*, which are the ancestors, but not equivalents, of our own words *prophet* and *theory*. These designations, as we shall see, maintained the inherited sacral links between poetry and inspiration.

In the Homeric *Hymn to Hermes*, the god Hermes is represented as singing the first theogony ever, thereby *krainōn*, 'authorising', the gods, that is, confirming their authority (427).[53] In this respect, Hermes is analogous to Hesiod as an undifferentiated poet/prophet. Later, Hermes enters into an agreement with Apollo, where he cedes to that god the lyre with which he had sung the theogony, along with all the powers that go with it (434–512); in return, Apollo gives Hermes a *rhabdos*, 'staff', described as *epi-krainousa*, 'authorising', the ordinances that Apollo had learned from Zeus (531–2). Again we see an analogy with Hesiod, who received the *skēptron*, 'sceptre, staff', of authority to proclaim the *Theogony*. But we must note carefully that, while Hermes is allowed this much authorisation, he is explicitly excluded from the sphere of prophecy that is associated with the Oracle of Apollo at Delphi (533–49), being restricted to the sphere of prophecy that is associated with the Bee Maidens of Mount Parnassus (550–66). These Bee Maidens also *krainousin*, that is, 'authorise' (559), but only if they are fed fermented honey: then they are in ecstasy and tell *alētheia*, 'truth' (560–1), though they *pseudontai*, 'lie', when deprived of this stimulant (562–3).

In this 'exchange' between Hermes and Apollo, myth formalises the specialisation of Hermes and the generalisation of Apollo. The division of attributes between Apollo and Hermes re-enacts the evolutionary separation of functions that are pictured as still integral at the time when Hermes sang the theogony. But then Hermes cedes the lyre to Apollo and confines himself to the primitive shepherd's pipe (511–12). In this way, Apollo can take over the sphere of the poet. Apollo also takes over the sphere of the prophet on a highly evolved pan-Hellenic level (his oracle at Delphi), leaving Hermes the more primitive sphere of the prophet as a local exponent of the sort of 'truth' that is induced by fermented honey. The affinity of Hermes with an undifferentiated stage of poetry/prophecy and his actual inauguration of Apollo's poetic art by way of singing a theogony suggest that Hermes is an older god than Apollo, and that his 'authorising' staff and his 'authorising' Bee Maidens

---

[52] Ford, *Terms for Poetry*.

[53] On this value of *krainō*, see Benveniste, *Vocabulaire*, I, pp. 35–42.

are vestiges of an older poetic realm. From a historical point of view, Apollo and his Olympian Muses are the newer gods: they represented a streamlining of this older realm into the newer one of pan-Hellenic poetry.

It bears stressing that the words 'old' and 'new' apply respectively to Hermes and Apollo from a diachronic standpoint: it is a matter of *Religions-geschichte* that Hermes presides over older institutions and Apollo over the newer ones.[54] From the synchronic point of view of the myth itself, however, Hermes *seems* to be the 'younger' god and Apollo the 'older': in terms of the narrative, Hermes is after all a newborn infant when he discovers the tortoise, constructs the first lyre out of its shell, and sings the first theogony ever. And yet, even in terms of the myth, Hermes is latently 'older' than Apollo, though he is overtly 'younger', for he is conventionally represented in the Archaic period as a bearded adult, Apollo as a beardless ephebe.[55] Just as Hermes presides over older institutions by comparison to Apollo, so also Apollo by comparison to the muses. He is their *khorēgos*, their leader in the choral context of singing, dancing, and instrumental accompaniment (e.g., Homeric *Hymn to Apollo* 189–203). While he dances and plays the instrument, the muses' function is more specifically that of singing or reciting. In the realm of prophecy, as in the realm of poetry, it is Apollo, not the muses, who presides over the older functions. Whereas the muses can be described in general as guarantors of prophetic powers to tell the future (Hesiod, *Theogony* 32), it is Apollo in particular who presides over prophecy, within such overarching frameworks as the Oracle at Delphi.

The differentiation between Apollo as a specialist in prophecy and the muses as generalists in poetry is reflected in Plato's treatment of the distinction between *mantis*, 'seer', and *prophētēs*, a word that can best be described in the passage that follows as 'declarer':

For the authors of our being, remembering the command of their father when he bade them create the human race as good as they could, that they might correct our inferior parts and make them attain a measure of *truth* [*alētheia*], placed in the liver the seat of mantic power [*manteion*]. And herein is a proof that the god has given mantic skill [*mantikē*] not to the wisdom, but to the foolishness of man. No man, when in his wits, attains mantic skill that is *inspired* [*entheos*] and *true* [*alēthēs*], but when he receives [the mantic skill], either his intelligence is enthralled in sleep or he is demented by some distemper or possession [*enthousiasmos*]. And he who would understand what he remembers to have been said, whether in a dream or when he was awake, through a mantic and inspired nature, or would determine by reason the meaning of the apparitions which he has seen, and what indications [verb *sēmainō*] they afford to this man or that, of past, present, or future good and evil, must first recover his wits. But, while he continues demented [*maneis*], he cannot discriminate [*krinō*] the visions which he sees or the words which he utters; the ancient saying is very true – that 'only a man

[54] Scheinberg, 'Bee maidens', p. 19.
[55] Burkert, *Greek Religion*, pp. 144–5, 158.

who has his wits can act or judge about himself and his own affairs'. And for this reason it is customary to appoint the lineage of declarers [*prophētai*] to be judges [*kritai*] over the inspired [*entheos*] mantic utterances. Some persons call them seers, being blind to the fact that they [*prophētai*] are only the expositors of riddles [*ainigmoi*] and visions, and are not to be called seers at all, but only declarers of what the seers say.

(Plato, *Timaeus* 71e – 2b, after B. Jowett's tr.)

In this passage, we must distinguish between the complex philosophical points being made and the relatively simple institutional reality upon which they are predicated: it is clear that the *mantis* is being recognised as one who speaks from an altered mental state, let us call it inspiration, while the *prophētēs* does not. The philosophical connection that is being made in this passage between *mantis* and *mania*, 'madness, dementia', is in fact etymologically correct: the etymology of *mantis* is 'he who is in a special [i.e., marked or differentiated] mental state' (from the root *men-, as in Latin *mens*, *mentis*), while that of *mania* is 'a special [i.e., marked, differentiated] mental state' (again, from root *men-).[56] The word *mantis* has been semantically specialised in conveying the altered mental state of a 'seer' or 'prophet' within the framework of Greek religious institutions, while the word *mania* retains the general notion of being 'out of one's mind', being in a state of mind other than the everyday one. From the standpoint of the Platonic passage, the inspiration of the *mantis* is a given, a matter of Greek religious institutions. The non-inspiration of the *prophētēs* is also a given, again a matter of Greek religious institutions, as we have seen in the explicit wording of Plato: 'and for this reason it is customary to appoint the lineage of declarers [*prophētai*] to be judges [*kritai*] over the inspired [*entheos*] mantic utterances [*manteia*]'. (Cf. Scholia A to *Il.* 16.235).

The prime example is the *prophētēs* of the Oracle of Apollo at Delphi (cf. Herodotus 8.36 – 7). The *prophētēs* declares, formalises as a speech-act, the words of the inspired *mantis*. In the case of the Oracle at Delphi, the office of the inspired *mantis* was traditionally held by a priestess, known as the 'Pythia'.[57] From stories about famous attempts to bribe the Pythia (e.g., Herodotus 6.66.3, 6.75.3), we know that it was the Pythia, not the *prophētēs*, who controlled the content of the mantic utterance. The *prophētēs* thus controlled the form. The standard transmission of this form, as we see most clearly in the numerous quotations of the Delphic Oracle in Herodotus, was the poetic form of dactylic hexameter. The *prophētēs* was involved in the poetic formalisation of prophecy.

The *mantis* is the 'middle man' between the source of inspiration and the *prophētēs*, the recomposer of the inspired message in poetic form. Alternatively, in the realm of myth, there are situations where we see no 'middle man'. Thus, the seer *par excellence*, Teiresias, who declares the will of Zeus, is the

---

[56] Chantraine, *Dictionnaire*, p. 665.

[57] For a minimalist survey of the Pythia's role, see Fontenrose, *Delphic Oracle*, pp. 196 – 228.

'*prophētēs* of Zeus' (Pindar, *Nemean* 1.60). Here we are witnessing a relic of an earlier and undifferentiated stage, in that Teiresias is generally known as a *mantis* (e.g., *Od.* 11.99). In other words, the figure of Teiresias represents a stage where the *prophētēs* is the *mantis*. The diction of poetry preserves further relics of such an undifferentiated stage, where the prophecy of the *mantis* and the poetry formulated by the *prophētēs* are as yet one: there are instances where the word *prophētēs* designates the poet as the one who declares the voice of the muse (Pindar, *Paean* 6.6; Bacchylides, *Epinician* 8.3). A particularly striking example is Pindar fr. 150: 'be a *mantis*, Muse, and I shall be the *prophētēs*'. The very form *mousa* (< *mont-ya; possibly *month-ya) may well be derived from the same root *men- as in *mantis* and *mania*.[58] If this etymology is correct, then the word for 'muse' reflects an earlier stage where not only the one who is inspired and the one who speaks the words of inspiration are the same, but even, further, the type of mental state marked by *mania* is not yet differentiated from the type of mental state marked by formations with *mnē-*, 'have the mind connected with, remember, remind'.

There is yet another pertinent use of *prophētēs*: as the herald who declares the winner at athletic games (e.g., Bacchylides, *Epinician* 9.28). This usage is crucial for our understanding of another word, *theōros*, 'he who observes the vision (*thea*)', in the specific sense as designating the official delegate of a given city-state who is sent out to observe the athletic games and to bring back the news of victory (Herodotus 1.59.1, 8.26). Thus the *prophētēs* is the one who declares the message of victory at the games, while the *theōros* is the one who witnesses the message and takes it back to the polis, where he declares it to the polis. Similarly, the *theōros* is the official delegate of a given polis who is to bring back the message of the Oracle: there are many examples, the most famous of which is Creon in Sophocles (*Oedipus Tyrannus* 114).

The word *theōros*, to repeat, designated a person who was specifically assigned by his community to go to Delphi in order to consult the Oracle about a given matter that concerned the community. After the consultation, the *theōros* was to return to his community, where he would impart the communication of the Oracle. There were severe sanctions against any *theōros* who would divulge the message of the Oracle to outsiders before returning home. This message was a privileged kind of communication. As Heraclitus declares (fr. 93 Diels-Kranz), the god at Delphi neither *legei*, 'speaks', nor *kruptei*, 'conceals': rather, he *sēmainei*, 'indicates'. The verb *sēmainō* is derived from the noun *sēma*, which means 'sign' or 'signal' and which in turn derives from a concept of inner vision (as attested in the Sanskrit cognate *dhyāma* derived from the verb *dhyā-*). Correspondingly, as we have seen, the word *theōros* means literally 'he who sees (root *hor-*) a vision (*thea*)'. Thus the god Apollo of the Oracle at Delphi, when he 'indicates', is conferring an inner vision upon the

[58] Chantraine, *Dictionnaire*, p. 716.

theōros, the one who consults him. Both the encoder and the decoder are supposedly operating on the basis of an inner vision. Greek usage makes it clear that the *prophētēs*, who communicates the words of Apollo to those who consult the god, likewise *sēmainei*, 'indicates' (cf. Herodotus 8.37.2).

In Greek usage, someone *sēmainei*, 'indicates', that is, 'makes a *sēma*', when he or she speaks from a superior vantage point, as when a scout goes to the top of a hill and then comes back down to indicate what can be seen from there (Herodotus 7.192.1, 7.219.1).[59] By extension, someone 'makes a *sēma*' when he or she speaks from a metaphorically superior vantage point, as when an authoritative person makes a pronouncement that arbitrates between contending points of view (Herodotus 1.5.3). But the ultimate voice of authority belongs to the god of the Oracle at Delphi, whose supreme vantage point confers upon him the knowledge of all things, even the precise number of all grains of sand in the universe (Herodotus 1.47.3).

Thus it is most appropriate for the poet, when he speaks with the voice of authority, to compare himself to a *theōros*, one who consults the Oracle and to whom the Oracle 'makes a *sēma*' through the intermediacy of the priestess of Apollo, the Pythia. Here is an explicit example, from the poetry of Theognis of Megara:

> A man who is *theōros* must be more straight, Kyrnos, being on his guard,
> than a carpenter's pin and rule and square
> – a man to whom the priestess of the god at Delphi makes a response,
> as she indicates [*sēmainei*] the *omphē* [Voice] from the opulent shrine.
> You will not find any remedy if you add anything,
> nor will you escape from veering, in the eyes of the gods, if you take anything away.
>
> (Theognis 805–10)

Just as the priestess, through her intermediacy, 'indicates' the message of the god, so also the poet speaks authoritatively, as if he were a lawgiver. Again from Theognis:

> I must render this judgement, Kyrnos, along [the straight line of] a carpenter's rule and square,
> and I must give to both sides their equitable share
> with the help of seers, portents, and burning sacrifice,
> so that I may not incur shameful reproach for veering.   (Theognis 543–6)

By implication, the poet is a *theōros* who 'indicates' to his community what the god indicates to him. To be a *theōros*, as he declares, you may not change for your audience one iota of what the god has imparted to you, just as the man who consults the Oracle must report to his community exactly what the priestess has told him. In these examples from Theognis, there is no 'middle man', no *prophētēs*, between the Pythia and the *theōros*, because the *theōros is*

---

[59] Hartog, *Miroir*, pp. 368–9.

the *prophētēs* as well. The poetry here collapses the attested differentiation between the one who formulates the inspired word as poetry and the one who takes it back to the community. That the poet is truly speaking here in the mode of a lawgiver is clear from the traditions reported by Herodotus (1.65.4) about Lycurgus, the lawgiver of Sparta: it is the Pythia of the Oracle of Apollo at Delphi who indicates to Lycurgus the law code of Sparta.

By now we have seen the following differentiations:

1. *mantis*: 'he who is in a special mental state', he who is inspired (*entheos* = having the god within), he who communicates in a sacred medium;
2. *prophētēs*: either no. 1 (e.g., Teiresias) or, more specifically, 'he who communicates the message of the *mantis* in a poetic medium' (e.g., the official who turns the inspired message of the Pythia into dactylic hexameter or the poet who turns the inspiring message of the muse into a variety of metre);
3. *theōros*: either no. 2 (e.g., Lycurgus or Theognis in the stance of a lawgiver) or, more specifically, he who is officially delegated by the city-state to communicate the message of the *mantis/prophētēs* to the polis, or in the case of athletics, the sacred message of the victory.

From the sacral standpoint of its Archaic Greek etymological legacy, 'theory' must take the place of the long-lost poet who speaks as an author, that is, with the authority of the *theōros*. Theory, then, must recapture exactly what was intended by the poetry. To put it another way, theory must recapture the very essence of the communication between the poet and the poet's community, as proclaimed by the *prophētēs*.

6 Myth, truth and pan-Hellenic poetics

Having surveyed the concept of inspiration in early Greek poetry, we may now consider thought-patterns concerning the truth-value of such inspiration. Again, the two crucial factors of the development of the Archaic Greek city-state and the tendency of pan-Hellenism are the context for an evolution of the concept of poetry into the concept of *alētheia*, 'truth', as distinct from *muthos*, 'myth', and for the evolution of the concept of the poet or *aoidos*, 'singer', into the concept of the master of truth.

The key to this evolution is that the 'singers' are *dēmiourgoi*, 'artisans in the district (*dēmos*)', and are socially mobile. Accordingly, the contents of what they sing are conditioned by the forces of pan-Hellenism, in that the pan-Hellenic perspective detaches these contents, that is, myth, from ritual. For myth to travel from city to city, the ritual grounding has to be screened out. What sacred tradition is accepted as *etumon/etētumon*, 'genuine', in one community will be deemed *pseudos*, 'a fallacy, lie', in another. This dilemma for the repertoire of the itinerant singer is dramatised in the allegro recounting in *Homeric Hymn* 1.1 – 6 of the multiplicity of versions telling the story of where the god Dionysus was born. A myth that serves as truth to one community will be a lie to another. From the standpoint of an itinerant singer, who is exposed to variant myths in varying communities, the concept of *muthos* becomes destabilised. Whereas this word used to stand for a given local myth corresponding to a given local ritual and reinforcing a given community's truth-values, it now comes to stand for whatever is variable, whatever has to change in the repertoire as the singer's performance shifts from one locale to the next. The pan-Hellenic impetus, then, is the development of a critical faculty in response to the crisis of variants, leading to a streamlined process of selectivity or criticism. What must be selected are those aspects of myth that are common to all locales visited by the singer. The diffusion and concomitant streamlining of myths can in fact be symbolised by the *topos* where a given poet offers a catalogue of all the places he has visited. A prime example is the 'signature' of the blind singer from Chios, surely a self-reference to the figure of 'Homer', who is represented as travelling throughout the city-states of mankind in the Homeric *Hymn to Apollo* (172 – 6).

The pan-Hellenic tradition of myth-making is like a least common denominator, where convergent features of diverse traditions are highlighted and divergent features are shaded over. The word *muthos*, to repeat, becomes associated with the divergent features. By contrast, the word that comes to express the convergence of features, the least common denominator, is *alētheia*, 'truth'. This word *alētheia* is predicated on the poetic concepts in the roots *mnē-*, 'have the mind connected with', and *lēth-*, 'have the mind disconnected with'. The concept of *lēthē*, 'forgetting', however, is not only negative. *Lēthē* is not only the opposite of *mnēmosunē*, 'remembering': it can also be an aspect of *mnēmosunē*. For example, the goddess Mnemosyne is described in the *Theogony* of Hesiod (53 – 5) as giving birth to the muses, divine personifications of the poet's power, so that they, through their poetry, may provide *lēsmosunē*, 'forgetting', of sadnesses and of worries for humankind; whoever hears the muses no longer 'remembers' his own ills (*Theogony* 98 – 103). By implication, the highlighting of the glory of poetry is achieved by shading over anything that detracts from it. A bright light needs a background of darkness. Such a concept of *mnēmosunē* can only be achieved through an ever-present awareness of its opposite, *lēthē*. Without the obliteration of what need not be remembered, there cannot be memory – at least, from the standpoint of Archaic Greek poetics.

Let us reformulate these thought-patterns in terms of an opposition between 'unmarked' and 'marked' categories. In the opposition between *mnē-* and *lēth-*, *mnē-* would be the unmarked member and *lēth-* the marked, in that *lēth-* can be included by *mnē-* as an aspect of *mnē-*. In the ritual of incubation connected with the cult of Trophonios, the initiate has to drink from the springs of both *Lēthē* and *Mnēmosunē*; this way, the undesired mental state can be shaded over while the desired mental state is highlighted (Pausanias 9.39.8).

These relationships can be conceived as a larger circle of 'remembering' that includes an inner area of 'forgetting' surrounding a smaller circle of specialised 'remembering' that excludes the outer area of 'forgetting'. The area of forgetting is visualised as the ongoing erasure of things not worth remembering, erasure by way of *lēthē*; the smaller circle of remembering, within the larger circle, is highlighted by the area of darkness surrounding it, the area of forgetting. In fact, there is a special word in the diction of Archaic Greek poetry that formalises this specialised and exclusive kind of remembering: that word is *alētheia*, normally glossed in the English as 'truth'. The *alētheia* of the poet is the non-erasure of the poetic glory that is his to confer. The same concept is evident in the periphrastic expression *oude me / se / he lēthei*, 'it does not escape my / your / his-her mind', which conventionally reinforces injunctions to be *memnēmenos*, 'mindful, remembering'.[60] In the surviving texts of Greek poetry and song we find the ultimate extension of this principle – to the point where the latest version becomes the last version, a canonisation that brings to a final state of crystallisation what was becoming an ever-less fluid state of variation in performance. This canonisation is to be attributed not to the phenomenon of incipient literacy but to the broader social phenomenon of pan-Hellenisation. From the standpoint of an outsider to the tradition, the phenomenon is relative in that some compositions will be more pan-Hellenic in scope than others. From the standpoint of the insider to the tradition, however, in the here-and-now of performance, the pan-Hellenic perspective is the absolutist perspective of *alētheia*, 'truth'.

While the *alētheia* of the poet is a marked and exclusive kind of memory where the erasure of *lēthē* is negated, the unmarked and inclusive kind of remembering, *mnē-*, is compatible with the notion of the muses, who can help humans forget what is bad in order that they may remember that which is good. Moreover, the very word *mousa*, 'muse', seems to be etymologically connected with *mnē-*, which means, fundamentally, 'have the mind connected'.[61] In which case, the muse is one who connects the mind with what *really* happens in the past, present, and future (e.g., Hesiod, *Theogony* 38).

The evolution of the concept of the muse, as will now be argued, is connected with the evolution of the professional *aoidos*, and this evolution happens, again, in the context of a pan-Hellenisation of song and poetry.

---

[60] Nagy, '*Sēma* and *noēsis*', p. 44; Cole, 'Archaic truth', p. 12. For a critique of Heidegger's celebrated explanation of *alētheia*, see Cole, pp. 7–8, and Detienne, *Maîtres de vérité*, p. 48, n. 107.

[61] The etymological connection is certain if *mousa* is to be derived from the root *men-*, expanded as *mon-t-* (or *mon-th-*), which is one of several possibilities entertained by Chantraine, *Dictionnaire*, p. 716.

A prime example is the transformation of the local Heliconian Muses[62] into the pan-Hellenic Olympian Muses, as dramatised in the *Theogony* of Hesiod. The local theogony of the Heliconian Muses is sung and danced by them (*Theogony* 3-4), not recited like the dactylic hexameters of the Hesiodic *Theogony*. This local theogony has a different narrative structure, starting with the differentiated gods of Olympus and working its way down to the un-differentiated primordial forces of nature, like Earth, Okeanos, and Night (*Theogony* 11-20). The pan-Hellenic *Theogony* proper, by contrast, adopts the reverse sequence (116 and following). Similarly, the *Theogony* proper explicitly rejects any lingering over localised stories of anthropogony, how mankind had its beginnings from this or that local oak or rock (35). Such variant myths would merely serve the purposes of various local interests. The Hesiodic *Theogony*, in distinguishing itself from local theogonies, is marking its pan-Hellenic distinctness. Moreover, the *Theogony* is thereby revealing its own evolution from an epichoric to a pan-Hellenic medium. Similarly, we have already seen an idealised description in *Odyssey* 9.3-11 of the singer's performance at an evening's feast, with its programmatic reference to the spirit of *euphrosunē*, 'mirth', that holds sway on such an occasion, serving as a 'signature' for the evolution of poetic performance from the occasionality of the *ainos* to the universality of the epic of Homeric poetry.

The pan-Hellenic truth-value of the Hesiodic *Theogony* is dramatised in the encounter of the muses with Hesiod:

> One day, they [= the Muses of Helicon] taught Hesiod[63] a beautiful song
> as he was tending sheep at the foot of holy Helicon.
> This is the first thing that the goddesses said to me,
> the Olympian Muses, daughters of aegis-bearing Zeus:
> 'Shepherds abiding in the fields, base objects of reproach, mere bellies!
> We know how to say many false things that are just like genuine [*etuma*] things.
> But we know also, whenever we are willing, how to announce things that are true
> [*alēthea*]'.
> Thus spoke the daughters of great Zeus, they whose words fit together.
> And they gave me a sceptre, a shoot of thriving laurel,
> having plucked it. It was a sight to behold. And they breathed into me a voice
> that is divine, so that I could give glory [*kleos*] to the things that will be and the
> things that have been.   (Hesiod, *Theogony* 22-32)

Truth, which itinerant, would-be oral poets are 'unwilling' to tell because of their need for survival (*Od.* 14.124-5), is 'willingly' conferred by the muses.

---

[62] Note the functional names of the Heliconian Muses, *Meletē*, *Mnēmē*, and *Aoidē* (Pausanias 9.29.2-3), corresponding respectively to three aspects of the poetic process: the three names mean 'practice', 'memory', and 'song' (= performance).

[63] The name *Hēsiodos* means 'he who sends forth the voice', corresponding to the description of the muses themselves at lines 10, 43, 65, and 67. The element *-odos*, 'voice', is apparently cognate with *audē*, 'voice', the word used at line 31 to designate what was 'breathed' into Hesiod by the Muses; see Nagy, *Best of the Achaeans*, pp. 296-7.

We see here what can be taken as a manifesto of pan-Hellenic poetry, in that the poet Hesiod is to be freed from being a mere 'belly' – one who owes his survival to his local audience with its local traditions: all such local traditions are 'lies' in face of the 'true things' that the muses impart specially to Hesiod. The conceit inherent in the pan-Hellenic poetry of Hesiod is that this over-arching tradition is capable of achieving something that is beyond the reach of individual local traditions.[64]

It must be understood, however, that pan-Hellenism is a relative criterion: for example, it is possible to say that the poems of the so-called Homeric Cycle are *less* pan-Hellenic than the *Iliad* and *Odyssey*. In a poem of the Cycle like the *Aithiopis*, as we shall see, the degree of pan-Hellenism is determined by the extent of the cultural sphere of Miletus. It must also be understood that local details may achieve pan-Hellenic prestige, but only at the expense of corresponding details from elsewhere. For example, the worship of Aphrodite is explicitly associated with Cythera and Cyprus in Hesiodic poetry (*Theogony* 192 – 3), and the historical pre-eminence of these two places as cult-centres of the goddess certainly justifies this association, but the result is that other places lose their claim to Aphrodite altogether, from the standpoint of Hesiodic poetry. There is no such thing, then, as absolute pan-Hellenism. Still, the Homeric and Hesiodic poems represent the historical limits reached by the exoskeleton of the earliest attested Greek poetic traditions.

The shift of the Homeric and Hesiodic traditions from local to pan-Hellenic purposes is reflected in their intertextuality. Both the Hesiodic *Theogony* and *Works and Days* are founded on social purposes that are fundamentally local in nature. A theogony is for the purpose of validating a given community by confirming the authority of a given power as the incarnation, the body politic, of that community. And yet, the Hesiodic *Theogony* is pan-Hellenic: it confirms the authority of Zeus over all Hellenic civilisation, and this authority is vested not in any political power but in the wisdom of the sage of the *Theogony*, Hesiod himself. The muses, to repeat, give him a *skēptron*, elsewhere reserved for kings.

So also with wisdom poetry: it is for the purpose of educating the local authority. In the case of the *Works and Days*, however, it is all the potential kings of all the city-states that are being addressed, and it is left open whether Hesiod's wise words to them will find their mark. The kings are called upon to arbitrate a dispute between Hesiod and his negative counter-part, the overacquisitive Perses, and we know from the *Theogony* that it takes an ideal king to arbitrate a great dispute. How the kings *should* rule in this ultimate case of arbitration is made clear by what happens to Perses while Hesiod addresses his words of righteousness to him: like the cicada, he loses all, while Hesiod, like the industrious ant, wins all. What we see,

---

[64] Nagy, 'Hesiod', p. 48.

in short, is a universalisation of the 'situation ethics' in the *Works and Days*.

The intertextuality between *Theogony* and *Works and Days*, and between *Iliad* and *Odyssey*, is not a matter of written text vs. written text. 'Text' here is used in the broader sense of text-fixation, where the process of composition-in-performance entails progressively less and less recomposition in every performance, in the pan-Hellenic context of ever-widening circles of diffusion. The intertextuality goes even further: as Herodotus says (2.53.1–2), Homer and Hesiod educate Hellas. But as noted above, they also have a contest.

Moreover, any poetic tradition other than that of Homer and Hesiod must have a contest of its own with these canonical standards, if it is to stand a chance at becoming canonical on its own terms. Such a contest can take the form of explicit criticism of older canonical models, even if these models happen to be the norms set by Homeric and Hesiodic poetry. Thus the poetry of Xenophanes, for example, which acknowledges Homer as the poet from whom all have learned this thing or that (fr. 10 Diels-Kranz), can also take to task Homeric as well as Hesiodic representations of the gods as deceitful or promiscuous (fr. 11).

Such criticisms are pan-Hellenic in intent, as we see from the attack made by the poetry of Xenophanes against the anthropomorphism of the Homeric and Hesiodic representations of the gods: by the same sort of standards that we see in Homer and Hesiod, the poet charges, the Ethiopians say that their gods are snub-nosed and black, and the Thracians, that theirs have light blue eyes and red hair (fr. 16). Here we see the absolutist impulse of pan-Hellenism reaching its ultimate limits, becoming a kind of universal humanism that rejects even the Hellenic element as provincial in comparison to the absolute universal. The absolute truth claimed by pan-Hellenic poetics is made to match an absolute standard for the gods. As far as concerns an absolute to be represented by the gods, even the human standard is seen as a limitation: would not animals, after all, represent *their* gods in *their* own image (fr. 15)? It follows, then, that there is but one god, absolutely independent of human conception, different from humans in both body and thought (fr. 23–4).

Like Homer and Hesiod before him, Xenophanes relies on the pan-Hellenic model of absolute poetic truth imparted by the all-knowing gods (fr. 18.1), but he stresses that this truth has in the past been only partially revealed, and that the full extent of this absolute truth can be achieved only through the process of human inquiry over the course of time (fr. 18.2). Going beyond the older traditions of poetry does not mean that Xenophanes rejects the *form* of poetry: like the poetry of Homer, which refers programmatically to the poetic occasion as the spirit of *euphrosunē*, 'mirth' (*Od.* 9.6), at a feast, the poetry of Xenophanes pictures that same spirit of *euphrosunē* (fr. 1.4, 8) as the setting for its own performance (1.7), to be inaugurated with established Hellenic ritual pieties towards the god who is presiding over the feast (1.6, 8–11).

Still, Xenophanes rejects the traditional *subjects* of this poetry: instead of talking about Titans and Centaurs, poetic creations of earlier generations (1.21 – 2), or about the social strife of today (1.23), it is better to follow in the tradition of the poet who can reveal the genuine truth (1.14).

7 The poet as author

Such a synthetic 'tradition' of early pan-Hellenic poetics requires a narrower definition than is suitable for the kind of oral song and poetry described by Albert Lord on the basis of his ethnographic fieldwork in the South Slavic oral traditions. The fundamental difference is that such a tradition is in the process of losing the immediacy of the sort of performer-audience interaction that we would expect in the context of ongoing recomposition-in-performance. The teleology of this loss is attested: in the historical period, Homeric and Hesiodic as well as old elegiac and iambic poetry is performed verbatim by rhapsodes at pan-Hellenic festivals like the Panathenaia. Each new performance is now aiming at a verbatim repetition – not at an act of recomposition. In other words, composer and performer are now distinct from each other.

The differentiation of composer and performer is attested in many cultures, as reflected in the incipient semantic split of *trobador* as 'composer' and *joglar* as 'performer' in Old Provençal usage. In the case of Homeric poetry, the notion of 'composer' is drastically retrojected, from the standpoint of the performers themselves, to a proto-poet whose poetry is reproduced by an unbroken succession of performers; Socrates can thus envisage the rhapsode Ion as the last in a chain of magnetised metal rings connected by the force of the original poet Homer (Plato, *Ion* 533d – 6d). More accurately, we may say that Ion is the next-to-last in the chain with relation to his audience, who would be the last link from the standpoint of the performance (*Ion* 536a). By implication, the magnetic force of the poetic composition becomes weaker with each successive performer. Ion, then, by virtue of being the last or at least the latest reproducer of Homer, would also be the weakest. By contrast, in phases of a given tradition where both composition and performance can be 'owned' by the same person at a given occasion, the advantage of the immediate composer/performer, as conferred by the occasion at hand, can be conventionally contrasted with the relative disadvantage of his predecessors, who are at this point of course deprived of their own occasion.

In the case of Plato's *Ion*, the myth-making retrojection of Homeric composition back to the strongest proto-poet belies the evolutionary progression of a tradition where the aspect of recomposition gradually diminishes in the process of diffusion entailed by performance in an ever-widening circle of listeners. The wider the diffusion, the deeper the tradition has to reach within itself: the least common denominator is also the oldest, in that a

synthesis of distinct but related traditions would tend to recover the oldest
aspects of these traditions. Given the ever-increasing social mobility of the
poet, who is teleologically evolving into the rhapsode, his cumulative exposure
to a multiformity of traditions in a plurality of places is analogous to the
experience of an ethnographer who attempts to reconstruct back to the
prototype the distinct but cognate versions of traditions in different but
neighbouring locales. A synthetic tradition is like a prototype of variant
traditions, and the diachrony of its evolution thus becomes its own synchrony.
Homeric synchrony, to take the clearest example, is like this: it operates on
the diachronically oldest recoverable aspects of its own traditions.

Let us take even further the notion of a single pan-Hellenic tradition as
opposed to a plethora of local traditions. It is clear that this notion of 'pan-
Hellenic' is absolute only from the standpoint of insiders to the tradition at
a given time and place, and that it is relative from the standpoint of outsiders,
such as ourselves, who are merely looking in on the tradition. Each new
performance can potentially claim to be the definitive pan-Hellenic tradition.
Moreover, the degree of pan-Hellenic synthesis in the content of a composition would correspond to the degree of diffusion in the performance of this
composition. Because we are dealing with a relative concept, we may speak
of the poetry of the *Iliad* and *Odyssey*, for example, as more pan-Hellenic than
the poetry of the Epic Cycle. To put it conversely: a Cyclic poem like the
Aithiopis, attributed to Arctinus of Miletus, is clearly less pan-Hellenic and
more regional, focusing on the local traditions of Miletus. Whereas both the
Iliad and *Odyssey* refer, each in its own way, to the immortalising *kleos*, 'glory',
of pan-Hellenic epic that is to serve as compensation for the death of Achilles
(e.g., *Il.* 9.413; *Od.* 11.489–91), the *Aithiopis* (p. 106, 12–15 Allen) is
concerned rather with the personal immortalisation of Achilles after death,
on the island of Leuke. This myth, as espoused by the *Aithiopis*, is anchored
in local cult: Leuke is not only a mythical place of immortalisation for Achilles
but also the ritual place of his hero-cult, localised in the territory of Olbia,
daughter-city of Miletus. The Cyclic epics are so different from the two
Homeric epics not because they are more recent or more primitive but rather
because they are more local in orientation and diffusion.

Myth can express the relationship between the Cycle and the Homeric epics
in terms of the genealogy of Homer and the Homeridae. According to one
myth, Stasinus, reputedly the poet of the *Cypria*, was not really the poet after
all, having instead received the poem as a dowry from his father-in-law,
Homer (Tzetzes, *Chiliades* 13.636–40; Pindar, fr. 265 Snell-Maehler).
Whatever succession of rhapsodes is left out of the direct genealogy of Homer
would presumably have to relinquish the central repertory of the Homeridae,
making do with what is left over. Hence the distinct repertory attributed to
Arctinus of Miletus, Lesches of Mytilene, Stasinus of Cyprus, and the other
poets of the Cycle.

To judge by the repertory of the Cycle, what was indeed left over was already finite, in that the pan-Hellenism of the Cycle, however less developed than that of the *Iliad* and *Odyssey*, would still entail the preservation of a few variants at the expense of the extinction of many others. Just as the *Iliad* and *Odyssey* had prevailed over the Cycle, so also the Cycle had teleologically prevailed over countless other epic traditions. In terms of myth, however, the loser, if the given tradition can somehow survive, can be presented as the winner, as if the surviving tradition, deprived of the repertory of the prevalent tradition, has won its own remaining repertory as a concession from the prevalent one. Such is the case in the myth that tells of the contest between Arctinus of Miletus and Lesches of Mytilene, which is won by Lesches.

A similar point may be made about the *Contest of Homer and Hesiod*, where Hesiod is represented as the victor on the basis of the specialisation of Hesiodic poetry: telling of peacetime pursuits is deemed superior to telling of wartime ones (by implication, the telling of wartime pursuits is not open to Hesiod, whereas it is to Homer). The myth of this victory compensates for the fact that the poetry of Hesiod is relatively less pan-Hellenic than that of Homer. For example, we hear only of Homeric poetry, not of Hesiodic, in connection with reports about recitations that are privileged by law at the Panathenaia. As we look at the narrative coverage of the *Little Iliad* as attributed to Lesches, it seems at first to be an intrusion that interrupts the narrative of Arctinus of Miletus. But it would be more accurate to say that the narrative of Arctinus envelops the narrative of Lesches at both ends, almost engulfing it.

The overarching pan-Hellenism of the Homeric poems, as we have seen, is evident from the differentiation of these poems from those of the Cycle. But the differentiation has to be asserted on the basis of whatever distinct traditions are offered by the Cycle. Without the actual assertion, the distinction between the Homeric poems and those of the Cycle poems can lapse into indifference in face of Homeric pan-Hellenism. Thus whereas the poems of the Epic Cycle could be attributed to individual poets like Arctinus and Lesches, they could also be attributed to the central figure of textual fixation, Homer. According to one particular myth, for example, it was Homer himself who was commissioned to 'dictate' the *Little Iliad*, along with another composition called the *Phokais*, when he travelled to Phokaia (Herodotean *Life of Homer*, pp. 202–203 Allen). In this version any attribution of the *Little Iliad* to Lesches of Mytilene is wanting.

In this sketch of the tradition that produced the Homeric poems, there is no implicit denial of the notion of 'poets within a tradition'. It is clear that the oral composer, in the context of performance, can execute considerable refinements in the act of recomposition. The composer can even appropriate the recomposition as his or her own composition, as if it emanated exclusively from an owned authority: 'this is my song'. But it is important to stress that the gradual replacement of divergences in local oral traditions by convergences in pan-Hellenic oral tradition leads to an internal idealisation of the very concept of the composer. If indeed pan-Hellenisation gradually eliminates opportunities for recomposition-in-performance, we should then expect a commensurate elimination of opportunities for successive generations of performers to identify themselves as composers. The argument is not that tradition creates the poet. Rather, it is that the pan-Hellenic tradition of oral poetry appropriates the poet, potentially transforming even historical figures into generic ones who merely represent the traditional functions of their poetry. The wider the diffusion and the longer the chain of recomposition, the more remote the identity of the composer will become. Extreme cases are Homer and Hesiod. To put it another way: the poet, by virtue of being a transmitter of tradition, can become absorbed by the tradition. Then, the poet as an exponent of his poetry can become identified and even equated with that poetry. Thus for example when Heraclitus (fr. 42 Diels-Kranz) says that Homer and Archilochus should be banned from contests in poetic performance, what is really being said is that rhapsodes (as suggested by the playful use of *rhapizesthai*) should not be allowed to perform Homer and Archilochus.

The appropriation of a historical person by the poetic tradition in which he is composing can be visualised hypothetically in the following general schema of progressive phases, which have been constructed from specific examples of performance conventions taken from a variety of societies.

1. At a phase of the tradition where each performance still entails an act of at least partial recomposition, performer 'L' publicly appropriates a given recomposition-in-performance as his or her own composition.
2. At a later phase of the tradition, performer 'M' stops appropriating the recomposition of the recomposition as his or her own composition and instead attributes it to the predecessor 'L'; this attribution is then continued by the successors '...NOPQ...'.
3. In the process of successive recompositions by '...NOPQ...', the self-identification of 'L' is itself recomposed often enough to eliminate the historical aspects of identity and to preserve only the generic aspects (that is, the aspects of the poet as defined by the poet's traditional activity as poet or by being the ancestor of those who continue in the tradition).

The key to loss of identity as a composer is control over performance. Once the factor of performance slips out of the poet's control, even if the performers of the poet's poetry have a tradition about what to say about the poet as a composer, nevertheless, the poet becomes a myth. More accurately, the poet becomes part of a myth, and the myth-making structure will appropriate his or her identity. Such is the case with the poetry of a Homer or a Hesiod or an Archilochus, as performed by rhapsodes such as Ion of Chios.

8 The poetics of singing

In Archaic Greece, the form of song or 'lyric poetry' was functionally divided into two distinct media of performance. This division is most explicitly formulated in a hypothetical discussion, as framed by Plato (*Laws* 764c – 5b), of an idealised system of festivals in an idealised polis; the presuppositions of this discussion, however, are based on the institutional realities of the polis. On the one hand, there is *monōidia*, 'monody' (764d – e, 765b), that is, performance by a single professional such as a rhapsode or *kitharōidos*, 'lyre-singer' (764d – e). On the other hand, there is *khorōidia*, 'choral song' (764e), that is, performance by a non-professional *khoros*, 'chorus', a singing and dancing ensemble of selected men, boys, or girls (764e), who represent some aspect of the polis as a whole. The essential context of performance, in both the monodic and the choral media, is competition – among rhapsodes, among lyre-singers, among choruses. This competition is called *krisis* (765b), and those who are officially chosen to select the winners are *kritai*, 'judges' (cf. 659a – b). Granted, there is no traditional distinction made between a monodic and a choral mode of *composition*. Still, the essential fact remains that the medium of both monodic and choral composition is public *performance*.

In Archaic Greek choral performance, we are dealing not with a single professional or non-professional performer but with a group of strictly non-professional polis-dwellers as represented by the chorus, who both sang and danced the song. In the choral medium of a figure like Pindar, however, the *composer* of the performances was clearly a professional, as we see explicitly in Pindar's own words (*Isthmian* 2.1 – 13). In this sense Pindar's medium was in fact professional, and it contrasts itself with the good old days when love-songs were sung to the lyre, spontaneously and without pay, in the setting of symposia (*Isthmian* 2.1 – 5). Pindar's diction describing the poetry of the good old days is suggestive of the grand old masters of sympotic love-lyric, such as Alcaeus, Anacreon, and Ibycus (cf. Aristophanes, *Women at the Thesmophoria* 160 – 3; Athenaeus 600d on Anacreon). But the spontaneity of non-professional performance by these figures of the past turns out to be an idealisation, once we take fully into consideration the special skills needed for the traditions of performing this and other kinds of monodic poetry. These skills were transmitted professionally, through the medium of professional *kitharōidia*, 'lyre-singing', either directly in performance or indirectly in the professional teaching of performance.

The story of Arion in Herodotus (1.23 – 4) is the classic example of professional performance in lyre-singing. Arion, who is described as the most prestigious 'lyre-singer' of his era, is represented as giving a monodic performance, in a ploy to save his life, for an audience of greedy sailors who had captured him in order to rob him of his great wealth; it is specified that Arion had amassed his riches, designated as *khrēmata*, 'property', on a musical tour through Italy and Sicily. In Pindar's *Isthmian* 2, this same word, *khrēmata*, is used in a context where one of the Seven Wise Men, in reaction to his personal loss of both property and friends, exclaims bitterly: 'Man is nothing more than *khrēmata*! Yes, *khrēmata*!' (2.11). Another variation on this bitter reaction is quoted in the monodic poetry of Alcaeus (fr. 360 Voigt), again in a context where the Wise Man is bewailing the equation of self-worth with purely material value. In other words, the ethic of sympotic monody, as presented by Alcaeus and represented by Pindar, is the transcendence of purely material value. But the anecdote about Arion suggests that the art of sympotic monody is nevertheless founded on the dynamics of material value. So too with choral poetry, as dramatised in Pindar's *Isthmian* 2: the poem is admitting that its art is founded on the dynamics of material value, but it proclaims an ethic of transcending the purely material, claiming the ethic of old-fashioned sympotic monody as a model..Pindaric poetry fuses the real art of monody, which is professional, into the transcendent ethic of monody, which rejects the superficial equation of 'possessions' with self-worth. Pindar's fusion of the professional into the ethical, so that the professional aspect of monody is no longer evident, is itself an ethical act, corresponding to a parallel fusion that is ongoing within his own choral medium. This ethic of fusion should not lead to our own confusion about professionalism and non-professionalism in monody.

Having recovered the reality of professional performance in the art of lyre-singing, we may turn to the professional *teaching* of performance in lyre-singing. In Aristophanes (*Clouds* 961 – 89) there is explicit reference to the schooling of young boys by professionals in the art of lyre-singing, back in those 'good old days' of the generation that had fought at Marathon. The comic allusions in this passage to an atmosphere of aristocratic pederasty that pervades such schooling (e.g., 966) is indicative of a common theme, typical of not only monodic song but also elegiac poetry, linking aristocratic *paideia*, 'education', and aristocratic *paiderastia*, 'love of boys', in the context of the symposium. In the comic vision of Aristophanes, even the schooling of the boys is pervaded by this dominant theme. In Pindar's idealised vision of non-professional monodic performance at the symposium, the songs being sung are called *paideioi humnoi*, 'songs of boyhood' (*Isthmian* 2.3), an expression that suggests *paideia* and *paiderastia* simultaneously.[65] The passage from Aristophanes about the old-fashioned schooling of non-professionals by professionals in this art helps put the spontaneity of the monodic moment into perspective.

The most we can say for non-professionalism in Archaic Greek songmaking is that the monodic medium, in contexts like the symposium, may at least allow for composition on a non-professional as well as professional level,

---

[65] Kurke, *Pindar's Oikonomia*.

whereas the choral medium of a figure like Pindar, according to his own words, has become restricted to the composition of professionals. Also, the monodic medium allows for performance on a non-professional as well as professional level, whereas the choral medium is restricted to performance by non-professionals. Moreover, even choral compositions can be reperformed by non-professionals at symposia as solo pieces, but they are then expected to accompany themselves on the lyre, and that in turn requires professional education in the specialised art of 'lyre-singing'. In fact, such solo performance was the ultimate sign of education, of direct access to the old traditions of song. In a word, the symposium was a last stand for non-professional performance of both monodic and choral compositions. Still, the choral medium was already professionalised in the dimension of composition, and the monodic in the dimension of transmission through such specialised skills as 'lyre-singing'.

Given these patterns of differentiation between the choral and monodic media, we may ask about their diachronic relationship to each other. As the discussion proceeds, we shall be seeing a series of indications that the direction of long-range development proceeded from choral lyric to monody as a differentiated offshoot. Further, monody can be seen as a mid-stage in the differentiation of *song* into *poetry*.

At the very start, we may already observe the patterns of restriction, in the Archaic choral lyric form, to performance by non-professionals, for whom such performance was a ritual act of community. This restriction is a fundamental indication that we are dealing here with a less differentiated institution. From the standpoint of later standards in the more differentiated world of poetic and musical professionalism, the inherited necessity of performance by a chorus of non-professionals imposed limitations on the virtuosity of both performance and composition (cf. Aristotle [?], *Problems* 19.15). Moreover, the references to non-professional choral performance in Homeric and Hesiodic poetry, combined with cross-cultural comparative evidence, make it clear that the social institution of what we call the chorus even antedates the institution of the polis.[66]

In the Archaic and even the Classical period of Greece, it appears that the greatest diversity in local oral traditions was on the level of song, with a wide variety of different melodic patterns native to different locales.[67] Because of the diversity of localised traditions in melody, it was not oral song but oral poetry that was better suited for pan-Hellenic diffusion, in that rhythmical (metrical) and phraseological regularisation would not violate localised perceptions of what is 'correct' as readily as would the synthesis of diverse melodic patterns. Granted, the melody of song would have promoted diffusion

---

[66] Calame, *Les choeurs*, is fundamental in this regard.
[67] Comotti, *La musica*, pp. 15–25.

from the standpoint of mnemonic utility. Still, melody would also have impeded diffusion from the standpoint of contextual sensitivity. For this reason, it can be argued, the process of pan-Hellenisation took effect relatively later for oral song than it did for oral poetry.

The pan-Hellenisation of song required an ongoing synthesis of patterns in vocal and instrumental traditions. Within the actual traditions of song, however, the synthesis is treated rather as if it resulted from inventions by prototypical figures, and the two names most commonly associated with these inventions are differentiated in terms of instrumental accompaniment: Terpander in the realm of string instruments, to which we shall refer with the general term *kithara*, 'lyre', and Olympus in the realm of wind instruments, that is, the *aulos*, 'reed'.[68] The most comprehensive direct account of the relevant traditions is to be found in the anonymous work, *On Music* 1032cd – 4b, preserved in Plutarch's *Moralia*.

Let us begin with Terpander, that is, *Terpandros*, 'he who gives pleasure to men'. Tradition has it that he was a singer from Lesbos who moved to Sparta, where he was the first of all winners at the Spartan festival known as the *Karneia* (Hellanicus in Athenaeus 635e). The Feast of Karneia was reportedly founded in the twenty-sixth Olympiad, that is, between 676 and 672 BC. In other words, the inception of the Karneia, an institution that was recognised by tradition as the oldest established festival of the Spartans, was reckoned in terms of Terpander's victory in a contest of singing to the accompaniment of the lyre. That Terpander was conceived as a solo-singer is clear from his being regularly designated as a *kitharōidos*.

Tradition also has it that Terpander 'invented' what are called the *nomoi* of *kitharōidia*: Boeotian, Aeolian, *Orthios*, *Trokhaios*, *Oxus*, *Kēpiōn*, *Terpandreios*, *Tetraoidios* (*On Music* 1132d; cf. 1132c; supplemented by Pollux 4.65). For the moment, the word *nomoi* may be left untranslated. It is enough to observe at this point that Terpander's 'invention' is traditionally seen as the forerunner of a specific genre known in the time of Plato as the 'citharodic nome' (*Laws* 700b). In this context, the word *nomos* is specific to the given genre, which is to be compared with the tradition, as reported in Herodotus (1.23), that ascribes to Arion the 'invention' of the dithyramb. Arion is described as the premier 'lyre-singer' of his era, who was the first to name, compose, and teach the dithyramb at Corinth in the era of the tyrant Periandros. That the strict taxonomical distinction between 'citharodic nome' and 'dithyramb' may be relatively late is indicated by a detail in the story of Arion: when he is abducted by pirates and performs for them a solo lyric composition that ultimately saves his life, this composition is described as an *orthios nomos* (Herodotus 1.24.5). This naming of Arion's tune corresponds to one of Terpander's *nomoi* in the list of his 'citharodic nomes' (Pollux 4.65). Still, for Plato, the 'citharodic

[68] Barker, *Musical Writings*, pp. 14–15.

nome' and the 'dithyramb' are to be treated as parallel genres inherited from the Archaic period (*Laws* 700b).

Let us now move beyond the use of the term *nomos* in the Terpander tradition, in the context of Terpander's having supposedly 'invented' the various categories of *nomoi* just listed. In this context, to repeat, *nomos* is a matter of a specific genre and reflects a specialisation of usage. In other contexts, however, the word *nomos* refers more generally to various types of local melodic patterns. In general references to song within song, *nomos* has the sense of 'localised melodic idiom' (as in Aeschylus, *Suppliants* 69); such a usage meshes with the basic meaning of *nomos*, which is 'local custom'. Just as *nomos* as 'local custom' refers to the hierarchical distribution or apportioning of value within a given society (root *nem-, as in *nemō* 'distribute'), so also *nomos* as 'localised melodic idiom' refers to the hierarchical distribution or apportioning of intervals within the melodic patterns of song.

The various Greek systems of *nomoi* evolved in symbiosis with the patterning of pitch-accent in the phraseology of song. As a melodic pattern that is characteristic of distinct speech in distinct habitats, *nomos* serves as the ideal metaphor for conveying the distinctiveness of birdsong, as when the voice of Alcman declares that he knows the *nomoi* of all the different kinds of birds in the world (fr. 40 Page). This theme can best be understood in the context of Alcman (fr. 39 Page), where the poet names himself as the 'discoverer' of melody and words that put into human language the voices of partridges. In other words, the song of Alcman is a mimesis of birdsong, and the varieties of birdsong resemble the varieties of *nomoi*. Thus song, as a mimesis of speech, can extend into a mimesis of the 'speech' of birds.

In the context of Terpander's invention of *nomoi*, however, *nomos* takes on more restricted meanings. From the standpoint of our main source, *On Music*, the *nomoi* of Terpander are the result of a systematisation of pre-existing melodic patterns. The figure of Terpander represents the common denominator of these patterns, and the fitting of these patterns into a system attributed to Terpander is formalised in the tradition that attributes to this figure the invention of a seven-note scale that accommodates 'his' *nomoi* (Aristotle [?], *Problems* 19–32; *On Music* 1140f; 1141c).

Corresponding to Terpander's invention of this scale is his invention of the seven-string lyre, displacing the older four-string type (Strabo 13.2.4; *On Music* 1141d). The iconographical evidence of the eighth and early seventh centuries BC corroborates this testimony: the norm during this period is a four-string instrument, which is replaced after this period by a seven-string instrument. It has been said that the spread of the seven-string lyre in the seventh century 'betokens a revolution in music'.[69] In terms of the pan-Hellenic synthesis here proposed, the older four-string lyre would be adequate

---

[69] West, 'Singing of Homer', p. 120.

for any single local *nomos*, while the newer seven-string lyre, which represents the 'revolution' of the seventh century, could fit a wide variety of *nomoi*, irrespective of local provenance, within a new interrelated system. In the diction of Pindar, Apollo himself is represented as leading the choral performance of 'all sorts of *nomoi*' (*Nemean* 5.24–5) as he plays on the seven-string lyre, which is described as 'having seven languages'.

Just as Terpander is a prototype of the *kitharōidos*, so Olympus is presented as a parallel prototype of the *aulōidos*, 'reed singer' (*On Music* 1137b, 1133d–f; Aristotle, *Politics* 1340a). Like Terpander, Olympus is credited with the invention of specific *nomoi*. Olympus is a decidedly mythical figure, a disciple of the mythical *aulos*-player Marsyas of Phrygia. Besides Olympus, there are later figures who are less remotely mythical in appearance and who tend to be synchronised with Terpander. One such figure is Clonas, described as an inventor of *nomoi* for *aulōidia*, 'reed (*aulos*)-singing', who supposedly lived shortly after the time of Terpander (*On Music* 1132c–3a).

The earliest attestations of a critical mass of actual compositions in Greek song – which we may also call lyric poetry – are represented by the surviving texts attributed to Alcman, Stesichorus, Alcaeus, Sappho, Ibycus, Anacreon, Simonides, Bacchylides, and Pindar; in the era of Alexandrian scholarship, these nine names constituted the inherited canon of lyric poetry (*Palatine Anthology* 9.184, where all nine are enumerated). The relative dating of these poets covers a period stretching roughly from 650 to 450 BC. These attestations of song are the reflex of a new wave of pan-Hellenisation, achieved through an ongoing synthesis as represented by the myths about the inventions of *nomoi* by the likes of Terpander and Olympus. As in the pan-Hellenisation of oral *poetry*, the relatively later pan-Hellenisation of oral *song* would entail a progressively restricted series of recompositions, in ever-widening circles of diffusion, with the streamlining of convergent local traditions happening at the expense of divergent ones. In this way, a pre-existing multitude of local traditions in oral song could evolve into a finite tradition of fixed lyric compositions suited for all Hellenes and attributed by them all to a relatively small number of poets. The smallness of their number is due to the pan-Hellenisation of pre-existing traditions in oral *song*, just as the comparably small number of canonical Archaic poets who are credited with compositions in hexameters (predominantly two, Homer and Hesiod) or in iambics (Archilochus, Hipponax, Simonides, Solon, *et al.*) and elegiacs (Archilochus, Callinus, Mimnermus, Tyrtaeus, Theognis, Solon, Xenophanes, *et al.*) is due to the pan-Hellenisation of pre-existing traditions in oral *poetry*. It can be argued that the very evolution of what we know as the Classics – as both a concept and a reality – was but an extension of the organic pan-Hellenisation of oral traditions. In line with this reasoning, the evolution of an ancient Greek canon in both *poetry* and *song* need not be attributed primarily to the factor of writing. Granted, writing would have been essential for the ultimate preservation of any canon once the traditions of performance were becoming obsolete; but the key to the actual evolution of a canon must be sought in the social context of performance itself.

In considering the internal and external references to the performance of compositions attributed to the canonical nine poets of lyric we can find clear traces of pan-Hellenic systematisation, as we have already seen in the example taken from Pindar: the seven-string lyre, presented as a symbol of systematisation, allows Apollo to lead the choral performance of 'all sorts of *nomoi*' (*Nemean* 5.25). The word *nomos* itself, however, is hardly adequate for designating the actual process of systematisation, since its basic meaning of 'local custom' retains a built-in emphasis on the local origins of the constituents of the system. A more adequate word is *harmonia*, in the specific sense of a 'tuning' or *accordatura* that fits a given melodic idiom, as in Aristophanes, *Knights* 994. In a more general sense, *harmonia* can be understood as a 'system of intervals in pitch', as in Plato, *Republic* 397d, where the point being made is that the traditional *harmonia* and rhythm of song is regulated by the words of song. Plato's usage in this passage, it has been observed, 'points to the fact that the existence of melody depends on the prior existence of an organised scheme of pitches standing to one another in determinate relations, on the basis of whose relations the selection that generates a melody is made.'[70] We must distinguish this notion of *harmonia* from the later notion of *tonos*, especially as developed by Aristoxenus, pupil of Aristotle, who was himself the son of a professional musician from Tarentum (*Suda*, s.v. 'Aristoxenos'). The difference has been formulated as follows: 'each *tonos* had the same pattern of intervals: they differed one from another, as modern keys do, only in respect of pitch';[71] by contrast, the *harmoniai*, as Plato understands them in the passage under consideration, 'were distinguished from one another primarily by being constituted out of different sequences of intervals'. Correspondingly, 'rhythm' in this passage means 'the element of rhythmic organisation that any composition must possess, an individual rhythm being the formal rhythmic structure underlying an individual piece or type of piece, its overall pattern of movement'.[72]

The various *harmoniai* were distinct enough from each other to require considerable effort in the development of a performer's repertoire. In the comedies of Aristophanes, we see the ridiculing of a character on the grounds that he could learn only the Dorian *harmonia*, to the exclusion of the others, when he had been a boy in school (*Knights* 985–95). The context for such learning can best be observed in the *Clouds* of Aristophanes, with its informative description of old-fashioned Athenian education, the kind that purportedly produced the men who fought at the Battle of Marathon, where

---

[70] Barker, *Musical Writings*, p. 130, n. 18.
[71] Barker, *Musical Writings*, p. 164.
[72] Barker, *Musical Writings*, p. 164.

boys learn selected compositions of old lyric masters in the house of the *kitharistēs*, 'master of the kithara' (964), who teaches them to learn by heart the performance of famous lyric compositions and who insists on their adherence to performing these compositions in the proper *harmonia* that had been 'inherited from their forefathers' (968; cf. 969–72).

With this glimpse of melodic traditions in Greek song serving as background, we are ready to pursue further the notion of a canon in our ongoing discussion of pan-Hellenisation in poetry and song. The formation of a canon in *song* – which we can also call lyric 'poetry' – started relatively later than the formation of a canon in non-lyric *poetry* proper. Once the pan-Hellenic breakthrough of song did happen, however, its transmission would have been facilitated to rival that of poetry not only because of the mnemonic utility of melody but also because of the relative brevity of song as opposed to the potentially open-ended length of poetry. In any inherited distinction between singing and speaking, we would expect that the pressures of regularisation in singing would tend to delimit the length of production in contrast with the potentially open-ended length of speaking everyday speech. So also in any differentiation of singing into *song* as distinct from *poetry*, we would expect that song would be more clearly delimited in length of production by contrast with the potentially open-ended length of poetry in its imitation of speaking.

If indeed the transmission of pan-Hellenised song coexists with that of poetry, it stands to reason that the professional performers of such song, the *kitharōidos* or 'lyre-singer' and the *aulōidos* or 'reed-singer', would be valued on a scale comparable to that of the professional performer of poetry, the rhapsode. In fact, the epigraphical evidence shows that *rhapsōidoi*, *kitharōidoi*, and *aulōidoi*, as they perform in competition at festivals, are awarded comparable sums for their prizes.[73]

In what follows, we shall have occasion to observe a recurrent pattern where the composer/performer of song or 'lyric poetry' is eventually differentiated into a mythical proto-composer on the one hand and a contemporary professional performer, the *kitharōidos* or *aulōidos*, on the other. But this pattern is just one of many other possible patterns of evolution. The category of lyric poetry includes performance not only by a single professional or non-professional performer but also by a non-professional group of specially selected natives of the polis, the chorus, who both sang and danced the song. In Pindar's time the non-professional chorus would be performing, on commissioned occasions, songs composed by professional poets of pan-Hellenic prestige, such as Pindar himself. As we shall see, the institution of the chorus plays its own role in the emerging concept of authorship in Archaic and Classical Greece.

---

[73] Cf. *Inscriptiones Graecae* II², 2311, and XII, 9.189.

9 Mimesis

In a context where the performer and the composer are distinct, the *persona* of the composer can be re-enacted by the performer. In other words, the performer may impersonate the poet. The word for such re-enactment or impersonation is *mimēsis*. In general, the noun *mimēsis*, as well as the corresponding verb *mimeisthai*, designates the re-enactment, through ritual, of the events of myth (e.g., Lysias 6.51). In the case of a highly stylised ritual complex like Athenian drama, the re-enactment is equivalent to acting out the role of a mythical figure (e.g., Aristophanes, *Women at the Thesmophoria* 850). The acting out can take place on the level of speech alone, or on the level of speech combined with bodily movement, that is, dance. By extension, however, mimesis can designate not only the re-enacting of the myth but also the present re-enacting of previous re-enactments. In that the newest instance of re-enacting has as its model, cumulatively, all the older instances of performing the myth as well as the 'original' instance of the myth itself, mimesis is a current 'imitation' of earlier re-enactments. This is the sense of mimesis in the Homeric *Hymn to Apollo* (163), where a choral group called the Deliades are described as being able to 'imitate', *mimeisthai*, the voices and musical sounds of a wide variety of Ionians who are described as assembling for a festival on the island of Delos.

The sense of wonder about the mimesis performed by the Deliades has to do with the accuracy or exactness of their re-enactment: everyone will say, when they hear their own voices and sounds re-enacted by the Deliades, that they are hearing their own voice. This line of thought corresponds to the celebrated description of *mimēsis* in the *Poetics* of Aristotle as the mental process of identifying the representing 'this' with the represented 'that': 'this *is* that' (1448b17). Such a mental process, Aristotle goes on to say, is itself a source of pleasure (1448b11 – 18). This pleasure is not incompatible with an anthropological understanding of ritual: 'Fixed rhythm, fixed pitch are conducive to the performance of joint social activity. Indeed, those who resist yielding to this constraining influence are likely to suffer from a marked unpleasant restlessness. In comparison, the experience of constraint of a peculiar kind acting upon the collaborator induces in him, when he yields himself to it, the pleasure of self-surrender'.[74]

Such a formula of equating 'this' with 'that', as implied by the use of the verb *mimeisthai* in the *Hymn to Apollo* and as explicitly linked with the concept of mimesis in the *Poetics* of Aristotle, is a fundamental expression, in many languages, of assent: besides the many attestations in Greek (e.g., 'this is that' = 'yes' in Aristophanes, *Lysistrata* 240), there is a particularly striking example in the Latin combination *hoc illud* 'this is that', which is the ancestor of the

---

[74] Tambiah, 'Performative approach', p. 113.

French *oui*, 'yes' (and of the Southern French *oc*, as in *Languedoc*). Such a 'yes' can serve as the 'amen' of a participant in a given ritual, who assents to the realities of myth as retold in the context of ritual.

The concept of mimesis, in conveying a re-enactment of the realities of myth, is a concept of authority so long as society assents to the genuineness of the values contained by the framework of myth. Correspondingly, the speaker who frames the myth, or is re-enacted as framing the myth, is an 'author' so long as he or she speaks with the authority of myth, which is supposedly timeless and unchanging. The 'author' has to insist on the timelessness and unchangeability of such authority, which resists the pressures of pleasing the interests of the immediate audience by preferring the pleasure of timeless and unchanging values transmitted to an endless succession of audiences by way of mimesis. These thought-patterns are particularly evident in two passages from Theognis of Megara. In the first, the *persona* of Theognis declares that only the one who is *sophos*, that is, 'skilled' in the decoding and encoding of poetry, can execute a mimesis or 're-enactment' of Theognis:

> I am unable to decide what disposition it is that the townspeople have towards me.
> For I do not please them, either when I do for them things that are advantageous
> or when I do things that are disadvantageous.
> There are many who find blame with me, base and noble men alike.
> But no one who is not skilled [*sophos*] can re-enact [*mimeisthai*] me.
>
> (Theognis 367–70)

In the second and related passage, we shall see that the notion of mimesis is an implicit promise that no change shall occur to accommodate the interests of any local audience of the here-and-now, the 'townspeople'. The re-performance of a composition, if it is a true re-enactment or mimesis, can guarantee the authenticity of the 'original' composition. In the second passage, where the *persona* of Theognis actually identifies himself by name, thereby authorising himself, there is an explicit self-description of the 'author' as someone who practises *sophia*, the 'skill' of decoding or encoding poetry, and as one who therefore possesses the authority of timeless and unchanging value, resisting the necessity of having to please merely the audience of the here-and-now:

> Kyrnos, let a seal [*sphragis*] be placed by me, as I practise my skill [*sophia*],
> upon these my words. This way, it will never be undetected if they are stolen,
> and no one can substitute something inferior for the genuine thing that is there.
> And this is what everyone will say: 'These are the words of Theognis
> of Megara, whose name is known among all mortals.'
> But I am not yet able to please all the townspeople.   (Theognis 19–24)

The composer has to risk alienation in his own here-and-now in order to attain the supposedly universal acceptance of the ultimate audience, which is the cumulative response of pan-Hellenic fame, achieved through the authority and authenticity of mimesis. Implicitly, only the pleasure of exact re-performance, the ongoing achievement of mimesis, is truly lasting. The pleasure elicited through change in response to an immediate audience is ephemeral. Needless to say, the notion of unchangeability is merely an ideology. The tradition may insist that it is unchanging, but it represents in fact an ever-changing cumulative response to the evolving society that it addresses.

In the case of poetry, we have seen the eventual differentiation of a composer/performer into a mythical proto-composer on the one hand and a contemporary professional performer, the rhapsode, on the other. The task of the performer is to re-enact the composer. In the case of song, there is a parallel task to be performed by the *kitharōidos* or *aulōidos*. But there are other possible patterns of re-enactment, as we now turn to the medium of choral song, performed by a group of strictly non-professional polis-dwellers, the 'chorus', who both sang and danced the song, and whose non-professionalism imposed limitations on the virtuosity of both performance and composition (cf. Aristotle [?], *Problems* 19.15). The chorus is a group that represents, by way of singing and dancing, a given community. In attested choral lyric poetry, the community is generally represented as the city-state, the polis itself. A given chorus in a given polis may perform a wide variety of compositions related to various local or civic rituals. The range of this variety is apparent from the book titles in the Alexandrian edition of Pindar. There are, for example, the maiden-songs or *parthenia* related ultimately to local/civic rituals of coming of age.[75] There are also of course choral odes connected directly with cults of the gods, such as Pindar's *paianes*, 'paeans', in honour of Apollo. The list could be extended, but the point has already been made: choral lyric is public, a thing of the polis.

In the songmaking traditions of choral lyric poetry, one of several possible patterns of evolution results in the attested differentiation between a proto-composer who is grounded in myth and a succession of contemporary non-professional performers, selected by age-groupings, who sing and dance a proto-composition grounded in the ritual of seasonally-recurring festivals. Needless to say, such a 'proto-composition' would be subject to potential ongoing recomposition with each seasonally-recurring performance. Striking examples of this pattern of evolution can be found in the available testimony about the festivals of Sparta, which were the occasion for seasonal reperformances, in the ritual setting, of the lyric 'proto-compositions' of Terpander, Thaletas, Alcman, and others.[76] The first *katastasis*, 'establishment', that is, ostensibly the first phase of songmaking institutions at Sparta, is traditionally attributed to Terpander (*On Music* 1134b). The second *katastasis* is attributed

[75] Calame, *Les choeurs*, I, pp. 18–20, 117, 249.
[76] On the strict preservation of performance-traditions in song in Sparta, see Athenaeus 633f.

to Thaletas of Gortyn, Xenocritus of Locri, and Polymnestus of Colophon (*On Music* 1134bc). These composers are associated not only with the Feast of the *Gumnopaidiai* at Sparta but also the Feast of the *Apodeixeis* in Arcadia and the Feast of the *Endumatia* at Argos (*On Music* 1134c). There is a striking description in a fragment of Sosibius (Athenaeus 678bc) of choral events at the Spartan Feast of the *Gumnopaidiai*, featuring reperformances of compositions attributed to Thaletas, Alcman, and Dionysodotus.

In order to understand the progressive reshaping, over time, of the *persona* who claims the composition of a choral lyric performance in societies like that of Archaic Sparta, we must first come to terms with the fundamental characteristics of the Archaic Greek *khoros*, the singing and dancing ensemble or chorus. To begin, we must note that the *khoros* is by nature a microcosm of society. The Spartans, for example, actually referred to the interior of their civic space as the *Khoros* (Pausanias 3.11.9). As a microcosm of society, it is equally important to note, the *khoros* is also a microcosm of social hierarchy. Within the hierarchy that is the chorus a majority of younger members act out a pattern of subordination to a minority of older leaders; this acting out conforms to the role of the chorus as an educational collectivisation of experience, including various forms of institutionalised or stylised homosexual experience serving as an initiation into the heterosexual status of marriage.[77] The concept of older leaders, within the hierarchy of the chorus, is in most instances embodied in the central *persona* of the *khorēgos*, 'chorus-leader'. There is a pervasive choral convention of emphasising the superiority of the *khorēgos* and the subordination of the 'I' that speaks for the choral aggregate; while the collectivity of the choral aggregate is itself egalitarian, the superiority of the *khorēgos* is a fundamental model of hierarchy.

A splendid example of the choral form as a hierarchical construct is the Spartan song that is sung and danced by the chorus of Spartan girls as dramatised in Alcman (fr. 1 Page), where a chorus-leader called Hagesikhora, focal point of admiration for the aggregate (e.g., 45–57), is described as *khorēgos* (44); her very name, *Hagēsikhora*, recapitulates the meaning 'leader of the chorus'.[78] Similarly in Aristophanes' *Lysistrata* (1296–321), a choral song of the Spartan women, Helen in her role as major cult-figure of Sparta is pictured by the chorus as the leader of their group, as the ultimate *khorēgos*. Likewise in Theocritus 18, a composition known as the *Epithalamium for Helen*, a chorus of Spartan girls pictures Helen as a resplendent chorus-leader, in terms that resemble strikingly the description of Hagesikhora in Alcman.[79] It is clear from such evidence that a figure like Hagesikhora, as leader of the chorus, is represented as performing a re-enactment, a mimesis, of a given divinity in a given role.

[77] Calame, *Les choeurs*, I, pp. 437–9.
[78] Calame, *Les choeurs*, II, pp. 46–7.
[79] Calame, *Les choeurs*, II, pp. 123–6.

Like *Hagēsikhora*, the feminine name *Agidō*, which occurs in the same composition, seems to be generic: in this case, it fits into the naming pattern owned by the Spartan royal lineage of the Agiadai, as best known from the name of a particularly distinguished member of this dynasty, Agesilaos.[80] From this example, we can see that the role-model defined by a choral leader can be expressed in terms of royalty as well as divinity. An analogous case is to be found in Alcman (fr. 10b Page), where the figure of a yet-beardless youth called Agesidamos, meaning 'leader of the local population', is addressed specifically as *khorēgos*.

That the roles of choral leadership indicated by names such as Agido or Agesidamos demand to be filled, in performance, by real royalty or aspiring royalty is shown indirectly by narrative traditions that tell of aberrant situations where an individual Spartan of genuine royalty is denied a prominent position in a choral group, thus affording him the opportunity to assert a wise saying, to the effect that it is after all the man in question who determines the status, not the status the man. In one such story (Plutarch, *Sayings of Spartans* 208d – e), the focus of the story is none other than King Agesilaos of Sparta, of the royal patriliny of the Agiadai, who is pictured as still a boy when, one day at the Spartan Feast of Gymnopaidiai, he is assigned an inconspicuous choral position. The narrative emphasises that, at this moment, as Agesilaos utters the wise saying about man and status, it is not yet clear that he will indeed become the king of Sparta; as Plutarch notes elsewhere, the young Agesilaos was brought up as a private citizen before he became king (*Life of Agesilaos* 596a; 597b). The fact that other variants of this story are assigned to other kings of Sparta is yet another indication that kingship could and did determine pre-eminence of status in the choral groups of Sparta. In short, whoever performs the role of a choral leader in a given seasonally-recurring Spartan festival would be performing a mimesis of a mimesis. The performers in the here-and-now would be experiencing a personal mimesis of choral characters with choral names like Hagesikhora and Agesidamos. Such characters or characterisations would be, in turn, part of a seasonally-recurring institutional mimesis of authoritative role-models like divinities or royal ancestors.

The more generic and impersonal the content of such a composition, in the eyes of the local Spartan community, the more pan-Hellenic prestige the presentation of this composition can have in the eyes of whatever Hellenes from the outside may be looking in, as it were, on Sparta. The local community's public self-esteem, in order to live up to the proper degree of admiration both from outside and consequently from within, must seek the least occasional and most catholic aspects of its seasonally recomposed choral self-presentation. The impulse of pan-Hellenism in Archaic Greece begins at home.

---

[80] Calame, *Les choeurs*, II, pp. 140–1.

10 The singer as author

It remains to ask what relationship exists between the authority of the role-model who is represented as leading the choral group and the authority of the composer who is credited with the representation. To put it another way: how does the authority of the *khorēgos*, 'choral leader', as the focus of potential pan-Hellenic prestige for the local community, relate to the authority of the composer, real or re-created, who speaks through this *persona*? The answer should help define the concept of authorship that emanates from such authority.

To begin, it is important to notice that, in a choral composition like Alcman, fr. 1, the two chorus-leaders who are being represented, Agido and Hagesikhora, do not have speaking parts: rather, it is the aggregate that speaks *about* them, represents them, in all admiration. It is as if the chorus-leaders were dancing only, while the choral group was all along singing and dancing. The potential differentiation of the chorus-leader from the singers and dancers can in fact proceed in various different directions. The *khorēgos* may become specialised as a virtuoso singer, a virtuoso dancer, or a virtuoso player of a musical instrument. The ultimate model is the god Apollo himself, who is conventionally represented by poetry as the leader of the choral group as he performs, in his capacity as leader, various combinations of the three components of choral lyric, that is, song, dance, and instrumental music. Perhaps the most undifferentiated picture can be found in the Homeric *Hymn to Hermes* (475 – 6), where Apollo is represented as simultaneously singing, dancing, and playing the lyre. Elsewhere, the specialties become clear. In the *Hymn to Apollo* (182 – 206), Apollo dances and plays the lyre (201 – 3), while the muses sing (189 – 93) and the rest of the gods dance (194 – 201), most notably the Graces (194). The emphasis here is on Apollo's specialty, the lyre. In other references (e.g., *Il*. 1.603 – 4), only the specialties are mentioned: Apollo plays the lyre and the muses sing. A similar situation holds in the Hesiodic *Shield of Herakles* (201 – 6), where again Apollo plays the lyre while the muses are described as choral leaders in song, by way of the verb *exarkhō*, 'lead the chorus', in combination with *aoidē*, 'song' (205).

In a composition like Alcman, fr. 1, as we have noted, the figures of the choral leaders Agido and Hagesikhora do not have a speaking part in the song. Presumably, they are instead simply in the forefront of the dancing. It is explicitly the choral aggregate who speaks for the chorus-leaders, and it is implicitly the composer who speaks through the chorus-members. In another example (Alcman fr. 39 Page) the chorus-members actually identify the composer of their song: they refer to the figure of Alcman by name, in the third person, as the one who composed what they sing. Or again, in Alcman, fr. 38, the chorus-members praise the *kitharistēs*, 'lyre-player', a performer on the musical instrument who may or may not be visualised as distinct from the composer.

There are, however, other situations where the singer/lyre-player may differentiate himself from the choral group by speaking in his own *persona* instead of theirs, as most dramatically illustrated by the declaration in Alcman, fr. 26, where the singer says that he is too old and weak to dance with the chorus. Such conventions of stylised separation and self-introduction may help explain the distribution of roles in *Iliad* 18.567–72, the description of a lyre-playing boy who sings the Linus-song in the midst of a festive chorus of boys and girls: here the singing is apparently subordinated to the lyre-playing and dancing. So also in *Hymn to Hermes* 499–502: Apollo first struck up the lyre, and then 'he sang beautifully, in accompaniment [*hupo*-]'. Just as subordinated dancing required heightened virtuosity and could be described in terms of choral leadership, so also here: the subordinated singing of Apollo is a virtuoso performance. The distinction between the patterns of subordination in *Iliad* 18.567–72, where the boy's song responds to the lyre, and in *Odyssey* 8.256–65 and 367–80, where the dancing responds to the song, seems to be missed by later generations in the post-Classical era, as for example in Athenaeus (15d).

The archetypal virtuoso performance of Apollo is morphologically a *prooimion*. The *prooimion* is a framework for differentiated virtuoso singing by the individual *kitharōidos*, 'lyre-singer', and it literally means 'the front part of the song [*oimē*]'. The prooemium took the form of a prayer sung to a given god who presided over the occasion of a given seasonally-recurring festival where the song was performed, in competition with other songs. A clear reflex of this form can be found in the actual structure of the *Homeric Hymns*.[81] In fact, Thucydides (3.140.4–5) uses the word *prooimion* in referring to the version of the Homeric *Hymn to Apollo* that he knows. That the dramatised context of these *Hymns* is one of seasonally-recurring festivals where contests in song are held is clear from the use of *hōra* in *Hymn* 26.12–13 and of *agōn*, 'contest', in *Hymn* 6.19. That these *Hymns* are morphologically *preludes*, with the inherited function of introducing the main part of the performance, is illustrated by references indicating a shift to the performance proper, such as 'I will shift to the rest of the song [*humnos*]' at *Homeric Hymns* 5.293 (cf. 9.9; 18.11). Quintilian (4.1.1–2) sums up the essence of the *prooimion* thus: '*oimē* is song and the *kitharōidoi* refer to those few words that they sing before their contest proper, for the sake of winning favour, as *prooimion* ...'.

Quintilian's reference to 'those few words' sung by the 'lyre-singers' is of course belied by the proportions of some of the larger *Homeric Hymns*, which had evolved into magnificent extravaganzas that rival epic itself in narrative power, as in the case of the *Hymn to Apollo*. It is in fact legitimate to ask whether the *Homeric Hymns*, especially the larger ones, were functional preludes. For now, however, it is enough to stress that they were formally just that, preludes.

---

[81] Koller, 'Das kitharodische Prooimion', pp. 174–82, 195–206.

To repeat, Thucydides refers to the *Hymn to Apollo* as a *prooimion*. Even the Hesiodic *Theogony*, with its still more imposing proportions, is morphologically a *prooimion*. So also is the representation of the first theogony ever sung, an archetyal performance of lyre-singing by the god Hermes himself, as described and paraphrased in *Hymn to Hermes* 425–33. The crucial concept here is *anabolē*, 'prelude', closely parallel to the concept of *prooimion*. Hermes sings his theogony 'in the manner of a prelude' (426), just as the song started by Apollo's lyre is described in Pindar (*Pythian* 1.4) in terms of 'the chorus-leading prooemia'.

We can perhaps go one further step. It has been argued persuasively that the entire body of Archaic poetry as composed in dactylic hexameter, including Homeric and Hesiodic poetry, evolved out of the monodic medium of the *prooimion* in *kitharōidia*, 'lyre-singing'.[82] For such an argument to be taken further, we would have to look back to the close formal affinities that exist between the Homeric and Hesiodic hexameter on one hand and, on the other, the metres of such figures as Stesichorus, Sappho, and Alcaeus. It so happens, as we shall see presently, that these figures are in fact early exponents of the medium of *kitharōidia*. Before we can turn to Stesichorus and the others, however, it is important to explore still further the question of the chorus and the relationship between choral and monodic forms. In particular, we must ask how poetry may have become differentiated from monodic song, much as monody had earlier become differentiated from choral performance.

We had started our survey of the prooemium with the vision of Apollo as he had struck up the lyre for the very first time and then 'sang beautifully, in accompaniment [*hupo*-]' (*Hymn to Hermes* 502). And yet, singing in response to the musical instrument of Apollo is a feature not only of Apollo himself as archetypal player of preludes. There are also specialists in the art of the prelude: those supreme experts in song, the muses, as they execute their special skills. As we have already seen in the Hesiodic *Shield of Herakles* (201–6), the muses are described as choral leaders in song by virtue of their responsiveness to the lyre of Apollo. Paradoxically, the subordination of the muses to the choral leadership of Apollo in the overall domain of choral performance, where Apollo controls all three components of song, dance, and musical instrumentation, is a key to the choral leadership of the muses in the specific domain of song. It is Apollo who generally dances and plays the lyre, while the muses' function is more specifically that of singing or reciting. It is after all a muse, not Apollo, who inspires a 'song' like the *Odyssey* (1.1). To put it another way: the specialisation of the muses as experts in the words of song, as differentiated from Apollo who is overall master of all the components of song, is comparable to the specialisation of Greek *poetry* as differentiated from a general category of singing. As the overall authority of singing, Apollo is the ultimate

[82] Koller, 'Das kitharodische Prooimion', pp. 203–6.

chorus-leader of the muses, their leader in the choral integration of singing, dancing, and instrumentation. As for the muses, they are specialised chorus-leaders of song, in stylised descriptions such as we have seen in the *Shield of Herakles* (205).

Another way of expressing the divine model of choral leadership is the verb *exarkhō*, 'lead, lead off, lead the chorus' and its derivatives. We have already seen it applied to the muses in their role as specialists in singing at a choral performance. The word conveys the fundamental theme of a differentiated individual initiative, followed by an undifferentiated response or reinforcement by the group that joins in (cf. *Il.* 24.721–2). This theme helps explain the choral metaphor built into the extended meaning of the Greek verb *hēgeomai* which means not only 'take the lead' (e.g., *Il.* 9.168) but also 'think, have an opinion', in the sense of 'think authoritatively', as often in Herodotus; it is from this verb that the name Hagesikhora, 'she who leads the chorus', is derived. The verb *exarkhō* can take as its object the given genre in which the performance is happening, as in *Iliad* 18.51, where Thetis begins her *goos*, 'lament'. In such instances of spontaneous individual initiative as dramatised by the narrative, we can see an ultimate model for the *khorēgos* as the organiser of the spontaneous occasion, the one who gives it a form, a format, for the group to follow and join. To the extent that the *khorēgos* gives the occasion its form, the occasion *is* the genre.

With these divine models of individual initiative in mind, it is now time to extend the proposal, articulated in the specific case of Alcman, fr. 1, that a lead character like *Hagesikhora*, 'she who leads the chorus', is a substitute on the level of ritual for a corresponding cult-figure who exists on the level of myth. The analogous name of a figure like Stesichorus, 'he who sets up the chorus', implies that a poet, like a lead character in a chorus, may somehow function as a ritual stand-in for the divine models of choral lyric poetry, Apollo and the muses. The generic poet in Archaic Greek traditions is by definition a ritual substitute, as conveyed by the word *therapōn*, in relation to the muses explicitly and to their leader Apollo implicitly.[83] Further, the concept of ritual substitute is closely associated with that of cult-hero. There is a pervasive symmetrical pattern of god–hero antagonism on the level of myth and of god-hero symbiosis on the level of cult. A prime example is the figure of Archilochus. As we have already seen, the compositions ascribed to Archilochus take a specialised form of poetry that is differentiated from song: he belongs to the repertoire of a *rhapsōidos*, not a *kitharōidos*. Still, the figure of Archilochus retains a choral personality, as evidenced by his self-description as an *exarkhōn*, 'choral leader', of the specific genres known as the dithyramb (Archilochus, fr. 120 West) and the paean (fr. 121). Again we see that the genre *is* the occasion in such instances of dramatised individual initiative.

---

[83] Nagy, *Best of the Achaeans*, pp. 279–316.

Given that the figure of the poet Archilochus remains a choral personality, we may now move on to observe the tradition that represents Archilochus as a ritual substitute of his divine choral models: the story has it that Archilochus was killed through the indirect agency of Apollo, who at the same time promotes his status as cult-hero, pronouncing the dead poet to be the minister (*therapōn*) of the muses.[84] The theme of the poet as ritual substitute could be pursued further, but we must stay on track with the topic at hand by trying to understand better the role that the poet – let us call him or her the 'author' – actually plays in the chorus.

What needs to be shown is that the authority of Apollo over song, as formalised by his function as *khorēgos*, is the fundamental model for the concept of authorship in choral lyric, as embodied in figures like the poet Alcman. A crucial passage in this regard is Herodotus 5.83, with its description of a local festival on the island of Aegina, where female choral groups perform in worship of two *daimones*, 'spirits', called Damia and Auxesia, whose wooden statues or *agalmata*, 'cult-representations', are the centrepieces of the ritual event. From independent evidence, we know that both these names reflect epithets applied in the cults of the goddess Demeter.[85] We may compare in this regard the name Hagesikhora in Alcman, which as we have seen is an appropriate epithet for visualising, through a choral substitute, a cult-figure as the focal point of a choral group. Even more important is a detail in the description of the Aeginetan festival concerning the nature of the leadership over the female choral groups who perform at the Feast of Damia and Auxesia: 'there are ten men who are chorus-leaders making public presentation [= verb *apo-deiknumai*] for each of the *daimones* [Damia and Auxesia]'. The noun that corresponds to the verb *apodeiknumai* is *apo-deixis*, which we have seen is the name of a major festival of choral song in Arcadia. This seasonally recurring festival thus featured the public presentation of ten, presumably competing, female choral performances, each one being 'presented' by a male *khorēgos* whose relationship to the female group corresponds to the stylised relationship of Apollo to the muses. Such a relationship also corresponds to the relationship of the figure Alcman to the female choral groups at Spartan festivals who dance 'his' compositions. In the description of the Aeginetan festival, it is specified that the worship of the cult-figures takes the form of ritual strife, where the characters in the chorus engage in mutual mockery (cf. Herodotus 5.83.3).

It seems that each of the ten choral performances at this local festival on the island of Aegina entailed two rival choral subdivisions, assigned to each of the two figures Damia and Auxesia. We may compare the internal dramatised rivalry of Agido and Hagesikhora in Alcman. We may also

---

[84] Nagy, *Best of the Achaeans*, pp. 301–2.

[85] Nilsson, *Griechische Feste*, p. 414.

compare the 'setting up' of two distinct female cult-heroes, Hippodameia and Physkoa, by a collegium of sixteen women at the Feast of Heraia at Olympia in Elis, as reported by Pausanias (5.16.6 – 7). Tradition has it that this feast in worship of the goddess Hera was established by Hippodameia to celebrate her marriage to Pelops (Pausanias 5.16.4), a fundamental model of power and authority. There is a detail in this tradition that bears special emphasis: the number sixteen here stems from the fact that two women are chosen from each of the eight *phulai*, 'tribal divisions', of Elis (Pausanias 5.16.7). Perhaps we are to understand that each of the two representatives of each *phulē* was assigned to one or the other of the two cult-figures, Hippodameia and Physkoa. It may well be, then, that there were eight choral performances entailing two rival choral subdivisions, assigned to each of the two figures Hippodameia and Physkoa, with each of the sixteen women assigned as *khorēgos* to each of the sixteen choral subdivisions. Whatever the precise nature of these configurations may have been, the actual patterns of division were modelled on the patterns of division that make up the whole society, that is, the eight *phulai*. Such patterns of division in the setting up of the rival choral performances, where the notion of 'setting up' is expressed by the traditional combination of the verb *histēmi*, 'set up', plus the object of *khoros*, can be connected with the attested negative meanings of *stasis* as 'conflict'. This noun, *stasis*, derivative of *histēmi*, means not only 'setting up, establishment, standing, station, status' both in general applications (e.g., Herodotus 9.21.2; Euripides, *Bacchae* 925), and in more specific applications to the chorus (e.g., *Suda* s.v. *'khorodektēs'*) but also 'division, conflict, strife' in general applications to the community at large (Theognis 51, 781; Herodotus 3.82.3; etc.).

In sum, the ritual essence of the choral lyric performance is that it is constitutive of society in the very process of dividing it. For this reason, the concept of *stasis* is simultaneously constitution and division. The notion of constitution is the unmarked member of the opposition, in that it includes and integrates *division*, which is the marked member. Constitution is integration, and this unmarked–marked opposition can be rephrased in terms of unmarked integration and marked division.

The very constitution of society, as visualised in the traditions of a polis like Sparta, is choral performance. We have already seen that the name for 'civic space' in Sparta is in fact *Khoros* (Pausanias 3.11.5). Moreover, Spartan myth insists that Chorus had to precede Constitution: in Plutarch's *Life of Lycurgus* (4.2 – 3), we see that Lycurgus, the lawgiver of Sparta, who is the culture-hero credited with the institutional totality that is the Constitution of Sparta, brought his laws from Crete to Sparta only after he had already sent ahead the lyric poet Thales/Thaletas, whose songs had in them the qualities of *kosmos*, 'order', and *katastasis*, 'establishment'. It is this same Thaletas who figures in the so-called second *katastasis* of Spartan traditions in songmaking (*On Music* 1134b – c). The Spartan tradition stresses that the social effects of the lyric poet are like those of the most powerful *nomothetēs*, 'lawgiver' (*Lycurgus* 4.2). In this particular tradition, poet and lawgiver are differentiated as Thaletas and Lycurgus respectively. But in other traditions, the two roles are represented by one *persona*, as in the case of Theognis: he speaks not only as a choral lyric personality, singing and dancing to the lyre (Theognis 791) or singing to the lyre and reed (531–4), but as a lawgiver (Theognis 543–6, 805–10). In the case of a differentiated choral lyric personality like Thaletas, to repeat, his affinities with the constitution of his community are made explicit.

The key to choral performance, then, as we have seen primarily with the help of the description of an Aeginetan festival by Herodotus (5.83.3), is the public presentation, the *apodeixis*, of the *khorēgos*. With further help from such actual compositions as Alcman, fr. 1, we have also seen that the authority of the *khorēgos* is presented through the performance of the 'I' that is the chorus. It is from this authority that the authorship of the *khorēgos* emanates. And the presentation through the chorus is the representation that is mimesis. The 'I' of the choral ensemble is not just the collectivisation of persons who are singing and dancing at the ritual: it is also the impersonation of characters that belong to whatever myth is being represented in the ritual.

We have seen how, in compositions like Alcman, fr. 1, a differentiated *khorēgos* who is composer and who is off-stage, as it were, makes the collectivised 'I' of the chorus speak about another differentiated *khorēgos*, the alter ego of the composer, who is the mute virtuoso dancer and who is centre-stage, the focus of collectivised experience, either male or female. But there are other kinds of 'I' besides the collectivised 'I' of the chorus. Given that the *khorēgos* is the choral expression of the individual who momentarily stands out from among the collective, we have yet to see how the *persona* of the *khorēgos* itself would speak if it found a voice to go with the role of chorus-leader as a composer and performer on the model of Apollo as he simultaneously sings, dances, and plays the lyre. One way for such a voice to be present can be found in the 'I' of a *khorēgos* who engages in a dialogue with the rest of the chorus, as in Bacchylides 18, where the *khorēgos* represents Aigeus, the father of Theseus. Another way for the voice of the *khorēgos* to be activated can be found in the 'I' of a personality like Sappho, whose *persona* speaks as a *khorēgos* both to and about members of an aggregate of female characters who are bound together by ties that correspond to the ties that bind a chorus together. In such a reversed situation, the 'I' is not the group through whom the authority of the *khorēgos* finds a voice: rather, the 'I' who now speaks is the individual whom we have seen in another situation, at centre-stage, so to speak, as the mute virtuoso dancer. In that other kind of choral situation, as illustrated in Alcman, the 'I' is spoken by the aggregate while the 'I' of the *khorēgos* as individual and as composer is mute. But as soon as the 'I' of the *khorēgos* as individual starts singing, as it were, this same figure stops dancing and, even more, the aggregate stops both singing and dancing. This figurative and diachronic scheme of reassigned parts is the essence of what we have been calling 'monody'. It should be clear from what precedes, then, that the monodic form is not antithetical to the choral but rather derived from it. A figure like Sappho speaks as a choral personality, even though the elements of dancing and even the very presence of a choral group are evidently missing from her compositions. Still, these compositions presuppose or represent an interaction, off-stage, as it were, with a choral aggregate.

As for the corpus of Stesichorus, it may be considered a monodic mimesis of choral performance. True, even the name *Stēsikhoros*, 'he who sets up the chorus', projects a choral personality. Still, the compositions that are credited to this figure are of such enormous dimensions that they seem to defy any sustained singing and dancing by a choral aggregate. For example, we learn from *Oxyrhynchus Papyrus* 2617 that the *Geryoneis* of Stesichorus contained at least 1,300 verses. The repertoire of Stesichorus, as also most of the repertoire attributed to Ibycus, Sappho, Alcaeus, and Anacreon, finds expression in the monodic medium of *kitharōidia*, 'lyre-singing'. Alternatively, the monodic medium is *aulōidia*, 'reed-singing'. Just as the proto-composer of a choral performance can be impersonated by the chorus-leader, so also the proto-composer in non-choral lyric is impersonated by a contemporary performer such as the *kitharōidos*.

The varieties of mimesis in monody correspond to what we have already seen in the choral form. To begin, the monodic form can have the performer impersonate individual figures *other* than the composer or proto-composer. A clear example is the first-person feminine in Alcaeus (fr. 10 Voigt). As for cases of direct self-presentation, there are particularly arresting examples in Sappho and Alcaeus. Alternatively, self-presentation in the form of first-person interaction and narrative can step back stage, as it were, while the self simply tells a third-person narrative, as in numerous examples from Stesichorus. Moreover, the lyric poetry or song of monody is not far removed from the ultimately differentiated forms of poetry, as in the compositions attributed to Archilochus or Theognis. Here singing is replaced by stylised speaking, but the choral personalities persist. We may note again that the characterisation of a *khorēgos*, 'chorus-leader', which persists even in poetry, fits the pattern of ritual substitution. Just as the chorus-leader in the song of choral performance enters a force-field of antagonism with the divinity who is being represented in choral performance, so also the figure of the author in poetry, as in the case of Archilochus, is ultimately locked into a force-field of antagonism with the god Apollo himself.

There are traces even in Homer and Hesiod of choral personalities. The very name of 'Hesiod', 'he who emits the voice', corresponds to the characterisation of the muses as *ossan hieisai*, 'emitting the voice' (*Theogony* 10, 43, 65, 67), which applies to them in a choral context (7–8, 63). So also

the name of Homer, *Hom-ēros*, 'he who fits the song together', corresponds
to the characterisation of the muses as *arti-epeiai*, 'having words [*epea*] fitted
together' (*Theogony* 29) and *phōnēi homēreusai*, 'fitting [the song] together with
their voice' (*Theogony* 39), again in the same choral context. Also, we may
consider the quasi-choral performance of Demodokos in *Odyssey* VIII. Or
again, the contest won by the figure of Hesiod at the Funeral Games of
Amphidamas, described in Hesiod, *Works and Days* (654–8), is presented as
if it were a choral competition. The performance with which Hesiod won
is actually called a *humnos* (*Works and Days* 655). Alternatively, the self-
characterisation of the poet in Homer and Hesiod can suit the more differentiated figure of the 'lyre-singer', appropriate to the differentiated format of
poetry. Such is the description of generic poets in Hesiod, *Theogony* 94–5.
Another example is the image of Hesiod as holding a lyre, as attested by a
statue seen by Pausanias at Helicon (9.30.3).

Before we leave the topic of solo singers or poets who speak as choral
personalities even though their *persona* has become detached from the chorus,
let us consider a remarkable case where the solo singer is represented as
potentially becoming attached to a chorus as their *khorēgos*, only to stay
detached in the end. In the Homeric *Hymn to Apollo* (149–78), there is a
description of a festival on the island of Delos where contests in choral
performance take place. In this context, the figure of Homer describes a choral
ensemble known as the Deliades, who can *mimeisthai*, 'make a mimesis', of
anyone who comes to the festival where they perform. By implication, they
could make a mimesis of Homer as well. That is, they could be the speakers,
the 'I' of the performance, with Homer as their *khorēgos* and speaking through
their identity. They would be like the girls in Alcman, through whom Alcman
speaks when they sing his words in choral ensemble. More fundamentally,
they would be like the muses, through whom Apollo speaks when they sing
the words of choral performance. But the figure of Homer indirectly declines
the occasion, bidding the Deliades farewell in the same way that the performer
of a prelude bids farewell to the god who is the subject and occasion of the
prelude, so that he may go on to the rest of the performance. He promises
to sing about them as he proceeds on his way to give performances throughout
the various cities of the Hellenic world. Instead of staying in Delos as a choral
personality who finds expression through the local quasi-muses, the Deliades,
he will be a pan-Hellenic personality whose 'I' speaks for itself, and it will
be through him that the pan-Hellenic muse of the *Iliad* and *Odyssey* finds her
own self-expression.

Although the 'I' of Homer is not taken over by the Deliades, it is their voice
that is quoted in the glorification of Homer: asking the Deliades to keep him
in mind even as he moves on (166–7), the figure of Homer instructs them
about what to say to anyone who comes to Delos and should ask a question
about the *aoidoi* who have come to the island, 'which one has delighted you the

most?' What the Deliades should 'answer' in this hypothetical dialogue is expressed as a direct quotation of what they would indeed say: he is a blind man, from Chios, whose songs will win universal approval in the future (172–3). And the word here for 'answer' is *hupokrinomai*, from which is derived the agent-noun *hupokritēs*, 'actor'. In this way, the Deliades are true to their choral function of serving as speakers, mouthpieces, as it were, of the composer, even though the composer declines, in this case, to stay as their chorus-teacher.

Similarly with the figure of Hesiod: it is through him that the pan-Hellenic Olympian Muses find expression, transforming themselves from the local Heliconian Muses that they had once been at the beginning of the *Theogony*. It is through the encounter of Hesiod with the Heliconian Muses that he gets his power to speak *alēthea*, 'true things', that is, to speak with a pan-Hellenic authority that reciprocally transforms the Heliconian into the Olympian Muses. Similarly, it may be that it is through the encounter of Homer with the Deliades, who can represent anyone who comes to Delos, that Homer gets his own pan-Hellenic authority. The centripetal model of the Deliades, who assimilate all the different languages that come their way from all the Hellenes converging at their festival at Delos, is the foundation for the centrifugal model of Homer, who leaves the island to spread their fame, their *kleos*. The *kleos* of the Deliades is not only what Homer sings about them but also, reciprocally, what they themselves say through Homer about Homer, which turns into the *kleos* of Homer. And their repertoire is that of all the Hellenes, who have come to Delos and who have all been represented by these all-versatile muses.

Let us return to our basic observations about the chorus as a formal expression of the simultaneity of hierarchy and egalitarianism in the polis. As we have seen, it is implicit that the chorus-leader is diachronically a combination of composer and leading performer, while the rest of the *khoreutai*, 'chorus-members', are performers. The key to choral performance, as we have also seen, is the public presentation, the *apodeixis*, of the *khorēgos*. The authority of the *khorēgos* is presented through the performance of the 'I' that is the chorus, and it is from this authority that his authorship emanates. The presentation through the chorus is the representation that is mimesis. The 'I' of the choral ensemble is not just the collectivisation of persons who are singing and dancing at the ritual: it is also the impersonation of characters that belong to whatever myth is being represented in the ritual. We have seen in Alcman how a differentiated *khorēgos* who is composer and who is off-stage, as it were, makes the collectivised 'I' of the chorus speak about another differentiated *khorēgos*, the alter ego of the composer, who is the mute virtuoso dancer and who is centre-stage, the focus of collectivised experience, either male or female.

Moving forwards in time, we come to another complex pattern of choral tradition, where the *khorēgos* as proto-composer/performer remains a contemporary composer: he is a professional whose compositions are occasional, ostensibly performed by a chorus consisting of contemporary non-professionals. Here again it is the chorus as a group that serves as the impersonator, the actor, of the *khorēgos*. Such is the case with the epinician or victory odes of Pindar, commissioned as choral compositions or perform-ances that celebrate the victories of athletes in pan-Hellenic games, notably, the Olympian, the Pythian, the Nemean, and the Isthmian Games. In this case, as in the other examples that we have seen before, the composer is no longer necessarily a performer, although his *persona* keeps speaking of himself as not only a composer but also a group of performers, maintaining the impersonation of his choral functions as *khorēgos*. In this way, the 'I' of Pindar speaks in a diachronic mode that reflects in content the evolution of the *khorēgos* from 'proto-composer/performer' into a differentiated contem-porary composer. In Pindaric as in other choral poetry, it is the chorus who performs the 'I', but this 'I' can at will refer to the composer. For example, since the chorus at any given epinician occasion consists of local polis-dwellers, the references in Pindaric poetry to an 'I' who comes to the polis from afar must be the mark of the poet.[86] Moreover, there are six Pindaric compositions addressed to non-Thebans that bear clear 'signatures' of Thebes as the poet's native polis,[87] just as Bacchylides of Keos is surely referring to himself in attributing one of his choral compositions to 'the nightingale from Keos' (Bacchylides 3.96).

In Pindaric poetry, as a choral medium, it is not only the references to the 'I' of the occasion that reveal the control of the figure who is diachronically the *khorēgos* and synchronically the poet. Even the references to the occasion itself reveal that control, in that they are all orchestrated to convey the 'absolute present' of the performance. At the end of Pindar's *Nemean* 2 there is a self-reference to the prelude that is supposedly getting under way at the poem's beginning. This kind of time-warp absolutises the occasion, as also in general the numerous conventional futures and imperatives in Pindaric diction, the purpose of which is 'to collapse into themselves the whole tem-poral sequence of the epinician occasion'.[88]

Having come to the end of this rapid survey of various different patterns in the development of traditions in the composition and performance of song, it is time to recapitulate. These different patterns reveal different models for the distinction or potential distinction of performer and poet. By now we may note not only the model of the *rhapsōidoi* in the realm of poetry but also the various different models of *kitharōidoi*, *aulōidoi*, *tragōidoi*, and *kōmōidoi* in the realm of song. In all these models, the common point of departure is that the *persona* of the composer can be re-enacted by the performer or performers.

---

[86] Mullen, *Choreia*, p. 28, who cites Pindar, *Olympian* 7.13–14; *Pythian* 2.3–4; *Isthmian* 5.21–22 and 6.20–21.

[87] Mullen, *Choreia*, p. 28, citing Pindar, *Olympian* 6.84–86, 10.85; *Pythian* 2.3–4, 4.299; *Isthmian* 6.74–6, 8.16.

[88] Mullen, *Choreia*, p. 27.

In other words, the performer may impersonate the composer as well as the characters represented as speaking within the composition. The word for such re-enactment or impersonation, to repeat, is *mimēsis*.

11 Iambic and comic poets as critics

In the *Poetics* (1449a9ff.) Aristotle says that both tragedy and comedy had a beginning that is 'improvisational' and that tragedy was derived from the *exarkhontes*, 'choral leaders' of the *dithurambos*. Aristotle seems to have had a passage of Archilochus in mind.[89] In Archilochus (fr. 120 West) the *persona* of the composer declares that he knows how to be the *exarkhōn* of the dithyramb, while his mind is thunderstruck with wine. The metre of this passage is trochaic tetrameter catalectic, and Aristotle says explicitly that the metre of dialogue in early tragedy, before it was replaced by iambic trimeter, was trochaic tetrameter catalectic (*Po.* 1449a22ff.). In short, what Aristotle claims about the evolution of comedy and tragedy implies that he thought that Archilochus was a typical 'choral leader' of dithyramb. Moreover, the claims of Aristotle imply that he considered Archilochus an exponent of primitive blame poetry (*Po.* 1449a and 1448b23). It is important to stress, however, that the 'blaming' side of Archilochus was part of this poet's overall function as a socially redeeming exponent of song and poetry, one who blames what is ostensibly bad while he praises what is good. This socially redeeming value, as we shall now see, is a traditional civic function, viewed as integrating the community.

From the testimony of the Mnesiepes Inscription[90] we learn of a traditional myth, native to the island of Paros, that represented Archilochus as a chorus-teacher of his community. This myth, preserved in the context of his hero-cult in Paros, dramatises the social function of Archilochean poetry in the civic life of the polis. In the wording of the inscription we are witnessing a cognate of the source of Aristotle (*Po.* 1449a and 1448b23), claiming Archilochus as an exponent of primitive blame poetry. According to the story Archilochus improvises a composition, which he teaches to some of the citizens of Paros. From the standpoint of the narrative, Archilochus seems to be represented here as a 'chorus-teacher'. The Mnesiepes Inscription then proceeds to quote the words of the composition; the text is fragmentary, but we can see clearly that Dionysus figures prominently in the context of the epithet *Oipholios*, a derivative of the obscene verb *oiphō*, 'have intercourse (male subject)'. The polis finds this composition 'too iambic'. Archilochus is put on trial and apparently condemned. But then the polis is afflicted with a plague that affects the genitalia. Emissaries of the polis consult Delphi, and the Oracle

---

[89] Else, *Aristotle*, pp. 157–8.
[90] Tarditi, *Archilochus*, pp. 4–7.

tells them that the plague will not abate until the polis honours Archilochus. The connection here of Archilochus with Dionysus and the notion of *Oipholios* institutionalises the 'iambic' composition of Archilochus. The inscription offers testimony concerning the practice of worshipping various gods, along with the cult-hero Archilochus, in the sacred precinct of Archilochus, the *Arkhilokheion*: among the gods listed, Dionysus is accorded a position of particular prominence.

The narrative pattern of the story of Archilochus and the punishment of the Parians is typical of aetiologies concerning the founding of a hero-cult: (1) some hero is dishonoured, sometimes even killed, by a community; (2) the community is then beset by some plague; (3) the Oracle is consulted, who prescribes the hero-cult of the given hero as the remedy.[91] In such aetiologies, the well-being of the community, as threatened by the plague, is visualised as fertility of crops and inhabitants alike – a fertility which is then restored and guaranteed to continue through the proper maintenance of the hero-cult. In the Archilochus story as well, the fertility of the polis is connected, in general, with the hero-cult of Archilochus, which is after all the context for the telling of the story, and, in particular, with the institutionalisation of Archilochus as 'chorus-leader'. Here we have the nucleus of the civic function of Archilochean poetry, in that the chorus is the traditional medium for the self-expression of the polis.

The theme of fertility is explicit in the story of Archilochus in his stylised role as chorus-teacher, which is connected, as we have seen, with the cult of Dionysus. The same theme of fertility is implicit in the connection of Archilochus with the cult of Demeter, in his stylised role as a participant in the *panēguris*, 'festival', of the goddess and her daughter, Kore (fr. 322 West). The given festival is that of the *Iobakkhoi*, and the very name expresses the complementarity, in terms of the festival itself, of Demeter with Bacchus, that is, Dionysus.[92] Moreover, the fertility of the polis is connected with the 'iambic' nature of what Archilochus teaches to the community. According to Aristotle (*Po.* 1449b8), the notion of 'iambic' is inherited by the synthetic genre of Athenian comedy.

The 'iambic' nature of comedy, and Aristotle's claims about the evolution of tragedy from the medium of *exarkhontes*, 'chorus-leaders', ostensibly like Archilochus, whose message was too 'iambic' for the people of his own time, reinforce the general notion that comedy and tragedy were once undifferentiated, becoming distinct in the specific context of the City Dionysia at Athens. Which brings us to the *aition* that motivates the City Dionysia, closely parallel to the *aition* that motivates Archilochean poetry. According to Athenian tradition, the Feast of the City Dionysia was instituted in honour of Dionysus

---

[91] Nagy, *Best of the Achaeans*, p. 285.
[92] Hephaestion, *Encheiridion* 15.16; see Archilochus, fr. 322 West.

Eleutherius, whose image had been brought over from Eleutherai in Boeotia to the theatre precinct of Athens; there the god was not given his due honours, and the men of Athens were accordingly punished with some sexual affliction, from which they were freed only on the condition that they make ritual *phalloi* for Dionysus.[93] The undifferentiated tradition represented by the complex of dramatic contests as the City Dionysia, like the Archilochean 'iambic' tradition, has a symbiotic relationship with the entire cult of Dionysus.

This general notion of 'iambic', with its emphasis on fertility, is analogous to the concept of 'carnival' as applied by M. M. Bakhtin to the traditions inherited by François Rabelais in the sixteenth century. In the generations that followed the time of Rabelais, that is, in the pre-classic times of the seventeenth century preceding the reign of Louis XIV, 'Rabelais did not as yet appear exceptional'.[94] Soon thereafter, however, 'the atmosphere in which Rabelais was understood vanished almost entirely, and he became a strange and solitary author who needed special interpretation and commentary'. A similar judgement looms over both Archilochus and Aristophanes.

To an author like La Bruyère, writing in 1690, Rabelais is to be condemned for his crude obscenity and vulgarity, though he is to be praised for his exquisite genius and originality in the use of language; Bakhtin comments that La Bruyère sees the work of Rabelais as 'two-faced' because 'he has lost the key that could have locked together its two heterogeneous aspects'.[95] That key, in Bakhtin's terms, is carnival. Without insisting on the term, which lends itself to overextended use, we see here a striking analogy with the figure of Archilochus and the institution of Old Comedy as represented by Aristophanes.

For Bakhtin, 'carnival' is a synthetic description that accommodates a wide range of actually attested European carnivals, as celebrated, on a seasonally recurring basis, at various times of the year at various places. The synthetic description is particularly apt in view of the synthetic nature of carnivals: 'This word combined in a single concept a number of local feasts of different origin and scheduled at different dates but bearing the common traits of popular merriment.'[96] It is not inaccurate to say that the very concept of carnival is a synthesis: 'These celebrations became a reservoir into which obsolete genres were emptied.' For Bakhtin, carnival is not a safety-valve that helps prevent revolution, as was held to be political dogma at the time that his work on Rabelais was taking shape; rather, carnival is revolution itself. Its target is whatever happens to be current, the here-and-now, the differentiated, and it will profess nostalgia for the past, the Golden Age, the undifferentiated.

[93] Scholia to Aristophanes, *Acharnians* 243.
[94] M. M. Bakhtin, *Rabelais and his World*, tr. H. Iswolsky (Bloomington, Indiana, 1984), p. 107.
[95] Bakhtin, *Rabelais*, p. 108.
[96] Bakhtin, *Rabelais*, p. 218.

The very themes of carnival recapitulate the undifferentiated structures of the past, temporarily overthrowing the differentiated structures of the present.[97] The feast of Saturnalia yearns for the *ancien régime* of Saturn and resists whatever régime is current. Bakhtin argues that carnival attacks the differentiated present by recapitulating the undifferentiated past, with an emphasis on the grotesque, thus celebrating the renewal of fertility. Similarly with the tradition common to Archilochus and Old Comedy: it will attack whatever happens to be current, the here-and-now, while all along celebrating the theme of fertility.

In the case of Archilochus, the 'iambic' function is manifested in his dramatised alienation from his own here-and-now. This fact of alienation can be accepted, as part of the undifferentiated past, by the community that embraces Archilochus as the present guarantor of its fertility. In the case of comedy, especially the Old Comedy of Aristophanes, there is an analogous stance of dramatised alienation from everything that happens to be current. And that includes the conventions in the craft of poetry as it was current in the time of Aristophanes.

The criticism of current poetry in Aristophanes operates on a solid foundation: a thorough education in the classics of poetry is presupposed, as we can see from the parodic references to such canonical masters as Archilochus (*Birds* 967–88), Alcman (*Lysistrata* 1248–320), Stesichorus (*Peace* 796–816), and Anacreon (*Birds* 1373–4). But the critical area for criticising what is current in terms of the classical is the theatre itself, the medium *par excellence* for the composition and performance of poetry in the time of Aristophanes. The theatre, as it developed within the City Dionysia, had absorbed the repertoire of epic, as we can readily see from such individual tragedies as the *Seven Against Thebes* of Aeschylus and, more generally, from the overwhelmingly epic themes of most of the tragedies composed by Aeschylus and others who followed in his wake.[98] As with epic, so also with lyric: the evolving predominance of Athenian theatre as the primary poetic medium played a major role in the obsolescence of lyric poetry in other media and, by extension, in other genres. From Plato's writings, we hear of complaints about *theatrokratia*, 'the dominance of the theatre' (*Laws* 710a) and about the intoxication of pleasure in the poetry of the theatre (*Laws* 700d), leading to 'transgressions' of genre (*paranomia*, *Laws* 700e). To be contrasted are the good old days, as in the earlier era that followed the Persian Wars (*Laws* 698b), when there were still distinct *eidē*, 'types', and *skhēmata*, 'figures' of song (*Laws* 700a), five of which are specified as examples: 'hymn', 'lament', 'paean', 'dithyramb', and 'citharodic nome' (*Laws* 700b). These genres, as well as other genres left unspecified, are the structurally distinct aspects of

[97] Bakhtin, *Rabelais*, pp. 334–6.
[98] Herington, *Poetry into Drama*, pp. 138–44.

mousikē (that is, for all practical purposes, lyric poetry), parallel to the structurally distinct aspects of *aristokratia* in Plato's good old Athenian society (*Laws* 701a). By contrast, the progressive levelling by Athenian theatre of generic distinctions in lyric poetry is for Plato parallel to the levelling by Athenian democracy of class distinctions in society.[99] An infusion of lyric genres into theatre, and their concomitant atrophy elsewhere, is seen by Plato as an illegitimate mixing of genres (*Laws* 700d), a degeneration into a superseding genre of lyric traditions in Athenian drama. By contrast, Athenian drama is seen by Aristotle not as the product of degeneration but rather as a teleological organic development in the evolution of poetic traditions (*Po.* 1449a14–15). From either point of view, in any case, the lyric poetry of Athenian theatre is the final productive phase of a medium that had otherwise become unproductive, and canonical, already by the second half of the fifth century.

Given that the Theatre of Dionysus at Athens is the predominant context of poetry as current poetry, it follows that contemporary comedy will single out the current poetics of theatre as the main target of its criticism of poetry. Specifically, the current comedy of theatre attacks the poetics of current tragedy. One of the clearest examples is in the great *agōn*, 'contest', between Aeschylus and Euripides in Hades, as dramatised by Aristophanes in the *Frogs* (905–1098), first performed in 405 BC. That tragedy is the craft of poetry *par excellence* is the one given that is held in respect by both sides in the contest. What is at issue is the superiority or inferiority of the old and current ways of practicing that craft, as represented by Aeschylus and Euripides respectively:

The two great professionals are made to discuss the correct proportion of song to dialogue, and the character of that dialogue (905–91); then the moral impact of tragedy and poetry (1003–98: the two arts are not distinguished, at least by Aeschylus, who invokes the precedents of Homer, Hesiod, and other early epic composers); iambic prologues, together with the questions of clarity in diction (1119–99) and of the avoidance of metrical/syntactical monotony (1200–47); choral lyric technique (1248–329); solo lyric technique (1329–64); and weight of diction (1365–414).[100]

Needless to say, the old-fashioned Aeschylus wins over the innovative Euripides in the judgement of the god Dionysus himself (1467ff.), who is after all the *raison d'être* of the City Dionysia. Still, even the older features of the craft, perceived by comedy as old-fashioned, reveal earlier stages of poetic innovation in the theatre. The stage-Aeschylus may be ridiculed by the stage-Euripides for his old-fashioned and monotonous lyric rhythms, as parodied by the lyre-strumming onomatopoeia *tophlattothrat tophlattothrat* (*Frogs* 1286, 1288, 1290, 1292, 1294), and yet the very form of these rhythms, from an

---

[99] Svenbro, 'Découpe du poème', p. 225.
[100] Herington, *Poetry into Drama*, p. 106.

earlier perspective, represents an innovative appropriation, by the poetics of theatre, of the distinct genre of the 'citharodic nome'. The stage-Euripides himself says that these old-fashioned Aeschylean rhythms are taken from 'citharodic nomes' (*Frogs* 1282). It is precisely the appropriation and hence domination of such genres by the poetics of theatre that led Plato to condemn innovations as a degeneration of genres. Thus the Aeschylean use of the *kitharōidikos nomos* may be old-fashioned synchronically; but it is an innovation diachronically. It represents an earlier stage of the same sort of innovations practised by Euripides, who is accused by the stage-Aeschylus of freely appropriating to drama such non-dramatic forms as *skolia* and *thrēnoi* (*Frogs* 1301–3).

In short, the fundamental reason for the loss of Euripides to Aeschylus in the *Frogs*, and in general for his being singled out as a special target for the comedy of Aristophanes, is that his poetics are *current*. The definitive statement on what is current in the poetics of tragedy is treated as a foil by the poetics of comedy. That it is Aeschylus who wins the contest in the *Frogs*, thus winning the chance to be brought back to the contemporary world of the living by the god of theatre himself, is the wish-fulfilment of a nostalgia for the undifferentiated Dionysiac essence of Drama.

The contest of Aeschylus and Euripides in *Frogs* takes the form, to repeat, of an *agōn*, and this word is actually used in self-references at lines 785, 867, 873, and 882. The very format of the *agōn* is indicative of an undifferentiated phase of drama as it must have existed before the differentiation of the City Dionysia. It has been argued that the functional part of comedy known as the *agōn* resulted from an undifferentiated choral *agōn* consisting of two antagonistic *antikhoria*, 'each combining the aggressive entrance of the parodos with the primitive features of the parabasis: self-presentation and self-praise, invocation and invective, "literary" polemics'.[101] Ironically, however, the notion of *agōn* as 'contest' is the basis for the ongoing differentiation of poetics in the theatre. The *agōn* of a poetic contest requires a judgement, the word for which is *krisis*, and the two words actually occur together at *Frogs* 785.

At the very beginning, we observed that the Alexandrian concept of *krisis*, in the sense of 'separating', 'discriminating', 'judging' those works and those authors that are to be preserved and those that are not, is crucial to the concept of 'canon' in the Classical world. The Alexandrian scholars who were in charge of this process of separation, discrimination, judgement, were the *kritikoi*, 'critics', while the Classical authors who were meant to survive the *krisis* were called the *enkrithentes*. We also observed that the *krisis* of the *enkrithentes* starts not with the Alexandrian scholars, nor even with the likes of Aristotle: that the 'crisis' of this *krisis* is already under way in the Archaic and Classical periods of Greece, where songs and poetry were traditionally

[101] Seaford, '*Hyporchēma*', p. 86.

performed in a context of competition. What we see in the *agōn* of the *Frogs* of Aristophanes is a dramatisation of that competition between drama and drama, and this time the competition is happening *within* drama. This way, the ontogeny of drama is recapitulating its own phylogeny as a competitive medium, an *agōn* calling for the *krisis* of selection.

12 *Poetry as education*

In Aristophanes (*Clouds* 1353–8), the old-fashioned Strepsiades complains about his son Pheidippides, the product of modernist trends that have eroded the traditions of old-fashioned liberal education in the 'Classics'. On the occasion of a symposium, Pheidippides refuses a request to take up the lyre and sing a famous lyric composition by Simonides. The composition was an epinician, that is, a victory ode, akin to the choral medium of Pindar. Moreover, Pheidippides ridicules the singing of Simonides' lyric poetry as something passé. It is clear that Pheidippides is not well-versed in the art form of this kind of performance. Then he is asked at least to perform something from the compositions of Aeschylus, while holding a branch of myrtle (*Clouds* 1365). Of course it is not the lyre but the *aulos*, 'reed', that serves as the medium of accompaniment for the lyric compositions of Attic Drama. Singing to the lyre implies potential self-accompaniment, whereas singing to the *aulos* does not. Thus there is a lower degree of education required for performing in the chorus of an Aeschylean tragedy or for reperforming at a symposium selections from the choral songs of such a tragedy. Even this kind of performance is refused by Pheidippides, who elects to recite a passage from a speech in Euripides (*Clouds* 1371). The word *rhēsis*, 'speech', makes it clear that the modern Pheidippides opts for a medium that is devoid of the lyric element.[102] The formulation of Plato (*Laws* 802c–d) is apt: 'For when someone passes his life from childhood up to the age of steadiness and sense among temperate and ordered music, then when he hears the opposite kind he detests it, and calls it unfit for free men [i.e., not liberal education]: but if he was brought up amid the sweet music that is generally popular, he says that the opposite kind to this is frigid and unpleasing.'

The inability of Pheidippides to perform a lyric composition by Simonides, a master of the choral medium and a contemporary rival of Pindar, is bad enough: but even worse is his refusal to perform a lyric composition by Aeschylus, which does not even require self-accompaniment to the lyre and which is part of the civic heritage of Athens. In the *Frogs* of Aristophanes, the victorious Aeschylus, as he is returning to contemporary Athens after having defeated Euripides in the judgement of Dionysus himself, is called upon to save the polis and 'educate' his ignorant contemporary audiences (1502).

---

[102] Reitzenstein, *Epigramm und Skolion*, pp. 32–9.

Clearly, the contemporary youth of Aristophanes' time is deemed impervious to the choral education, the civic formation, provided by the traditions of Archaic lyric. Long gone are the Archaic days of old-fashioned Athenian *paideia*, the kind that purportedly produced the men who fought at the Battle of Marathon (*Clouds* 961), when boys learned selected compositions of old lyric masters in the house of the *kitharistēs*, 'master of the *kithara*' (964), who taught them to learn by heart (966) the performance of famous lyric compositions (967), and who insisted on their adherence to performing these compositions in the proper *harmonia*, 'mode', that had been 'inherited from their forefathers' (968; cf. 969–72).

The last securely-datable poem of Pindar, *Pythian* 8, was composed for performance in 446 BC (for Bacchylides, the last datable compositions are *Odes* 6 and 7, performed in 452 BC). With this date of 446, we have an imprecise but revealing terminus in the history of Archaic Greek poetry. What this terminus reveals is the fact that the canon of lyric poetry excludes poets who flourished in the second half of the fifth century or thereafter. This fact is perhaps the single most telling point in favour of the argument already advanced to the effect that the canon of lyric poetry results from patterns of pan-Hellenisation in oral traditions of song. Although there is ample evidence for the existence of poets who composed song in the second half of the fifth century and thereafter, there is also evidence that their song was a medium that had evolved beyond the lyric poetry represented by Pindar and the other canonical lyric poets.

It has been argued that the later lyric forms, predominantly nome and dithyramb, were non-stanzaic and thus not regarded by Alexandrian critics as in the same genre as melic poetry.[103] A different reason for the exclusion of these poets in the canon of the Alexandrians may be that the likes of Timotheus and Philoxenus, unlike the earlier masters of lyric, were already being excluded from the canon of traditional Athenian education in the 'classics', mainly on the grounds that the innovative virtuosity characteristic of such poets, and of the new genres that they represented, tended to restrict their *oeuvre* to performance by professionals and to defy the traditions of 'liberal education' for non-professionals, that is, for the future citizens of the polis. Any eventual patterns of exclusion in fifth-century Athens, however, need not have affected the adoption of these poets as 'Classics' at a later time, in the context of revivals of 'old masters'. For example, there is the report of Polybius (4.20.8) concerning the choral education in the second century of Arcadian youths who were being brought up on the compositions of Timotheus of Miletus and Philoxenus of Cythera: for these Arcadians, at least, these poets represent the 'Classics'. The phenomenon of shifting perceptions, where a given style is perceived as 'modernistic' by one generation and 'classical' by another, is illustrated by the attitudes dramatised in Plato (*Laws* 803c – d). As for Plato himself, when he rejects the modernisms of Timotheus and the like, he is rejecting trends that were by then some eighty or more years old. Plato's tastes are a matter of nostalgic retrojection into the Classical period. Such prescriptions as three years of liberal education, starting with the age of thirteen, in the art of the lyre (*Laws* 810a), are surely a mere exercise in idealisation from the standpoint of Plato's own era. In the fourth century, even in Athens, the rapidly increasing specialisation of music had increasingly restricted it to the professionals, as we see from the revealing discussion in Aristotle's *Politics* (1341a9 – 36; 1341b8 – 18). The specialisation is even more pronounced in a place like Sparta (*Politics* 1339b1 – 4).

With regard to the crucial era of the second half of the fifth century and thereafter, alongside the emergence of new media of song as represented by the 'new' *nomos* and *dithurambos*, there is a concurrent obsolescence of the old media of song as represented by lyric poetry proper. In fact, the traditions of composition in lyric poetry, as once practised by Pindar, seem to be becoming extinct in this era of the 'new' nome and the 'new' dithyramb. Such a trend of extinction is most evident from the standpoint of traditions in performance. For example, in Eupolis (fr. 366 Kock) the complaint is made that the songs of Pindar have for some time been covered over in silence, ignored by the audiences of the day (Eupolis was a contemporary of Aristophanes). In another fragment of Eupolis (139 Kock) we see a parallel theme: the speaker is complaining that the songs of Stesichorus, Alcman, and Simonides are considered out of date by contemporary audiences, who prefer the 'modern' poets.

There is still, however, an important 'last stand' of old-fashioned lyric poetry in the second half of the fifth century and thereafter, and it is to be found in the choral traditions of Athenian tragedy and comedy. The poets of Old Comedy, as we have just seen, even ridicule the new poetry that purports to displace the old poetry. Of course, on another level, Old Comedy could also ridicule the old poetry of lyric traditions, as in the parody of Pindar in Aristophanes, *Birds* (926 – 30; 941 – 5) (note too the adjacent reference to Simonides in *Birds* 917 – 19). But the point remains that the old traditions of lyric are obsolescent, and in fact the *Birds*, presented in 414 BC, is the last attested comedy of Aristophanes that mentions or parodies the poetry of Pindar. The only other Aristophanic references to a Pindaric composition where we know the identity of the intended audience is in *Acharnians* (637 – 9) and in *Knights* (1329 – 33), both referring to a passage from a famous *dithurambos* composed expressly for the glorification of Athens. It is noteworthy that these Aristophanic references to recognisably Pindaric passages, one the *huporkhēma* for Hieron and the other the *dithurambos* for the Athenians, both focus on the beginning of a Pindaric composition. It seems that the allusion is being made to the most famous parts of famous compositions. Besides these two cases, there seems to be only one more where we can be reasonably certain that the reference is to a well-known passage of Pindar: *Knights* 1264–6, alluding to a *prosodion*, 'processional song' (fr. 89a Snell-Maehler). It has been observed that these three Aristophanic references to three passages that were apparently familiar to an Athenian audience can give us an indication of the kind of repertoire that was being taught to young Athenians in the years roughly between 450 and 420 BC.[104] This repertoire is decidedly limited in scope, which converges with what we have observed about the canon of nine 'classics' of lyric poetry.

Plato's portrait of nostalgia for those earlier days when lyric poetry had not yet been absorbed and ultimately usurped by Athenian theatre brings us back to the era of Pindar, last in the canon of lyric poets. Let us consider the genres in which Pindar composed. It is best to begin with the inventory of an Alexandrian edition of Pindar as reported in the *Vita Ambrosiana*, according to which Pindar's poetry is subdivided into seventeen books corresponding to specific genres of his poetry. We are struck by the fact that, of the distinct genres of lyric poetry mentioned in Plato's partial list, namely the *humnos*, the *thrēnos*, the *paian*, the *dithurambos*, and the citharodic *nomos* (*Laws* 700b), all but the last one are also represented in the *Vita Ambrosiana* inventory of Pindar's poems.

The inventory of seventeen books attributed to Pindar contains ten distinct genres (an asterisk marks those genres that correspond to Plato's list): (*1) hymns; (*2) paeans; (*3–4) dithyrambs; (5–6) *prosodia*; (7–9) *parthenia* (maiden songs); (10–11) *huporkhēmata*; (12) encomia; (*13) laments; (14–17) epinician odes. It is difficult to be certain whether or not such an editorial organisation of Pindar's poems goes back further in time than the Alexandrian era – back to the time of Plato, for example. But we do know for certain that Plato was familiar enough with Pindar's poems to refer to them at least sixteen times in the attested Platonic corpus.

It remains to ask exactly how these references came about. One readily available explanation, of course, is that Plato was citing from a hypothetical edition of Pindar that was circulating in Athens.[105] Most likely such an edition would have been a school text going back to an earlier time when youths had still been well-educated in the actual performance of old-fashioned lyric compositions. In Plato's time, however, it was becoming less and less likely that performers of *kitharōidia* or *aulōidia*, especially the amateurs, could still have had in their repertoires selections from Pindar and other grand masters of lyric poetry. A musicologist summarises the situation thus:

[104] Irigoin, *Pindare*, p. 14.
[105] Irigoin, *Pindare*, pp. 19–20.

The classic Athenian comedy had been made for a society which talked music as it talked politics or war. But in Aristophanes' post-war plays, a shrunken chorus gives us only a last flash or two of his musical parody; and his successors substituted *entr'actes* by variety artists. The Alexandrian era still has excellent stage gossip on performers, but a first-hand judgement on the style or quality of music is hardly to be found after the fourth century. Aristotle already prefers received opinions. His master Plato and his pupil Aristoxenus are the last who speak to us with the authority of musical understanding.[106]

Here we return once again to the problem of the Classics. The very evolution of what we know as the Classics – both a concept and a reality – was but an extension of the organic pan-Hellenisation of oral traditions. In other words, the evolution of ancient Greek canons in both song and poetry need not be attributed primarily to the factor of writing. Granted, writing would have been essential for the ultimate preservation of these canons once the traditions of performance were becoming obsolete. Still, it is important to recall the observation, made earlier, that the key to the actual evolution of canons must be sought in the social context of performance itself.

It can be argued that the performance-traditions of the Classics, as an extension of the pan-Hellenisation of oral traditions in poetry and song, were preserved in the social context of what the Greeks called *paideia*, 'education'. For illustration, we shall examine two passages in particular, one from the *Clouds* of Aristophanes and another from the *Protagoras* of Plato. Before we proceed, however, it is essential to note the direction of evolution in both the composition and the performance of the Classics. We can posit an earlier stage of old oral traditions of composition-in-performance, which would have to survive from one generation to the next through performance. Then comes a later stage, where the traditions of composition-in-performance were breaking down, and the need for sample performances as models was becoming ever more pressing. Thus education would in time become transformed: from the activity of learning the techniques of composition-through-performance, all the way to the activity of learning sample compositions through reading; once the performance tradition becomes obsolete, the text becomes simply a sample piece of writing, potentially there to be imitated by other sample pieces of writing.

Let us begin with the *Clouds* of Aristophanes already discussed above, with its informative description of old-fashioned Athenian *paideia*, the kind that purportedly produced the men who fought at the Battle of Marathon (961 – 89). This precious glimpse of old-fashioned education in Athens provides us with a model for understanding the metamorphosis of oral traditions into the institutions of schooling in the 'Classics'.

With the increasing complexity of society in the context of the polis comes

---

[106] Henderson, 'Greek music', p. 340.

a pattern of differentiation in the passing on of traditions from generation to generation, and the institution of schools, as we see it described in the passage from the *Clouds* about the good old days of education, may be considered a reflex of this pattern. Already in this era, schools are not a phenomenon merely confined to Athens but seem to appear on a pan-Hellenic scale. The earliest attested mention of schools is in Herodotus (6.27.2), alluding to an incident that occurred in Chios around 496 BC, where a roof collapsed on a group of 120 children as they were being taught *grammata*, 'letters'.

That these 'letters' are the 'belles-lettres' of poetry and song is made clear if we compare the portrait of old-fashioned education by the figure of Protagoras in the *Protagoras* of Plato, to which we may now turn. In this dramatisation of the way things supposedly were in the second half of the fifth century, we can see how schooling is a matter of differentiations in the passing on of traditions from generation to generation. The subject is introduced as we find an old Protagoras debating with Socrates in a company of young Athenian intellectuals that pointedly includes two sons of Pericles himself. In his description of *paideia*, the figure of Protagoras specifically says that the wealthy can afford more of it: they extend the education of their children by starting it earlier and continuing it longer (326c). There are at least three stages to what Protagoras describes. First, there is a period of education at home, where father, mother, 'nurse', and *paidagōgos*, 'tutor', all play a role in one's early ethical formation (325c–d). Second, the child is sent to school, where he is taught letters for the explicit purpose of memorising poetry (325e–326a). That this memorisation is for the explicit purpose of performing and interpreting this poetry is made clear in Protagoras' description of the third stage of schooling, where the child is taught to sing compositions of lyric poets while accompanying himself on the lyre (326a–b).

Whereas the poetry that is taught in the earlier stage when the child is still learning his letters is described only generally as *diexodoi*, *epainoi*, and *enkōmia* concerning 'noble men of the past' (326a), it is clear that the poetry taught at the later stage is specifically lyric poetry (the compositions of *melopoioi*, 'lyric poets'). From the standpoint of Protagoras, the most important aspect of *paideia* (his word) is to acquire skill in the performance and interpretation of poetry (339a), and it is clear that he is thinking in particular of song, that is, lyric poetry. Illustrating his point about the primacy of poetry in education, he begins his debate with Socrates by citing and then interpreting a lyric composition of Simonides (339b), having just made an earlier reference to a famous lyric passage from Pindar (331d). After Protagoras and Socrates have a contest of wits in interpreting the meaning of the composition by Simonides, Alcibiades challenges Protagoras to continue his debate with Socrates by abandoning the use of poetry as the framework for the discussion (347b and 348b), in the context of a particularly significant remark of Socrates: to use poetry as a framework for the debate between Protagoras and himself is analogous, says Socrates, to the hiring of girl-musicians, either string or wind, or girl-dancers to entertain at symposia. Such symposiasts reveal their lack of *paideia*, whereas those who are noble and 'educated' (*pepaideumenoi*) can entertain themselves with their own conversations (347d).

Plato could have had Socrates say, as does the poetry of Aristophanes, that the educated symposiasts can also entertain themselves by performing and interpreting lyric compositions, as opposed to the ill-educated symposiasts who hire girl-musicians to play for them. But of course Plato is the champion of a new education where dialogue supplants the primacy of poetry, and Socrates in fact goes on to set up 'the poets' as a bad thing, parallel to the girl-musicians (347e). In other words, instead of having girl-musicians as a foil for 'the poets', Plato has both the girl-musicians and 'the poets' serving together as a foil for the medium of the dialogue that Socrates and Alcibiades are advocating. The stance of Alcibiades here is particularly suggestive: his is the generation ridiculed in the *Clouds* of Aristophanes for abandoning the ideals of old-fashioned *paideia*. According to these ideals, as we have seen, a sign of the highest achievement was the performance, at a symposium, of a lyric composition by one of the old masters. There is a vivid contrast to these ideals in the *Alcibiades* of Plutarch (2.6), where the young Alcibiades refuses to learn how to play the *aulos*: let the Thebans, says he, play the reed, since they do not know how to have a conversation at a symposium.

Given the obsolescence, lamented already in the days of Aristophanes, of the old-fashioned *paideia* at Athens, it follows that the survival of the Classics in old lyric poetry, with their antiquated traditions of composition and even performance, was severely threatened. Other cities, such as Thebes in the anecdote that precedes, would doubtless have held on to the antiquated traditions for a longer period, given their more conservative traditions of education.

We cannot rule out the possibility that some of the better schools, even in Plato's time, insisted on extensive memorisation of the *libretti* of the lyric masters, but it is clear that most schools limited their requirements to a small repertoire of selected passages to be memorised for recitation (cf. Plato, *Laws* 810e). As for professional musicians, there is evidence that they still had access, even at as late a time as the era of Aristotle, to the melodic traditions of Archaic masters like Pindar. There is a revealing report in *On Music* (1142b) attributed to the theorist Aristoxenus, pupil of Aristotle: according to Aristoxenus, who as we have seen was the son of a professional musician from Tarentum, there was a composer, one of his own contemporaries, who in the course of his career reverted from the musical idiom of Timotheus and Philoxenus back to that of the Archaic poets, among whom Pindar is mentioned first. Clearly, the musical tradition of Pindar had survived until then. Still, the point remains that there would have been no chance for any major ongoing recomposition of Pindar's poetry through performance, in that contemporary traditions of choral lyric composition would have been sufficiently differentiated from Pindar's old-fashioned traditions. In fact, as we have seen, the very traditions of performing Pindar's compositions had become obsolete.

In Pindar's own time, by contrast, his compositions could still be readily reperformed, not by a chorus but by individuals at symposia, simply as 'Classics'. As we have seen, Old Comedy represents the mode of re-performance at the symposium in the format of a solo song with self-accompaniment to the lyre. By implication, there was a time when a choral composition could be actively converted into a solo performance. Such interchangeability between choral and solo contexts is a clear indication, however indirect, of the flexibility of the choral lyric form as a still-living tradition in the era of Simonides, Bacchylides, and Pindar. In the later era of Timotheus and Philoxenus, as we have also seen, this flexibility had broken down.

As 'Classics', the compositions of a Pindar could be reperformed at will, but they would have to be grounded in an awareness of the situations and ideologies in which Pindar was commissioned to give public poetic testimony. These 'situations and ideologies', let us call them 'occasions', may strike us at first as potential obstacles to the pan-Hellenisation of such poetry. Still, these occasions were of pan-Hellenic importance, with an impact that was meant to be lasting in prestige. Each of Pindar's compositions was indeed originally commissioned for a specific occasion, to be performed ostensibly by a chorus assembled and trained for that one original occasion. But the prestige of such an occasion was meant to reverberate indefinitely in time and space. This transcendent occasionality of Pindar's poetry is most evident in the only genre of his poems to survive almost intact – the four books of *epinikia*, 'victory odes'. Commissioned as *ad hoc* choral performances in celebration of victories won by athletes at the great pan-Hellenic games, each of Pindar's victory odes was a composition centring on a single performance, each containing details grounded in the historical realities of the time and place of performance. And yet, each of these victory odes aims at translating its occasion into a pan-Hellenic event, a thing of beauty that can be replayed by and for all Hellenes for all time to come.

It is clear that there would have been no rationale for recommissioning a chorus to reperform such a composition, since the original occasion would have been archetypal from the standpoint of the poetry. Or, to put it another way, the original occasion would have gone forever from the standpoint of us outsiders who are critics of this poetry. For us, any reperformance of such a composition in, say, Aristophanes' time seems at first sight to be just a performance of a canonical poet. From the internal point of view represented by the poetic tradition itself, however, a reperformance in an old-fashioned symposium is a remaking of an original poetic event. There is no 'chorus', no 'chorus-leader' present, and instead it is a soloist performer who has to reconstitute their roles, while all along accompanying himself on the lyre. The example of the young Pheidippides in the *Clouds* of Aristophanes, however, suggests an incipient failure of liberal education, even by the time of Old Comedy, to produce anyone to take up such a challenge.

These historical developments in differentiation and crystallisation, in local traditions and pan-Hellenism, and in the practice of mimesis, the role of the poet as author, and the concepts of genre and canon, constitute the background against which the beginnings of systematic literary criticism in the fourth century should be viewed. The body of poetry we have been considering remained, and remains, the central corpus of Greek literature, texts which critics have interpreted, or misinterpreted, ever since.

2

LANGUAGE AND MEANING IN ARCHAIC AND CLASSICAL GREECE

Inherent in any literary criticism are assumptions about the nature of language and about what constitutes valid interpretation. This chapter will set out briefly what some Greek philosophers have to say on these and related subjects, but it should be recognised that we are often viewing their thought on the basis of modern assumptions about the implications of what they say, rather than entering into their own epistemic system. Until the fourth century BC we should probably grant that the Greeks saw language as a natural map of reality; they sought more often to understand reality with the tool of language than to try to understand the nature of language itself. Yet the discussion can provide a substratum of thinking which lies beneath the literary criticism of Aristophanes, Plato, and Aristotle, and a background for the discussion of the theories of Hellenistic philosophers in chapter 6, or for later Greek hermeneutics in chapters 10 and 11. Readers whose interests in criticism are not theoretical may, however, prefer to skip to chapter 3 and continue at this point with the applied literary criticism of Plato.

1 Early Greek hermeneutics

The Homeric poems already reveal a society grappling with interpretative problems.[1] Nestor in *Iliad* 1 is represented as a wise old man whose insight, based on experience of situations and people, allows him to interpret and reconcile opposing views, and whose words 'flowed sweeter than honey' (249). Odysseus in both poems is astute and in the *Odyssey* often veils his thought, either as a form of self-protection or to test the attitudes of others. The scene with Penelope in *Odyssey* 19 is a particularly subtle example of indirect communication, culminating in Penelope's description of a real or feigned dream and Odysseus' interpretation of it, which is validated by the subsequent action. The interpretation of dreams has close analogies with literary criticism, as we will see in the discussion of Artemidorus in chapter 11, section 1.

[1] The history of hermeneutics begins 'if not with Nestor in the *Iliad*, then at least with Odysseus', Hans-Georg Gadamer, *Philosophical Hermeneutics*, tr. D. E. Linge (Berkeley, 1976), p. 22.

A specific problem throughout the Homeric poems and in Greek society was the interpretation of omens and prophecies from the gods. An *oiōnos* or *ornis*, 'bird', is often a 'sign' (*sēma*) from the gods, but it is a valid sign only if it is recognised as such. Hector can reject Polydamas' interpretation of a bird flight as an evil omen, claiming 'one bird-sign is best, to fight for one's country' (*Il.* 12.243), and Zeus confirms this position by sending the wind to blow dust against the Greeks. The validity of a bird-sign is again debated in *Odyssey* 2.146 – 207. In the Archaic and Classical periods the problem was most acute in the interpretation of oracular responses. Croesus of Lydia staged a test of several oracles, judged the Delphic Oracle the best, and after cultivating the good will of the priests there asked for advice about his plan to attack the Persians. He was told that if he crossed the Halys river a great kingdom would fall (Herodotus 1.46 – 53). He interpreted this to mean the kingdom of his enemies, but it was his own. Oracular responses were often couched ambiguously so as to be self-validating. If the oracle were an old one, there might be the problem of the correct 'text'. During the plague at Athens an old prophecy of a Peloponnesian war accompanied by 'death' was remembered, but some said the prophecy was for a 'dearth'. Thucydides wryly comments that if there is a famine during some future war the verse will be understood in the latter sense: 'for men adjust their memory to what they experience' (2.54.3).

Pious Greeks, Socrates among them as seen in the *Apology* (21b6), felt that oracles did not lie. The problem was to work out what the oracle really meant. Socrates tests the literal interpretation of an oracle that he is the wisest of men and concludes that his wisdom consists in a unique appreciation that he knows nothing. The oracle is true, but understanding of it requires effort, and this effort is a valuable one philosophically or religiously, a feeling shared by later interpreters of the obscurity of sacred texts. Truth is often revealed darkly in the sacred language of proclamation.

The style was cultivated by religious sects, such as the Orphics, and by some philosophers. Heraclitus (*c.* 480 BC) wrote 'The Lord who owns the oracle at Delphi neither speaks nor hides the meaning, but indicates it by a sign [*sēmainei*]' (fr. 93 Diels-Kranz). He imitated the style in his own prose and acquired a reputation as 'the riddler' and 'the dark'. What we know of his work suggests that it was aphoristic, but the original context may have had an argumentative progression.[2] Most famous, though not most obscure, is his proclamation 'you cannot step twice into the same river' (Plato, *Cratylus* 402a9 – 10). The effect of Heraclitus' discourse is to challenge the hearer (for his writings were intended to be heard rather than read) to a new awareness of external order in the universe and the powers of human understanding. He seems to have attributed to God the signifying power of the eternal

---

[2] Jonathan Barnes, 'Aphorism and argument', in Robb (ed.), *Language and Thought*, pp. 91 – 105.

logos, of which the deep meaning appears to man implicit in the sign.[3]
Martin Heidegger thought that in Heraclitus 'the essence of language
flashed in the light of Being … but the lightning abruptly vanished. No one
held onto its streak of light and the nearness of what it illuminated.'[4]
This perhaps goes beyond anything of which Heraclitus can be said to have
been aware. His essential interest was in *logos* as human thought, rather than
as linguistic expression, and as the divine force giving order to the universe,
creating the harmony or ratio between hot and cold, dry and wet, and other
opposites, but in common with the other pre-Socratics, Heraclitus had to
invent a terminology to describe the external world. Thus the frequent
presence in his and their work of polemic against ordinary language and
also against the traditional poetry of Homer and Hesiod.[5] Xenophanes of
Colophon (second half of the sixth century BC) had attacked the anthropomorphism and immorality of the Homeric and Hesiodic gods (fr. 10–18 Diels-
Kranz); Heraclitus in the next generation broadened the attack: Homer and
Archilochus deserve to be expelled from poetic contests and clubbed (fr. 42);
Hesiod is regarded as a teacher, but in fact is quite ignorant (fr. 106); the mob
is persuaded by bards, but the good are few (fr. 104). At the root of the problem
is *logos*.

   Logos has many different meanings in Greek: 'word', 'speech', 'story',
'narrative', 'mention', 'reputation', 'conversation', 'cause', 'argument',
'pretext', 'due measure', 'proportion', 'principle', 'the faculty of reason',
'definition', are all common in the Classical language.[6] The meaning has to
be determined from context, and just as *pharmakon*, 'drug', can mean both
'cure' and 'poison', *logos* has two opposed connotations, for it can mean both
the truth and a lie. One of its most common uses is in antithesis to *ergon*, 'deed'
or 'fact': 'in word and not in deed'. There is thus in words both the potentiality for revealing and the potentiality for disguising reality, the possibility
that they are directly reflective of nature (*phusis*) and the possibility that they
are matters of convention (*nomos*). The problem for a philosopher, as for a
literary critic, is the discovery of a criterion. The early philosophers had no
epistemology and were interested in explaining the nature and stuff of being,
largely on an intuitive basis and through what amounts to metaphor; for
Thales all things were water, for Anaximenes air, condensed or rarefied.
Heraclitus is a possible exception to this in that, judging from the very limited
fragments preserved, he may have relied on certain logical principles to
validate his thought in contrast to his predecessors and especially in contrast

---

[3] J. Baille, 'Epistémologie présocratique et linguistique', *Etudes philosophiques* (Paris, 1981),
   pp. 1–8.
[4] *Early Greek Philosophy*, tr. D. F. Krell and F. A. Capuzzi (New York, 1975), p. 78.
[5] E. A. Havelock, 'The linguistic task of the Presocratics', in Robb (ed.), *Language and Thought*,
   pp. 15–20.
[6] Guthrie, *Greek Philosophy*, I, pp. 419–24.

to the poets and popular opinion. It has been argued that for him experience is the basis of interpretation, but interpretation must account for all experience, must introduce no extra-sensibles, must be holistic, and must be given by the experience, not imposed on it.[7] He thus sought to conceptualise universals and abstractions, of which particulars were manifest in experience.[8] He is pessimistic, however, about an audience's ability to grasp reality through words. Behind human *logos* ('a word') stands divine *logos* ('the Word'). 'Of this *logos*, as it is always, men have no understanding, both before hearing it and when they have once heard it. For though all things came to be according to this *logos*, they are like people of no experience when they experience such words and deeds as I set forth when I distinguish each thing according to its nature and showing how it is' (fr. 1 Diels-Kranz) and 'Listening not to me but to the *logos*, it is wise to concur that all is one' (fr. 50).[9] Yet relationships between spoken words indicated to Heraclitus profound truths, often through contradictory meanings which reflect the strife characterising all of life. For example (fr. 48): 'The name of the bow [*biOS*] is life [*BIos*], but its work is death.' It was perhaps Heraclitus who first recognised that a word, or a text, could have more than one valid meaning, which he seems to have thought of as resulting not from conventional association, but from the nature of words as motivated signs. (A considerable amount of our knowledge of Heraclitus comes from early Christian writers, especially Clement of Alexandria who himself has an important place in the history of hermeneutics, to be discussed in chapter 11, section 1.)

A rather different tradition can be said to stem from Heraclitus' younger contemporary, Parmenides. Heraclitus, and his Ionian predecessors, had written in prose; Parmenides, in southern Italy, and his successor Empedocles used hexameter verse, and though the effect is less riddling, the result is cumbersome and no less obscure. In Parmenides' poem an unnamed goddess rebukes those who think that there can be thought about that-which-is-not; men are deaf and blind and believe that to be and not to be are the same and not the same (fr. 6 Diels-Kranz). The cause of this is habit (*ethos*), born of experience (*polupeiron*) (fr. 7). That is to say, common thought and speech are conventional and contradictory. There are signs (*sēmata*) of the truth, but Parmenides, unlike Heraclitus, leaves no place for any belief at all in the world our senses reveal to us.[10] Men have made up names and falsely assigned signs (*sēmata*) to them (fr. 8). Support for Parmenides' philosophical view was provided by Zeno of Elea in a prose work which drew contradictory

[7] Edward Hussey, 'Epistemology and meaning in Heraclitus', in Schofield and Nussbaum (eds.), *Language and Logos*, pp. 35–6.

[8] J. M. Moravscik, 'Heraclitean concepts and explanations' in Robb (ed.), *Language and Thought*, esp. pp. 142–7.

[9] See Hussey, 'Epistemology', pp. 56–7.

[10] Kirk, Raven, and Schofield, *Presocratics*, p. 256; contrast the name Parmenides gives to Being, Leonard Woodbury, 'Parmenides on names', *HSCP*, 63 (1958), pp. 146–60.

conclusions from the premises of his master's opponents. Aristotle is said (Diog. Laert. 9.25) to have called him the inventor of dialectic. The most famous of Zeno's arguments is what came to be known later as the parodox of Achilles and the tortoise: Achilles can never overtake the tortoise in a race, for at any moment of time he will always reach only a point the tortoise has just left. The ability to manipulate language paradoxically was an intoxicating discovery and helped pave the way to sophistry.

2 *Sophistry*

The sophists of the fifth century – Protagoras, Gorgias, Prodicus, Hippias, and others – were itinerant lecturers who created a lucrative profession by teaching, chiefly through example and imitation, modes of discourse useful in civic life or in dialectical discussion. The best brief picture of what sophists taught is found in Plato's *Protagoras* (316c – 19a), where Protagoras, the first acknowledged sophist, sums up the goal of his instruction as prudence (*euboulia*) in private affairs and those of the city, 'that the student may be most able to act and speak' (319a1 – 2). In their teaching sophists opened up epistemological questions. As a group their stance was relativistic, sceptical of the possibility of knowledge, content with exploiting opinion, and celebratory of the practical utility of speech. While Parmenides had thought that reality could not be known from words, Protagoras believed that to each individual appearance is reality (*Cratylus* 386a1 – 4) and *logos* is the tool by which we control it. His relativism is summed up in the famous statement: 'Man is the measure of all things; of things that are, that they are, and of things that are not, that they are not' (fr. 1 Diels-Kranz); his scepticism in the assertion that he could not know whether or not the gods exist, 'for there is much to prevent knowledge: the obscurity of the subject and the shortness of life' (fr. 4). On every issue he claimed there were two opposed arguments (fr. 6a).

An outline of a discussion of nature by Gorgias carried this further: nothing exists; if it exists it cannot be apprehended by men; even if it is apprehended it cannot be expressed or explained (fr. 3 Diels-Kranz). The thesis has some philosophical significance, but for Gorgias and his students it primarily provided an opportunity to practise verbal skills of argument, which might be applied to other situations. Gorgias developed a striking prose style which makes great use of sound, rhythm, and play on words; as we shall see, in large part it is intended for an emotional effect on an audience, playing with the assumption that similarities of words and sounds reveal deeper meanings. Antiphon, in a treatise *On Truth*, argued that there is no permanent reality behind words, nothing comparable to the results of seeing and knowing.[11]

[11] Morrison, in Sprague (ed.), *Sophists*, p. 212.

The sophists as a group thus privileged *nomos*, or convention, over *phusis* or nature, and did so with *éclat*. In their work there is nothing of the bitterness of Heraclitus or Parmenides. The debate between nature and nurture is a common feature of Greek writing in the late fifth and fourth centuries as sophistry was applied to political and ethical discussions. For example, the Melian dialogue in Thucydides (5.87 – 111) and the discussion in Plato's *Gorgias* and *Republic*, Book I, show the concepts applied to the topic of justice in society. The sophists also adumbrated an anthropology of human development, including the historical origin of speech as conventional and arbitrary signs, seen in Plato's *Protagoras* (322a). Thinking on this subject was continued by the Epicureans and Stoics, though among the latter accommodated to a theory of natural signs. There are important later discussions of the origin of speech in Cicero's *De inventione* (1.3), Lucretius (5.1028 – 90), and Diodorus Siculus (1.8).

Sophists sometimes used myth as a form or a subject of discourse, either creating new versions of traditional stories to illustrate their views, as Protagoras is shown doing in Plato's dialogue of that name (320c – 2d), or taking a situation from epic as material for the illustration of their technique. The best known example of the latter is Gorgias' *Encomium of Helen of Troy*.[12] Gorgias here does not provide an interpretation of the myth, nor does he reveal radical scepticism;[13] he treats Helen as an historical figure and seeks to demonstrate that whatever reason is given for her departure from her husband, Menelaos, she is morally blameless. The most interesting passage considers the possibility that Paris persuaded her by words to go with him. The following translation seeks to preserve a sense of Gorgias' highly artificial style:

But if speech persuaded her and deceived her soul, not even to this is it difficult to make answer and to banish blame, as follows. Speech is a powerful lord that with the smallest and most invisible body accomplishes most god-like works. It can banish fear and remove grief and instil pleasure and enhance pity. I shall show how this is so. It is necessary for it to seem so as well in the opinion of my hearers.

All poetry I regard and name as speech having metre. On those who hear it come fearful shuddering and tearful pity and grievous longing as the soul, through words, experiences some experience of its own at others' good fortune and ill fortune.

Listen as I turn from one argument to another. Divine sweetness transmitted through words is inductive of pleasure, reductive of pain. Thus by entering into the opinion of the soul the force of incantation is wont to beguile and persuade and alter it by witchcraft, and the two arts of witchcraft and magic are errors of the soul and deceivers of opinion. How many speakers on how many subjects have persuaded

---

[12] Text in Diels-Kranz, *Vorsokratiker*, B 11; tr. by G. A. Kennedy in Sprague (ed.), *Sophists*, pp. 50 – 5.

[13] John M. Robinson, 'On Gorgias', in E. N. Lee (ed.), *Exegesis and Argument* (Assen, 1973), pp. 49 – 60.

others and continue to persuade by moulding false speech? If everyone, on every subject, had memory of the past and knowledge of the present and foresight of the future, speech would not do what it does, but as things are it is easy neither to remember the past nor consider the present nor predict the future; so that on most subjects most people take opinion as counsellor to the soul. But opinion, being slippery and insecure, casts those relying on it into slippery and insecure fortune. What is there to prevent the conclusion that Helen too, when still young, was carried off by speech just as if constrained by force? Her mind was swept away by persuasion, and persuasion has the same power as necessity, although it may bring shame. For speech, by persuading the soul that it persuaded, constrained her both to obey what was said and to approve what was done. The persuader, as user of force, did wrong; the persuaded, forced by speech, is unreasonably blamed.

To understand that persuasion, joining with speech, is wont to stamp the soul as it wishes one must study, first, the words of astronomers who, substituting opinion for opinion, removing one and instilling another, make incredible and unclear things appear true to the eyes of opinion; second, forceful speeches in public debate, where one side of the argument pleases a large crowd and persuades by being written with art even though not spoken with the truth; third, the verbal wrangling of philosophers in which too a swiftness of thought is exhibited, making confidence in opinion easily changed. The power of speech has the same effect on the condition of the soul as the application of drugs to the state of bodies, for just as different drugs dispel different fluids from the body, and some bring an end to disease but others end life, so also some speeches cause pain, some pleasure, some fear; some instil courage, some drug and bewitch the soul with a kind of evil persuasion. $(8-14)$[14]

Speech, in Gorgias' view, is a material substance and a form of magic.[15] It operates at the level of opinion, not knowledge, whether applied to science, to public life, or to philosophical debate, and it works upon the emotions, rather than upon reason. Gorgias' own style illustrates the process:

The rhetor, then, capable of distortion, and aware of the flexibility of human *doxa*, commands a *technē* which can directly touch the psyche through a process of aesthetic and emotional excitation, and hence guide or control human emotion. Reason is thus ultimately made the master of emotion, but not, as Socrates taught, by completely over-powering it; but rather by channelling and directing emotional energies to preconceived ends. It is now the emotional potentialities of the *logos* which are exploited, and not the intellectual, though the methods of exploitation are still rational.[16]

Gorgias' discussion of *logos* is a valuable background for Plato's criticism of rhetoric and poetry and may have anticipated Aristotle's theory of *katharsis*.[17] The sophists also took the first steps toward the conceptualisation of grammar. Protagoras defined four classes of sentence: wish, question, answer,

---

[14] Translation revised on the basis of the edition of Francesco Donadi (Rome, 1983), pp. 13–17.
[15] The implications are explored by de Romilly, *Magic and Rhetoric*, pp. 3–22.
[16] Segal, 'Gorgias', p. 133; on Gorgias' doctrine of *logos*, see further Kerford, *Sophistic Movement*, pp. 78–82.
[17] W. Süss, *Ethos* (Leipzig, 1910), pp. 85ff., and Segal, 'Gorgias', pp. 130–2.

and command (Diog. Laert. 9.53–4) and criticised the opening of the *Iliad* as cast in the form of a command when it should have been the expression of a wish (Aristotle, *Po.* 15.1454b15). He thus recognised the existence in Greek of grammatical moods. He also first identified grammatical gender (*Rh.* 3.1407b6). Prodicus examined distinctions between actions identified by kindred terms such as 'to wish' and 'to desire', 'to become' and 'to be' (Plato, *Protagoras* 340a). These observations contributed to the understanding of diction and thus provided a basis for a theory of prose style among the rhetoricians. It was long, however, before the Greeks clearly differentiated all parts of speech. In Plato (e.g., *Cratylus* 431b) only nouns and verbs are differentiated; Aristotle added *sundesmos* (preposition, conjunction, or particle) (*Rh.* 3.1407b12) and *arthron* (article) (*Po.* 20.1457a6).

By the late fifth century a crisis had been created in philosophy and public life. Oracular and poetic statements, derived from intuition, could neither be refuted nor substantiated. Equally persuasive arguments could be advanced for and against any thesis, and the 'worse' made to seem the 'better' cause. As viewed in the plays of Aristophanes, especially *Clouds*, philosophy had been reduced to idle quibbling or the encouragement of immorality and seemed to be undermining traditional values of Greek culture. The situation was ominous for literary criticism as well, in that the traditionally accepted reference of terms – especially moral or evaluative terms – could be extended to cover almost any kind of self-interested behaviour, as Thucydides (3.82) notes of his own time with dry despair. Yet he implies hope 'that things could somewhere, sometime, be different'.[18] A new beginning was made by the Platonic Socrates, with his consistent demand for definition, and by Democritus, with his atomic theory. Socratic dialectic led to Aristotelian and Stoic logic; Democritean scientism to Epicurean physics, including an atomistic view of language to be discussed in chapter 6, section 7.

3 Allegorical interpretation

There is some allegory in early epic (e.g. *Il.* 9.502–12), lyric (e.g., Alcaeus fr. 1), and philosophical writing (e.g., the opening of Parmenides' philosophical poem). Allegorical interpretation may have begun with Theagenes of Rhegium in the sixth century as a response to the criticisms of the representation of the gods in the Homeric poems by Xenophanes and others and was continued by Pherecydes of Syros, who regarded the Homeric gods as representations of cosmic forces.[19] It was further developed in the fifth century by Metrodorus of Lampsacus, who extended interpretation from the gods to the heroes: Agamemnon represented the air; Achilles the sun; Hector

[18] White, *When Words Lose their Meaning*, p. 90.
[19] Pfeiffer, *Classical Scholarship*, pp. 9–10; on the motivations for allegorical interpretation, see J. Tate, 'On the history of allegorism', *CQ*, 28 (1934), 105–14.

the moon (fr. 61A4 Diels-Kranz). As a pupil of Anaxagoras, he seems to have been seeking an exposition of a philosophical system by finding it in epic texts, and throughout antiquity allegorical interpretation remains largely a tool of philosophical or religious rhetoric, as well as a technique to rescue the Homeric poems from the strictures of critics, of whom Plato emerged as the most powerful. Prodicus' *Choice of Herakles* (Xenophon, *Memorabilia* 2.1, 21 – 3) is the most famous sophistic allegory, but the sophists show no interest in allegorical *interpretation*. The closest to it is perhaps Antisthenes, a follower of Gorgias, who drew moral doctrines from the Homeric poems without regard to the literal sense and was the first to note a contrast between 'seeming' and 'truth' in them (Dio Chrysostom 53.5). Plato's myths are often allegories, but he was opposed to allegorical interpretation of traditional myths as part of education, since the young cannot tell what is allegory and what is literal (*Rep.* 2.378d), and in the *Phaedrus* (229d – e) Socrates criticises allegory as a game for the ingenious that opens up flood gates of imagination and wastes time that ought to be given to more serious things. Aristotle shows no interest in it either, and it is not a tool of the Alexandrian literary scholars, but the Stoics resurrected allegory on a large scale as a way to teach their philosophical views, and it had an important future in the interpretations of neo-Platonists and Christians. The term 'allegory' is not used in Greek of the Classical period. Plato, in the *Republic* passage cited above, speaks of *huponoia*, 'an underlying meaning'. 'Allegory' as a technical concept cannot be securely attested before the first century BC, though its occurrences in Demetrius' treatise *On Style* may be earlier; as used by the rhetoricians it is a figure of speech in a specific context where the words say one thing and mean another (e.g., Demetrius 99).

4 Etymology: Plato's 'Cratylus'

An interest in etymology, and especially the etymology of proper names, is found in all periods of Greek literature, reflecting a popular assumption that names are or should be somehow significant. The *Odyssey* plays on Odysseus' name as meaning 'man of wrath' (1.55) or 'man of sorrows' (1.62), and compound names such as Astyanax, Telemachus, Megapenthes are often given contextual significance. The Greek poets continued to play on names, as when Aeschylus derives dire compounds from the name of Helen of Troy (*Agamemnon* 681 – 90). A more theoretical interest emerged in the late fifth century in the philosophical and sophistic schools described above. For us, the major statement of the controversy is in Plato's *Cratylus*.

In this dialogue, the date of which has been much disputed, three basic positions emerge. One, that of Heraclitus' follower Cratylus, is that names (and all words) originated with a divine name-giver, exist by nature (*phusis*), and reveal a necessary relationship between a sign and a signified. A name that does not have such a relationship is not a name at all: Hermogenes, since he is not 'born of Hermes' has no right to that name (383b). A second view is that of Hermogenes himself, perhaps a follower of Parmenides (Diog. Laert. 3.6), that names are matters of custom and convention (*nomos*), and their relationship to reality is thus arbitrary (384d). He rejects the position of Protagoras, that appearance is reality (386a). A third position, suggested by Socrates (414d, 425d–6b), perhaps ironically, is that some basic, original names are divine in origin and significant, but that they have been corrupted, altered, or expanded over time, often for the sake of euphony, producing conventional language in which the sign often bears little apparent relation to the signified (435c). The dialogue is aporetic, for no final conclusion is reached, and a good example of dialectic as practised in the Socratic schools: Socrates is first seen arguing against Hermogenes, then against Cratylus. Probably he should be viewed as regarding etymological interpretation with the same scepticism he voices towards allegorical interpretation. Plato uses the subject of etymology, however, to introduce some of his central ideas about reality, divinity, and imitation, and toward the end of the discussion (438eff.) Socrates is made to reveal a deep distrust of imitation, asserting that reality may be learned without names. 'No man of sense will put himself and his soul under control of names and trust in names and their makers to the point of affirming that he knows anything' (440c).

In the course of the discussion with Hermogenes, Socrates, whose mood throughout is playful (cf., e.g., 421d), suggests many fanciful etymologies. In so far as a pattern is discernible, it is to get back to a few basic terms, often reflecting the Heraclitan principle of flux (424a–b), in which particular ideas are associated with particular letters and sounds. A name is 'an imitation with the voice of that which is imitated' (423b). The letter rho imitates motion, iota indicates everything subtle, delta and tau represent binding and rest, gamma a gliding motion, and so on (426c–7d). The correspondence of sound and sense in Greek poetry is not mentioned, but the passage is evidence that in the Classical period there was a conscious awareness of it.

5 The oral and the written word

The period from the mid-fifth to the mid-fourth century is the turning point in Greece from a predominantly oral to a predominantly written basis of intellectual life. Though the Phoenician alphabet, improved by the invention of signs for vowels, had been introduced into Greece in the eighth century BC and written texts of poetry existed already in the seventh century and of philosophical works in the sixth, it does not seem accurate to speak of a 'reading' public until the late fifth century. Until then literature was known chiefly through performance: epic poetry from the performance of rhapsodes; lyric from choral performances, for which young people were given training by teachers; tragedy and comedy were primarily known from the dramatic

festivals; even early prose was given performance, for Herodotus is said
(Eusebius, *Chronicles*, 445/4 BC) to have recited portions of his *History*, and
the fame of the sophists came from their speeches. But in the *Apology* (26d – e)
Socrates says that the works of the philosopher Anaxagoras could be easily
bought by anyone who wished, written versions of epideictic speeches by
sophists were circulated for study, as is clear from the opening of Plato's
Phaedrus, Euripides was thought of as a bookish man who amassed and used
a library (Athenaeus 1.3a), and Aristophanes' parodies of tragedy seem to
imply a knowledge of the plays from reading texts as well as from attending
performances. There was opposition to the new development, as seen in
the work of Alcidamas, *Against those Writing Written Discourses* (pp. 135 – 41
Radermacher), and in the remarks of Socrates toward the end of the *Phaedrus*,
where writing is represented as destructive of memory and in contrast to
dialectic productive of a text which cannot answer back. This passage will
be discussed in chapter 3, section 6, below.

The change from oral to written publication of literature has been compared to the revolution brought about by the introduction of printing in the
fifteenth century and to the introduction of the computer in the twentieth.[20]
The analogy to printing is most striking in that both innovations greatly
increased the dissemination of texts. Writing facilitated the spread of formal
education throughout the Greek-speaking world, reduced the importance of
Athens as the leading centre of literary activity, and made possible the eventual
foundation of research libraries, such as that at Alexandria. The existence
of a written text as a basis of literary criticism certainly potentially changed
the nature of the critical act. It facilitated comparison of contexts, either in
two or more works or within a single work, encouraged re-reading with
knowledge of the text as a whole, allowed a greater accuracy of citation, and
helped to ensure a greater integrity of preservation of the original. A 'word'
became an entity, clearly distinguishable from and intermediate between
authorial enunciation and reader reception. A written text may have implied
a gradual privileging of the visual over the aural, seen for example in the theory
of *loci*, 'places', in rhetoric, in the development of mnemonic systems on the
basis of images and backgrounds, in alphabetisation in scholarly works, in
the writing of poems in visual shapes on the page (*technopaignia*), in the growing
importance of the epistle, and in the development of a substantial bureaucracy
based on the use of documents and archives. But it is easy to exaggerate these
potentialities. Throughout antiquity, texts continued to be read aloud, rather
than silently. Sound remained an integral part of the literary experience. The
major goal of formal education remained an ability to speak. Texts written
on papyrus scrolls, the usual form of the book until the Roman Empire,
were cumbersome to consult, compare, and collate. Like oral speech,

[20] Ong, *Orality and Literacy*, pp. 78–116.

they emphasised the linear quality of a work. Throughout antiquity, most literary criticism is either concerned with the rhetorical qualities of particular passages, or takes the form of running commentary. Though unity was to Aristotle and his followers an important literary quality, the average critic and average reader were often indifferent to it. Lines and short passages were enjoyed for themselves and were often quoted out of context and from memory. The common recourse to the written word did, however, produce a new level of imitation and a new function of signs in language. It was commonly believed that the written word was a conventional sign of the oral word, which in turn was a sign, whether conventional or natural, of some more remote signified. To this another level of signs was added: Aristotle introduced the use of letters of the alphabet rather than words as logical symbols to express the generic nature of the syllogism: 'if all A is B, when B = C, all A is also C'.

6 Aristotle on interpretation and topics

A discussion of Aristotelian logic would take us too far from purely literary criticism, and Aristotle's *Poetics* and *Rhetoric* will be discussed in subsequent chapters, but brief mention can be made here of two Aristotelian works which have some critical implications. A short, elementary treatise *On Interpretation* (*hermēneia*) follows the *Categories* and precedes the *Analytics* in the Aristotelian logical corpus, *Organon* (Tool). It is probably a genuine work of Aristotle and certainly a part of the traditional teaching of his school. No explanation of the term *hermēneia* is offered; Plato had used it (e.g., *Rep.* 524b1) to mean 'explanation' in a non-technical sense; the later treatise attributed to Demetrius, *On Hermēneia*, uses it to mean style or expression. It is related to the verb *hermēneuō*, which had been used to mean 'translate' from a foreign tongue or simply 'to put into words' (cf. Thucydides 2.60.5). The Aristotelian treatise is concerned with the expression of thought in words, sentences, and logical propositions.

Aristotle begins by defining words as vocal symbols (*sumbola*) of affections (*pathēmata*) in the soul, written words as symbols of spoken words. Neither written nor spoken words are the same for all men, but *pragmata* (realities) are. Words are primarily (*prōtōs*) signs (*sēmeia*) and the affections which they signify are themselves likenesses (*homoiōmata*) of things. Not every thought (*noēma*) in our minds is true or false nor is every expression in sound. A noun (*onoma* = 'name') is a conventional semantic sound with no reference to time. No sound is by nature a noun; it becomes one when it is a symbol for a thing. A verb is a sound which conveys a meaning with time value, but no part of the verb has meaning in itself. A verb is always a sign of something that is said about something else. Verbs by themselves are nouns and signify something; in uttering one, the speaker stops his thought and the mind of the hearer acquiesces – a view foreign to a modern critic who often sees the action in a text inherent in the verbs, whereas for Aristotle they are predicates of nouns. A *logos* (here = 'sentence') is a significant sound, of which the separate parts are semantic units, and it too is conventional. A sentence is not an *organon*, a tool or instrument of nature, and not all sentences are propositional (*apophantikos*); a prayer, for example, is not a proposition. The study of non-propositional sentences, Aristotle says (17a7), belongs to rhetoric and poetic, of propositions to logic. The rest of the treatise is concerned with propositions.

A few observations: words are regarded as one, but only one, species of symbol. Affections, or states of mind, are 'likenesses' and thus, in modern terminology, motivated signs; sounds and words are conventional and thus unmotivated.[21] The assignment of non-propositional statements to rhetoric and poetics is a denial of the truth-value of such statements, but not of the possibility of truth in a rhetorical or poetic work. In so far as rhetoric is the counterpart of dialectic, as the first sentence of the *Rhetoric* claims, a rhetorical work may contain propositions and its thesis may be probable. Speeches in imitative poetry may take propositional form, and even though the fictional setting lacks truth-value itself, epic and tragedy have meaning in their representation of cause and effect, as discussed in the *Poetics*.

On Interpretation is followed in the corpus of the *Organon* by the *Prior* and *Posterior Analytics*, Aristotle's treatment of syllogistic logic, and then by the eight books of the *Topica*, his major discussion of dialectic. Dialectic is the art of probable reasoning from generally accepted opinions and is useful, Aristotle says (101a25ff.), as an exercise (so practised in his and subsequent schools to early modern times), in conversation, and in the philosophical sciences, in as much as the first principles of a science (geometry, for example) cannot be established by that science, but must be based on commonly accepted assumptions. The significance of the treatise for literary criticism lies in its provision of an orderly system of analysis. Its identification of *topoi*, literally 'places', here meaning strategies of argument, provides the logical basis for rhetorical proof, both in theory and in practice, and some of its categories (definition, property, genus, accident, essence, quantity, quality, relation, place, time, position, state, activity, and passivity) (103b22 – 4) are adapted to rhetoric as well. A judicial speech can be said to concern itself with demonstrating who did what act of what sort where at what time under what conditions and with what degree of responsibility. A person trained in seeing these categories might be expected to apply them not only to argumentative, but to narrative discourse, or in the criticism of such passages. Aristotelian dialectic and its Stoic successor lie behind, and are occasionally evident in, Hellenistic criticism.

[21] Todorov, *Theories of the Symbol*, pp. 16–18.

We will return to some subsequent developments relating to language theory in the discussions of Hellenistic literary scholarship, of the work of Varro on the Latin language, and of interpretation as practised in late antiquity. It is time now, however, to turn to the most striking and most controversial of all Classical literary criticism, that found in dialogues of Plato and in Aristotle's *Poetics*.

3

PLATO AND POETRY

The great challenge for any interpreter of Plato's views on poetry is to appreciate why he is so uncompromisingly hostile towards it.[1] That he should seek to subordinate poetic to philosophic measures of expression and understanding is not in itself surprising. Philosophy has long had a need to keep poetry in its place – as Plato, alluding to the 'ancient quarrel' between the two, was among the first to tell us (*Rep.* 10.607b). But what is striking in Plato's attitude is that even when he comes to acknowledge a usefulness in poetry – its role in educating the young, in civil celebration, in persuasion of many sorts – he is not content (as is, say, Aristotle) to grant its virtues, unstintingly, while nevertheless delimiting their scope; rather, he regards poetry at all times and in all its uses with suspicion, as a substance inherently volatile. He recognises that human society is not possible without some form of poetry, but discerns in this fact a mark, so to speak, of our fallen state. Many philosophers have measured their distance from the poets; but Plato would put them beyond hierarchy altogether; would banish them – at least, would banish those he confesses to represent poetry at its greatest – from his ideal society.

1 Poetry as performance: the example of Ion

We shall not appreciate the reasons for Plato's hostility towards poetry unless we bear in mind how poetry would typically reach the public in Plato's day.[2] In a modern culture our most frequent direct contact with the literature deemed important in our society (and in the West this would of course include the very poets on whom Plato targets his attack) comes either through private and (at least potentially) reflective reading, or in the context of the classroom; and is supplemented in the case of drama by visits to the theatre, to see actual performance. In Plato's culture, live performance was the norm. Private reading and study of literary texts, to the extent that it was practised at all,

---

[1] In this chapter 'poetry' will often be a translation of μουσική, and this includes music and dance, as well as metrical language.
[2] Havelock, *Preface*, chs. 2 and 8.

92

seems to have been confined to a tiny minority of enthusiasts and intellectuals. Most citizens experienced poetry – not drama merely, but also the Homeric epics and lyric poetry – as members of an audience (or, indeed, as performers themselves) in various well-defined social settings: seeing tragedy and comedy at the annual dramatic festivals, hearing their Homer performed by professional rhapsodes, taking their turn with a song or two at drinking-parties. And all would have felt these (rather than reading or study) to be the proper contexts for poetry – oral memorisation and recital dominating even the schoolchild's poetic training. So that in order to gauge Plato's critique we must first banish any image of the serious reader curled quietly in an armchair with the *Iliad*, and think rather of the audience at a performance by the rhapsode Ion, tears in their eyes as they listen to Hector bidding Andromache farewell (*Ion* 535b–e). For Plato, the typical experience of poetry is never anything like private contemplation; and our most appropriate context for comparison is the experience of the theatre-going or, it may be, film-going public.

This aspect of poetic experience, its 'theatricality', is a major target of Plato's hostility; above all because poetry has at least the appearance of human talk, of saying something; and Plato believes that its theatricality, so far from strengthening poetry's voice, has a tendency to hamper its ability to speak to us. In his earlier dialogues he makes this point by turning traditional claims about poetry to his own purpose: most especially the claims that the poet is divinely inspired, and that he is a kind of teacher to his audience (in the *Republic* and later dialogues we will find him setting up a more innovative critical apparatus and linking it more explicitly and technically with his metaphysics and psychology). These claims are not unconnected, of course. When Hesiod promises to instruct Perses about going to sea for trade – while admitting that he himself has been to sea only once, and has no personal skill in sailing – he warrants his confidence by appeal to the poetic voice which the muses breathed into him on Helicon (*Works and Days* 646–62). In order to see how Plato attempts to break this connection between poetic inspiration and understanding, let us consider his most important treatment of poetry prior to the *Republic* (indeed, the only dialogue entirely devoted to the topic of poetry): the *Ion*.

Socrates' strategy in conversation with the rhapsode Ion is to get him to see that poetic inspiration is not a prerogative of the poets alone (although only to poets is it traditionally assigned), but is transmitted by them to intermediaries, such as actors and rhapsodes, enabling them to perform the poetry; and so the contagion spreads to its final carrier, the enthusiastic audience. Perhaps we wish, reading this dialogue, that Socrates could have had his discussion with a real poet, not a 'poet's interpreter' (as Ion is called at 530c3–4). Indeed, our unease may be compounded by the fact that the rhapsode occupied a niche to which no single modern calling corresponds; for not only was he something of an actor, giving emotional recitations of the Homeric poems at public festivals, but also something of a literary critic, able to discourse at length on the virtues of his chosen poet, Homer (Socrates twice has to restrain Ion from launching into his stump lecture, at 530d9 and 536d8). But on reflection we see that, for the twist Plato wishes to give to the concept of inspiration, a rhapsode rather than a poet makes the best choice as conversational partner. Poets, after all, then as now, were not judged on how well they could talk about their poetry, but on the quality of the poetry they produced. Rhapsodes, by contrast, win garlands not just by performing Homer, but by praising him (530d6 – 8); for which it seems necessary that they should penetrate the poet's thought (530b10 – c6). But if their supposed penetration can be revealed as a meagre affair, and moreover if its meagreness is shown to derive from its reliance on the same capacity for inspiration that empowers not only their own performance but also the creativity of the poets they perform and the receptivity of their audience, then we will be led to doubt whether poetry ever transmits anything more than inspiration; whether the understanding which the poets claim to transmit by virtue of divine *afflatus*, and which seems to be embodied in the rhapsode's interpretation of the poet's thought, is anything more than an appearance of understanding. This is the pattern of argument in the *Ion*, and its target is a rhapsode rather than a poet because only the rhapsode made his understanding of poetry an object of professional discourse distinct from the performance of the poetry itself – thus laying that understanding bare to Socrates' attack.

But let us look more closely at how Socrates presses his case. As a rhapsode, Ion specialises in the poetry of Homer to the exclusion of all others, and announces himself satisfied with this limitation (531a). But he cannot justify his satisfaction by comparing Homer with other poets; for he admits that he is quite unable to talk of other poets, nor to listen to talk about them without falling asleep. Only Homer stirs him to loquacity (532c). Well then, Socrates responds, it cannot be 'through art and understanding'[3] that Ion becomes so prolix; otherwise he would have something to say about the other poets too, just as a knowledgeable critic of arts such as painting or sculpture or indeed of rhapsody would have something to say about all its famous practitioners: not simply an Orpheus or Phemius but Ion of Ephesus as well (532c – 3c). What is more, the same can be said about the verbal fluency of Homer himself; since the readiness with which Homeric *trouvailles* come to Ion's lips, claims Socrates, is due to none other than that divine inspiration which Homer and other poets cite as the well-spring of their own poetry. And Socrates imposes a new psychological shading on that traditional concept.[4] If the poets insist that they get what they have to say direct from the muse, we must take them at their word, and consider them not responsible for what

---

[3] τέχνῃ καὶ ἐπιστήμῃ, 532c6.

[4] It may be that Democritus anticipated Plato's conception of poetic inspiration: fr. B18 and 21 Diels-Kranz (and further Verdenius, 'Principles', nn. 133 and 134).

they say. They should be compared with ecstatic Corybants, who can dance well only when 'possessed'[5] by their god; no longer in full control of their actions, but 'out of their minds'[6] (533e–4e). And inspiration in this sense is passed on from poet to performer; for Ion admits under questioning that when performing Homer he is taken out of himself and possessed by the narrative, so that his eyes brim with compassion and his hair bristles with fear – emotions which he transmits in turn to the audience (535b–e). Socrates compares this to the way a lodestone can magnetise an iron ring, which in turn magnetises another ring, until a whole chain is formed; so the power of the muse passes through her poet and his rhapsode to the audience (533de; 535e–6b). And that is why Ion bubbles over with opinions about Homer but is empty of ideas about other poets; and why the poets themselves tend to be good at only one genre of poetry, not all; or why poor Tynnichus should have produced only one worthwhile poem in his entire output, but that one a song that all sing and love: because neither Ion nor Homer speaks with 'art and understanding' but rather through the happy chance of 'divine gift and possession'[7] (534b–e; 536b–d).

Socrates does not actually deny that poetry and rhapsody are arts; he denies that what poets and rhapsodes say (as professionals) is said with art and understanding on their part. Thus, it is striking that Socrates should first deny Ion's Homeric disquisitions the status of art and then include rhapsody among the 'arts'[8] of which there are connoisseurs. But he seems to be driving a wedge between Ion's undoubted artistry as a theatrical performer (he comes to the dialogue fresh from victory at Epidaurus, 530b1) and his less than artistic understanding of what Homer's poems have to say. The need for this distinction is set by the following crucial fact: that a poem is both a product of theatrical skill or art and a stretch of language, in which things get said. Unlike the painter or sculptor, poets and rhapsodes create and perform through talk. But talk (not paint or stone) is also the medium through which non-performers express and communicate their non-theatrical understanding of things. Hence (Plato argues) we have a tendency in our estimation of poetry to confound the values of performance with the values of understanding, and not see how the former undermine the latter. When Socrates drags Tynnichus' name in the mud, this is not a low blow or a merely *ad hominem* argument, but makes a quite general and valid point: that it is perfectly possible (even if we think it unlikely, or believe that it has never actually happened) for a good poem to be produced by a bad poet. That is, we can appreciate what is said in poetic language quite without regard for its conditions of production. Not that we do not use our understanding in appreciating what a poem says,

---

[5] κατεχόμενοι, 533e7.

[6] οὐκ ἔμφρονες, 534a1; ἔκφρων, 534b5.

[7] θείᾳ μοίρᾳ καὶ κατοκωχῇ, 536c2.

[8] τεχνῶν, 532d3. So too, poetry is described (by implication) as an 'art' (τέχνη) at 532c8–d2.

but that, precisely, we *use* our understanding – use it only as a means towards appreciating the poem as a theatrical product, as performance.

Plato concludes that poetry does not properly engage the understanding – the criticism encapsulated in his description of poets, actors, and audience alike as inspired and out of their minds. But it is important to see that he is not accusing anyone in this magnetic chain of being actually crazy. This is clear from the fact that he allows Ion to note (without challenge from Socrates) that even as his eyes brim with inspired tears of sympathy he is paying sharp attention to the reactions of the audience, intent on making them weep so that he can laugh all the way to the bank (535e – 6). Ion is not actually lost in a world of his own; but his mind is lost to its proper function of understanding. It is a slave to the theatrical event (the image of the chain is especially appropriate here[9]): merely instrumental to his need to place himself imaginatively in the narrated scene, and to make the audience do likewise.

This point is developed through the curious discussion in the second half of the dialogue (536d – 42b), which is designed to show that even when Ion is at his most professorial, he is still running on 'inspiration' rather than understanding. We recall that Ion not only recites the Homeric poems but delivers encomia of their poet; and he now insists that in the latter role he is hardly 'possessed' or 'mad' (536d4 – 7). Lecturing, we might agree, is a lot different from acting. In reply, Socrates presses the issue of what in Homer Ion is best able to praise, eventually securing his agreement to the absurdity that generalship alone is what study of Homer qualifies a rhapsode to talk about, and that rhapsody and generalship are identical (540d – e). The reason Ion proclaims himself expert in generalship is that he 'knows what is suitable for a general to say' (540d5); and the reason he finally opts for generalship as the rhapsode's *métier* rather than any of the many other skills that Socrates first proposes (540b6 – c8) – despite his initial claim that rhapsody gives him knowledge of what is suitable for anyone, in whatever social role, to say (540b3 – 5) – seems to be that warfare is thought of as Homer's major theme,[10] and the scenes and projects of generalship, accordingly, make up the domain in which Ion's imagination is trained to roam most freely, and with which he most readily identifies himself. The point, then, is that Ion's lectures are not so different from his acting after all. In both cases he is not talking about something, but merely performing through talk. He thinks he knows how to talk about Homer, but Socrates has shown that he knows this only in the sense that he claims to know about generalship. He knows what is suitable for one talking about Homer to say. But he knows this through the same capacity for enthusiastic and imaginative identification (what Socrates calls 'inspiration') that he employs to perform the *Iliad*; which is why

---

[9] Notice the pun to this effect at 536a7 – b1.
[10] See 531c4; cf. *Rep.* 10.599c7 – 8.

he falls silent when other poets are in question. He knows what to say only to the extent that he knows what the words should be in this case; he does not understand why those words, not others, should be said (he knows Homer's poems, but does not know their place as poetry). In that sense, a rhapsode (and, by implication, the poet and the audience too) is, as it were, always acting, even when the person he acts is himself.

Perhaps we feel that Plato has given Socrates too easy a time in this encounter. Ion is a self-important and transparently silly creature; and the satire at his expense inclines us to dismiss the argumentation of this dialogue as something of a skit. Let us grant that Ion himself employs his understanding no more properly in speaking about Homer than in performing him; why should we therefore accept as a general point that inspiration disables understanding in the poetic chain, and not rather conclude that Ion is a poor specimen? And why does Plato allow Socrates to beat Ion down from the rather promising position (at 540b3–5) that as rhapsode he learns what it is appropriate to say across the whole gamut of social roles, to the patently absurd claim that, no, he learns only what a general will say? The discussion had seemed on the verge of isolating what we would call the 'fictionality' of poetic discourse; of declaring outright that when Homer makes his swineherds speak he is not bent on giving a lesson in pig-keeping but on adding a plausible voice to the full and varied choir of the *Odyssey*'s fictional world – not knowing what the swineherd knows, but knowing what he will say.

But to be dissatisfied in this way would be to miss Plato's point. Just as Tynnichus is not after all the hapless butt of an *ad hominem* argument, but his case allows us to derive a quite general conclusion, so Plato's satirical portrait of Ion is no mere indulgence of animus against poetry, but a weight-bearing pillar in the structure of his argument. It is not that a poet of Homer's stature would not have done better in discussion with Socrates than does his wretched epigone. The point, rather, is that only in discussion with a philosopher does Ion's wretchedness show; in other words, that poetry, being oriented towards the values of performance, is by its nature indifferent to the wisdom of its practitioners. Ion, do not forget, is a *good* rhapsode – a first-prize winner. Whether or not Ion had held on to his position about what he knows would make not the slightest difference to the fact that he does indeed know how to speak as a man or woman should speak, or as citizen and slave should, or ruler and ruled – and can come up with the quotations to prove it (as he does, for example, at 537a4). It is to make us appreciate the irrelevance of Ion's shallowness to the quality of his theatrical achievement, that Plato makes him so shallow. Provided that, in performance, what strikes the audience's eyes and ears has at least the appearance of being wrought with understanding (that the characters speak as such characters *should* speak), it does not matter how, exactly, either rhapsode or poet has brought the thing off, whether their ability to create and evoke the appearance of a living world in performance stems from genuine understanding or merely from a gift for capturing the look and feel of a world, for saying the appropriate words in the appropriate tone – the gift upon which Ion relies to lecture on Homer as well as to perform him, thus clarifying the limitations of that talent for readers of this dialogue.

The chief indictment laid against poetry in the *Ion*, then, is simply this: that since poetry in its proper form is theatrical performance, it can be fully appreciated and evaluated in terms of its effects alone (of how it comes across in the moment of performance) and without regard for how those effects are brought about – the source from which they derive their power. Hearing it put thus, we may not think of this as an indictment at all. That is because it is a point we tend now to make by invoking the concept of 'fictionality'. Any 'fiction' has a certain life of its own. We could become enthralled by *Hamlet* even if the script had somehow been worked up by monkeys; or by the *Iliad* even if its medium is a monkey like Ion. And we tend not to see anything wrong with this, because fictionality is a concept that applies primarily to artistic language as such, or in a larger sense to artistic creations in general (insofar as paintings or sculptures can be thought of as fictions). Questions of right and wrong in the practice of art (hence the possibility of censorship) we consider mostly in terms of how we as audience are affected by such creations: whether we learn from them, are emotionally enriched by or otherwise benefit from exposure to them, or the opposite. But the fictionality of the work we take for granted; poems, plays, novels just *are* fictions; and whether, as such, they are good or bad for you is a quite separate question.

Plato thinks of this differently. It is significant that the discussion in the second part of the *Ion* verges on isolating the concept of fictionality but stops short; for as we shall see, Plato never in fact works with this concept, and still less does it have any verbal equivalent in his Greek. What dominates his thinking about poetry (and art in general) is not fictionality but 'theatricality': that capacity for imaginative identification which inspired poets and performers and satisfied audiences alike employ. Fictionality belongs to the artistic product; theatricality belongs to the soul. And by thinking of poetry in terms of theatricality rather than fictionality, Plato makes poetry through and through an ethical, not an aesthetic affair. There are not two separate domains of inquiry for Plato here: the fictionality of literature (its aesthetic status) and the psychology of literary production (its ethical effects). Theatricality promotes in poet, performer, and audience alike a psychological stance that is not to be confined to aesthetic contexts but occupies an important place in our regular ethical lives. But Plato further believes that in this ethical role it is liable, if not carefully circumscribed, to have a pernicious effect. In order to see how this can be so, we want above all to hear more about the audience, and how theatricality stirs their souls. But in the *Ion*, Plato takes aim primarily at poetic professionals, and does not dwell on the larger ethical context set by their audience – although he prepares the space into which his theory can grow, in Socrates' all too brief description of the audience as the final link in the magnetic chain of inspiration (535e). The fuller theory arrives, we shall find, when the concept here called 'theatricality' crystallises around a term in Plato's language: *mimēsis* – 'imitation'. The crystal blooms in the *Republic*; but in preparation for considering that work let us range a little further among the dialogues.

2 Poetry and the professors

We have seen how in the *Ion* Plato seizes upon the traditional inference from the poet's status as an inspired performer to his ability to teach and inform his listeners, and how he disables this inference by contrasting inspiration with understanding and verbal performance with genuine communication. Various points to which the *Ion* devotes concerted attention are mentioned in some other early dialogues more briefly, or else developed further, by comparison to their treatment in the *Ion*, but tangentially to a dialogue's major topic. In the *Meno* Socrates is at something of a loss to fathom the success some political figures have undoubtedly achieved in managing the city's affairs, while nevertheless not meeting the criteria he thinks appropriate for those who can be said truly to understand what they are able to do; and he has recourse (at 99c–e) to comparison with inspired poets and prophets, and the now familiar claim that since their words are not their own responsibility but are vouchsafed them by divine gift, they speak without properly understanding what they speak about. In the *Apology* Socrates mentions the poets alongside politicians and craftspeople as one of the groups in the city whom he sought out because they seemed to possess various kinds of knowledge that he did not, but in whom he was disappointed. We have seen Socrates distinguish Ion's artistry as a performer from his shallow understanding of the momentous subjects he evokes; so in the *Apology* (22b–d) he declares that the poets he questioned seemed to understand less than anyone about the matters raised in their poems, and that they were like craftspeople in presuming that their skill in crafting objects of beauty gave them wisdom in the most important things also. And in the *Gorgias*, (501d–2d) the poet's skill (demoted in the schema of this dialogue to a mere empirical knack) is invoked in yet a different comparison, with the practice of rhetoric – the practice upon which the dialogue is centred. Poetry, being speech directed at large audiences, is a kind of 'public oratory' (*dēmēgoria*, 502c12), and like the orator, the poet aims primarily not to improve his audience, but to satisfy them. We recall that Ion's critical intelligence was employed most intently on giving his audience a good cry.

However, Plato is also concerned to show that, if poetry in its traditional manifestations is not a trustworthy medium of teaching, neither is it worthily used in the new style of teaching introduced by the sophists. This becomes

apparent from a survey of the scene in the *Protagoras* (338e6–48a9) in which
Protagoras and Socrates interpret and discuss a poem by Simonides. We
encounter here a kind of literary criticism quite different from the unrelieved
praise that an Ion would lavish on his Homer. Protagoras insists no man can
call himself educated unless he can take what the poets say and assess how
'correctly' (*orthōs*, 339a2) it is said; and he further claims that by turning to
poetry in this way he and Socrates can continue their discussion of virtue,
only with reference to a different medium (339a). Plato invites us to judge
this proposal by the exegesis he then has the sophist give of a poem addressed
by Simonides to his patron, the tyrant Scopas. From the forty-line poem[11]
Protagoras selects the opening couplet, in which the poet avers how difficult
it is to become a good person; he secures Socrates' agreement that the poem
as a whole is a fine and 'correct' piece; and then produces a later couplet in
which Simonides appears to contradict himself by taking issue with the sage
Pittacus for an apophthegm much the same as Simonides' own opening lines.
With that, his exegesis is done. He sits back, amid the praise and applause
of his audience, to savour Socrates' confusion (339b–d). Plato's satire of the
kind of literary criticism indulged in by the sophists, then, is transparent.

But it is important to see that Plato also measures a certain distance from
Socrates' own handling of the poem. He warns the reader to cast a critical
eye on Socrates' procedure by having Socrates confess to somewhat shady
tactics in his immediate reaction to Protagoras' exegesis: telling Protagoras
that he thinks the poem consistent, but admitting to the companion to whom
he narrates this conversation that at that moment he felt far less assured than
he allowed himself to sound (339c8–9); and admitting also that he provoked
the long and fruitless intervention of Prodicus for no better reason than that
he needed to play for time while he thought up a worthwhile response
(339e3–5). Thus alerted, we are the less surprised to find that with the
interpretation he eventually does produce, Socrates exploits the poem for his
own purposes quite as much as Protagoras – nobler though those purposes
might be.

To begin with, he gives no serious, impartial consideration to the possibility
that Protagoras might be right. He is 'afraid' that the sophist might be onto
something (339c8), and his next move is to buy time to consider 'what the
poet meant' (339e4–5). His immediate feeling, then, is that Protagoras ought
to be wrong, that Simonides is consistent, and that his task is to wrest a
consistent sense from the poem. We might think to justify his reaction as based
on a principle of literary-critical generosity: of assuming the author innocent,
as it were, until proven guilty. But it is hardly appropriate thus to attribute
an established code of literary-critical investigation to the man whom we will
later find recommending that the exegesis of poetry should simply be dismissed

[11] Fr. 542 Page.

from any discussion aiming at truth, since no one can settle a poem's sense (347e–8a). Socrates is motivated not by literary-critical, but by ethical principles. When he claims to have looked into the poem sufficiently (339c1) and to know it by heart because it has been a matter of special concern to him (339b5–6), his assurance is not supported by his having worked up a careful interpretation of the piece; for he is unpleasantly surprised by Protagoras' accusation, and has to invent his own exegesis from scratch.

What he means (we are led to suspect) is that he has been much concerned not with the poem as such, but with what he takes the poem to be about: the difficulty of becoming good. The poem's value for him is emblematic: this is the point of his quoting the appeal of the 'besieged' Scamander to his brother Simois when he calls on Prodicus to help prevent the 'sacking' of Simonides (340a). Simonides represents their cultural heritage, their home (Socrates chooses to emphasise that Prodicus is a fellow-countryman of the poet, 339e6); and there is something no less sacrilegious in the *parvenu* Protagoras' opportunistic carping at the famous singer (with whom Socrates, acting as bulwark, here identifies himself, as Scamander did with Troy) than there was in Achilles' hand-to-hand combat with a very god (*Il.* 21.315). In effect, Socrates is adopting towards Simonides the stance that, in the course of his exegesis (345e–6b), he says Simonides and praise-poets of his sort adopted towards their patrons. In both cases, there is a presumption of piety. Simonides is not going to make a point of Scopas' imperfections (although one hopes they were not gross); and Socrates will not go out of his way to denigrate his cultural forebears, any more than (to use the analogy he applies to Simonides) he thinks we should gloat over and trumpet the faults of our fathers, or of our fatherland – any more than he would allow Crito, in the dialogue of that name, to entice him into railing at his native Athens. Protagoras, we can see, is just such a gloater, amazing his audience by scoring points off the greatest names. Socrates, by contrast, prefers to allow Simonides the same monumentality that the poet himself helps confer on the subjects of his praise (indeed, by one modern reading of this much-contested poem its opening lines constitute a claim to just this artistic power[12]).

But if we look askance at Protagoras' ethic, we can hardly fail to be troubled also by the consequences of Socrates' piety when he is called upon to deliver a full-scale interpretation of the poem. Most readers are struck by its perversity. Whenever Simonides appears to say something that Socrates finds ethically unacceptable, he refuses to believe that the poet could have meant what he, Socrates, wants him not to have meant and is prepared to reinterpret syntax and sense in the most unlikely directions in order to get his way (as at

---

[12] Svenbro, *Parole*, pp. 144–61. For an English-language survey of scholarship on the poem consult Walter Donlan, 'Simonides, Fr. 4d and *P. Oxy.* 2432', *TAPA*, 100 (1969), 71–95.

343d6 – 4a6, and 345d7 – e6).[13] Precisely because Socrates wears this poem
like a badge of honour, he cannot bring himself to unpick its thread. He
interprets the poem as if it were a proto-philosophical argument between
Simonides and Pittacus (for it was through such lapidary mottoes as Pittacus'
'it is hard to be good', that philosophy was conducted in those days); but an
argument in which Simonides sounds suspiciously like Socrates himself.
Which is why his prefatory story of how the Spartans – renowned throughout
Greece for philistinism – are in fact, in their brusqueness, crypto-philosophers
of the lapidary Pittacan sort (342b – 3c), can be read as a parable of literary
criticism. These traditional slogans ('Know Thyself', 'Naught in excess') do
indeed contain a philosophy, but only if unpacked through the philosophic
activity of one who lives by them, as Socrates does. He knows as well as anyone
that the Spartans are no philosophers; but the point is, from their pithy mottoes
alone, who can tell? Everything and nothing can be built on such generously
pregnant phrases. Moreover – and here we come to Plato's, in contrast to
Socrates', purpose in this scene – much the same (within less extreme limits)
can be said of poetry. What Simonides' poem has done for Socrates is stoke
his enthusiasm to cope with the problem of which it speaks, as have the Delphic
mottoes. This emblematic, inspirational function, Plato thinks, is poetry's
raison d'être; for poetry is performance, and as such, we have seen, will involve
argument (if it does) not for its own sake, but for the sake of the performance.
But Protagoras, wearing his literary-critical cap, has assessed the poem as if
it were an argument, pure and simple. Thus pressed, Socrates has had to
follow suit in Simonides' defence, and has reinterpreted the poem as if it were
itself the kind of philosophic argument to which it provokes him – as well
as re-moulding the social and historical context in the shape of the archaic
'philosophy' his interpretation requires. But he cannot bring himself to treat
Simonides' sentences with the care that he would generally devote to
examining the opinions of a partner in argument (his interpretation, we saw,
is quite irresponsible), and with his exegesis complete, pleading now with
Protagoras to have done with poems and get back to their original discussion
of virtue, he explains why: because Simonides cannot answer him back. Treat
poetry as argument, and you will quickly find that it only appears to have
a voice; for your neighbour thinks the poet means one thing, you think he
means another, and a new argument begins: not over what the poet says, but
over what he means. And it is an argument to block the progress of all others;
for since a poem, unlike a poet, cannot answer our questions, the argument
will be interminable (347c – 8a).

The moral of the scene is certainly not that literary exegesis is worthless
and should be abandoned; indeed, Plato demands that his readers think
through their own understanding of the poem, and of poetry, if they are to

[13] Consult the commentary by C. C. W. Taylor, *Plato: Protagoras* (Oxford, 1976).

appreciate the inadequacy of the interpretations that his characters propose. The moral is rather that analysis of poetry, even of poems about virtue, cannot do the job that Protagoras claimed it could: to continue the investigation of virtue in another mode. For all that the sophists have found a way to include the poet's voice in their new, contentious style of teaching, Plato here implies that any impetus they may have given to the traditional view of poets as teachers is only spurious.

It is important to understand that Socrates' piety towards Simonides is not the piety of intellectual acquiescence. Given what we have heard him say about poets in the *Apology*, that would be strange indeed. So too in the *Hippias Minor*, another dialogue in which Socrates steers a sophist away from appealing to poetry on the grounds that the poet is not there to explain what he meant, Socrates makes no bones about disagreeing with what he takes to be Homer's opinion once he can get Hippias to espouse it as his own (365c–d) – indeed, the great advantage of being aware of his own ignorance, he insists, is that he is never afraid to disagree with the wise, knowing that he is likely to learn from his mistakes (369d, 372c). Translate a poem into a set of opinions, and Socrates will be as argumentative about them as you please. But a poem is not meant to be a set of opinions (this, surely, is the point of the repeated claim that poetry cannot answer back); it is meant for performance. And it is in the face of poetry's value as performance, the inspiration it can be, that Socrates is genuinely acquiescent and modest.

And not without good reason, it must be said. The Socrates of the earlier dialogues especially, as we have seen, is just not very good with poetry, at least in the technical sense. Moreover, the loving satire of Socrates in these dialogues opens a distance between Socrates as character and Plato as author. Socrates does well to be pious and to attempt simply to leave the poets out of his kind of discussion, but the Plato who shows us this Socrates in dramatic fictions is more a poet and a literary critic than such a character could ever be, and need not be bound by modesty. Moreover, if his ambition is to draw the blueprint of the ideal society as a whole, he cannot just set the poets aside, but must brace himself, given his beliefs, for confrontation with them. The theory that emerges still comes, of course, from Socrates' lips; but a Socrates to whose idosyncrasies rather less attention is paid than in such dialogues as the *Protagoras*.

3 The Dionysian chorus

From Plato's treatment of poetry in his earlier dialogues, as well as of the literary criticism of his day, two main rubrics of complaint have emerged. On the one hand he is disappointed by the intellectual quality of those reputed wise in a practice traditionally thought not merely to entertain but also to teach, and he subjects characters representative of the current scene to comic persiflage. On the other hand he traces the particular behaviour of his satirical butts to its roots in the nature of poetry, in order to make the general point that, since poetry as such is not thought and feeling but the performance of thoughts and feelings, the poet or performer need have no proper understanding of what he says, but may as it were be aping the appropriate words; and further that the literary critic who construes poetry as direct opinion is therefore mistaking its nature. However, it is one thing to show that poetry does not positively require from its participants a proper understanding of what is performed, and quite another to show that it is not even hospitable to such understanding. The example made of Ion supports only the former point. And although Socrates' description of inspired poets as out of their minds certainly suggests the latter claim, taken by itself it is hardly more than an exaggerated insult. It is only in the *Republic* that Plato offers theoretical arguments to sustain that second claim, and so justify the exclusion of Homer and the tragedians from his ideal society.

Consider here a few pages from the last work that Plato wrote, the *Laws*. This chronological skip will prove convenient because in the *Laws* Plato tends to declare his philosophic beliefs quite flatly, as if summarising them for posterity (for which purpose the Athenian Stranger proves a more amenable mouthpiece than Socrates), but often without the fullness of argument that supported similar views in previous dialogues. By turning now to the passage in Book II (667b–71a) in which he considers how poetry should be judged and by whom, we will therefore be able to compare a somewhat textbook-like statement of Plato's later position with the opening sallies that have occupied our attention so far, and so register developments with special clarity. It will then be time to consider the *Republic*, which is home to the strongest arguments instrumental in that development.

Rather than begin from the failings of poetry's practitioners and infer characteristics of the practice in order to explain those failings, Plato here begins from assumptions about the nature of poetry and draws inferences about its practitioners and judges – in particular, about what they need to know in order to practise and judge. All poetry is mimetic (668a7), and the correctness of an image in general depends on its 'equality' (*isotēs*, 667d5) with the original, that is, its faithful recreation of what the original is like. As such, the judgement of poetry is not to be left to taste; for from the mere fact that a poem pleases us nothing follows as to whether it is a faithful imitation or not (667d–8b). Rather, with any artistic creation one must first know 'what it is', that is, 'what it intends and of what it is in fact an image'. Only so can we judge whether the intention has been correctly or incorrectly followed through; which itself is a precondition for the third and highest stage of judgement, distinguishing what is good from what is bad (668c4–d2). The Athenian clarifies his remarks by appeal to the visual arts. If we did not even know that the painting or sculpture before us represented a man, we would be hard put to assess its correctness – whether it conveys the appropriate proportions and shape and general appearance of a man. But knowing the one and the other, we would also be in a position to judge how fine the work was (668d2 – 9a4).

That poetry is imitation is presented as a matter of common agreement among poets, audience, and actors alike (668b9 – c2). It is not, however, a notion of which we have heard anything in the earlier dialogues. There, poetry was the topic of farce, and Socrates seemed anxious to dismiss it from serious colloquy. Here poetry is set apart from the mere 'game' of harmless pleasure (667e) and given serious standards to meet, in order to take its place in the well-run society – for the Athenian at this point is establishing the importance of a 'Dionysian chorus' of older men whose task it would be to select and perform the best sort of poetry for the benefit of the entire city. Yet things are not as changed as they may seem. The standards to be met by poetry are not distinct standards of its own, but are constraints of truth and understanding imported from the kind of serious discourse in which Socrates wished to be engaged. Imitation is parasitic on what is imitated; it is from our understanding of what humans are like that we judge the sculpted man. In the case of the visual arts, Plato seems to think, this understanding need be nothing too difficult, a familiarity with and appreciation of how things look; whereas poetic image-making aims to capture what is far more difficult to understand and far more important: not just how people look, but how they act, and how they are motivated to act. Hence the Athenian says that lack of understanding in poetry can dispose us to look kindly on the wrong sort of behaviour (669c1). That is, through poetry we can misrepresent and misunderstand what is ethically appropriate – as when in drama, complains the Athenian, language suited to men is given a woman's melody, or the gestures of freemen are set to rhythms appropriate for slaves (669c – d).

Clearly, then, the goodness of the imitation is being thought of as inseparable from the goodness or appropriateness of what is imitated, and poetry would ideally demand nothing less than an understanding of how an entire society should regulate itself. But while we all know what proportions are appropriate to the human body, and therefore (at the simplest level) what a painting or sculpture of a man should look like, our knowledge of what constitutes appropriate behaviour in human society is considerably less secure and far more a matter of dispute, so that even at the simplest level we may be mistaken about how a dramatic imitation of human ways and actions should go.

Thus, whereas we can hardly imagine a person so benighted as not to recognise what a (realistic) painting of a man is intended to represent, with poetry even this first step is problematic. This, says the Athenian, is because most people learn their songs and dance-steps through compulsory drill, as a result of which they are able to perform without understanding the several elements of their performance (670b8 – c6). In other words, in the case of poetry (but not in the visual arts) it is possible to participate in a performance or enactment of its various images without appreciating what they are images of, but merely mouthing the words and going through the motions. And the problem is compounded by the fact that, although (in Plato's view) the different musical rhythms and modes to which words were set correspond as images to different ethical dispositions (a topic developed at length in the third book of the *Republic*), it was no easy matter to say which correspond to which – hence the Athenian deplores the latest practice of elaborating music without words, in which it is 'very difficult to say what is intended and what, among the worthy imitations, it is meant to be' (669e1 – 4). As a first step, then, the Dionysian chorus must not merely be drilled into performance but must willingly and capably 'follow along with' the rhythms and melodies they perform: that is, they must appreciate and understand[14] what the musical images are images *of* (670c8 – d4) (the analogy with painting shows that this, rather than a knowledge of musical theory, is meant).

We recall that there were two higher stages of artistic judgement: judging the correctness of an image, and whether it is good or bad. Here again the issue is presented as more complex in poetry than in the visual arts. The Athenian had asserted that, knowing everything about a man's appearance to be correctly represented in a painting or sculpture, we can then 'necessarily' and 'readily' tell how fine or beautiful it is;[15] to which his interlocutor, Cleinias, had been allowed the surprised response that, at that rate, we should all be connoisseurs (668e7 – 9a6). This may be Plato's way of acknowledging the short shrift he gives to the ambitions of painting and sculpture as art forms; but more importantly it makes the point that even in real life, let alone in painting, a person's bodily beauty is a beauty of *appearance*. It would make no obvious sense to say: 'he looks very handsome, but actually he isn't'. By contrast, it makes all too much sense to say of someone that he only seems a fine person, but in reality he is not. Hence this difference: to capture the appearance of a beautiful person in a visual image (and here we should bear in mind the tendency to idealism in the visual arts of the time) can be readily thought of as the creation of something visually beautiful; but to capture ethically fine behaviour through poetic image-making is not for that reason to produce something ethically fine, since beauty of soul (unlike physical beauty) can properly belong only to people, not to their products; nor is it (necessarily) to *do* something ethically fine, since the poet may work from a knowledge of the appearance of virtue merely, not of its reality.[16] Accordingly, it is in the case

---

[14] The Greek term συνακολουθεῖν (670d2) has a similar semantic stretch in this respect to our 'follow along with'.

[15] The Greek term καλός (see 669a3 – 4) ranges the semantic domain of both 'fine' and 'beautiful'.

[16] In Xenophon's *Memorabilia* 3.10.1 – 8, where Socrates talks with sculptors, the discussion brings out the limitations of the means available in that art for the portrayal of character and the soul.

of poetry above all that the second and third levels of artistic judgement become importantly distinct. The poet ought certainly to know more than the rote-learning public, for he must at least intend an object for the images that he makes; and if he is to avoid the dramatic hybrids that now bedevil the stage, he should attain to the second level, that of correctly matching image to object. But he can do this without reaching the third level, without being able to judge whether or not his image is 'fine', where that means ethically fine in its effects (670c4 – 1a1). This is a task for the Dionysian chorus, who must not only be able to select from the panoply of poetic devices those appropriate for whatever is to be represented (the second level) but also (the third level) to make a judgement of what is appropriate for men of their years and character – that is, for model citizens – to sing (670d4 – 6).[17] They do not simply know the poetic means that best captures each ethical pattern – something a poet could know while being acquainted only with what seems or is generally thought to be virtue – but, insofar as they are models for the community, in judging what is appropriate for themselves to sing they are judging for themselves where virtue lies – not only for their own satisfaction, however, but in order to 'lead the young' (here usurping the poet's didactic role) 'to embrace worthy patterns of behaviour' (670d6 – e2).

What emerges most clearly from this passage of the *Laws* by comparison with the earlier dialogues, then, is that while on the one hand Plato is taking poetry more seriously than he seemed prepared to in the earlier works, and granting it an educative purpose in society, on the other hand he is still much concerned to keep poets and poetry in a subordinate position. Elsewhere in the *Laws*, indeed, we find versions of the accusation that poets are crowd-pleasers (700d – 1b), as seen in the *Gorgias*, and of the familiar claim that poetic inspiration is a kind of madness (719c – d). Nor should we be misled by the importance we have seen accorded the 'intention' of the artistic work (at 668c6 and 669e4) into comparing it with the modern literary-critical notion of the recovery of authorial intent – as if Plato were now proposing that in order to evaluate poetry we should carefully unpack the contents of those poetic skulls which previously he had told us were empty of rational thoughts. It is not what the author but what the *work* 'intends'[18] that the Athenian insists we should know; not an elaborate scheme in the poet's head but (as the examples in this passage and the previously translated gloss at 668c7 together show) simply an answer to the question: 'What is this image an image *of?*'

---

[17] ἐκλέγεσθαί τε τὰ προσήκοντα refers to the second level of competence and the specification ἃ τοῖς τηλικούτοις τε καὶ τοιούτοις ᾄδειν πρέπον encapsulates that sense of what it is to be a model citizen which only those at the third level of competence possess. That there are two distinct levels to be discerned in these lines is supported by the otherwise otiose collocation of προσήκοντα with πρέπον.

[18] βούλεσθαι ('to want'). A further example of its use with an inanimate subject ('myth') comes at *Theatetus* 156c3, where its sense approaches that of 'to mean', 'to signify' (compare the French *vouloir dire*).

The answer may not, indeed, be simple to give, at least in the case of poetry; but its difficulty will not derive from the hopelessness of the attempt to inspect a poet's inner purpose; and it makes for only the first and most straightforward stage of poetic judgement, not its ultimate criterion. That criterion is rather the constraint imposed by the actual nature of the subject-matter than by the poet's intentions towards it. And that is why Plato aims to put poetry under the control of those who understand and actually live the good life. He does not even exclude the possibility that poets could be among their number; but what he does think crucial is to establish that, if so, it would not be as poets that they figured there. He acknowledges, to put it another way, that a poet is not a moralist *manqué*, is not trying and failing to come up to the standards that the Dionysian chorus imposes; and for that very reason he imposes the Dionysian chorus upon the poet.

Underlying that acknowledgment and justifying this imposition is the analysis of poetry as *mimēsis*. The poet has a skill all his own: not understanding, but capturing the appearance, the look and feel of human life. But just as an image is, or rather should be (in Plato's view), for the sake of its original, the art of image-making is destined to be the helpmate of the art that seeks truth. Poetry cannot, so to speak, be trusted on its own, but as the ward of a philosophic guardian can put its talent to good use.

4 'The Republic': a poetic training

The dominant theme of the critique of poetry in the earlier dialogues, we saw, is that poetry is theatrical performance, and for that reason dangerously independent of the understanding by which it may or may not be informed. The theme of the account just perused in the *Laws* is that poetry is imitation, and has for that reason a potentially important role in education, provided that it is controlled by those best qualified to judge the models that education should set before us.

The two themes are connected in the following way. The theatricality of poetry does not reside in the poem considered as a stretch of language but in an aspect of the psychology of those who participate in the performance of that stretch of language (a description that includes the audience): namely, in their capacity for imaginative identification with what is to be represented. Theatricality contrasts in this respect with what we call the 'fictionality' of poetry, although the two notions can be brought to bear on the same issue of the independence of a poetic creation from the understanding of its creators (and appreciators). Now, it may seem that when Plato comes to construe all poems as imitations he is shifting his emphasis from the psychology to the properties of poetic discourse itself, hence in the general direction of fictionality. This thought might be encouraged by the analogy with the visual arts, since the status of painted or sculpted 'imitations' of a man is presented as depending (not on psychology but) only on the fact that the image, while clearly not a real man, is related in a certain way to real men. But here we must bear in mind the Athenian's warning that things are not so simple with poetry. Certainly, the actor on stage is as clearly not Oedipus or Agamemnon in person as the painting is not actually a man; but let us recall this difference: that whereas a painter (at least as Plato understands painting) attempts to capture only how people and things look, a poet captures how people behave. The result is that in the case of poetry the image and that of which it is an image are not so clearly distinct from each other as in the visual arts. A poetic performance (the image) engages its participants not simply in the look but, as we say, in the whole 'feel' of the human action it portrays; and since emotions and ethical attitudes are a crucial part of that action, by allowing ourselves to identify with what is depicted (by participating, that is, in the performance) we come in some sense to reproduce those emotions and attitudes, that 'feel', within ourselves – as opposed to reproducing or considering the look of a thing in a material image outside ourselves. Not that a painting of, say, some harrowing scene, vividly executed, cannot move or shock us; but a canvas on a wall tends to invite sustained and relatively detached meditation rather than sympathetic participation in the portrayed scene.

Imitation in poetry, it turns out, is therefore accomplished by just that theatricality on which the earlier dialogues were focused. For if poetry in Plato's scheme is imitation, it is not for all that conceived of as a merely mechanical snapshot of life, which could as it were be held up alongside its object of comparison ('imitation' as a theoretical term is not to be rejected, then, on the strength of the criticism which would now accrue to such a conception). In our passage from the *Laws* the old men of the Dionysian chorus do not check prospective poetic works against an itemised list of the merits in their own lives; rather, they choose to perform what feels right for them, and the 'pleasure free from side-effects' which they take in their performance (the pleasure of identifying with the models they represent) is itself a part of the example they set for the young in how to 'embrace worthy behaviour' (*Laws* 2.670d6 – e2). Rather than produce a snapshot of the virtuous life, they enact a representative component of it. In a poetic performance, then, the image and what is imitated become, in a sense, one. Therein lie both its potential benefit and its danger. And it is just insofar as the visual arts maintain a stricter demarcation between image and what is imitated that Plato is inclined to think of them as relatively trivial.

But this is to state in general terms what requires elucidation from the detailed text of the *Republic*; for it is there that the transition between the earlier and the later stance is made out. Let us turn first to the recommendations for training the new generation of Guardians, the ruling-class of the ideal society: a training in which poetry plays a considerable role. The discussion of that role begins towards the end of the second book and takes up most of the third; and its structure reveals what is truly new about Plato's mature critique of poetry in relation to the tradition. After all, by acknowledging once more the didactic function of poetry (after the violent break of the earlier dialogues) Plato was to that extent returning to a traditional position; and his disapproval of a gamut of poetic topics and themes, although more radical than any that came before, had both philosophic and more conventionally poetic precedent (for example in Xenophanes and Pindar).[19] But censorship of the content of poetry, of what is and is not to be said, makes up only the first part of his critique (2.376c – 3.392c). He follows this with an analysis of the manner in which a poet says what he has to say, introducing the issue of poetry's mimetic nature as evinced by its use of imitative verbal techniques (3.392c–8b); after which he considers how melody, rhythm, and choreography are to fit with this enterprise, both ethically and mimetically (3.398c–403c). And in his account of verbal technique he judges the value of poetic imitation not only by appeal to the worth of what is imitated but also in terms of the worth of the activity of imitation itself – in terms of the effect of its use on the character of the user (394a–8b). But that effect, at least if our imitative bent is allowed to go its natural way, he finds to be pernicious. Thus poetry is to have its wings clipped not only for the ethical content it happens to have but – far more radical and unavoidable a challenge – for the ethical effect of the imitativeness that is in its very nature. This is the truly path-breaking aspect of Plato's critique (although his case for it is not made out in full until Book X, for reasons which we shall consider).

But let us look first at the rather less controversial part of the critique, Plato's proposal to set limits on the content of poetry for educational purposes. I say 'less controversial' because his primary and repeated concern throughout this account of the Guardians' education is the question of what should be allowed to reach the ears of the impressionable young;[20] and the general aim of his restrictions, that of not exposing the young to fictional models of behaviour (to use the modern term) that might be a bad influence on them, would be shared by many today – as attested, for example, by calls for scaling down the violence shown on television.[21] However, the example from television offers an illuminating contrast as well as a parallel. The modern fear is, often enough, that the impressionable viewer will simply ape the actions portrayed on the screen; that if beating up old men is made to look thrilling, some among the thrill-seeking young will be tempted to beat up old men. The nearest Plato comes to this notion is in talking of the very youngest children, those of an age to listen to their mothers' or nurses' fairy-stories (377c) and who cannot tell what is allegorical from what is not (378d), when he worries

---

[19] Xenophanes fr. B1, B11, B12 Diels-Kranz, and Pindar, *Olympian* 1.28–36.
[20] See 377a4, 378a3, 378d6–7, 388d2, 389d7, 395d1, 401c6, 402a2.
[21] Nehamas, 'Imitation', pp. 50–1.

that to tell them the story of what Cronus did to Uranus is tantamount to inviting them to take pleasure in the prospect of extreme revenge on their oppressive parents (378b). But Plato is hardly envisaging that the little mites have no sooner heard the story than they go looking for daddy's scythe. He is saying that such stories influence childhood fantasy, and fantasy has an effect on the development of character. The sway of poetry over actions, then, is only indirect, insofar as action stems from character.

This pattern becomes firmly established as Socrates moves on from stories of the gods to stories of heroes, and to the inadequacy of the model they provide for virtuous conduct. General attitudes and emotional poses, rather than particular types of action, are what he fears the young Guardians will emulate; shuddering along with Achilles at the bleakness of death and so softening themselves for their task of defending the city in war (387c); weeping unabashedly with the same hero over Patroclus, thus sapping their endurance of future grief (388d); and, in general, learning to condone unacceptable behaviour in themselves on the grounds that they find it exemplified by heroes and by gods – that is, by beings thought of as greater and better than mere mortals, hence as role-models (391c–e; cf. 378b4–5). Thus what Socrates imagines traditional poetry to encourage, and what he warns against, is not so much the spectacular violence or exotic sexuality that is the fodder of modern censorship – behaviour more likely to be entertained in fantasy than enacted – as certain weaknesses of character to which we are all prone, and which are, so to speak, only a movement of the soul away.

The ground for so stringent a censoring of poetry is prepared in the speech of Adimantus towards the beginning of the second book (362e–7e). The burden of the speech is roughly that, with the poets for friends, Justice has little need for enemies. The poets tend to exalt virtue so high that the path to reach it comes to seem impossibly arduous, while the wheeling and dealing that goes on below they attest (even as they condemn it) to be more practicable and more likely to bring pleasures and rewards in this life (364a–b). For this reason they and we can more readily identify with what they condemn than with what they exalt. Small and weak as we are, we can at least beg mercy of the gods, they say, and make up in foxiness what we lack in strength (364e, 365c) – how we learn to love our little selves! And even the rewards of justice are imagined as just that: rewards, as if the aim of a superior breed of fox (366e). The effect of the speech, then, is to disarm the temptation to think of the poets as honest realists, painting human frailty and the bitterness of life in its true colours. To describe human nature in this way is rather – perhaps despite the poet's best intentions – to make a self-fulfilling prophecy of ethical doom. It is not to face facts, but, as it were, to create them – to turn out an audience in the poet's own pessimistic image.

Accordingly, when Socrates comes to censor poetry for his own ethical purposes, we are not to see him as imposing an ethical agenda on what was previously innocent of any such thing, but as adjusting and controlling a poetic effect that previously occurred more haphazardly. While admitting that we find it sweet to indulge and pity our faults and frailties – in theatrical guise no less than in our own actions (387b2 – 6, 390a5) – Socrates refuses to accept that we cannot be brought up in such a way as to find that sweetness in justice, and in the images of justice (401c6 – d3). If the poets tell stories of the stony road to virtue and the rewards of opportunism, Socrates will counter by disseminating a 'Phoenician Tale' that will make it positively attractive for the citizens of his ideal society to be civic-minded (414b1 – 6, 415d3 – 5); not, however, by offering vulgar rewards, but by instilling a confidence in the social arrangements that will have the effect (as we eventually discover) of permitting all to take pleasure in what is worthy of pleasure (9.586d – 7a). And in the *Laws* this theme of using the sweetness of poetry to promote the sweetness of justice becomes still more explicit.[22]

This need to make a matching but corrective *riposte* to the poets underpins Socrates' aggressive advertisement of the place of 'falsehoods' and 'lies' in the Guardians' education.[23] The Phoenician Tale itself would be a 'noble lie' that we were telling the citizens (414c); and all education, he startles Adimantus by saying, should begin with falsehoods – although he quickly soothes him by explaining that a child's education should begin with myths, which 'taken as a whole, are false; though there is some truth in them' (377a). We are being asked to understand Socrates' censorship as an extension of a use of 'falsehood' that we would all recognise as noble. Indeed, what Socrates intends to disseminate is in the deepest ethical sense not false at all, but true. Thus he is careful to say, as he rejects each unsatisfactory myth and portrayal of character, that not only is it morally harmful but also 'untrue' (or 'inconsistent').[24] Yet he also asserts that even if the unsavoury myths *were* true we should not tell them, not casually at least, to the young (378a; and cf. *Laws* 2.663d6 – e2). Plato allows the moral impulse to show from behind the arguments of falsehood because, while believing he can construct theological and cosmological arguments that confute the cosmic perspective which he attributes to the poets (and in which they find the ground for their ethical views), arguments of which Socrates offers us a glimpse at the end of Book II, he nevertheless does not want to rest his ethical case on such speculative reasoning alone.

This point needs explanation. The whole purpose of Socrates' pruning and manipulation of the poetic environment in which his Guardians mature is to bring them up in the belief and the sentiment that the just life is also the most truly pleasant life – the belief which the argument of the *Republic* is designed

---

[22] *Laws* 659d, 663 – 4a, 802c – d.

[23] The Greek term ψεῦδος and its associated verbal forms can refer to both intentional and unintentional falsehood.

[24] See 378c1, 380c3, 381e5, 386b10, 391b7.

to vindicate for us. We can readily see why such a 'noble lie' is noble; but in what sense is it a lie? Not because Socrates believes it false; on the contrary. It is a lie only because it is the kind of truth to which we can 'give the lie' in our souls – whatever the cosmic way of things may be, and however neat the theological arguments that Socrates produces. Conversely put: not only is it a truth, but it is a truth that we must make for ourselves. But we shall be unable to make it come true unless we are sheltered while impressionable from the full knowledge of how we can also give it the lie (thus the good judge must be a 'late-learner' of the nature of injustice, 409b4 – c1). And it is in this sense that Socrates would tell lies: in that he would consciously suppress the full complexity of what he knows in order to manipulate the young towards ethical truth (as he insists all mothers attempt to do, although perhaps not so consciously, 377b – c). His strategy thus combines the two acceptable types of intentional falsehood which he says humans must use to the extent that they do not have the perfection of gods (382c6 – d3): first, the medicinal lie, by which the natural weakness and lack of sense in children is adjusted and tempered.[25] (The foundation for this point was laid in the example from the first book, at 331c, of how one would not return a dangerous weapon to a friend, and would resort to lying to prevent this, if the friend had lost his wits in the meantime; cf. 389b – d); and second, the mythological lie, in which, not knowing 'what the truth about ancient things actually is', we construct a story as like the truth as possible – that is, the kind of merely plausible and/or ethically appropriate account that even the most philosophic cosmology, as in the *Timaeus*,[26] let alone the tales we would tell to children, cannot rise above. Notice, again, that Socrates is not here isolating the fictionality of poetic myth; rather, he emphasises that it is speculative. Whereas fiction for us has positive and autonomous value, a speculation, while useful (382d3), remains a second-best, a stab at truth. We might compare – however trivial the comparison – the 'lie' that today's children are told about Santa Claus. Insofar as it is not simply an adult indulgence – the desire to live vicariously in a kinder world, as seen through the eyes of one's children – it has the worthy purpose of giving children a breathing-space in which to develop values appropriate to a kinder world, values resistant to the tarnish of cynicism that the world will attempt to impose, and from within which the historical falsity of the story, when unmasked, will seem an unimportant matter: the story itself all the more deeply true for that.

But this comparison may seem not just trivial, but misleading. For none but children believe in Santa Claus, whereas Socrates with startling ease extends the purview of his censorship in several casual-sounding statements (and for all that young people remain the focus of his concern in these books)

---

[25] See 377b1 – 3, 378a3.
[26] See e.g., 29c4 – d3, 48d1 – e1.

to include the adult audience.[27] Moreover, the Phoenician Tale is to be told
to all, even the rulers themselves (414c1 – 2). It seems that no one in Plato's
ideal society would, in the terms of the comparison, ever grow out of a literal
belief in Santa Claus; and this offends (as it should) our liberal belief that at
some stage people must be considered sufficiently adult to be left as the best
judges of whether the poetry to which they expose themselves does them harm
or not. The matter is complicated by the fact that the 'rulers' at this point
in the argument of the *Republic* are not yet the 'Philosopher-Kings' who eventually emerge as the ruling class. Still, we must bite the bullet here and not
conceal from ourselves that Plato believes that some – most – adults remain
in an important sense children throughout their lives. It is not just for children
but also for the benefit of 'men who must be free, and fear slavery more than
death' that morbid visions of Hades are to vanish from poetry (387b4 – 6).
In the *Phaedo* Cebes requests Socrates to pile on the arguments for the
immortality of the soul not so much for Cebes' own sake as for that of the 'child
inside' of him who fears the bogey of death (77e3 – 7). In the psychology of
the *Republic* the soul is divided into three parts; and the lowest part is made
up of impulses and appetites which, if allowed to dominate over the other
parts, will emerge, in extreme cases, as the worst kind of childish indulgence.
It could also be described, we shall see, as by nature the most 'theatrical' part
of the soul. We all carry this theatrical child and its potential tyranny around
inside us through life; and this fact has two consequences: first, that the
theatrical stimulus of poetry must be carefully monitored even for adults, and
second, that being adult (in the conventional sense) does not automatically
qualify one to do the monitoring.

The argument is not fully made out in these terms until the tenth book;
but it is expressed in a preliminary way in the next stage of the critique in
Book III – the stage at which we first encounter the more radical and
innovative aspect of the critique, its potshot at poetry's mimetic nature. The
account is preliminary in the sense that it remains at a somewhat limited,
technical level, not straying from the mechanics of poetic expression, since
it cannot extend its range (as happens in the tenth book) by appeal to a
psychological and metaphysical apparatus that at this point in the *Republic*
has yet to be established. But it is worth digging a while around the technical
roots of that fuller growth.

Plato flags both the technical level of the passage and the fact that something
rather new is afoot by having a puzzled Adimantus request a gloss first of
Socrates' distinction between content and 'diction' or form (*lexeōs*, 392c6),
and then of the example he gives to illustrate what he means by diction: the
contrast between 'simple narrative' and 'narrative through imitation'
(392c6 – d7). Adimantus' puzzlement need indicate no more than that the

[27] See 378d1, 380c1, 387b4.

terms have a technical air, not that they are Platonic neologisms. What is distinctively Platonic is rather the focus on the ethical aspect of such technicalities. For although our key term, 'imitation', is here made the focus of attention (and this is the first time in the *Republic* that it has come to the fore) in what may seem a rather specialised, almost syntactic application – to denote narrative couched in direct rather than indirect speech – nevertheless we swiftly discover that far more important distinctions than the merely syntactic are at issue. The desire to speak in a voice other than one's own becomes fraught with unwelcome implications.

Consider how Socrates explains himself to Adimantus. With reference to the opening lines of the *Iliad*, he first describes how Homer shifts from plain narrative of Chryses' embassy to the Atreids, in which the poet does not attempt to make us think 'that anyone other than himself is speaking', to delivering the priest's indignant appeal to the kings 'as if he himself were Chryses'; and Socrates then goes so far as to offer an actual sample, with a view to pre-empting Adimantus' further puzzlement, of what Homer might have composed had he decided not to 'hide himself' but to express the whole passage without imitation – a sample which he speaks in prose rather than verse because he is 'no poet' (392e–4b). In effect, Socrates impersonates Homer; that is, he says what he imagines Homer might have said had he couched the opening of the *Iliad* in indirect prose – but how differently from the way in which Homer impersonates Chryses! Socrates resorts to impersonation only as a teaching-aid, to clarify the unfamiliar for Adimantus (392d8–e1, 393d2–3), and even then he can speak in no way other than his own ('I am no poet'). By contrast, impersonation is the very backbone of Homer's achievement: witness how laughable and lifeless Socrates' paraphrase sounds (not for nothing does he warn us of his lack of poetic talent).

In this long preamble, then, Plato is concerned not only to familiarise his audience with certain technical distinctions but, more importantly, to illustrate (rather than describe) the ethical dimension of these technicalities (and for the same reason that the character Socrates has recourse to illustration over description). For consider how Socrates proceeds. Having established his technical terms he next asks whether the young Guardians should be allowed to be 'imitative' (*mimētikous*, 394e1), a term which, we discover, has both a quite formal reference and an ethical connotation. Formally, the Guardians are to perform poetry which contains little direct speech, and then only that of good characters (396c–e). Thus they are not to be 'imitative' in Socrates' sense, since he means by this word not just 'engaging in' but *prone* to imitation (at 395a2 he glosses the phrase 'will be imitative' as 'will imitate many things'). Ethically, Socrates assumes that the use of direct speech in poetry will engage the Guardians' 'desire to speak as if they were that person' (i.e. the speaking character), with the result that they 'would not be ashamed of such an imitation' if the character were good, whereas they would not want 'seriously

to liken themselves' to a bad character (396c7 – d5). Here it is especially crucial
to recall how far the modern model of the contemplative reader is from Plato's
thoughts. The Guardians are to *perform* this poetry; imitation is as much what
they do as it is what the poets do (e.g., 395d7); so that the responses of an
actor rather than of a reader offer a better analogue, however approximate.
It is this anticipated seriousness of ethical engagement that underpins Socrates'
claim that imitations, if performed regularly from childhood, tend to become
established in our own habits and behaviour, both in our bodily demeanour
and our patterns of thought (395d1 – 3). 'Imitation', indeed, is too pale a word
in English for what Socrates evidently speaks of here: 'identification' or
'emulation' would be closer to the mark.

Looking again at the little parable of imitation that Socrates' own preamble
provides, we can now see that it follows the pattern he lays down for his
Guardians. He employs imitation only as a tool to advance understanding
(as the Guardians are to imitate only as an aid to living the reflective life) and
the voice he produces (as the Guardians should limit themselves to voices to
which they would wish to own up) remains recognisably his own – Homer
becomes Socrates, not vice-versa. And just as Socrates' limp metaphrase
showed imitation to be the very life of Homer's verse, so the Guardians are
contrasted with a type who, through bad upbringing (396c2 – 3), would think
no topic unworthy for imitation, but would attempt to 'imitate everything
seriously and before large audiences', not only villains and madmen but also
dogs and sheep and the sound-effects of such things as thunder or wagon-
wheels or blaring trumpets (397a – b, 395e – 6a).

Superficially, we are some distance from Homeric poetry here; for these
are the theatrical tricks of tragedy and comedy, while Socrates seems to judge
the epic style closest of any current type to the poetic discourse a Guardian
would employ (396e4 – 8) (similarly in the *Laws*, at 2.658c – d, the Athenian
judges tragedy to be the preference of 'educated women, youths, and pretty
much the public at large', Homer and Hesiod the preference of old men such
as himself). Nevertheless, imitation is as constitutive of Homer's ambition
as it is of the ambition of this vulgar ventriloquist. For although epic poetry,
with its single metre and generally elevated tone, approaches the even and
relatively unchanging style declared fit for a Guardian (397b6 – c1), comparison with Socrates' metaphrase shows (if such a demonstration were
needed) that Homer is not simply out to impart information about what
happened at Troy (information which Socrates' version adequately encapsulates) but is intent as it were to give us the whole Troy, to surround us
with the panoply of its leading voices. This is to use imitation not as the
Guardian would use it, as an aid to make vivid his ethical ideal, but rather
as a way of understanding the ethical implications of a complete series of
events, wherever it leads. We are to judge Agamemnon's offence by hearing
the indignation in Chryses' voice; but so too we are to come to terms with

the larger tragedy of the events at Troy by hearing Achilles cry out in anger, in grief, in moments of despair. In an essential respect, then, Homer is akin after all to our 'vulgar' imitator (397a1). For notice that Socrates does not criticise this latter because the models he chooses to imitate are disreputable (although some will be), but simply because he does not discriminate between what is and is not reputable in choosing his models, but imitates anything and everything in all seriousness (397a2–4). That is, he treats imitation as an activity good in itself rather than dependent for its value on the goodness of what is imitated. But no less does Homer, in treating imitation as his favoured procedure of understanding. Socrates, by contrast, although he holds that imitation of good models is a proper part of the Guardians' education, insists that bad models can and ought to be understood without imitation (thus his Guardians are to 'know and recognise' mad and wicked characters, but not to perform or imitate them, 396a4–6).

Imitation thus emerges as inherently suspect. It is valuable only when directed towards overcoming its own limitations, that is, as practised by Guardians who intend to become in life what they begin by merely imitating. The moment it is held to be valuable in its own right it begins to weaken the imitator's grasp of the best kind of life. At this stage in the argument of the *Republic* Socrates supports the point by appeal to the principle on which he is establishing the ideal society: that each person can do one task well, but if he or she attempts to be good at many, is likely to fail at all. So too, he begins by saying, we find that in the field of imitation one dramatist or actor will specialise in tragedy, another in comedy, and so on (394e2–5b1). However, the analogy will not go through in these terms, because of a peculiarity in poetic activity: namely, that the poet speaks mostly of others' tasks rather than his own; that he is, as it were, a professional busybody. Thus the tragedian only appears to have a single task; while at the ethical rather than purely technical level he will, as we have seen, attempt to be many people at once – to take on the perspective of a multiplicity of characters, in all seriousness, as a means of understanding the patterns of human life. In this sense the 'single' task of poetic imitation is in its very essence opposed to the principle of 'one person, one task'. (Recall that for Socrates the phrase 'is imitative' means 'imitates many things', 395a2.) The Guardians, even though they will imitate a plurality of characters – the brave, the self-controlled, the pious, 'and all such' – are imitating only what conduces to their one task of building a free society (395b8–c5); but for poets the imitation of human multiplicity, even if thought of as eventually conducive to a unified ethical purpose, is a good just in itself – a path of understanding. Hence, although Socrates begins by pointing out a technical sense in which poets conform to his social principle, it is on the strength of this principle that he ends the discussion by excluding conventional poets from his ideal city, insisting that there would be no place for their talent in a society devoid of 'multiplex' characters (397d10–8b4).

What justifies his shift is that in the course of the discussion he has brought out the ethical consequences of poetry's technical procedures.

Thus, while he began by distinguishing three modes of poetic discourse on a purely mechanical basis – as narrative, 'imitation' (direct speech), and thirdly a style which employs both these (394c) – he ends by adjudicating (on the grounds discussed) between a different triplet of poetic resources, between the 'austere', the 'sweet', and the 'mixed' styles. And here the styles are correlated and imbued with the ethos of their characteristic users: the austere being that especially wary use of imitation combined with narrative which the Guardian should adopt, and the sweet the style favoured by our ventriloquial type (the mixed is not further specified, but Homeric epic would fall naturally into place at this point in the spectrum, 397b6 – e2). In mechanical terms, all three of these latter styles employ both narrative and direct speech, and so are to be classified under the third type of the former triplet. Plato's intent in this development is surely to stress that the important distinction in this domain is ultimately not syntactic, but ethical. The transition from the former to the latter triplet is potentially confusing to modern readers to the extent that we are less ready to correlate poetic styles with ethical dispositions; but some commentators have attributed the confusion to Plato himself.[28] Notice that Plato is careful to avoid such confusion as might arise between the third terms in either triplet, by referring to one as the 'mixed' type (397d3, 397d6), to the other as 'that which employs both' (394c4, 396e6), and never as a 'mixture'.

One further consequence of this development is that Socrates' restrictions on what the Guardians may imitate are looser than we might think; for we are not to think of him as denying them – at least, not by rigid application of a merely technical criterion – any and all poetry in which a corrupt character gives direct voice to his or her corruption. Socrates' crucial qualification is that good persons will not want 'seriously' (*spoudēi*, 396d4) to liken themselves to one worse than they (396d4 – 5). This is to be understood by comparison with the kind of response to poetry that Socrates precludes through censorship earlier in the book, the reception by the young of unworthy Homeric passages (388d2 – 7): such sentiments, he says, are dangerous if the young listen to them seriously and do not rather 'laugh them down' as unworthily spoken. The important point is not that the Guardians avoid at all costs either hearing or performing the direct speech of unworthy characters, but that they avoid any ethical engagement, any serious identification with such characters and their actions. That is why Socrates recommends (387e9 – 8a3) that laments not be assigned to male heroes but only to women – 'and not to serious

---

[28] E.g., Annas, 'Triviality', p. 27, n. 37: 'Plato finds it hard to make his mind up here'. Else, *Plato and Aristotle*, p. 36, thinks Plato is deliberately obfuscating things.

women either'[29] – or to men of low quality: because imitation of unworthy conduct in perceived role-models, rather than such imitation *tout court*, is what he is most anxious to pre-empt.

This also explains the two riders that Socrates adds to his prescription: first, that good persons may indeed imitate unworthy characters in all seriousness to the extent (and it will be minimal) that the character is doing something good (in other words, if the character is undergoing ethical reform, and to identify with this would be no bad thing); and second, that although a Guardian would be ashamed 'seriously' to imitate unworthy characters in their very unworthiness (as opposed to when they are doing good), he might yet imitate even these traits, but 'for play'[30] (396d3 – e2). In context, the phrase seems to make room for a satirical kind of imitation,[31] in which the good could attend to or enact the actual voices of the bad while yet remaining disengaged – not treating them as role-models – and 'laughing them down' in the manner that we have seen Socrates wish the young would adopt in the face of unworthy Homeric sentiments. Not that Socrates actually develops this option for his Guardians: as we have seen, he does not imagine that the young will take Homer in any other way but seriously, and so resorts to censorship. But the qualification is of special relevance to anyone attempting to configure Plato's own literary practice with Socrates' prescriptions in this work. After all, the *Republic* itself boasts in its opening book a lengthy and direct 'imitation' of Thrasymachus, an unworthy character acting unworthily. Would it therefore be unfit for a Guardian of that republic to hear? We should notice how the blustering, overbearing Thrasymachus is portrayed more as a caricature than a character (as rudeness incarnate, so to speak) – a quality of portrayal common to all Plato's villains and buffoons, such as Callicles and Ion. Indeed, almost the only fully drawn, complex character in the dialogues is Socrates himself. Perhaps, then, Plato was out to mimic the voice of the enemy in such a way that we, the philosophic audience, neither so young nor so unsophisticated as to require the extreme protection of censorship, would be unable to identify with it but would be prompted to laugh its venom off.[32]

---

[29] The Greek term σπουδαῖος means both 'serious' and 'good'; the more awkward translation keeps the echo of 'serious' imitation.

[30] παιδιᾶς χάριν, 396e2. Contrast the interpretation of Nehamas, 'Imitation', p. 49, who takes the phrase 'for play' to qualify the imitation of bad characters engaged in doing good.

[31] For this sense of παιδιά ('jesting', 'comedy', 'satire'), cf. Aristotle, *Nicomachean Ethics* 4.1128a19–24.

[32] Distinguish, however, Plato's attitude to theatrical comedy: esp. *Laws* 816d–e.

5 *'The Republic': poetry overcome*

Plato's fundamental criticism of poetic imitation, and thus of poetry as such, is that poets see imitation as good in itself, as a process of knowledge or understanding, regardless of what is imitated. But at this point we surely want to ask: what exactly is *wrong* with taking poetic imitation to be a process of understanding? Did we grant Plato too much by agreeing, in considering the Dionysian chorus of the *Laws*, that he had at least dismantled any necessary connection between the activity of poetic performance (that is, imitation) and proper understanding; for why not think of imitation as itself a kind of understanding – one among others, to be sure, but a fully fledged member of the species nonetheless? That is, by imaginatively participating in the represented situation we become familiar with it, through a 'sympathy' that implies no necessary approval of the actions or attitudes portrayed and therefore needs no censor, and so we come to understand it perhaps better than had we kept an analytic distance. Let us grant that poetic performance can be properly appreciated in terms of its effects alone, without regard for their source; but why worry over this, when the effects are effects of familiarity with expanded horizons? And if the portrayed situation has the breadth of an *Iliad*, the fullness of familiarity (greater than any Ion or trivial 'ventriloquist' could attain) offers scope for a lifetime. So we might reason. Plato's arguments to block this line of reasoning require him to build upon the foundation of nothing less than the psychology and metaphysics laboriously established in the ensuing books of the *Republic*, and to be invoked at the outset of his attack on poetry in Book X.

When discussing the Phoenician Tale that Socrates would disseminate among all members of his just society, including even the rulers, we noted that these 'Guardians' are distinct from the 'Philosopher-Kings' who emerge as heads of state in the subsequent account. These philosophers, by contrast, will be as aware of the conditions of their education as is the Socrates who lays down its pattern; for they are to accept voluntarily (if reluctantly) and in full conscience the requirement he enjoins upon them to descend (in the terms of the famous allegory) from unalloyed philosophic contemplation into the Cave of political life, and to govern in the ideal city (7.520d1 – e3). One way to see why they have advanced beyond the merely virtuous Guardians of the just society is to consider the comparison Socrates makes in Book III between learning to be a Guardian and learning to read (at 502a7 – c9). The Guardians must learn to recognise the 'forms' (*eidē*, 401c2) of courage and self-control and the other virtues as they crop up throughout social life, and no less in poetic imitations, just as we learn to read by recognising alphabetic letters as they crop up in an enormous variety of combinations, and would use the same skill to recognise images of letters encountered in mirrors. The point to emphasise is that the Guardians learn to read but do not learn about reading; changing the metaphor slightly, they learn the grammar of virtue by learning to speak its language, but they do not become grammarians. One can recognise the 'forms' of virtue entirely from within one's own sense of the virtuous life, just by living it; or one can attempt not only to live that life but to grasp its conditions; not only to recognise but to understand,[33] to study the system of virtue (something Plato and we may be venturing by talking *about* how the Guardians learn virtue) – and then we approach Platonic metaphysics, and the 'Forms' we study begin, as it were, to merit their capital 'F'.

Commentators have worried[34] that if the 'forms' of virtue mentioned here are taken to be fully fledged Platonic Forms, the poetic images also mentioned would have such Forms as their direct object; and this would contradict the account given in the tenth book, according to which poets imitate the Forms only indirectly, by imitating manifestations of Forms in the world. Let us grant that 'transcendent' Forms have not at this point yet made their appearance in the text; but let us also understand how closely they are related to these 'immanent' forms – forms of virtue recognised as they turn up in life. Platonic Forms – to be quick about it – are permanent standards that make up the furthest background against which we live, and since they are our background we cannot fully express our understanding of them in explicit propositions. Plato puts them to work in what we would call cosmology and epistemology as well as ethical theory; but confining ourselves to the ethical aspect most relevant to our purposes here we may say that they represent an attempt to ground the best human life in a sense that there is such a thing as human nature, and that it has constants. And we can (inadequately) express the transcendence rather than immanence of the Forms contemplated by the Philosopher-King by saying that he operates not only *against* their background but with a conscious sense of them *as* background; a sense which makes the world a Cave, to be lived in with a measure of alienation.

The purpose of alluding to the metaphysical postulates of the philosopher's activity is to get at the psychology associated with it and so by contrast to explain Plato's hostility to the psychology of poetic imitation. Again, let us approach the point through Platonic metaphor. It is striking that when Socrates comes to describe how philosophers will bring about the ideal society, he chooses an analogy from artistic image-making: the philosopher will be like a painter, first scrubbing the canvas of the city clean, then sketching on it the shape of a new constitution, and finally filling in the mixed colours of flesh, all the time looking to the divine model in an attempt to create as close a likeness as possible in human terms to the Forms of virtue (6.500e–1c; cf. 484c–d). Whereas the 'models'[35] with which the Guardians and their

---

[33] The verb meaning 'to read' also means 'to recognise' (ἀναγιγνώσκειν); cf. γνωρίζωμεν, 402c5.

[34] E.g., Adam, *Republic*, I, p. 168.

[35] παραδείγματα: see 3.409a7–b2, 3.409c4–d2.

fellow-citizens had worked were empirically assimilable patterns of virtuous (and unvirtuous) behaviour and character, the 'divine model'[36] to which the philosopher looks is nothing less than the pattern of how the society must fit together as a whole. For the young Guardian, the models of virtue are scarcely distinct from the actual human paragons whom he begins by emulating and whose ranks he can hope (no longer merely an imitator) to join. But there is a sense in which the Philosopher-Painter must remain an imitator, in that he aspires to and attempts to identify with something that he must nevertheless recognise is not entirely him, and from which he must measure his distance – the 'godlike' element within him.[37] (We recall that painting is to be contrasted with poetry as an art in which the image and what is imitated are most evidently distinct from – distant from – each other.) It is akin to the thought that Plato conveys in the *Laws* by calling the social arrangements in the just city, in so far as they are an imitation of the best life, the finest and most genuine 'drama'.[38] Nevertheless, the imitation in which the philosopher engages is decidedly not a type of artistic imitation, nor (conversely) is Socrates making room here for a reformed kind of art that would imitate the Forms directly; this, in part, is the force of resorting to an analogy with artistic imitation in order to describe the philosophic. To imitate justice in poetry is to produce an actual imitation – a poem, or a performance of a poem; to 'imitate' the Form of justice is to live justly and aspire, in a self-consciously philosophic manner, to the just society.[39]

But what exactly are we to understand by Socrates' reference to the 'godlike' element within a person, and therefore to what the poet fails to emulate? Here we must consider the account of the three 'parts' of the soul, especially as developed immediately prior to the return to poetry, in Books VIII and IX. Plato's analysis of the psychology of human action develops from a focus on the frequent conflict between our reason (or better judgement) and our desires (in Book IV) into something less familiar. The soul is to be thought of as having three parts – three characters, almost – which in ascending order of worthiness are: one which loves 'gain' (in a wider sense than that of material profit; we might say rather that it is the part which 'loves to get its way'), one which loves honour, and that in us which loves wisdom (this being the godlike part). From the interplay of these three characters derive, not particular actions primarily, but rather the shape (or, it may be, shapelessness) of a whole life. That is why they do not represent simple

---

[36] τῷ θείῳ παραδείγματι, 6.500e3; cf. 9.592b2–3.
[37] θεοειδές τε καὶ θεοείκελον, 501b7.
[38] *Laws* 7.817a–d; cf. 803b; *Philebus* 50b.
[39] Nehamas, 'Imitation', pp. 59–60; Sörbom, *Mimesis*, pp. 133–8; cf. Vernant, 'Naissance', pp. 133–6. A notable formulation of the view they oppose is made in the classic series of articles by Tate, most explicitly in 'Maritain', pp. 116–17: 'like the genuine painter, he [the Philosopher-King] uses the "divine paradigm"' – to which we can object that Plato's analogy makes no mention of a 'genuine painter'.

'faculties' (such as reason or desire) but rather are characterised by (but have no monopoly over) the exercise of such faculties in the pursuit of their respective goals. Thus the wisdom-loving part (also called the 'commanding' part) has the special power and function of caring for the soul in its entirety; it does not want simply to further its own desires across the life of the person, but cares also that the other two centres of desire in the soul should find their proper place in that life (esp. 9.586d – e). It thus earns its title to be called the 'calculating' or 'reasoning' part in so far as it is devoted to a cause for which deliberation is essential: the ordering across a lifetime of impulses which are in natural contention.

So too, the Philosopher-King – in whom the wisdom-loving part is dominant – cares for (looks to the model of) the society as a whole, in contrast to the Guardian (a military type, and representative more of the honour-loving part) who is qualified to rule the city just in so far as he furthers his own natural interest in the virtuous life. But such a blinkered pushing of one's interest is a characteristic *par excellence* of the 'lowest' part of the soul, the lover of gain. This earns its title to be called the 'appetitive' part because it deliberates (if it deliberates) exclusively about the means of fulfilling its wants, whatever they may be, and never (unlike the wisdom-loving part) about those wants as such. It will manoeuvre as elaborately as need be to bring the others around to its own interests, but only in so far as they stand in the way of those interests; it does not care by what means their cooperation is secured, nor does it care what happens to their interests in the process. In this sense, as mentioned when considering Cebes' fear of the bogeyman, it is the 'child' within us.[40]

All this is vividly brought out in Books VIII and IX, in the narrative of how a philosophic life can degenerate through various stages into a tyrannical one. and given what we have just learnt about the parts of the soul, we can now understand better why Socrates should express the philosopher's alienation from the Cave by saying that its denizens seem to him to be dreaming, pursuing shadows (7.520c; so too those who cannot understand the Forms are said at the end of Book V to be 'living a dream', 476c). The metaphor becomes incarnate in the figure of the tyrant. He allows himself to be completely consumed by the desires of the lowest part of the soul, desires which, says Socrates, come into their own even for the best of us when we are asleep (9.571c – 2b); so that the tyrant becomes in real life what the rest of us are only in our most unhealthy dreams (574e, 576b). And the pleasures to which he is addicted are for Socrates mere 'wraiths' (586c), or 'shadow-paintings' (583b, 586b) of genuine pleasure – this last a term commonly applied to illusionistic scene-painting in the theatre. The tyrant lives a dream,

---

[40] Jon Moline, *Plato's Theory of Understanding* (Madison, Wisconsin, 1981), ch. 3, and Annas, *Plato's Republic*, ch. 5.

we now see, because he is overwhelmed by that part of him which, in as much
as it deliberates only about the means to its goal, but not about the goal as
such, seeks only effects. The tyrant cares only to satisfy his addiction, but he
does not care (for his appetite does not care, and he has become his appetite)
what means he must employ, what path he must follow, to gain satisfaction.
But the path of satisfaction has become his very life; and thus he cannot care
about his life. From the perspective of one who can still care, this life is
meaningless, a dream.

And here we have come back to the topic of poetry and theatre – as the
metaphor from scene-painting will have suggested. For a constant theme of
this account has been that poetic imitation is performance, and as such can
be fully appreciated in terms of its effects in the moment of performance,
regardless of its conditions or source. But to be content with mere effects is
the mark of that in us which will steer us towards the least worthy pattern
of life. Plato's strategy in the tenth book, then, is to take what we might think
of as poetry's miraculous capacity to broaden our imaginative horizons and
sympathetic understanding by means of the mere representation or appearance of a character or situation, and paint it in the unappealing colours of
the tyrannical personality; of that in us which delights in 'appearances' in
the loaded metaphysical sense that contrasts with the 'reality' – the meaning-
fulness – of a life lived in an attempt to know the Forms.[41] We are to see
that this part of the soul is not only childish and appetitive, but quintessentially
theatrical.

This is a tall order; for what can a Homer or his audience have even
minimally in common with such a sick character as the tyrant? And if
truth it be, it is an unpleasant truth: small wonder that Socrates, daunted
by his ingrained respect for Homer, is reluctant to speak (10.595b9 – c3).
But let us move now from this general background to the detail of his
argument.

That these preliminaries are necessary, Plato's own words clearly indicate;
for Socrates announces as his reason for returning to the topic of poetry the
intention to clarify and reinforce his previous criticism by appeal to the
psychological distinctions that have now been set up (595a5 – b1). In particular, we are to see why we must reject 'such poetry as is imitative'.[42] This
statement has proved a persistent source of puzzlement and contention; for
Socrates seems here to accounce an attack on all poetry that employs imitation;
yet in Book III we saw him actually recommend for the Guardians a style of
poetry that 'imitates' worthy characters (397d4, 398b2), involving imitation
in both the technical and the ethical sense – and which, moreover, he seems
to be recommending at the conclusion of his critique in Book X, in the shape

---

[41] Notice in this connection the slur in Book VIII on Euripides as a friend of tyrants, 568a–b.
[42] αὐτῆς ὅση μιμητική, 595a5.

of 'hymns to the gods and encomia of the virtuous' (607a4).[43] Yet the problem is only apparent, and can be dispelled entirely if we bear in mind that when Socrates asked in Book III whether the Guardians should be 'imitative' (394e1) he was asking whether they should be *prone* to imitation. The Guardian can be an 'imitator' of good characters without being 'imitative', because by confining his imitation (in both the technical and ethical sense) to characters such as he himself intends to become, he never has to make himself other than he is and become a double or multiplex personality (see 397e1), unlike the less worthy type who imitates indiscriminately and thus is truly 'imitative'. We should understand Socrates' reference to 'imitative' poetry at the beginning of Book X in just this sense: as poetry which values imitation as such, and so promotes the ethos of the unworthy imitator to whom we were introduced in Book III.[44] There is no contradiction with that book, nor even much of an enlargement from the sense in which imitation was spoken of there (which is why Socrates does not remark on any change of position); for we saw that the ethical sense (imitation as 'imitativeness'), of which the technical ('direct speech') is a symptom, was already present in Book III – only, now we are to focus exclusively on that ethical sense, and with the more sophisticated psychological apparatus that the intervening metaphysics has provided.[45]

Socrates begins with metaphysics: with an appeal to the Forms, applying what he calls 'our usual method' (596a5 – 6) to the question at hand. His only other appeal to this method as the means of resolving an issue under discussion had come at the end of Book V, when he had presented an argument to support his claim that in the ideal society philosophers should rule, in which he demonstrated that other enthusiasts who might appear equally devoted to learning new things were disqualified by their lack of understanding of such Forms (esp. 475e – 6a). And the prime example of such enthusiasts had been the 'devotees of spectacle' (*philotheamones*, 475d2): avid theatre-goers who never missed a show, but wanted nothing to do with philosophic discussion, and saw no need for it. So here in Book X Socrates appeals again to the Forms in order to defuse the claim of a closely related group of pretenders to wisdom: the poets, whose imitations are thought of as a mode of understanding. He is out to show that they live in as much of a 'dream' as their willing audience, the devotees of spectacle: in contact only with 'appearances', not with the

---

[43] Keuls, *Painting*, p. 30, and Annas, 'Triviality', p. 7, provide modern versions of the view that the puzzle weakens Plato's argument. Even Nehamas, who wants to downplay its importance, thinks it cannot be completely resolved, 'Imitation', p. 51.

[44] The suggestion is not new: cf. Tate, 'Imitation', pp. 18 – 19; Belfiore, 'Theory of Imitation', pp. 126 – 7.

[45] There is no compelling reason to believe that Book X is an afterthought or appendix or in any sense insufficiently integrated with the body of the *Republic* as claimed by Else, *Structure and Date*.

reality of the Forms (5.476a4 – 7, 5.476c2 – 7). However, the poetic context introduced by the theatre-goers in Book V was only one example of an inadequate forum of understanding; Socrates there illuminated by contrast the understanding required to compass the rule of an entire society, and the Forms to which he appealed were correspondingly weighty: the just, the good, the beautiful. Here the focus is entirely on poetry. Socrates' question is 'what is imitation as a whole?' (595c7); and since he is thinking of imitation in the first instance as a kind of 'making', the making of images,[46] and since it is this activity that he wants to investigate, he directs Glaucon's attention to Forms of made objects: of artefacts such as couches and tables (596a10 – b1).[47]

Fastening on the example of the couch, Socrates points out that there are three distinct levels at which such an object can be understood or apprehended, to which correspond three distinct kinds of 'making'. A particular wooden couch may be taken primarily as a representative of its type, of 'what a couch is' (597a2) – the Form of a couch. This Form is what the carpenter had to 'look towards' or consider as he made the material object now before us. That is to say that he had to bear in mind at every stage what a couch is *for* – that people would be *using* it.[48] Clearly, in making the wooden couch the carpenter does not also make what a couch is for. If anyone can be said to have 'made' this, it will be the same character that made human beings with the need to recline and a hankering for comfort: a creator-God of some sort. (This seems to be the sense in which Socrates can talk of apparently transcendent Forms of couches and tables that – as he made a point of telling us at 2.373a2 – were not even around in the earliest city but were a mark of the luxurious society that came after. These artefacts arose from permanent dispositions to luxury in human nature; were not so much 'invented', as 'discovered'.)[49] But if the carpenter's making is therefore parasitic on what the creator-God has made, there is a third kind of making, namely artistic imitation, which is parasitic on the creations of the carpenter. Thus if a painter, for example, makes a painting of a couch, he does not attempt to look at what a couch is for, but rather looks to the couches that carpenters make; these, moreover, he does not imitate as they are but rather as they seem: that is, he attempts to capture the 'look' of a couch. If the Form is what properly merits the title of 'reality', then what the painter and indeed any artist produces (the poets no less) is therefore 'at a third remove from reality' (596b – 8d).

---

[46] See 596e5 – 11; cf. *Sophist* 265a – b.

[47] Socrates' manner of appeal to the Forms in Book X has provoked much controversy; cf. Nehamas, 'Imitation', pp. 72 – 3, n. 32.

[48] Notice 596b8: the carpenter looks to the Form in order to make the tables and couches 'which we use'.

[49] Noted and developed along different lines by Griswold, 'Ideas'.

This passage is easily misunderstood, and its model of the artistic process can then seem extremely crude.[50] Encouraged perhaps by Socrates' comparison of the painter to someone strolling the world with a mirror (596d8 – e6), and by his reference to children and foolish adults confusing paintings seen from a distance with the real thing (598c1 – 4), we might suppose that Plato thinks of the painter as finding a couch, setting up his canvas before it, and proceeding to produce a slavish copy to serve ambitions of *trompe-l'oeil*. Bad enough as a conception of what painting involves, this model seems still less applicable to poetry – yet Socrates never actually says or even suggests that the painter is out to produce as exact a copy as possible of some particular couch. He says that the painter (when he chooses to paint artefacts) imitates, not the Form, but 'the products of craftsmen'; and even then he looks to such material objects not as they are, and as they remain regardless of the angle from which we view them, but rather to just that aspect of them which changes along with our angle of view: 'the way they look' (598a1 – b5). In other words, what occupies in the painter's mind an analogous place to that occupied in the carpenter's mind by thoughts of the Form (as they produce their respective creations) are not thoughts of material couches or of some particular couch, but thoughts about how couches (typically) 'look'.[51] And these thoughts may be as 'abstract' as you please – at least as abstract as those the carpenter employs. That is, although the painter might be trying to evoke the look of some particular couch that he either remembers or has before him, and certainly the image he produces will present the couch from some particular angle, still, nothing in what Socrates says constrains the painter's ambition to mechanical reproduction of the world around him.

On the contrary, in pulling off the 'look' of an object or scene the painter would be striving as much to have this look come across as such to potential viewers as he strives to capture the object or scene; the former goal, indeed, is partly constitutive of the latter; with the result that it is not even a condition on his image (and Socrates never says it is) that it should be especially accurate, in a photographic sense, provided that viewers accept it as accurate – as conveying the look of a couch. The look of a thing depends as much on the psychology of the viewer as on the nature of the object viewed; and the concept thus provides considerable scope for sophistication in the artist. Socrates' appeal to the man with the mirror should not mislead us: its function is only to isolate the notion of making images of things as opposed to the things themselves (the focus is not on the 'making'; it is not an analogue for how the painter actually goes about his task: see 596e4 – 6). And as for *trompe-l'oeil*, the fact that Socrates specifies children and weak-headed adults as the dupes shows that this is not what is intended; for *trompe-l'oeil* is designed to fool

[50] Annas, 'Triviality', pp. 4–7; Keuls, *Painting*, esp. p. 43.
[51] Nehamas, 'Imitation', p. 58.

everyone. The statement draws on no more than the contemporary assumption that painting should be realistic; that a 'good painter' (598c2) will produce life-like images,[52] which will therefore have the potential to trick a sufficiently unsophisticated audience in favourable conditions of viewing. This is to prepare us for how poetry can trick a far more sophisticated audience – can satisfy the childish part within them – and with far more dangerous consequences.

Plato's view of painting is not the unacceptably crude position that it may seem. (Nevertheless, anyone disposed to think that when Van Gogh paints his wicker chair he captures not just its look but its very 'chairness' will still want to resist Plato's view. It seems a fact that painting has changed more radically than poetry since Plato's day; that certain developments in it go beyond what Plato could perhaps even have imagined. However, the more sophisticated view is at least arguable; and the position taken by Van Gogh's promoter at least debatable.) But let us understand that painting – indeed, this whole passage – is being used as an illustration on a simpler level of what in poetry is more difficult to grasp (a practice we have seen to be something of a habit with Plato).[53] If painters capture 'only' the look of their objects and scenes, poets capture, on this view, a fuller gamut of what they represent: the entire 'feel' of human behaviour. That is why the carpenter is no less simple an example of what it is to imitate the Forms than is the painter an example of what it is to imitate the world. The carpenter occupies the place in the hierarchy that, if we turn to more important matters, would be occupied by the Philosopher-King, who we have seen is also an imitator of the Forms: the just, the good, the beautiful. But in the measure of its greater importance the philosopher's task is also more difficult to explain. Both painter and carpenter produce material objects, indubitably distinct from themselves. But we have seen (when considering the Dionysian chorus) that in poetic performance the barrier between imitator and product of imitation is far less clear; and now we can see that this applies also to the philosophers, the product of whose imitation of the Forms is nothing less than their own lives, and life in the ideal society.

That this is Plato's thought emerges clearly when Socrates comes to complete his account of why artistic imitation grasps only appearance, not reality (announcing that he will not leave this 'half-said', 601a9–c4). For here he cuts manual craftsmanship back down to size. We recall that in looking to the Form of couch the carpenter was bearing in mind the use to which his product would be put. But it is no intrinsic part of his craft that he should

---

[52] In the analogous domain of sculpture cf. Xenophon, *Memorabilia*, 3.10.7.

[53] Most notably in the account of the Dionysian chorus in the *Laws* (esp. 2.668d2–9b3); cf. *Ion* 532e–3c; *Sophist* 234b–c (painting deceives only the youngest children in the way that sophistry deceives older youths); *Politicus* 285d8–6b3 (there are no visual images for the most important things in life).

himself be a user of his product. When it comes to couches, of course, he could hardly fail to be in practice; which is why Socrates chooses different examples to make the point: those of the bridle-maker and flute-maker (601c – e). For the maker may indeed be no horse-rider or flute-player (the obverse of the fact that it takes no great skill to use a couch). And Socrates' point is this: that in so far as the craftsman must look to the use of his product he must also look to its users. His skill is subordinate in this sense to the skill of the user; craftspeople comprise, we could say, a service-industry. By contrast, if Philosopher-Kings are makers at all, they are intrinsically the users of what they make. Alternatively put: they are makers only in the sense in which their task can be called imitation of the Forms, and compared to the act of painting the image of the ideal society; but what this amounts to is a user's skill, the skill of living and organising the good life.

None but the childish confuse the average painting with the real thing; and the role of the manual craftsman is clearly demarcated from that of the user of his products. Accordingly it poses no threat that a painter can paint or a craftsman make what they do not know how to use. But what makes poets so dangerous is that not only can they transport us into scenes, convey the feel of human behaviour, without being possessed of the understanding from which such behaviour would arise in life, but also, since their images do indeed convey an accurate feel of the entire situation, and because they are composed in a medium – talk, primarily – not obviously distinct from that through which the actual situation would find expression, poets, unlike painters or craftspeople, can readily convince us that what they produce springs from a full understanding of the user's skill to which it corresponds. And since the imitative scope of a Homer extends to nothing short of how the greatest communities are led by their princes, the user's skill he can appear to arrogate is the very highest: that which Socrates would reserve for the Philosopher-King (599c – d). Poetry is thus in direct competition with philosophy for the education of the ruling class.[54]

Socrates also offers social considerations in support of the contrast between different types of skill and its metaphysical basis when he confronts the imagined objection that surely a good poet, such as Homer, simply could not compose fine poetry on his chosen topic unless he had some worthwhile understanding of what he was talking about (598d8 – e5). Socrates' response is to suggest that 'fine' poetry for such an objector is no more than poetry that is found convincing, and the objector is not allowing for the possibility that he has been too easily convinced – taken in by the appearance of understanding (598e5 – 9a4). Socrates backs up his response by pointing out that the social institutions of poetry are just what we should expect to

---

[54] A similar contrast between the respective place of craftspeople and poets in the ideal society was later drawn by Proclus, *In Rem Publicam*, I, pp. 48, 26 – 49, 12 Kroll.

accompany the imitator's as opposed to the user's skill. That is, for all that Homer seems to talk about how cities are to be governed, and for all that his poetry is esteemed as a public good and an education, neither Homer nor his successors, the rhapsodes, ever acted as lawgiver to a city, like Solon, nor contributed inventions of practical value, as did Thales, nor even, on a more private scale, established a sect devoted to a certain way of living the good life, as did Pythagoras (599d – 600c).

It is easy to find this criticism grotesque. What is to become of poetry, we want to protest, if it is to be measured by the yardstick of such grossly practical results? But Plato is not saying that we should apply so practical a yardstick to poetry; he is saying that, indeed, we should not, but that, if we suppose poets to have a user's rather than an imitator's skill on the question of how to live in society, we would be compelled to do so; for that is the yardstick we customarily apply to those we hold to be so endowed. And mention of the institutions that Homer did not establish reminds us by contrast of his actual social legacy: the guild of Homerids, the circuit of performance by travelling rhapsodes (599e6, 600d5 – 6). Poetry had its established portion in the life of the city, in the time of festivals and celebrations and of preparation for adulthood; and it perpetuated itself as an institution not by attempting to change society to its own genetic advantage, but by transmitting the (imitative) skill which entitled its practitioners to their allotted place in society (even though that skill might be used to say things which, if attended to, could bring about social reform). Poetry, in short, was an autonomous profession; whereas philosophy, in Plato's day and as Plato thought of philosophy, was not. Plato's Academy, we know, was politically active; philosophers, in his view, were to seek ultimately to change society, and at least (in Pythagorean fashion) to establish their own way of living the good life; but not, like poets, to be content to perform within society. In claiming for philosophers the user's skill in 'political' life he could not abjure, then, the practical yardstick. That Socrates never wrote a law is to be seen as a failure, both on Socrates' and society's part. The point is: it is at least not absurd for Socrates, still less for Plato, to have aspired to such an ambition; whereas it would be absurd – socially, professionally absurd – for a Homer.

But there is a further point in Socrates' appeal to practical success, namely an acknowledgment that, however worthy a part of one's ambitions it may be, it is an unreliable index of wisdom. This can be seen in Socrates' un-favourable comparison of Homer's reception to that of the sophists Protagoras and Prodicus, who managed to surround themselves with a coterie of enthusiasts convinced that they had found the only sages capable of telling them how to live their lives (600c – e). We hardly need to be acquainted with Plato's general suspicion of these figures – who were threatening to professionalise philosophy in much the way that he found a weakness in poetry – to sense the irony in the hyperbolic language of this comparison. The pair of sophists offer a prime example of the ability to give an audience the impression of understanding how to live, without possessing or imparting the actual skill (cf. *Sophist* 234c – d). And this is directly relevant to the objection that Homer could not have composed as well as he did without properly understanding how to live the kind of life he spoke of. Socrates' reply is, in effect, that, however plausible this may seem, there is no use in simply insisting on it; for we all know of examples such as those of Protagoras and Prodicus which demonstrate that a guru can win unmerited conviction from his audience; and who is to guarantee that Homer is not the beneficiary – at a less sensational level, to be sure – of this type of response? The objector, then, must at least provide further argument to support his objection; and Socrates meanwhile is engaged in the further argument needed to show that poetic imitation not only need not be hospitable to the user's understanding, but if given its head is positively inhospitable to it; and moreover that what it offers does not deserve to be classed as a kind of understanding in its own right.

So far, then, Socrates has reasoned on both metaphysical and social grounds that the imitative artist has no intrinsic understanding – no understanding just by virtue of being an imitator – of the user's skill to which his imitations correspond; and that our epic and dramatic poets are imitative artists in the required sense (602b6 – 10). Put another way: the success of a good painting or poem can be completely explained without reference to the Forms. What painters produce is the look of a scene; but this 'look' (in an abstract rather than concrete sense) is also all that they need refer to as they work. Similarly, what poets produce is the feel of a situation, and all they need refer to as they work is this 'feel' – how human behaviour comes across. A poet could be entirely successful and yet remain trapped within the circle of social appearances, which would provide both the object and the outcome of his imitation.[55]

This argument would not be properly compelling, however, unless Plato can make it out in terms of the reception of poetry, in addition to its production. For what would it matter, really, how poets bring off their creations, if the effect of those representations on the audience were to provide them with the means of uncovering the very springs of the human behaviour represented? Here Socrates must call upon the resources of psychology, as elaborated in the preceding books; and it is the move that clinches his argument. His question now is: given the imitative nature of poetry, what in us – what element of our psychological make-up – is the target of its power (602c1 – 5)? And he represents his (psychological) answer as a direct elaboration of what he meant in demoting imitative art to the 'third remove from reality' (603a10 – b2).

---

[55] Socrates uses the word φάντασμα, 'appearance' (in a sense that encompasses both 'look' and 'feel'), to describe both what the imitative artist produces (599a2) and the object he imitates (598b3): a point developed by Nehamas, 'Imitation', p. 62.

Socrates begins with a simpler illustration of what he wants to say, taken
again from the visual arts (and making his method explicit at 603b9 – c2).
Painters, theatrical scene-painters especially, make much use of optical effects
such as that of distance on apparent size, or of how a surface can appear
concave or convex depending on the arrangement of its colours (602c7 – d5).
This 'trickery' works on us in a special way. To the extent that we are familiar
with its operation, we are not fooled into thinking the distant object is actually
smaller, or that the plane surface is actually convex; we are able to make
comparisons, to 'measure' and judge in such a manner that 'the apparently
larger does not hold sway within us' (602d6 – 9) – which is to say that we
do not act on a belief that the man in the distance is a midget, nor would we
attempt to get inside a stage-flat. Nevertheless, it often happens that even to
one secure in this judgement 'the opposite appears at the same time about
the same object' (602e4 – 6); that is, the man in the distance persists in looking
smaller, the stage pillar we know to be flat still looks round (and by having
Socrates say that this happens 'often' rather than 'always' Plato presumably
alludes to the fact that in certain cases, especially on stage, our knowledge
of how the effect comes about can actually kill the illusion). Appealing to the
principle by which he first distinguished the parts of the soul (4.436b), Socrates
points out that whatever in us judges the proper size of the object in the
distance cannot be the same as that which contradicts it – that to which the
distant object seems small, and which disposes us to insist that it does at least
look small (602d8 – 3a2). The task of judging correctly he assigns to the
highest, wisdom-loving part of the soul, the part which Socrates here recalls
in its devotion to 'measure and calculation' and applauds as the 'best' element
within us (602d1 – 2, 603a4 – 5). He does not further justify the equation, but
Plato's thought is that insofar as the wisdom-loving part cares for the entire
soul and has as its greatest task the organisation of all impulses in the soul,
including its own, across the course of a life, so on the more mundane level
of vision it would fall to this part to take into critical account our impulse to
discern a particular look in an object when seen from a particular distance
or angle, an impulse that would put blinkers on us and lead us into all sorts
of trouble if we were to follow its call exclusively (that is, if we were to believe
that the man in the distance really is a midget), although, when adjusted for
by our life-long experience of the effects of distance on size, it not only causes
no trouble but provides essential information about where we stand in the
world. Left to itself, however, it opposes the 'best' in us and so merits Socrates'
disapproval of it as 'one of the base things in us' (603a7 – 8). This it is that
painting 'consorts with' and targets itself upon (602d1 – 4, 603a10 – b2).

But Socrates does not dwell on how the base part merits its title in the
workings of vision, nor on what we are to think of painting for consorting with
it, but passes on to the parallel workings of human action (of which vision
is but a small component) and its representation in poetry; and it is here that

he dwells on the attendant dangers (a contrast which suggests that Plato thought of painting not only as an art that was easier to comprehend, but also as comparatively trivial). Socrates adduces the example of psychological conflict in a man grieving over the loss of a beloved son. Grieve he certainly must, but to the extent that he is led by the best part of him, the part which looks to the long-term and has a sense of the man's place within society as a whole, he will 'be measured' in his grief (603e – f), and work to heal the wound that sequesters him from his fellows. He must resist wallowing in his grief; refuse, that is, to be *ruled* by the impulse to grieve (as opposed to avoiding grief altogether) – an impulse of the lowest part of the soul, which reacts immediately, almost as a reflex, to the situation at hand, and seeks satisfaction blindly. (This is a paraphrase of 603d – 4d).

The example is taken from life, not fiction; Socrates has yet to say how poetry exploits such situations. This corresponds to his order of presentation in speaking of the visual arts, when he first described optical effects that apply in the world (effects of distance on size, of refraction through water), and only then turned to how scene-painting exploits similar effects (indeed, one of the effects mentioned, that a stick appears bent in water, scene-painting presumably did *not* exploit; the examples are primarily to illustrate the psychological process of vision) (602d1 – 2). The correspondence between the merely visual and the fully ethical types of psychological conflict is clear enough.[56] Once we have used our eyes in this world for but a little while, we understand that the person in the distance is not actually tiny, that the stick in water is as straight as it ever was; nevertheless, the stick does still look bent, the person still looks tiny, and no amount of understanding will (or even should) stop this effect, for it is part and parcel of how we apprehend the world. What we must avoid, however (and here we introduce the element of conflict), is being 'ruled' or led by the appearance, being inclined to throw the stick away because it is broken. So too, at a level of conflict vastly more difficult to cope with, the bereaved father who has lived long enough to see his way around life understands that this grief will pass and can console himself by taking the large view of human frailty – knows, as it were, the true size of his bereavement when measured against the fullness of a life. This knowledge will not stop him grieving (the stick still looks bent, the bereavement is still painful), nor should it; such reactions are part and parcel of how we actually register vicissitudes (as opposed to dismissing them, refusing even to apprehend them). But this knowledge will prevent the immediate reaction from ruling or obsessing him, and mourning from becoming the purpose of his life. Hence, Socrates sees fit to mention (604a) that the man would let himself go far more if alone than if in sight of others, for grief threatens to make him a world unto himself; makes him want to throw the stick of his life away, we might say, because it is broken.

---

[56] The correspondence has, however, worried some commentators, cf. Annas, 'Triviality', pp. 7 – 9; Murphy, *Plato's Republic*, pp. 239 – 43; Nehamas, 'Imitation', pp. 64 – 6.

Now consider what Socrates says of the poet's task at 604e–5a. That in us which is prone to complain, the lowest part of our souls which, given its head, would have us not merely grieve but indulge our grief, offers many and varied opportunities for imitation; but the thoughtful and steadfast character manifest in the father who is measured in his grief, being equable and relatively unvaried, is neither easy to imitate nor so readily understood by the audience, especially an audience as kaleidoscopic as that found at dramatic festivals. For both these reasons, poets incline to appeal through their imitations to our baser part.

Plato makes the point with tantalising brevity, but let us follow his lead (at 605a8–b2) and elaborate it through configuration with the example from scene-painting. Scene-painters aim above all at getting their props recognised, and since we recognise scenes not by virtue of what they are but by how they look, they tailor their efforts to that in us which picks up on the look of things rather than that which judges things as they are. So too poets, as imitators, aim at drawing us into their presentation by making us imagine ourselves as participants in the action, whether by identifying with one or more characters or simply by thinking of ourselves as bystanders, and just as by recognising a prop to suggest a house we can imagine ourselves entering it. But as we recognise stage-scenery by how it looks rather than by what it is, so we recognise poetic action by how it feels (which in the case of staged drama will include how it looks); only so can we be drawn into the imitation. Hence, poets will appeal to that in us which dwells upon the particular flavour of a human situation rather than to our capacity to minimise it; being vivid, after all, is what the medium of imitation both invites and excels at. It has an inbuilt tendency, then, to heighten the particular, to focus upon crises. But what is most characteristic of the better role-models is that insofar as they must adopt a particular perspective, it is one which would emphasise the particularity of a whole life at the expense of the particularity of its crises (the father grieves without dwelling on his grief); its crises will be less critical. Thus poetic imitation will centre on sensational characters, sensationally presented. There is something in this of Brecht's complaint that the 'hypnotic magic' of realistic drama works by 'drawing each trait of character from the narrow field within which everyone can say at once: that is how it is'.[57] Brecht worried that for as long as theatre remains dependent on the recognisable it would be impotent to challenge bourgeois complacency and so awaken our critical faculties; Plato is saying that by its dependence on the process of recognition and identification imitative poetry feeds our appetite for surrender to the moment (by offering like characters for our delectation), and dulls our more reflective part.

Here, despite what the comparison with Brecht may do to give us pause,

---

[57] See 'A short organum for the theatre', esp. sections 28–33, in John Willett (ed.), *Brecht on Theatre* (London, 1964).

we will surely want to protest at what may seem Plato's intolerable cheapening of tragic poetry. Let us grant that a poet will gravitate towards the portrayal of crisis; still, why must we think of this as an appeal to our baser part, and suited to the worst kind of audience? To become involved in Oedipus' struggle as he thrashes at the tightening nets of fate and finally, in a supreme moment, in an agony of understanding, comes to accept responsibility for who he is – surely this can be to experience through the narrow focus of a moment the epiphany of a whole life, a perspective as all-encompassing as any could be? And surely such crises will be suited to a wide audience not because they touch the lowest common denominator, but because they invite a full range of exploration, from the shallowest thrill of shock to the most Nietzschean 'joy in the annihilation' of the hero.[58] And why can the model of an Oedipus not offer us food for reflection without tempting us somehow to emulate its undesirable aspects? This is a version, made specific to Plato's argument at this point, of the more general objection voiced at the beginning of this section: granted that to create poetry is by no means simply to teach or convey information in an especially lively fashion, still, why should we not regard the benefits of imaginatively partaking of an imitation in quite as positive a light as we do the sharing of information? Why should we not regard imitation as itself a kind of understanding? Perhaps the worthiest benefits yield themselves only to the worthiest among the audience, but at least at that level there is surely room for an experience far deeper than the sensationalism that Socrates here indiscriminately attributes to serious poetry.

Plato faces this, the most serious challenge, quite squarely; for the last and what Socrates calls the 'greatest' of the counts against poetry is precisely that even as experienced by the worthiest among the audience – never mind that tragedians and rhapsodes must in fact appeal to a wider public – it retains the tendency to exploit their worst part, and so corrupt them (605c6–8).[59] The response deserves step-by-step examination. Socrates keeps to the example of grief, and considers the reaction of even 'the best of us' in the audience while a hero draws out a long speech of bereavement or a group sings, beating the breast in mourning. 'We feel pleasure', he points out, 'and give ourselves over, following along sympathetically, and we praise in all seriousness, as a good poet, the one who can most readily put us in this condition' (605c10–d5). He contrasts the reaction that he and Glaucon had agreed would characterise the best of us when faced with actual bereavement; such a person, acting out of self-respect, would seek to behave in just the opposite manner of the characters on stage, that is, would attempt to still and quieten himself, believing this to be 'manly' conduct, whereas 'the other kind

---

[58] The phrase is from section 16 of *The Birth of Tragedy*.

[59] At 605c7 Socrates announces only that poetry is 'sufficient' to corrupt even the worthiest, but the conclusion to which he argues is stronger: that it actually 'nourishes' our worst part, and that this effect is 'not easy' to escape (606b7–8, 606d4–7).

of behaviour, which we were then praising, is womanish' (605d7 – e2). Seen from a modern perspective, Socrates has shifted his ground here. He first pointed out, quite impeccably it seemed, that the object of our praise, when we take pleasure in being moved to sympathetic grief, is the skill of the poet; but now he is saying that what we were praising 'then' – when we were a part of the audience – was not the poet for his portrayal of the 'womanish' behaviour, but the unacceptable behaviour itself. Can Plato not see the difference between praising a representation and praising what is represented? Apparently not, for Socrates proceeds to compound what we would think of as the confusion. How can it be right, he goes on, to witness a man acting as we ourselves would be ashamed to act and yet not to feel aversion but rather take pleasure in and praise his behaviour (605e4 – 6)? Not only our praise but also the pleasure we feel while in the audience would be pleasure at the behaviour portrayed rather than at the dramatic portrayal.

But let us look more closely. Plato has not selected just any example of behaviour that the best of us would shun in ourselves, but an example in which the unacceptable act is an act of expression. It is not the hero's grief that is found unacceptable – for the bereaved father also grieves – but the fact that the hero and others give full expression to their grief. This, and not grief as such, is the behaviour that stands in natural contrast with the attempt to endure and keep silent (at 605d8 – e1). Seen with this emphasis, Plato's apparent refusal or incapacity to acknowledge what we would call 'aesthetic distance' – that the pleasure the audience takes is not at the sorrow represented but at the representation of the sorrow[60] – becomes not only understandable but, we may even think, justifiable. When we praise the tragic poet for his 'imitation' of the grieving hero, and take pleasure in that portrayal, the object of our praise and pleasure is not the grief itself, but the poet's expression of grief. Yet this same behaviour – giving expression to grief – is what we witness in the figure of the grieving hero; and how better, after all, can the poet imitate grief directly than by showing us characters who themselves express their grief? Thus Plato does not shift his ground in this argument; for the behaviour we praise and savour in both the poet and his character is of the same type.

It is not that tragic poetry is somehow doomed to portray characters who indulge their 'complaining part' in an utterly exorbitant fashion. Rather, it is that tragic poetry must at least, of its very nature, air the complaint. Tragic poetry, we can say, just *is* the expression of human sorrow. And in this it stands intrinsically opposed to the ethos of the enduring soul, for whom sorrow is, precisely, to be endured, but not expressed. This is not a stricture tragic poets could evade (even if they wanted to) by portraying less extravagant sorrowers. Any expression of sorrow in so prominent and, as it were, well-lit an arena as

---

[60] The accusation is forcefully made by Nehamas, 'Imitation', p. 69.

the stage is too much: not because sorrow is to be denied, but because it is to work its way out in silence, in the background. To pluck it from the background and give it expression is to turn towards it, instead of working to get over it; to give it a value all its own and become hypnotised by its voice, rather than register and learn from what it has to say. That is why the type of troubled and breast-beating hero whom Socrates in Book III actually recommends the young Guardians should hear (390d) is Odysseus admonishing his heart to endure. Odysseus is not denying his wretchedness; but he is giving expression only to his endurance. We would not get very far with Plato, then, even if we could take him to one side and point out that it is not the represented sorrow that we in the audience are praising or pleased by, but the representation or expression of the sorrow; for what he takes to be bad, and to make tragic poets and audiences guilty equivalents of the self-indulgent hero, is just that: not the sorrow, but the expression of the sorrow.

That this is Plato's point becomes clear from the psychological analysis of the audience's response that Socrates proceeds to establish. The part of the soul to which tragic poets appeal when they give expression to human suffering and induce us to shed sympathetic tears is indeed the lowest part, which is 'hungry to weep and to get its fill of bitter lamentation' (606a4 – 5); for we saw it defined as the centre of immediate, unreflective reaction in the soul, and the urge to weep and lament – not just to grieve, but to express grief – is our immediate reaction to great sorrow. It is this urge that tragic poets 'satisfy and delight' (606a6 – 7). The audience feels pleasure not in that they are moved to sadness – sadness is no pleasure, after all – but in that they are allowed to give vent to their sadness by participating sympathetically in its poetic expression. Similarly, at a comedy we vent in laughter the urge to indulge a kind of buffoonery that we would be ashamed actually to play at ourselves (606c2 – 10).[61] Outside the theatre, as we have seen, our better, reflective part – at least in the best among us – would act to restrain the urge to give grief full expression. As members of an audience, however, our second thoughts take a different form. We reason that it is no shame to us, personally, to witness or hear of others giving vent to grief in a shameful way; yet by pitying them we are able vicariously to 'gain the profit' of pleasure – the pleasure of relaxing our guard on the tear-hungry part and giving it its fill (606a7 – b5). We cream off the pleasure of letting ourselves go, but with no fear of suffering the pain of remorse. Put so disagreeably, it is no wonder that Socrates attributes this calculation (606a7 – 8) to a lack of proper education (by which he means an education from which, for one thing, such poetry would be absent). And in our eagerness not to be deprived of this pleasure if we can enjoy it with impunity, few of us pause to reflect that by allowing our plaintive

---

[61] In the *Philebus* (at 47e – 50e) there is an analysis of comedy even more closely parallel to that of tragedy here.

part to wax strong in such contexts we make it harder for ourselves to resist its blandishments in our own personal sorrows (606b5–8).

We see, then, that so far from ignoring the phenomenon we know as aesthetic distance, Plato is in fact directing his attack upon it. The category of the 'aesthetic' only came to prominence, of course, in a later age; but in its appropriation of a zone of pleasure divorced in principle from ethical consequences Plato would surely have little difficulty discerning the line of reasoning he here attributes to the lack of proper education in even the best of us. Crucial to his argument, we have seen, is the premise that with certain feelings, such as the grief central to the experience of tragedy, shame attaches not to the feeling itself but to its expression. And shame is a public sensibility; it ties us to our fellows (recall that the grieving father was the more likely to let himself go if left alone than if in company, 604a2–4). But if public venting of grief is itself the shameful thing, then why should we think it makes a difference that what causes us to vent our grief in the public theatre is no private trouble of our own, but rather a fictional situation with which we allow ourselves to become collectively engaged? The public expression of grief takes place just the same; indeed, with a greater licence; hence Socrates insists we are nourishing exactly that part of us which hungers to lament over our private sorrows. From this perspective, the fact that by the conventions of performance we agree to suspend the sense of shame that would operate outside the theatre seems no better than a collective abdication of social responsibility. Plato is not denying the existence and power of these conventions; he is not pretending that the audience simply indulges in an orgy of losing itself in the fiction, and is not also measuring its distance from the feelings it allows to well up; this he acknowledges in describing the conscious acquiescence of our better part. But what he describes is truly the distance of 'spectacle' in the worst sense; for by allowing the plaintive appetite to have its head, the more reflective part is allowing it almost literally (as we might say) to *make a spectacle* of itself.

The premise crucial to Plato's argument at this point is clearly an ethical rather than what we would call an aesthetic premise; and if we grant its consequence, and wish either to controvert or to bolster the conclusion, we would have no option but to widen the focus from poetry to the entire ethos of Plato's ideal society. The implication of Socrates' conclusion (that poetic imitation brings about in our souls the rule of the lowest, appetitive part and so corrupts and makes us wretched, 606d4–7) is that we thereby start on the degeneration towards the tyrannical personality, in whom the rule of the lowest part has become unshakeable and whose life is the most wretched possible (9.578b). Socrates' assertion here that the rule of the lowest part will make us wretched is not warranted by the argumentation of Book X but rather by that of Books VIII and IX.

We saw that the tyrant's life is described in the ninth book as a waking dream. The description is based on Socrates' account of sleep at the beginning of the book, in which he explains that our lowest urges come into their own when we sleep; that what we call sleep is really, for most of us, the sleep only of the highest part of the soul; for it is then that the lowest part 'wakes up' and does not hesitate to commit, 'so it thinks', the most shameless acts (571c–2b). Whereas our best part, being devoted to the needs of the whole, is concerned primarily with the waking person, with our active and therefore 'actual' lives, our lowest part can 'wake up' – can fully manifest its nature – even in dreams.[62] It can do so because it has no care for the other elements in the soul, hence for the waking person, and can accordingly be satisfied by merely 'thinking' itself satisfied. As the source of immediate wants in the soul it seeks only satisfaction, however obtained. If a dream will satisfy, then a dream is as good as the real thing.

We can surely see, then, why this part of soul – the part which consumes the life of the tyrannical personality and turns it to waking fantasy – should be the 'theatrical' part. Just as in sleep our immediate urges slip the leash of reflection and cavort across the dreamscape, so we in the audience collectively agree to let loose and give expression to the impulses we would normally restrain, whether these are cheap and voyeuristic or appropriate to the deepest struggles and sorrows in life. Certainly, an audience is not asleep, but is able to monitor the course of its impulses. However, this is only to say that we are not just experiencing the impulse but dwelling upon it; not just 'feeling along' in a manner appropriate to the situation, but having the 'feel' presented to us through the magic of poetic imitation. And what we fail to reckon with is that if our lowest part comes into its own in dreams, so too is it being allowed to show its true colours in the collective dream that takes place in the theatre. It makes no difference that our reflective part is awake and watching while the other part cavorts; for by joining in the expression and imitation of grief or anger or lust (606d1) we do not simply grieve or feel angry or sexually excited but also dwell upon the feeling of these states of the soul. But just this is what it is for the lower part to rule in the soul: that its impulses are not restrained or kept in the background but find full expression. It does not matter that the audience-member has not actually been deprived of a son or frustrated by Agamemnon; the impulses that would come into play are given their head as if these things had actually happened, and to be given their head is all that they seek. They do not, so to speak, stop to ask after the cause of their freedom. Thus we cannot – at least, not with safety – join an audience for the purpose of extending our imaginative horizons beyond what we have ourselves experienced. The distinction between simulation and the real thing just does not apply to our immediate impulses.

[62] At 571d6–2b1 Socrates describes a regimen preparatory to sleep for the purpose of 'stimulating' our highest part and putting the other two truly to sleep. See Adam's commentary at 572a7.

We may be deterred from accepting this type of analysis, as some philosophers have been, by considering the particular audience-reaction of fear. As I sit in the audience and watch Frankenstein's monster march towards me on screen, or (in Plato's world) see the Furies rush onto the orchestra, can it be that the impulse gripping me is actual fear, and not to be distinguished from what I would feel in real life? Perhaps my skin crawls, my fingers tighten on the arm-rests – but still, if I were really afraid, would I not have to think that I were really in danger, and simply run for it? Surely, then, it is a 'make-believe' fear that I feel – and so too with the gamut of our reactions?

This objection can be successfully resisted even as an account of our reaction to horrific effects,[63] but it misses the high tone of Plato's account. When Socrates discusses how poetry can induce fear, at the beginning of Book III, the focus of his worry is that the bleak and pessimistic evocations of Hades in Homer will foster and indulge our fear of death, and only as a secondary matter does he add that since the very words used to name the place and its denizens can cause listeners to tremble, they should be expunged (386a–7b). It is not the passing tremor caused by the sound or appearance of the imitation that he considers most dangerous, but the deeper fear of which it is a symptom – a fear which can hold sway over an entire life. So too what he seeks to induce by tampering with stories of the gods is no fleeting glow of piety but a sense that the harmonious life (as represented by such role models) is valuable or worthwhile, and a determination to live it; while what he seeks to avoid is a creeping contempt for the very fabric of our social life (see 3.386a1–4). The tenseness of the audience at a horror-show pales into triviality by comparison.[64] Plato is thus directing his criticism at the sort of poetic performance that arouses in the audience what we ought least to be inclined to dismiss as a merely 'make-believe' or 'fictional' reaction. And this will be performance of the noblest sort. For if my heart swells as I watch son part from mother, or lovers lose their chance of happiness, it swells not only for the characters but for the human situation to which the performance gives me access: I weep that sons must part from mothers, that things should be so. But so too when we part from our own mothers, or lovers; our feelings brim not simply at the moment, but at the consciousness that this moment has importance for a lifetime; that it is somehow exemplary. Our life at that moment, we might say, feels like a tragedy; and indeed, in Plato's view our heart swells no differently in the theatre than in real life. The difference comes in how we act on its promptings. In real life I would not sit and luxuriate in my fear of an approaching monstrosity, but would run; in real life I would not prolong and wallow in the grief of parting, but would help my partner to bear up under its strain.

---

[63] Alec Hyslop, 'Emotions and fictional characters', *Australasian Journal of Philosophy*, 64, 3 (1986), esp. p. 294.

[64] Aristotle makes a similar point, *Po.* 1453b.

Readers can now, perhaps, feel something of the force of Plato's challenge. It is this: that poetic tragedy, despite what we may think, cannot help us cope with or even more richly appreciate the tragedies of life. It cannot do so because the way to cope with and appreciate and learn from the tragedies of life is to live them; and that means – if we are to live successfully – to bear up under their strain and not allow them to dominate. But that they should dominate is just what poetic tragedy does allow, by giving them full expression. Let me put this to the reader directly. Have you never felt, sitting there in the audience, or even perhaps through deep study of great tragic literature, that this after all – the vulnerability, the fragility of human life that tragedy portrays – is what is, at least in part, truly valuable in a human life, and to be embraced as intrinsic to our humanity? That life would be less if tragedy were absent from it? If so, you – we – have been prey to the temptation on account of which Plato would banish the greatest poetry. It makes no difference that the characters of the drama are perhaps shown learning from their struggles, coming to terms with them as Oedipus does; for by allowing full expression to the pain and sorrow with which he must come to terms, poet and audience risk making a fetish of it. Put brutally: we learn to kiss the boot that kicks us. And that is why it is not absurd for Plato to give poetry the unhealthy complexion of so addictive a personality as the tyrant. We would never be prepared to part with poetry, as Socrates by contrast declares himself ready to part from the poetry he loves, as if parting from a lover (607e4–5); for we prefer the tragedy of parting – the bitter thrill of it – to the sadness of having parted.

Let us, finally, not disguise from ourselves that it is the very greatest poetry that Plato would banish. A place will remain in the ideal society for 'hymns to the gods and encomia of the worthy' (607a3–4), with which we should compare the material to be sung by civic choruses of various ages, culminating in the Dionysian chorus, as instituted in the second book of the *Laws*. But no place is made for a kind of poetry, or poet, who could be any rival for the philosopher. These civic choruses are merely celebrating and confirming themselves in the shared values of the city: values for which philosophy is their guide. But the greatest poetry is that which threatens to become a value in its own right, and so an obstacle. Plato banishes tragedy from the stage for fear that it will prevent us coping with the drama of life.

6 Plato as poet

To what extent, if at all, does Plato envisage the possibility of a reformed and truly philosophic sort of poetry? Certainly, no one can claim to understand Plato's views on poetry without formulating a response to these questions. The matter can only be addressed briefly here, and consideration of it involves a shift from Plato's views on poetry to his views on a certain way of doing philosophy. The nub of it is that for Plato there is no such thing as philosophic poetry, only (at closest) a poetic sort of philosophy.

We should begin by asking whether Plato leaves room in the *Republic* itself for a poetry that would not be confined to the inculcation of good habits in the young and to civic-minded celebration. At the outset of Book X Socrates declares that tragic poetry is harmful to 'all except those who have as remedy [*pharmakon*] an understanding of what it actually is' (595b3 – 7); and later (at 606b6) he alludes to 'those few' who are able to forsee its dangers. But we are surely not to think that the greatest poetry will have a place in the ideal society as the preserve of these 'few' – as if by coming to it forearmed they can appreciate it with impunity. For one thing, Socrates banishes the greatest poets 'from the city', without qualification (607b2 – 3). His talk of a 'remedy' is related to his closing description of his arguments as the 'spell' (*epōidē*, 608a4) that he sings to counteract the seductive pull in poetry, a pull instilled in him by his upbringing (607c6 – d2, 607e4 – 8b2). The word translated as 'remedy', after all, also bears the more particular meaning of '(love)-philtre' or 'spell'. Being able to cast this remedial spell would not render Socrates immune to the effects of imitative poetry if he were to go ahead and participate in the imitation; rather, it enables him to hold aloof, unlike the rest of the audience, from indulging his inclination to participate.

The true account of these matters is expressed in the analogy of the Philosopher-Painter discussed at the beginning of the previous section. Plato's ideal is this: that imitativeness shall nowhere flourish, but that imitation, by contrast, is to be considered essential to human development both in the lesser guise of poetry (in educational and civic contexts) and in its highest manifestation as the philosophic life that imitates the Forms, emulating what is divine in us. The best sort of imitation is not poetry at all, but philosophy – an activity which cannot be distinguished, either in its products or procedures, from the practice of a certain kind of life. This position does not shift in any essential way (although it does undergo development) in dialogues thought to have been written after the *Republic*. In particular, we might think that the *Phaedrus* represents something of a change of heart, since Socrates there seems prepared to acknowledge that the 'divine madness' or inspiration characteristic of poets, as well as of prophets and ritual healers, should find a place in the philosophic life also, in the special kind of erotic love that philosophic characters conceive for each other (244a – 5c). Has Plato perhaps returned here to the aspect of poetry which first aroused his hostility – poetic inspiration – in order to set the record straight? Yet in the same speech that begins with this generous acknowledgement Socrates proceeds to issue a ranking of types of life in which that of the philosopher, a 'follower of the muses and a lover', is at the top and that of the poet is in only sixth place, after statesmen, businessmen, doctors, and prophets and just before such clearly inferior lives as those of the demagogue and the tyrant (248d – e). On closer scrutiny, we see that in the proem of his speech Socrates is casting the inspirational arts he names more in the light of their ancient achievements than of their future potential.[65] When he turns from such traditional piety to the new myth of the after-life (246a – 9d) on which he is to ground a radical revision of the moral psychology of love (249d – 57b), philosophers come into their own as the 'followers of the muses' *par excellence*. Philosophy is being portrayed as the inheritor of the role of poetry (and of other arts), not as its partner.

Certainly, then, we find a shift in position here by comparison to the treatment of poetic inspiration in the earlier dialogues; but the crucial element in that shift – the recognition that poetry can be put to positive use as the ward of philosophy – was already in place, indeed is the heart of the account, in the *Republic*. In the *Phaedrus*, by comparison with the *Republic*, Plato turns from the place of poetry in society at large to the life of the individual philosopher, and the place in that life of something comparable to poetic inspiration: the inspirational force of the philosopher's falling in love. For in his direct encounter with beauty, in the shape of the beloved, the philosopher is confronted with something more than he can either properly articulate or fully understand, but which he aspires to make sense of – and this amounts to discovering himself as a philosopher – by building a philosophic life in partnership with the beloved. The 'divine madness' of philosophy is related to that of poetry much as imitation of the Forms is related to poetic imitation. While the poetic activity issues in a performance that has its place within life, philosophy issues in a 'performance' that simply *is* a life.

Nevertheless, to judge from those scenes from the philosophic life provided by Plato's dialogues, the philosopher is not to scorn the resources of poetry. In the *Phaedrus* itself Socrates constructs an elaborate 'mythic hymn' (265c1), which he explicitly qualifies as 'poetic' (275a5), in order to give expression to the very difficulty that the philosophic lover encounters in understanding and articulating his love. As philosopher, after all, Socrates is no more exempt from this difficulty than is the philosophic lover of whom he speaks; hence his recourse to the confessedly inadequate medium of mythic allegory (246a3 – 6). Moreover, in several dialogues Socrates famously brings the discussion to an end with myths of the after-life: in the *Phaedo*, the *Gorgias*, and the *Republic*. We have seen that Socrates makes a place in his ideal society for the 'mythological lie' (*Rep.* 382d); a necessary place, given our need for speculation beyond the limits of what we can securely understand.

But there is more than this to the philosophic use of myth. In none of the dialogues is Socrates talking to citizens of the ideal society; rather, he talks to those interested in philosophy, or defends philosophy from its detractors. By propounding new myths of the after-life, Socrates is in a sense painting

---

[65] 244a8 – c5 (esp. 244b6 – 7, 244c4 – 5), 244d6, 245a4.

a background for a new and philosophic culture – offering the frightened
disciples he leaves behind in the *Phaedo*, for example, a vision on which to fix
their shared aspirations when he is gone. He calls that myth a 'spell' that they
must repeat to encourage themselves (114d7), as we have just seen him call
the arguments of the tenth book of the *Republic* a 'spell' to counteract the
temptation to participate in tragic performance, and as in the *Phaedo* (77e8)
itself he refers to the series of arguments for the immortality of the soul by
implication as a 'spell' for Cebes to cast each day on the child within his soul
until the fear of death is lulled. Both argument and story have the power to
change our lives, and Socrates accordingly uses both, provided the change
is for the better. However, the type of life towards which he would direct us
is nevertheless characterised by its dissatisfaction with myth. Socrates
concludes the arguments of the *Phaedo* with the caveat that we should follow
them up and clarify their assumptions (107b) – with the sense, then, of an
ongoing programme of inquiry; but concludes his myth quite otherwise, with
the caveat that no sensible person would insist on its details, but that to believe
that something of this sort is true would be a 'noble risk' (114d). There is no
implication that myth could provide a cutting edge for shared inquiry. In the
Phaedrus, similarly, Socrates pushes discussion forward by turning from his
mythic hymn to a more discursive investigation. The discussion is partly
driven by dissatisfaction with myth, yet the effect of the dialogue as a whole
is to recognise the human necessity of myth, together with the corresponding
limitations of argument; much as the philosophic lover of the mythic hymn
is driven to the philosophic life by struggling with the mystery of what is
happening to him, a mystery he can never fully articulate, but can render less
mysterious – can make his home in, his new culture.[66]

We can regard Plato's own use of the dialogue form in much the same light.
Not only is he careful to mark with caveats the various poetic resources to
which he is nevertheless driven within the dialogues (myths, allegories, and
images), but his decision to adopt dialogue as the mode appropriate to his
philosophic writing is itself a way of marking that entire written corpus with
a warning for the reader or audience. We do not know how the dialogues were
disseminated. At one point in the *Laws* the Athenian suggests that the
discussion on which he and the others have been engaged might stand as a
paradigm for what the young should hear at school (7.811c–e). But this does
not necessarily imply that Plato would recommend the *Laws* itself as some
kind of textbook; and the *Laws* is in any case an uncharacteristic dialogue.
More illuminating is the opening scene of the *Theaetetus*, in which Euclides
and Terpsion, two of the companions of Socrates mentioned in the *Phaedo*
(at 58c2) as present at his death, are shown arranging for a servant to read

---

[66] The *Phaedrus* offers Plato's most concerted examination (as well as being itself, of course,
a fine example) of a 'poetic' kind of philosophy (as opposed to philosophic poetry); cf.
Ferrari, *Listening to the Cicadas*.

to them from Euclides' record of the Socratic conversation that then appears as the main body of the dialogue.

But regardless of whether Plato's dialogues were themselves performed in a dramatic fashion,[67] there was that about them which would render their realisation quite distinct from a performance of conventional drama or even the recitation of epic: namely, that whereas these latter are an imitation of people's actions,[68] of which the activity of talk is only a part, in a Platonic dialogue the talk *is* the action, the whole of it. Even when Antigone is constructing a plea for justice, her arguments are motivated by what she has done (her burying Polynices), and elicit from Creon not merely a response, but punishment. In Plato's dialogues, by contrast, the talk of the characters not only expresses the ideals of the philosophic life but puts those ideals into practice (at least, when the character is a role-model). It is expression and action all at once. Its particularity as a (fictional) action or event is as a conversation between people who believe (and challengers who do not) that thoughtful talk in itself is among the most important actions of our lives, and is important just in so far as it attains to a truth not tied to the particularity of any one conversation. Witnessing Antigone's tragedy, hearing of the struggles of Odysseus, we are privy to actions which, however exemplary or revealing they may be, in some sense stand on their own. These things are happening, we tell ourselves in imagination, and what, now, shall we make of them? But as the audience of Platonic dialogue we hear talk which, just to the extent that we imagine ourselves present as it is spoken and identify with the ideals it expresses, directs us out again to the world beyond such fictions, telling us that the only reaction to its message which has value in itself is to recreate its ideal in our own lives. The written dialogue itself, then, has, strictly speaking, only instrumental value towards that end.

This point is made explicit in the *Phaedrus* (274c – 7a).[69] The 'living discourse' of philosophic discussion is there contrasted with its written 'image', which can serve at best as a 'reminder' of what is to be understood in the philosophic life (276a8 – 9, 275c8 – d2). Socrates compares the written word to a painted portrait, which may seem to be alive but cannot answer back if questioned; so speech, once written down, can say only the same thing over and over (275d4 – 9). Yet while fixed in this sense, it is extremely fluid in another; for a script will circulate indiscriminately among all audiences, incapable of selecting those who can receive it with understanding (275d9 – e5). A living speaker, by contrast, and especially the philosophic discussant,

---

[67] Gilbert Ryle, *Plato's Progress* (Cambridge, 1966), pp. 23–32.
[68] See the description in *Rep.* 10.603c4–8, and compare Aristotle's famous definition of tragedy in *Po.* 6.1449b24–8.
[69] A similar point is made in the *Seventh Letter* (341b3–5a1) and in the *Second Letter* (314b–c). Scholars have doubted the authenticity of both works, but most especially the latter.

can choose an appropriate conversational partner, can answer when questioned and so can expect to sow the seeds of fresh speech in the soul of the hearer (276e4 – 7a4).

All this is akin to the point Socrates made when bringing discussion of Simonides' poem to an end in the *Protagoras*. Let us not become locked in an interminable discussion over what the poet meant, he pleaded. The poet is not here to tell us what he meant; we are left only with what he said. So too, any speech that gets written down is prone to divide along these two channels: it becomes something that has been said, quite apart from something that was meant. And the division is accentuated – as it is not in speech – by the sharp contrast between the fixity of the former, the actual text, as against the extreme plurality of interpretive guesses at what the latter might be. But this is not a counsel of despair. Plato is not suggesting that philosophy should not be written, and therefore that what he writes is somehow not philosophy, any more than he suggests in the *Protagoras* that literary exegesis is valueless. Rather, he is anxious to ensure that philosophic writing and reading should not become an end in itself, but should be practised with the sense that what ultimately matters is the way of life in which it can find a worthy place. It is to be approached, says Socrates, in the spirit of a 'game' (276d1 – 8).

Plato holds that practitioners of writing are especially liable to lose sight of this goal. However, it is important to see that not only does he not think this an inevitable outcome of writing, but that he is also quite aware that oral discourse is not automatically free of such hazards. For one thing, writing is not directly in question in the discussion of Simonides' poem in the *Protagoras*. The poem is introduced orally, and its impotence to answer back derives from its canonical status and the absence of the author: conditions which would apply even if the poem had never been written down but had been orally transmitted. But there is a fine illustration of Plato's sensitivity to this issue in the opening scene of the *Phaedrus* itself, in Phaedrus' characteristic shenanigans with the written scroll of a speech by the orator Lysias. Phaedrus is a great fan of all manner of intellectual talk, rhetorical as well as philosophical, and in the hope of a chance to give his personal re-creation of the rhetorical performance he had heard from Lysias on the morning of this conversation, he attempts to conceal from Socrates that he has managed to borrow the actual script of the speech from its author. But Socrates uncovers his ruse, and insists on having the written text read to him instead (227a1 – 8e5). Not that Socrates, as we have seen, is any friend to the written word; but he wants to preclude a mere pretence at living speech on Phaedrus' part. In re-creating Lysias' speech, Phaedrus would not have been intent on conveying what Lysias had said, for all his praise of its cleverness (227c5 – 8). Had this been his primary intent, he would have produced the script without further ado. Rather, what he longs for is to reproduce its effect of cleverness; to make himself over in the image of an artificer of words (as he tells us at

227d6 – 8a4). Phaedrus treats Lysias' script not as a simple tool of verbal transmission but as something magical: the bottled essence, as it were, of the performance that thrilled him so, and a potion which can transform him into his ideal. That is why he spared no effort to secure it from its author, yet is so ready to disown it before Socrates.

Phaedrus' behaviour illustrates two points. First, that the dangers Socrates later attributes to writing can also be run in spoken discourse; for had he let Phaedrus have his head, we would have heard *extempore* speech that took as its goal not the generation of fresh discussion, but the re-prompting of old applause. Indeed, to suppose that the medium of *extempore* speech is by its very nature invulnerable to these hazards would be to treat it with just the superstition that Phaedrus brings to the written word. The second point illustrated is that the written word is nevertheless especially apt to promote this problem. As a tool for capturing words in a permanent form external to and potentially independent of their user, writing encourages Phaedrus' fetishist illusion that it can somehow preserve and transmit the very power by which authors write, and through the possession of which they have something to say. In other words, the practice of writing and reading is prone to take us in with its appearance of autonomy and lull us into not feeling the need to step beyond its confines in order to seek the way of life that makes that practice meaningful. So it is significant that when Socrates later (at 264c1 – 5) uses the metaphor of a 'living creature' to describe the properly scripted composition, with head and feet and torso all in place and forming an organic whole, he emphasises only the external aspect of the organism, its array of limbs. Contrast the 'life' subsequently attributed to oral discussion: talk that 'has soul in it' (*empsuchon*, 276a8), and in comparison to which the formal completeness of the organic composition seems but an external 'portrait of life' (*zōgraphia*), not life itself. Indeed, Plato may here be out to show the limits of what amounted to a commonplace of technique (albeit one he accepted for his own writing), since he has Socrates announce the recommendation of organic composition as something that Phaedrus, the rhetorical enthusiast, would say (264c2).

In sum, neither writing nor speaking matter just in themselves; both draw their value from their use in a way of life. Despite this, there is no reason to suppose that Plato's devaluation of writing in comparison to speaking is not seriously meant. Certainly it is not undermined by the irony that it itself is couched in writing; for Socrates does not say that writing inevitably lies, but only that its truth is liable to get lost. We are offered neither a self-defeating nor a self-overcoming text, but a serious warning.[70]

But to speak more generally in conclusion: when we consider Plato's use

---

[70] This brief allusion must suffice in response to the 'ironic' interpretations of Derrida, 'Pharmacie', and Burger, 'Plato's *Phaedrus*'. For further discussion see Ferrari, *Listening to the Cicadas*, ch. 7.

of the dialogue form in conjunction with the content of the dialogues in this way, we see that consideration of the dialogues' merely instrumental value is being continually urged upon us, independently of any explicit statements to that effect, by the simple fact that what we hear are philosophic voices in action. Plato's dialogues are not philosophic poetry; for poetry is of its very nature content when it has presented us with human action (however sophisticated a task such presentation may be, however suggestive the presentation), and leaves us then to cope, or meditate. The dialogues are, rather, a poetic and philosophic call to the philosophic life.

4

ARISTOTLE'S POETICS

When, towa[...] ury after Christ, the rhetorician Dio of Prusa cal[...] whom they say that criticism [*kritikē*] and the st[...]] took their origin' (53.1), it was not the *Poetics*[...] udgement he was citing, had in mind. Dio men[...] any dialogues' in which Aristotle had discusse[...] Homer, and the phrase indicates that it was the [...]rs, to which he was referring. The three books of *On* [...] re books of *Homeric Problems* (presumably not in dialogue form), w[...] t the two chief works in which Aristotle's ideas on poetry were disseminated in the ancient critical tradition; while the *Poetics*, originally produced for use within the philosophical school, never became at all readily available or widely known. Our own view of Aristotle the literary critic is therefore bound to differ substantially from that of antiquity; and it is the more inward voice of the philosophical theorist of poetry which the *Poetics*, if incompletely, allows us to hear. But it is a useful first step in a fresh approach to the surviving text to consider briefly what can still be discerned of its relation to the lost works on poetry which Aristotle intended for a more public audience.

1 'On Poets' and 'Homeric Problems'

The use of the dialogue form in *On Poets* places this work with fair likelihood in the first period which Aristotle spent at Athens (367 – 347 BC), up to the time of Plato's death. For *Homeric Problems* there is no helpful chronological evidence, though *Poetics*, chapter 25, appears to contain a summary of the principles which had been worked out at greater length, and with fuller application, in this separate work on Homer. Since the *Poetics* was a document designed for Aristotle's own teaching purposes, it is unlikely to have been entirely compiled in one short period, and then left permanently unrevised. Some parts of the treatise, particularly the chapters on language and style (20 – 2), can reasonably be dated early in the philosopher's career; but other sections seem to reflect later and more mature views, and it is

149

plausible to suppose that the work was at any rate in use in the Lyceum in Aristotle's second Athenian period (335–323 BC). If so, the *Poetics* ought to represent an essentially philosophical statement of the latest stage of his thinking on poetry which Aristotle felt it worth at least delineating in writing.[1]

The major stimulus behind this thinking, however, was undoubtedly Plato's adverse critique of poetry, and this fact justifies the assumption that Aristotle developed at any rate the rudiments of his critical position while Plato was still alive. Among a number of later neo-Platonic references to an Aristotelian doctrine of *katharsis*, we find Proclus's statement that Plato's opposition to tragedy and comedy gave Aristotle 'much cause for complaint'.[2] The suggestion of an explicit, even polemical response to Plato makes highly unlikely the common view that Proclus is referring to the lost second book of the *Poetics* – a hypothesis which would also leave us with the improbability that Aristotle relegated to his treatment of comedy the contentious exposition of a concept which first occurs in the definition of tragedy. If the allusion can instead be taken to *On Poets*, then we may attribute to this work the forthright declaration of an anti-Platonic idea on the implications of which Aristotle later, in the surviving version of the *Poetics*, seemingly no longer feels much pressure to dwell.

A somewhat different instance of continuity of thought combined with a shift of emphasis in presentation, can be discerned in a comparison of fr. 70 of *On Poets* with chapter 1 of the *Poetics*.[3] In the dialogue, Aristotle praised Empedocles' stylistic virtues, including metaphor; in the *Poetics*, he avers (despite the unquestionable debt of Empedocles' style to Homer) that Empedocles and Homer have 'nothing in common except their metre'. Since fr. 72 of *On Poets* seems to indicate that Aristotle argued in this work for mimesis, not metre, as the criterion of poetry, the reference to Empedocles in fr. 70 surely belongs to a context analogous to that in *Poetics*, chapter 1. The significant difference lies in the formulation. Whether because *On Poets* was intended for a wider audience, or perhaps because the *Poetics* represents a more uncompromising phase of Aristotle's thought, the treatise presses the separation of poetry from other types of discourse to a firmer conclusion than the dialogue appears to have offered. Elsewhere, the distance between the two works may have been greater. Both the title and some of the fragments of the dialogue intimate a concern with the biography of poets (an established and relatively popular topic). While the loss of context prevents us from deducing Aristotle's attitude to the evidently anecdotal biographical material attested in the fragments, the very fact of a willingness to discuss such things contrasts

---

[1] On the dating of the *Poetics*, Halliwell, *Aristotle's Poetics*, app. 1.
[2] For Proclus's and other neo-Platonic references to *katharsis*, see Kassel's ed. of *Po.*, p. 52; tr. in Smith and Ross, *Works*, XII, pp. 74–5.
[3] Fr. in Rose, pp. 76–81; tr. in Smith and Ross, *Works*, XII, pp. 72–7.

with the severe exclusion of them from the purview of the *Poetics*, within which the history of poetry is conceived in a much more theoretical spirit.

Between the *Poetics* and *Homeric Problems* the important differences were, by contrast, probably more a matter of detail than of principle. If chapter 25 of the *Poetics* now has a compressed and somewhat rebarbative character (as well as being in a partially garbled state), that is because it offers a concise summary of critical standards and criteria which were applied in *Homeric Problems* to a multitude of individual passages and interpretative issues. Responding to a wide range of earlier criticisms of Homer, as well as to the moral and epistemological force of Plato's views on poetry, Aristotle worked his way towards a fundamental insight: a qualified recognition of poetry's status as an independent art with its own distinctive potential, to be evaluated with a grasp of appropriate critical axioms. The typically terse pronouncement that 'correctness in poetry is not identical to correctness in politics [*politikē*] or in any other art' (25.1460b13 – 15) stands as an expression of the most basic of these axioms, and the fragments of *Homeric Problems* allow us some glimpses of its implications put into critical practice for the solution of various factual, technical, historical, and moral 'problems'. The bulk of material examined in this work gave Aristotle copious opportunities to elaborate and clarify the principles which also came to be embodied in the spare philosophical formulations of the *Poetics*.[4]

2 Theoretical components of the 'Poetics'

If the dialogue *On Poets*, as we have seen, may have made some concessions to popular interests, and if *Homeric Problems* tackled a host of specific exegetical questions raised by mostly non-philosophical writers, the *Poetics* was produced as a measured *résumé* of a theory of poetry which could both come to terms with the challenge set by Plato, and conform to the standards of philosophical rigour which Aristotle sought in other areas of his thought. This context does not match the still common opinion that the treatise was designed to impinge on practising poets in contemporary Athens. Although at certain points (particularly in chapters 17 – 18) Aristotle turns briefly to direct consideration of the processes of poetic composition, the work's general prescriptivism has a sharply theoretic not a pragmatic slant. A telling instance of this occurs at the end of chapter 18, where Sophocles' use of the tragic chorus is recommended against the practices prevalent around the middle of the fourth century: the brevity and detachment of this passage, despite the explicit contradiction of contemporary dramaturgy, negates any idea that Aristotle seriously hoped to sway Athenian tragedians in his own day.

---

[4] Fr. of *Homeric Problems* in Rose, pp. 120–37; tr. (selection) in Barnes, *Complete Works*, II, pp. 2431–3.

A deeper reason for seeing the *Poetics* as a work of theoretical or philosophical criticism is its steady focus on a conception of genres and their intrinsic nature, rather than on the individual poet and his work. The framework for Aristotle's disquisition on poetry is given by 'the art itself and its species' (or genres), to quote the programmatic opening sentence. Aristotle's response to the potent but unsystematic drive of Plato's ethical, psychological, and epistemological criticisms of poetry was to offer a stable theory of poetry's true nature, and with it a defensible sense of what could and could not be expected of the art. In proceeding now to an assessment of the tenets of this theory, it is desirable to try to do justice to the implicitly comprehensive scope of the ideas which underlie it. This essay will respect Aristotle's own priorities by first examining the wider and more abstract components of the *Poetics*.

The *Poetics* purports to follow a 'natural procedure from first principles' (1.1447a12 – 13). While close attention to the laconic style of exposition may find that basic assumptions are not always announced (for the treatise belongs in and with a larger philosophical course of study), the central principles have been conceived as elements of a coherent system. The approach to poetry as a distinctive art, and therefore a distinct area of inquiry, entails both a positive attempt to define its essential attributes and a negative separation of poetry from other types of discourse. Besides the analytical character of Aristotle's own philosophical temperament, two major factors encouraged a more acute demarcation of poetry's domain than had previously existed in Greek culture or criticism. One was the rapid diversification, in the course of the fifth and fourth centuries, of regions of thought and activity which in retrospect came to be categorised in terms such as history, rhetoric, science, scholarship, and philosophy itself. Most of these subjects involved elements shared with at least certain sorts of poetry, and we have already seen the resulting ambiguity confronted by Aristotle in his refusal to regard Empedocles' verse-writings as poetry proper. In addition to this cultural issue, there was the particular challenge of Plato's assault on poetic standards of truth and morality, posing for Aristotle the task of finding criteria which could do justice to poetry's intrinsic nature and values.

Aristotle's response to these promptings centres around a concept inherited from Plato: mimesis. But while adhering to Plato's premise that mimesis is essential to poetry (as well as to the visual arts, music, and dance), Aristotle suggests some important specifications which cut across Plato's thinking on the subject. 'Since the poet is a mimetic artist like a painter or any other image-maker, he must use mimesis to portray, in any particular instance, one of three objects: things such as they once were or now are; things such as men say and believe that they are; or things such as they ought to be' (25.1460b8 – 11). Aristotle's position has an affinity with Plato's, in that he accepts that all art offers images of possible reality; but at the same time it is remote from it in spirit, since the qualification expressed by 'possible' involves a crucial relaxation of the demands that Plato, at his most exacting (or dismissive), had brought to bear on mimesis. While sharing with him what might loosely be termed a 'correspondence theory' of mimesis, Aristotle circumvents the implications of Plato's view of art by holding that the content and meaning of mimetic works cannot justifiably be tested against any fixed criterion of truth or reality.

It is tempting to argue that passages such as the one quoted above from *Poetics* 25 allow for a notion of poetic fiction or imagination; but the need for some reservations on such a conclusion serves well to illustrate the difficulty of bringing Aristotle's ideas properly into relation to later aesthetic attitudes. It is especially important to avoid a facile assimilation of the poet's relative freedom of invention, as characterised in the *Poetics*, to romantic conceptions of creative imagination. The difference resides partly in the fact that Aristotle does not conceive of the poet himself as possessing any special imaginative faculty or powers. The philosophical interpretation of mimesis is concerned with the status of mimetic *works*, and stands above all in resistance to the Platonic subjection of poetry to extrinsic and objective standards of truth and goodness. If we are not to attribute to Aristotle a subjectivist aesthetic which is entirely alien to him, we must perceive the strength of the assumption, perhaps latent in the general Greek concept of mimesis, that the understanding of poetry is aligned with the axis which runs between the work of art and the world, not that between the artist and his work. Once such a caveat is grasped, a suitably cautious use of terms such as 'fiction', 'imagination' and 'invention' can still help to characterise the significance of Aristotle's rejection of a simple truth-to-fact model for mimetic art.

It is an implicit idea of fictionality which gives Aristotle a basis on which to distinguish the nature of poetry from activities such as history and philosophy, with which it shares an interest in the world of human action and experience. The practitioners of history and philosophy are taken to strive for direct truths about reality: particulars about the past, in the one case, and universal or general truths in the other. The relative affinity between poet and philosopher posited in *Poetics* 9 does not affect the assumption, declared most insistently at the end of the same chapter, that the poet must 'make' his own material, even in cases where he takes its data from history: that is, he must select, organise, and shape it, so that the resulting design is a product of art, not a statement or description of existing reality. These contentions raise a further question about the truth-status of poetry to which we shall shortly return.

A cognate, if more elusive, factor in Aristotle's development of the concept of mimesis is its gravitation towards the notion of the *dramatic*. Although in chapter 3 the narrative mode holds an equal place alongside dramatic enactment, elsewhere – in the praise of Homer's dramatic qualities

(4.1448b34 – 8), in the prescription of dramatic plot-structures for epic in general (23.1459a18 – 19), and above all in the assertion that mimesis is incompatible with the poet 'speaking in his own person' (24.1460a5 – 11) – Aristotle intimates, without fully tying himself to, a concept of poetry as preferably and properly dramatic. Here too we can detect the pressure of a desire to define the boundaries between poetry and other types of discourse. The historian's and philosopher's direct commitment to truth makes it necessary for them to rely on the modes of statement, description, and argument. It is these and similar modes which Aristotle wishes to eliminate from the poet's resources (except in so far as they can be incorporated in the dramatic portrayal of agents), since it is not the purpose of poetic art to offer express affirmations about the world (cf. *On Interpretation* 17a5 – 6), but to show 'images' of possible human life and experience. The dramatic mode suits poetry best, on this view, because it comports with the status of poetic material as an enactment, an imaginative presentation, of patterns of action: the notion of poetic fictionality which emerges from the *Poetics* therefore coordinates the logically 'non-committal' standing of poetry (its exemption from the Platonic requirement of veracity) with the ideally enactive or dramatic mode of presentation. Both these factors are present in the judgement on Empedocles, whose verse-writings are classified as 'natural philosophy', not poetry, because they offer categorical claims about the world (including the larger sphere of nature, which Aristotle excludes in *a priori* fashion from poetry's distinctively human subject-matter), and because they are consequently not concerned with the hypothetical or fictional dramatisation of action.

If our own cultural readiness to separate philosophy from poetry makes it easy to see Aristotle's point in the case of Empedocles, this should not be allowed to disguise the radical implications of the *Poetics* for Greek poetry in general. The passage from chapter 24 cited above indicates that Aristotle is prepared to entertain doubts about the mimetic, and therefore the poetic, status even of some uses of narrative in epic – uses which carry too strong a sense of the poet 'speaking in his own person'. Elsewhere, Aristotle's doctrine would appear to entail at best an equivocal attitude towards those poetic genres (conventionally accepted as such within the culture) which made extensive use of non-dramatic utterance. Since this latter category should embrace, on the *Poetics'* criteria, all first-person statements which are not dramatically attributed within a poem, we might expect doubt to be cast on the poetic qualifications of much of the work of such writers as Hesiod (didactic), Archilochus (iambus), Solon (elegy), Sappho and Alcaeus (personal lyric), and Pindar (choral lyric). Though such an inference is startling for the student of Greek poetry, it is borne out by the fact that none of these poets is ever mentioned or cited in the *Poetics*, and the genres to which they belong are largely ignored. If Aristotle is the first Greek critic to essay a precise conception of what constitutes poetry and differentiates it from other types of thought and writing, it must also be said that the result is severely and limitingly normative, and that it takes little or no account of many major figures in the culture of Archaic and Classical Greece.

This restrictive aspect of the notion of mimesis operative in the *Poetics* is counterbalanced by the fresh and serious attempt which is made to define the cognitive value of poetry. Plato's impugnment of the authority of poetic texts in Greek life rested, like those of the earlier philosophers Xenophanes and Heraclitus, on the assurance of philosophy's own access to the universal truths which were traditionally attributed to the wisdom of poets. Aristotle shared the assurance but, perhaps because of his non-Athenian origins, lacked Plato's sense of a vital rivalry between poetry and philosophy. Whereas Plato's metaphysics had induced him to demote poetry to a very low epistemic level, Aristotle's view of the relation between particulars and universals allowed him to incorporate poetry positively within his scheme of values. Poetry is 'more philosophical and more ethically serious than history', according to *Poetics* 9, because the actions and characters in its images of life come closer to the universals of philosophy than to the discrete particulars of real events.

It is a task of some urgency for any interpretation of the treatise to try to disentangle the implications of this principle from the later aesthetic ideas with which it has sometimes been confused. To do so, we need to grasp that Aristotelian universals are the categories and concepts which enable the mind to move beyond concrete sense-perception to the comprehension of essential and permanent features of reality. The first risk to be avoided, therefore, is the reduction of these universals to the level of the merely typical or normal, as happened with the shallower neo-classical paraphrases of Aristotle's theory. The formulation at 9.1451b8–9 – 'the sorts of things which a certain sort of person may say or do, according to probability or necessity' – only superficially justifies a principle of normative *vraisemblance*, as the final clause makes clear. Verisimilitude might be satisfied precisely by vividness of particulars, and therefore cannot serve as a description of the doctrine of *Poetics* 9. Aristotle's point is no more and, given the Platonic challenge, no less than that poetry's dramatisations of life are constructed, and have their intelligibility, in terms which conform to the conditions of general thought and reasoning, terms which are at least related to those employed at a higher level by the ethical and political philosopher.

It is equally important, however, to avoid a false inflation of Aristotle's position into the ideas of what may broadly be called the neo-Platonic tradition in aesthetics, with its faith in poetry as the expression or manifestation of 'higher' or transcendent truths.[5] Faced with an overtly metaphysical poetics of this kind, it becomes obligatory to stress by contrast the limitations

---

[5] Cf. Plotinus 5.8.1, where Pheidias's conception of Zeus's physical form is said to show him 'as he would be'; cf. *Po.* 9.1451a37, 9.1451b5.

intimated by the comparative phrasing of the juxtaposition of poetry and philosophy in *Poetics* 9. Poetry is not in any deep sense philosophical in Aristotle's eyes; it tends towards the status of universals, but it falls far short of philosophy since its structures are mimetic or fictive, and do not offer systematic truths. We have no warrant to extract from Aristotle's remarks an idealist aesthetic of the kind influentially stated in Butcher's essays at the end of the nineteenth century. In particular, it is a mistake to confuse what the *Poetics* has to say on the general cognitive status of poetry, which is exemplified in chapter 9 by a reference to comedy (whose characters are nonetheless 'worse than us'), with the specific observations (in chapters 2, 15 and 25) on the idealising or heightening of characterisation – the portrayal of men 'better than ourselves' – which is found in epic, tragedy, and certain sorts of visual art. Generic features of the latter kind do nothing to endow the universals of poetry as a whole with a metaphysical force or potential.

The concept of poetic universals must be taken with, and can be clarified by, Aristotle's canons of artistic form and unity. Since the decisive rejection of the neo-classical, spuriously Aristotelian, trio of Unities, the *Poetics'* cardinal doctrine of unity of plot-structure has managed to retain critical respectability. But respect does not guarantee understanding, and certain misconceptions are persistent. Particularly to be rebutted is the belief that Aristotle expounds a strictly formalist notion of unity as independent of poetic meaning. How erroneous this belief is we can see if we turn directly to the clearest formulation of the principle of unity: 'just as in the other mimetic arts a unitary mimesis is a representation of a unitary object, so the plot-structure, since it is the mimesis of an action, should be the representation of an action which is unitary and entire' (8.1451a30–2). As this passage shows, unity is grounded in the mimetic nature of a poem (or other work of art) and cannot be divorced from its signifying power. So the unity of plot-structure (*muthos*), which is the essential life ('the soul') of a poem for Aristotle, derives from the unity of the action which is the content or object of the representation.[6] And if poetic unity is justified in the terms of a wider aesthetic theory of perception, as it is in chapter 7, that is because the philosopher sees a cognitive foundation – the apprehension of significant structure – underlying all experience of beauty and formal unity.

Poetics 7 and 8 elaborate the requirements and criteria of unity of plot (specifically, here, of tragic plot-structure): they entail a construction which has sufficient size or scope to contain a complex organisation of parts, and within this construction an ordered progression from beginning to middle to end. Two further factors help us to make fuller sense of the latter idea, one of which applies to poetic form in general, while the other depends on the nature of the individual genre. These factors combine in the case of tragedy

---

[6] Aristotle endows the term *praxis* with the new sense of a coherent set of events; see esp. 8.1451a19 and 8.1451a28. This usage appears never to have been taken over by later critics.

(7.1451a11 – 15), where Aristotle prescribes that dramatic scale should allow for a change of fortune (which is the pattern of action conducive to the tragic emotions) in a sequence of events occurring according to, and given coherence by, probability or necessity. The first factor, then, concerns the kind of action (pitiful and fearful) which must be shaped and completed in order to constitute a properly *tragic* plot, while the second represents the essential point of reference, repeatedly cited in the course of the work, for the unity of all poetic mimesis. The distinctively tragic configuration of events will have to be considered later, as part of the wider theory of the genre; but the canon of 'probability or necessity', which we have already met in connection with universals, needs immediate elucidation as a key component in Aristotle's understanding of poetic form and significance.

Probability and necessity are closely conjoined concepts throughout Aristotle's system of thought, since they bear both on the causal relations between things and on the logical relations between propositions. In both areas necessity stands for relations which are invariable or unavoidable, while probability represents a degree of likelihood which falls short of certainty, but nonetheless holds 'for the most part'. These principles enter into the theory of poetry partly because of Aristotle's conviction that poems should be products of rational art, whose success depends above all on their formal coherence, and partly because of the premise that poetic mimesis is the representation of possible human action, and must be intelligible as such. Probability and necessity are normally invoked in the *Poetics* in connection with the causal links between the successive stages of a plot-structure. The resulting emphasis on a coordinated nexus of events can be most strikingly, because paradoxically, demonstrated from the notion of a 'complex' tragedy (chapters 10 – 11), in which a startling twist of fortune is mediated through the elements of recognition and reversal. Yet even here, where one might expect allowance to be made for a degree of tragic inscrutability, the indispensable function of probability or necessity is reaffirmed.

Aristotle does not regard the unity which derives from these principles as a mere basis or prerequisite for poetic achievement; he values it as the highest virtue of the most important genre of poetry, tragedy (7.1450b21 – 3). This fact affords an insight into his understanding of mimesis not as a mirroring of ordinary reality (which often precisely lacks unity: 8.1451a17 – 19) but as artistically designed images of possible reality whose intelligibility depends on their unity. From the discussion of unity in chapters 7 – 8 emerges the conclusion: 'it is not the poet's task to tell of actual events, but of things that might happen and are possible according to probability or necessity' (9.1451a36 – 8). Unity and mimetic significance are mutually supportive elements within this theory; unity – the mimesis of a unitary object – yields intelligibility, which resides in what might be called clarity of dramatic logic, embodied in the cohesive significance of the plot-structure. Just as propositions might stand to one another in a relation of necessity or probability, so Aristotle requires the components of a dramatic action to display an analogous degree of explanatory coherence.

The abstraction of this doctrine reflects the philosopher's interest in elaborating a serious formulation of poetic art, but it opens Aristotle to the charge of projecting his own intellectual needs onto the work of the poet. While the causal unity and perspicuity of dramatic action is a powerful critical requirement, it is stated in the *Poetics* with an uncompromising spareness which shows no interest in other means or resources of poetic unity. Moreover, by precluding any role for ambiguity or causal uncertainty within a structure of action, Aristotle's notion of unity carries us – as any serious concept of poetic form ought to do – into issues of causation and responsibility within the world of tragic drama; and to these we will later have to return.

The doctrine of unity put forward in the *Poetics* can serve to illustrate Aristotle's recognition of poetry, in the face of its devaluation by Plato, as a rational art whose procedures are objectively specifiable. Unity is the prime virtue of a plot-structure, and it is the plot-structure for which the poet, as 'maker', is above all responsible (9.1451b27 – 9). Hence, in one of his more pragmatic moments (chapter 17), Aristotle envisages the composing poet setting out the general scheme of his work before elaborating the details. Unity, incorporated into the poet's material by conscious selection and design, is fundamental to the 'rationality' of the art, and Aristotle repudiates traditional notions of poetry as inspirational or beyond clear comprehension. Instead, he systematises the equally traditional notion (present in the very term *poiētēs*, 'maker') of the poet as a craftsman in possession of a controlled, teachable skill. The poet's craft or artistry is a variety of *tekhnē*, which comprises the whole range of activities that harness human skill and intelligence to productive effect, and all those capacities which use rational procedures to bring predetermined objects into being. It was as a comment on all such productive activity, and not as the formula for the fine arts which it later became, that Aristotle enunciated the principle that 'art imitates nature', linking the purposive and intelligible methods of artistry with the teleological workings of the natural world.[7] By giving full force to such a principle in the case of poetry, Aristotle takes perhaps his single most important step away from the Platonic stance towards the subject.

Aristotle's poet, then, is a rational 'maker' of artifacts – mimetic structures of action – in the media, or materials, of language, rhythm, and music (chapter 1). For the post-romantic reader of the *Poetics* it is essential to grasp how this understanding of poetic activity subordinates the poet to his art by positing a teleological relation between them: the true locus of the art lies

---

[7] E.g., *Physics* 194a21 – 2, 199a16 – 17; for a later instance, Seneca, *Ep.* 65.3. In the course of time the idea became confused with the 'imitation of nature' in the mimetic arts: e.g., Horace, *AP* 317 – 18; Pliny, *Natural History* 34.61, 35.103; Longinus 22.1; Plotinus 5.8.1.

not in the personal springs of the poet's mind, nor in the subjective impulses of his imagination, but in the end towards which he works, the finished poetic structure. On a spectrum of possible views of poetic intentionalism, the *Poetics* is close to one extreme: the poet's individual intentions are immaterial; his function is to give fresh mimetic embodiment to principles which exist independently of him in the nature of his art.[8] Aristotle's presuppositions on this point are exemplified by his remark, cited above, that the poet abandons his status as mimetic artist when he speaks 'in his own person' (24.1460a7–8). We can see here how the concepts of artistry and mimesis complement one another: the first subordinates the poet to the objective or intrinsic attributes of the works he produces; while mimesis defines the poems themselves not in terms of an inward relation to the poet's mind, but as the (preferably dramatic) representation of patterns of possible reality.

There is also a larger, cultural dimension to Aristotle's interpretation of poetic art. In his general thinking, art is not simply assimilated to nature by analogy, but can itself be located within the framework of nature by virtue of its part in man's own natural capacities. By contrast with Plato, who often treats mimesis as a matter of deceptive contrivance, Aristotle was convinced of the natural roots of mimetic activity, and this conviction is reflected in his explanation for the very existence of poetry, as well as his schematic reconstruction of its development. In *Poetics* 4 poetry in general is attributed to two natural causes. The first is a human instinct for mimesis – a universal characteristic of man, illustrated by the place of mimesis (here embracing various imitative and make-believe activities) in the learning of children. The second is a human capacity to take pleasure in the products of mimesis (even where their content is intrinsically painful), which Aristotle interprets, with typical economy, as due to the enjoyment of learning and understanding. The illustration given from visual art is, it should be observed, a deliberately rudimentary instance of what must be taken to have much more complex forms; so while the illustration concerns no more than familiarity with the particular subject of a portrait, the essential point touches the wider relationship between cognition and pleasure in the experience of mimetic art. If the various parts of the theory are properly to cohere, then in the case of poetry whose significance lies on the quasi-universal level for which Aristotle later argues, it is only the grasping of universals, not particulars, which can provide an adequate basis for the spectator's or reader's cognition of the work. In this way, the pleasure of tragedy can be seen as a species of the general pleasure which Aristotle supposes to be derived from apprehending the structure of meaning embodied and dramatised in the action of a poem.

The 'natural causes' of poetic mimesis are used in *Poetics* 4 as the

---

[8] He may do so, however, either from conscious artistry or from natural aptitude: 8.1451a24. The possibility of such an aptitude only confirms how the principles of art are ultimately grounded in nature.

starting-point for a diagrammatic sketch of the development of Greek poetry
from its origins. In this condensed passage, nature remains the key principle
throughout, and the work of individual poets is subsumed and evaluated
within a teleological framework of quasi-historical reconstruction. Here the
Poetics presents us with the first in a long tradition of quests to find patterns
of natural or organic growth in the data of cultural history.[9] For Aristotle,
the major lines of evolution in Greek poetry are provided by the discovery
and elaboration of genres, stemming in the first place from a basic and natural
dichotomy between serious and humorous poetry, or the poetry of ethically
elevated subjects (eventually epic and tragedy) and the poetry of ethically inferior men and actions (iambic satire and comedy). It is these principal
branches which interest the theorist in Aristotle, and the poets themselves are
considered chiefly as possessors of natural aptitudes for the refinement of the
particular forms taken by man's mimetic instinct. This claim remains valid
even for the epoch-making significance attributed to Homer in both the serious
and the comic spheres. Homer is not regarded, in this scheme, as an isolated,
self-sufficient genius, whose achievement was simply *sui generis*. His poems
have their true historical value for Aristotle only when placed in the context
of a continuing poetic evolution, for Homer was, above all, 'the first to show
the form' of both tragedy and comedy; and when these had been revealed,
further generic progress was able to occur, culminating in the eventual
superseding of epic by the later dramatic forms (4.1448b36–9a6).

It is not Aristotle's intention to limit Homer's greatness by placing him
in the perspective of literary teleology. But recognition of this greatness is
subordinated to the conviction that the finest poetry brings to fulfillment the
inherent, the natural, potential of its genre, and that the long-term history
of poetry is to be understood as a 'genealogy' of genres, rather than a record
of the contingent achievements of outstanding poets. Aristotle carries this
conviction to the point of allowing *a priori* conceptions of generic nature to
take precedence over the raw data of literary history, and it is principally for
this reason that literary historians have encountered so many problems in
trying to use his remarks for their own reconstructions.

The heavily theoretical character of what is outlined in *Poetics* 4 (and the
first part of chapter 5) can be briefly indicated for each of the two main
branches of poetic evolution, both of which are traced back to primitive
'improvisations'. For serious poetry the following stages and types are posited:
'hymns and encomia' – narrative epic – Homeric, 'dramatic' epic, prefigur-
ing tragedy – dithyramb – Attic tragedy (which itself unfolds through a
whole series of phases). There is a powerful organising impulse behind this
conception of an evolutionary cultural pattern, but Aristotle does not actually

---

[9] See J. J. Pollitt, *The Ancient View of Greek Art* (New Haven, 1974), pp. 73–84, with later
analogues in the work of Vasari, Winckelmann, and others.

attempt, and it is doubtful whether he was in a position, to integrate these various stages into a single, coherent historical series. His primary aim is to contend for the decisive progression from Homeric, 'tragic' epic, to Attic tragedy itself, but he leaves it perhaps necessarily uncertain what relation exists between this progression and the immediate emergence of tragedy from dithyrambic antecedents, as indicated, with what is surely revealing brevity, at 1449a10 – 11. One can be forgiven for bringing away from the chapter a sense of a double explanation for the birth of tragedy – a contingent juxtaposed with an essential explanation. And there can be no doubt which belongs at the heart of Aristotle's theory of poetry.

A similar observation will hold for the second branch of poetry's evolution, whose components are: early, hypothetical 'invectives'; iambic satire; comic epic (the *Margites*, attributed to Homer); phallic festivities; Sicilian comedy (Epicharmus); Attic comedy (which itself moves from an 'iambic' phase towards true comic drama). Here, in fact, the picture is even more complex than for serious poetry, and even less reducible to a congruous historical scheme; but again we can discern how Aristotle's theoretical position involves him in teleological judgements which operate on a different level from the discrete historical data. Homer is once more set up as the forerunner of a later genre, and the *Margites* represents progress from iambic invective, which concentrates on particular targets, towards comedy proper, which replaces scurrilous satire with the use of generalised characters and actions. But, as with tragedy, so Attic comedy has its specific antecedent in festive celebration, and there is the further, awkward factor of the putative influence of Sicilian comedy on Attic. Yet, despite the grave obscurities lurking here (and Aristotle is not interested in disguising them: 5.1449a38 – 9), we are not left in any doubt about the significant direction of change: it is a movement towards a genre that will best embody the universals which *Poetics* 9 identifies as poetry's proper material.

In Aristotle's entire outline of poetic growth from primitive improvisations to the final perfection of individual genres, reference to nature is entailed at various points: in the basic supposition of a mimetic instinct in man; in the pleasure associated with the experiences of understanding and learning; in the natural use of rhythm and music (which gives rise, for example, to metrical adaptation in the course of poetic history); in the grounding of poetic species in basic emotional responses (admiring or adverse) towards ethical distinctions which are, for the philosopher, aspects of reality; and in the tendency of human productive activities to develop towards the regularity and proficiency which are contained in the idea of artistry (*tekhnē*). The climax of these processes is the attainment by a genre such as tragedy of its true 'nature', its consummate fulfilment (1449a14 – 15). And it is this whole complex of principles which explains why Aristotle chooses to frame his treatise around the examination of epic, tragedy, and comedy: these are the genres he judges to have employed the poetic media most successfully so as to satisfy the human impulse to represent and dramatise the world in fictional forms, and thereby to provide at its finest the natural pleasure of mimesis.

The question of poetic pleasure now calls for a little further scrutiny before we can proceed to examine the details of Aristotle's treatment of each of his major genres. The proposition put forward in *Poetics* 4, that the pleasure derivable from mimesis rests on the enjoyment of learning and understanding, constitutes the foundation on which the specific and appropriate pleasures of individual genres can be defined. When we are later told that tragic pleasure arises 'from the experience of pity and fear through mimesis' (14.1453b12–13), the species confirms and illuminates the genus of poetic pleasure by not only adapting it to, but also enriching it with, the distinctive character of the particular genre. The case of tragic pleasure consequently shows how the bare formula of chapter 4 needs to be expanded so as to encompass an experience in which cognition and emotion are fused.

In apprehending a work of mimetic art, whether a poem or a visual image, the mind 'understands and reasons what each thing is' (4.1448b16–17), and Aristotle remarks (with obvious relevance to tragedy) that the pleasure involved applies even to the representation of painful objects. In the latter case, as is later confirmed by the definition of tragic pleasure, the paradox presupposes a sense of the mimetic work's artistic and fictional status, without which painful objects, such as human suffering, would arouse nothing but painful emotions. It is therefore legitimate to suggest that the Poetics presents us with the kernel of a theory of specifically 'aesthetic' pleasure; but the use of this term needs careful regulation in such a context.

In the *Politics* (8.1341a23–8), Aristotle states that our feelings towards mimetic works are closely aligned with those experienced towards the equivalent aspects of reality. It follows from this that the pity and fear elicited by tragedy are not wholly distinct from these emotions as felt in real life. To the extent that these emotions become associated with pleasure from tragic poetry – 'the experience of pity and fear *through mimesis*' – they belong, on Aristotle's premises, with the sense that poetry offers us dramatic images only of possible, not of actual, reality. By the same token, however, the *Poetics*, corroborated by the passage cited from the *Politics*, suggests that the major elements of this experience – the understanding of the mimetic content, and the emotional response induced by it – stem from the reader's or spectator's grasp of the kinds of reality (the 'universals') which the work presupposes. This is, then, no doctrine of an autonomously aesthetic pleasure; and it may be worth adding that Aristotle appears to have understood even the pleasures of rhythm and music to be essentially tied to their mimetic potential.[10]

---

[10] Halliwell, *Aristotle's Poetics*, p. 68, n. 29.

It is important to stress that the emotional element in the pleasurable experience of tragedy is not something which supervenes on the cognition of a poem's content, but an integral part of the total experience. Aristotle's psychology of the emotions is itself cognitivist: emotions are a natural and appropriate dimension of the mind's perception of, and response to, certain features of the world (and, correspondingly, to mimetic representations of those features). Within the theory of poetry, therefore, the emotions are not treated separately or independently from the analysis of poetic structure and content, for the theory as a whole assumes a direct alignment of its affective principles with the larger conception of the nature of each genre.

The *Poetics* has, however, often been thought to go beyond such an intrinsic notion of the emotional potential of poetry, and to offer, in *katharsis*, an independent psychological view of the effect of tragic drama on the mind of the spectator or reader. *Katharsis* merits consideration here, rather than in the specific discussion of tragedy, for two reasons: first, because it stands in close relation with poetic pleasure (in tragedy, *katharsis* is *of* the pity and fear *from* which, according to chapter 14, tragic pleasure arises); secondly, because there are good reasons to suppose that the doctrine of *katharsis* was meant to apply to poetry in general, not exclusively to tragedy. The evidence cited above for a polemical statement of *katharsis* in the dialogue *On Poets* points to the application of the concept to comedy as well as tragedy, while the *Poetics* itself treats epic as possessing the same emotive potential as tragedy, and so presumably as being equally capable of affording a kathartic experience.[11]

In order to serve as a justification of poetic emotion against Plato's severe stricture (that poetry 'nourishes and waters' feelings which ought to be 'dried up': *Rep.* 10.606d) we would expect *katharsis* not just to be relevant to all the major genres mentioned, but also to be an intrinsic function or aspect of the experience of poetry, rather than a factor active only in the case of people of a particular susceptibility, as has often been supposed. Only if *katharsis* has this wider applicability can we understand why it finds a place in the definition of tragedy's essence (though the lack of an explanation for the concept in the surviving book of the treatise may reflect a diminishing sense on Aristotle's part, in his later years, of the need to produce a specific riposte to Plato's puritanical psychology).

The problem of making sense of *katharsis*, therefore, ineluctably remains. Our best hope of doing so lies in the combination of four pieces of evidence: first, the general view of the pleasurable experience of mimesis which emerges from the *Poetics*; second, the Aristotelian tenet that to feel emotion in the right way and towards the right objects is integral to virtuous living; third, the reference to *katharsis* in *Politics* VIII, where the alleviation of a state of emotional

---

[11] *Katharsis* is mentioned in connection with comedy in the neo-Platonic texts cited in the second note to this chapter; cf. Janko, *Comedy*, pp. 143–4. Epic *katharsis* is surely entailed by the comparison with tragedy at *Po.* 24.1459b7–15.

disturbance is the immediate point;[12] and finally, the idea of an affective mean or balance found in the neo-Platonic references to *katharsis* already cited. Producing a coherent reconstruction of poetic *katharsis* from these slender clues is taxing, but a reasonable case can be made for an interpretation which moves away from the idea of sheer emotional release (which has been the prevailing view on the subject for the past century) in the direction of a notion of psychological refinement whose implications are in part ethical.

The passage from *Politics* VIII supplies us with a basic pattern of emotional 'dynamics' which contradicts Plato's belief that the experience of strong emotions will tend to produce a permanent heightening of emotional capacity. Our other sources of evidence supplement this with Aristotle's recognition of the legitimately cognitive and ethical dimensions of the emotions. In comprehending the implicitly universal terms of a mimetic structure of events in poetry, we are drawn into a strong affective response towards the moral features of the action portrayed, as the definitions of pity and fear in *Poetics* 13 make clear for tragedy. It is plausible to suppose that, for Aristotle, the emotional energies released in such a response are not simply drained or 'purged' away, but tend to improve our capacity to feel these emotions 'in the right way and towards the right objects'. This process of refinement, of *katharsis*, is, moreover, inextricably connected with the particular pleasure yielded by each genre. That pleasure rests, as we have seen, on the understanding involved in the contemplation of mimetic representations of reality. *Katharsis* may after all, therefore, be less extraneous to Aristotle's theory of poetic significance than has often been believed.

This necessarily curt suggestion of a line of approach to *katharsis* perhaps offers a way of seeing how the doctrine may originally have embodied not just a claim about the psychological consequences of the experience of poetry (though it certainly needs to do that, in order to counter Plato's charge) but also a more intimate part of Aristotle's view of how the mind responds to the fictional plot-structures of poetry. As such, *katharsis* provides a conclusion to the examination of the conceptual foundations of the *Poetics*, and supplies a further, if incomplete, illustration of the treatise's aim of defining a respectable place for poetry within the purview of the philosopher. Against this background, we can now turn to the assessment of Aristotle's treatment of tragedy, epic and comedy.

---

[12] *Politics* 8.1341b32–2a16. The reference to a further discussion in connection with poetry clinches the relevance to the *Po.*, but what the passage describes need not apply without qualification to poetic *katharsis*; see Lord, *Education*, pp. 119–38.

3 Aristotle on tragedy

Although (or, in fact, because) Attic tragedy arose historically later than, and was in some degree indebted to, Homeric epic, Aristotle's teleological theory gives poetic primacy to the younger genre (5.1449b16–20). Not only is tragedy discussed before epic, and at greater length, but when we reach the treatment of epic we find that it depends integrally on reference to the principles already laid down for tragedy. No earlier Greek critic is known to have perceived the relationship between the genres in quite this way, and it is an aspect of Aristotle's thinking about poetry which must have formulated itself gradually after his first arrival in Athens in 367 BC. The few fragments of *On Poets* do not suggest much direct concern with Attic tragedy, and it is likely that at this stage Homer and other early forms of poetry received more attention from Aristotle.[13] But for the two decades which he spent in Plato's Academy, Aristotle was in a position to experience and reflect on the dominant poetic phenomenon of the preceding two centuries in the Greek world, the growth and establishment of dramatic tragedy at Athens. The genre was by this date old enough to encourage attempts to survey and interpret its history, a fact which was eventually to lead to the research into theatrical records conducted by Aristotle in the latter part of his life.[14]

Tragedy had, however, also borne the brunt of Plato's philosophical attack on poetry, and it stood arraigned for deep immorality, for falsehood, and for the arousal of dangerous emotions in its audiences. In the dialogue *On Poets* Aristotle probably confronted at least some of these criticisms polemically; but it is significant that the *Poetics* prefers to argue an alternative case without engaging in direct rebuttal of Plato. It is consequently appropriate that the nature of Aristotle's response should be allowed to emerge gradually, rather than being stated in reductive formulae. It should be clear at once, nonetheless, from the elevation of Attic tragedy to superiority over Homeric epic, that Aristotle's mature views convinced him of the possibility of a complete justification of the major species of poetry within Plato's own Athenian culture.

Whether one approaches Aristotle's view of tragedy from the direction of Plato, or from that of modern theories of the genre, it is striking that a similarly negative observation is pertinent in either case. Whereas Plato's critique hinges on metaphysical assumptions about truth and goodness, and while the dominant modern (German) line in the theory of tragedy has tended to interpret the literary genre as the expression of a comprehensive *Weltbild*, the analysis of tragedy presented in the *Poetics* is, by contrast, wholly lacking in metaphysical aspirations, or even in any strongly existential implications for

---

[13] Apart from the discussion of *katharsis*, the only ref. to tragedy attested for the dialogue is fr. 74 (Euripides).

[14] Pfeiffer, *Scholarship*, pp. 81–2.

the understanding of 'the tragic'. To warn against the expectation of such
an ambitious or speculative level of ideas is not to exclude the possibility of
serious philosophical import from Aristotle's theory of tragedy, but we shall
find that any significance of this kind belongs to the sphere of ethics, not to
a metaphysical perspective.

One reason for this contrast with modern conceptions of tragedy is that
the *Poetics* considers the genre not entirely for its own sake, but also as the
finest embodiment of the standards and principles of the art of poetry as a
whole. This aim is reflected by the dependence of the later analysis of epic
upon that of tragedy, by the incorporation of important generalisations about
all poetry (concerning unity and universals, for example) into the chapters
on tragedy, and by the elaboration of principles for tragic drama many of
which could with equal force be applied even to comedy. If we consider the
weighting of elements within the very definition of tragedy at the start of
chapter 6, three of the five primary ideas exist on the level of general poetics:
the notion of an action (of a certain scale and unity) as the object of mimesis;
the inclusion of stylistic embellishments; and the stress on mimetic enactment,
rather than the use of the narrative mode. This last point emphasises the
ideally dramatic status of poetic fictions, while the concept of action incorporates a canon of unity whose applicability embraces not just poetry, but
all mimetic art in whatever media (8.1451a30–5). As for poetic style, the later
chapters on the subject (20–2) show that Aristotle does not suppose tragedy
to have any unique resources in this respect.

This leaves us, then, with two components in the definition: the idea of
an ethically *serious* action; and the formula 'pity and fear effecting *katharsis*'
for the emotional potential of the genre. Of these, the first is both a point
shared with epic, and also a defining characteristic of one of the two major
branches of the entire poetic tradition sketched in *Poetics* 4. It is only with
the final clause of the definition of tragedy, and its references to pity, fear,
and *katharsis*, that we reach features likely to be regarded by a modern reader
as distinctive of the genre (though these too are common to epic, as we shall
see). Yet Aristotle does not develop the implications of his premise concerning
the emotional effect of tragedy until chapter 10 and onwards, and he does so
only after first breaking the genre down into a scheme of six 'parts' or
elements, none of which directly specifies a peculiarly tragic attribute. This
adds confirmation that the *Poetics* aims to examine tragedy within a steady
framework of poetic analysis, rather than for any intensiveness or exclusiveness of existential interest. To follow the rationale of Aristotle's approach,
therefore, we must attend to the ground plan set out in chapter 6, before
considering how he advances from that to a conception of the characteristic
heart of tragic drama.

The significance of this ground plan lies not in the mere elaboration of a
group of critical categories or instruments, but in the evaluative force behind

the enterprise. Nowhere is the prescriptive motivation of the work plainer than in chapter 6, where Aristotle ranks the parts of tragedy in descending importance: plot-structure; characterisation; thought; style; lyric poetry; and spectacle. The priorities indicated by this arrangement are reinforced by the very slight attention later paid to the last two items, by the rather diffuse nature of the chapters on language, and by the assignment of 'thought' to the province of rhetoric (19.1456a34 – 5) – all of which leaves Aristotle free to concentrate on plot-structure and characterisation. The basis of this uncompromising strategy (whose implications, to reiterate, extend to other forms of poetry) is teleological: 'the plot-structure is the end [*telos*] of tragedy, and the end is what matters most of all' (6.1450a22 – 3).

Entailed in this principle is the relative dispensability of the remaining five elements. This is stated (though not as a recommendation) even for characterisation, immediately after the above quotation; and we can extrapolate to the diminishing value of the other 'parts', until we reach the wholly inessential factor of theatrical spectacle, which probably denotes chiefly the visual presentation of the agents, rather than the wider *mise-en-scène*. By the same criterion, if the use of any element is to be poetically effective and justified, Aristotle presupposes that it will be so in virtue of a contribution to, or enhancement of, 'what matters most of all', the plot-structure. Thus, even spectacle, as we gather from the early sentences of chapters 14 and 17, can be properly made to heighten the intrinsic properties of the dramatic action, rather than offering an independent, and consequently a distracting, pleasure.

The evaluative scheme of tragedy's parts represents, from one point of view, a powerful and cogent critical perspective. Combined with the standards of unity which Aristotle goes on to elaborate for plot-structure, and which we have already considered, it supplies a strong sense of central dramatic values, and so a sharp focus for the analysis and judgement of individual works. But this strength has also an inflexibility which brings limitations with it, as emerges perhaps most immediately from the *Poetics'* neglect of lyric poetry (*melopoiia*), or the choral element, in tragedy. This neglect is compounded by the difficulty of making sense of the injunction found at the end of chapter 18 that the chorus should be handled 'as one of the actors', so as to be a 'part of the whole' or an integral component in the structure of action. We can assent to Aristotle's negative strictures, in this same passage, on the dramatic irrelevance of 'interlude' choral entertainment, but there remains no clear and consistent way of understanding the positive function which he assigns to the chorus. The fundamental reason for this is precisely the treatise's intense but narrow concentration on dramatic action, which nowhere makes any allowance for the special lyric status – the shifting 'voice' and dramatic ambiguity – of the chorus of Greek tragedy. While the surviving plays include individual points of choral impingement on the dramatic events, which may appear to satisfy the precept offered in chapter 18, this ideal of active choral integration remains out of harmony with the lyric practices of all the major tragedians, for whom in various ways the handling of the chorus is irreducible to the progression of the action proper.

Aristotle's overriding concern with unity of dramatic action also helps to explain, though in a somewhat different way, the rather low value placed on poetic style (*lexis*, which applies only to the spoken, not the lyric, portions of a play). Here we encounter a further disparity between the *Poetics* and modern (as well as much ancient) criticism, for which questions of poetic language and style are often central. In view of the principle (6.1450b14–15) that style or verbal expression has the same force whether in prose or in verse (verse being, we recall, anyway inessential to poetry), it is not surprising that when Aristotle eventually develops his doctrine of style in chapter 22 ('clarity without meanness') its effect is towards the levelling down of important stylistic distinctions of register to be found in the plays themselves. This is partly because the whole of chapters 20–2 (which may be of an earlier date than the rest) seems designed to create a framework for discussing poetic style in general, rather than to probe the particular stylistic features of tragedy, from which only a minority of the examples are taken. Two leading ideas can be identified in this framework: first, that stylistic analysis may be conducted primarily on the lexical level (through the categories of standard term, dialectal term, metaphor, and so on); second, that stylistic differences, especially between genres, can be understood as divergences from a norm represented by standard spoken usage (and by those prose writings which reproduce it). Hence Aristotle's final, and apparently approving, verdict on the spoken verses of tragedy (and comedy), that they come as close as possible to the mimesis of ordinary speech (22.1459a12) – a conclusion which is impossible to reconcile with so much of the poetry of the fifth-century tragedians.

While there may be other factors involved in this seemingly reductive view of tragic style, the chief one is surely the nature of Aristotle's entire theory of poetry. 'The poet ought to be more a maker [*poiētēs*] of plot-structures than of verses' (9.1451b27–8). The poet's art and *raison d'être*, in other words, are not primarily located in a distinctive use or quality of language (and certainly not in the power of language to create a special tragic tone), but rather in the capacity to conceive and shape a pattern of action for mimetic representation. This is especially true of the tragedian, whose genre is capable of the highest degree of unity and integration. Thus the evaluation of poetic style, like the marginalised treatment of the chorus, points us back in the direction of the work's central emphasis on structure of action, which Aristotle envisages as enriched by the characterisation of the agents and, to a lesser degree, by the (rhetorical) presentation of their persuasive and emotive arguments ('thought'). If we ask bluntly why action and character are judged to be the most important components of tragedy, or, for that matter, of poetry in general, the answer lies in the concept of mimesis. All poetry, for the philosopher, is a mimesis of action (2.1448a1), and tragedy is a mimesis of 'serious' action – of action which involves true ethical gravity. In the serious matters of life, action and its ethical motivation, character, are the factors of most significance: they must consequently be so, according to the *Poetics'* premises, in the dramatisation of such matters too.

This principle, when combined with the quasi-universal significance which chapter 9 attributes to poetry, warrants us inferring that Aristotle recognises in tragedy the power to afford an understanding of certain types of human experience, and thereby repudiates the Platonic charge against the tragedians of presenting a false picture of reality. To clarify this hypothesis requires us now to move closer to the centre of Aristotle's theory of tragedy, approaching first the relation between action and character. Twice in the treatise, in chapters 6 and 15, character (*ēthos* or *ēthē*) is delimited as the sphere of 'ethical choices' and 'dispositions'. The concept is therefore not to be assimilated to more indefinite, and more psychological, notions of individuality or subjectivity. Once Aristotle's conception of characterisation is properly taken, it becomes easier to grasp why he subordinates it as a dramatic element to action. Action, constituting the poetic structure of events, is primary because without it the imperative requirement of a mimesis of unitary action will remain unfulfilled; while the demonstration of the moral intentions of the agents, though important, will only make full sense, and therefore justify itself poetically, if it can be seen as an enhancement of the plot-structure. Aristotle's poetic theory reflects here his wider ethical philosophy, within which character is intelligible only in terms of clear dispositions to act in certain ways.

Though bearing the philosopher's own stamp, the *Poetics'* restrained notion of character is nonetheless arguably closer to the general practice of the tragedians (and of Homer, to whom it equally applies) than we can expect the nuances of psychological criticism to bring us. This is not to deny the existence of psychological subtleties in Greek tragedy, but rather to suggest that they do not furnish a consistent means of dramatising character which could be set as an alternative to the Aristotelian model. Tragedy, like epic, takes its material from a corpus and tradition of myth in which clear-cut ethical distinctions between agents are a fundamental and pervasive assumption, and in which such distinctions are normally determined or marked by action and objective achievement. If, in the world of poetry, character does not depend quite exclusively on active excellence, it does at any rate centre firmly on qualities which can be socially recognised and sanctioned, not on peculiarities of individual behaviour (still less of consciousness). Aristotle's view of poetic characterisation closely matches a play such as Euripides' *Iphigenia in Tauris*, in which it is the dimension of ethical choice and purpose which affords us the only criterion to categorise the status of the individual agents. Character here exists as little more than a 'colouring' of the major figures' moral merits and innocence, and a broad suggestion of the opposing forces of good and evil to sharpen the delineation of the central action. This is, in type if not necessarily in degree, representative of much Greek tragedy.

But if Aristotle's theory operates on the same level – the ethical rather than the psychological – as the predominant mode of characterisation in the genre, a question must still be raised about the deeper relation between the critical model and the playwrights' practice. This question can be formulated around two connected issues: first, the heroic standing of the major figures of tragedy; second, tragedy's scope to dramatise the disparity between (ethical) character and the experience of affliction. Superficially, Aristotle seems to allow for heroic characters in tragedy and epic by his references to men 'better than ourselves' (chapters 2 and 15), and by the stipulation of goodness as the primary requirement of character in chapter 15. This would appear to commit him, in the face of Platonic disapproval, to a view of tragedy's subject-matter as the sufferings of the good. Yet in *Poetics* 13 the person of outstanding virtue is specifically rejected, though not without some equivocation (1453a16–17), as unsuitable for the ideal tragic plot. It is in fact this chapter which proves that Aristotle is prepared to apply to tragedy his wider philosophical separation of intrinsic ethical factors (character proper) from extrinsic matters of social or material standing (the 'great esteem and prosperity' of the tragic figures). We should consequently be prepared to see in the idea of men 'better than ourselves' a compound reference to both types of attribute. In describing the general features of the genre, that is to say, Aristotle's formula loosely embraces the possibility of heroic values; but in elaborating his own precise ideal in chapter 13 he finds it essential to limit what he regards as the strictly ethical qualities of tragic figures, in distinction to non-ethical attributes of status or stature.

If this is right, then it casts a little further illumination on the theory of character and action in poetry. Aristotle's model of tragedy is built around a drastic change of fortune between the poles of prosperity (*eutuchia*) and affliction (*dustuchia*). Such a change is a matter of external states, not character. This confirms the idea, found in chapter 6, that tragedy can, at an extreme, dispense with characterisation altogether. It remains evident, though, that characterisation does have a contribution to make to a plot-structure in which a discrepancy exists between the agent's ethical deserts and the vulnerability of his non-moral existence, which is subject to external forces. Implicit in this disjunction, then, there is indeed an acceptance of what had so deeply disturbed Plato about tragedy's images of the world. But at the same time, by placing constraints on the type of character required for his ideal tragedy, Aristotle seems to restrict the genre's scope in this respect. These constraints must now be more closely examined, for they lie at the heart of the *Poetics'* understanding of tragedy.

The exclusion from the ideal tragedy of the sufferings of the ethically pre-eminent person is formulated twice in chapter 13: the first formulation (1452b34 – 6) indicates that our response to such a case would be one of revulsion, not pity or fear; the second (1453a8) that what Aristotle has in mind is a figure of *outstanding* virtue. It is sometimes suggested that this line of argument rests on strictly aesthetic considerations, but the context shows that the tragic emotions – defined here in terms of our sense of undeserved suffering on the part of a figure with whom we can sympathise – themselves imply an ethical aspect to the tragic action. Nor is it adequate to suppose that what Aristotle rejects is a degree of innocent tragic misfortune which would not in any case appeal to a tragedian. Although it is difficult to be sure what would qualify in the philosopher's mind as a dramatic pattern of the kind precluded, it is at any rate arguable that both Homer and the Attic playwrights supply instances that come close to it; and it is certain that Plato, for one, thought that in their own terms they did so.[15] Moreover, while Plato ultimately did not accept the true possibility of tragic suffering and unhappiness, Aristotle's outlook allowed him to recognise a potential disparity between ethical merits and states of fortune. We can therefore say with confidence that from his own point of view Aristotle is rejecting in *Poetics* 13 some types of possible reality as outside the sphere of tragic poetry and drama.

Why should this be so? Within the Aristotelian view of the world, extreme affliction of a kind which can obliterate any possibility of happiness (or complete human fulfilment) may on occasion befall even the most virtuous of men. But this same world-view can supply no explanation for such suffering beyond the brute fact of uncontrollable fortune or chance. Now chance falls into the category of the 'irrational' or unintelligible, and this is something which the *Poetics* repeatedly and emphatically holds to be inconsistent with the primary requirement of a unified plot-structure. Tragedy, the supreme genre of serious poetry, exemplifies to the highest degree the canons of artistic unity and coherence; as such it must, on Aristotle's premises, dramatise actions and events which constitute an organised whole, and this means that its material has to conform to the connective principles of probability or necessity, so that each stage in the action carries forward a dramatic 'logic' which the mind of a reader or spectator can fully grasp. Unity and dramatic intelligibility are mutually explicable within this theory, and between them they equally rule out the play of the irrational or incomprehensible. It is implicitly on this basis that chapter 13 finds the affliction of the exceptionally virtuous figure unsuitable for tragedy: such events, while certainly representing a possible extreme on the scale of undeserved misfortune, fall quite outside the scope of the intelligible; and it is because of this that they could, Aristotle believes, move us only to a sense of moral shock or revulsion (*miaron*: 1452b36).

---

[15] See esp. Plato, *Rep.* 3.387d – 8b, 10.603e, where tragedy is condemned for showing the afflictions of supposedly noble figures. On the problems, see Nussbaum, *Fragility*, pp. 387 – 8.

But to put the point this way is to be brought to see that the philosopher's whole stance towards the substance of tragedy poses a question about the nature and limits of what is humanly intelligible. For within the world of tragedy as we know it from the plays, there is in fact a source of significance – the religious – that can encompass events for which Aristotle's critical theory leaves no room. At this juncture one cannot shirk the observation that the *Poetics* in general largely ignores the place of religious ideas and beliefs in the fabric of poetry, tragic as well as other kinds, despite an evident willingness on Aristotle's part to dissent from Plato by countenancing popular religious presuppositions within poetic fictions.[16] What is at issue, however, in the case of tragic plot-patterns is not the incidental inclusion of religious notions, but the bearing of religious thought on the fundamental meaning of dramatic action. Since it is a pervasive assumption of the outlook incorporated in the myths of Greek tragedy that the dynamics of human action are not self-sufficient, but need to be set against an obscure though potent background of divine influence, it is hardly conceivable that Aristotle could have left a positive attitude to tragic religion simply to be inferred from his theory, given his pervasive stress on lucidity and coherence of dramatic action. The treatise's minimal concern for religion should, in other words, be taken at face-value as a virtual rejection of any central role for modes of religious understanding or explanation within the scheme of a poetic plot-structure.

But if the religious mentality is excluded from the critic's attitude towards tragic myth, with what is it to be replaced? While aberrant in other respects, the traditional intuition that *hamartia* forms the crux of the Aristotelian view of tragedy evidently retains a strong plausibility. *Hamartia* and its cognates are terms of demonstrably wide application both in the philosopher's own works and in general Greek usage: ideas of error, wrong-doing, moral failing, mistake, misjudgement, and fallibility are all possible meanings in particular contexts. In *Poetics* 13 one may be struck by the fact that *hamartia* belongs to a cautious and largely negative argument, in which more is ruled out than is positively approved. Rather than pressing for a specificity of reading which Aristotle's words do not readily yield, it is more instructive to observe that *hamartia* here functions indeterminately as a term for the type of causal factor which remains available for tragedy after the elimination of various basic possibilities of plot-structure.

In the larger framework of the argument, the two most important exclusions are, firstly, 'irrational' elements (including divine influence) which are incompatible with a coherent pattern of dramatic causation, and, secondly, any positive guilt on the part of the major agents, for this would remove the

---

[16] Aristotle has popular religion in mind at 25.1460b35–1a1, but the liberal premise expressed there, as a means of defending poets, has not found a positive place in his own general attitude to poetry. When he objects (*Po.* 15.1454b2) to Athena's intervention in *Il.* II, one could quote his own later 'solution' against him.

conditions of pity and fear. If we look to *Poetics* 14 for further elucidation of Aristotle's ideal, we find there a prevailing emphasis on cases of tragic ignorance, and this is consonant both with the line of argument in the preceding chapter, and with the larger theory of the complex tragedy (in which both recognition and reversal presuppose a factor of ignorance). Without identifying *hamartia* directly with ignorance, we can infer that Aristotle's tragic ideal requires some causal involvement of the agents in the events which bring about their change of fortune, but without thereby importing any strong moral culpability.

Hamartia posits, then, a disparity between moral intention (and therefore character) and the consequences of action; but it equally presupposes an element of dramatic equipoise between the agents' implication in, and their ultimate innocence of, the tragic events. A plot-structure which conforms to this ideal will be, in the technical sense, 'complex', and so will entail some form of active ignorance that is exposed at the point of recognition or discovery. But it is difficult to go beyond this essentially negative setting for the doctrine of *hamartia* to reach a positive insight into the underlying implications for tragic patterns of action. The model of the complex tragedy can certainly stand as a perceptive statement of certain formal features of some of the finest tragic myths, and in particular of the way in which their effect is constructed around nodal moments of discovery and paradoxical trans-formation. But this formal correlation between theory and practice cannot mask doubts about the relation between the crucial role of *hamartia* in Aristotle's model and the fundamentally religious significance of the typical material of Greek tragedy.

The indeterminacy of *hamartia* lies in the fact that while strongly precluding personal guilt as a cause of tragic events, and replacing it with a notion of human fallibility, it leaves the roots of this fallibility unspecified. If the *Oedipus Tyrannus* is to be thought a clear illustration of Aristotle's ideal, the reading of the play involved in such a view is one which cannot probe beyond the mere fact of Oedipus's ignorance and consequently deluded actions, nor beyond the superficial 'probability' of the dramatic sequence of the play. When, to take just one critical instance, the messenger who will be the occasion of Oedipus's reversal arrives from Corinth, after Jocasta's prayer to Apollo for a solution to the King's troubles, it makes indeed a world of difference whether we can acknowledge a motive force that lies outside the immediate sphere of the human agencies involved. What is at stake here will arise again and again in any attempt to interpret tragic action (in the Greek genre) solely on the level of the humanly plausible. And *hamartia*, which locates the cause of tragedy purely in relation to human responsibility, is emblematic of just such an attempt.

This argument can be reinforced by reference to *Poetics* 14, which has received much less attention than chapter 13. In chapter 14 Aristotle concentrates on two factors in the plot-structure: firstly, the relation between the major figures, which he takes to be ideally one of kinship or some similarly close bond; secondly, the place of *pathos* or 'suffering', which he earlier defined as an action involving pain or destruction (11.1452b11 – 12). *Pathos*, in the damage which it causes to the fabric of the characters' lives, gives a strong focus to tragic transformation; and its role in Aristotle's theory legitimately reflects the preoccupation of the heroic-poetic tradition with death and the extremes of distress. Likewise, the vital importance to tragedy of kinship and other bonds is readily borne out by the surviving plays, and Aristotle is here essentially codifying the finest concerns of the playwrights. But what remains remarkable about *Poetics* 14 is its final recommendation of a type of play in which *pathos* is closely approached but averted: the perfect tragedy, on this premise, depends on the imminent prospect of tragic 'suffering', not on its actuality.

Poetics 14 has often troubled readers of the treatise, both because it seems to offer a recipe for melodrama, and also since it ostensibly contradicts the premise of chapter 13 that a tragedy should end in misfortune. But both these judgements require some qualification. If a play such as *Iphigeneia in Tauris*, which conforms to chapter 14's prescriptions, is to be regarded as melodrama (which may be debated), it does not follow that Aristotle's argument necessarily points in that direction. The central insight – that tragedy's essence does not require an ultimate act of pain or destruction – is one that might be fruitfully developed in various ways.[17] Nor does the conclusion of which it forms a part radically contradict Poetics 13: all that really separates the train of thought in the two passages is the difference between prospective and actual pathos; but the underlying shape of action is consistent in both cases.

It is for this reason that the limitation which chapter 14 does in fact impose on tragedy can be discerned, on closer inspection, to reproduce the rationalising impulse already identified in chapter 13. The central factor of ignorance in chapter 14's ideal plot-structure must be equated in such a case (though not necessarily in general) with *hamartia*, and this confirms that what the two chapters have in common is an insistence on interpreting tragic causation purely on the level of human fallibility. While chapter 13 gives a final preference to the *Oedipus Tyrannus*, and chapter 14 to *Iphigeneia in Tauris*, it remains clear that Aristotle believes both types of play to conform to the major requirements of his 'complex' model; and we are equally entitled in both cases to question the sufficiency of his critical premises for an interpretation of the works' full tragic significance.

Aristotle has attempted to come to terms with tragic poetry without

---

[17] Even where sufferings form part of a tragic myth, Aristotle does not consider it important that they should occur within the play; cf. *Nicomachean Ethics*, 1.11.1101a31 – 3.

surrendering the philosophical ground on which all his thinking is based. The perhaps inevitable consequence of this is an unconsciously concealed divergence between the poetry and the theory at the deepest level of thought and belief. This final assessment leads us back to the Platonic antipathy to tragedy. This antipathy was uncompromising precisely because of Plato's realisation of the gulf between his own idealist metaphysics and a tragic vision which allowed, among much else, for insoluble problems of evil and suffering. In accordance with his larger view of poetry, Aristotle's *rapprochement* with tragedy was made possible in part by a much weaker sense of poetry's affirmative power than Plato had attributed to it: tragedy simply does not loom large enough to seem a rival to philosophy – the role in which Plato had perceived it. Aristotle allows the genre the power to stir deep emotions of pity and fear by displaying human fallibility and instability in the setting of actions whose momentum is one of ethical seriousness. But in doing so, he deprives it of the scope to move to the edge of, and even outside, the realm of rational understanding, or to dramatise events whose meaning cannot be encompassed by the logic of probability or necessity.

4 Aristotle on epic

This conclusion, together with a number of earlier points, needs to be carried over into consideration of Aristotle's treatment of the genre which he regards as tragedy's prototype, Homeric epic. The preliminary statement of epic's theoretical subordination to tragedy (5.1449b16–20) is later borne out by the much briefer scale of the analysis which it receives and by its clear dependence on the principles already enunciated for tragedy. In its consummate Homeric form, epic is viewed as aspiring to, and virtually achieving, dramatic status, and its primary element is therefore the same as tragedy's: plot-structure, the unified representation of a pattern of action. Epic's poetic nature is open to the same categorisation into 'parts' as was applied to tragedy, save only for epic's lack of lyric poetry and theatrical spectacle, which are in any case the components of tragedy rated as least important by Aristotle. Moreover, the *Iliad* and *Odyssey* not only belong with tragedy in the 'serious' branch of the poetic tradition, but they can be placed within a scheme of specifically tragic plot-types (24.1459b7–15). Once we allow for adjustments regarding metrical form and the use of narrative (which Homer minimises), we can see that a definition of epic is not provided because it can so readily be extrapolated from that of tragedy.

This assimilation of epic to tragedy is more than a means of critical economy. It is above all an expression of Aristotle's teleological conception of poetic history, according to which epic was superseded, not just followed, by tragedy, in a process whereby the newer genre made possible the finer realisation of poetic ends which the earlier had revealed. The strongly

Aristotelian cast of this view helps to explain why it was never absorbed by the subsequent tradition of criticism in antiquity, nor even in the later movement of neo-classicism: in both periods, orthodoxy placed epic at the pinnacle of the poetic hierarchy, essentially by reference to rhetorical criteria of stylistic, and sometimes ethical, elevation.

The philosopher's final verdict on tragedy's superiority to epic rests on two main tenets: that tragedy possesses greater unity and concentration than epic; and that it better achieves the particular pleasure (itself incorporating an emotional and cognitive experience) appropriate to serious poetry. It is probably legitimate to regard the second of these points as dependent on the first, for it is the combined issues of poetic scale and unity which point us to the nub of Aristotle's determination to judge epic within the same evaluative framework as tragedy. The topic is addressed twice, in chapters 24 and 26. In the first passage, epic's length is treated positively (if curiously) as an attribute arising out of its narrative possibilities, and as one which allows special scope for both grandeur and variation. When we reach chapter 26, however, epic length is seen as standing in the way of the achievement of complete poetic unity, even though the two Homeric poems are once more singled out for commendation.

But Aristotle's admiration for Homer should not be permitted to obscure the fact that it is precisely the *Iliad* and *Odyssey* which, because of their exceptional scale, are ultimately deemed inferior to dramatic tragedy at its best. About the shorter epics of the Cycle, Aristotle could afford to be curt: twice in the *Poetics* these lesser works are disparaged for a clear failure to realise the true nature of poetic unity, which does not reside in concentration on a single hero or period of time. It is certainly an astute observation on Aristotle's part to discern the force of Homer's choice of potentially unitary actions from the great blocks of available mythical material. Yet it was also the exceptional scale of his two epics which posed the question of epic unity for Aristotle's theory in such an acute form.

There are no doubt considerations which can be adduced in explanation and mitigation of Aristotle's attitude to epic scale, including the simple factor that the *Iliad* and *Odyssey* went well beyond the practical limits of recitation in a single performance. But this hardly seems to have troubled Greek audiences or readers in general, and it certainly will not account in full for the convictions of a theorist who is prepared to separate even dramatic works from the requirements of performance. In both its strengths and its shortcomings, Aristotle's position is, as always, essentially the product of his own presuppositions about poetry, and this means that epic length is in the end assessed by reference to the canons of sequential unity laid down in the course of the analysis of tragedy. In chapters 23 and 24 these canons are brought to bear tactfully on epic, and Homer's combination of a unified plot-structure with deliberate means of variation through episodes is acknowledged as a consummate achievement which exploits to the limits the possibilities of the genre. It is only in the final adjudication between epic and tragedy, in chapter 26, that the shorter scope of tragedy is deemed a matter of superior coherence and concentration, with the necessary corollary that the subordinate and digressive episodes of the *Iliad* and *Odyssey* must now be held to detract from the poems' otherwise admirable singleness of structure.

The prescriptive drive behind Aristotle's theory here leads him not just to an arguably redundant judgement of one genre's superiority over another, but also to a narrowness of critical vision. Despite the earlier acknowledgement of the distinctive capability of epic's scale, chapter 26 presses the concept of unity of action to an unimaginative and ungenerous extreme, on the assumption that the cohesion which arises from singleness of action can in the last analysis override all other poetic strengths. We are faced at this juncture, it would appear, with an unavoidable facet of Aristotle's critical position and sensibility, namely a virtual obsession with the integrated structure of the action dramatised in a poem. One might suggest that the principles applied in chapter 26 would best be satisfied by an *Iliad* which wholly isolated an action from the saga of the Trojan War, whereas Homer's provides such an action set in significant relief against the vista of the war as a whole.

Aristotle's understanding of form and unity is based on a concern with intelligibility. This same concern is also relevant to what is perhaps the chief qualitative distinction drawn in the *Poetics* between epic and tragedy. The latter part of chapter 24 is given over to an attempt to define the place in epic of 'the marvellous', and its source 'the irrational'. We learn in chapter 9 that 'the marvellous' encompasses a psychological and emotional effect which goes beyond the immediate causal logic of the action. In the case of tragedy, it is closely conjoined with pity and fear, and it appears to hinge on dramatic events which happen 'unexpectedly yet on account of one another' (9.1452a4): that is, on patterns of action whose underlying causation is not immediately perspicuous, but emerges only after the first powerful response to the events. The sense of wonder which arises in such cases does not, therefore, exclude the possibility of intelligible unity of action, though it may seem to pose a challenge to it. Hence the association stated in chapter 24 between the marvellous and the irrational, the latter entailing a direct clash with 'probability or necessity' and so representing actions which cannot be reconciled with a final coherence of plot-structure. But the dividing line between acceptable and unacceptable cases of the marvellous remains ambiguous, as can be seen from Aristotle's equivocation in this section of argument: having suggested that epic offers greater scope than tragedy for the irrational (on the curiously pragmatic and surely irrelevant grounds that we do not see the agents), Aristotle goes on to caution that irrational points should as far as possible be kept 'outside the plot-structure' (1460a29).

This equivocation alerts us to a deeper tension surrounding the *Poetics'* criterion of probability. In some passages of the work, Aristotle appears to allow a generous freedom to the poet's choice and handling of material, as in the sentiment that 'impossible but plausible events should be preferred to possible but implausible ones' (24.1460a26 – 7, cf. 25.1461b11 – 12). Again, at times the canon of probability or plausibility seems to encompass the breadth of 'what people say and think', even where this may clash with what philosophers or others hold to be the truth; and in chapter 25 Aristotle specifically uses popular religious ideas as an illustration of this point.[18] Yet against all this must be set both the general fact that traditional religious convictions, of the kind present in both epic and tragic poetry, posit divine powers whose operations characteristically do not conform to consistent expectations, and also the explicit recognition of this fact by Aristotle in *Poetics* 15, where divine interventions in human action are clearly equated with 'the irrational' (1454a37 – b8). If the notion of probability inevitably involves presuppositions, or standards of belief, then Aristotle's basic requirement of probability in poetry (or, even more strongly, of necessity) poses the question: *whose* sense of probability, of the believable, counts?

Seen in this context, the uncertainty discernible in chapter 24 over the scope of the marvellous in epic can be better understood. Aristotle is well aware of epic's successful use of material which cannot be reconciled with anything like his own naturalistic view of reality, and he is prepared to admire the way in which Homer can carry off what in other poets might be simply absurd (1460a34 – b2). But the fact remains that the *Poetics* as a whole presses the related principles of unity and intelligibility to an extreme which makes them inimical to the full imaginative freedom of poetry, at least to the extent that such freedom may carry the level of poetic significance beyond the range of the rational probability which Aristotle himself would be predisposed to accept. In the case of tragedy, the rationalising thrust of the theory brings it into implicit conflict with the religious assumptions of the genre's mythical material. While this point applies equally to epic, the latter also raises a wider problem for Aristotle in what he regards as its extra scope for 'the marvellous'; here too the underlying tension can be traced to the philosopher's unwillingness to compromise to any serious degree his commitment to the clarity and intelligibility of poetry's dramatic logic.

The greater diffuseness of epic, and its employment of a less tightly knit structure of action, draw Aristotle to the conclusion in chapter 26 that epic affords a less concentrated and effective pleasure than tragedy. Following, but carrying further, Plato's view of Homer as 'the first of the tragedians',

---

[18] 25.1460b35 – 1a1; even irrationalities can be defended by ref. to 'what people say': 25.1461b14. Yet Aristotle's strongest view is that the irrational should be kept out of the plot: 15.1454b6 – 8, 24.1460a28 – 30. Where popular religious ideas are concerned, it is difficult to see how Aristotle's sense of probability could ever be entirely reconciled with 'what people say and think'.

Aristotle identifies the psychological experience of the *Iliad* and *Odyssey* with that of tragedy, as is intimated particularly by the alignment of epic and tragic plot-types (24.1459b7–15). This passage looks back to the special emotional power earlier attributed to the crucial and climactic components of the complex plot-structure, reversal and recognition (especially at 6.1450a33–5). While equivalent junctures of supreme poetic and dramatic importance can certainly be located in the Homeric poems, it is questionable whether the much larger framework in which they are set is comparable with the more compact plot-structure of tragedy. Yet once this difference is conceded, there seems to be no convincing basis for Aristotle's judgement that the more concentrated poetic form offers greater or purer pleasure. The judgement assumes, as does the whole account of the genre given in the *Poetics*, that epic effectively aspires to the condition of tragic drama, and it leaves out of account the particular strengths which are inseparable from the monolithic construction of the Homeric poems. But to make this negative point is to be reminded that Aristotle simply does not aim at a comprehensive treatment of Homeric epic: his self-defined task is to place the genre theoretically in the teleological perspective of serious poetry whose central focus is Attic tragedy.

5 Aristotle on comedy

In turning finally to Aristotle's view of comedy, we face the massive impediment of the loss of the work's second book, but we can assume with some confidence that for this genre too there will have been much reference back to basic poetic principles established in the treatment of tragedy and in the preliminary chapters of the treatise. This likelihood, together with a handful of points made about comedy in the surviving pages, enables us to glimpse at least a few features of Aristotle's conception of the subject. Some would argue that these hints can be supplemented from the *précis* of a theory of comedy found in the Byzantine document now known as the *Tractatus Coislinianus*: we shall return shortly to this claim. From the sparse evidence of the extant book, two directions of inquiry can be suggested, neither of which can be pursued very far on firm ground: the first is the polarity between serious poetry's concern with men 'better than us' and comedy's dealings with base or inferior characters and their actions; the second is the equally sharply drawn distinction which Aristotle makes between 'iambic' humour (aimed at individuals) and the truly comic, which he takes to employ material of generalised or universal significance.

Comedy's agents are characterised as 'base' or 'worse than us' more than once in the *Poetics*, in pointed contradistinction to those of epic and tragedy. In the case of tragedy at least, Aristotle wavers between a broad formula for the elevation of the genre's characters, and the desire, shown in chapter 13, to separate ethical from other, extrinsic attributes of the agents. Would some analogous qualification have played a part in his theory of comedy? At the start of chapter 5, the inferior nature of comic characters is restricted so as to exclude the sphere of 'complete evil', and the distortion of the comic mask is instanced as the kind of ugliness or shamefulness (the Greek term, *aischron*, covers both) which furnishes suitable comic 'failings' (*hamartēmata*). The language of this passage warrants the inference that Aristotle has in mind a wide range of comic possibilities, encompassing physical, social and material, as well as specifically ethical, 'failings', provided only that 'pain and destruction' (the domain of tragedy) are avoided. He would thus withhold from comedy those vices and faults whose gravity is incompatible with laughter, but beyond this we are given no positive intimation, either here or elsewhere, that comedy needs to differentiate carefully between failings for which their possessors are morally responsible and those for which they are not.

Lacking anything like an Aristotelian paradigm of comic plot-structure, we cannot be finally certain on this point; but it remains likely that Aristotle was at least as interested in delimiting a characteristic comic tone or ethos – a general counterpart to serious poetry's concern with exceptional or elevated figures – as in specifying a particular role for *hamartēmata* in the action of comic drama. *Poetics* 5 links the spirit of comedy with the basic Greek concept of shame, which revolves around public or social attitudes of disapproval. The factor of shame might help to explain why Aristotle's category of comic 'faults' extends beyond the strictly ethical. Even a non-ethical feature such as ugliness could become legitimately comic once brought into a public context, particularly if combined with, say, an element of self-ignorance. It would certainly be misguided to suppose that Aristotle accepted the free licence of comic laughter to turn itself against *any* human deficiency, and we shall shortly meet some evidence of an ethical dimension to his view of comedy. But it remains implausible that the category of *hamartēmata* in chapter 5 is designed to narrow down the scope of the genre.

Since the surviving book of the *Poetics* refers to comedy largely for the purpose of indicating the grand dichotomy of the poetic tradition, it is not surprising that the formulation of comedy's characters as 'inferior' is broad and unrevealing. But in sketching the development of comedy, in chapters 4 and 5, Aristotle introduces a further distinction, between the iambic and the properly laughable or ridiculous (*geloion*). The iambic mode represents, according to chapter 4, the earliest attempts of poetic mimesis to deal with defective aspects of human life and behaviour. Such attempts naturally fastened onto particular individuals, just as serious poetry celebrated the deeds of named heroes and gods. There is an *a priori* element in this scheme of Aristotle's, though it is also in part derived by extrapolation from early iambic poetry such as Archilochus's, and from the type of personal satire associated with phallic rites which Aristotle assumed (as *Poetics* 4.1449a11 – 13 intimates) to retain primitive customs.

Both in its foundations and in the lines of growth which it goes on to posit, the pattern discerned in the history of comedy is problematic in ways already noted. Its guiding principle is not documentary but teleological: underlying the multifarious data of poets, genres, and changes of convention, Aristotle detects a movement away from the personal emphasis of early satire or invective (which, however, preserves some vestiges in later poetry) towards a generalised and more refined style of comedy which presents us with universal embodiments of the faults and deficiencies that can arouse laughter. It is clear from his ethical writings that Aristotle shared with Plato and others a certain mistrust of the power of laughter and ridicule, sensing that it could be abused by use against undeserving targets, or simply by excessive indulgence.[19] The putative evolution of comedy is therefore approved as involving a civilising process in the ethics and sensibility of humour, and Aristotle's history of poetry produces a notable symmetry by attributing a key role in this process to Homer, matching his discovery of the true nature of tragedy in his serious epics.

The comic epic to which Aristotle assigns such significance, *Margites*, was probably not the work of Homer at all, and our interpretation of the philosopher's view of it is obscured even further by its meagrely fragmentary survival. But three points about the poem seem to have been paramount for Aristotle: the fact that its central figure was blatantly fictional, a kind of exaggerated 'anti-hero'; the likelihood that it had a consequential plot-structure (though we cannot reconstruct this); and, finally, the foolishness and self-ignorance of Margites himself. Self-ignorance had been singled out by Plato as a suitable target for comic ridicule, and Margites apparently suffered from it to an immoderate and absurd degree. A glimmering of some gently ethical implications in the humour of *Margites* can perhaps be glimpsed, but it would be equally reasonable to infer a liking on Aristotle's part for a comic ethos detached from anything potentially disquieting – far indeed from 'pain and destruction', in the terms of *Poetics* 5. Consistent with this is the reference to comedy at the end of chapter 13, where a final reconciliation of even the gravest enemies, such as Orestes and Aegisthus, is used to illustrate an apt *dénouement* for comedy ('and no-one is killed by anyone', 1453a38–9). But a burlesque on the antagonism between Aegisthus and Orestes, if that is what Aristotle has in mind, might at least be expected to skirt close to possibly serious matters, and it would certainly be rash to suppose that the philosopher could have advocated a wholly frivolous or innocent theory of comedy.

Comic triviality would conflict with the point which emerges clearly in *Poetics* 9, that comedy at its best should conform to just the same standards of universality and unity of plot-structure that Aristotle expects of serious

---

[19] *Nicomachean Ethics* 2.7.11–13, 4.8; *Eudemian Ethics* 3.7.7–9; *Politics* 7.15.

poetry. This passage makes it hard to doubt that plot-structure would be considered the 'soul' of comedy in precisely the same way as it is of tragedy. But it is just at this point that our paucity of evidence halts us, since we can do nothing to translate such a hypothetical tenet into concrete observations on particular types of Greek comedy: nothing, at any rate, beyond a basic acknowledgement that Aristotle's ideal would lie closer to fourth-century developments in the genre (developments on the way to Menander) than to the scurrilously satirical and fantastic plays of Aristophanes and his time. Nor can we make any real progress with the affective or psychological aspect of comedy, since the concept of comic *katharsis*, which was probably originally elaborated by Aristotle alongside that of tragedy, is now a matter for the sheerest conjecture.

These negative remarks would call for some qualification if it were to be accepted that the *Tractatus Coislinianus* preserves remnants of the lost book of the *Poetics*.[20] It is arguable, however, that this curious document raises more interpretative problems than it solves, and traditional scholarly scepticism about its credentials remains well justified. The *Tractatus* offers two main sets of ideas or suggestions: first, a definition of comedy, and a statement of its 'parts', which are closely modelled on the analysis of tragedy known from the *Poetics*; secondly, a catalogue of types and sources of humour under the two broad headings of 'language' and 'things'. The definition and related analysis emphasise comedy's dramatic structure in a way which makes it a counterpart to Aristotle's theory of tragedy, while the scheme of comic sources concentrates on discrete means of arousing laughter by verbal and practical techniques, including forms of discontinuity, anomaly, and incoherence. The *Tractatus* does nothing to explicate how such comic means are to be integrated into a plot-structure, and suspicion on this score is increased by the fact that it is precisely in connection with the key idea of plot-structure that the work is so conspicuously lacking in substance: apart from the near-replication of the Aristotelian definition of tragedy, we are offered no more than the statement that a comic plot is built around 'laughable actions'. The *Tractatus* appears to represent the mentality of someone who knows how to imitate Aristotle mechanically in constructing the barest framework of a theory of comedy, but who lacks a positive conception of the genre to place at the heart of this framework.

Nor is confidence in an Aristotelian source raised by the feeble formula for comic *katharsis* ('through pleasure and laughter accomplishing the *katharsis* of such emotions'). It is wholly incredible that Aristotle could have called pleasure and laughter 'emotions', and equally so that a theorist concerned to attribute appropriate pleasures to individual genres could have been content

---

[20] For text and tr. of the *Tractatus*, see Janko, *Comedy*, pp. 22–41; another version in Russell, *Criticism*, pp. 204–6.

to assign pleasure *tout court* to comedy. Aristotle's response to the Platonic charge that comedy could be psychologically harmful may have involved an ethical element, perhaps on the lines of a salutary excercising and tempering of emotions such as *phthonos*, a malevolent feeling which Plato (*Philebus* 49b – e) had regarded as the core of our reaction to comedy. But this is a speculation in the dark.

If we glance once more at the end of *Poetics* 13, the reference there to the proper pleasure of comedy appears to be connected with a final sense of moral resolution or equilibrium: whether by an equitable reckoning, or simply by the benign defusing of potential seriousness, the kind of play to which Aristotle alludes seems to close with an easy and gratifying settlement of problems (of enmity and evil) at which the comedy must at least have hinted. No far-reaching interpretation can be built on this passing remark, but it is at least worth suggesting that Aristotle here has in mind a containment of the force of laughter within the bounds of a moderate view of human failings. We can conclude, at any rate, by reminding ourselves that, to find its place in the theory and justification of poetry which the *Poetics* was designed to offer, comedy must have been regarded by Aristotle as a form of mimesis capable of affording a cognitive and emotional experience that might bring its audiences and readers a little closer to the imaginative understanding of universal human realities.

5

THE EVOLUTION OF A THEORY OF ARTISTIC PROSE

Literary prose first emerges in the middle of the fifth century BC in writings in the Ionic dialect, including the *Histories* of Herodotus, then in the Attic dialect in the oratory of the Sicilian Gorgias and the Athenian Antiphon, and is seen at the end of the century in Thucydides' *History*. Oratory and history, throughout antiquity, remain privileged prose genres, to which is added as a third the philosophical dialogue, developed by Plato in the fourth century. Except for a very few references to the literary epistle, ancient critics ignore all other prose forms as sub-literary. History, with its mixture of narrative and set speeches, may be thought of as corresponding to epic in poetry, the dialogue to drama; epideictic oratory, seen in the display speeches of sophists, such as that attributed to Lysias in Plato's *Phaedrus*, or in funeral orations or speeches at festivals, has some relationship to lyric forms, such as the hymn, but the chief poetic antecedents of deliberative oratory are found in the debates in epic.

Aristotle claims (*Rh.* 1.1404a20 – 39) that prose became artistic in the first instance by borrowing stylistic features from poetry; a more accurate statement might be that analogies were created to the effects of poetic sound and rhythm, seen in the so-called Gorgianic figures of isocolon, paronomasia, homoeoteleuton, and the like. These are flagrantly indulged by Gorgias himself and found in more restrained form in Thucydides and elsewhere. As pointed out in chapter 1, section 3 above, 'prose' assumes the prior existence of 'poetry'. Poetic diction, the use of metaphor, patterns of sound, and rhythm are qualities which helped make prose literary to the Greeks, and Gorgias and his successors realized that they contributed to persuasive effect by inducing some of the emotional force of poetry. Gorgianic mannerism finds a partial analogy in the appearance of Gongorism and Euphuism in early stages of Renaissance vernacular prose. The critics, beginning with Aristotle, counselled restraint, and in practice judicial oratory, as seen in Antiphon, Lysias, and Andocides, not to say the Socratic dialogue, achieved literary quality more by purified mimesis of everyday speech: elegance of diction, clarity, and power of thought.

1 Sophists and rhetorical handbooks

A theory of artistic prose is first set forth in Book III of Aristotle's *Rhetoric*. That work reflects his teaching of the subject in Plato's Academy in the middle of the fourth century. The extent to which a conceptualised theory of rhetoric existed before Aristotle is difficult to define. Plato (*Ph.* 266d – 7d) gives a survey of rhetorical handbooks (*tekhnai*) of the late fifth century which described parts of a judicial speech (*prooimion, diēgēsis,* etc.), useful for a novice in addressing a lawcourt, and also outlined how to employ argument from probability. This survey of what became 'invention' and 'arrangement' in later rhetoric clearly represents a response to the needs of the democratic state where citizens were expected to conduct their own litigation before large, popular juries. But Plato also mentions other works in the same passage which seem to be examples of diction and style, such as the 'Museums' of Gorgias' pupil Polus. Gorgias himself was certainly a teacher of rhetoric, including argument and style, but to judge from Plato's dramatisation of him in the *Gorgias* he had not analysed his own views, and so far as we know he taught only by example. Aristotle complains (*Sophistici elenchi* 183b37 – 4a1) that the training offered by Gorgias was unsystematic, as if shoemaking were taught by showing the student different kinds of shoes. Yet in his *Helen*, as discussed in chapter 2, section 2 above, Gorgias advanced a theory of discourse: the view of *logos* as a tiny and invisible material force which is a powerful lord, capable of bewitching an audience.

2 Isocrates

Isocrates (436 – 338 BC) had been a follower both of Gorgias and of Socrates; he admired rhetoric and gave it an increased conceptual base and an improved method. In the process he made significant contributions to criticism, rhetoric, and education.[1] About 390 BC, even before the opening of Plato's Academy, Isocrates established a school in Athens that offered advanced instruction in something like the liberal arts, the *enkuklios paideia* as the Greeks came to know it, with an emphasis on rhetoric. Its function was to teach young aristocrats from Athens and abroad the arts of speech in such a way that they could become leaders of society. The programmatic early speech *Against the Sophists* provides (16–17) an outline of his intended method. The student was to acquire a knowledge of *ideai*, by which he seems to mean the topics of a subject, how to arrange them, and how to adorn them appropriately with 'enthymemes', not logical arguments as in Aristotle, but striking expressions of thought. These were then to be cast into rhythmical and melodious words. Thus style follows and is separate from invention. The student needs natural ability, developed by understanding of the different species of discourse,

[1] Jaeger, *Paideia*, III, pp. 46–155.

and should practise himself in their use. Nature, theory, and practice become the trinity of later teachers of rhetoric.[2] The teacher, Isocrates says, should expound these matters accurately, thus apparently should lecture on rhetoric or engage in the explication of texts, and should himself furnish examples of composition, as had the sophists. It is the latter duty which produced most of Isocrates' extant works. He wrote extended speeches on contemporary issues, read them or had them read to his students for their edification and criticism, and after further polish published them, that is circulated copies in hopes of influencing public opinion. This is the first publication of civic oratory, part of the transition from speech to writing in the society of the time. During the following centuries rhetoric continued a process of *letteraturizzazione*, or slippage from a phenomenon of speech to the art of written composition.[3]

Twenty-one of Isocrates' discourses survive, including the *Panegyricus* on the role Athens should play in the leadership of Greece around 380 BC, the *Antidosis* (355 BC), in which the rhetor defends his ideals and methods, and the *Philippus* (346 BC), in which he urges Philip of Macedon to seize political hegemony in the Greek world. Isocrates' own personality is everywhere evident in his work, marking the emergence of an authorial voice and an individualism seen before chiefly in lyric poetry. He often digresses to point out what he is doing in the text or to celebrate the power of speech. Thus he introduces into the political context of the *Panegyricus* (47 – 50) his theory of discourse. *Logos*, he says, is what differentiates human beings from other animals and makes it possible for them to develop in all other respects. In activities other than speech chance prevails, so that the wise fail and the foolish succeed, but speech is the work of an intelligent mind, the surest sign of culture, and the source of power. Carrying on the theme in the *Antidosis* (274) he says:

> I think that the kind of art which can implant honesty and justice in depraved natures has never existed, neither in the past nor now, and that those making promises about this will grow weary and stop speaking before such an education can be found, but I believe that men become better and worthier if they are anxious about speaking well and if they desire to be able to persuade their listeners and moreover if they set their hearts on their advantage, not what the ignorant think is advantage, but what is advantage in the true sense.

This might be paraphrased to say that ethics and politics cannot be taught; speech can be, and by developing noble themes the speaker ennobles his own mind and values and increases his ability to influence society. Isocrates' favourite noble theme was the superiority of Greek culture to that of the barbarian and the application of this doctrine to the cause of union among the Greek states against the Persian empire. In pressing this theme he may

---

[2] Shorey, '*Phusis*', pp. 185–201.
[3] Kennedy, *Classical Rhetoric*, pp. 109–19.

be thought to seek a reply to Plato's strictures against rhetoric in the *Gorgias*: rhetoric has an appropriate subject matter in political and social life; it has a method; and it has moral value. But in practice Isocrates' treatments often lack logical rigour, distort historical precedent, and seem isolated from reality. He is a closet orator and the first example of the academic mind.

The choice of a noble theme was the first criterion in composition. The second was style. Isocrates developed and taught a distinctive prose style, less poetic than that of Gorgias, or even Plato, characterised by fullness, periodicity, and smoothness. He is fond of asserting the positive as well as denying the negative, of amplifying clauses of cause and result, or composing in extraordinarily long sentences made up of long units, and of giving attention to smooth-flowing sound. There is an obsessive avoidance of hiatus, the oral gap resulting from ending one word and beginning the next with vowels. The effect of the style, combined with the elevated but conventional thought, is extremely bland, especially if contrasted to the much more forceful style (*deinotēs*) of his younger contemporary, Demosthenes. To later Greek critics Isocrates is often the example of the 'middle' style, characterised by smoothness, lacking the passion of the 'grand' style or the naturalness of the 'plain', and he has remained the great model of epideictic, or display, oratory, even though most of his speeches are not technically in the epideictic form.

Like Gorgias, Isocrates composed an *Encomium of Helen*, which is indeed a true epideictic speech. In the prooemion he attacks contemporary eristic philosophers, criticises sophists who composed orations on trivial themes, like bumble-bees or salt, and though he praises Gorgias for choosing a noble theme in Helen, objects that the sophist has left not an encomium but an apology, limited to refuting charges against Helen. His own speech praises Helen as a symbol of beauty and an incentive for great deeds on the part of heroes of the past. This criticism suggests an emerging sense of rhetorical species within the genre of oratory, each with its own conventions. The *Rhetoric to Alexander*, a late fourth-century handbook largely the work of Anaximenes of Lampsacus, lists (in section 1) the species as protreptic, apotreptic, encomiastic, invective, categoric or accusational, apologetic, and investigational, and describes the conventions appropriate to each.

One of the most unusual critical contexts in Greek is found in Isocrates' last speech, *Panthenaicus*, completed in 339 BC when he was ninety-six years old. The passage should interest modern critics as a Greek example of self-reference, where the text folds back and comments upon itself ambiguously, and it shows an awareness of hermeneutic questions. Isocrates says (200) that when his discourse was lacking only a conclusion he reviewed it with his students and gave it to a former student to read. The latter praised the speech as a whole, but objected to the treatment of the Spartans in it. The criticism was rather brusque, and Isocrates replies sternly with a justification of what he has said. The other students praise Isocrates and rebuke his critic, but

Isocrates says they did not understand either. He then comes to feel that what he has said about Sparta is not right, summons the students, and asks whether the speech should be destroyed or published (233). The former student speaks, within Isocrates' text, questioning the master's motives and providing an extended exegesis of Isocrates' intent (*dianoia*), with what amounts to an awareness of reader-reponse theory (235–63). The most interesting passage is that in which the critic claims that Isocrates built a double meaning into the text (*logous amphibolous*, 240) and attributes to Isocrates the deliberate (*proelomenon*) intent of composing a speech like no other that the casual reader will superficially understand, but which to those going through it 'accurately' (*akribōs*) will appear difficult. 'You will say', the critic continues, 'that in explaining the force of your words and expounding your intent I do not realise that I make your speech less glorious to the extent that I make it more clear and intelligible to readers'. To this pointed observation about his own text Isocrates makes no reply, leaving open the question of his intent and the meaning of the speech as well as the possible 'reductionist' effects of analysis.[4]

3 Plato on rhetoric

Isocrates and Plato were close contemporaries, and their writings often seem to be reactions to each other, though Isocrates does not name Plato and Plato only once refers to Isocrates by name (*Ph.* 278e10). Socrates there is allowed to speak of the young Isocrates' talent and potential for philosophy, perhaps ironically on Plato's part. Plato has often been regarded as the archetypical enemy of rhetoric as of poetry, but neither claim is entirely fair and his attitude toward the two arts is rather similar. Socrates loves speeches as he loves poetry, but he recognises great danger in both and proposes purified forms appropriate to a more just and beautiful society.

Negative criticism of rhetoric is most forcefully stated in the *Gorgias*, a relatively early dialogue. Socrates seeks to elicit from Gorgias and his follower Polus a definition of rhetoric; he easily shows that they are unduly impressed by its powers and have not thought out its true nature, but some of his criticism is unfair. He insists that to be an art rhetoric must have a distinct subject matter, as do other arts, and that the rhetor must have knowledge of that subject. Gorgias ill-advisedly suggests justice and injustice as its subject (454b7), and on that score Socrates easily shows that the rhetor has only opinion. That rhetoric might be, as Aristotle will claim, a faculty analogous to dialectic, applicable to any subject, is not seriously considered in the dialogue, and throughout the first third Socrates seems to be taking an extreme position to challenge the sophists, somewhat tongue-in-cheek. In response to

---

[4] Kathy Eden, 'Hermeneutics and the ancient rhetorical tradition', *Rhetorica*, 5 (1987), 59–86.

Polus' request for his own definition he says that rhetoric is no true art at all, but an empirical knack, a branch of flattery, and a counterpart to cookery that dresses up bad food to make it palatable (463a – 6a). In his discussion with Callicles he again provocatively suggests that rhetoric might be useful in helping a guilty man convict himself and thus secure needed punishment (480b – d). Poetry is rudely dismissed as a rhetorical kind of public address, used like rhetoric to flatter an audience of the ignorant (502b – d). Much of Socrates' opposition to rhetoric, as to poetry, is clearly dependent on his negative reaction to how it was being used in Greek society. Athenian orators have not made their audiences better by their skill at words, he claims (515c – 17a). Yet in one passage Socrates does seem to grant the possibility that an orator, artist, and good man might use rhetoric to lead the souls of his listeners to justice and virtue (504d5 – e3). This possibility of a philosophical rhetoric was to be taken up again in greater detail ten years or so later in the *Phaedrus*.

The *Phaedrus* is structurally perhaps the most complex of all the Platonic dialogues. It has an elaborate introductory section setting a beautiful scene in which many of the motifs of the dialogue are delicately introduced, it has three epideictic speeches which are criticised on artistic and moral grounds, a theoretical discussion of composition, which touches on matters of invention, arrangement, and style, and the interpretation of a myth on the value and danger of writing, discussed in chapter 3, section 6, above. The picture of philosophical rhetoric, or of good literary composition, which emerges is that the speaker or writer must have knowledge of, not opinion about the subject, an understanding of logical definition and division and orderly arrangement of material, and a knowledge of the souls of the audience. 'It is necessary for every speech to cohere like a living thing having its own body so that nothing is lacking in head or foot, but to have a middle and extremities suitable to each other, sketched as part of a whole.' (264c6 – 9). Rhetoric is 'a kind of leading-the-soul (*psuchagōgia*) through words, not only in lawcourts and public assemblies, but also in private gatherings' (261a7 – 9).

Until someone knows the truth of each thing about which he speaks or writes and is able to define everything in its own genus, and having defined it knows how to break the genus down into species and sub-species to the point of indivisibility, discerning the nature of the soul in accordance with the same method, while discovering the logical category which fits with each nature, and until in a similar way he composes and adorns speech, furnishing variegated and complex speech to a variegated and complex soul and simple speech to a simple soul – not until then will it be possible for speech to exist in an artistic form in so far as the nature of speech is capable of such treatment, neither for instruction nor for persuasion, as has been shown by our entire past discussion.

(277b5 – c6)

This is Plato's developed view of rhetoric; it is the programme on which Aristotle based his teaching of rhetoric, including the necessary preliminary study of logic, and it probably can be taken as a summation of Plato's view of poetry as well and thus of literature as a whole. It raises, of course, many practical problems. How is it to be applied to discourse addressed to a multitude of differing individuals? Aristotle's application of it to the real world, and all later applications, have necessarily involved some debasing of Platonic idealism. Plato preferred the 'simple' soul, and Aristotle seems to follow this in his remarks on the 'simplicity' of popular audiences (*Rh.* 1.1357a1 – 4).[5] But the Platonic passage is remarkable for its focus on communication and on the central role of the audience in the speech or literary act. Until early modern times rhetoric and criticism all too often lost this clarity of vision. That tendency will be seen even in Aristotle. Sophistic emphasis on the speaker rather than on speech or audience remained strong, and alienation of speaker from audience was increased by the loss of political significance in public address in times of despotism and barbarism.

4 Aristotle's 'Rhetoric'

Philodemus (II, p. 50 Sudhaus), Cicero (*De or.* 3.141), and other later writers say that Aristotle began to lecture on rhetoric in reaction to the teaching of Isocrates. The treatise we read today is largely a product of his teaching before he left Athens in 347 BC, but may have been given its final form around 340 BC when he was tutor to the young Alexander the Great. It seems to have been among Aristotle's books which were lost from the time of the death of Theophrastus (*c.* 284 BC) to after 80 BC, but its contents were known to the early Peripatetics and through them some of his ideas were known to others.[6] Though used by Cicero, the subsequent direct influence of the *Rhetoric* was rather slight until modern times. The primary reason for this is that it does not deal, at least not specifically, with a number of features of theory which were regarded as especially important in later centuries: stasis theory, the characters of style, and figures of speech. Yet it seems appropriate to speak of an Aristotelian, dialectical tradition in rhetoric.[7] In the first century BC Cicero says (*De inventione* 2.8) that the Aristotelian and Isocratean traditions were merging, and his own later writings on rhetoric contributed much to this synthesis.

The opening chapter of the *Rhetoric*, with its declaration that rhetoric is the counterpart of dialectic and its rejection of the interest of handbooks writers in the parts of the oration or elements external to the speech, makes a sharp break with rhetoric as it was being taught, influenced by Aristotle's study of logic and dialectic as seen in the works we call the *Organon*. In fact, these

---

[5] Trimpi, *Muses of One Mind*, pp. 235 – 6.
[6] Strabo 13.54; Plutarch, *Sulla* 26.1; Carnes Lord, 'On the early history of the Aristotelian corpus', *AJP*, 107 (1986), 137 – 61.
[7] Solmsen, 'Aristotelian tradition'.

subjects are eventually discussed, for Aristotle, like Plato, moves from an extreme theoretical stance taken in his original lectures to practical considerations as the subject unfolds.[8] In chapter 2 rhetoric is defined as the faculty of discovering, on every subject, the available means of persuasion (1.1355b25 – 6). There are three and only three modes of persuasion: logical argument, the impression of the speaker's moral character (*ēthos*) as reflected in the speech, and the awakening of emotion (*pathos*) in the audience by the speaker. The speaker or writer – for Aristotle includes written discourse – is in control, imposing his will upon an audience through the power of words. To a much greater extent than the *Poetics*, the *Rhetoric* is a prescriptive treatise, even sometimes using the second person singular address of a handbook, but it can be turned inside out to provide a system of rhetorical criticism. If this is done, the basis of critical judgement becomes authorial intent and how that is transmitted by artistic techniques through the text to the audience. Here rhetoric stands in sharp contrast to poetics, as understood by Aristotle, for in the *Poetics* the primary function of art is to allow the *muthos* to emerge, with its connections of cause and effect and its potentiality to accomplish a catharsis of pity and fear. A poet, according to Aristotle, should speak in his own person as little as possible (24.1460a5 – 6), and to manipulate a text to resolve the plot, or by implication to give it topical meaning, is 'inartistic' (16.1454b31). Rhetoric has a place in poetry in the rhetorical exposition of the thought of characters (19.1456a35), not in the thought of the poet. But in rhetorical composition it is just the other way around. Documents, witnesses, and evidence, the materials of the case, are inartistic, and art consists in the speaker's own invention and manipulation of argument, in his portrayal of his own ethical character, and in his ability to stir the emotions of his audience in order to get them to accept his proposition (*Rh.* 1.1355b35 – 6a20). In trying to give practical application to Socrates' requirement that the rhetor know the souls of his audience, Aristotle views the latter as types based on their emotions, ages, and fortunes (2.1388b30 – 1), suggestive of the characterisation found in Greek New Comedy or later in Roman comedy and Greek romance. He classifies the various kinds of emotion, such as anger or envy, which can be awakened in an audience, with advice as to what statements stir which. It is all a very deliberate process on the part of the author, and used as a critical system it is also a very deliberate and specific analysis of technique.

These characteristics of rhetoric – authorial intent as the basis of criticism, teaching of a method of composition applicable to varied situations but within a standardised notion of oratorical genre and form, interest in argumentation, character portrayal, and emotion – remain features of classical rhetoric. Some, as we have seen, do not originate with Aristotle, though he adds a great

---

[8] For an effort to demonstrate the unity of the *Rhetoric*, see Grimaldi, *Studies*, pp. 18 – 52.

emphasis on logical argument, especially through use of the enthymeme, by which he means a rhetorical syllogism. Of his other concepts, the one most permanently influential, and most consistently attributed to him, is the division of rhetoric into three and only three species: judicial, which is concerned with judgement of past action and centres on the topic of justice; deliberative, concerned with the judgement of a future action and its expediency; and epideictic, in which the audience is not called upon to take an action, but is a spectator of praise or blame (1.1358a36–b8). Later rhetoricians came to think of poetry as a form of epideictic, thus bringing it within the sphere of rhetoric. Rhetorical argument, according to Aristotle, is formed from probabilities and from signs, some of the latter being necessary, others only possible indications (1.1357a30–4). There is a connection between what is said here and the discussion of 'recognition' in *Poetics*, chapter 16.[9]

Rhetoric employs 'topics', Aristotle continues, identifying for the first time a part of compositional theory that remained important until it was rejected in the seventeenth and eighteenth centuries. A topic is a 'place' where a writer looks for subject matter or logical strategy. Aristotle discusses both 'special topics', characteristic of one species of oratory such as ways and means, war and peace, defence, imports and exports, and legislation as the topics of deliberation (1.1359b19–23), and 'common topics' found in any species, such as past fact, future fact, possibility, and size (2.1391b22–2a7). There is also a long chapter (2.23), apparently not an original part of the work, on topics in the sense of strategies of argument, drawing on the discussion of dialectic in the *Topics*. 'Commonplace' is not used in the *Rhetoric* in the sense of ornamental passages, digressions, or moralising, though the chapters on epideictic (1.9) and amplification (2.26) show some awareness of this phenomenon of rhetorical composition. Though Aristotle does not point it out, all literary genres utilise common topics and each has its own special topics which help to define a tradition. The special topics of epic in the tradition of the *Iliad* or *Aeneid*, for example, could be said to include intervention by the gods, councils, embassies, arming, single combat, the death and burial of a hero, and the like. Though they do not construct a systematic list, later critics show sensitivity to the appropriate topics in particular works. Longinus, for example, criticises (9.7) battles between gods as inappropriate unless allegorically interpreted.

In Books I and II Aristotle resists any tendency to identify rhetoric with style, but Book III sets forth a theory of style which through Theophrastus and Cicero influenced later discussion. At the outset we are told that 'it is not sufficient to know what one ought to say, but one must know how to say it' (3.1463b15–16). Invention and style are viewed as separate, though related, stages in composition, a characteristic attitude of rhetoricians. Although the

---

[9] Eden, *Poetic and Legal Fiction*, pp. 10–16.

distinction is not specifically spelled out, Aristotle treats first diction, or word choice, then composition into sentences as two separable processes. The appropriate diction for prose is that used in conversation, but this includes metaphor, which thus becomes the most acceptable way to give distinction to discourse (3.1404b26 – 37). 'To learn easily', he says (3.1410b10 – 13), 'is naturally pleasant to all and words signify something [*sēmainei*, 'give a sign'[10]] so that those words which make knowledge in us are most pleasant. But glosses [strange words] are obscure, and we already know proper words. It is metaphor which most produces knowledge.' Metaphors should be derived from what is beautiful in sound, in signification, to sight, or to some other sense (3.1405b17 – 18). Appropriate metaphor is to be thought of as a mean between what is prosaic and what is poetic. The characteristic Aristotelian principle of the mean occurs also in the consideration of prose rhythm, where patterns should be sought that are not metres of poetry but yet impose some sense of limit (3.1408b30 – 1). A sense of limit rests the reader and is pleasant; that is why the periodic style is preferred to a running or paratactic style (3.1409a31 – 2). By periodic is primarily meant a short antithetical construction, not the enormous periods of Isocrates. In prose composition, we are told (3.1410b35 – 6), it is necessary to aim at three things: metaphor, antithesis, and what is called *energeia*, or the 'actualisation' of a scene in the reader's mind.[11] Aristotle has no terminology for tropes and figures, which is a development of the following centuries, but he does discuss a rather miscellaneous set of techniques, including *asteia*, or 'urbanities', similes, proverbs, and hyperboles.

The whole discussion of diction and composition is set in a larger theoretical context which again reveals the emphasis on a search for a mean and which was to have, through Theophrastus, an important future development. This is the effort to identify a 'virtue' (*aretē*), or characteristic excellence, of good prose style. At the beginning of the chapters on style the virtue is defined as clarity (3.1404b1 – 2), a position clearly consistent with the view of rhetoric as a counterpart to dialectic. But the statement is immediately qualified to say that clarity must not be 'mean' or 'coarse' on the one hand, nor on the other above the dignity of the subject, which would make the style poetic; the word choice must be 'appropriate' (*prepon*). Subsequently (3.1407a20) we are told that the basis of diction is found in speaking correct Greek; still later (3.1407b26) we are given rules for creating *ongkos*, 'loftiness' or 'bulk', as well as further advice about propriety (3.1408a10). The virtues of style are thus foreshadowed, to be given more specific discussion in later writers.

Although Aristotle has no theory of the characters or registers of style, which are a major part of later theory, his emphasis on propriety may be said

---

[10] On Aristotle's theory of the sign, see above, ch. 2, section 6.

[11] Distinguished by its root, *ergon* = 'act' from the later rhetorical term for visual description, *enargeia*, (*arges* = 'bright'), e.g., Quint. 8.3.89; see Eden, *Poetic and Legal Fiction*, pp. 71 – 2.

to have contributed to that development, as did his remarks on the differences between spoken and written discourse (3.1413b2 – 1414a28). The latter should be precise, should avoid repetition, and should use connectives, but in delivery this will seem 'meagre', whereas a speech which has been effective in delivery, filled with repetitions and disjunctions, may seem 'silly' when read. A deliberative speech should resemble a rough sketch; a judicial speech can be more finished, the argumentation worked out in greater detail. An epideictic speech is closest to the written style. Except in this chapter, style in the *Rhetoric* is considered in terms of short contexts, not of the work as a whole. This anticipates some features of Alexandrian poetics and is endemic to much of ancient criticism, which had a poor grasp of issues important to modern critics, such as unity (though that was stressed in the *Poetics*), textuality, and programmatic imagery, even though those qualities are found in Greek literature. The failure to find ways to speak about whole texts may have begun with the difficulty of turning back and forth within a text when written on a papyrus scroll, worsened by the custom of ancient teachers of reading works of poetry line by line, and not ameliorated by the development of the running commentary as the preferred form of exegesis in the Hellenistic period. It is remarkable that no practising poet strongly protests against this tradition; we must wait for the neo-Platonists to find a different attitude.

5 Theophrastus

Aristotle's successor as head of the Peripatetic School in Athens was Theophrastus (*c.* 370 – *c.* 284 BC). He wrote monographs, now lost, on the Art of Rhetoric, the Art of Poetry, the Ludicrous, and Comedy, as well as a long work *On the Species of the Rhetorical Arts*, which perhaps resembled Aristotle's *Topics* (Diog. Laert. 5.42 – 50). Little is known about their contents. More can be said about two other works, *On Lexis* and *On Hupokrisis*. *Lexis* properly means diction, but was sometimes extended to style as a whole. According to Dionysius of Halicarnassus (*Isocrates* 3), Theophrastus claimed that 'dignity' in style was attained by diction, arrangement of words, and use of figures, and all three of these may have been discussed. The word for 'figure' here is *skhēma*, not so used by Aristotle, but the standard word in later writers. We should probably understand a rapid growth in the naming and defining of figures during the two centuries after Aristotle, encouraged by the systematic teaching of grammar and rhetoric in the schools. *On Lexis* discussed the excellence or virtues of style. According to Cicero (*Orator* 79), Theophrastus said that style should be pure (grammatical) Greek, clear, appropriate, and ornamented. This has been much discussed, but probably can be taken to mean that good prose style should exemplify all four of these qualities and should be a mean between style which is meagre and that which is excessively poetic, a systematisation of Aristotle's position.[12]

More difficult to specify is what Theophrastus may have said about the 'characters' or kinds of prose style, which by the late Hellenistic period are commonly defined in terms of a grand, a middle, and a plain style. He spoke of the style of the sophist Thrasymachus as 'mixed and composite', between the grandiose manner of Thucydides and the plainness of Lysias (Dion. Hal., *Demosthenes* 3). Does this imply three registers, available to a writer on the basis of the subject, occasion, and audience? The consensus of modern scholarship is that it does not, that Theophrastus is again expressing a preference for a mean.[13] Nevertheless, the statement may have constituted a precedent for three characters, taken up by later rhetoricians who found more variety to admire in Greek prose than the philosophical approach of Aristotle or Theophrastus allowed. A very ornate, frigid style, often called Asianism, was much affected by some Hellenistic orators and rhetoricians,[14] while at the same time the *Koinē*, or 'common' non-literary Greek of the eastern-Mediterranean diaspora was developing. With the neo-Atticism of late Hellenistic and Roman times it became clear that a variety of stylistic registers existed in practice; as the schools became more classicising, that is, as they increasingly found literary excellence in the imitation of models of the past, it was obvious that these differed considerably and various ways of categorising them were tried by Demetrius, Dionysius, Hermogenes, and others.

The contents of Theophrastus' monograph *On Hupokrisis* is more problematic. In the beginning of the third book of the *Rhetoric* Aristotle had suggested that the subject of rhetorical delivery, which he associates with acting on stage and calls *hupokrisis*, could be given systematic treatment. Theophrastus probably carried this out, as he developed other Aristotelian views. A recent study concludes that *On Delivery* 'was an inclusive work that discussed voice and motions appropriate not only to orators but also to musicians, actors, and rhapsodes'.[15] If so, it may be associated with an interest evident elsewhere in Theophrastus in the effect of language, composition, thought, and performance on an audience. This is seen in the most often quoted critical fragment of Theophrastus, perhaps from *On Lexis*: 'You must not state everything with precise and lengthy elaboration; leave some things for your hearer to infer and work out for himself. When he grasps what you have omitted he will be more than a hearer, he will be a witness on your behalf, and a friendly witness because he thinks himself rather clever and you have given him a chance to exercise his intelligence. To say everything is to convict your hearer of stupidity, as if you were talking

---

[12] Innes, 'Theophrastus', pp. 225–60.
[13] Grube, 'Thrasymachus, Theophrastus', pp. 251–67; Innes, 'Theophrastus', pp. 225–60.
[14] Wooten, 'Style asiatique', pp. 217–22.
[15] Fortenbaugh, 'Delivery', pp. 269–88.

to a fool.'[16] Plato's call for a knowledge of the audience on the part of a reader, remarks in Aristotle, including the theory of catharsis and metaphor, and the hermeneutics of Isocrates thus show for a limited time some awareness of reader reception, but an interest in this important topic fades in subsequent rhetorical treatises.

6 Demetrius, 'On Style'

Another student of Aristotle was Demetrius of Phaleron, who ruled Athens for ten years at the end of the fourth century and subsequently had a role in the establishment of the Library at Alexandria. As an orator, according to Cicero (*Brutus* 37), 'he walked into the bright sun and dust of the city as though coming not from a soldier's tent, but from the shady school of the learned Theophrastus'. He thus was taken as the representative of the beginning of post-classical oratory. An extant treatise *On Style* was long attributed to him, but is now believed to be the work of some later Peripatetic. We continue to call him Demetrius, though there is no proof that was his name. There is no consensus as to the date of the treatise; suggestions have ranged from the third century BC to the first century of the Christian era or even later. A possible compromise is the view that, though written much later, the work is highly anachronistic, drawing on fourth and third-century sources and ignoring or ignorant of late Hellenistic theories.[17] Whatever its date, the nature of its contents justifies treating it among works of the early Peripatetics.

Demetrius' treatise reads like a series of notes on certain aspects of composition, chiefly periodicity, prose rhythm, and the characters of style. The word used to mean style is *hermēneia*, the expression of thought in words. The author rejects (36–7) the view of some unnamed source that there are only two characters, the plain and the grand, and instead defines and describes four: the grand, the elegant, the plain, and the forceful. Each has characteristic content, diction, and arrangement, and each has its vitiated counterpart: the frigid, the affected, the arid, and the coarse, respectively. Consistent with Peripatetic values, the treatise stresses the need for all features of style to be appropriate to the level of seriousness of the content and for sound to be related to sense. Though not given full development, a concept of 'taste' is inherent in many passages (e.g., 67, 137, 287). Most examples cited come from prose writers, but poets are cited too, especially Sappho, who is greatly admired by the author. Yet she is a critical problem for him in that 'she extracts great charm from devices which are in themselves questionable and difficult' (127). Differences in style among her poems are great, and deliberate (*ek tēs proaireseōs*,

---

[16] Demetrius 226, quoted from Grube, *Critics*, p. 105.

[17] Schenkeveld, *Demetrius*, pp. 135–48. There are possible references to the treatise in Philodemus (*Rh.* I, p. 165, Sudhaus; cf. Grube, *Demetrius*, pp. 53–4) which would date it before the first century BC.

168). As this suggests, Demetrius shares the common rhetorical attitude that a poet or prose writer is in complete, conscious control of material, and conversely his criticism takes the form of trying to grasp authorial intent and the technique by which it is transferred to the reader. He makes frequent use of *metathesis*, the device of recasting a line or sentence into different words or different word order to show the difference of effect. Plato had done this with the opening lines of the *Iliad* in *Republic* III and it is also found in Dionysius of Halicarnassus.[18]

The treatise devotes considerable space to naming and illustrating figures of speech (*skhēmata*). Clearly this part of rhetorical theory had undergone development between the time of Aristotle and the date at which the author was writing. A concerted, if not always successful, effort is made to identify the specific effect of a particular figure in its context. An example of the problems encountered is that both the omission of connectives (here called *dialusis*; in modern terminology *asyndeton*) and the repetition of connectives (*sunapheia*; *polysyndeton*) can create impressiveness (61 – 3). For this and similar situations the author has no explanation to offer, contenting himself with pointing out the possibilities.

A feature of the work which deserves mention is that, alone among major rhetorical treatises, it contains a discussion of the appropriate style of letter-writing, citing letters of Aristotle and others (223 – 35). Letters, we are told, should be written in a mixture of the plain and elegant styles and are like one side of a dialogue. The literary quality of the epistolary form thus results from its approximation to a more canonical genre. The discussion doubtless reflects the increased role of the epistle, both public and private, in the Hellenistic period, but why other rhetoricians did not take up this practical subject is a difficult question. Perhaps letter-writing was taught by some grammarians, but scorned as beneath the dignity of rhetoricians who took as their goal the composition of civic oratory. Cicero's letters show some awareness that epistles may be classified into types on the basis of their function, such as a letter of recommendation, and that their style will vary with content. Handbooks on letter-writing were eventually produced for the use of students.[19]

The development of artistic prose came to be regarded as analogous to the historical development of style in painting and sculpture. This was already noted by Aristotle in the case of poetry (*Po.* 6.1450a25 – 9), and Demetrius says that the early prose style had polish and neatness, 'like old statues whose art seems to have a plain spareness, whereas the later style resembles the statues of Pheidias with their combination of splendour and precision' (14). The topos was further developed by Cicero, Dionysius, Quintilian, and others. The rhetoricians thus show a sense of the evolution of style, parallel

[18] Greenberg, 'Metathesis', pp. 262–70.
[19] Cicero, *Ep. ad familiares*, esp. 2.4, 4.13, 12.30; Kennedy, *Greek Rhetoric*, pp. 70–3.

to other cultural phenomena. By the first century BC they came to feel that they lived late in the history of culture and that the teaching of composition should concentrate on describing and imitating the great features of the Classics, thus resisting decay rather than seeking further development or innovation. Demetrius does not lament the decay of style in his own times, one reason for giving his treatise an early date, but his cultural stance is already one of classicism, of seeking to maintain the excellence already attained. Criticism for him consists not in developing new literary theory, but in working out, sometimes correcting, details already adumbrated by Aristotle, Theophrastus, and others.

7 Hellenistic rhetoric

An important feature of rhetorical theory in the Hellenistic period relates to invention. This is the elaborate system of determining and describing the *stasis* (Latin *status* or *constitutio*) of a speech, attributed to Hermagoras of Temnos around 150 BC.[20] *Stasis* is the 'stance' which opposing orators or writers take toward a question at issue and can be found in any argumentative discourse, though most easily described in a case at law. There is first a distinction between 'general questions', or dialectical theses (e.g., is it right to kill a tyrant?) and specific cases, or *hupotheses* in which individuals are named (e.g., did Brutus murder Caesar?). The latter may be argued on the basis of one or more of four issues. Is the question one of fact, one of definition, one of the quality, motivation, or circumstances of an action, and one within the jurisdiction of an audience or tribunal to judge? Or does it rest on the inter-pretation of some statement, text, or law, where again hermeneutics enters into the sphere of rhetoric? Hermagoras' works are lost, but his theories may be found in Cicero's *De inventione* and in the *Rhetorica ad Herennium*, both products of the early first century BC. The theory, with its many stages of formulation of a question and formidable jargon, was chiefly applied to helping a student formulate issues and compose a speech, but it has some critical significance in that it is a way of understanding the treatment of a subject in a piece of argumentative writing.[21] Thus it is used by late Greek commen-tators in analysing speeches by Demosthenes and other orators, as seen in the scholia, and continues in modern times as a sometimes useful tool of rhetorical analysis.

Though the reading and analysis of texts was a feature of the grammatical and rhetorical schools, the emphasis of instruction was on acquiring practical arts of written and oral composition, in which the students were given extensive exercise. We are ill-informed about the nature of grammatical

[20] Matthes, 'Hermagoras', pp. 58–214.
[21] On the significance of stasis for literary theory, see Trimpi, *Muses of One Mind*, pp. 245–84.

exercises (*progumnasmata*) until the first century of the Christian era when we find them set forth in a Greek handbook by Aelius Theon, but they are probably in some form much older (cf. *Ad Herennium* 1.13). In the developed system of the empire they are graded in difficulty, usually beginning with the simple retelling of a fable, then an easy narrative to be recounted in the student's own words, and a *chria*, or the retelling of an anecdote about someone saying or doing something, with the drawing of a moral. More complicated are *ekphrasis* (the description of some place, work of art, or other object), *prosōpopoeia* (a speech in character for an historical or mythological personage), *enkōmion* (praise of a person, place, or thing), and *synkrisis* (comparison of two things or persons). The student was also taught to amplify a commonplace about vice or virtue and to argue a thesis and practise refutation and confirmation.[22] One result of such studies is the appearance of set pieces derived from the exercises as compositional units in works of literature. Epic composition, for example, involves narrative, prosopopoeia, ecphrasis, and sometimes other such units, and elegiac and lyric poetry often take these forms, at least in a general way.[23] Thus Ovid's *Heroides* are versified prosopopoeia. Progymnasmata continued to be practised in Greek throughout the Byzantine period and continued to influence attitudes toward literature. They were somewhat less influential in the West, but the short handbook attributed to Hermogenes was translated into Latin by Priscian about AD 500, and the handbook of Aphthonius was introduced to teachers of the Renaissance through a translation by Rudolph Agricola in the late fifteenth century.

Rhetorical exercises, or declamation, by the first century BC came to take the form of *suasoria*, a deliberative speech recommending some course of action to an historical or mythological personage, or *controversia*, a fictitious speech before a jury in which specified laws are posited and a situation given which will test the student's ability.[24] We know these exercises best from the Latin work of the elder Seneca, to be discussed in chapter 9, section 1 below, but Seneca includes reference to Greek declamation as well. In all the exercises, amplification (*auxēsis*) of prescribed material was fundamental to the compositional process, and this attitude is taken over into literary composition where most writers work with traditional materials, often within traditional styles and traditional verse forms, but seek originality in new combinations, new details, allusion, and rhetorical conceit.

[22] Kennedy, *Greek Rhetoric*, pp. 54–73.
[23] Cairns, *Generic Composition*, pp. 89–90.
[24] Bonner, *Declamation*, pp. 1–26.

6

HELLENISTIC LITERARY AND
PHILOSOPHICAL SCHOLARSHIP

Philip of Macedon defeated the Greek city states at the Battle of Chaeronea in 338 BC. Though they retained some control of their internal affairs, their political importance largely comes to an end. Between 336 and 323 his son, Alexander the Great, extended the Macedonian empire beyond anything the world had seen through Asia Minor, Egypt, Mesopotamia, and into the Middle East, and with it the Greek language, education, literature, and religion. Under Alexander's successors, the political, commercial, and cultural centres within fifty years became Alexandria, the capital of Egypt, Pergamum in Asia Minor, and other eastern cities, though Athens remained the home of the philosophical schools established there in the fourth century: the Academy of Plato (which evolved into a school of scepticism); the Peripatetic School, founded by Aristotle; the Stoa of Zeno and his successors; and the Garden of the Epicureans. The emergence of the Hellenistic monarchies had an effect on literary life in that the focus of writers' attention was often drawn to the royal courts. The institution of patronage, important for early Greek poets but largely forgotten in Classical Athens, re-emerged and with it an impulse to flattery. A famous example is Callimachus' elegy on the apotheosis of the 'Lock of Berenice', Queen of Egypt, the ancestor of Pope's 'Rape of the Lock'. For the history of criticism, the most striking developments are the establishment of the great Museum and Library at Alexandria, which became a centre for textual criticism and exegesis of texts based on literary, historical, biographical, and linguistic scholarship, and the phenomenon of Alexandrianism in poetic composition, which combined learning with artistic craftsmanship, often favouring the shorter poetic genres such as elegy, hymns, epigrams, and idylls. The two developments, scholarship and Alexandrianism, are closely interconnected, and were sometimes affected by teachings of rhetoricians and philosophers who dominated secondary and advanced education respectively.

1 The Alexandrian Museum and Library

At the death of Alexander the Great in 323 BC, his Greek general Ptolemy seized Egypt and ruled there for the next forty years. He was an administrator of genius and a man of letters who wrote a biography of Alexander. Among the institutions created by Ptolemy were the Museum and Library, adjacent to his palace in Alexandria. The Museum was a community of scholars, headed by a priest named by the king, and it functioned much as do modern institutes of advanced study. Poets and scholars were appointed to the staff, supplied with facilities for their work, and well paid; they were free to devote their time to research, though some took students and thus supplied a kind of graduate education. The central subjects were scientific, for example the geographical studies of Eratosthenes, and literary: the collecting, collating, editing, and interpretation of Classical texts. Books were collected from all over the Greek world, including Athens, catalogued, and preserved in the great Library, which came to include hundreds of thousands of scrolls. Eventually a second library was built for the over-flow. According to Plutarch (*Caesar* 49), the Library was burned in the Roman siege of Alexandria in 47 BC, but other references indicate the damage was only partial. As Rudolf Pfeiffer, the great modern authority on Hellenistic scholarship, has written, 'The unprecedented interest in books was kindled by the new scholar poets, who were in desperate need of texts; by a notable coincidence the royal patrons and their advisers immediately fulfilled these imperative demands in a princely way. We shall find a similar sequence of events when in the Italian Renaissance the ardent zeal of the poets and humanists from Petrarch to Politian led to the recovery of the Classics and the setting-up of great libraries.'[1]

2 Callimachus and Alexandrianism

Philetas of Cos, who wrote elegiacs, short epics, and epigrams in the late fourth and early third centuries, is the first to be described as 'poet as well as critic' (Strabo 14.657). He marks the abandonment of the great public genres of the city state – epic, tragedy, and comedy – and of their heroic and ethical themes, aiming instead at 'artistic perfection in limited space'[2] for the aesthetic pleasure of an educated and sophisticated readership. As such, he became the model for the 'new poets' (neoterics) of Alexandria, including Callimachus and Theocritus, and for their Roman successors, including Propertius and Ovid. The favoured themes of Alexandrianism were mythology, especially incidents in myth not previously given classic treatment, 'scientific' subjects such as the constellations, religious cult, the pastoral world,

[1] Pfeiffer, *Scholarship*, p. 103.
[2] Pfeiffer, *Scholarship*, p. 89.

erotic love, and occasionally urban social life. These themes often represent
a turn from public issues into an imagined world of the past or into the sphere
of personal emotion. They parallel the attempts of the Hellenistic philosophical
schools to discover a basis for personal contentment and freedom from troubles
and fears. Though in Athens the production of comedies continued, this is
the New Comedy of Menander and his contemporaries, later imitated by the
Romans Plautus and Terence, which is again primarily concerned with the
emotions and the relationships of private citizens, and which emphasised
elegance of diction and realistic characterisation.

Alexandrian poetry is highly self-conscious; the poet's voice is often heard
through the poem. The most important example, and the Alexandrian poet
with the most developed critical theory, is Callimachus (*c.* 305 – *c.* 240 BC),
who worked on the staff of the Library and produced its *Pinakes*, or *catalogue
raisonné* in 120 volumes. Works were classified by genre or subject, authors
were listed alphabetically within each category, and brief biographies were
supplied as well as the *incipit*, or first line, of each known work. Callimachus
was also a major poet; his most famous work was the *Aetia*, or *Causes*, a
narrative elegy in four books in which he described himself as transported
to Mount Helicon. In the first two books he interrogated the muses about
myth, history, and ritual.[3] The use of question and answer, unprecedented
in poetry, was borrowed from scholarship where it is seen, for example, in
the *Problemata* attributed to Aristotle. Callimachus made significant innovations in narrative technique, to be imitated by later poets, including
variations in tempo and the insertion of tales within tales. Except for a series
of literary *Hymns*, Callimachus' extensive poetic work is largely known to
modern readers from fragments of papyri discovered in Egypt during the last
hundred years and still increasing in number.[4]

Callimachus' most quoted remark is 'a big book is a big evil'.[5] The quip,
for which no context is preserved, may have been a librarian's reaction to the
length of papyrus scrolls. His own practice shows that he did not object to
long works if subdivided into smaller units. Yet the words have been, and
can be, taken as symbolic of his opposition to the writing of traditional epic
poetry, such as the *Argonautica* of his contemporary, Apollonius of Rhodes.
His own treatment of myth is often light-hearted, and he apparently felt that
the heroic spirit, and thus serious epic, could no longer be evoked with success.
The precision of language and polish of verse which his age could attain were
best applied to shorter incidents, which could, however, be given loose
connections or set in a narrative framework. Ovid's *Metamorphoses*, Alexandrian in spirit, well illustrates the principle. Although Callimachus greatly

---

[3] P. J. Parsons, 'Callimachus. *Victoria Berenicis*', *Zeitschrift für Papyrologie und Epigraphik*, 25 (1977),
1–50.

[4] Survey by Bulloch, 'Hellenistic poetry', pp. 549–70.

[5] Callimachus, fr. 465, ed. Pfeiffer, from Athenaeus 3.72a.

admired the Homeric poems as the greatest monuments of the past, the works of Hesiod seemed better models for his own times. What Hesiod lacked, and what could now be supplied, was more careful diction and much greater control of imagery and connotation. As the rhetoricians too had come to believe, literature was a reflection of the age in which it was written, and as in rhetoric, appreciation of style was now to be found in the scrutiny of short units, rather than in the sweep of the work as a whole. Vision narrows, but becomes sharper.

Callimachus' views are best summed up in lines preserved from the first book of the *Aitia*:

> Away, Jealousy's destructive brood. Henceforth
> judge poetry by its craft and not the Persian league;
> don't seek from me the thumping song:
> thunder is not my part, that is for Zeus.
> The very first time I put the tablet on my knee
> Apollo said to me, the Lupine god,
> 'Poet, let your sacrifice be fat as you can,
> but your muse, my friend, keep her slim.
> This too I say: where the waggon does not trample
> there you should tread, not by others' common tracks
> nor the broad highway, but on unworn paths –
> no matter that you take a narrower course'.
> Amongst those we sing who love the clear note
> the cicada makes, not the uproar of the ass;
> like the long-eared beast others may bray,
> I would be slight, the winged one.[6]

The passage alludes to the opposition Callimachus provoked from traditionalists; within the Alexandrian circle critical ideas were highly controversial and created personal animosity. Callimachus' stance is one of superiority and élitism. Apollo speaks, and gives authority to Callimachus' views, but this is no longer to be taken as the inspiration experienced by early Greek poets; it is an artful convention, treated with some humour. The chief critical positions advanced are that the themes of the Classic poets are now sterile and should be avoided and that the characteristic excellence of poetry, corresponding to the 'virtue' of style in rhetoric, should be slimness, avoiding epic or inflated language, seeking to be thin (*leptos*), precise, disciplined, not fat, coarse, and gross (*pachus*). The modern age requires dieting. Physiological metaphors are often found in subsequent Greek and Latin discussions of style.[7]

---

[6] Tr. by Bulloch, 'Hellenistic poetry', p. 559.
[7] Quadlbauer, 'Genera dicendi', pp. 65–6.

3 Neoptolemus of Parium

Opposition to Callimachus' views can be seen in the continued writing of epic, as by Apollonius. A middle-of-the-road, more Aristotelian theory of poetry which called for unity, but accepted stylistic polish had a spokesman in Neoptolemus of Parium, probably a contemporary of Callimachus who had been trained as a Peripatetic and came to work in Alexandria. His writings are lost, but can be partially reconstructed by references in Philodemus' *On Poetry* and by the use of them in Horace's *Ars poetica*. According to Porphyrion, a late Latin commentator on Horace, 'not all' but the 'chief' principles of Neoptolemus are found in the *Ars poetica*. There is less than perfect scholarly agreement about what Neoptolemus taught and the extent to which Horace followed him, but three concepts seem to have been central to his theory: *poiēma*, *poiēsis*, and *poiētēs*.[8]

Poiēma in Neoptolemus' theory seems to refer to the technique of writing in verse and may be thought of as corresponding to *lexis* or *hermēneia* in rhetoric; it is poetic diction, composition, and style. The term was also sometimes used to refer to a short context in a longer poem, which is consistent with Callimachus' emphasis on the workmanship of small units of composition and also with the rhetoricians' way of looking at style as separable from, but appropriate to content. But Neoptolemus regarded discussion of *poiēma* as inadequate for a complete poetics and proceeded to discuss as well the more Aristotelian concept of *poiēsis*, which involves content, thought, plot (*hupothesis*), and characters. Thirdly, according to Philodemus, he added 'the person who possesses the art of writing poetry and has the power to do so as a species of the art along with *poiēma* and *poiēsis*'. The discussion of the poet, reminiscent of the rhetoricians' emphasis on the power of the rhetor, may have been influenced by Aristotle's dialogue *On Poets* and may be reflected in Horace's *Ars poetica* (295 – 476), where the poet's equipment, knowledge, and materials are discussed. Fragments preserved by Philodemus, if correctly reconstructed, indicate that Neoptolemus stressed the moral function of poetry: 'It is necessary for the complete poet to benefit the audience in regard to virtue, with enchantment of the soul [*psuchagōgia*] and to speak usefully, and Homer pleases and even more benefits.'[9] *Psuchagōgia* is the word we met in chapter 5, section 3, in Plato's definition of rhetoric and provides some awareness that the reader has a presence in literature. We seem to have here, developed out of Aristotle and given classic statement in Horace (*AP* 343), the nucleus of what became the orthodox view of later times that the poet should both please and edify. Its analogy in rhetoric is the Ciceronian doctrine (*De or.* 2.115; *Orator* 69), developed out of Aristotle's argument, ethos, and pathos, that the orator should teach, charm, and move.

[8] Brink, *Horace*, I, pp. 43–150.
[9] P. 33 Jensen; cf. Pfeiffer, *Scholarship*, p. 166.

4 The Peripatetics and biographical criticism

Aristotle's interest in the historical development of poetry and in the solution of critical problems (as in *Poetics* 25) was carried on by his successors in the Peripatetic School, including Theophrastus, Heraclides Ponticus, Aristoxenus (best known for his work on music), Dicaearchus, Chamaeleon, Praxiphanes, and others.[10] A distinguishing characteristic of Peripatetic criticism was its interest in biographical information about poets. Callimachus' *Pinakes*, of course, provided biographical notes, but Peripatetic interest in moral character encouraged an unprecedented interest in biography, and the works of authors were read as sources of information about their lives, personalities, and interests.[11] Some of this material was then used by later commentators and critics to explain passages in their works. The process becomes a circular one in that, though the Peripatetic biographers utilised external evidence where available, they had little to go on and quarried the texts for hints, the more startling the better. Biography became a product of rhetorical amplification, intended to entertain the reader. The best preserved Hellenistic example is the papyrus fragment of the 'Life' of Euripides by Satyrus, written in third-century Alexandria.[12] Out of the imagery of the sea in Euripidean lyrics and the tradition of the poet as a misanthrope, Satyrus constructs a story that Euripides lived alone in a cave by the sea; out of the death of Pentheus, torn apart by women in *Bacchae*, comes the story that Euripides was attacked by hunting dogs.[13] Once they gained currency, the stories could be used to explain the texts.

5 Alexandrian philology

A picture of the literary scholarship of the Museum and Library can be given by summarising briefly some of what is known about the work of four of the greatest Alexandrian scholars who worked there: Zenodotus, Eratosthenes, Aristophanes of Byzantium, and Aristarchus. Their research, and that of other scholars, is known to us chiefly from excerpts and citations found in Byzantine scholia and commentaries, such as that on the Homeric poems by Eustathius in the twelfth century. All four approached literary texts as aesthetic experiences to be enjoyed; they show little interest in moralising or allegorising, and their one concern was with the integrity of the text.

Zenodotus of Ephesus became the first head librarian about 284 BC. His edition of the *Iliad* and *Odyssey*, as well as recensions of Hesiod's *Theogony* and of works by Anacreon and Pindar, were the first efforts to recover an

---

[10] For a survey, see Podlecki, 'Peripatetics', pp. 114–37.

[11] Momigliano, *Greek Biography*, pp. 65–84.

[12] Ed., with Italian tr., Graziano Arrighetti, *Vita di Euripide* (Pisa, 1964).

[13] Lefkowitz, 'Euripides', pp. 195–6.

authoritative text. When he came to a line in the Homeric poems which he suspected to be spurious, he left it in the text for the reader's information, but 'athetised', or rejected its genuineness by marking in the margin a horizontal line (*obelos*). Since he wrote no commentary, he gave no reasons for his editorial decisions. They seem to have been based primarily on readings he found or did not find in what he regarded as the oldest and best manuscripts, sometimes influenced by his study of word usage, for he also compiled an alphabetic *Homeric Glossary*. Though he did not set forth a theory of textual criticism, Zenodotus may be said to be the father of that sub-discipline of literary research. Similar work was begun about the same time on the tragic poets by Alexander the Aetolian and on comedy by Lycophron.

Zenodotus' successor as head librarian was the poet Apollonius of Rhodes. Little is known about his scholarly work and his theory of literature must be inferred from his epic poem, *Argonautica*. It attempts the heroic spirit, but also shows Alexandrian attention to diction and develops the love story of Jason and Medea with psychological insight. Apollonius' successor (*c.* 245 BC) was Eratosthenes of Cyrene. Though the first to call himself a *philologus* (Suetonius, *De grammaticis* 10), and said to have written a treatise on comedy, his major work was in mathematics and geography, where he calculated with consider-able accuracy the circumference of the earth and the distance of the sun. But his *Geographia* also discussed Homeric geography and in the process rebuked those who thought that Homer intended to teach geography, theology, ethics, or anything else. The wanderings of Odysseus, he thought, were purely imaginary, and the aim of the poet was to give pleasure to an audience. 'Every poet', he said (Strabo 1.15), 'aims at *psuchagōgia*, not at teaching.' *Psuchagōgia* in contrast to teaching clearly means 'enchantment', an elevated form of entertainment. Neoptolemus' use of the term in the passage quoted earlier suggests that he may have been responding to his contemporary Eratosthenes, insisting on entertainment as subordinate to instruction.[14]

Aristophanes of Byzantium became head librarian around 200 BC and continued editorial work on epic, lyric, and dramatic poetry. He further developed the system of marginal signs, adding for example the asterisk to denote a line repeated from another context in which it seemed more appro-priate, he was perhaps the first to give systematic attention to punctuation, and he began the custom of marking the accent on Greek words, an effort to preserve the original sound of the verses despite changes in pronunciation in contemporary language. Until Aristophanes' time lyric poetry was written continuously, like prose; he first divided it into metrical *cola*. Like Zenodotus, he was a conservative editor, but his judgements were more influenced by study of the use of words. For example, Zenodotus had athetised the fourth and fifth lines of the *Iliad*, presumably because they were lacking in some early

---

[14] Pfeiffer, *Scholarship*, p. 166.

texts, realising that the syntax led easily from line three to line six. Aristophanes marked the lines as questioned by Zenodotus, but as genuine, and emended the word *daitos*, 'food', in line five to *pasi*, 'all', on the ground that *dais* in Homeric Greek is a shared, human meal, not appropriately used of animal food, which the context demands. He marked *Odyssey* 23.296 as the *telos*, or 'end', of the poem; we do not know why. Perhaps he felt that the poetic power of the work fell off at that point.[15] Although he did not write commentaries on the texts, he composed monographs on literary subjects, collected proverbs, and provided *hypotheses*, or simple introductions to tragedies and comedies. These, the ancestors of hypotheses in our manuscripts and modern printed texts, outlined the plot, identified other treatments of the story, and gave some information on the initial production of the play. He also compiled an important lexicographical work which identified earlier and later meanings of words, classified words on the basis of subject signified, and for the first time conceptualised the inflexion of Greek nouns and verbs, seeking general rules of morphology on the basis of analogy. This was subsequently attacked by the Stoic Chrysippus, who claimed that words are not in harmony with the things they express and that grammatical usage is dominated by anomaly. The analogy-anomaly debate long continued; we will return to it in chapter 7, section 6 below.

Although Aristophanes' studies were devoted to the Classical writers of the past, he was an admirer of the New Comedy of Menander, summed up in the epigram 'O Menander, O Life, which of you imitated the other?'[16] This paradox reflects a Peripatetic view of comedy as imitation of real life; that there is a sense in which life can be said to imitate art is probably a modern conceit. Aristophanes is also the first critic known to have concerned himself with plagiarism, for he 'gently rebuked' Menander's borrowings from other poets and drew up a list of them.[17]

Aristophanes and his successor, Aristarchus, established literary canons as understood throughout the rest of antiquity and still influential today. The Homeric poems had long enjoyed pre-eminence in epic, and by the end of the fifth century, as seen in Aristophanes' *Frogs*, Aeschylus, Sophocles, and Euripides were already recognised as the greatest of the tragedians. Aristophanes of Byzantium and Aristarchus now gave canonical status to three early iambic poets, led by Archilochus, and nine lyric poets, led by Pindar, establishing them as classics to be read in schools. No contemporary writers were included in their lists. Their feelings that the greatest literary works were creations of the past, and their willingness to judge what was best, what not quite so good, made of the critic the authoritative arbiter of quality as well as the judge of the authenticity of texts. In so doing, they defined the corpus

---

[15] Pfeiffer, *Scholarship*, pp. 175–7.
[16] Syrianus, *On Hermogenes*, ed. Rabe, II, p. 23; Pfeiffer, *Scholarship*, p. 190.
[17] Pfeiffer, *Scholarship*, p. 191.

of literature. Roman, Renaissance, and modern successors have only too
willingly followed their lead. The best ancient picture of the results is the
survey of literary genres, Greek and Latin, author by author, in the first
chapter of Book X of Quintilian's *Institutio oratoria*, which includes references
to the judgements of Aristophanes and Archilochus. Their canons were
apparently limited to poetry; the rhetoricians at some later time extended the
process to include prose as seen in the canon of the 'Ten Attic Orators', of
whom Demosthenes emerged as pre-eminent. Canonisation of books of the
Bible, though based on a judgement of religious authenticity rather than
literary quality, may perhaps be thought of as an analogous process. Until
very recent times teachers of literature, like their Hellenistic predecessors,
have tended to exclude contemporary works from the curriculum, though they
have added a rationale not stated in Alexandria, that survival over time is
a criterion of literary excellence.

Aristarchus of Samothrace succeeded Aristophanes as head of the library
about 153 BC and earned the reputation as *grammatikōtatos*, the greatest of the
students of literature (Athenaeus 15.671). His textual criticisms and editing
of the poets reached new heights of science; like Aristophanes he composed
monographs on literary problems and most important of all, he began the
writing of running commentaries. According to the Byzantine encyclopedia
Suda, these amounted to more than 800 books. Large excerpts from his
commentary on the *Iliad* are included in the great Venetian codex 454 of the
tenth century. These illustrate the critical principle that each author is his own
best interpreter, which has often been attributed to him, though it was perhaps
first stated in so many words by Porphyry 400 years later.[18] It is descriptive
of his method in that he carefully examined parallel passages to determine
the poet's usage and thought. To a greater extent than many ancient critics
he kept in mind the composition of the poem as a whole, he emphasised the
relationship of speech to character, explained the function of metaphors and
similes, and, though his admiration of the text is often evident, he sometimes
criticised passages as inappropriate or overwritten. Among his other commentaries was one on Herodotus, the first scholarly treatment of a prose
author.

Hellenistic scholars sought to understand the language and society of the
heroic period, but they do not seem aware that the *Iliad* and *Odyssey* stand at
the end of a long tradition of oral composition. They viewed inconsistencies
in the texts as largely the result of interpolation by later rhapsodes or scribes,
and they believed in Homer as the poet of genius who composed the works.
A partial exception are *hoi khorizontes*, the 'Separatists', who anticipated some
modern philologists in claiming that the two Homeric poems were the work
of two separate poets. One such separatist was Xenon, against whose

---

[18] Pfeiffer, *Scholarship*, p. 226.

'paradox' Aristarchus wrote a monograph. The question was later taken up by Longinus, who suggested (9.11–14) that differences between the two poems could be resolved by regarding the *Iliad* as the work of the poet's youth, the *Odyssey* of his old age.

One of the last of the succession of Hellenistic scholars was Didymus 'the Brazen-Bowelled' (*c.* 80–10 BC), said to have written as many as 4,000 works which were largely compilations of the critical and exegetical writings of his predecessors. Medieval Greek scholia to Pindar and the dramatists are probably derived from his work. A papyrus fragment of his commentary, largely historical, on Demosthenes' *Philippics* is a unique example of the method of an Alexandrian scholar in its original form.[19] In Latin, the only example of the commentary form surviving from the Classical period is the valuable discussion of the historical background and allusions in five orations of Cicero, written by Asconius Pedianus about AD 55.

The methods of the Alexandrian critics made an eventual contribution to biblical studies. According to later tradition, the Septuagint, the Greek translation of the Old Testament, was made in the Alexandrian Library by seventy-two scholars brought there from Jerusalem at the request of Ptolemy II.[20] Biblical commentators of the imperial period adopted some techniques of Alexandrian scholarship, such as the citation of parallel passages to determine meaning. Allegorical interpretation, which became characteristic of neo-Platonic and of Alexandrian Christian exegesis, has, however, a different antecedent. It represents a continuation of a method developed primarily at the school and library in Pergamum, Alexandria's rival in the second and first centuries BC. Some allegorical interpretation of the Homeric poems can be found as early as the sixth or fifth centuries, as noted in chapter 2, section 3 above. It was regularly inspired by a desire to see in a text some particular philosophical doctrine or the religious views of Orphism. Neither Plato nor Aristotle encouraged it, but the Stoics of the Hellenistic period found it a convenient way to teach their view of nature and life. Probably the most important of the Stoic allegorists was Crates of Mallos, who was working in Pergamum at the same time as Aristarchus in Alexandria. His treatment included an interpretation of the Shield of Achilles in *Iliad* XVIII in which its ten parts represent the ten circles of the sky.[21] Allegory required seeing passages in poetry as figurative and coincided with Stoic grammatical interests in identifying figures of speech.[22] Among those basic for allegorical interpretation were *catechresis*, where a term is used to name something that has no proper name of its own, *metalepsis*, where a non-synonymous word

---

[19] Ed. Hermann Diels and Wilhelm Schubert, *Didymus Kommentar zu Demosthenes* (Berlin, 1904).

[20] Sources in Pfeiffer, *Scholarship*, pp. 100–1.

[21] Pfeiffer, *Scholarship*, p. 240.

[22] Barwick, 'Stoische Sprachlehre', pp. 88–111.

implies a middle term giving it contextual meaning, and especially *emphasis*, defined as a figure by which words imply more than their literal meaning.

As one looks back over the great achievements of Hellenistic literary scholarship, not equalled until the philologists of the nineteenth century, it is difficult not to escape the conclusion that the factors which most made it possible were the existence of great libraries and the provision of support for scholars, resulting in a professional commitment to preserving, under-standing, and transmitting texts, and largely protected from political or religious ideology. It should also be remembered that the fourth-century philosophers, Aristotle and Theophrastus in particular, had laid the foundation for logical method in objective research applicable to a wide variety of phenomena, including literary studies. The philosophical schools continued to provide an environment for literary criticism, but in the case of the Stoics and Epicureans conditioned by doctrinaire assumptions about language, meaning, and the nature of Being.

6 The criticism of the Stoics

Stoicism, as formulated by Zeno and Cleanthes at the end of the fourth century BC, continued by Chrysippus, Diogenes of Babylon, Panaetius, and Posidonius down into the first century, and later expounded by Seneca, Epictetus, and others, was probably the most popular philosophical movement of the Hellenistic and early imperial period, and it made a number of contributions to literary criticism.[23] The best known are the development of grammatical theory, including the doctrine of anomaly, and the use of allegorical interpretation. Less well known, but of some importance for the view of literature is that part of Stoic epistemology and logic which dealt with *phantasia*, or the 'presentation' of images to the mind of a thinker or writer and through a text to a reader. Stoic theory here owed some debt to Aristotle's discussion of psychology in the third book of *De anima* and that in turn to concepts in Plato's *Philebus* and *Timaeus*.[24]

In his dialogue on epistemology, *Academics* (1.40–1), Cicero attributes to Zeno of Citium (335–263 BC) the theory that sensation results from the combination of an impact offered to the mind from some outside source and a mental assent, recognising the validity of the presentation. One is reminded of early Greek views of omens as discussed in chapter 2, section 1 above. Mental assent is a voluntary act, residing within us, which can be given or withheld. The impact is a 'presentation' (*phantasia*; Latin *visum*), but all presentations are not valid, only those that have clarity of manifestation (*enargeia*; *declaratio*) peculiar to themselves and which thus permit *katalēpsis*

[23] DeLacy, 'Stoic views', pp. 259–61.
[24] Imbert, 'Stoic logic', pp. 182–216; Eden, *Poetic and Legal Fiction*, pp. 67–111.

(*comprehensio*), a 'grasping' of the image. Although the Stoics generally held to a view of art as imitation, their theory eventually provided an alternative to the Platonic and Aristotelian theories of imitation. According to Philostratus (*Life of Apollonius of Tyana* 6.19), speaking of works of art by Pheidias and Praxiteles, '*phantasia* wrought these works, a wiser and subtler art by far than imitation; for imitation can only create as its handiwork what it has seen, but *phantasia* equally creates what it has not seen; for it will conceive of its ideal with reference to the reality, and imitation is often baffled by terror, but imagination by nothing'. An example of how this process worked, transmitted from Stoic sources, is the story of the painter Zeuxis' creation of an ideal portrait of Helen of Troy based on an imaginative combination of the best features of five young women of Croton (Cicero, *De inventione* 2.1–3). All the sciences, arts, and crafts were regarded by the Stoics as demonstrating the same principle, 'for what can be accomplished by art unless he who practises art has perceived much?' (*Academics* 2.22).

Also attributed to Zeno (Diog. Laert. 7.49) is the statement '*phantasia* comes first, then thought, "being capable of talk" [*eklalētikē*], expresses in speech what it experiences from *phantasia*'. The Stoics added brevity to the four Peripatetic virtues of style (Diog. Laert. 7.59), and their professional writing was often notorious for its lack of literary quality, but Zeno's successor Cleanthes was an exception, as seen in his *Hymn to Zeus*, which both visualises the god and celebrates his rule, and he is said (Cicero, *De finibus* 2.69) sometimes to have begun his lectures with a picture drawn in words. The most specific application of *phantasia* to writing is in ecphrasis, a literary description of a work of art, object, or place, which was a common motif in Hellenistic and later literature and was practised as an exercise in the grammar schools, as noted in chapter 5, section 7 above. Emphasis is regularly put on the action which is going on in the picture, and the speaker often loses his identity and becomes an interpreter to an audience, as does the goatherd in describing a cup in the first *Idyll* of Theocritus, but Roman examples are sometimes more subjective, as is Aeneas' description of the reliefs on the temple at Carthage in the *Aeneid* (1.453–93). A visual presentation can be made the basis of an entire work, as seen in Longus' novel *Daphnis and Chloe*.[25] The concept of *phantasia* became a part of the rhetorical and critical vocabulary of Greek and Latin.[26]

The Stoics accepted the view of Cratylus in Plato's dialogue that names exist by nature and that sound imitates things.[27] In contrast to the Alexandrian scholars, their interest in etymology was not an historical interest in the usage of words, but a philosophical interest in meaning, related to their physics and ethics. Posidonius (*c.* 135–50 BC) defined *poiēma* as 'diction [*lexis*]

---

[25] Imbert, 'Stoic logic', pp. 198–209.
[26] E.g., Quintilian 6.2.29, 8.3.88, 10.7.15; Longinus 15.1.
[27] DeLacy, 'Stoic views', pp. 256–8.

that is metrical and rhythmical with ornamentation going beyond prose' and *poiēsis* as 'significant poetic diction' (Diog. Laert. 7.60). A poem as a whole imitates life, and the words, actions, and characters must be appropriate to real life. But as applied in allegorical interpretation this imitation may be symbolic, not literal. There was some difference of opinion among Stoics about the basis of criticism. Zeno's pupil Aristo and his followers seem to have placed the criterion for good poetry primarily in the ear, stressing the need for euphony, whereas Crates and others took a more rationalising view, emphasising contents and philosophical interpretation.[28] The Platonic expulsion of the poets reappears in Chrysippus in the form of ordaining that citizens of an ideal state will do nothing for the sake of pleasure (Plutarch, *Stoic Self-Contradictions* 1044b).

Much of what is known about Hellenistic philosophy comes from Cicero. Out of many passages of interest, two may be cited here as examples of Stoic criticism. In *De oratore* (1.225–6) Antonius, making use of Stoic values, criticises an emotional outburst in a speech by his friend Crassus: 'Snatch us from miseries, snatch us from the jaws of those whose cruelty cannot be filled except by blood; do not allow us to be the slaves [*servire*] to anyone except to all of you' (i.e., the Republic). The term 'miseries' is objectionable, Antonius says, for a brave man cannot admit to them; the term 'jaws' and the context with it is equally objectionable, for this cannot befall a wise man (*sapiens*, the Stoic 'sage'), but worst of all is *servire*; how can Crassus dare to say not only that he but that the senate is a 'slave'? One influence of Stoicism was thus to censure shrillness in rhetoric, strong metaphor, and emotional appeal, and this attitude was consistent with traditional, if unphilosophical, Roman ideals of virtue and decorum. The classic models were Socrates in the *Apology* and the Roman Rutilius Rufus, convicted on an unjust charge because he refused to make emotional appeal to his jury (1.227).

In *De natura deorum* Cicero presents a discussion of the nature of the gods between the Epicurean Velleius, the Stoic Balbus, and the Academic Cotta. Balbus' remarks (2.60–71) provide a summary of Stoic interpretation of myth and poetry. The name of a god may be metonymy for a thing that comes from the god, as Ceres for grain. Or virtues, forces, and emotions may be deified ('Faith', 'Concord', 'Desire'), or a human benefactor like Hercules may be deemed a god. Myths may represent scientific facts: Saturn devouring his sons means that time eats up the years. Here etymology is useful, since Kronos, the Greek name of Saturn, is taken as related to *khronos*, 'time'. In conclusion, Balbus rejects the literal interpretation of myth in favour of symbolic meaning. The doctrine that pagan gods were men, deified by their human admirers, is called Euhemerism and had originated in a fictitious travelogue entitled *Sacred Scripture* written by Euhemerus of Messine around 300 BC. Cotta's reply

[28] DeLacy, 'Stoic views', pp. 252–6.

(3.38–64) is sceptical, as one would expect from the Hellenistic Academy. His main points are that the myths cannot be worked out to give consistent meaning, and thus the interpretations are always arbitrary and imposed by the Stoics from their other beliefs. The deification of abstractions is to him only a figure of speech (3.41). Between these two views there is no real possibility of reconciliation or compromise unless the text itself contains a key or unless it can be endowed with some authoritative status as divine revelation rather than the product of human art.

The eclectic Jewish philosopher Philo of Alexandria (*c.* 20 BC – AD 40) was strongly influenced by Stoic thought and by Platonism. His extensive surviving writings occasionally touch on questions of literary criticism and interpretation. Some of what he says has relevance for the discussion of Longinus in chapter 10, section 3 below; for example, he uses the term *hupsōs* ('sublimity') and applies its cognates to utterances of Moses and Jehovah.[29] Philo believed that every word of the Old Testament, which he read in the Septuagint Greek translation, was divinely inspired, but he also believed it to be a divine allegory of the human soul and its relation to God. His writings are the earliest extended allegorical interpretations in Greek, and provided some model for later Christian hermeneutics. In most cases Philo accepts a literal meaning in the text and adds an allegorical, figurative meaning as well (cf. *Legum allegoria* 2.14), but sometimes he regards a literal meaning as impossible.[30] The degree to which he is willing to go in freedom of interpretation is seen in his claim that creation cannot have taken place in six natural days (1.2) and in his description of the story that Eve was born from Adam's rib as 'mythical' (*muthōdes*, 21.9). He claims in his interpretation to follow 'the chain of logical sequence, which does not admit of stumbling but easily removes any obstruction and thus allows the argument to march to its conclusion with unfaltering steps' (*De confusione linguarum* 14). Drawing on the Stoic theory of *phantasia* he speaks of the biblical accounts as 'modes of making ideas visible' so that he resorts to allegorical interpretation to find 'what lies beneath the surface' (*De creatione* 154–7).

Great interest attaches to a passage in Philo's *De plantatione* (156–9), which seems to have some relationship to the *topos* of the decline of eloquence, which we will meet in Seneca the Elder, Petronius, Tacitus, Quintilian, and Longinus. It indicates that interest in the subject already existed among Greeks in Alexandria in Philo's time. Men of the present day, Philo claims, do not resemble men of the past, either in language or in action. They have substituted sickly speech for a sound style, full of the vitality of an athlete's frame. The passage continues with the medical or physiological metaphor and introduces as well the theme of masculinity vs. effeminacy. Philo is apparently

---

[29] Russell, in his edition of Longinus, pp. xi–xli.
[30] Rollinson, *Allegory*, pp. 8–9.

thinking of Asianism, criticised by Dionysius of Halicarnassus in Rome slightly earlier (see chapter 8, section 3 below). He concludes:

Consequently, in their times poets and prose writers flourished and all those who were seriously devoted to other aspects of literature, and they did not at once charm and enervate men's ears by the rhythm of their language, but they revived any faculty of the mind that had broken down and lost its tone, and every true note of it they kept in tune with the instruments of nature and of virtue. But in our days chefs and confectioners flourish, and experts in making dyes and concocting unguents. These are ever aiming at sacking the citadel of the mind, by bringing to bear upon the senses some novelty in shade of colour or shape of dress or perfume or savoury dish.[31]

The analogy to cookery is surely ultimately derived from Socrates' discussion with Polus in Plato's *Gorgias*, as discussed in chapter 5, section 3 above.

7 Epicurean language theory

Stoic doctrine on most subjects was questioned by followers of the Academic School and by Epicureans. Epicurus himself (342 – 270 BC) had little interest in literature, but he did outline a theory of language (*Letter to Herodotus* 75 – 6). Names, he thought, were not deliberately given to things, but originated in the feelings and impressions of human beings in different places and thus in different languages. Meanings were later made more specific by common consent and convention, and additional words were created by reasoning in accordance with the prevailing mode of expression.

This position was somewhat developed by Epicurus' successors who saw poetry as combining the emotional value of words with cognitive values developed in society.[32] They generally scorned rhetoric as a misapplication of poetic devices to prose, but in the first century BC some changes in attitude are evident. The poetics and rhetoric of the Epicurean Philodemus will be discussed below. About the same time the Latin poet Lucretius composed his great philosophical epic, *On the Nature of Things*. His account of the origin of language (5.1028 – 90) follows Epicurus, but modern scholars have noted an interesting application of Epicurean atomic physics to language in Lucretius' use of puns. He points out (1.901 – 20) that just as physical objects contain atoms arranged in different ways, so words contain elements, sounds, or letters, arranged differently. Atoms of fire are contained in wood, and the elements of the Latin word *ignis*, 'fire', are in the same way contained within *lignum*, 'wood'. This natural principle is applied in a significant word-play throughout the poem, creating what has been called an 'atomistic' poetics.[33]

---

[31] Tr. Colson and Whitaker, *Philo*, III, p. 395.
[32] DeLacy, 'Epicurean language', pp. 85 – 92.
[33] Friedlander, 'Patterns of sound', pp. 16 – 34; Snyder, *Puns*.

8 Philodemus

Philodemus was born in Gadara *c*. 110 BC but lived in Italy from *c*. 75 to *c*. 40 BC. He had a Roman patron, Lucius Calpurnius Piso, and instructed young Romans, among them Virgil and Virgil's friends Varius and Quintilius,[34] in Epicurean philosophy. His literary criticism is, however, written within and for the Greek scholarly world. It is appropriate that he seems to have lived mostly in Campania near Naples, then still a Greek city and a centre for Epicureans.[35]

Philodemus is peculiarly difficult to interpret. Papyri of his works, including treatises *On Poems* and *On Rhetoric*, have been partly recovered from the lava of Herculaneum, excavated from what seems his own personal library. They are charred, brittle, and often fragmentary; some have now since disappeared and survive only in copies. In both works there is the further problem that Philodemus does not primarily expound his own views, but follows a method of argumentation traditional in Epicurean polemic, quoting extensively the views of opponents, then turning their arguments against them in a refutation which can ignore the original context and supporting premises. This makes him a valuable source for otherwise obscure Hellenistic critics; for example Book V of *On Poems* attacks successively Neoptolemus and the Stoics Ariston and Crates; but it is hard to get a coherent picture of Philodemus' own theories. The result does, however, suggest a critic of a sensitivity and originality which is unexpected in an Epicurean, though his link with Siro and the debt he acknowledges to his teacher Zeno of Sidon suggest he was not unique.

On Poems, to Gnaeus, was in at least five books, of which we have part of Book IV, much of Book V, and substantial other pieces. Some of the untitled fragments on poetry may come from a different work. A collected edition is urgently needed to give easier access to what is Philodemus' most original and stimulating work. He is, for example, somewhat unusual among critics of his time in asserting that poetry is morally neutral, in itself not exemplary or didactic but intended for pleasure. Any usefulness is incidental, and morally beneficial passages are not as such superior (pp. 5–11, 33–7 Jensen). Allegorising of 'immoral' passages is misplaced effort, and he ridicules Stoic interpretations of Homer, where for example Achilles is the sun, Hector the moon (II, p. 225 Sbordone). Similarly the poet does not need expert knowledge of all he presents; Homer for example need not know geography (pp. 11–13 Jensen): this is reminiscent of the view of Eratosthenes discussed above, but contrast the Augustan geographer, Strabo, who describes Homer as the first expert in geography (1.1.2).[36] Again the obvious targets are the

---

[34] But not Horace; see F. Della Corte, 'Vario e Tucca in Filodemo', *Aegyptus*, 49 (1969), 85–8.
[35] On Philodemus and Piso see Cicero, *In Pisonem*, ed. R. G. M. Nisbet (Oxford, 1961), pp. 183–6. Rawson, *Intellectual Life*, pp. 22–4.
[36] See Schenkeveld, 'Strabo on Homer', pp. 52–64.

Stoics. Nor need poetry represent real life. Truth and fiction are equally valid, the criterion is aesthetic, the poetic handling (p. 21 Jensen). Fiction includes the fabulous, *alogos muthos*: much of Philodemus' theory of poetry will fit his theory of prose, but he here recognises the poet's imaginative power, a quality which may well be specific to poetry.

In what is perhaps his greatest claim to originality, Philodemus argues that style and content are inseparable (e.g., pp. 27ff. Jensen). A poem must be judged as a whole and we cannot judge specific aspects in isolation. There is sharp antithesis of form and content in Hellenistic criticism, and even when the need for their combination is recognised, they are formally analysed under separate categories, with style an adornment or dress which will be chosen to suit the content. But for Philodemus change of form, even of single words, will change the subject. It is therefore wrong in his view to isolate and demand any single quality such as brevity or grandeur, since you must look at the whole (pp. 13ff. Jensen). What is essential is knowledge of poetry's general principles and goals (*skopoi*), the style should imitate that of simple exposition, the thought should avoid the extremes of the erudite and the uneducated (p. 53 Jensen), and the poet will choose his theme carefully (p. 21 Jensen).

Philodemus' theory of organic unity also underpins his isolation of what is unique to a poet, *idion*, from what he shares with other poets, *koinon*. It is irrelevant whether the theme is new or borrowed from another, like the stories of Troy and Thebes. When Sophocles and Euripides take the same myth, each produces a unique treatment; poets are not to be judged better or worse from priority of theme, and later poets are often better than their predecessors (II, pp. 205 – 9 Sbordone). Homer and other early poets are recognised as good poets (p. 41 Jensen), but it is not enough to imitate a predecessor or to equate good poetry with the poetry of any specific model. On that basis we cannot explain how Homer and others are good, since they did not imitate themselves (pp. 67 – 9 Jensen). In any case, no poet is consistently good, even in a single genre (p. 75 Jensen).

Genres also have individuality, as he argues in Book IV, where he attacks an early Peripatetic view of *mimēsis*. This, he claims, does not discuss tragedy and epic as such, but only elements which epic shares with tragedy. But tragedy scarcely has some of the subjects of epic, such as natural philosophy, tragic narrative is not confined to messenger speeches and disjunct from action, *to praktikon*, epic is not always narrative, and epic narrative is richer and intrinsically different from tragic narrative. Philodemus also criticised Peripatetic theories of *katharsis*, as seen in a fragment of Book V.[37]

Word-arrangement is the subject of much polemic, as Philodemus attacks those who hold that originality lies not in the thought or words but in

---

[37] See C. O. Brink, 'Philodemus, *Peri poiēmatōn*, Book IV', *Maia*, 24 (1972), 342–4; cf. M. B. Nardelli, 'La catarsi poetica nel *P. Herc.* 1581', *Cronache Ercolanesi*, 8 (1978), pp. 96–103.

word-arrangement (pp. 31 – 49 Jensen; II, pp. 245 – 65 Sbordone). He agrees with them that poetry is properly judged on the aesthetic ground of *psuchagōgia*, and that bad arrangement entails a bad poem, but for him good arrangement cannot alone produce a good poem – unless we redefine arrangement to mean the whole poem in its fusion of all aspects. He similarly attacks metathesis, a standard method of criticism, favoured for example by Dionysius, where a critic redrafts a passage to prove a point, usually the superiority of the original.[38] But for Philodemus arrangement cannot be isolated in this way, since the rearrangement changes the subject. So too an otherwise unknown group he calls 'the critics'[39] wrongly asserts that euphony is the sole essential, to the lengths of asserting that only the practised ear can judge poetry. But euphony cannot be isolated, poetry is an art, to be evaluated by reason, *logos*, and in any case there are no absolute criteria, no naturally beautiful or ugly words. It is nonsensical to say 'either that the same sounds or that different sounds please or annoy', and he lengthily attacks an opponent called 'the Milesian', who distinguished three types of combination: smooth, harsh, and compact or harmonious. These are combinations of letters, not words, e.g., successive long vowels give smoothness, and many consonants, especially r, s, z and x, give harshness, but they are parallel to and suggest the tradition behind the three types of word-arrangement in Dionysius, *On Composition* (21 – 4).

Philodemus' own surviving poems in the *Greek Anthology* are elegant trifles, fitting his theory of poetry. His Epicurean orthodoxy on the uselessness of poetry might seem questioned by *On the Good King According to Homer*[40] where he offers his patron Piso examples from Homer to illustrate desirable behaviour in rulers. Such use of poetry is familiar, especially among the Stoics, but contrast what Philodemus says elsewhere (*Rhetoric* I, p. 262 Sudhaus): 'Why should a philosopher heed Euripides, especially since he cites no proof and the philosopher does?' It would seem that in this popularising work Philodemus is not offering literary criticism of Homer's purpose, but exploits passages where Homer is incidentally beneficial as a convenient framework to give, as he says at the end, 'starting-points [*aphormai*] which can be taken from Homer for instruction in rulership'.

On Rhetoric was written in Italy to a young Gaius (I, p. 223 Sudhaus), perhaps as early as the 70s BC. It partly restates Philodemus' earlier *Hypomnē-matikon*, much of which survives (II, pp. 196 – 303 Sudhaus). Since that earlier work circulated anonymously and was misattributed to Zeno, its views were probably shared by Zeno, including, explicitly and tantalisingly, the most

---

[38] Greenberg, 'Metathesis', pp. 262 – 70; cf. e.g., Demetrius 45 – 6; Cic., *Orator* 214 – 15; Longinus 39.

[39] See Schenkeveld, '*Hoi kritikoi*', pp. 176 – 214.

[40] Oswyn Murray, 'Philodemus on the Good King according to Homer', *JRS*, 55 (1965), 161 – 82.

original theory, on the status of what Philodemus calls 'sophistic' oratory: epideictic oratory or display speeches. For under the hackneyed topic whether rhetoric is an art (*tekhnē*), the subject of Books I and II of *On Rhetoric*, Philodemus argues that although forensic and political oratory depend on guesswork, sophistic oratory is an art, since, like poetry and medicine, even if it is not an exact science, it is largely subject to rules 'conjecturally' (*stokhastikōs*). This theory is clearly heterodox, though he and Zeno captiously and unconvincingly attribute it to Epicurus and Metrodorus against criticism from other Epicureans (I, p. 12 and especially pp. 77ff.). Apart from Book IV, which has an analysis of style, much of the rest is both traditional and Epicurean. Book III is lost, but argued that the schools of the sophists do not produce statesmen and are often harmful; Book V contrasts the unfortunate rhetor and the fortunate philosopher; Book VI attacks the schools of philosophy which support the teaching of rhetoric, and what may be Book VII attacks Stoics and Aristotle, ending with another comparison of rhetoric and philosophy.

The sophistic art is the art of beautiful speech, a 'useless' art, which, like poetry, aims to give pleasure from its beauty. Ethics and politics are irrelevant, and the good man and the good (sophistic) orator are to be judged by different criteria. The 'good' grammarian or musician can be a villain (II, p. 75), just as Isocrates, Philodemus' principal literary model, can write a *Busiris* or *Helen* as well as *Panegyricus* and *Panathenaicus* (I, p. 127, cf. 216ff.). This theory may well derive from his view of poetry (also music), and it contrasts the usual search to reconcile oratory and morality, seen for example in Cicero's slightly later *De oratore*. Moreover, although Philodemus is concerned only with oratory, the theory has the potential to suggest a new category of autonomous literary prose.

The art of sophistic oratory concerns 'display speeches which orators make and the arrangement of words which they write or improvise' (I, pp. 122–3), and like the doctor or pilot, the prose-artist may not always succeed but will fail less often than the layman (I, pp. 27–8). It is less clear what kinds of knowledge justify his status as an artist from 'the observation of shared principles which apply to the majority of cases' (I, p. 69), but he will know when and how to use standard topics for eulogy and invective (I, p. 213), psychology in terms of suitable *ēthē* and *pathē* (I, pp. 193, 199–200, 370), and especially stylistics, such as knowledge of the meaning of words (e.g., II, p. 192; I, pp. 159–60). He will use a naturally beautiful style, close to the use of words in their proper meaning (I, p. 149), just as his gestures and voice will reflect the natural expression of emotions (I, p. 196). It will be the style of the philosopher, not the orator or sophist, nor the specific style of any individual model, whether Isocrates, Demosthenes, or Thucydides. This naturally beautiful style will be clear, avoiding obscurity whether it is unintentional from ignorance of grammar and subject or intentional to hide lack of content;

it will also be appropriate, and although the tropes and figures of what he calls the artificial style are sometimes suitable, speech is satisfactorily moulded in accordance with vulgar speech (I, pp. 148–164). Philodemus knows of a theory of four styles,[41] which we can contrast with the styles in Demetrius, *Ad Herennium*, and Cicero, and more dubiously a list of virtues moving beyond the four in Theophrastus towards the elaborations which we find fully developed in Dionysius,[42] but he clearly prefers a simple style, similar to the usage of ordinary speech and avoiding stylistic luxuriance.

Editor's comment

During the period from 323 to 30 BC there developed a variety of ways of looking at language and literature and a variety of institutional settings in which criticism was practised. The approach to literature became much more technical and was accompanied by a proliferation of technical terminology, some of which is still in use today. Teachers of grammar and rhetoric concentrated on describing the stylistic phenomena of Classical texts and encouraging their imitation, but there was some increased articulation between views of the nature of language and the composition or interpretation of literature. The ancient quarrel between poetry and philosophy continued, chiefly in the difference between those who saw the primary function of poetry as entertainment, pleasure, or enchantment, and those who saw it as a vehicle of philosophical thought. Meanwhile a second language, Latin, was beginning to develop a literature of its own, largely by imitation of Greek models, and for the first time opened up some critical questions of a comparative nature.

[41] *Rhetorica*, I, p. 165 Sudhaus: grand, plain, middle (read *mesotēta*), and elegant.
[42] Gaines, 'Qualities'.

7

THE GROWTH OF LITERATURE AND
CRITICISM AT ROME

If the Greeks were first in Europe to create and record literature, to develop
literary genres and define their natures, and to evolve critical systems for
describing and prescribing forms of rhetoric and poetry, the Romans,
paradoxically, scored a different first. They were the first cultural community
to inherit literary models – those set up for them by the Greeks – before
they began to compose their own literature. It might be claimed that they
practised literary criticism, however rudimentary, before they practised
literature, for they were faced with questions of what to imitate and how. The
emergence of a relatively developed, highly imitative, national literature in
the third century BC has some analogies to the appearance of new criticism
and national literatures in the Renaissance; in both cases critical theory,
adapted from the prototype literature, helped to mould form and content and
in both cases formal education in grammar and rhetoric provided norms for
literary expression. But Renaissance writers in the vernacular had a richer
tradition of native poetry on which to draw than did the Romans, richer lexical
resources, and greater ambition for literary originality.

1 Livius Andronicus, Naevius, and Ennius

Of Rome's three earliest poets, two were professional teachers and both were
culturally as much Greek as Italian. The few relatively secure facts about
Livius Andronicus are representative of Rome's literary beginnings. He came
from Tarentum in Greek-speaking south Italy, which had been captured by
Roman forces between 280 and 275 BC. He probably knew little Latin when
he first came to Rome, but from time spent in instructing young Romans in
Greek acquired sufficient command of Latin to produce a translation of the
Odyssey, not into quantitive Greek hexameters, but into Archaic, accentual
Saturnian verse. His text was probably intended for school use and remained
a school-text in Horace's youth, but it gave him the reputation to become the
first Latin playwright, when he was commissioned by the magistrates
supervising the Great Games of 240 BC to make translations of a Greek
tragedy and comedy for stage production. These unidentified plays are the

landmark with which Cicero opens his account of Latin literature in the *Brutus* (72), our best source for the early phases of literature at Rome. A generation later, in 207 BC (Livy 27.37.7) as an old man he was invited to compose an original work, a hymn celebrating Roman successes in the war with Hannibal. In return he was honoured by the grant of membership to himself and his fellow poets in the guild of the professional clerks (*scribae*) in the temple of Aventine Diana. So Livius' first compositions in Latin were translations, and his professional livelihood the teaching of Greek poetry, to which Suetonius (*De grammaticis* 1), writing 350 years later, adds the reading and explanation of Latin poetry which he or his associates had composed. Both translating and teaching would direct emphasis to the actual language of composition; when plot and narrative sequence, character and dialogue are predetermined by the model, composition becomes very much a matter of choosing (or creating) the right word for the context. Hence Roman poetry began with concern for diction but with scope for linguistic creativity. The Roman inferiority complex in relation to Greek was compounded by the quest for dignity, and much Latin criticism would take the form of carping at single words thought unworthy of the writer's genre.

How did Livius and his successors teach poetry? The *praelectio* (*explication de texte*) was the *grammaticus'* stock in trade in the Roman Empire, and Suetonius assumes it was already practised by the first Roman *grammatici*. Since it was adapted from Hellenistic school practice it may have been fully developed when first introduced to Rome. The teacher would define the genre of the work, describe the poet's life and circumstances, and then analyse the form of the poem. Although serious analysis may only have been introduced to Rome by Crates of Mallos around 170 BC, we can assume Livius also pointed out the moral application of what was read and identified Greek deities and mythological figures; there is little reason to expect an evaluation of broader aesthetic elements than what was inherent in grammar, diction, and figures of speech.

Early Latin poetry – epic, drama, or hymn – was intended to be heard, not read. Even the dramatic scripts of Plautus, two generations after Livius, survived as property of theatre companies, and Ennius and Terence were the first poets whose texts were preserved for study. The Romans' own outline of their early literary history could not take shape until the scholarly researches of Aelius Stilo and his pupil Varro in the last century of the republic established a relatively firm chronology, and our chief source, Cicero, shows in the *Brutus* (72) that around 100 BC a serious student of Roman theatre production, the poet Accius, could be as much as two generations out in dating the first poets.

Naevius, Livius' successor, was more remarkable, because he did more than adapt Greek tragedy and comedy. He was an original composer of Roman tragedy and historical epic, the latter a heroic narrative of the first war with Carthage (in which he himself fought). But little of his work is preserved, and apart from his alleged imprisonment for insulting a powerful family, the Metelli, we know virtually nothing of his personality and literary methods. Only with Quintus Ennius does a fully rounded man of letters emerge, though it is probably his versatility and popular success that eclipsed both Naevius and Livius before him.

In his great epic *Annales*, designed to follow the history of Rome from her foundation to the current warfare with Greece, Ennius asserted a new kind of status. No one, he declared (line 209 Skutsch), had been *dicti studiosus* before him. The phrase, in which *dicti* cannot be given any of its regular connotations, translates the Alexandrian value-word *philologus*, which lies halfway between scholar and critic and denotes a man with sufficient learning in language and literature to evaluate and give permanent form to the poetic text. Ennius is affirming his qualifications as a critic, though his greatest pride was as a *poeta* (*Satirae* 3 and p. 64 Vahlen). The Calabrian poet spoke three languages, Oscan from birth and Greek and Latin as languages of education. He declared that this gave him three personalities (Gellius 17.17.1). Finding the accentual Saturnian metres uncouth, 'verses once changed by woodland sprites and bards' (207 Skutsch), he modified the Homeric hexameter to match the heavier rhythms of Latin. His standards were Greek, and he opened his poem, like Homer, with an appeal to the muses on Olympus, creating the symbolic fiction of a dream to match the dream of Hesiod, who met the muses on Helicon and was given water from the sacred spring Hippocrene. But there is no evidence that he simply copied Hesiod's dream and claimed his own encounter with the muses. Instead he reports (2 – 10 Skutsch) a vision of the poet Homer who explained that a single soul, after passing in Pythagorean metempsychosis through Homer into later men, was now possessed by Ennius himself: thus he was literally a second Homer, a critical claim that Roman nationalists would repeatedly adapt to other aspiring counterparts of the Greek poets.

Did Ennius' appeal to the muses and his vision come from the influence of Callimachus' famous poem, the *Aetia*? We should be cautious about going beyond the fragmentary excerpts in order to match Ennius with the Callimachean poetic baptism, but Ennius' claim to inherit Homer's soul may be a device to escape Callimachus' reproach against mere imitators of Homer.[1] He had extensive knowledge of Hellenistic works, for he composed poems based on writings by Euhemerus, Epicharmus, Archestratus, and others. Surely, then, he also knew the great Alexandrian, and was writing in reaction to him. Certainly, the translator of Euhemerus will not have recorded Roman history in a spirit of simple faith, and Ennius probably belittled Naevius as much for his literal narrative as for his Archaic verse-form and diction. As protégé of Rome's élite – first Cato, then Scipio Africanus,

---

[1] Skutsch, *Annals*, p. 148.

later Fulvius Nobilior, the learned dedicator of a shrine to the muses – Ennius lived by his Hellenism: Suetonius includes him with Livius as one who taught as a *grammaticus* and explicated Greek poetry. But Cicero, who read them both, claims (*Brutus* 76) that he owed much to Naevius and passed over the first war with Carthage because Naevius had reported it. Taking the two statements together we would guess borrowing of diction rather than content, but the forty-odd lines left of Naevius' epic do not permit comparison.

We may blame Ennius and Naevius for squeezing contemporary history into epic and tragic form with the hazards of incongruity commonly recognised in, say, Cicero's epic poem *On his Consulate*. But Ennius' Council of the Gods before the apotheosis of Romulus (53 – 4 Skutsch), his personification of Discord flinging open the Gates of War (225 – 6), and his application of Homeric imagery to contemporary commanders show that a Latin writer could achieve epic sublimity: such passages as the dream of Ilia (34 – 50) or the silence of the people of Rome awaiting the competitive auspices of Romulus and Remus (72 – 91) provided generations of Roman historians and poets with language that added emotional depth to their texts through its allusive resonance. In this, Ennius long remained for Roman writers what Homer never ceased to be for the Greeks, and 600 years later the critics Macrobius and Servius would use a knowledge of Ennius, however derivative and fragmentary, to interpret Virgil's greater epic. Cicero's judgement of Ennius' relationship to Naevius as either debt or theft (*Brutus* 76), will be repeated by less perceptive critics. But Roman literature was built on conscious and acknowledged imitation. Beginning with the transfer of thought from Greek to Latin it progressed (with Ennius) to the transfer of techniques to report new content and (with Plautus, Ennius' older contemporary) to the reclothing of Greek content in a freer and more travestied verbal wardrobe.

2 Plautus and Terence

As the dramatic *ludi* (festivals) increased in popularity, audiences now attended several adapted Greek tragedies and comedies each year. The reflection of their tastes in Plautus' versions of Greek comedy suggests no critical demands beyond simple pleasure in humour and violence, and an elementary desire to see villains punished, young lovers forgiven, and social values reconciled. The two Plautine comedies that make least compromise with popular taste also have programmatic prologues. *Captivi* (*Prisoners*) presents the edifying tale of a slave prisoner of war sacrificing himself to win his master's freedom and rewarded by the recognition of citizen status. Plautus asks for approval because the play is not on a hackneyed theme: 'it has no foulmouthed verses unfit to quote, no dishonest pander or naughty courtesan or boastful soldier'. What is offered for popular appeal is the theme of disguise and deception and a guarantee of a happy ending. Many Romans were captured and ransomed during the wars of this period (*c.* 210 – 185 BC) and the subject may have been welcome for this reason. It is harder to see how Plautus made a popular success of *Trinummus* (*Three-bit Trickster*) which opens with a unique moral allegory: the prologue is spoken by Luxury to her daughter Poverty, announcing the imminent ruin of a young spendthrift. It is also unusual in refusing any hint of the action to come. What is exceptional in Plautine comedy will not become regular practice until he is succeeded by a more sophisticated writer.

For our purposes the chief significance of Plautine comedy is in demonstrating how far a 'translator' can go in changing the form and content of his model. This is the first explosion of linguistic virtuosity in Roman· literature, and Plautus' cavalier liberties taken with dramatic structure and characterisation are offset by the versatility of his lyric and dialogue metres and by every kind of play on sound and sense in extravagantly stylised verbal fantasy. Translation as imitation has been superseded by exploitation of the model as vehicle for the Roman poet's personal idiom.

For several generations the verbal pyrotechnics of Plautus blinded Roman scholars to his carelessness as a playwright, so that Varro repeated his master Aelius Stilo's claim that if the muses had spoken Latin they would have spoken the language of Plautus (Quint. 10.1.99). But it would not be fanciful to read implied criticism of Plautus into the polemical prologues of Terence, which offer the first body of systematic dramatic criticism in Latin. Terence's premature attempt to refine Roman taste must be seen as the product of extraordinary circumstances. How did a nineteen-year-old of Carthaginian or African origin come to fuse two similar plays by the Greek Menander (*Andrian Girl* and *Perinthian Girl*) into one classically elegant Roman piece? We are told in the Life by Suetonius[2] that he was the slave of a Roman senator, won the friendship of the younger Scipio (Aemilianus, *doyen* of Roman culture in the next generation), and died at the age of twenty-five on a trip to Greece in search of more Menandrian scripts to translate. His achievements and associates can only be explained if he was educated with these or comparable Roman nobles. The rhetorical accomplishment of Terence's prologues points to a training alongside future politicians whose careers he might also be expected to serve, and the expulsion of Greek rhetoricians and philosophers from Rome in 161 BC[3] suggests that Greeks had probably been teaching or serving as private tutors at the city of opportunity since the first Macedonian war. Only bilingual education and rhetorical training could explain Terence's fastidious language and standards of dramatic decorum, ideals he could practise but not preach without overt criticism of old favourites

[2] The 'Life of Terence' found with Donatus' commentary on the plays is generally believed to be abridged from Suetonius' *De poetis*, to which we also owe lives of Virgil, Horace, Lucan, and others.

[3] Kennedy, *Art of Rhetoric*, pp. 151–3.

like Plautus that would be unacceptable from an upstart foreigner. Instead, Terence exploited a man of straw, the obscure Luscius of Lanuvium, whose jealous attacks on his rival's scripts justified Terence in composing polemical prologues to articulate his principles. This introduction of the voice of the dramatist into a play, commenting on his own work, has its chief precedent in the *parabasis* of Old Comedy.

We do not find in Terence explicit claims for the superiority of one type of comedy over another, or appeals to propriety. He had to disguise his beliefs and provide diplomatic reasons for his procedure. None of his prologues forecasts the course of the dramatic action or identifies the mysterious heroine, but in the prologue to *Andria* he treats such revelations as the proper purpose of prologues, which he has had to sacrifice in order to defend himself against unfair criticism. In this first play he departed from convention in three ways: by blending elements from a second play, *Perinthia*, into his main model; by replacing the wife of the borrowed exposition scene by an invented role – the trusty freedman Sosia – and by introducing into the action a subordinate plot based on a second master-and-slave pair. The last change was most extensive, entailing patchwork reconstruction at the beginning of two acts and the end of two others, but he is silent about this, as he is about suppressing the wife. We owe our knowledge to the commentator Donatus. In the prologue Terence stresses the first change, claiming his enemies accused him of 'contaminating' the Greek plays (like adulterating wines) whereas he is following the inspired creative licence of Naevius, Plautus, and Ennius, models more worthy of imitation than his pedantic rivals. *Contaminatio* seemed a threat to dramatists in that it 'spoiled' two Greek originals for Latin adaptation, a measure of the deep-seated feeling that action and character could only be found in the Greek versions. In this and other prologues Terence appeals to the audience over the heads of his rivals, affirming the freshness of his comedies. He did not change his practice: his two most successful comedies, *Eunuchus* and *Adelphoe*, are also based on more than one model, and the latter actually imports material from a different playwright. The secondary model, Diphilus' *Synapothneskontes*, had already been adapted for the Roman stage by Plautus, which laid Terence open to the charge of plagiarism, but he can deny it because Plautus had omitted the one scene he took over.

The terms of production seem to have required that a play be *novus*, not previously adapted; it is less clear whether the term *integer*, 'fresh' or 'unused', has the same meaning in the prologue to *Heautontimoroumenos* (*Self-Tormentor*). Both the Greek and Roman plays are called *integer*, probably in a different sense; the Greek is 'not previously adapted', the Terentian script is 'complete', 'unmodified'. This prologue adds to the issue of originality a question of comic standards, the basic conflict between high comedy and farce. Terence's chief actor, who speaks the prologue, calls the play 'static' and praises its refined language. He makes a pretext of his advanced age to justify the quiet type of action: 'give me permission to put across a quiet comedy in silence, so that we don't always have to have a Running Slave, an Angry Old Man, a Greedy Parasite, an Impudent Sycophant, a Miserly Pander – all acted with the greatest noise and the maximum effort' (35 – 40). Terence deprecates the standard comic roles because his own interest lay in the subtle psychology of well-bred citizens. Before the *Self-Tormentor* he had already produced a family-based play, *Hecyra* ('Mother-in-Law'), which failed to get a hearing, and the absence of a Terentian production in the following year suggests that the quiet *Self-Tormentor* was also a failure. His next plays stressed low-life roles, importing action scenes and earthy humour, as in *Eunuch* with its boastful parasite, its mock siege, and its titillating rape-narrative.

What other literary principles or tastes emerge from his appeals to the public? His criticism of his opponent's plays singles out three episodes, criticising two in terms of decorum. In one play Luscius had made the crowd give way to a slave as he ran on with urgent news. Terence sees it as quite wrong that the crowd 'should play slave to the crazy fellow' (*Self-Tormentor* 6 – 10). In another play Luscius had presented his young hero hallucinating that a stag chased by hounds was crying to him for help: the extravagant paratragic behaviour offends Terence (*Phormio* 6 – 10). The third play reveals a conflict between the needs of drama and legal convention. In the arbitration scene of *The Treasure* Luscius had made his defendant speak before the adversary suing him. This might be incorrect procedure, but it was dramatically more effective that the successful party speak last, and doubtless Luscius was keeping the order of his Greek models. (The reversal of order had already been used by Euripides, *Trojan Woman*, 895 – 1059.) What these criticisms show is that verisimilitude and social decorum were recognised as dramatic issues, distinguishing high comedy from farce. Not only Luscius, but Plautus and those Terence professed to respect would have been liable to the same reproach.

Terence is important to the history of Latin because, though writing in verse, he created the language of artistic prose, contributing as much to future oratory and prose dialogue as to drama itself. His fastidious exclusion not only of extravagance and vulgarity, but even of everyday allusions to food and furnishings (in this contrasting with Menander) drained the colour from comedy but produced an idiom flexible and elliptic. From a narrow lexical base he gave Latin both *sermo*, informal conversation, and *contentio*, discourse streamlined for swift and forceful argument. This achievement was supported by the work of two very different men of letters, the elder Cato – orator, politician, and historian – and Lucilius, the gentleman satirist. Cato was nearly seventy when Terence died: his oratory ranges from broad prolix deliberative speaking to pungent personal invective rich in irony and humour and figures of thought.[4] He asserted the dignity of Latin as a medium for

---

[4] What remain of Cato's speeches are collected in Enrica Malcovati (ed.), *Oratorum Romanorum fragmenta* (2nd ed., Pavia, 1955), pp. 12–97.

national history and mocked a younger contemporary, Postumius Albinus, for writing history in Greek and apologising for his inadequate command of the language (Gellius 11.8.2).

3 Lucilius

Lucilius, a generation younger than Terence, is familiar with Greek rhetorical terms, and uses them to tease Hellenophiles like Titus Albucius for their affected concern with rhythm and artificial word order: 'how daintily his diction is artfully arrayed, like mosaic cubes in an inlaid floor!' (fr. 84–5 Krenkel). Lucilius mocks himself (fr. 184) for an involuntary rhymed ending in the fashion of Isocrates, finding the homoeoteleuton hollow and adolescent (*meiraciodes*). In sharp contrast, he writes seriously on matters of grammar and orthography and takes time to distinguish the concepts of *poema* and *poesis*: the latter, like the *Iliad* or Ennius' *Annals*, is a unity in theme (*thesis*) and form (*epos*) (fr. 376–85). Criticism of Homer, he says, will not be of the whole poem, but of one verse or phrase or argument or passage. Here, however, he is not concerned so much with literary criticism as with determining the text: his verb *culpare* corresponds to the Alexandrian *stigma* placed against lines of a passage deemed spurious. Along with this concern for purging the text, Lucilius shows the traditional veneration for the 'real' authors. Roman respect for the past quickly turned revered poets into *auctores*, 'authorities', whose diction was a model for the next generation and who could be held up as a reproach against attempts at new styles and standards by younger poets, just as followers of Varro angered Horace by their preference for the dead primitives over the living innovators. As a medium for reflection on personal experience or moral and social issues, Lucilius' verse carried further the range of colloquial Latin. Thus by the end of the second century Roman culture had moved beyond the primitive nobility of Ennius and early tragedy, and the uninhibited peasant vigour of Plautine comedy. Greek rhetoricians and philosophers were there to stay, and the intellectuals around Scipio Aemilianus or the Gracchi, educated in Hellenistic ideas and techniques of expression, were transplanting into Latin new genres of prose like the dialogues on jurisprudence of Junius Brutus (Cic., *De or.* 2.224) and history and biography.

4 Rhetoric at Rome

Latin literature was pragmatic: what philologists call *Gebrauchsliteratur*. As the first century began, poetry was either an increasingly politicised tragedy or the leisure occupation of the aristocrat, a form of exercise for the wits. Plutarch (*Lucullus* 1.5) illustrates Lucullus' love of literature (*philologia*) with the story that he, the orator Hortensius, and the historian Sisenna tossed dice to see who should record the Marsic War in Latin verse, who in Greek prose, and who in Greek verse. The first works of literary criticism at Rome would have to emerge from rhetoric, the art of words applied to the purposes of the forum, and rhetoric itself would have to escape from the dominance of the most recent utilitarian contribution to the art – the *stasis* theory of Hermagoras of Temnos, with its programmed analysis of a legal situation so as to choose the appropriate defence and draw on the full range of favourable arguments to fit the case.

The earliest complete work of rhetorical theory at Rome is based on this system, and although medieval writers would find guidance for composing narrative verse and prose from its discussion of *narratio* and outlines of circumstantial sources of argument, none of its instruction is based on literary values. Had Cicero continued his youthful *De inventione* to include the theory of expression (*elocutio*) like the contemporary author of the anonymous *Rhetoric for Herennius*, we might have had a better picture of the aesthetic standards of the 80s BC. As it is, the author of *Ad Herennium* presents in Latin a code of styles and a classification of ornament which originated in Greek. Its most distinctive feature, not repeated in later rhetorical manuals, is its parade of models for the three recognised styles of discourse, the grand style, the middle or mixed style, and the plain, with parallel samples of unsuccessful passages in each idiom. We meet a recognisable heir to Terence in the vivid and swift plain narrative, with excerpts of conversation (4.14), and two excerpts from formal speeches, a grand denunciation from the peroration of a political prosecution (4.12) and a defence counsel's reasoned analysis of the motives of a rebellious colony in the calmer, symmetrical, middle style (4.13). The tone of the last is conciliatory, whereas the grand passage aims to fan the emotions, a contrast that Cicero will later identify and formalise. *Artes poetriae* of the Middle Ages, such as those by Geoffrey of Vinsauf, John of Garland, and Matthew of Vendome, will apply the three-style system to new definitions of narrative genres, in which grand, middle, and plain will be seen as the modes for narrative about the court, the town, and the world of shepherds and peasants. But for this to evolve the three styles had to pass through further modifications and applications by Varronian and post-Virgilian criticism.

Both Cicero's *De inventione* and the manual for Herennius come closest to concern with creative literature when they discuss types of narrative (*De inventione* 1.27; *Ad Herennium* 1.13f.): both quote the Hellenistic tripartite division of subject matter based on the two polarities of fact versus fiction and realism versus fantasy. Thus events neither true nor probable are seen as the material of tragedy (*fabula*), events imaginary yet probable are assigned to comedy (*argumentum*), and events which did take place, but at a time remote from the recollection of our age provide the subject of historical writing (*historia*). Concern with vividness and psychological interest in narrative, as with the variety and excitement produced by 'reversals of fortune, unexpected disaster, sudden joy' (*Ad Herennium* 1.13) show how aspects of tragedy singled out by Aristotle's *Poetics* were adopted by Hellenistic historians in the service of romanticising history. Polybius, the most scientific of the Hellenistic historians, lived at Rome for a generation under the patronage of Aemilianus, and (e.g., 12.25) denounced (but sometimes practised) the dramatisation of history. His influence will be apparent two generations later in Cicero's distinction between the required features of continuous history and of the more rhetorical monograph.

The Roman nobility was a governing class which subordinated both education and cultured leisure to the interest of the state or more often of their own political careers. They embraced the applied art of rhetoric, but were indifferent to its epideictic or ceremonial branch, from which Greece had developed the taste for artistic prose, rich in rhythm and evocative imagery. In the quarrel between rhetoric and philosophy in the time of Plato and Isocrates, the philosophers' fundamental objection had been the indifference of rhetoric to the truth, whether known or unknown, and its substitution of emotional pressure for argument. Isocratean teaching had stressed moral context, but was essentially an art of embellishment, not of reasoning. Aristotle and his successors, whether Peripatetic or Stoic, developed the topics – categories of reasoning – and established a complete system of argumentation. Cicero, with the advantage of training in both the Academic and Stoic systems, could improve the quality of oratory, but lacked the intellectual tools for a critical study of imaginative literature such as epic or tragedy. Stylistic and structural analysis would not suffice, since perceptive criticism should also concern itself with the author's choice of theme and event, and with his handling of psychology and ethics – largely the domain of the ancient philosopher. This was the gap that even the highly educated Cicero would have had to leap if he consciously sought to be a literary critic, but the Romans did not have such a profession. Even the Alexandrian *kritikos* was more editor than critic; his primary job was to examine a text as a Roman censor would the citizen body, expelling what was unworthy. The criterion was one of technical authenticity, and we can see how Cicero exploits this expectation to mock his enemy Piso Caesoninus, when Piso condemned Cicero's verse *cedant arma togae*, 'Let warfare give way to words'. 'Surely', he asks the audience, 'this is not an Aristarchus, but a Phalaris to mark a verse for excision because he doesn't like its subject matter?' (*In Pisonem* 73)

Piso was unusual in his deep interest in philosophy and poetry; usually Cicero had to adjust his words in the senate or forum to conciliate a philistine public. He need not conceal his knowledge of Roman law, but he had to play down his training in ethics and dialectic with the Academician Philo and the Stoic Diodotus, as he had to play down his love of poetry. We get a fair picture of public taste from his speech *For Archias* (62 BC), defending the claim to citizenship of a Greek poet. Archias himself illustrates what the Romans of the mid first century expected of poetry. From Antioch in Syria he had come to Italy, supporting himself by poetry and perhaps teaching in the Greek cities of Campania. He won the patronage of the Luculli and Lutatius Catulus the younger and was taken abroad by them to commemorate their campaigns in verse. Poets, as Cicero pointed out, are necessary if our deeds are to be immortalised. In society Archias could extemporise with amazing fluency on any topic, changing the metre or treatment of the theme to produce a second or third versification of the same material. Here is the dichotomy between occasional epigram and military epic which we noted earlier. And although Cicero does not say so, these poems were in Greek. Cicero's speech associates the pursuit of poetry with *humanitas* and *doctrina*: the former assimilates it to morality and good breeding, the latter to knowledge, as if poetry were an educational tool. When he surveys what poetry has to offer society, Cicero begins with its power to enrich public oratory, then moves to its service as relaxation after the serious business of life. But its greatest service is to inspire men to heroic achievement, providing them with models of behaviour, and preserving the memory of great deeds in history which would otherwise be neglected and forgotten. In this way poetry offers men personal survival in a verbal likeness comparable to honorific statues, and it celebrates national achievements. Cicero's antithesis of utility and pleasure (*For Archias* 16) anticipates Horace's prescription that 'poetry scores highest when it mixes utility and sweetness' (*AP* 343). Thus poetry is justified by its moral benefits, and the poet is recognised as a useful member of society. Cicero is modelling his portrait of the poet on Ennius, and cites him as authority for the most extravagant claim, that poets are specially inspired, privileged by the gods and so *sancti poetae*. This is a far cry from the technical versatility of a professional versifier like Archias. But we cannot blame Cicero's utilitarian approach entirely on his audience, since he himself used poetry for relaxation, translating Aratus' astronomical poems from the Greek, and for political self-advertisement, when he composed a three-book epic on his consulship.

5 Cicero's dialogue 'On the Orator'

The culture of Cicero's generation would have been impossible without ownership of, or access to, libraries. Scipio Aemilianus, a century earlier, was probably unique among his generation in enjoying a private library – his share of his father Aemilius Paullus' spoils from the palace of the defeated Perseus of Macedon. Sulla exercised the same right of conquest after the siege of Athens in 85 BC, acquiring from the wealthy Andronicus the esoteric library of the Aristotelian school containing Aristotle's *Rhetoric* and other major works. This library then passed into the hands of Cicero's friend Faustus Sulla. The nucleus of Cicero's own collection came more conventionally by gift from his friend Papirius Paetus, whose cousin, the grammarian Servius Clodius, died in Athens leaving a Greek and Latin collection. Cicero's letters of 60 BC show him negotiating with Atticus to have the collection shipped back to Rome. Thus in his first mature work of literary and rhetorical theory, *De oratore* (55 BC), he could draw on his own resources and the library of Faustus. More important, he was on good terms with the Greek scholar-grammarian Tyrannio of Amisos, who was then editing the texts of the Aristotelian library for Faustus. This is one reason why we should not doubt that Cicero drew for the composition of *De oratore* on Aristotle's *Rhetoric*; the other is the close coincidence of his theory of invention with the system of Aristotle's first two books (his speaker Antonius claims to have read rhetorical works by the philosopher) and further affinities between Cicero's treatment of tropes in Book III with Aristotle's discussion in the third book of the *Rhetoric*.

Vivtruvius (9. pr. 17), writing in the Augustan age, includes *De oratore* with Lucretius' *De rerum natura* and Varro's *De Lingua Latina*, as one of the three learned monuments of the previous generation. The work reflects Cicero's lifelong concern to defend rhetoric against the criticism of philosophy, especially the moral and epistemological criticisms of Plato's *Gorgias* and Plato's appeal for a new philosophical rhetoric in the *Phaedrus*. Both Isocrates and Aristotle had tried to meet this challenge, and Cicero draws on their separate traditions, relying on Isocrates for the pedagogic and stylistic theories of the first two books[5] and on Aristotle for the theory of invention and expression. But the work is more than a synthesis of the Greek traditions. Cicero's own interest as an artist drove him to explore every aspect of personal style: its growth, its adaptation to context, and its relation to the evolving styles of different generations of oratory. Throughout his argument he recognises that the orator *qua* performer is an actor, but *qua* composer is closer to the poet. Hence his analogy (1.69) to the metaphrastic poets Aratus, writing on astronomy, or Nicander on snakebites, because they present other men's material in verse as the orator must do in prose. Yet he recognises the different licence of the poet and orator in the use of language; the poet is more restricted in rhythm but correspondingly freer in vocabulary and phraseology.

A recurring theme in *De oratore* is personal idiom. The Isocratean tradition taught by model passages and claimed that the best student was the one who came closest to the model (*Against the Sophists* 18). How could the young writer achieve his own style while copying the admired teacher? Cicero points to the need to choose a teacher suited to the pupil's natural talents and represents the pupil's mature work as a fusion of his own idiom and that of the model (2.89–90). In the third book (19–35), when form becomes the dominant issue, Cicero begins by affirming two principles which are as much literary as rhetorical: the first is that style and sense, form and content, must be matched so that ideal form gives brilliance to significant content. The second

---

[5] The treatment of natural ability, exercise, and imitation up to 2.98. The discussion of rhythm (3.171–98) blends Isocratean with Aristotelian theory.

principle is respect for diversity, for the difference of idiom between Aeschylus, Sophocles, and Euripides within the spectrum of tragedy, or for the distinct idiom of orators trained in the same generation by the same teacher, whose differing personalities shape their discourse. In this important section Cicero treats oratory simply as one of several literary genres and takes as his starting point the whole field of literature.

Cicero's adaptation (2.115) of the three Aristotelian modes of rhetorical proof stresses means of persuasion: the logical or quasi-logical proof, the power to move pity or anger, and the art of winning over the audience by a congenial self-portrayal. In his modification of the formula in *Orator* (69), written ten years later, the substitution of the art of pleasing (*delectare*) for the art of winning over reflects his growing interest in the aesthetic aspects of discourse. Perhaps too he felt that for the Roman advocate, who defended his client in person rather than ghost-writing a speech, the psychological techniques of conciliating the audience were not essentially different from the emotional mode of proof, and that Aristotle had not taken into account the power of charm, wit, and imagination to beguile the public. Roman rhetorical theory had been slow to adapt itself to the more varied opportunities for ethos and pathos offered by the Roman courts, but Cicero's speeches show him fully exploiting them.[6]

As a legacy of his concern with the orator as performer, Cicero often measures style by its effect on the ear, yet whatever he has to say about the expectations of the listener is valid in appreciating literature read in silence today. The reader is affected by the same perception of rhythm, diction, imagery, and verbal music as the ancient listener, although his reaction may be weaker. Cicero was acutely aware of audience reaction, and the orator's need to improvise or modify his text in response, but he cared even more for the higher standards which only written preparation of the speech could achieve, and his recommendations for control of expression mix what we might see as aesthetic criteria with the rhetorician's focus on persuasion. One particularly important passage (*De or.* 3.96–101) defines *ornatus* as something organic rather than superficially applied. The text is a body that must be well-proportioned. Whether taken from the human body or its sculptured likeness, the analogy is visual, and Cicero declares that dignity, charm, culture, breeding, refinement, and emotional depth are manifest not in the individual limbs, but in the body as an organic whole. Local or applied ornament makes its effect by contrast and should not be sprinkled throughout the text but spaced at calculated intervals, like ornamental motifs in a public display. This Isocratean principle of *kosmos* (both ornament and harmonious ordering) is reinforced by analogies from other senses and arts. The audience should be charmed without surfeit, just as sober old-fashioned paintings with simple

[6] George Kennedy, 'The rhetoric of advocacy in Greece and Rome', *AJP*, 89 (1968), 419–34.

colouring appeal to us longer than modern works loaded with cloying and brilliant colour. From painting, from music, from perfumery and cookery, Cicero argues the counterproductive effect of excessive sweetness or ornament too prominently patterned and unrelieved. In poetry or prose, he insists, contrast is essential. It is all the more necessary because writing, unlike painting, occupies not just the ears (we would say eyes) but the mind, and false flourishes are quickly spotted. Just as the speaker's delivery should rise and fall in volume, pitch, and stress, so the writer must vary the intensity of his diction. This amazingly synaesthetic paragraph, which may well go back to a Hellenistic source, perhaps Theophrastus' *Peri lexeōs*, points to the twin criteria of taste: discretion and variety in the successful work of art.

A Greek origin for Cicero's argument is suggested by its interest in visual analogy. Cicero knew Greek art, but is more likely to have drawn the principles from his studies of Greek rhetoric than from the examples of music, painting or sculpture. Since he uses the fourfold analysis of the 'virtues' of style attributed to Theophrastus throughout the third book of *De oratore* (36 – 212) and explicitly later in the *Orator* (79), it is possible that this illustrative material also comes from Theophrastus. When he considers added ornament based on word selection and arrangement, and the tropes and figures, Cicero seems close to Aristotle's analysis. Both in *Poetics* 22 (1458b17f.) and *Rhetoric* 3.2 (1404b5f.) Aristotle had classified words into basic vocabulary ('proper' words) and three deviations: exotic or archaic (*glossai*), compound words, and coinages. These three categories gave poetry elevation appropriate to its inspired effect, but in prose only metaphor was an admissible variation on the dignity of basic vocabulary, giving speech novelty (what Aristotle calls *to xenon*, 'exoticness') without affectation. For metaphor uses basic vocabulary in a strikingly new context. Cicero echoes Aristotle's interpretation of the psychology of metaphor. As in the *Rhetoric*, the pleasure received from imagery is partly stimulus to the imagination, challenged to note a resemblance between one sphere and another, and partly the release of mental travel from the continuing theme to a different field. 'The listener without actually straying, is led in his thought in a new direction – and this is a source of the greatest pleasure ... every apt metaphor is directed to the senses, particularly that of the sight, the keenest of all' (3.160). He notes images drawn from the other senses, but singles out the visual images because 'they almost place within the mind's eye things that we cannot see and perceive in fact ... the single word that contains the likeness will bring the brilliance of metaphor to the language' (3.161).

We may contrast Cicero's impatient dismissal of the figures of speech that depend on repetition and arrangement, and even of the figures of thought by which we vary syntax to avoid the monotony of continuous statement. These were the staple of traditional rhetoric and the *Rhetoric for Herennius*, Book IV, does not go beyond them to consider the problem of consistency and harmony of style. Although Cicero alludes to the three-style system of the manual (*De or.* 3.177, 3.199, 3.212) he prefers to stress the infinite gradations of idiom from person to person. His aesthetic sense strides ahead of his analytical vocabulary, but even the relatively rough account of prose rhythm (3.171 – 98) pays the same attention to the need for variety of phrase length and the hasards of too obtrusive symmetry in the so-called Gorgianic figures which Isocrates perpetuated. Here again Cicero insists on the primacy of thought. Rhythm should seem a spontaneous by-product of meaning, and the architecturally admirable periodic sentence, first rousing then satisfying suspense, should be varied by shorter sense-units, just as prose should not reiterate rhythmic patterns like actual verse. At the centre of his discussion of rhythm is a teleological section comparing the written or spoken word to an organism or artistic construct. Cicero argues that like the heavenly bodies in orbit, like trees or ships or even temples, the ideal discourse will derive its beauty from the very features introduced of necessity or for convenience: meaning and the need of speech for breath determines the proportion of units within the sentence and the length of the whole. Here again he may be drawing on Theophrastus.

> Columns and porticoes serve to support temples, but they are as imposing as they are functional. It was not beauty but necessity that designed the gable-end of the Capitoline temple and others too, for in devising a means to drain water from the roof to either side, the magnificence of the gable followed from the temple's requirements, so that even if the Capitol were to be set up in heaven, where there is no rain, it would have seemed undignified without its gable ... this happens in the same way in all the parts of a speech.
> (3.180)

To raise aesthetic demands in this way when considering the oratory of the senate house and forum shows how far Cicero had taken over the values of epideictic discourse into the practical genres. But *De oratore* itself embodies an entirely new standard of artistry, not only in its style, varying easily between conversation and forceful argument, but in its proportions and elaborate structure, held together by thematic imagery, cross-reference, and dramatic form. A composition designed on this scale is the product of increased familiarity with Hellenistic technological writings, and of training in dialectic, in arguing both sides of the case and synthesising conclusions.[7] The quality of organisation in the prose writings of Cicero's generation will be lost in the next century under the negative influence of declamation, with its cult of the momentary aphorism.

Both by its precepts and its example *De oratore* ensured that artistry was now expected from prose, and Cicero makes a special digression (2.51 – 64) to give recommendations for a different kind of prose: historical writing,

---

[7] Elizabeth Rawson, 'The introduction of logical organisation in Roman prose literature', *Papers of the British School at Rome*, 46 (1978), 12–34.

intended to be read, not declaimed, a genre in which practice at Rome had proceeded without sufficient concern for scientific or artistic principles. It is useful to measure his judgement of open-ended historical writing in *De oratore* against the nearly contemporary letter to the historian Lucceius requesting special treatment in a historical monograph. The discussion in *De oratore* approaches history as a species of epideictic and is more concerned with its form than its content: thus the early Roman chroniclers are compared unfavourably with the great writers of Greek history, not for their intellectual limitations but for their baldness, while the work of each Greek historian is given its *character* (stylistic portrait). Although Cicero admits the requirements of accuracy (the truth and nothing but the truth like a witness in court, 2.62), freedom from bias, background knowledge of the places and persons to be described, and scientific analysis of causality, Cicero's prime concern is stylistic: the need for a flowing and varied discourse precedes and follows his recommendations for the treatment of history itself. But his recognition of the appropriate, even, forward-flowing style for historical writing, distinct from the sharper idiom of the forum, opened up the way for *belles lettres*, treatises, dialogues, essays, and epistles in prose.

While *De oratore* focuses on continuous history, the letter to Lucceius (*Ad familiares* 5.12) addresses an annalistic historian and tries to divert him into the rhetorically freer world of the monograph. The criteria of drama and encomium are mingled in Cicero's vision of the projected separate work which he compares to a play: Rome was the originator of the *fabula praetexta*, historical drama in verse centred on a national hero, and this form provided another precedent for the monograph. Cicero points to the self-contained unit created by his consulate, exile, and recall, to its variety, its scope for moral judgements, and the appeal of 'a fine man's vicissitudes offering wonder, suspense, joy, distress, hope and apprehension' (5.12.5). Setting aside the historical precedents, we see here the same elements commended in the rhetorical manuals' prescription for narrative. But clearly Cicero knows the difference between imaginative encomium and veracious historical record. The charm and the power to immortalise which he predicates of this imagined work are the attributes of poetry, as his comparison with Homer's service to Achilles, found here and in *Pro Archia*, shows beyond doubt.

6 Cicero's 'Brutus' and 'Orator'

Despite its primary concern with education, *De oratore* reflects principles of genre-criticism and aesthetics, and in its surveys of Greek oratory and historiography show a grasp of the evolution of literary forms. But in the second phase of his rhetorical works, during his withdrawal from public life under the domination of Julius Caesar (48–44 BC), Cicero re-examined his assumptions to answer the challenge of changing tastes in the younger

generation. If practice comes before theory in rhetoric (as Cicero declared
in *De oratore* 1.88f.), then his own speeches and *De oratore* exhibit standards
which he only systematised when he was provoked to defend them. M. Junius
Brutus, the future assassin of Caesar, was not himself an 'Atticist', advocating
imitation of the chaste simplicity of early Athenian oratory, like his friend
Calvus, but he was a purist, morally austere and deprecating either pomp
or charm in oratory. The two works dedicated to Brutus in 46 BC, *Brutus*,
'On distinguished orators', and *Orator*, 'On the best style of discourse',
apply Cicero's critical ideals first descriptively to literary history, then
prescriptively as he reconciles conflicting approaches to personal style
and shows how all levels of style can and must be combined in the supremely
gifted speaker. If *Brutus* is more concerned with performance than composition, including the gesture and delivery of orators of Cicero's day,
yet the work is based on a new sense of the evolution of literature at Rome.
The chronological work of his friend Atticus, like the contemporary researches
of Varro and Cornelius Nepos, gave the perspective and framework to
measure Roman progress against that of Greece. Comparative criticism
is Cicero's chief tool in the *Brutus*: comparison of Roman with Greek,
in a spirit of emulation which we also see in Nepos' extant lives; comparison
of each new generation at Rome with its predecessors; and repeated contrasts
between the orators representing the grand and the plain style in each
generation. We should add comparison between the rise to technical perfection
of oratory (embodied with more truth than modesty in Cicero himself)
and the evolution of painting and sculpture. Cicero almost certainly adopted
ready-made from Greek criticism the canons of artists representing the
birth, growth, and acme of each art, but applies them effectively in vindicating
the present achievement of Roman oratory by comparison with the early
primitives. When he wrote this dialogue, oratory was already politically
endangered, and it is possible to see the entire work as an obituary for
his own art, but it is not until after Caesar's death, when he composes
the *Tusculans*, that Cicero will describe oratory as 'sinking into senility
and soon to pass away' (2.5).

Cicero's history of his own genre falls short of what we might expect in
a history of tragedy or the novel because development can be limited largely
to style and sentence structure. There is no evolution of the form, such as
Aristotle perceived when the second actor was introduced into tragedy, or
even of content, such as can be marked in the rise of the 'recognition' play,
or the change from naturalistic to formal Euripidean prologue. Alert to the
social and political conditions that stimulated oratory, Cicero nonetheless
marks growth by noting increasing command of the medium of discourse:
Isocrates is a great figure because he perceived and taught the need for rhythm,
periodic structure, and attention to the hearer's rhythmic expectations.
When Cicero comments on other genres in the introduction to *De finibus*

and (if it is a genuine work)[8] in *De optimo genere oratorum*, it is still a competition between Greek originals and their Roman adaptations: a Roman content to read Ennius and Accius is depicted as reluctant to read Latin versions of philosophical works or Greek oratory. Rome did not have the creative writers to stimulate criticism, and Cicero can record the early history of epic, comedy, and tragedy in the *Brutus* without asking why Terence had no successor, nor Ennius, nor even Accius, who died in Cicero's youth.

The best poetry of Cicero's day was esoteric: Catullus writing for his refined smart set, whom Cicero (*Tusculans* 3.45) called 'Chanters of Euphorion' (a sort of Hellenistic Swinburne, now lost) and scolded for their disrespect towards Ennius, or again Lucretius' solitary poem, mentioned by no contemporaries except in a private letter from Cicero to his brother who had apparently passed on the text for comment. Cicero finds it has 'many strokes of natural inspiration, but also quite a few technical successes' (*Ad Quintum* 2.9.3). Drama had been a popular art, drawing on audiences like that of oratory, and Cicero recognises the different public of non-dramatic poetry in a passage discussing the response of the crowd and the connoisseur to standards in oratory. *Brutus* (183–200) describes how the crowd which had initially admired a competent orator was overwhelmed by the skill of the great L. Crassus and admired him as enthusiastically as did the expert. The learned poem, Cicero adds, needs only the approval of a few, but a speech must rouse the crowd and needs their response to maintain its momentum. He cites the discomfiture of the fourth-century Greek Antimachus, author of epic and elegy on a grand scale, whose recitation of his own work was soon left with only Plato as audience. Did Cicero admire this poet whom Callimachus and Catullus' circle (cf. *Carmina* 95b) despised for his inflated style and scale? The orator judges poetry either by rhetorical or moral standards, seeing its purpose as protreptic, to move the listener by its emotive power to admire and emulate noble deeds. Ulysses cried out in pain in the lost *Niptra* of Pacuvius because of his wound; Cicero, writing on fortitude in the face of pain (*Tusculans* 2.48) reproaches the poet for showing weakness in a supposed hero. As an orator he was equally alert to what we might call reader-response, but the moral effect took priority over the aesthetic.

His last major critical work, *Orator*, a sort of utopian counterpart to the historical account of *Brutus*, was in many ways his most influential study (on Quintilian and St Augustine, for example), and its many shifts of approach show him struggling to leave an aesthetic testament as he calibrates the concept of personal style within a multi-dimensional measuring system, taking into account the genre, the immediate context and circumstances, the author, and every change of theme that invited a change of tone or dynamics within the discourse. He had to reconcile the quest for an ideal of versatility with the

---

[8] Fantham, 'Genus-terminology', pp. 441–59.

three-style system. Among the problems was the ill-defined status of the middle style: to say it stood halfway between the plain and grand in degree of ornamentation gave it no distinctive features: a more promising approach associated it with the symmetrical antithesis of Isocratean composition, the flowing sweetness of epideictic ornamented with figures and rich vocabulary. The tripartite analysis may have gone back to Theophrastus' work on diction (used by Cicero at *Orator* 79) since Theophrastus seems to have developed references in Aristotle's *Rhetoric* (3.12) to specific qualities of styles like the sweet or the grandiose. Cicero himself may have distrusted this finite labelling, and he had based his rhetorical character sketches in *Brutus* on a simpler polar antithesis between the plain argumentative mode and the grand poetic style.[9] Returning to the issue in *Orator* (20) he no sooner introduces the three standard levels of style than he subdivides them; the plain speaker, it appears, can be shrewd and pointed without artistry of form, or neat and well-turned; each stylistic mode can occur in a rhythmic or unrhythmic version. Again (26), the orator Demosthenes can raise or lower the level of his diction, increasing in ardour and boldness of imagery as his audience warms up. Between the different genres of prose outside oratory styles will again be distinct. It was Cicero who first recognised the scope of the third, negatively defined, branch of oratory: the residue after court and political speeches had been defined and prescribed for. History, philosophy, and all formal prose can be sheltered under the rubric of epideictic. Early in *Orator* (37) he illustrates this category from the sophists and Isocrates and notes that the relative artificiality of this kind of figured display-speaking is the best training for the more covert art required in senate and forum. Its deliberate symmetries and periodisation train the speaker to refine technique, giving him a more subtle control of rhythm and form.

In the central section (*Orator* 60–112) Cicero starts from genre classifications in our sense, between sophistic, philosophic, historical, and poetic discourse, and isolates the sense of taste and propriety which a speaker must apply in both sentiment and language to match every circumstance: the audience, his adversary, his own role and the seriousness or triviality of the issue. It is this most relative of all criteria that Cicero singles out as the key to the successful control of style, and it is something we today begin to notice when we compose a formal utterance, such as an apology or letter of condolence, but would not normally consider when composing or criticising imaginative poetry or fiction. In fiction we are more interested in characterisation – what rhetoric called *ethopoeia* – than in variation of tone and tempo in narrative which may affect the reader by its relaxation or tension, irony, or commitment. But what concerns Cicero is tonal variety, the need for the artist to use the whole spectrum of colours from the plainest argumentative

[9] Douglas (ed.), *Brutus*, pp. xxxiv–xxxv.

style to the impassioned grandeur of a denunciation or plea for mercy. It is significant that his three sketches of style linger longest over the plain idiom (75 – 90). His first specifications are negative, rejecting self-conscious euphony and embellishment or Gorgianic figures, but he gives most attention to illustrating the use of imagery, wit, and pithy sayings as the real ornament of this idiom. He knows the difficulties of apparent simplicity, yet ultimately cannot rest content with speech that ranges only from the simple to the charming, and his ideal master of oratory specialises in the grand treatment of great issues. If Cicero does not give us an analysis of the Sublime, he still reflects the same hierarchy of values as will Longinus.

But there is a hidden item on Cicero's agenda. He is initially reticent about rhythm, but takes pains to mark off the rhythmic from the unrhythmic orator in outlining the plain and grand styles. The theme of rhythm and patterned speech recurs in the first half of *Orator* before it is formally introduced in the second. It is noted, for instance, as the differential between the narrative mode of history (66) and the expository mode of philosophical dialogue (62 – 4). To define prose rhythm and identify its effects demands more subtlety than simply advocating attractive cadences like the notorious Ciceronian *esse videatur*. Rhythm is as much a component of successful prose as metre of classical verse; indeed, what we call free verse is free simply in the sense of substituting non-recurring prose rhythm for regular metre. While Cicero was preoccupied with the spoken word and with persuasive as opposed to ceremonial oratory, he was struggling to define a feature common to all polished literary texts. He realised that certain logical or syntactical forms, like the antithetical sentence, generated their own rhythm, and in an inflected language symmetry of syntax produced rhythm or metrical equivalence in parallel form: the units of utterance were balanced in sound as in sense.

After tracing the origin of prose rhythm to the desire to please the ear and explaining the basis of quantitative metre that underlies the listener's reaction to rhythmic prose, Cicero relates this strictly musical element to the arching syntactical forms which give the periodic sentence its suspense and final release with the completion of the thought. His account of the periodic sentence is pioneering: a new if awkward step forward in aesthetics.

The periodic sentence should flow from its source so that when it reaches its goal it comes spontaneously to a halt. This will not be difficult, since well-trained students who have written much will make anything they utter, even without a written text, seem like a regular composition. For the mind encompasses the thoughts, and the words come together instantly released by the mind, swiftest of all things, so that each word falls into position, and their ordered sequence ends with a different cadence in different places. Indeed all the words from the beginning through the middle should point forward to the last. The pace is now accelerated, now held back, so that you must consider from the start how you want to reach the finish. (*Orator* 199 – 201)

Thus his analysis of composition allows for three elements: arrangement, symmetry, and rhythm. He concludes that what is called rhythmic prose often springs not from deliberate rhythm but either from symmetry or from the natural order of words. One senses in Cicero's recognition of the greater freedom of epideictic to indulge in rhythm and ornament some regret that the fighting world of the forum imposed a more sober style, and that rhythm used to excess undermined the plausibility and pathos of the discourse. Certainly his own aesthetic sensibility leads Cicero to devote far more time in this work to aspects of technique which he had to play down in their practical context. At the time of *Orator* his only non-forensic prose (other than the private letters) were his rhetorical dialogues; *Orator* itself was not a dialogue but something more like the philosophical genre called protreptic (exhortation), and Cicero must already have conceived his plan of composing a philosophical corpus, just as the preface to *De legibus*, usually dated to 50 BC, shows that he seriously considered writing history. He was fully aware of the potential of prose discourse and had acquired practice in the quasi-drama of dialogue as well as some philosophical exposition. His account of the features required in artistic prose composition does not offer the common rules of rhetoric; these he could take for granted, nor would they have taken the student beyond the limit of professional oratory. What he did offer was seldom in the form of direct precept, but more often a complex blending of factors to be taken into account.

It is harder for the modern reader to look beyond Cicero so as to recover a picture of other rhetorical or linguistic movements in this fertile generation. The stimulus to Cicero's later work had been a reform movement objecting to 'Asianism' in oratory and grouping Cicero himself as an 'Asianist' alongside his predecessor Hortensius: but Asianism was a Greek term, applied by mainland Greeks to stigmatise the new trends of the rhetoricians in Asia Minor. The most famous instance of a Greek Asianist was Hegesias, whose surviving fragments show a jerky dislocation of thought into minute syntactical units. Cicero in *Brutus* (325) reports two varieties of Asian diction, the pointed style full of neat and patterned aphorisms, and the voluble style, excited, ornate and smart, but with more speed than symmetry. *Orator* adds to this description only the caution against sing-song delivery which Latin speakers would with typical prejudice denounce as unmanly, and he was eager not to be reckoned Asianist, carefully explaining that his own Rhodian training retained the good taste of the Athenian tradition, while Demosthenes was to emerge as his favoured model.[10] But his account of the new reform movement, the so-called Atticists, is not straightforward. Greeks of his time suffered from the inferiority complex of the post-classical period, and a nostalgia for the age of independence associated with the great speakers. Thus the earliest form of Atticism, a classicising return to the grace of Lysias and the fastidious

[10] C. W. Wooten, *Cicero's Philippics and their Demosthenic Model* (Chapel Hill, 1983), pp. 46–57.

vocabulary of the fourth century, could be seen as a refining of vulgarity. We do not know how Calvus spoke, but the *Commentaries* of Caesar exemplify in their ostensible plainness and restrained vocabulary a similar refinement in Latin. But Cicero reports other Atticists who made the oblique and often abrupt idiom of Thucydides their model for Latin oratory (*Orator* 287 – 8): that such people existed is borne out by the historical prose of Sallust and Asinius Pollio, men of Brutus' age group who cultivated brevity, asymmetry, and sentences that seemed to end prematurely, frustrating the rhythmic expectation of the reader. They were memorable historians, but Cicero may not have been unfair to suggest that Thucydides was no model for public oratory, and that audiences would find the mannerisms of his imitators indigestible. It would seem that reaction had moved from purism to a new kind of affectation, while carrying the same banner of return to Attic standards.

6 *Grammatical scholarship in the Late Republic*

Purism also manifested itself in other ways during this generation. Focus on the word had moved since the deaths of Pacuvius and Accius (about 90 BC) from adventurous expansion of vocabulary to increasing restriction. Poets now coined words only on well-established precedent. The *grammaticus* Aelius Stilo objected to the superlative *novissimus* (Varro, *De lingua Latina* 6.59); Lucretius and Cicero, who need new vocabulary to express Greek physical and logical concepts, often complain of the poverty of Latin; the innovative orator Sisenna was treated as eccentric for his new formations (*Brutus* 259), and his *Histories* did not survive, because his style was not admired. When Cicero wants to systematise the Latin words *genus* and *species* as equivalents for Greek *genos* and *eidos* he has to use *forma* to supplement the cases of *species* which were not acceptable in Latin (*Topica* 30). This conservative language never imitated the syntactical flexibility or inventive power of Greek, although every well-educated Roman had learned to write in Greek and read most serious material in that language. Prose discourse was intended for a broad public, and Cicero knew that it was essential to use only familiar, even traditional, language. And there were no more great dramatic poets to convert the public to new flights of diction.

One factor was the rise of *grammatici*, another the philosophical preoccupation with etymology, as though the Word manifested the value of the Thing. Etymology appears intermittently in Ennius or Lucilius, and Lucretius argues (1.871 – 4) that the relationship between wood and fire is expressed in the way Latin *ignis* (fire) is found in *lignis* (logs), while Cicero explains the nature of the gods in *De natura deorum*, Book II, by etymologies. The Stoics saw the names of things as part of their nature and led the way to a quasi-philosophical analysis of word-roots, aiming at tracing word families to their origins. The grammarian Crates of Mallos, who came to Rome from Pergamum, and

Aelius Stilo, Varro's teacher, will have followed this theory, but the doctrine known as *analogia* does not seem to have been a problem at Rome until the fifties, when etymological theory was polarised between the Alexandrian trained advocates of *analogia* in determining word formation and the Stoic influenced supporters of *anomalia*. Both sides were committed to the importance of words as expression of the nature of what they named, but the anomalists saw merit in maintaining the inconsistencies of usage in word form and word inflexion, whereas the analogists believed language was based on consistent relationships (*to analogon*, 'ratio'), and inconsistent formations or declensions should be eliminated from the language. How was the individual to proceed? The conservatives would merely avoid inconsistent forms by using synonyms; the radicals seem to have advocated coining new by-forms, like Sisenna's active *adsentio* or Caesar's *frustro*, for the passive endings of everyday usage.

Caesar himself wrote two books *On Analogy* shortly after the publication of *De oratore* and dedicated them to Cicero, perhaps in reaction to Cicero's too brief dismissal of the issue of correct Latinity: certainly in his preface he affirmed the importance of correct speech even at a less glorious level than the formal public discourse in which Cicero excelled. So we find in the *Brutus* (252) the statement that Caesar set right bad usage by replacing it with good usage. Cicero stresses the difference between the usage of the ignorant and men of culture, but as a public speaker he was committed to accepting the anomalies that had grown up with usage, and he has adjusted his account of Caesar's views to suit his own. One famous remark attributed to Caesar shows his conservatism in choice of words; 'you should', he declares, 'steer clear of an unfamiliar word like a reef' (Gellius 1.10.4), and his own *Commentarii* keep a small conventional vocabulary.

The other scholar-critic who addressed himself to Cicero was the more learned but less gifted Varro, who studied and reproduced theories of language as he did every other kind of antiquarian research. Some ten years older than Cicero, Varro survived the triumviral period and died in 27 BC, the year that Augustus earned his honorific title by the Restoration of the Republic. Politically and intellectually conservative, he turned to antiquarian scholarship in earnest in 47 BC, and must have begun *De lingua Latina* at that time. The first four books (now lost) adopted the Hellenistic form of *Eisagōgē*, or Introduction, first establishing the claim of etymology to be an art, then defining its nature. Like Cicero in *De oratore*, Varro presented both sides of the argument, giving successively the case against and the case for etymology. Oddly it was not these fundamental books of theory but the more particular catalogues of etymologies and the triad of books on the controversy between the Analogists and Anomalists that he dedicated to Cicero. In the introduction to Book V he claims to have studied Aristophanes of Byzantium (the Alexandrian advocate of analogy) and Cleanthes, representative of the Stoic support for anomaly, and explains that although there are four levels of etymological interpretation (common knowledge, grammatical tradition, philosophical explanation, and religious mystery), he himself will aspire to the philosophical level. The three books covering the dispute between the two theories are organised on the same principle as the first three, arguing first against analogy, then for it, and then in Book X synthesising conclusions.

What interests us most is Varro's recognition of the special status of poetry. Following Aristotle's distinction between regular vocabulary (*kuria onomata*), foreign and obsolete words, he separates poetic from ancient words with the artificial distinction that he derives much more pleasure than utility from the poetic vocabulary, but more use than pleasure from ancient words (5.9). This confusion of argument seems to arise because he has tried to combine discussion of glosses with the conventional literary dichotomy between pleasure and usefulness. To Varro, poetry offered two great benefits: the poets, unlike the orators, bound to normal usage, could be innovators; 'such new inflectional forms as are introduced by the analogical theory but are rejected by the speech of the forum, these the good poets, especially the dramatists, ought to force upon the ears of the people and accustom them to them. For the poets have great power in this sphere' (*De lingua Latina* 9.17). As he had said earlier, 'the poet can with impunity leap across all the boundaries'. But the second merit was fundamental to almost all of Varro's researches: the poetry that he loved celebrates and preserves national institutions. Thus the seventh book starts with the glorious line of Ennius promising the deification of Romulus and with the use of *templa* for the regions of the sky, a meaning associated with augury and the consecration of Rome's kings and magistrates. Most of the illustrations, even in fragmentary form, are recognisable as rich poetry, and most come from the now lost poets of epic, tragedy, or comedy.

For Varro's greatest contribution to Roman literary history was not through etymology, nor certainly through the merit of his own prose. He makes a significant appearance in the opening dialogue of Cicero's *Academics*. There Cicero compliments Varro on the breadth of his research into the national inheritance: 'It is', he says, 'as though we were strangers in our own city, and you made it known to us' (1.9). Varro has questioned the value of Cicero's decision to translate Greek philosophical works into Latin; students of philosophy can after all read the original works in Greek. Always alert to literary form, Cicero answers that men who read Roman adaptations of Greek tragedy and comedy for pleasure should derive equal enjoyment from the study of philosophy in their own language. In this courteous disagreement are embodied the limitations of the Roman educated class. While Catullus and Lucretius were creating original poetry, cultured Romans occupied themselves with gathering precious information about their country's past – like Varro, who for all his study of the Greeks imitated neither their elegance of language nor clarity of argument – or else, like Cicero, they accepted Greek superiority and aimed chiefly to provide Romans with a body of derivative theoretical writings equal to those of Greece in interest and beauty of form.

Caesar had planned to make Varro director of the great library he would build: the library, in two parts, a Greek and a Roman collection, was finally inaugurated just before Varro's death, but we cannot tell whether he actively selected the contents of either collection. Indirectly at least he determined the Roman canon, through works begun in the fifties and certainly known to Cicero when he composed the *Brutus*. Varro's researches probably began with his investigation of the archives of the magistrates who supervised the dramatic festivals, recovering performance details for the plays of Plautus, Terence, and others. The information printed as *didascalia* in modern texts of Terence and surviving for two plays of Plautus, like the canon of twenty-one authentic Plautine comedies, goes back to Varro and his continuation of his master Stilo's work. Two other lost books, *De poematis* and *De poetis*, are the main source for the history of republican poetry transmitted by Horace, Suetonius, Gellius, Macrobius, and Jerome. The organisation of these works has been reconstructed.[11] While *De poematis* followed the traditional pattern (also evident in the first fifty chapters of Cicero's *Brutus*), defining the art and its function and tracing its origin and evolution through adolescence to the acme, *De poetis* was essentially historical, marking the inventor of each poetic genre, starting at Rome with the tragic playwright Livius. It is to this work that Cicero owes his landmark, pinning the first dramatic production to the year 240 BC. This work too signalled the birth and development of the art of poetry at Rome, and in both works Varro associated the prime with Ennius, who had already been dead over a century. Yet it seems unlikely that he acknowledged the corollary of this early acme and considered the question of decline, or the rise and fall of different genres as they emerged at Rome. He had the model of Greek literature, with its Classical phase now some 300 years in the past, to suggest what might be expected at Rome. But we have no evidence of Varro's attitude to contemporary authors and poets, and it is only with Velleius Paterculus, two generations later, that the comparative chronology of genres, each with its heyday and decline, is outlined for the arts and literature of Greece and extended to the literature of his own society.

[11] Hellfried Dahlmann, *Studien zu Varro De poetis* (Wiesbaden, 1963).

8

AUGUSTAN CRITICS

The Augustan period includes two major critics, Horace and Dionysius, both important in themselves but also in part conveniently complementary and typical. Horace is both poet and critic, a Roman deeply conscious of Rome's literary debt to Greece, yet also a champion of new Roman poetry. The historian and rhetorician Dionysius of Halicarnassus is also practitioner as well as critic, but he is primarily concerned with prose, especially oratory, though poetry has an important place in his most original work, *On Composition*. A Greek, he too is conscious of the Greek past, yet within a framework of Classicism in his assertion of canons of past greatness he displays a confident optimism about the present. But though living in Rome by 30 BC and in some works addressing Romans, he shows no interest in Roman literature; quite exceptionally in the preface to *On Ancient Orators* he refers to the influence of good Roman taste on the victory of Greek Atticism over Asianism.

Dionysius is here entirely typical of Greek lack of interest in Roman literature. By the late Republic and Augustan period Rome was a magnet to Greek men of letters as a centre of power and patronage; almost every Augustan Greek writer was in Rome for a substantial part of his life, and Greek works were often dedicated to Roman patrons. But Greek literary criticism expounds Greek theory and literature, and the basic relationship is of Greece instructing Rome, sometimes explicitly so, for example when Dionysius dedicates *On Composition* to the young Metilius Rufus, promises him the gift of a second work on diction so that he will be better instructed, and refers to their daily instruction together (*Comp.* 1, 20, 26). Similarly the pre-Augustan Philodemus dedicates *On Rhetoric* to a young Gaius and *On Poems* to a Gnaeus, and the post-Augustan Longinus (whatever his date) offers *On Sublimity* to the young Roman Terentianus with whom he has been reading Caecilius' work on the same subject. The Romans saw themselves as heirs to the Greeks and culturally bilingual, but as Cicero admits in his defence of the Greek poet Archias (23), Greek literature is read throughout the world, Latin only by its own speakers. Greek intellectuals may flatter Roman cultural pretensions and taste, as Dionysius does (cf. Strabo 9.2.2), but Greek recognition of Latin literature is rare. It may be significant that when Horace imagines the world-wide fame of his poetry, his list of places ranges the frontiers and beyond of Roman rule but does not include any centre of Greek culture such as Athens (*Odes* 2.20).

Caecilius of Calacte, a rhetorician who was roughly contemporary with Dionysius and came from heavily Romanised Sicily, provides our only evidence of Greek analysis of a Roman writer in the Augustan period, in his lost comparison of Demosthenes and Cicero. Just such a comparison is also Longinus' only acknowledgement of a Roman author, given with the reservation 'if we Greeks are allowed to make a judgement' (12.4), and Plutarch, who refuses to compare their literary styles, describes Caecilius' presumably notorious comparison as inept, like a dolphin on dry land (*Demosthenes* 3). Since Caecilius was an Atticist, preferring Lysias to Plato (Longinus 32.8), we may assume that he failed to appreciate Cicero's richness of style and compare Roman Atticists' attacks on Cicero's style as Asianic. If so, the Atticist/Asianist controversy is perhaps significantly the one area where Dionysius attests Roman influence on Greece. Its origins are obscure, though it may have begun among Greeks, probably primarily in terms of linguistic purity, and was then influenced by mutual cross-fertilisation between Greeks and Romans. Atticism was in any case related to the growth of Classicism, as the one inevitably entailed the other in the case of oratory, even if the canon of ten Attic orators was established later and was wrongly attributed to Caecilius.[1] Most of Caecilius' surviving fragments suggest a narrow interest in oratorical style, particularly Demosthenes and figures of speech, but as a champion of Atticism he may have been an important influence on contemporary taste.

1 Tradition, originality, and the Callimachean legacy in Latin poetry

One of the most striking features of Latin and later Greek literature is the pervasive imitation (*mimēsis*) of previous authors. Originality is found within an awareness of a past tradition, authors name and adapt their predecessors, and audiences are expected to recognise these allusions. Literature is for the educated, and in the case of the Romans it is effectively bilingual.

A theory of imitation is discussed by Cicero (*De or.* 2.87–97) and was probably already familiar to Callimachus, who praises Aratus' excellent remodelling of Hesiod (Epigram 27), and to Crates of Pergamum, who advises good imitation of authors like Homer (Philodemus, *On Poems* 5, p. 30 Jensen). To the Augustan age belongs one of our main sources, the partly surviving *On Imitation* by Dionysius of Halicarnassus: Book I on what it is; Book II on

---

[1] A. E. Douglas, 'Cicero, Quintilian and the canon of the ten Attic writers', *Mnemosyne*, 9 (1956), 30–40.

who should be imitated; Book III on how to do it. This is the apparent source for the list of Greek models and probably much of the theory in Quintilian 10.1–2. Surviving theory has little by way of concrete examples, but the general conceptual framework is uniform. What we imitate must become our own,[2] plagiarism is wrong, and we must produce what is, like Ovid's use of lines of Virgil, 'not theft but an open borrowing with the intention of being recognised' (Seneca, *Suas.* 3.7). We must choose our model carefully according to genre and our own capacities, we need a discerning understanding of our predecessor's virtues and his purpose in the original context, and crucially we must avoid merely verbal imitation and imitate the spirit (Quint. 10.2.27–8). In short, 'the man who imitates Demosthenes is not the man who speaks words of Demosthenes but the one who speaks in the manner of Demosthenes' (Pseudo-Dion. Hal., *Ars* 10.19). So Horace attacks servile imitators of his poetry (*Ep.* 1.19.19) and prescribes originality: 'You will not make efforts to copy word for word, a faithful translator, nor will you in your imitation leap down into a narrow prison from which timidity or the rules of your poetry give no escape' (*AP* 133ff.). We should feel a competitive spirit of emulation (*zēlos*), which Longinus (13–14) sees as a path to independent sublimity of thought, as we move from emulating the spirit of, for example, Plato (as Plato himself emulated Homer) to testing our own independent compositions by the criterion 'and how would Homer judge it?' But although it was possible and desirable to improve on the predecessor, the burden of the past could be heavy, especially when, as often, the predecessor was an acknowledged master. The combination of Classicism and imitation could be stultifying, yet it is within these confines that the Roman writers found stimulus to their greatest success.

As noted above in chapter 6, section 5, the Alexandrians had established acknowledged canons of great Greek writers, but although the Alexandrian poets were later added (there was a convention to exclude contemporaries), the Greek canon then remained virtually closed; Quintilian's list of Greek writers names only one post-Alexandrian, the Augustan historian Timagenes (10.1.75). For Horace and his contemporaries, the best Greek writers are the oldest (*Ep.* 2.1.28–9). Even linguistic change was denied, as imitators aimed to reproduce the Greek of their predecessors, and in prose the grip of linguistic Classicism tightened in the late Republic, probably as part of the Atticist/Asianist controversy, and Dionysius and others call for the return to the 'pure' standards of Classical Attic prose.

The Romans accept both the Greek theory of imitation and the admiration of acknowledged Classical models, the *Graeca exemplaria* which Horace says should be studied day and night (*AP* 267–8), but they use the theory both to acknowledge the debt and to assert originality as the first equivalent Roman.

---

[2] Cf. Horace, *AP* 121: 'communal material will come under one's own private jurisdiction.'

They often name and imitate specific Greek authors who are models for their genre. Virgil's *Eclogues* call on the Sicilian muses of Theocritus, in the *Georgics* he proclaims 'I sing Hesiodic song through Roman towns' (2.176), and the opening lines of the *Aeneid* recall Homer by their imitation of the beginnings of both *Iliad* and *Odyssey*. Propertius (3.1) is proud to be the first Roman bard to enter the groves of Philetas and Callimachus, and Horace claims for his *Epodes* that he was the first to introduce Archilochus, 'following his metre and his spirit, but not the content and words which savaged Lycambes' (*Ep*. 1.19.23 – 5). In prose too, Cicero calls his speeches against Anthony *Philippics* to signal his claim to emulate Demosthenes, and he mocks Roman Atticists for restricting their choice of model to Lysias (*Orator* 28 – 9). The Romans have an obvious ambition to establish their own comparable status as great writers, and Horace revealingly complains that this Roman zeal to compete with the Greeks had led too soon to the establishment of unjustified canons of Roman authors: Ennius, for example, is 'wise, martial, a second Homer, as the critics say' (*Ep*. 2.1.50ff.). He fights for the rights of contemporary poets with their new standards and champions the idea of growth and change in language (e.g. *AP* 48ff.). He and his contemporaries in fact became canonical almost in their lifetime, and though Quintilian's Roman list of models continues to give hospitality to newcomers, it is a victory of the Augustan age, following on the earlier success of the Ciceronian age in oratory, that the Romans could legitimately claim that their literature rivalled the Greeks.

Ovid heralds this victory in the last poem of his first book of *Amores* (1.15), where he drops his usual playfulness to assert his own immortality as a poet, producing two successive lists of famous Greek and Roman poets, each of the same length. The Greek list follows tradition in beginning with epic, Homer and Hesiod, and ending with Menander, and Ovid introduces only these three with the word 'he will live' (*vivet*), which he then applies to himself, 'I shall live' (*vivam*), marking his own succession within this great Greek tradition. The Roman list also begins traditionally with Ennius, but ends with the Augustan poets, Virgil and Ovid's pre-decessors in elegy, Tibullus and Gallus. Ovid's lists are also not merely lists of fame, but bring out what we will find to be interrelated pre-occupations of the Augustan poets, the contrast of major and minor genres, genius (*ingenium*) and technique (*ars*), and old and new Roman poetry. By including the minor genre of elegy in both lists, Ovid claims parallel fame for his own poetry, and the Roman poets progress from Ennius 'who lacks *ars*' to the 'polished' Tibullus. This is why Callimachus is so important, symbolically central in the Greek list, 'weak in *ingenium* but strong in *ars*', yet 'he will always be sung all over the world', words which repeat those Ovid used of his own ambition. Ovid also imitates Callimachus both before and after the lists, when he complains against contemporary envy, and asserts élitist scorn for the masses since he has Apollo's support.

Nor is Ovid unique in this focus on Callimachus.[3] Callimachus holds a peculiarly important position in the poetics of the Roman poets, less as a role-model for elegy, though he can be (cf. Propertius 3.1, 4.1; Horace, *Ep.* 2.2.100), but because he provided the poets of the late Republic and Augustan period with an aesthetic framework for a new direction in Roman poetry. His poetry may or may not have been widely read, but Roman poets repeatedly echo his programmatic statements since they influenced and gave respectable precedent for their own similar ambitions to move away from an outmoded form of epic and achieve a more sophisticated 'slender' style. Disparaging words such as 'small', 'slender', 'finely-spun', and 'delicate' (*parvus, tenuis, gracilis, deductus, lepidus, mollis*) become a roll-call of honour, and poetry is the result of erudition, work, polish, and nights of revision (*doctrina, labor, lima, evigilatio*).

If we look back to the last generation of the Republic we find little literary criticism in Catullus,[4] but Callimachean polemic is strong. He rejects sheer reams of verse and annalistic epic in favour of his friend Cinna's *Smyrna*, a work which took nine years and will last through the centuries, and he enjoys small works against the people's mistaken pleasure in swollen Antimachus (95). Such lengthy annals are rustic and lack wit (36); Catullus' own book of poems is elegant, new, small, and freshly polished with dry pumice, a mere trifle, yet he prays it will last more than one century (1). A translation of Callimachus is a compliment to the addressee (65.16, 116.2), the muses are 'learned' (65.2), metrical experimentation with Calvus a passionate delight for sophisticates (50). Little survives of Calvus and Cinna, but the *Smyrna* was so erudite it soon needed a learned commentary, and four lines of Cinna offer a gift of Aratus' poem with a clear echo of Callimachus' praise of Aratus: it is 'the product of many night-lamps, written in a dry little book of smooth paper' (like Catullus, he uses the book's physical appearance to describe its poetry). It is also significant that Calvus is the leading figure in the parallel polemic on prose-style, where he attacked Cicero's rich style and supported a plainer, more refined style as true Atticism (and again a contemporary issue is given authority from the Greek past). Further evidence of a group of poets with the same literary standards comes from Cicero (*To Atticus* 7.2.1; *Tusculans* 3.45). He parodies 'the new poets', the neoterics (Greek *neōteroi*), with a line he calls 'spondaising', because it ends with a fifth foot spondee, an Alexandrian mannerism which has Catullan parallels, and (presumably referring to the same group) he scorns the poets who are devotees of the learnedly obscure Euphorion and unappreciative of Ennius.

Literary polemic in the Catullan generation is obvious, artistry (*ars*) is the dominant issue, and the typical new poem is what modern critics call the

[3] Walter Wimmel, *Kallimachos in Rom* (Wiesbaden, 1960); W. B. Clausen, 'Callimachus and Latin poetry', *GRBS*, 5 (1964), 181–96.
[4] R. O. A. M. Lyne, 'The neoteric poets', *CQ*, 28 (1978), 167–87.

epyllion, or short hexameter narrative. Cinna's *Smyrna* and Calvus' *Io* are lost, but from Catullus 64 we can see the new level of sophistication in Roman poetic technique, with its carefully polished diction, elaborate patterning of single lines and intricate, many-layered structure. Narrative avoids the orthodox to focus on descriptive tableaux (*ecphrasis*) and direct speech, and Catullus continually surprises us with changes of mood and theme, as he misleadingly opens with an echo of Ennius' *Medea* and, exploiting a description of the wedding coverlet, a typical Alexandrian technique, moves us abruptly from the frame story of the glamorous wedding of Peleus and Thetis into the inset story of Ariadne betrayed by Theseus.

This late-Republican group may well include Virgil's friend, the poet Gallus, who imitated Euphorion (see Servius on *Ecl.* 6.72 and 10.50). Links forward are also provided by two shadowy but influential figures, Valerius Cato and the Greek Parthenius, both significantly poets and scholars in the Callimachean tradition. Parthenius was brought to Rome by Cinna's family, is said to have helped Virgil study Greek, includes two 'spondaising' lines in a group of six, and wrote a still surviving prose collection of obscure love-stories, which was intended to serve as a source-book for Gallus to turn into short epics and elegies. Cinna (fr. 14 Morel) praises Valerius Cato for his erudite poetry, a newly discovered fragment of Gallus looks to his expert literary judgement,[5] and for the poet Furius Bibaculus he is as scholarly as Zenodotus or Crates and is the arbiter of poetry, 'the Latin Siren, who selects and makes poets' (fr. 2 and 17 Morel). Pollio is another bridge figure, a youth of sophisticated wit in Catullus 12, honoured with a *bon voyage* poem (*propemptikon*) by Cinna, and for Virgil a patron who both appreciates and writes new (neoteric?) poetry (*Ecl.* 3.86). Virgil himself gives high praise to Cinna in *Eclogue* 9.35, and Callimachean stylistics are particularly evident in 6.3ff. with the appearance of Apollo to warn Virgil off martial epic, just as he had Callimachus, telling him 'to feed his sheep fat but his song thin'. Pastoral too fits neoteric affiliations, since it is small-scale poetry modelled on an Alexandrian, Theocritus, and Horace calls the *Eclogues* 'delicate and witty' (*molle atque facetum*, *Sat.* 1.10.44). Virgil's *Georgics* are more ambitious, but they follow Hesiod, whom Callimachus admired, and conclude (4.387–558) with an aetiological epyllion with typical inset story of love (Orpheus and Eurydice). Virgil fulfils the role of the poet he attributed to Gallus, claiming the muses give him the pipes of Hesiod to sing an aetiological poem (*Ecl.* 6.64ff.).

But there is one crucial difference between the neoterics and Virgil: Virgil's poetry includes a serious awareness of Roman political and moral issues. Already in the first *Eclogue* pastoral peace is shadowed by land eviction, and in the fourth his usually lowly pastoral explicitly attempts something 'a little greater' (4.1), with a prophecy of a babe bringing Rome a new Golden Age.

---

[5] R. D. Anderson *et al.*, 'Elegiacs by Gallus from Qaṣr Ibrîm', *JRS*, 69 (1979), 125–55.

The *Georgics* too include the suffering of civil war and hopes for a better future under Augustus, and they advocate moral worth and the need to work in a hard world. Virgil nowhere says so, but like Horace and unlike Propertius and Ovid, he rejected the Callimachean attitude of 'art for art's sake' which we find explicitly proclaimed by Eratosthenes.[6] This return to the mainstream of ancient literary criticism was probably influenced particularly by the Stoics and Lucretius, who both emphasised the useful function of poetry and saw it as a means to an end, in Lucretius' imagery the honey on the cup to sweeten the doctor's bitter medicine (1.936ff.). Lucretius was also a precedent for selective use of the Callimachean aesthetics. He champions the sweetness of poetry over mere quantity, 'I shall expound with sweet rather than many verses, just as the small note of the swan is better than the clamour of cranes' (4.180–2), but he writes in grand style a morally protreptic epic on the traditionally noble theme of the nature of the universe.[7] All this makes it less surprising that Virgil moved up the hierarchy of genres to produce the paradox of the *Aeneid*, a martial epic of refined polish and elusive ambiguity, Homeric narrative of the aetiology of Rome herself, telling her imperialist destiny with all its heavy cost in human suffering.

As the traditional 'top' genre, epic was also in any case an obvious challenge if the Romans were to rival the Greeks, and successful emulation of Homer, '*the* poet' of the Greeks, would be the most glittering prize, even if Callimachus had thought Homer inimitable. The Augustan hope of conquering epic at least partly explains the typical stance in their refusal to attempt epic, the *recusatio*.[8] The Roman poet imitates Callimachus' rejection of epic, but he does so not because epic is outmoded but because he lacks the ability – and sometimes he claims he will attempt it in the future, a promise which is usually only a polite evasion but is fulfilled in Virgil's *Aeneid*. No doubt the popularity of the *recusatio* in Augustan poets reflects some pressure to praise famous deeds in the old poetic tradition, honoured by Cicero in *Pro Archia*, a pressure particularly likely in the circle of Maecenas with its closeness to Augustus. Tibullus has no *recusatio*; the early Ovid wittily plays with it as a convention in the first of his *Amores* (1.1), where Cupid appears instead of Apollo to steal a foot and turn Ovid's hexameters into elegy. The apparent refusal to praise Augustus' deeds also allows a more sophisticated form of oblique eulogy as the poet lists the sort of deed he cannot or will not tackle (as in Virgil, *Georgics* 3.16ff. and Horace, *Odes* 4.15). But often, as in Ovid, the *recusatio* is only formally a defensive stance. There is irony, for example when Propertius

---

[6] Poetry is for enjoyment (*psuchagōgia*), not instruction (*didaskalia*), cf. Strabo 1.2.3 and above, ch. 6, section 5.

[7] D.C. Innes, 'Gigantomachy and natural philosophy', *CQ* 29 (1979), 165–71.

[8] On the *recusatio* see Nisbet and Hubbard on Horace, *Odes* 1.6. On the Ennian passage see above, ch. 7, section 1. It is a sign of changing taste and standards that Ennius, who prided himself on his learning (*dicti studiosus*), is now seen as deficient in technique and 'shaggy' (*hirsutus*), cf. Propertius 4.1.61; Ovid, *Tristia* 2.424.

wittily plays with Callimachean terminology as he links his 'narrow couch',
the battle-field of love, to the 'narrow lungs' of Callimachus who cannot
'thunder' on Jupiter's battles against the Giants (2.1.39ff.), and he promises
to attempt epic, but only if Maecenas will, as of course he knows Maecenas
will not (3.9.45ff.). There is an assumption that the minor genres are a
respectable and even preferable alternative, small but choice. For Horace (*Odes*
4.2) Pindar is inimitable, a mighty swan to Horace's small bee, but the bee
labours hard and feeds on sweet thyme (and he implicitly undercuts the
contrast by his own imitations of Pindar, which show that Pindar can be
emulated but only in the minor key of monody). For Virgil's *Georgics* the bee
is also small, yet 'my efforts [*labor*] are on a slender theme [*tenuis*], but the
glory is not slender' (4.6). What matters and is the permanent legacy of the
Callimachean battle of books in the late Republic is the new standard of *ars*,
technical polish.

Curiously combined with the Callimachean terminology and imagery of
ars we also find much use of the language of religion to dignify the poet as
more than mere craftsman but heir to the tradition of inspired bards like
Orpheus. Modern critics speak of the *vates* concept, and here again Virgil's
Eclogues are seminal. Virgil revives the term *vates*, 'seer' or 'priest-poet' (7.28,
9.34), as a term of praise against Ennius' mocking use to describe his crude
predecessors.[9] It has been argued that *vates* refers specifically to Virgil's
concern with moral and political ideas, but *vates* has a wider role, signifying
the poet's claim to innate genius (*ingenium*), a connotation which fits one of
Varro's etymologies (he derives it 'from the force of the mind', p. 213
Funaioli). On this view Virgil neatly turns the Ennian antithesis of art and
art-less into one of art and inspiration. Inspiration was more naturally
associated with poets attempting the major genres in elevated style, so Horace
(*Sat.* 1.4.43–4), where the true poet has 'genius, a more divinely inspired
mind and a style which will resound with grandeur', like Ennius (*ibid.* 60–2),
and it is suitably Lucretius who describes himself as 'inspired with a vigorous
mind' (1.925). The miniaturist Callimachus, on the other hand, was thought
to have only *ars* (as we have seen from Ovid), and his use of priestly language
merely reinforces his élitist scorn for the vulgar when he compares good poetry
to pure, untainted water offered to Demeter from a holy spring (*Hymns* 2.100).

The Augustan poets, however, also claim *ingenium* for themselves, for
example Horace: 'Truthful fate has given me a small portion of countryside,
a slender genius [*tenuis spiritus*] from the Greek muse and a scorn for the envious
populace' (*Odes* 2.16.37–40); and 'Apollo gave me *spiritus*, Apollo gave me
the *ars* of song and the name of poet' (4.6.29–30). Propertius and Ovid also
frequently refer to their *ingenium*, for example Propertius 2.33.57–8: 'By my
genius I am as a king feasting among a throng of girls'; 3.2.25–6: 'But fame

[9] On the Ennian passage see above, n. 8, and ch. 7, section 1.

sought by genius will never fall from eternity, glory from genius stands deathless'; Ovid, *Ars amatoria* 3.545ff.: 'Genius is softened by peaceful technique ... there is a god in me'. *Vates* and sacral imagery make precisely the same claim to inspiration in more poetic terms, as in Virgil's *Georgics* (2.476), where the poet carries sacred offerings of the sweet muses, significantly adding the religious image to an imitation of the Alexandrian Aratus, and Propertius (3.1ff.), where the poet formulates his debt to Callimachus and Philetas in rich imagery of sacred groves and rites.

So too Bacchus connotes inspiration, Callimachus was a water-drinker (*Palatine Anthology* 9.406, 11.20), and Ennius drank wine (Horace, *Ep.* 1.19.7 – 9). But although the Augustan poets drink water from Callimachean clear, pure springs, they also serve Bacchus, for example in Propertius (2.30.37 – 8), where the poet draws his power from his mistress, Cynthia, and Bacchus, who significantly also has *ars*: 'You, Cynthia, will be set in the forefront of the dancing muses, and Bacchus will be in the middle with his learned [*doctus*] wand; then shall I allow the holy clusters of ivy-berries to garland my head: for without you my genius has no strength' (cf. 3.2.9 – 10; Ovid, *Tristia* 5.3). The epiphany of Bacchus in Horace (*Odes* 2.19), however tinged with ironic self-deprecation, similarly reveals Horace as a true poet, filled with inspiration. Callimachean mastery of technique is not enough for the Augustan poets, and Horace can speak for more than himself: 'There is controversy whether praiseworthy poetry comes from nature or art. I see no advantage either from effort without a rich natural vein or from crude genius. Each requires the help of the other and they form a friendly conspiracy' (*AP* 408 – 11).

As for structure, we have virtually nothing outside Horace's *Ars poetica* on the problems of unity raised by the wish to avoid what Callimachus called 'single, continuous' narrative, though we can deduce lively interest from poetic practice: the interweaving of themes in Catullus 64 and 68, the latter with an elaborate annular structure; the clustering of related themes in Tibullus; or the careful architectonic designs of Virgil. Ovid lifts the veil slightly in his *Metamorphoses*, paradoxically a finely-spun, continuous narrative from the creation of the world till his own day (1.3 – 4). He sets up a weaving competition between Minerva and Arachne, where Arachne wins with a structure recalling Ovid's own (6.53ff.).[10] Such symbolic allegory fits the stock analogy of literature and the arts (cf. Horace, *AP* 361: *ut pictura poesis*, 'poetry is like painting'), and the use of a description of a work of art to encapsulate a major theme of the rest of the poem, as in the shield of Aeneas (Virgil, *Aen.* 8.626ff.). Literary polemic is also transparent in Ovid's immediately preceding story, a competition between the muses and the Pierians

[10] H. Hofmann, 'Ovid's Metamorphoses: *carmen perpetuum, carmen deductum*', *Papers of the Liverpool Latin Seminar*, ed. Francis Cairns, 5 (1986), 223 – 41.

(5.294ff.). There the learned muses report their easy victory, with a carefully structured epyllion, over the boastful Pierians, who think quantity an argument (they are nine, like the muses, 311), lack originality ('imitating everything', 299) and tell ineptly and impiously the theme of the battle of gods and giants which needs the power of Orpheus and is too grand for poets like Ovid (*Met.* 10.143ff.; *Amores* 2.1.11ff.). Callimachean poetry wins.

But the contest between Minerva and Arachne is between equals in Callimachean skill, as both select slender threads (*gracilis*), ply learned hands with a zeal which hides the work (*labor*), use subtle shades (*tenues*) with a rainbow effect of countless bright colours, and the traditional story each depicts 'is finely spun' (*deducitur*). Minerva's design is both morally didactic and strictly unified: a central picture which is a symbol of her victory over Arachne, the aetiology of Athens, as Athena/Minerva defeats Neptune with her gift of the olive to become the name-deity of Athens and the gods watch 'augustly grave', four small corner pictures which all explicitly exemplify divine justice, and a framing band of her own victorious olive. But this is matched by Arachne, who has vivid realism ('You would think it real', 104), amoral gods, a rich medley of stories linked loosely by love and characters changing shape, like Ovid's own *Metamorphoses*, and a thin border (*tenuis*) of flowers interwoven with ivy, the poet's symbol of inspiration. This is no contrast of old and new, of an Ennius and an Ovid, but Ovid challenging Virgil. Note also that Minerva has a central main scene, as does Virgil's shield (*Aen.* 8.675) and his temple of poetry (*Georgics* 3.16). Within shared standards of skilful technique, Ovid justifies his own large-scale poetry which is not tightly structured and morally conscious but shows Callimachean variety and allegiance to poetry as 'art for art's sake'. To do so, Ovid neatly uses the Virgilian technique of symbolism but for aesthetic, not moralising purpose.

But by their nature much of the poetics in Catullus and the Augustan poets is selective and often oblique. Much is absent. There are, for example, only a few hints that a poet might have his own individual style (Ovid, *Tristia* 1.1.61; *Ex Ponto* 4.3ff.), or that apparently personal poetry need not be autobiographical (*Tristia* 2.354: 'My life is respectable, my poetry is playful'; cf. Catullus 16). For a fuller picture we turn to Horace.

2 Horace

Horace is our single major author on poetics among the Augustans, and he is both poet and critic, defending his own poetic practice and advocating the same high standards for others. In particular he demands a combination of polished artistry and moral responsibility and, often within a contrast of Greece and Rome, justifies the best new Roman poetry against older Roman poetry and fashionable amateurism. But he avoids abstract, systematic argumentation, an unqualified note of seriousness is rare, and we have to reckon with irony, mock-humility, and tactical exaggeration of one half of an antithesis. His range of genres also produces some differences of theme and stance, as we might expect: 'If I lack the ability or knowledge to observe the set rules for changes of genre and style [*colores*], why am I acclaimed as a poet?' (*AP* 86 – 7).

In the *Odes* (Books I – III published 23 BC, Book IV, a decade later) Horace sets himself within the Greek tradition. He aims to join the canon of Greek lyric poets (1.35 – 6) and asserts his originality as the first to Romanise a Greek genre: 'I have completed a monument more lasting than bronze ... the first to have adapted Aeolian song to Italian metres' (3.30; cf. *Ep.* 1.19.21ff.). He also immortalises, as Homer had: 'There lived many brave heroes before Agamemnon, but all are unlamented and unknown, buried in the long night, because they lack a sacred bard' (4.9.25 – 8). Yet he claims that the *Odes* are light erotic, an unconvincing pose in view of the many ethical and political poems and the similar variety of theme he admires in his Greek model, Alcaeus (1.32, 2.13). It is because eroticism is a necessary part of the genre that Horace can humorously exploit the stock contrasts of love and war, of light and serious genres to avoid writing epic or, at the end of unusually serious poems to warn that he will not maintain the seriousness (e.g., 1.6, 2.1, 3.3). The pose also fits his view that poetry is 'born and invented to give pleasure' (*AP* 377), and for Horace, as we shall see, lyric is his 'real' poetry. He only obliquely hints at the moral content of the *Odes*, as when he couples his own poetic gift and upright character: 'I have a sense of duty [*fides*] and a generous vein of talent' (2.18.9 – 10); and when in the Roman Odes he takes up a public role as a priest-poet to sing to the young (3.1.1 – 4).

The *Satires*, published a decade earlier than *Odes* I – III, are by contrast a Roman genre, invented by Lucilius,[11] and though Greek influence is not absent (*Sat.* 1.4.1ff. looks to Greek Old Comedy), Horace is concerned with the development of Roman poetry, criticising Lucilius for being slipshod and prolific, an example of the lack of polish which made older Roman poetry inferior to that of new poets like himself and Virgil: 'In an hour he often dictated two hundred verses, as if it were a great achievement, standing on one foot; in his muddy flow, there was much that you would want to remove' (1.4.9 – 11); and 'Granted that Lucilius is humorous and urbane, granted he is more polished than the poet producing rough verses unacquainted with the Greeks,[12] than the mob of older poets; yet, if he had been transported by fate to our time, he would refine much, he would delete all that dragged past the point of completion, and in writing his verses he would often scratch his head and bite his nails to the quick' (1.10.64 – 71).

Horace calls the *Satires* conversation pieces, *sermones*, a 'muse on foot' or

[11] Rudd, *Satires*, pp. 86ff.; Brink, *Prolegomena*, pp. 153 – 77.

[12] Translation uncertain; see Niall Rudd, 'Horace on the origins of *satura*', *Phoenix*, 14 (1960), 36 – 44, esp. 40 – 4.

prose-poetry (2.6.17), not perhaps poetry at all, 'I shall exclude myself from the category of those I would agree to be poets' (1.4.39ff.), but the more prosaic level allows Horace, like Lucilius, to include more technical literary criticism of a type alien to the *Odes*. For example, clearly describing his own practice and probably influenced by Cicero on the style of *sermo* (*De officiis* 1.136), he advises brevity and variety of tone 'sometimes severe, sometimes humorous, sometimes impersonating the orator and poet, sometimes the man of wit who deliberately constrains and restricts his force' (1.10.9ff.). Diction too should be good Latin, and he attacks those who admire Lucilius for his mixture of Greek and Latin words (1.10.20–1). So too Messalla was scrupulous in his Latinity, Pollio mocked Livy's *Patavinitas*, Po-valley provincialism, and the exiled Ovid feared that his Latin would be infected with barbarisms.[13] But technique is not everything. Lucilius was associated with strong personal abuse, but Horace allows attack only against those who deserve it (1.4) and in counter-attack (2.1). Poetry must then be both highly polished and morally acceptable, and Horace foreshadows his later praise of poetry which can both delight and be useful (*AP* 343–4): 'Yet what prevents telling the truth with laughter?' (1.1.24–5).

In the *Epistles* (Book I published 20 BC), Horace even claims to abandon poetry for philosophy, but he presents poetry in the suspiciously narrow terms of what delights, 'the play' of lyric (1.1.10). He exploits the old quarrel between poetry and philosophy to emphasise his total concern with moral content, and undercuts the formal disjunction in the following poem where he is reading Homer, 'a more lucid and better teacher of ethics than Chrysippus and Crantor' (1.2.3–4).[14] Homer presents moral paradigms, the *Iliad* of vices, the *Odyssey* of Odysseus as 'a useful model for the meaning of virtue and wisdom' (1.2.17–18). This type of interpretation was familiar in the schoolroom and among the Stoics,[15] but Horace also describes his own *Epistles*: Maecenas is a patron who knows how to give gifts, just as Odysseus' son knows how to refuse inappropriate gifts (1.7.14 and 40ff.). Similarly in the *Satires* he claimed to follow his father, who taught him to avoid faults by pointing out examples (1.4.106). This exemplary role of literature is not unique to the Augustans, but we can compare Livy's claim that his history will provide examples to imitate and avoid (Prologue 10), and it is no doubt part of what Virgil saw as imitation of Homer that he presents characters so often in a moral role, such as Aeneas in terms of *pietas*, Turnus of uncontrolled *furor* and *violentia*.

---

[13] Seneca, *Contr.* 2.4.8; Quint. 1.5.56; Ovid, *Tristia* 3.4.49–50.

[14] The Stoic Chrysippus wrote a lost work on how to read poetry (Diog. Laert. 7.200), presumably on moral lines similar to those of Plutarch's similarly titled work; the Academic Crantor was an admirer of Homer (Diog. Laert. 4.26).

[15] Bonner, *Education*, pp. 212–48, esp. 241–4; J. Tate, 'Horace and the moral function of poetry', *CQ*, 22 (1928), 65–72.

Poetry also appears when Horace asks a group of young Romans about their poetry, gently deflates pretensions to attempt epic, tragedy, and Pindaric odes, and warns one to avoid plagiarism, 'in case the birds flock to claim their own feathers and the crow is jeered when it is stripped of its stolen colours' (1.3.18–20). Traditional ideas of creative imitation support Horace's own claim to originality (1.19): his prescriptions on poetry are misunderstood; poets do need wine (= inspiration), but this rule has produced drunken imitators, who follow him slavishly and superficially. Implicit is the comment that poets also need the water of technique. Horace by contrast exemplifies original emulation of Greek models in his *Epodes* and *Odes*. Yet his lyric is privately praised, publicly denigrated because he does not look for popularity (an echo of Callimachus), and disdains the mutual flattery of other poets and influential critics in the literary circuit of the recitation hall.[16] So later he attacks the flattery of mutual compliments (*Epistles* 2.2.87ff.), and contrasts the true critical friend with the empty flatterer (*AP* 434ff.). The ethical framework of friend and flatterer is clear, and the *Epistles* as a whole see poetry in moral terms as part of a way of life. Slavish imitation, for example, of superficials such as beard and lack of washing (*AP* 298) marks the false philosopher just as much as the poet.

It is in the three latest and longer epistles that we find Horace's most mature reflections on poetry. Probably the earliest (*c.* 19 BC?) is *Ep.* 2.2 to Florus, which continues the apparent antithesis of poetry and philosophy, and does so all the more easily since it makes almost no reference to the social function of poetry. Horace no longer writes lyric: this is because he no longer needs the money; he is too lazy and old; different people want different types of poetry; Rome is too noisy; poets have to flatter each other and the fickle crowd. (There seems to be a hit at Propertius: the two poets, lyricist and elegist, compliment each other as an Alcaeus and a Callimachus or Mimnermus.) His reasons are ironically unconvincing, and he seems an example of one ignorant of poetry's true demands, until the key central section where he sets the standards of a *legitimum poema*: like a Roman censor, the poet will carefully prune inert words, 'even if they withdraw reluctantly and still hover in the inmost sanctuary of Vesta', will add new life from select archaisms, 'unearthing and bringing into the light beautiful words long hidden ... buried by ugly mould and the neglect of years', and admit neologisms as needed.[17] The 'play' of poetry is painful work (109ff.).

Epistles 2.1 to Augustus (published *c.* 13 BC) defends new Roman poetry (just because the best Greeks are the earliest, it does not follow that the earliest Romans are the best), contrasts the childlike frivolity and artistic enthusiasm

---

[16] A recent phenomenon, see Alexander Dalzell, 'C. Asinius Pollio and the early history of public recitation at Rome', *Hermathena*, 86 (1955), 20–8; Quinn, 'The poet and his audience', pp. 76–180, esp. 158–60. Horace recited only to friends, under pressure (*Sat.* 1.4.72ff.).

[17] Less probably 'subject to usage', see Brink on *AP* 72.

of the Greeks with the upright, practical, uncultured Roman of the past, contrasts the recent amateurist craze with poetry's disciplined demands, and criticises the technique of older Roman poetry to praise contemporary poets who combine the best of Greece and Rome. Appropriately in a letter to Augustus, Horace stresses that the poet is 'useful to society' (*utilis urbi*, 124), and ends with a deft compliment to Augustus, fortunate to have the services of Virgil and Varius, though, in typical *recusatio*, Horace himself is too small, *parvus*, to celebrate Augustus in epic grandeur. Through this series of contrasts Horace synthesises his ideals for Roman poetry. It began with Greece, 'captured Greece made captive her fierce conqueror, and introduced the arts to rural Latium' (156–7). Now there are Virgil, Varius, and Horace himself.

The usefulness of the poet occupies the centre of the poem (118–38). He is a poor soldier, but free from greed and *utilis urbi*. He teaches the young, a reminder of the important place poetry had in the school curriculum,[18] and a fate Horace had already foreseen for his first book of *Epistles*, 'teaching the boys their letters' (1.20.17). 'The poet shapes the boy's soft, faltering voice, turns his ear from indecent talk, soon proceeds to form his character with friendly precepts, a corrector of harshness, envy, and anger; he relates fine accomplishments, instructs the years of growth with familiar examples, and consoles the helpless and ill.' The state also gets choral hymns and prayers, and these are given unusual emphasis by the sonorously balanced conclusion, 'by song the gods above are placated, by song the gods of the dead' (138). Even Plato had accepted hymns to the gods in the *Republic*, but Horace also gently hints at his own *Carmen Saeculare*.[19]

But the two most prominent genres are drama and epic, partly because they cover the early Roman poetry praised by the critics (50ff.), and the final section on epic provides a compliment to Augustus. Drama has a particularly strong exemplary role, a significant parallel to the *Ars poetica*, which also shares a new interest in literary history, probably showing the influence of Varro.[20] The history of Roman drama mirrors the growth of Roman literature: it began with Fescennine verses at rustic festivities (where unrestrained freedom led to abuse and the need of rules), was captivated by Greek influence, but still now shows signs of rusticity (139–60). Tragedy illustrates the literary genius of Greece (98), and its possible usefulness attracted the Romans to their own first literary attempts (161ff.); the Romans have a natural talent for tragedy (*spirat tragicum satis*, 165), but from ignorance and pride have been afraid to revise, both in tragedy and in the apparently easier genre of comedy. As proof that he does not criticise from envy, Horace points to his appreciation of the power of dramatic illusion, 'the poet who causes me imaginary anguish, anger,

[18] Brink, *ad loc.*; cf. n. 14 above.
[19] Fraenkel, *Horace* (Oxford, 1957), p. 391.
[20] Brink, *ad loc.* and, on the parallel origins of Greek drama, at *AP* 275ff.

calm, fills me with false terrors, and like a magician sets me now in Thebes and now in Athens' (211–13). But there must also be space for poetry which will satisfy a reader if Augustus is to fill his new national library (216–17).[21] So too in the *Ars poetica* Horace highlights a reading public for poetry which will live (345–6), and traditionally the written style required more polish than that for performance. Drama was popular, Augustus himself enjoyed watching old Roman comedy,[22] but although Horace encourages further attempts, it looks as though, despite Varius' *Thyestes* and Ovid's *Medea*, he saw no contemporary Roman drama comparable to the triumphs in epic.

Ars poetica, a title already familiar to Quintilian (8.3.60), is probably Horace's last work,[23] and is a novel experiment in form, our first known poem on poetics and a fusion of epistle and technical treatise. As in Lucretius and Virgil's *Georgics*, brief passages in prescriptive style alternate with rich set-pieces, and Horace evades the unilinear structure of textbook headings by apparently abrupt transitions, producing overall unity from the interweaving of key ideas such as unity and propriety. It is his most systematic analysis of poetry but also his most elusive. He makes little open reference to Roman poetry, and his main model is drama, yet it is intrinsically unlikely that his analysis is irrelevant to the Roman literary scene and mere 'art for art's sake', a virtuoso versification of a technical treatise, developing topics according to their potential for poetic colouring. In fact much is familiar from his other works, and although drama is prominent to fit the Aristotelian tradition, Horace is brief on points unique to it such as the five-act structure. As in *Epistles* 2.1, drama is exemplary, and although he does not, as there, directly focus on Roman poetry as a product of the Graeco-Roman tradition, this is because he is analysing the universal standards of good poetry. The resulting picture is similar, and *Epistles* 2.1 and the *Ars poetica* are the two sides of a single coin. But many problems remain. Most puzzling of all, why does Horace appear as a dramatist of satyr-plays?

Porphyrio tells us that Horace took 'not all but his main precepts' from Neoptolemus: *praecepta ... non quidem omnia sed eminentissima*. From the little we know of Neoptolemus, these will include unity, attention to large-scale poetry, and the poet's dual function to delight and be useful; and, though evidence is lacking, it would hardly surprise if he included propriety and the need for technique. But the only major concern unfamiliar from earlier writings of Horace is unity. Horace also uses Neoptolemus' tripartite structure of *poema* (details and small poems), *poesis* (whole poems and large-scale poems), and *poeta* (the poet). The section on the poet is explicitly introduced (306ff.),

---

[21] Opened in 28 BC, in two sections, Greek and Latin, one of the first public libraries in Rome; see Quinn, 'The poet and his audience', pp. 127–8.
[22] Jasper Griffin, *Latin Poets and Roman Life* (London, 1985), pp. 198–210.
[23] Between 14 and 8 BC; see Brink, *Prolegomena*, pp. 239ff. and *Epistles, Book 2*, pp. 554–8; Ronald Syme, 'The sons of Piso the Pontifex', *AJP*, 101 (1980), 333–41.

while *poema* and *poesis* are to be identified in the roughly equivalent disjunction
of form and content (*verba* and *res*) (40 – 1), though Horace disguises the move
to content with an unobtrusive glide from metre to drama to characterisation
and plot.[24] *Res* opens the account of metre (73ff.): 'Deeds [*res gestae*] of kings
and leaders and grim warfare have been shown the appropriate metre by
Homer'. The genres are listed according to their match of metre and content;
then *res* (89) signals the transition to drama, a transition masked by the
continuing emphasis on propriety: 'comic content does not wish to be
expressed in tragic verses'. Since he regards them as inextricably linked,
Horace deliberately blurs the distinction between form and content, and the
disinterring of the Neoptoleman structure of *poema* and *poesis* is in fact a disadvantage to the understanding of Horace's own more elusive structure, based
on interlocking key concepts such as propriety.

Ars poetica begins with an analogy from painting, a grotesque monster of
disunity. The need for unity recalls Aristotle, but Horace does not look for
tight plot unity. He assumes a wish for a fusion of unity and variety, and the
call to avoid disunity from unrelated parts and the need of more than mastery
of isolated detail suggest what could go wrong in the contemporary experi-
ments in structure by Horace and other poets. He illustrates the 'purple patch'
(*purpureus pannus*, 15 – 16) by descriptions of places, and though the Rhine in
particular may suggest epic, such descriptions of places are standard examples
of *ecphrasis* in schoolroom exercises, and Horace shows the wider application
by illustrating his own advice with an integral description followed by skilful
variety from the interweaving of themes as he turns to the need for limits on
poetic freedom and introduces a second major keynote, the need for the
constraints of *ars*. He also produces unity from ring-composition at the end
of the poem (453 – 76) with a balancing tableau of the unrestrained mad poet.
'Let it be what you will, provided it is single and unified', *'simplex et unum'* (23),
but Horatian unity includes organised interweaving.

We are told to choose content to match our power; diction and lucid organisation will then follow (38 – 41). This is a *partitio* or table of contents, but it is
framed to remind us that poet, content, and style are interconnected. After a
rapid dismissal of organisation (say what is immediately suitable and
postpone much, advice he then follows), Horace moves to diction. This
is a very selective account (nothing on the usually important topic of metaphor), but the unusual first demand to be *tenuis* in itself indicates the need
for Callimachean polish and concision, and there may be further polemic
in the next item, the combination of words: 'You will have spoken excellently
if a known word is by clever combination [*callida iunctura*] rendered new'
(45 – 8). We can compare the attack on Virgil for 'a new type of affectation
[*cacozelia*] which is not from excessively grand or arid diction but from

---

[24] See Brink on *AP* 119 as the disguised beginning of *poesis*.

a new use of ordinary words, and for that reason unobtrusive' (Donatus, *Vita Virgili* 44).

Next come neologisms (48 – 59), which must be used in case of need (as with unity, he rejects unrestrained freedom) and taken sparingly 'from a Greek source' (*Graeco fonte*).[25] He vigorously claims the freedom of the old Roman poets to enrich the Latin tongue for Virgil, Varius, and himself: 'There has been freedom and there will always be freedom to bring forth a word minted with a new mark' (58 – 9). As one of the few references to Roman poets, this is an important passage, and since it recalls Horace's championship of new Roman poetry elsewhere, it is tempting to see neologism as a symbol also of the wider topic of originality, especially since Roman originality derived from the Greek tradition, *Graeco fonte*. If so, he himself illustrates such originality in the following set-piece on the way words flourish and decay like leaves and men, an adaptation to the theory of language of Homer's famous comparison of the generations of men to leaves (*Il.* 6.146ff.). Horace exploits the poetic potential: for example, 'The works of men will die, far less will the splendour and charm of words stand with enduring life' (68 – 9). But like the opening tableau on unity, this is no mere purple patch. The need for growth and change in language is an important point, which he similarly emphasises in the set-pieces on new life from archaisms quoted above from *Epistles* 2.2. The combination of change and ethical content also foreshadows later passages, the four Ages of Man and the history of music and drama (156ff., 202ff.).

The traditional authorial role in a treatise is critic, not practitioner. But in the earlier part of the poem Horace appears as both critic and poet, introducing himself first in both roles: 'we ask and grant in turn this permission' (11). On the dangers of neighbouring faults he cites himself for the fault appropriate to his own style: 'I take pains to be brief, I become obscure', but not for the faults to which he is less vulnerable: 'tautness fails the pursuer of smoothness, and the claimant to grandeur is turgid' (25ff.; cf. *Sat.* 1.10.9). He gives his own backing to the need for unity 'if I were to compose anything' (35), and he claims for himself the right of modern Roman poets to invent new words (53ff.). He ends the following list of genres and matching metres with lyric, his own genre, and exclaims that he must himself know the appropriate genres and styles (*colores*) if he is to be a poet (86 – 7).

In the long middle section on drama and epic, genres he never tackled, Horace is suitably audience, not poet. He moves gradually to tragedy and comedy, using their differences to show how diction should match the emotional level and character of the speaker, a standard rhetorical point, as in Aristotle, *Rhetoric* 3.7. In *Epistles* 2.1 emotional impact is not the only criterion: here Horace reverses the emphasis: 'it is not enough for poems to be

---

[25] The meaning is disputed, probably neologism where a Greek meaning is added to a Roman word; e.g., *dominantia verba* in 234 means 'ordinary words' on the analogy with Greek *kuria onomata*.

beautifully crafted, let them be attractive and drive as they wish the audience's emotion, ... if you want me to weep, you must first yourself feel grief, only then will I share the pain of your disasters' (99ff.). In contrast to Aristotle's *Poetics*, Horace moves freely between tragedy and comedy, and after initial advice on differentiation, he illustrates emotional level from tragedy, though comedy can rise in style to almost tragic anger, and tragedy descend to a plainer style for grief, an indication of an interest in the overlap between tragedy and comedy which marks his analysis of satyric drama. On character he turns first to comedy, but then epic/tragic characters illustrate how to follow tradition or invent consistently (119ff.: 'let Medea be fierce and indomitable'). Yet again avoiding analysis by genre, Horace also shifts to epic, probably because of the polemic on structure prompted by Callimachus, and advocates originality from the imitation of Homer. Only later do we recognise that line 119 is a disguised move to plot and originality (119–52).

Horace permits the invention of new characters, but creative imitation is preferable: what he calls the difficult task of appropriating traditional material, avoiding the crowded path and merely verbal imitation. Homer is our model; he begins well, speeds to the end, introduces striking fantasies like the Cyclops, catches the reader by plunging *in medias res*, omits whatever could not 'gleam' poetically, and 'lies so skilfully, mingling false and true, that the middle fits the beginning, the end the middle' (151–2). Horace supports Callimachus, champion of the narrow path, but sets up Homer as the model for imitation; he ends with Aristotle's theory of unity, but couples it with praise of Homer's fiction. The whole mixture is original, and Horace adds a characteristic comic note when he deflates grandiose openings: 'mountains will labour and give birth to a ridiculous mouse' (*ridiculus mus*, 139).

With another abrupt twist, Horace returns to drama and characterisation (153ff.). Characterisation must fit the age-group, a prescription which introduces an elaborate and often ironic description of the Ages of Man: child, youth, man, and old man. Horace here moves beyond drama, though drama in any case influenced other genres, for example New Comedy characters enter Roman elegy, such as the bawd, prostitute, and penniless lover in Ovid (e.g., *Amores* 1.8). But Horace's source is significantly oratory, as in Aristotle's *Rhetoric* (2.12–24), with the addition of childhood. Age too is the standard first example of differences in the schoolroom exercise called 'speech with characterisation', a type which was thought important for the future poet and historian as well as orator.[26] Horace in short universalises, and this is in keeping with the moral exemplary role of literature which we saw in *Epistles* 1.2 and which he here makes explicit only later (312ff.). It is also this exemplary role which helps to explain why Horace, unlike Aristotle, gives more prominence to character than plot.

[26] Cf. *Rhetores Graeci*, ed. Spengel, II, pp. 60, 115–16; Quint. 3.8.49; Russell, *Greek Declamation*, pp. 87ff.

There follow (179–201) contrastingly brief prescriptions specific to drama: stage action is more vivid than reported speech, but avoid actions implausible on stage, such as Medea killing her children; have five acts (a practice already seen in Menander and Roman comedy); end with a god's intercession only if the plot requires it; let no more than three characters speak on stage; let the chorus be part of the plot, and give good advice, soothing the angry, praising what is right, and praying to the gods. The moral role is not Aristotelian, and combines the educational and choral functions of the poet *utilis urbi* which we saw in the Augustus letter (2.1.124–38). Morality also shapes the treatment of music (202–19): the simple, serviceable flute of the past suited its rustic audience but, as prosperity brought corruption, music degenerated into dissolute licence. Horace could draw on a rich Greek tradition for music as a sign or cause of corruption in society,[27] but it is interesting that the Romans saw a similar degeneration in musical changes of the first century BC (cf. Cic., *De legibus* 2.39). Roman civilisation was often thought to develop as Greece had, only centuries later.

Music has introduced the theme of historical change, which Horace next (220) applies to the history of drama. Diverging from Aristotle (*Po.* 1449a9ff.), and presumably using Hellenistic theory, Horace tells us that tragedy began with a competition for the prize of a goat, and satyric drama came later, a mean between tragedy and comedy, blending seriousness with play.[28] The section on the satyr-play occupies the centre of the poem, the position for key ideas in *Epistles* 2.1 and 2, yet the genre is not of contemporary relevance. Even more surprisingly, Horace suddenly and emphatically appears in the role of poet:

In my case, Pisones, it is not merely unadorned and ordinary vocabulary that I shall want as a writer of satyr-plays nor shall I struggle so hard to be unlike the style of tragedy that it makes no difference whether the speaker is Davus and bold Pythias when she has rooked Simo of a talent or Silenus, guardian and servant of the god he fostered.[29] I shall aim at a poem formed from the familiar, so that anyone else might hope to do the same, but his boldness will fail after much sweat and effort: such is the importance of arrangement and combination, such is the distinction added to what is open to all. (234–43)

It is a false trail to assume the addressees were particularly interested in satyric drama, nor does Horace himself intend to write it. Use of an addressee fits the prescriptive mode of didactic, but most of the poem has the usual anonymous 'you', and the Pisones are not made prominent as poets. In 366ff. Horace tells the elder son that there is no room for mediocre poets, but he

---

[27] Cf. Plato, *Laws* 700a–1b; Aristoxenus, fr. 124 Wehrli.

[28] Cf. *tragōidia paizousa*, 'playful tragedy', in Demetrius 169.

[29] Slave Davus, prostitute Pythias, and old Simo are typical New Comedy characters; Silenus accompanies Dionysus, the god of tragedy.

warns rather than encourages; the son has a typological role as a young Roman, and the address reinforces a point of importance to Horace. So too in 291–2 by the emotive vocative 'o blood of Pompilius' (i.e., descendants of king Numa, ambiguously the Pisones or the whole Roman people) Horace emphasises his own *credo*, the need for polish. Nor is Horace likely to follow a source slavishly to share some Alexandrian fascination with an obscure form.[30] As a theorist, he may well have been attracted by its complexity, but the other passages where Horace appears as poet support a practical application to his own poetry. He uses satyric drama to repeat and encapsulate many of his main ideas: the importance of appropriate style (*color*), suitable characterisation, originality achieved from the ordinary and from skilful arrangement, and the effort which seems no effort. Its style, however, and blend of seriousness and humour come close to Horace's own *Satires* and *Epistles*, and perhaps 'I, the writer of satyric plays' can suggest Horace's *Satires*. A false etymology (probably from Varro) linked 'satire' and 'satyric', and the historian Livy refers to a mysterious early form of dramatic satire. Horace associated Lucilian satire with Greek Old Comedy, but his own *Satires* and still more the *Epistles* are more serious. Did he see their analogue in satyric drama?[31]

Emphasis on Horace himself as a poet also prepares the transition from *poesis* and drama to the final section on the poet, and in the following passage on metre (251ff.), which symbolically illustrates the technical weakness of old Roman poetry (Ennius' metre thuds down, 260), Horace again appears as poet: 'Am I to wander and write with total freedom? ... Am I to play safe? ... Study the Greek models day and night!' (265ff.). The dilemma is resolved if we emulate the Greek canons. Yet Greece too knew progress and the need for rules as tragedy and comedy grew to achieve their proper nature, a point Horace leaves us to deduce from his examples: Aeschylus (illustrating technical progress) taught tragedy its appropriate grandeur of style and stagecraft (the high boot), developing tragedy from the rustic waggons of Thespis; comedy (illustrating moral progress) fell into unrestrained licence, but (contrast the example of music) restraint was legally imposed: 'and the chorus fell silent once the shameful right to harm was removed' (283–4).[32] The Romans have all the necessary boldness and originality, witness tragedy and comedy about Roman characters, 'daring to abandon the footsteps of the Greeks' (286–7), and all that is needed now is 'the labour of the file and delay' (*limae labor et mora*, 291).

---

[30] E.g., *Lityerses* of Sositheus; see Brink, *Prolegomena*, p. 149; Kurt Latte, 'Reste', *Hermes*, 60 (1925), 1–13.

[31] Cf. Diomedes 1, p. 485 Keil: *Satura autem sive dicta a Satyris*; Livy 7.2.4–10, probably reflecting a (Varronian?) attempt to make Roman drama develop analogously with Greek drama from the satyr-play in Aristotle. See Coffey, *Roman Satire*, pp. 11ff.

[32] Similarly Italian Fescennine *licentia* is restrained by law from personal attack in *Ep.* 2.1.145–55, and Horace himself restrained Lucilian satire.

After this reprise of themes familiar from his other poems, Horace suddenly turns to his final section, the poet (295ff.): Democritus allowed only mad poets. The need for *ars* as well as *ingenium* is clear from all that precedes, and with biting sarcasm Horace finds the price of madness too high and abandons poetry. Instead, 'I will serve as a whetstone, able to sharpen the knife, even if it cannot itself cut, ... writing nothing myself, I shall teach the poet's function and duty, the source of his power, what feeds and shapes him, what is appropriate, what is not, and where excellence and error lead' (304–8). Though predictably blurred by interweaving of points, this table of contents is probably fulfilled: first, content: ethical (309–32); second, aim: *utile* and *dulce* (333–46); and third, excellence: *ars* and *ingenium* (347–476).[33]

The poet needs knowledge (*sapere*); style will follow if he knows philosophy, 'the books of Socrates' (309–10), and learns social obligations to country, family, and friend, the duties of senator, judge, or leader in war. In short he will know appropriate characterisation and give realistic moral examples. Characterisation and morality go together, and 'the skilled imitator will scrutinise the models of life and manners and give them realistic expression' (318–19). Unobtrusively Horace links style to content (as in 40–1). Two apparently abrupt antitheses follow: unskilful plays with sound morality are more popular than skilful trivialities; Greece has genius, command of style, and 'is greedy only for fame' (324; cf. *Ep.* 2.1.119–20), while Roman boys are educated in arithmetic. We are left to deduce that moral content is rightly preferred, but Rome needs to learn the full Greek ideal of poetry, with all its artistry, commitment, and disdain for money. Then the oblique suggestion that poetry should be both useful and attractive is made explicit: 'poets aim to be useful or to give delight or to combine together what is pleasant and serviceable' (333–4), but 'every vote goes to the man who combines the useful with the attractive [*qui miscuit utile dulci*], delighting and at the same time advising the reader'; his is the book which sells, goes overseas, and gets lasting fame (343–6).

How far can a good poet fall short of such perfection? Some flaws are venial: we aim and miss the mark. But the habitual flaws from lack of effort by a Choerilus have no excuse, and Horace personally feels indignant even when 'good Homer nods' (*bonus dormitat Homerus*, 359).[34] He has to remind himself to excuse a short nap in a long work (presumably perfection is required for short works like those of Horace himself). Longinus (33.3–4) similarly, though less reluctantly, allows the few flaws of great writers like Homer; they are the result of a carelessness which necessarily accompanies that grandeur of mind which wins over flawless craftsmanship. A painting analogy follows, *ut pictura poesis*: some paintings please if you stand near, some if you are far off,

---

[33] Norden, 'Die Composition', pp. 481–528.
[34] 'Homer nods' was adapted by Cicero to Demosthenes, the comparable figure in oratory, Quint. 10.1.24, 12.1.22; Plutarch, *Cicero* 24.

some if seen dimly, some if in the light, unafraid of the critic's sharp judgement, some please only once, some withstand ten viewings (361–5). Horace gives no value judgement, but he will obviously prefer what will stand up to repeated and close study.[35]

Addressing the elder son of Piso, Horace pulls his points together. The boy has the ethical knowledge (*sapis*, 367) but is warned that, in contrast to utilitarian oratory, there is no room for mediocrity in art-forms designed to give pleasure, that talent needs also technique: so submit your writing to a critical ear, such as Horace's, and wait nine years before you publish (338).[36]

After the emphasis on poetry's link with pleasure, Horace redresses the balance with solemn praise of the social and sacral role of poets in an earlier age (391ff.). Poets founded and civilised society, Orpheus tamed beasts (Horace endorses an allegorical explanation: he stopped the eating of meat); Amphion's music moved stones to build the walls of Thebes; poets of old had *sapientia* (wisdom), produced laws, stirred men to war, gave oracles and moral advice, and in lyric mode pleased kings and gave relaxation. Such ideas go back to at least Aristophanes, *Frogs* (1030–6) and the claims of the sophists that they, not the poets, were the true inventors and educators. The strength of Roman prejudice against poetry is clear from the very emphasis Horace lays on the poet's historical status in Greece, to show a young Roman like Piso that it is no shame to write poetry.

Finally Horace turns to the question of genius and technique. The need for both, which has underpinned the whole poem, is now explicit: they form a partnership (408–11, quoted above). He gives two contrasting cameos, the ideal of *ars* and the warning caricature of untutored madness. First the young Piso is told to avoid flatterers and submit his verses to the judgement of a Quintilius.[37] 'If you ever recited anything to him, he would say "please correct this and that"' (438–9). If you dismissed his criticism, he wasted no more time on you. Such a critic will not say: 'Why should I offend a friend over a trifle' (450–1). Poetry submitted to scrupulous criticism is followed by the mad poet wandering uncontrolled, a figure to be avoided and left alone when he falls into a well. It is a splendid caricature, a counterpoise to the opening grotesque of uncontrolled disunity, and Horace ends as he began on a note of humour. It is one of the memorable vignettes which together with the abrupt transitions hide the underlying abstract thought and logical connections, but the apparent inconsequentiality is itself the result of infinite art. This has not always been recognised. Scaliger called the poem 'an Art written without art', but there has been an increasing appreciation of Horace's

---

[35] Brink, *ad loc.*, against R. W. Lee, '*Ut pictura poesis*: The humanistic theory of painting', *The Art Bulletin*, 22 (1940), 199.

[36] An allusion to the nine years of Cinna's *Smyrna*, see above, section 1.

[37] Friend of Horace and Virgil, his death is lamented in *Od.* 1.24.

own skill, and the way in which he attempts not merely a poem on poetics but a poem which itself embodies those poetics.[38]

3 Dionysius of Halicarnassus

A close contemporary of Horace, though so far as we know not personally acquainted with him, Dionysius came to Rome *c.* 30 BC and there composed a major historical work, *The Antiquities of Rome*, published in 8 BC. In addition he produced a series of important rhetorical essays. Their order of composition is not entirely certain,[39] but the earliest seem to be the first part of *On Ancient Orators* (*Preface*, *Lysias*, *Isocrates*, and *Isaeus*), *To Ammaeus I*, and perhaps *On Imitation*, then come *On Composition*, *Demosthenes*, *To Pompeius*, *Thucydides*, *To Ammaeus II*, and *Dinarchus*.

Dionysius is perceptive and sensible, unusually aware of the usefulness of comparative criticism and the close textual analysis of examples. He employs traditional classifications such as the theory of virtues, but he claims to be the first to isolate the characteristics of specific authors and to make a detailed study of word-arrangement (*Preface* 4; *On Composition*, 1). His aim is practical, to provide models for imitation, and he quotes extensively from a wide range of authors. He analyses style from the viewpoint of a moderate Atticist and approves morally or politically useful content. He criticises, for example, to modern minds wrongly, the focus on Greek sufferings in Thucydides' choice of the Peloponnesian War and prefers the pan-Hellenism of Herodotus and Isocrates (*To Pompeius* 3; *Isocrates* 5). He combines a historian's care for evidence with literary scholarship in his interest in biography and authenticity. Two essays belong here. *To Ammaeus I*, on the chronological impossibility of influence on Demosthenes from Aristotle's *Rhetoric*, and the *Dinarchus*, on the biographical evidence for Dinarchus and the genuineness of his speeches. So too internal chronological evidence proves two speeches are not by Lysias (*Lysias* 12). But in the last resort the test of authenticity is trained literary sensitivity, the final criterion the reader's own emotional reaction, his perceptiveness unaided by reason, *alogos aisthēsis*. Lysias, for example, is identifiable by the presence of a charm which Dionysius feels but cannot define (*Lysias* 11; cf. e.g., *Demosthenes* 24). Sensitivity to literature is important, and Dionysius strikingly reveals his own responses in *Demosthenes* 22: he reads Isocrates in tranquillity but is transported by Demosthenes, as if a celebrant in ecstatic rites; he relives each successive emotion as it is evoked, and reflects on the still greater impact on the original audience.

Dionysius also has a sense of historical development, recognising that style, for example, evolves from predecessors. The basic premise for the choice of six

---

[38] For its enormous later influence, see Russell in *Horace*, ed. Costa, pp. 126–32, and n. 32.

[39] Bonner, *Dionysius*, ch. 2; Usher, I, pp. xxii–xxvi; Germaine Aujac (ed.), Dion. Hal. (Paris, 1979), I, pp. 22–8.

orators in *On Ancient Orators* is chronological: they are the three most significant
of the earlier and later generations of Attic orators; the former originate styles
(Lysias, Isocrates, and Isaeus), the latter perfect them (Demosthenes,
Hyperides, and Aeschines). This plan is particularly clear in the unusual
choice of Isaeus: he is important as the link between Lysias and Demosthenes
(he introduces a technical precision which influences Demosthenes), but,
unlike the others, he is not a model for our imitation (*Isaeus* 2 – 3; 20).

The *Lysias*, *Isocrates*, and *Isaeus* were published together with the *Preface* and
share the same pattern of biography, style, content, and typical sample pieces.
Style is assessed by use of the traditional theory of qualities or virtues, *aretai*,
a list of the desirable qualities a writer achieves or lacks. These qualities are
subdivided as 'necessary' and 'additional' or ornamental (e.g., *To Pompeius*
3; *Thucydides* 22), and the latter expand the fourth Theophrastean quality of
ornamentation, the former match the other three, with the Stoics' addition
of brevity. The theory is important as a standard critical framework, it
influenced the still greater elaborations of the theory of ideas in Hermogenes,
but without application to texts it becomes a mere checklist of approved critical
labels, as in Dionysius' *On Imitation* to judge from the quotations in *To Pompeius*
3 – 6; for example, Thucydides lacks lucidity and charm but has grandeur and
force, Herodotus has lucidity, charm, and grandeur, but lacks force.

The essay on *Lysias* gives lengthier treatment but similarly cites examples
without comment. Thus Lysias has good, ordinary Greek, and lucidity,
brevity, compression, vividness, power of characterisation, pleasantly simple
word-order, propriety, persuasiveness, and most essentially charm, but he
lacks force and grandeur (*Lysias* 2 – 11). Analysis of examples begins in the
Isocrates: this essay is more concerned with Isocrates' life and thought than
style, but specific texts illustrate the excessive use of balanced periods, and
we have the first example of Dionysius' favoured method of *metathesis*, the
recasting of an example in a different form (14; 20). It is perhaps significant
that Dionysius is analysing word-order: compare already *Lysias* 14, where a
passage of Lysias is cited within a quotation from Theophrastus for its balance
and antithesis. (Dionysius considers it spurious on grounds of style.) The *Isaeus*
rapidly lists Isaeus' qualities of style but then develops a long comparison of
Isaeus and Lysias. Close study of the texts of each will show their different
styles (2), and contrasting examples are cited from each and analysed in some
detail (3 – 12). Isaeus and Demosthenes are then briefly compared (12 – 3),
again with detail: both use asyndeton and rhetorical questions. Dionysius'
characteristic methods of detailed analysis and comparison are already
evident, and are openly asserted in the *Demosthenes*: no author can be satisfactorily analysed in isolation (33); judgement is tested by the analysis of
examples (9).

The *Preface*, praising the victory of Atticism over Asianism, might lead us
to expect an Atticist bias in favour of Lysias, the prime Atticist model. But

Dionysius' attitude to the Attic orators is similar to that of Cicero: Demosthenes is agreed by all to be the best (e.g., *Isaeus* 20); there are different types of good style (*Lysias* 11); and though Lysias is unsurpassed in some areas, particularly his apparent naturalism, he lacks that grandeur and force which reveal an orator's full powers (*Lysias* 5, 13). So too Isocrates uses periodic structure, symmetry, and rhythm to excess, but they are not condemned as such and Dionysius avoids an appearance of contemporary polemic by linking his criticism to that of much earlier critics (*Isocrates* 13). Later works show similarly balanced treatment of Thucydides and Plato against uncritical devotees (*Demosthenes* 23; *To Pompeius* 1–2; *Thucydides* 2).

The *Demosthenes* is much longer, as fits Demosthenes' status as the best orator. In chapters 1–34 Dionysius adopts the theory of styles as a useful framework to show the sheer range of Demosthenes, master of all styles (compare Cicero's *Orator*). There are three styles, the grand (model: Thucydides), the plain (model: Lysias) and the middle, invented by Thrasymachus, nearly perfected by Isocrates and Plato, perfected by Demosthenes. The historical perspective of the earlier essays continues, but Isaeus is no longer an originator (8) and Demosthenes is set against all the best earlier writers as 'the ideal eclectic'.[40] He adds vigour to the Lysianic style, lucidity to the Thucydidean, and within the middle or best style he is superior to Isocrates and Plato. The styles are not an entirely satisfactory system, since the middle style lacks individuality, covering everything between the other two, which are seen as polar extremes like the top and bottom notes in a musical scale (2). But Dionysius' proof of Demosthenes' superiority is an excellent example of comparative criticism. He is weakest on Plato, deaf to his irony in the *Phaedrus* and testing his style off the *Menexenus* – it is untypical and probably parodic – but it was then much admired, and his methodology is sound, the comparison of authors on the basis of their best passages (23).

There is an abrupt new start on sentence-structure in chapters 35ff., and this second part may well have been composed at a later stage, since it mentions and largely repeats ideas from *On Composition*: Demosthenes is the best model of the intermediate type of word-arrangement. His skill in delivery is also stressed, and finely illustrated by the swift pace of *Philippics* 3.26–7 (53–4). Dionysius is in general too uncritical of Demosthenes (he denies him only wit, 54), but his acute and closely detailed textual analysis is a major contribution to ancient criticism.

The essay *On Thucydides* shares the same strengths but carefully balances Thucydides' virtues and weaknesses. Dionysius' assessments do not always convince but they reveal interesting assumptions. He was also himself a historian, as was the addressee, the Roman Tubero, one of Thucydides'

---

[40] Usher, I, p. 235.

admirers.[41] At the end Dionysius fears he may not have pleased Tubero (55) and he very carefully defends himself against charges of malice towards Thucydides (esp. 2 – 4). Contemporary enthusiasm for Thucydides is also seen by a further essay, *To Ammaeus II*, which meets a demand for Dionysius to amplify the excellent remarks on style in *Thucydides* 24.

In subject-matter (5 – 20) he praises Thucydides' wish to be useful and the rejection of myth (it does not fit contemporary history), condemns the annalistic structure by seasons (it fragments the narrative), and cannot see why he amplifies some episodes but not others, a criticism which reveals insensitivity to dramatic juxtapositions (e.g., the interweaving of the fate of two defeated cities in Book ,III). In style Thucydides surpasses earlier historians, and has four main characteristics: innovation in vocabulary, variety of figures, harsh arrangement, and compression of ideas. He is compact, vigorous and, above all, emotionally powerful, but excess leads to obscurity (21 – 4; cf. 49). This is well observed, and Dionysius' method of proof is new: he will analyse all these aspects together, using selected pieces to examine both style and content (25). He again balances success and failure. Predictably, for example, he admires the tragic narrative of the naval defeat at Syracuse but not the densely analytical account of civil strife at Corcyra (26 – 8).[42] The former, he notes, can be appreciated by more than the educated élite, a point he resumes in 50 – 1, where he rebuts the claim of 'some reputable sophists' that Thucydides writes only for a minority, who will find nothing strange in his style: but, if so, the many are deprived of a useful subject, we now need a linguistic commentary, and the style was eccentric even in Thucydides' own day. In short, for Dionysius obscurity is a fault which must be eliminated (as in his own recastings) if we are to imitate Thucydides. Some of the criticism may seem insensitive, but Dionysius is not analysing the uniqueness of Thucydides but assessing him as a model for others.

On Composition is a work of critical theory on the arrangement of words in poetry and prose. Dionysius' arguments for the importance of arrangement are traditional, for example that it can alone rescue a passage of 'ordinary' thought and diction, as in Telemachus' arrival at the swineherd's hut in Homer (3).[43] But his independence is quickly seen as he turns from the inadequacies of earlier textbooks to his own research and with characteristic empiricism refutes the then common notion of a 'natural' word-order, that it would, for example, be more naturally pleasing to put nouns before verbs (5) (cf. Demetrius 195). He aims instead to establish from observing the practice of ancient authors what combinations of letters, words, clauses,

---

[41] For recent Roman enthusiasm for Thucydides cf. Cic., *Orator* 30 – 2, and Sallust's emulation.

[42] C. W. Macleod, 'Thucydides on faction (3.82 – 3)', *Proceedings of the Cambridge Philological Society*, 205 (1979), 52 – 68.

[43] *Od.* 16.1 – 16; cf. Longinus 40.2 – 3 for such arguments; for Philodemus' rebuttal, see above, ch. 6, section 8.

and sentences are attractive, a programme which elicits interesting glimpses of linguistic and musical theory.[44]

The goal is pleasure and/or beauty (10; cf. *Demosthenes* 47), which is produced by the appropriate combination of melodious sound, rhythmical arrangement, and variety, and, as in music, we have an instinctive appreciation (11). Dionysius accepts the view that sounds and rhythms have 'natural' connotations, but in the identification of melodious sounds he is unusually exhaustive in assigning aesthetic values to each vowel and consonant; thus long vowels are more euphonious, S and R are rough, L is sweet (13 – 16). The system is too rigid, though it follows logically from the underlying Stoic assumption that sounds and words alike imitate nature,[45] but the supporting examples include some striking sound-effects from combinations of syllables and letters, such as the relentless sound of the sea in Homer (*Il.* 17.265): 'The foreshores boom to the echo of the salty brine',

ēiones booōsin ereugomenēs halos exō

-◡◡| - ◡ ◡| - ◡ ◡| - ◡ ◡| - ◡◡ | - ◡

Note the vowel sequences and monotonous dactyls. Rhythms and metres are similarly categorised (each is noble or base), and Dionysius may be the first critic to offer detailed scansion of lengthy passages of prose (17 – 18). Though some of his identifications of metrical feet appear arbitrary, prose-rhythm is rightly seen to be used differently by Thucydides, Plato, Demosthenes, and Hegesias. He then briefly proves the need for variety (19) and appropriateness (20), and in a particularly fine and detailed appreciation he analyses Homer's famous lines (*Od.* 11.593 – 8; cf. Demetrius 72 – 3) on the labour of Sisyphus, who in five dragging lines of long syllables and rhythms 'pushes up the stone',

laan anō ōtheske,

- ◡ ◡| - - | - ◡

only for it to 'spin away again to the plain' in a single fluid line of quick dactyls:

autis epeita pedonde kulindeto laas anaidēs.

- ◡ ◡|- ◡ ◡| - ◡ ◡| - ◡◡ |- ◡ ◡| - -

Three principal types of arrangement are then introduced: the austere, the elegant, and the well-blended (21 – 4; cf. *Demosthenes* 37 – 41). This triad is not to be confused with the triad of grand, plain, and middle styles; it derives from musical theory, and the austere and the elegant reflect the twin goals of beauty and charm. The austere type, illustrated by minutely analysed examples from Pindar and Thucydides, has harsh consonants, long syllables, hiatus,

---

[44] D. M. Schenkeveld, 'Linguistic theories in the rhetorical works of Dionysius of Halicarnassus', *Glotta*, 61 (1983), 67 – 94.

[45] Note also the reference to Plato's *Cratylus* in *Comp.* 16. On Philodemus' counter-view see above, ch. 6, section 8.

discordant juxtapositions, slow pauses, and abrupt and asymmetrical sequences of clauses and sentences. The elegant type, as in passages of Sappho and Isocrates, is characterised by the opposite: pleasant sounds and smoothly flowing clauses and balanced periods. In undiluted form both are extremes, but they blend together to provide the third and best type, which (like the middle style) will therefore cover a range of different mixtures, as in Homer, Demosthenes, and Plato. Finally (25–6) Dionysius considers how prose can be like poetry and poetry like prose, but he confines himself to rhythm and is most interesting in his characteristic strength, the deployment of examples.

4 Minor figures

Book I of the Stoic Strabo's *Geography* argues against Eratosthenes' claim that Homer is geographically unreliable and poets aim only to please.[46] Homer is the founder of geographical science, morally sound and concerned to present real life. But Strabo allows some compromise: fictions added to give pleasure can obscure the underlying truth, as in Odysseus' wanderings; and poetic licence sanctions a blend of the truth of history, vivid presentation, and the pleasure of myth. Strabo is hardly original, but he well illustrates the widespread acceptance of Homer's educational role.

Other figures of the period are shadowy. Rhetorical theory flourished, but rules and classifications dominated, as in the heated rivalry between the followers of Apollodorus of Pergamum and Theodorus of Gadara, which lasted into the second century.[47] Apollodorus (*c.* 104–22 BC) laid down strict rules for the organisation of speeches: thus every speech must include four parts, always in the order prooemion, narrative, proof, and epilogue; and emotion (*pathos*) is excluded from narrative and proof. Theodorus (*fl.* 33 BC) was more flexible: narrative is not always required; emotion may enter the proof. But for Quintilian the differences are technical and minimal, and both critics ignore the practical requirements of the lawcourts (3.6.1; 5.13.59), a fault we can link to the growing popularity of declamation. Figures of speech also loomed large, to judge from the lost treatises of Caecilius, Dionysius, and Gorgias the Younger (*fl.* 44 BC), whose four books on figures survive in a Latin abridgement by Rutilius Lupus and whose Asianist sympathies emerge from his unusual inclusion of Hellenistic examples, including Hegesias.[48] Augustan or slightly earlier, Tryphon's *On Tropes* is also lost, though its general outline is clear from

[46] See esp. 1.1.2, 1.2.3–19; Schenkeveld, 'Strabo on Homer'.

[47] Grube, 'Theodorus', rightly refutes wider claims that Theodorus was an empiricist who made emotion all-important; cf. Seneca, *Contr.* 2.1.36; Quint. 2.11.2, 4.2.32, 5.13.59.

[48] Seneca, *Contr.* 1.4.7; Quint. 9.2.102; text of Rutilius Lupus (first century AD) in *Rhetores Latini Minores*, ed. Halm, pp. 3–21; also ed. G. Barabino (Genoa, 1967).

its influence on later surviving treatises.[49] A few fragments survive of what sounds like a more original work, *On Wit* (*De urbanitate*) by the epigrammatist, Domitius Marsus,[50] who regarded wit as a pithy elegance of phrase which could be serious or humorous: 'a quality of compression into a brief saying suited to delight and move men to every emotion'.

The tradition of Hellenistic scholarship also continued, though we have little more than a parade of names and titles.[51] There were Latin works on philology by, for example, Messalla, *On the Letter S* (Quint. 1.7.23, 1.7.35), Cloatius Verus, *On Latin Words Derived from Greek* (Gellius 16.12), and Verrius Flaccus, *On the Meaning of Words* (a massive work on ancient and obsolete words which was abridged by Festus); and on critical exegesis we may note especially three freedmen: Caecilius Epirota, Crassicius Pansa, and Julius Hyginus.[52] Hyginus, librarian of Augustus' Palatine library from 28 BC, wrote commentaries on Cinna's *Propemptikon Pollionis* and Virgil; Crassicius wrote a commentary on Cinna's erudite *Smyrna*; and Epirota, 'the nurse of tender young bards' (Domitius Marsus, fr. 3 Morel), lived in the poet Gallus' household and after his death opened a school whose curriculum first introduced contemporary Latin poets such as Virgil. Greek scholarship on Homer also continued with Aristonicus, whose lost work on Menelaus' wanderings was used by Strabo (1.2.31).

There is no sharp break between the critical theory and methods of the Hellenistic and the Augustan periods, nor between that of the Augustan and imperial periods. Critical theory continued along the lines given it by the philosophical schools, while critical practice was dominated by teachings of the grammatical and rhetorical schools. In poetic criticism the most striking development is Horace's unique combination of traditional precepts, personal experience, and sensitive judgement; in prose the phenomenon of Atticism and Dionysius' efforts at a more subtle description of style. Atticism and the identification of qualities of style will remain major concerns of Greek critics of the Empire and also of the Byzantine period.

---

[49] M. L. West, 'Tryphon *De Tropis*', *CQ*, 15 (1965), 230–48, too readily ascribes *Rhetores Graeci* 3, pp. 215–26 Spengel, to Tryphon.

[50] Quint. 6.3.102–12; E. S. Ramage, 'The *De Urbanitate* of Domitius Marsus', *CP*, 54 (1959), 250–5.

[51] On these and others, see Duret, *Dans l'ombre*.

[52] Suetonius, *De grammaticis* 16, 18, 20; Charisius, *Grammatici Latini*, ed. Keil, p. 134.

9

LATIN CRITICISM OF THE
EARLY EMPIRE

The name 'Silver Latin' is often given to the literature of the first century
of the Christian era and is generally understood to imply its inferiority to the
Golden Age of the late Republic and Augustan era. Analogy with the five
Hesiodic ages, in which the silver age was both later and less worthy than the
golden, suggests the cliché of decline. To what extent did the Romans of the
early imperial period feel that they and their contemporaries were a falling
away from the previous generation? We will see that the change in form of
government, by denying opportunities for significant political speech,
trivialised the art of oratory. But was there any such external constraint on
poetry?

Modern critics have reproached Silver Latin epic and tragedy with being
'rhetorical'. Certainly it is clear from Tacitus' *Dialogus* that men thwarted from
political expression transferred to the safer vehicle of historical or mythical
poetry both the techniques and ideals of public oratory. But just as no one
suggests that Juvenal's satires were poorer compositions because of his
apparent rhetorical skill, so rhetorical colouring in the higher poetic genres
of tragedy and epic is not necessarily a fault. We would judge the individual
composition primarily by its internal coherence: but Roman critics like
Quintilian measured a work by its conformity to the characteristics of its genre
and defined those characteristics by a canon, which by his time consisted
largely of late-Republican and Augustan writers. Thus for classicising critics
of the first century 'different' meant worse, while the creative artists who
achieved significant poetry or prose did so largely in reaction against a norm
they could not usefully imitate.

Augustus himself was to some extent responsible for the hiatus between
the celebratory history and poetry of his early years and the renewal of creative
writing under Nero.[1] His old age made him intolerant not only of criticism
and independent judgements in history and oratory, but also of the last great
poet, Ovid, and his ironical indifference to official morality. The year of

---

[1] On the literary output and taste of the forty years between the death of Augustus and Nero's
assumption of power see Roland Mayer, 'Neronian Classicism', *AJP*, 103 (1982), 305–18.

Tiberius' adoption as successor, AD 4, has been marked as a turning point for society and for literature, on the evidence of increased suppression of free expression.[2]

1 Velleius Paterculus and Seneca the Elder

Two figures speak for the Romans of the immediate post-Augustan period, reflecting on the burst of achievement they had outlived. Neither of them, unfortunately, is an independent thinker or commands the critical terminology to analyse the standards by which past orators, poets, and historians are praised or found wanting, but each illustrates characteristic shifts of literary interest in the new generation.

First, the soldier-historian Velleius Paterculus, whose *Roman History* combines a swift compendium of events down to Rome's destruction of Carthage and Corinth in 146 BC with a progressively more detailed narrative culminating in the career of his patron, the emperor Tiberius (reigned AD 14 – 37). Roman historical writing, still undeveloped at Cicero's death, had flowered with the idiosyncratic monographs and *Histories* (now largely lost) of Sallust, composed before the Augustan principate, and the full-length national history of Titus Livius of Patavium (59 BC – AD 17), the first surviving Roman historian to compose his narrative as a literary synthesis of earlier sources, applying the arts of rhetoric as Cicero would have wished. These two contrasted stylists set the pattern for subsequent historians, but whereas Sallust remains an object of fascination to Roman literary critics and a school book even into the Middle Ages, it was Livy who initially provided the model for rhetorical history. Velleius takes over the form without the guiding convictions, and if he had not been the only Latin source for the rise of Tiberius, he would probably not have survived on his literary or historical merits.

When he comes to write on cultural history, however, he is clearly adapting the ideas of more sophisticated intellects than his own. Twice he offers an excursus on this theme, the first time after the fall of Corinth marking the onset of Roman hegemony at the end of his first book (1.16 – 18). Surveying the rise and fall of different arts, he concludes that great talents tend to concentrate in one art at a given time, emerging within a generation like the three Greek tragedians or the three greatest talents of Old Comedy or their counterparts in New Comedy. Philosophy and oratory resist his attempts to match this pattern, since he has to admit excellence in oratory from the rise of the long-lived Isocrates through the generation of his pupils to the time of their successors. He offers counterparts of his own from Roman literary history, with an acme for Roman tragedy around the lifetime of Accius (end

---

[2] Syme, *Tacitus*, p. 369, and in more detail, *History in Ovid* (Oxford, 1978), pp. 198 and 212 – 14.

of the second century BC) and for comedy around Caecilius and Afranius (spanning the second century); to history he assigns a period of eighty years culminating in Livy, and to oratory a flowering that includes with its central figure, Cicero, some speakers of the older generation and the group of younger orators who had learned by hearing him.

The inconsistencies of Velleius' Roman examples reflect not only his own prejudice against the early dramatists Ennius and Plautus, but also the difficulty of adapting the ideas of a fourth- or third-century Athenian source which had put forward the dramatic genres native to Athens, ignoring epic, didactic, and lyric poetry, which flourished over a wider period and the whole area of the Aegean. Cicero reflects a similar Isocratean emphasis in his more discriminating survey of rhetoric in the *Brutus*, but although Velleius seems to have drawn on the *Brutus* for the earlier Roman orators whom he explicitly excludes (1.17.3) from the period of acme, he is using his historical framework to argue a different point.

Velleius experiences difficulties both with the one-generation theory and in using the competitive aspect of imitation (*aemulatio*) to explain the transference of artistic interest from one genre to another.[3] Cicero had claimed that *aemulatio* fostered the arts, but he had not had to explain its relation to decline. Velleius instead argues that the perfection of classic artists in any art or genre deterred successors who therefore diverted their talents: he does not notice that this in turn contradicts the Atheno-centric claim that talent languished away from the competitive atmosphere provided by the city. There is here a real confusion between the agonistic rivalry of the Greek theatre and courtroom and a theory of imitation in which each generation advanced beyond its models in the process of learning its art from them. And it has not generally been noticed that while Velleius' statements imply the decline of Roman oratory in his own time, he does not acknowledge decline, but writes only in the most general terms, returning from his comment on the Roman orators to the *grammatici*, sculptors, painters, and modellers of his Greek source.

Indeed, far from being concerned with contemporary decline, he offers in his second excursus on the arts (2.36) a positive picture of subsequent achievement. Since the significant year of Augustus' birth (63 BC), he declares, Rome has produced the orators Pollio and Messalla Corvinus, Sallust – 'the rival of Thucydides' – Varro of Atax (translator of Apollonius' *Argonautica*), Catullus, singled out for special praise, Lucretius, Virgil – 'the prince of poets' – Rabirius, Livy, Tibullus, and Ovid, each credited with perfection in his own literary form. There are traces here of a 'neoteric' canon, but Velleius' own modifications, notably the omission of Horace and Propertius, reveal the same poor judgement that can include Rabirius' lost

---

[3] Heldmann, *Entwicklung und Verfall*, pp. 32–59.

epic alongside the *Aeneid*. The epitomator has left us little evidence of his sources' critical approach.

Seneca the Elder, born thirty years before Velleius, published his reminiscences of the Augustan declamatory schools at about the same time (AD 30–40). Although the great declaimers of his youth are the focus of his memoirs, he allows his readers to glimpse the reputations of Virgil and Ovid in formation, and in the preface to the *Controversiae* offers his own account of the decline of public eloquence. The world he considers includes only the lawcourts and the schools: he realises that the fictional cases and historical deliberative *suasoriae* of the schools are a new form of training, not practised in the Republic, and recognises the discrepancy between the virtuosity of public declamation and real contests of the courtroom. The auditorium was the centre of rhetorical interest in his youth, in which young Ovid declaimed, parents and teachers were obsessed with the displays, and Augustus and Agrippa came to hear the most famous performers, such as the rhetoricians Porcius Latro, Arellius Fuscus, Haterius, and Cestius, impersonate the defendant or accuser in imaginary cases, exploiting the paradoxes of adultery, incest, murder, and disinheritance. It was probably the popularity of these displays that led Asinius Pollio to innovate by reading his historical writings in public recitation (*Contr.* 4.pr.2). The Ciceronian age of reading and reflection was being replaced by an oral culture, with the inevitable corollary of a greater attention to clever epigram than to extended argument in composition.

Seneca's preface to Book I is much quoted as evidence for recognition of the decline of Roman oratory, but its style is surely fresher than its content. Its starting point is the superiority of these voices from the past as models for Seneca's own sons to imitate and the usefulness of their diversity; it is, he argues, always dangerous to base one's style upon a single model and more dangerous now than ever since Roman oratory has been in continual decline since the death of Cicero. In the moralist tradition, he blames the change of style for the worse on idleness and effeminacy in the young, invoking the same aspects of youthful fashion that his own hero Cato had denounced two hundred years before. To condemn effeminacy of style without specifying defects of vocabulary, rhythm, or sentence structure tells us little, and Seneca's son will offer a better demonstration when (*Ep.* 114) he compares Maecenas' luxurious life with his stylistic decadence and bad taste, illustrated from his prose and verse.

Although declamation has some interest for modern students of literary theory as a type of fiction,[4] Seneca's material has chiefly enjoyed the attention of historians of style, for he cites striking aphorisms and turns of phrase rather than techniques of argument or arrangement. In this respect the

---

[4] Trimpi, *Muses of One Mind*, pp. 306–27.

instruction in method offered by the *Minor Declamations* attributed to Quintilian gives a clearer picture of the training offered by the *Controversiae*. Yet Seneca's excerpts show that the pointed style which we associate with the Neronian age was already developed almost a hundred years before; short statements in basic prose vocabulary are made, by their very brevity or boldness of phrasing, to carry a load of irony or innuendo.

These memoirs, however, also show Seneca's appreciation of contemporary poetry and offer portraits of individual speakers that carry beyond Cicero's *Brutus* the art of descriptive criticism in which Dionysius of Halicarnassus excelled. Virgil is already a classic, beyond criticism to all but the perverse, and praised for his restraint in two similar physical hyperboles of the *Aeneid*; where Homer had depicted the Cyclops hurling a huge rock ('mountain is torn from mountain', *Od.* 9.481–2), Virgil is content with 'no small part of a mountain' (*Aen.* 10.128), and when he is conveying the scale of Antony's massive warships at Actium he softens his image: 'you might suppose there floated the Cyclades uptorn' (*Aen.* 8.691–2) (*Suas.* 1.12). Comparison between Virgil and Homer was made from the beginning, and in this case, ironically, Seneca seems to depend on Maecenas, who had praised Virgil for achieving grandeur without falling into decadence. Again, Seneca reports a discussion with Julius Montanus and Ovid on Virgil's adaptation from Varro of Atax in *Aeneid* 8.26–7: 'it was night, and over all the earth tired creatures, birds and beasts, were held in deep sleep'. Ovid's reaction was characteristic of the new pointed brevity: how much better it would have been if the last part of the second line were cut out and it finished thus: 'Everything was of night' (7.1.27–8).[5] Seneca provides a shrewd assessment of Ovid's gifts (2.2.8–12): his avoidance of the *controversia* in favour of the dramatic *suasoria*, because of a distaste for argument; his indifference to order in presenting commonplaces; his declamations with the qualities of poetry cast into prose (*carmen solutum*) and his restraint of vocabulary in oratory. With this Seneca contrasts the self-indulgence that made Ovid wilfully cherish in verse precisely his most extravagant conceits, and his inability to leave well alone. He shows us too the poet incorporating a Virgilian allusion, 'not as a literary theft but as an open borrowing to be recognised' (*Suas.* 3.7). It is with the canonical status of Virgil that allusion becomes a dominant ornament in Latin poetry, as poets either extend or redirect his poetic form. Seneca, though recognising Ovid's faults, can call his talent 'well groomed, becoming, and charming' (*Contr.* 2.2.8). How fine a boundary there is between approved elegance and the deplored effeminacy of the young!

These judgements are necessarily disjointed but suggest some of the critical issues of the day. To show Seneca's own critical repertoire and power of verbal characterisation we should look at his portraits of the great declaimers.

[5] Tr. by Winterbottom, *Seneca*, II, p. 49.

Arellius Fuscus embodies at the same time the confusion between the virtues of poetry and oratory that will increase in the literature of the first century, and qualities which have been recognised as Roman Asianism.[6]

Arellius Fuscus' developments [*explicatio*] were brilliant, but elaborate and involved, his ornament too contrived, his word arrangement more effeminate than could be tolerated by a mind in training for such chaste and rigorous precepts. His oratory was highly uneven, sometimes bare, sometimes because of its over-freedom wandering and discursive. Proems, arguments and narrations he spoke dryly, while in descriptions words were always granted a licence that went beyond the rules – the only requirement was that they should shine. There was nothing sharp, hard, or rugged. The style was brilliant, wanton rather than luxuriant. (*Contr.* 2. pr. 1)[7]

Without endorsing Seneca's diagnosis of stylistic corruption, we can detect in this cult of form both the concentration on the isolated sentence unit, which would undermine the organisation of prose works in the next generation, and the new goals of polish and smoothness (*cultus*, *nitor*), charming in verse but inimical to agonistic prose. It is as though epideictic form displaces that of fighting oratory when performance becomes theatre and the spectators of recitation and declamation replace the senate or political assembly.

2 Seneca the Younger and Petronius

It is not clear how far we should credit the elder Seneca for the literary achievements of his most famous son; the younger Seneca's oratory was submerged in his service as ghost-writer to Nero, but in almost every other literary genre he was a brilliant innovator: as satirist, essayist, and epistolographer, while in tragic poetry he dominated the new flowering of the Neronian age. It has been common to speak of a Neronian literary revolution, but despite the affinities between the work of Seneca and his nephew Lucan, no single literary fashion unites their work with that of the Stoic satirist Persius or the picaresque novel of Petronius.

The younger Seneca's philosophical principles did not interfere with his respect for poetry; passages from the early *De vita* (2.2.5–6) and the letters (108.10) show that he followed Aristotle rather than Plato in distinguishing the vicarious emotions of dramatic spectators from the damaging personal emotions to be avoided by Stoics, and he shared Cleanthes' recommendation of verse as a more vivid and memorable vehicle for moral instruction. Contemptuous of Ennius (as we know from Aulus Gellius cited below) he was respectful of Virgil and Ovid but resorted to them chiefly for moral texts rather than aesthetic or rhetorical analysis. Letter 88 illustrates the many forms of contemporary Virgilian criticism and explication, but the grammarians,

---

[6] Fairweather, *Seneca the Elder*, pp. 243–303.
[7] Winterbottom, *Seneca*, I, pp. 197–8.

like the moralists, tended to focus on the single line rather than the larger scale aspects of the epic. A typical letter (79) shows his approach as a prescriptive critic. His correspondent Lucilius had shown an interest in composing topographical poetry about Sicily. Surely, Seneca urges him, Lucilius will not hesitate to tackle the description of Mount Aetna, since his predecessors' achievements (Seneca has Virgil and Ovid in mind, perhaps also the unidentified author of the *Aetna*) have not pre-empted the theme but simply expanded its scope: 'The last man to write has the best circumstances: he finds the words ready to hand and they will take on a new look once rearranged' (79.5). He sees this as a challenge, arguing that the best can always be matched if it cannot be outdone. In another letter (84) Seneca considers the imitation of poetic models and develops Horace's Pindaric simile of the poet as a bee collecting pollen from many flowers. We ought, he claims, to read as the bees gather,[8] organising our material separately before amalgamating it into one single concentrated flavour; only food that is digested can truly be assimilated into the bloodstream, and intellectual food swallowed whole will merely be fodder for the memory, not nourishment for the intellect. Again, he sees the proper relationship between literary model and emulator as that between father and son, not the barren similarity of an inanimate portrait to the living face.

Despite his own pungent style of almost nagging questions, commands, and didactic analogies, Seneca inherited his father's mistrust of self-indulgent, effeminate diction, and his most famous letter (114) turns to the causes of bad taste in style, examining the fashion for different excesses such as hyperbole, cryptic brevity, or extravagance in metaphor. Here it is that the extravagant vocabulary, phrasing, and rhythms of Maecenas are held up as a dreadful warning that a man's style will reflect his way of life. The letter runs over the affectations of preceding generations: Sallustian brevity and archaism; roughness of composition and exaggerated hyperbaton to create suspense; or its opposite, a composition too smooth and sweet, closer to song than speech; or again aphorisms (*sententiae*), too disjointed, far-fetched, or flowery, with more sound than meaning. Behind the overt example of Maecenas it is easy to see the indulgences of Nero, who could not be criticised in person for his life or his art, but the supreme irony of this shrewd and amusing letter is Seneca's account of the trend-setter and his motivation: 'Once the mind has grown accustomed to despising the normal and feeling that the usual is stale, it looks for novelty in speech too ... Faults like these are introduced by some individual who at a particular time dominates eloquence; others imitate them, and pass them on to one another' (114.10, 114.17). Just so a generation later Quintilian would lament the pernicious influence of Seneca himself upon the younger generation:

---

[8] Cf. Horace, *Odes* 4.2.27–32: 'I, like a bee ...'; and note Seneca's word play on *legere*, both 'gather' and 'read'.

His admirers loved Seneca rather than imitated him: they fell as far short of him as he of the ancients ... He was popular for his faults alone. Everyone set himself to reproducing what he was capable of reproducing, and in boasting that they were speaking in the Senecan style his admirers slandered Seneca ... As far as his style goes, there is much that is corrupt and particularly dangerous just because the constant faults are so attractive. You might wish him to have written employing his own genius but someone else's judgement. (Quint. 10.1.126–7, 10.1.130)[9]

Quintilian was a Ciceronian, and his strictures on Seneca had some effect on standards in Latin prose in the next generation, and in the fifteenth century, but the anti-Ciceronians of the sixteenth century were again to be attracted to the model of Seneca.

Petronius, it has been suggested,[10] parodied Seneca's prose style in the moralising of his reach-me-down sage Eumolpus. Otherwise, it is not clear that the various pastiches in the *Satyricon* are parodies of specific authors, since Petronius has assigned his literary comments and compositions to absurd characters. Denunciations of the schools of declamation for their hollow themes, and of the bad upbringing of the idle and effeminate young by the pedantic rhetorician Agamemnon in the opening pages of the *Satyricon* come close to parodying Seneca the Elder, but the theme was still taken seriously by Quintilian or the conservative Messalla in Tacitus' *Dialogus* a generation after Petronius' death.[11] Indeed, some of Agamemnon's complaints, such as the 'recent' importation of corrupt style from Asia, could have been made by Dionysius or by Cicero's Attic opponents in the Republic.

The two extensive verse excerpts composed by Eumolpus are of a different order. The iambic trimeters narrating in dramatic verse the Virgilian theme of Laocoön and the Trojan horse (*Satyricon* 89) have been treated as parody of Senecan tragedy, but they have only generic features in common with Seneca. Pomponius, for example, also wrote a Trojan tragedy and these lines could as well be parody of Pomponius as of Seneca. The so-called *Bellum civile* (*Satyricon* 119–24) is a more complex problem still. Given its title, it is natural to assume that the work is related to Lucan's great epic of the Civil War. But there are both chronological and literary problems in this assumption. It is generally believed that Lucan had published only three books before his death in the same year as Petronius (AD 65) and that Petronius may have had very little time in which to know the work. There seems to be direct reaction to Lucan in Eumolpus' prefatory comment on his poetic effusion, which stresses the need for inspiration and reaffirms the Virgilian practice of including divine intervention in epic; as far as we know, Lucan was the first poet to abandon this element. But there were civil war poems by Cornelius Severus and Rabirius before Lucan's work, and many of the alleged echoes of Lucan owe

---

[9] Cf. what Anthony Trollope has to say about Dickens and his imitators, *Autobiography*, ch. 14.
[10] Sullivan, 'Literary feud', pp. 435–67.
[11] George Kennedy, 'Encolpius and Agamemnon in Petronius', *AJP*, 99 (1978), 171–8.

much to Virgil and cannot really be labelled more specifically than to call them post-Virgilian. The Petronian poem itself is overblown but not incompetent, apart from its excess of divine and daemonic figures – precisely the respect in which it differs from Lucan. Surely then Petronius is not attacking Lucan, but showing instead the limitations of those critics who would advocate a Virgilian epic with supernatural trappings in the current style. We should acknowledge that Latin satirists wrote burlesque rather than subtle parody; the author of the *Catalepton* burlesques Ventidius rather than Catullus' 'Phaselus' by applying the form of the latter poem to an incongruous and vulgar subject; Seneca by including a variation on his lament from the *Hercules Furens* in the sardonic lament for Claudius, the *Apocolocyntosis*, does not parody his own tragedy, but burlesques the dead emperor. What underlies Petronius' poetic exercises is rather the rejection of conservative dullness, a gesture that puts him on the same side as the innovators in the Neronian literary renaissance.

3 Tacitus' 'Dialogus'

Perhaps the single most impressive source of both literary history and literary criticism in the first century is the *Dialogue on the Orators* of the historian Tacitus. This subtle work exploits the form of the Ciceronian dialogue to recall or imagine a discussion at the home of the dramatic poet Curiatius Maternus from the early years of Vespasian, the time of Tacitus' youth. While scholars are now agreed that the dialogue was written more than twenty years after its dramatic date, there is still dispute about its date in relation to Tacitus' other minor works, the *Germania* and *Agricola*, and more importantly in relation to Quintilian's *Institutio* and Pliny's *Panegyricus*, which includes praise of contemporary eloquence in a speech of thanks offered to Trajan early in AD 100. The tragedian Maternus was probably the 'sophist' executed by Domitian, and the *Dialogus* was probably written after Quintilian's *Institutio*, but before the speech of Tacitus' friend Pliny, which it would otherwise contradict most discourteously.[12] Because the *Dialogus* is a radical work, which remained outside the mainstream of Roman criticism, and because it claims to describe conditions in the AD 70s, we should discuss it before considering Quintilian, whose work, completed about AD 92, is reflected in the later writers and critics of Rome.

The setting of the dialogue is pointed. Maternus has just given a public reading of his Roman tragedy when he is visited by two leading orators, Marcus Aper and Julius Secundus; later they are joined by the traditionalist Vipstanus Messalla, just as the speakers of Cicero's *De oratore* are joined in

---

[12] T. D. Barnes, 'The significance of Tacitus' *Dialogus de Oratoribus*', *HSCP*, 90 (1986), 225–44; and 'Curiatus Maternus', *Hermes*, 109 (1981), 382–4.

the second book by Catulus and his halfbrother. There is perhaps a deliberate contrast with *De oratore* in the plural 'On the Orators' of Tacitus' title, as the relativistic recognition of the many varieties of orator in Tacitus' day contrasts with Cicero's theme of the single, ideal, orator. Certainly the challenge is issued in the opening sentence: 'Why does our age in particular lack any distinction in eloquence, so that it has almost lost the name of Orator?' But in the first third of the text, before the entry of Messalla (14), the topic is rather the rivalry between oratory and poetry as professions for the man of words, with Maternus defending his choice of poetry despite his success as an orator. Since Maternus' poetry is avowedly political, even controversial, his defence of poetry, which rests on the innocent detachment from public life of a Virgil, must be measured by his own choice of material. Secondly Aper, in keeping with his own *arriviste* personality, praises oratory not for its defence of justice or liberty, but for the power, influence, and wealth it brings the speaker. Nothing is said in the first half of the work about deliberative political oratory, but the topics and audiences cited are those of the judicial pleader: senate, popular assembly, and courts have been replaced by courts and judicial hearings before the senate and emperor. Again, Aper's exemplars of modern success are the notorious 'informers', men of ignoble birth, limited resources, and undistinguished morals who have risen to the highest office and dominate society through the benefits they alone can confer upon the emperor. His description itself indicts the abuse of his art. In this socio-political context there is no scope for genuine political eloquence. Maternus simultaneously claims the innocence and divine origin of poetry, citing the achievements of Virgil, Ovid, and Varius in the Augustan age, and boasts of the political impact of his own tragedy, which broke the power of a vicious favourite of Nero. Aper charges Maternus with risking the hostility of the emperor; Maternus replies that Virgil enjoyed imperial favour *and* popular fame.

This prelude contributes little to the main issue besides setting the scene. But the arrival of Messalla, eager to champion the Old School – the orators of Cicero's day – against the new speakers triggers a powerful fighting defence by Aper (16–23). Political undertones continue: why, for instance, in proving how recent the *antiqui* really are, does he pointedly identify the year of Cicero's death with the beginning of Augustus' fifty years in authority? Aper's main assertion is that both forms and style of speaking naturally change with the times: he belittles the audiences of the previous century for their naivety in being impressed by the arid legal schematism of Hermagoras' system, by diffuse commonplaces, and by amateur philosophy. In contrast the sophisticated modern audience is impatient and expects to be entertained, whether they are passers-by, students, or busy autocrats who themselves determine the law and impose time limits on a defence. These listeners expect *cultus*, a smartness that pleases the ear with aphorisms and poetic trappings borrowed from Horace, Virgil, and Lucan. Much of Aper's argument seems to echo

Horace's recommendations in his pleas to Augustus (2.1) for the new poets against the *veteres*, and his demand for beauty and charm in dramatic and epic poetry. But the refinement and sublimity recognised as ideals for poetry in Horace[13] are less appropriate to judicial or deliberative discourse, and we can see, through the enthusiasm of Aper, why the old-fashioned critic saw these features as corrupt and unmanly. Again, some of Aper's arguments echo Cicero in *Brutus*; as Cicero demonstrated the diversity of the many fine Athenian orators, all entitled to the name of Attic, so Aper stresses the variety of the republican Roman orators; in his own eyes Aper is like Cicero, an innovator unjustly attacked and superior to his critics, for Cicero too, he claims (22), applied *cultus* to his speech and introduced telling aphorisms, at least in his latest speeches after he had found 'the best style of speaking'. The devil is quoting the scriptures of rhetorical orthodoxy to Messalla the believer.

What Aper rejects in earlier oratory, as in poetry and historical writing, is anything longwinded or lacking impact (*tardus*, *iners*) and above all the cult of archaisms from the first century of Roman literature. What he praises in his interlocutors is the refinement of their language, their invention, arrangement, and command of expanded or contracted form, their sentence structure, vivid aphorisms, and emotional effects, and especially their 'controlled candour', or as we would say, self-censorship.

The first brief section of Messalla's reply (25–6) contradicts Aper: the *antiqui*, however diverse in idiom, shared common standards and models. Earlier Messalla had denounced the Asianic traits of contemporary Greek speakers; now he selects as bad examples at Rome the effeminacy of Maecenas and the incantations of Gallio. In his judgement, present-day orators have the wantonness, frivolity, and licence of actors. This is a turning point. Maternus now dismisses the original question of whether the old orators were superior; the issue is only why this is so. Taking up Aper's phrase 'controlled candour' he politicises the discussion. We have, he declares, lost the ancients' freedom of speech even more than we have lost their eloquence (27.3). The remainder of the dialogue is divided between Messalla, with his theme of educational conservatism, and Maternus, who carries the political argument. Thus Messalla first (28–32) calls for a moral upbringing of the young, and revives the Ciceronian ideal of a broadly based education, rejecting the declamatory schools as training for real life, then in his last speech (33.4–35), under the traditional rubric of *exercitatio* (training) regrets the loss of the old republican practice of putting young men under the guidance of elder statesmen to see public life and observe the handling of political and judicial audiences. Messalla's reference to assemblies (34.2) is the first reminder of specifically deliberative oratory, and although the end of his speech and

---

[13] *Ep.* 2.1.165–6: *natura sublimis et acer*. This, the first use of *sublimis* in a context of literary criticism, applies to ethics rather than style but suggests the transference of Greek *hupsos* into Latin. The new ideal may have come from Caecilius, see below, ch. 10, section 3.

beginning of Maternus' reply are lost in our manuscripts, his argument is clearly leading back to Maternus' theme. Maternus has the ironic concluding speech, which acknowledges that by an unfortunate paradox oratory thrives on civil conflict, so that the disturbances of the last years of the Republic gave the stimulus for great judicial and deliberative oratory, awarding office and power to the eloquent: 'Great eloquence, like a flame, is fed by its material and excited by its motion and brightens as it burns' (36.1).

Those familiar with Tacitus' grim portrait of the principate and of a senate already servile and impotent at the death of Augustus cannot escape the irony of Maternus' apparent praise for his own times. We know from the historian's personal comment in *Annals* (4.34 – 5) that he saw the times he reported as inglorious material in comparison with the life-and-death national struggle and glorious victories of the expanding Republic. This passionate newcomer to the governing class cannot have believed that it was better for Rome that her oratory should atrophy while decisions were made by the single wise ruler without debate.

Given that oratory itself is marginal to our concept of literature, and no longer a significant strand in the rope of literary history, why is the *Dialogus* important? And what can we deduce beyond its courtly conclusion, looking at its premises and formulation? First, the recognition of genres. Tacitus the future historian never seriously puts forward history as an alternative literary career. Since Nepos' lament that Cicero had died without giving Rome a great work of history, Sallust and Livy had established the national achievement in the genre; yet Tacitus mentions history only briefly and obliquely in the *Dialogus*, when Aper blames archaisers for preferring Sisenna and Varro to his contemporaries Servilius Nonianus and Aufidius Bassus. He does not even name the genre, though he itemises tragedy, epic, lyric, elegy, iambic, epigrams, and other forms as parts of eloquence (10.4). Perhaps the advantage of presenting the dispute as a two-way fight between tragedy and oratory was their shared role as vehicles for public ideals: the one too direct; the other safer because more oblique. Their other kinship lay in the increasing cross-fertilisation of poetry and oratory of which we have spoken. Lucan the poet was marked by Quintilian (10.1.90) as more suited for imitation by orators than poets, but clearly the orators of this age were taking from poetry all that they dared. We must not forget that we are seeing the Roman literary world from a special perspective: our speakers are gentlemen, or at least public figures, and their opening approach is in terms of a gentleman's career and the power offered by competing literary forms. There was a tradition that history was written in the public man's years of retirement; hence it was hardly a career to compete with oratory. In fact, the greatest achievements of Roman literature were not composed with these motives or by men of this age and class, and we would do well to see Tacitus' splendid work primarily as a dialogue on the proper relationship between existing literary forms and public life in a depoliticised society.

Aper's periodisation of Roman oratory, juxtaposing the death of Cicero with the rise of the principate, and dating the beginning of the new style with Cassius Severus, last of the Augustan orators, has generally been taken as Tacitus' own perception, or the common interpretation of his generation. But even Messalla does not accept Severus as the turning-point in the acknowledged decline. We have probably been too ready in the past to transfer Aper's view to all the theorists of the first century, as if they associated the loss of eloquence with either the principate or a specific figure such as Severus.[14] Messalla too declares that when Asinius Pollio pleaded a testamentary case halfway through Augustus' principate 'a long period of peace ... unbroken tranquillity in the senate and particularly the restraining influence of the emperor had combined to pacify eloquence herself, like everything else' (38.2), but this interpretation is new and revolutionary, and the analysis of the decay of oratory at the end of *On Sublimity* should be seen as an echo of Tacitus' politicised account. Such is the power of this brilliant little book that it has redirected subsequent analysis of the so-called 'corruption of eloquence', substituting a political explanation for the traditional moralists' account. Neither explanation, however, will account for the apparent decline of poetry. Neither morality nor political liberty characterised the Neronian age, which produced poetry of originality and power; why then do we find in the next generation only derivative epic and the bread-and-butter epigrams of Martial? Literary history requires in the first instance a literary account of causality.

4 Quintilian

For posterity the most significant figure of this period is Quintilian, Rome's first public Professor of Rhetoric, whose teachings are reflected both in Tacitus' Messalla and in the writings of the younger Pliny. Quintilian's twelve books on the training of the orator (published about AD 95) are not all equally relevant to literary criticism. In the first two books, dealing with education in childhood and early adolescence, we meet only basic recommendations for the child's study of Homer and Virgil, with further reading of selected tragedies. At the next stage the young boy is recommended to read and learn excerpts from New Comedy and become steeped in the historical writing of Livy rather than the dangerously mannered Sallust, and of Cicero, or whichever orators most resemble Cicero (2.5.18–20). For the young, as for older students, Quintilian proposes a classical canon excluding both the primitive authors beloved of the archaisers and the new fashion for flowery and capricious display. Quintilian's table of contents at 2.14.5 organises

[14] Heldmann, *Entwicklung und Verfall*, pp. 255–86.

his theory in the tripartite Alexandrian form seen also in Horace's *Ars poetica*: he will write first about the art of rhetoric, then about the trained artist, and finally about the work of art. But these divisions have no importance until the final book, since the next nine books all deal with aspects of the art. Thus he opens with a doxography of definitions of rhetoric, and the analysis of its genres, also discussing the Hermagorean judicially-oriented analysis of legal issues. Books IV and V are devoted to argumentation in court cases, Book VI to the technique of opening and closing the speech, and the application of pathos and ethos, while Book VII considers the organisation of the parts of a speech. The treatment of pathos shows how much the teaching of rhetoric was now affected by poetry and especially by the predominance of Virgil. Quintilian invokes Virgilian passages to illustrate both pathos and vividness of representation (*enargeia*), analysing the poet's technique in terms that will reappear in the encomium of Macrobius' fourth-century rhetorician Eustathius (*Saturnalia*, Books IV and V). Horace's status is also authoritative, as when Quintilian (6.3.20) illustrates the meaning of *facetus* from Horace's praise of Virgil's *Eclogues* as *molle atque facetum* ('delicate and smart').

Books VIII and IX, discussing *elocutio* (diction and style), influenced the stylistic theory of the later Middle Ages, which adapted them along with recommendations of the *Rhetorica ad Herennium* into the Arts of Poetry, and influenced also the discussion and practice of prose style in the fifteenth century. Quintilian begins with the prerequisites of discourse – clear and correct speech; then he considers ornament both in the use of individual words and in their combination. This section is interesting for his presentation of types of fault in diction, loosely grouped under *cacozelia* ('affectation') and stress on *Romanus pudor* – a combination of restraint and outright prudery in the avoidance of sounds even vaguely suggesting obscenity. Here for the first time (8.3.60) Horace's Letter to the Pisones is cited as the *Ars poetica*, as Quintilian compares the incongruity of mixing sublime and humble words, old words and new, or poetic and colloquial vocabulary to the visual monster with which Horace opens his poem. There is a careful analysis of similes (8.3.72–82), distinguishing as most effective the Virgilian type in which correspondence between simile and context is fully developed. It is when discussing *affectus* and *ornatus* (emotional effect and ornament), that Quintilian most often invokes Virgil's example. Virgil is also cited as a model for the art of amplification, perhaps because Quintilian had inherited a similar reference to Homer in the Greek tradition; certainly he singles out, from *Iliad* III, Priam's statement that Helen is a worthy justification for the sufferings of war, noting how the circumstances and choice of speaker intensify the effect of Priam's words (8.4.21). The criteria of utility, moderation, and propriety guide Quintilian as is shown by another allusion to Horace; protesting against affectation (8.3.8) he anticipates that one of the modern 'corrupt' stylists may call him an enemy of *cultus*, and answers by opposing the real cultivation of a productive farm to the barren flowerbeds that Horace deplores in *Odes* 2.15.

In Quintilian's analysis of tropes and figures of thought and speech, it is worth isolating the elements that are peculiar to his own 'Silver' age. Many are tied to the new cult of irony, innuendo, and suggestion, such as *emphasis* which gives loaded significance to ordinary words, as in 'be a man!' (8.3.86); or *noema*, which aims to suggest the unspoken by its wording, a type illustrated from declamation and from orators now lost to us (8.5.12); or *ironia* and the whole concept of the *figurata controversia*, a discourse which carries its true reference below the surface. On this he shrewdly comments that it is adopted for three reasons: if it is unsafe to speak plainly; if it is indecent to do so; or purely as an ornament (9.2.66). The fictional eloquence of the declamations favoured the first type, for example when addressing tyrants, but Quintilian is quick to point out that the feared authority would see through such disguise and be as resentful of its obliquity as of open criticism: in real life such a mode is not prudent (9.2.69). Most character-istic of Silver Latin prose is the *sententia*, defined by Quintilian as a conspicuous saying, and often used to round off a unit of discourse (8.4.2). These could be pointed sayings specific to the subject, or general aphorisms, and a common form was the comment or 'moral' used to sum up an anecdote, the *epiphonema*. He warns against the hazards of this feature of oratory (8.5.20–5), the far-fetched word play, the excess of such pointed sayings, which can obstruct each other like trees in a forest, their disjunctive effect creating a break in the flow of speech after which the speaker must restart his momentum. Worst of all is the infectious tendency to utter whole speeches as if each sentence carried point, giving a false resonance to simple statement. Yet he recognises the importance of this ornament and cites its use by Cicero and Virgil to support its legitimacy when used with restraint; there is a proper degree of *cultus* which stops short of culpable excess.

Descriptive criticism and literary history alike have been sought in the critical survey of Greek and Roman authors contained in the first chapter of Book X, but we must remember that authors are considered only for their beneficial effect on the would-be orator. Quintilian first compares and con-trasts the styles of poetry, history, and philosophy as nourishment for prose style (10.1.27–36); readers of the *Dialogus* might note that Quintilian, like Cicero in *Orator*, recognises History as a literary form close to poetry with aspects of style that the orator should avoid; it is defined (10.1.31) as epic in prose, narrative, not demonstrative, composed as a record, not for con-troversy, and aiming at intellectual renown. Thus it avoids monotony with recondite words and daring figures. For orators its style is most suited to the digression, not the argument. The virtues shared by history and poetry appear in Quintilian's discussion of poetry itself as energy of content, sublimity of diction, emotional effect, and psychological interest from character drawing (10.1.27); its hazards for the speaker are boldness in vocabulary and expression unsuited to the courtroom.

In his assessment of specific authors, Quintilian's Greek listings (10.1.46 – 84) confirm the canon already known to us from *On Imitation* by Dionysius, but only the most favoured authors, Homer, Euripides, and Menander, are given detailed appreciation. Rhetoricians clearly had favourite passages in Homer, such as the embassy to Achilles, and had picked out the plums from the pie: speeches of consolation, exhortation, and encomium. Quintilian finds in Homer models for every part of a judicial speech from exordium to peroration. Hesiod in comparison is assigned to the middle style, praised for his useful aphorisms and easy language. Confronted by a later Greek writer such as Apollonius Rhodius, not included in the traditional canon, Quintilian's assessment is less specific than, for example, his praise of Pindar for his spirit, his great sayings, his command of figures, wealth of vocabulary, and flow of eloquence. But this may derive not from the Greek tradition but from Horace's great Ode (4.2): 'whoever strives to imitate Pindar ...' Euripides and Menander are recommended for the same qualities: their naturalism of diction and subtlety of characterisation. Menander is called the single most fertile source of invention and expression, and yet the plays commended are unknown to us apart from *Epitrepontes*. Finally it is his decorum, both in propriety and in appropriate characterisation, that wins Menander the emphatic final position balancing Homer in the evaluation of the Greek poets (10.1.69 – 72).

The Roman assessments (10.1.85 – 131) are more significant, in that they are not predetermined by the Alexandrian canon, though Quintilian couches his judgements in terms of a contrast between the two literatures, with one or the other winning each bout. As with Greek hexameter poetry, Quintilian makes no formal distinction between epic and didactic. Macer and Lucretius, whose form and purpose we would measure against the *Georgics*, are criticised simply for style, Macer for his dullness of diction, Lucretius for his difficulty. From Quintilian's viewpoint Ennius was more be be revered than imitated; Ovid, on the other hand is depreciated, as 'too much in love with his own talent' (10.1.88), and reproached with frivolity. We owe to Quintilian the recognition of satire as a Roman genre; in that context Latin wins by default (10.1.93). But though he includes Menippean satire, Quintilian's generic system only partially matches his material; Petronius is not mentioned either as an author of Menippean satire or of romance, whereas Ovid is treated under epic, elegy, and drama, and Seneca, ignored under the rubric of tragedy, rounds off the generic list in a way that may include him among the philosophers, or deliberately segregate his contagion to spare the student, as in the passage quoted earlier in this chapter. Elegy is regarded as a Roman success; so is historical writing – at last. Ovid and Varius earn the accolade of being a match for the Greeks in tragedy, but the same change of taste that turns

Quintilian away from Ennius makes him despair of comedy as Rome's biggest failure. His explanation lies in the nature of Latin itself in contrast with the charm of Menander's Greek, a theme expanded in the important chapter on style (12.10) to be discussed below.

Quintilian reserves his most detailed and loving analysis for the comparison of Cicero with his great model Demosthenes (10.1.105–12), attempting from his Roman point of view what Longinus presents from the Greek. He recognises their common excellence of structure and strategy in argumentation; he notes also the greater diversity and compression of Demosthenes' pungent wit, contrasted with Cicero's broader and heavier approach: Demosthenes is seen as pared to the effective minimum, Cicero as developed to the full. In the end Quintilian awards the prize to Cicero for his wit and power to stir compassion. He also includes Cicero's dialogues and letters (now for the first time treated as a literary text) in his evaluation. We may smile when he attributes to Cicero the power of Demosthenes, the abundance of Plato, and the charm of Isocrates, but the student of Cicero knows that he consciously trained himself to emulate precisely these merits of these authors. He was after all the continuing prose model of educated Latinists, even the Christians, Jerome and Augustine and the humanists of the Renaissance, just as he became the model for formal vernacular prose in the sixteenth and seventeenth centuries.

As the chapter on authors for imitation is concerned with their stylistic qualities, it is not surprising that there are overlaps of argument with the latter discussion of *genera dicendi*, or the levels of style (12.10). Only in this last book does Quintilian treat the artist as an individual, considering his moral character and education and proper behaviour in the profession before he moves to the finished composition, the third and shortest unit of his tripartite scheme. He opens with the acknowledgement that the level of achievement in oratory reflects both the taste of the speaker and that of his society: oratory is compared with painting and sculpture as arts that have passed through a primitive stage before youthful development and subsequent maturity. He takes over from Greek theory the tension between the ideals of realism (*veritas*) and beauty (*pulchritudo*), meaningful for sculpture depicting realistic men and beautiful gods, but not fully integrated into his own rhetorical application, where the sense of *veritas* as real life is always positive and often contrasted with the mere pretence of declamation. Relativism in taste is illustrated by the reception of Cicero, criticised by his younger successors as inflated, diffuse, sing-song and even effeminate, yet in later generations reproached as dry and bare. Quintilian owes to Cicero's *Brutus* and *Orator* most of his comments on the Atticists, but adds an interesting comment in answering Santra's explanation of Attic oratory: Santra claimed that Asiatic Greeks developed their verbosity and circumlocutory phrasing because they aimed at eloquence without adequate command of the language. Quintilian answers that this is rather the product of a taste for boasting and display in both speakers and audience (12.10.16 – 19): again the recognition that bad style is more often the product of bad judgement than of incompetence.

Quintilian adds to the traditional topics a fascinating comparison of the two languages (12.10.27 – 34), praising Greek for the beauty and musicality of Z and Y, and of the ringing terminal N in declension, while deploring in Latin the ugly roughness of F and consonantal U, especially after Q, and the mooing M termination of many Latin inflexions. He regrets the monotony of Latin accentuation, which always left the final syllable unaccented (equated with Greek grave accent) and if the penultimate syllable was short would leave two dragging unaccented syllables. Worse, Latin has too poor a vocabulary and writers have to use circumlocutions to substitute for missing concepts. No wonder Roman poets delighted to introduce Greek words for their musical appeal. The Roman orator must compensate with the positive assets of Latin, exploiting fullness of expression to offset lack of subtle precision; he must rely on emotional effect, imagery, weight, and energy of language, just as a large ship has to manoeuvre differently from a lighter craft. Quintilian realises that to the Latin speaker the greatest challenge was the simple style of the small-scale case, but commends the success of Cicero or Calidius in this plainer mode. He follows Cicero's *Orator* in matching each stylistic level to a function, the plain style for argument, the middle to win over or delight the audience, and the passionate grand style to sway men towards the desired decision. From Cicero again he derives the Homeric models of Menelaus for plain speaking, Nestor for charming conciliatory speech, and Ulysses for persuasive grandeur. Quintilian's refinement on this is to allow for a whole graded spectrum of ornament with which the orator can satisfy both the ignorant and the connoisseurs among the audience; for real superiority shows itself in two ways: the great orator will outclass the average performer when his turn comes to speak, and while others may win approval from many, there will be no one to find fault with the truly great speaker.

5 Pliny the Younger and Juvenal

Quintilian offered his pupils hope that their oratory would be both needed and a worthy continuation of the tradition. It is the exalted note on which his great treatise ends (12.11.25 – 30). Many of his themes are reflected in the letters of his pupil Pliny (AD 62 – 113), but somehow what is sound sense in Quintilian leads to self-conscious eclecticism in Pliny's theory and lack of economy in his practice. An early letter encloses a speech which Pliny has been composing with special stylistic care, imitating Demosthenes and the Roman Calvus in his use of figures but 'resorting to Cicero's paintpots wherever there is scope for an appealing digression' (1.2). In forwarding his *Panegyric* to a friend he notes the problems of the genre: the material is so familiar that the audience gives all its attention to the style, but most will miss his subtlety of organisation and the variation in ornament and tone without which a continuously elevated speech would be monotonous (3.13). A longer letter (1.20) pleads the case for copiousness against the advocates of Attic brevity: only fullness can achieve the two functions of pleasing and persuading, and great speeches were as long in actual performance as the written versions we admire.

Another letter (5.8) offers a fresh topic: the appeal and reward of composing history instead of oratory. The letter professes to answer a request from the historian Titinius Capito that Pliny compose a history. Yes, he is tempted, especially as oratory has to be consummate to endure, but 'History charms, however it is written'. His own incentive is not some political or moral message he is burning to offer, nor even an interest in a particular period, but the desire for immortality; he confesses that he is attracted by the glorious, lofty material, the scope for luxuriant ornament, the sweet smooth-flowing style with its wider vocabulary and different periodic form from that of oratory. But his request that Capito select a theme for him shows an indifference which suggests that the entire letter may have been planned as an exercise in comparative criticism.

Elsewhere certainly he is more confident of the immortal prospects of oratory. Let two more letters illustrate his principles in training the young orator and methods of preparing his own work. He urges (7.9) young Fuscus to practise translation and paraphrase, to exercise himself in short verse forms, and in composing a literary letter or a historical passage – the latter to develop descriptive skills, the former to cultivate economy and elegance. As for reading in each genre, there are the prescribed authors whom Fuscus will know without prompting. For his own work Pliny adopts the process of serial and collective criticism: 'I let no type of correction pass: first I go over what I have written by myself, then I read it to two or three friends; presently I pass it on to others for comment, and if I am in doubt reconsider their criticisms with one or two more. Finally I read it aloud to a larger group, and, believe me, it is then that I correct most zealously' (7.17.7). Pliny admits to hoping his speeches will give lasting pleasure to posterity, but his own diligence and the politeness of his friends could only increase or elaborate his text, and the *Panegyric* of which he was so proud reads as though he could not bear to omit any ingenuity that occurred to him. The nearest parallel in rhetorical history is the *Panathenaicus* of the aging Isocrates, product of the same gestational overkill.

The Roman poet of the second century was a far cry from the poet-teacher of Aristophanes, or the poet-spokesman of national aspirations whom Horace proposed. Literature had been socialised, falling between the truly public and the genuinely personal utterance. It was an accepted leisure occupation, and for epigrammatists or writers of commissioned lyric such as Statius it could be a source of support. But the idealist poet who lived to compose would be heard less often than the patron. Horace had complained that 'skilled and unskilled alike we all compose' (*Ep.* 2.1.111). Juvenal returns to this topic in his seventh satire, protesting that poets starved while a patron's verses occupied the muses' temple. His fine satire has a burst of resentment against recitations, ranging from an epic *Theseid* through tragedies on Telephus and Orestes (were these actual, and if so were they Euripidean?) to *togatae*, a form of Italianised comedy long obsolete, and even elegy; and the poetic *topoi* which he cites recall the purple patches of Horace's warning in *Ars poetica*. Pliny knew and admired men who composed comedy and elegy, and justifies his own hendecasyllables (5.3), not by their literary merit, but the social precedents of elder statesmen who had composed similar indelicate verse. Poetry was a diversion to vary the other types of rhetorical exercise. Technique came easily since it was borrowed from the creative Virgil or his contemporaries. Inspiration, since men did not wait for it, fled like Astraea to more innocent writers in other lands.

.

6 Fronto and Gellius

Juvenal should not always be taken at face value, and though he speaks of starving historians (7.98–104), Tacitus was still composing his greatest work in the second decade of the second century. Prose literature survived until the middle of the century, growing gradually more barren with the loss of purpose beyond its own creation. Quintilian had warned in the preface to his eighth book that 'some make no end of quibbling: they linger over almost every syllable, and even when the best words have been found, go on hunting for something more archaic, obscure, and unexpected, not realising that content is the loser when it is the words that are praised'. Did he anticipate the works of Cornelius Fronto?

Fronto, consul (AD 143) and imperial tutor to Marcus Aurelius and his brother Verus, continuously exhorts his charges to amass collections of synonyms, hunt out rare and splendid words, and distinguish between the place, rank, weight, age, and dignity of words (*On Eloquence* 1.1). Contemporaries of Sallust at the end of the Republic had derided him for employing Ateius Philologus to hunt up archaisms from the elder Cato. Fronto admires no writer more than Sallust, unless it be the early poet Ennius or Cato himself. Faced with the legitimate goal of persuading the philosophically inclined Marcus to produce inspiring imperial addresses, he cites the use of figures of thought by Chrysippus; elsewhere (II, p. 49 Haines) he classifies the poets according to the three styles: Lucilius is *gracilis* (plain), Lucretius sublime (the grand style), Pacuvius *mediocris* (the middle or blended style),[15] but passes on

---

[15] Cf. Gellius 6.14, where Varro is said to have assigned Terence to the middle style and Pacuvius to the grand.

to other types of characterisation which suggest some familiarity with the Greek theory of *ideai*, to be discussed in chapter 10, section 5 below. More original are the criticisms he directs chiefly at Seneca and his nephew Lucan in the letter *On Speeches* (II, pp. 101f.). Seneca, he admits, is rich in ideas but 'his thoughts go trot-trot, nowhere strain at a gallop under the spur, nowhere show fight or aim at sublimity'. He condemns the opening of the *Bellum Civile* for Lucan's repeated variations on the same point, turning the poet's cry 'shall there never be an end?' against his own sentence structure. Given Fronto's limited interest in Greek poetry it is surprising that he cites Apollonius Rhodius as a counter-example, for the economy of his opening lines. Despite traditional precepts such as 'the supreme eloquence is to speak of sublime things in the grand style, of homely things in simple language', his advice would merely produce the affectations he seeks to avoid.[16] The marvel is that Fronto's spiritual disciple, Aulus Gellius, escapes the fussy mannerisms and obsessions of the older man. Gellius has an intelligent approach to the old writers he loves, leaving us not only fragments of authors otherwise lost, but also critical comparisons more analytical and often more discriminating than in earlier sources.

Gellius' enthusiasm for early writers is combined with a moral sentimentality which has been aptly called 'socio-linguistic atavism';[17] it is the old Greece and Rome which includes poets and orators as milestones in literary growth, from Homer and Hesiod through Archilochus to Aeschylus and Empedocles, then (set in the next generation) Sophocles and Euripides, leading to the flowering of philosophy. On the Roman side his material reflects the sources of Cicero's *Brutus*, but in keeping with his own taste Gellius stops with Lucilius whom he admires both as poet and critic (17.21.49).

Gellius' enthusiasm for early writers is combined with a moral sentimentality which has been aptly called 'socio-linguistic atavism';[17] it is the old conviction of the moral superiority of the ancestors; yet for all his devotion to the elder Cato's oratory he can measure the difference between his beloved primitives and Cicero. In a comparison of excerpts from Gaius Gracchus and Cicero (6.3) he calls Cicero's speech brilliant, pleasing, harmonious, whereas Gracchus, despite the natural appeal and patina of antiquity, is rough, brusque, and unrefined. Citing Cato's great speech for the Rhodians, he concludes that Cato was not content with the eloquence of his own day, but strove for the effects which Cicero achieved (10.3). In another passage (12.2) he reacts violently against Seneca's criticism of Cicero and Virgil for adapting Ennian tags, 'harsh, irregular, and lumbering verses'. In a lost letter Seneca had accused Virgil of doing so to palliate, by apparent archaism, the shock of his new styled poetry for 'the people of Romulus'. Gellius notes that many

---

[16] In fairness to Fronto, note that only his correspondence survives, much damaged in a palimpsest manuscript.

[17] Baldwin, *Studies*, p. 52.

people in his day thought Seneca's diction low and vulgar, and condemned Seneca's phrasing and composition for its hollow, emotional urgency or empty cleverness of expression; yet there were others who recognised his lack of refinement in language but praised his learning and moral earnestness as itself a source of aesthetic appeal. What is significant here is perhaps less the see-saw of aesthetic preferences over three centuries than the vocabulary and framework of our critic. He has a formidably nuanced vocabulary for stylistic criticism, and although style still receives more attention than content, its traditional components – diction, composition, and ornament – are less prominent than aspects of tone and tempo. The age of Gellius and Fronto neither admired nor employed the pointed disjunctive urgency of Seneca or of Aper's friends, nor apparently did it cherish the rhythm and proportion of the Ciceronian period. Vocabulary is the focus of second-century prescriptive criticism and the most distinctive feature of its own writing.

Thus a typical sequence in Gellius, the chapters from 13.21 to 31, includes five literary discussions, all concerned with words: one discussion notes the relationship of variant word forms such as *urbes/urbis* to euphony, and scans the text of Virgil for his original practice; another (13.25) considers the distinction between certain synonyms and the literary effect of accumulations of synonyms in Homer and Cicero. Virgil's imitation of Parthenius in deploying Greek proper names with special metrical licence is compared with a Virgilian imitation of Homer (13.27), and the last three chapters deal respectively with Fronto, on the solemnity of the archaic expression 'with many mortals', with the changed semantics of the noun *facies*, and with the interpretation of the Varronian expression 'a dog's dinner'. A literary critic today would call this philology, but these niceties are certainly relevant to the appreciation of the ancient texts.

There is genuine literary judgement in Gellius' evaluation of Caecilius' comedy *The Necklace* in relation to its Menandrian model (2.23). Gellius demonstrates the crudity of the Roman version by citing three excerpts from both versions, showing how Caecilius has replaced or omitted subtle details and inserted the typical clichés of the mime, with wisecracks about bad breath and vomiting; he notes how Caecilius reduced eight swift, allusive lines to four lines of swollen tragic diction. Many of the critical discussions focus on Virgil; a sample (17.10) is criticism attributed to Favorinus of the description of Mount Aetna in *Aeneid* V, comparing it with Virgil's model in Pindar *Pythian* 3; Favorinus, who assumed Virgil had not reached the final version of his text, condemns the Latin version as inflated and hyperbolical, but also makes the same complaint against Pindar himself. We can understand his dislike for Virgil's conceit of flames 'licking the stars', but these are prosaic objections inimical to the spirit of epic or lyric poetry. In an earlier passage (9.9) on Virgil's adaptation of Theocritus, Gellius notes that Virgil did not try to incorporate what he could not convert into Latin, but adds praise for the poet's original contribution. There are in fact many changes from Theocritus' third *Idyll* to Virgil's fifth *Eclogue*. Gellius is also our witness (9.9.12f.) for Valerius Probus' criticisms of Virgil's adaptation (*Aen.* 1.498f.) of the Homeric simile comparing Nausicaa among her maids to Artemis (*Od.* 6.102f.). Probus had chiefly argued from propriety, but also objected that Virgil's description of Dido omitted the Homeric stress on the heroine's conspicuous beauty (although Dido's beauty could not have helped standing out against the elder statesmen around her). In this, as in Probus' criticism of the scene between Venus and Vulcan in *Aeneid* VIII, we sample the methods and excesses of Virgilian criticism, essentially a reaction against his preeminence. Gellius has the sense to repudiate Probus' prudishness about the word *membra*, but seems to accept the general censure of the scene.

We are in the world of *epigoni*; respect for their predecessors and a good grammatical and rhetorical training leads the educated men of the second century to preserve what is valuable and apply the knowledge they have to criticism of the specific text, but as literary criticism the formality and triviality is stifling. Nowhere do we find an interest in principles of organisation or characterisation, or even in allegory within the epic that was the Romans' greatest exemplar of creative literature. The work as a whole is revered without attempts to understand its form or value system, and these negatives apply even more strongly to second-century criticism of less canonical authors and texts. We leave the classical period of Latin literature with an impression of ingrowing methods, that can only repeat or elaborate themselves. But between Gellius and the next important Latin secular critics, Macrobius and Servius, six generations of political turmoil and literary infertility are best passed in silence. In the interim, Christian writers began to wrestle with the value of the Classics and the interpretation of texts, a topic resumed in chapter 11 below.

10

GREEK CRITICISM OF THE EMPIRE

Greek criticism of the first four or five Christian centuries presents a rich and diverse picture. It is not, however, one that can be complete in itself. Many of the basic concepts derive from Hellenistic or even earlier writings. The great elaborations of the rhetorical theories of types of issue (*staseis*) and types of style (*kharaktēres, ideai*) which we see, for example, in Hermogenes and his commentators, are firmly grounded in what was inherited from Hermagoras and Theophrastus and those who built on their work in the earlier period. The many attempts to discuss the relationship between literature and morals are still, in the main, a response to Plato. Furthermore, there was an important bilingual literary public – Romans who knew Greek, not Greeks who knew Latin, for these were few – and Latin literature had reached its classical acme and become a subject of study in its own right. There was thus a need to compare and contrast, to study the process of *imitatio*, but also to treat the two literatures as in an important sense one. In the late first and early second centuries the union seems particularly strong. Quintilian uses Dionysius' *On Imitation* as the source for his list of recommended reading in Greek, and the model for his corresponding advice about Latin (10.1). Aulus Gellius, reporting or embellishing the conversation of the elegant and pretentious academic circle of Antonine Athens, compares Virgil with his models in Pindar or Theocritus or Homer, and the comic poet Caecilius with his exemplar Menander. In the letters of the younger Pliny there are criticisms not only of Roman orators but of the Greek Isaeus (2.3) and a discussion of the dangers of the grand style (9.26) which uses Greek instances and reminds us very strongly of *On Sublimity*, the most important and influential book in all this period, itself addressed to a Roman reader, using Cicero as an example of a certain kind of grandeur (13.4), and (some would say) responding precisely to arguments advanced in Tacitus' *Dialogus*. But to mention *On Sublimity* here is to beg the question of its date; and the doubts about this central fact are a healthy reminder that many of the texts on which we depend are of uncertain authorship and date. The massive and enduring homogeneity of Greco-Roman higher education imposed a timelessness on its textbooks, very frustrating to the historian who looks for change.

But in fact change did occur. In these centuries we see the rise of two intellectual movements which had a great and long-lasting impact on the way in which literature was perceived; they are very different, and yet they had a basis of similarity which ensured the underlying homogeneity of which we are always conscious. The first movement is what is conveniently called the Second Sophistic. Its marks are an intense concern with correct Attic Greek in imitation of fourth-century prose, and the enormous prestige attached to 'sophists' who mastered this elaborate and difficult language and used their rhetorical skills not only in lawcourt or in council, but for the entertainment of their connoisseur public. One effect of this movement, which was both social and educational, was to develop a technique of close reading which exposed and explained the rhetorical moves of the great orators, especially Demosthenes. This technique could be used also for Homer and the dramatists, much read in the schools, and easily made to contribute to the formation of the orator. Later on it was used also for the basic texts of Christianity: to read St John Chrysostom's *Homilies* on the Pauline epistles can be uncannily like reading Hermogenes or Syrianus on Demosthenes. Another effect, due to the competitiveness among themselves of teachers of rhetoric, was proliferation of theory. Every teacher wanted to have his own system of *staseis* and *ideai*. Not all were foolish: one can unearth a good deal of suggestive theorising about the nature of literary discourse and its 'figures' (*skhēmata*). It is important to remember also that a great deal of the rhetor's effort went into *meletai*, exercises in declamation, including *plasmata*, imaginary speeches on invented legal themes, with or without an historical setting. These were a kind of fiction; giving instruction in them inevitably produced reflection on unity of plot and character as well as on style and the standard rhetorical strategies.

The second movement is the dominance of neo-Platonism in the third and fourth centuries. This had even more profound effects. It was very important for the neo-Platonists to reconcile Plato and Homer and somehow assuage the 'ancient quarrel', so as to free Plato, as far as they could, from the charge of despising poetry and banishing it from the ideal society. They proceeded, like many Stoics and others before them, by developing techniques of allegorical and symbolic interpretation. But they keyed these into their own special metaphysical systems – they inhabited, after all, a world in which everything, they thought, symbolised several other things – and thereby opened up possibilities of which both Medieval and Renaissance theorists availed themselves. This was a Greek, not a Latin, development; but it was a Latin writer, Macrobius, who ensured its future in Western culture, and it is his commentary on Cicero's *Dream of Scipio* to which we owe quite a lot of our knowledge of this kind of thinking.

There remains the similarity between the two movements, the rhetorical and the philosophical. Two common factors should be stressed. One is the sense, shared by all these teachers, that the trained mind is thereby admitted to a mystery and joins an élite whose success or salvation is assured. The second is the universal reverence for the authority of the Classical texts. Homer, Plato, and Demosthenes could not be wrong. If they seemed so, this must be explained away; if they differed, the differences must be reconciled. However much the philosophers and rhetors of the Empire attacked each other in set speeches or fought over the allegiance of the young, they were united in their conviction that the great texts of the past, properly interpreted, were the key to wisdom. Interpretation was thus the most vital of rhetorical and philosophical activities, as it was for the lawyers with their study of statutes and opinions and the doctors with their exegesis of Hippocrates. The process extended, not so much to contemporary creative writing (which the Greek schools tended to neglect), as to the interpreters themselves; what Plotinus or Hermogenes actually meant became an important issue to their successors. This common interest in interpretation made it easy for people of the right talents, like Syrianus, to excel in both professions and to comment with equal facility on Hermogenes and on Aristotle.

1 Dio of Prusa

Some men of letters of the first and early second centuries foreshadow the sophistic age and the rise of neo-Platonism. We begin with Dio and Plutarch, both of whom enjoyed the *felicitas temporum* (Tacitus, *Agricola* 2) which followed the death of Domitian in AD 96.

Dio of Prusa, nicknamed Chrysostomus, 'the golden-mouthed', was an accomplished mimic of Plato and a facile and amusing orator. He often takes the philosophic stance of a Socrates, sometimes even a Cynic pose. But his rhetorical and literary culture is never concealed. Several of his essays and speeches are relevant to our theme. *On the Practice of Speech* (*Or.* 18) has been thought spurious; indeed, it is the most explicitly rhetorical of his pieces. Like the author of *On Sublimity* and many another, the author sets himself up as the adviser of a man of substance and power who wants to improve his public speaking by a study of the best models. 'First, middle, and last, for child and adult and old' is Homer, who can never be read too much (18.8).[1] Since they make most use of debate, plays of Euripides and Menander are most to be recommended; Quintilian (10.1.12) thought the same. History is important, but for content rather than for style. Modern writers – and this is a somewhat unusual feature – are also on the list; Dio revealingly points out (18.12) that they have the advantage over the ancients that we do not come to them 'mentally enslaved', as we do to the classics, or reverence them to excess. But the most valuable author of all is Xenophon; he alone would be enough. The choice is interesting. If the author is Dio, it would indeed fit very well with

---

[1] Heraclitus, *Quaestiones Homericae* 1: 'man finishes with Homer when he finishes with life'.

what we know of his own enthusiasms. And the reason given – that the speeches in Xenophon provide models not only for public occasions but for private moments of persuasion – shows a concern also found in *On Sublimity* (17.1): rhetoric should give counsel appropriate to the political life of the Empire, in which authoritative individuals or small councils were more likely to be important audiences than the wayward assemblies of democratic city states.

This piece apart, Dio's comments on literature are mostly concerned with the poets. A short essay *On Homer* (*Or.* 53) takes up the poet's defence against Plato: Homer is inspired and also useful as a moral teacher, and his own poor wandering life (this was the common legend) demonstrates his courage and greatness of heart. Comparison (*sunkrisis*) is a common critical tool in this period, learned as an exercise in grammar schools and applied to historical subjects (as in Plutarch's *Lives*) as well as to literature. Dio's speech *On Homer and Socrates* (*Or.* 55) conducts a comparison between the two, drawing a parallel between Socrates' notorious use of vulgar instances and the abusive language of Antinoös in the *Odyssey*. It was appropriate that the glutton Antinoös should be shot 'through the gullet', as it is appropriate that Socrates should refute the leather-seller Anytus by examples from his trade, or the amorous Meno by talk of lovers. Nothing in either Homer or Plato is in vain. *Chryseis* (*Or.* 61) makes a fresh point: Homer is praised for a delicate understanding of female psychology. Unusually, the interlocutor in this little dialogue is a woman. It is surprising to find Dio in the *Trojan Oration* (11) taking quite a different line and demonstrating that Homer's whole tale of the Trojan War is a fiction, exhibiting all the traits of a clever liar. And so far from his simple life being a recommendation, nothing is more likely than that a beggar should lie to curry favour wherever he goes. All these speeches are designed for occasions; they lay no claim to consistency. It should not surprise us, then, to read in the speech reporting Dio's visit to the remote Black Sea colony of Olbia (*Or.* 36) that a moral couplet of Phocylides about the well-ordered city is worth more than all the *Iliad*, with Achilles' ranting and roaring. Even within this one speech, context demands different attitudes: Dio takes up the Platonic view that drama is inferior to epic, alleging that Homer and Hesiod were inspired, but their successors were not; themselves not initiated, they fraudulently claimed to initiate their audiences into theological truths.

Of Dio's discussions of tragedy, *Oration* 60 is a moralising treatment of the story of Nessus and Deianira as found in Archilochus and Sophocles. *Philoctetes' Bow* (*Or.* 52) is more important. It is a comparison of the versions of the Philoctetes story in the plays of Aeschylus, Euripides, and Sophocles. Dio reports himself as reading them while ill or convalescent, and pretending that he is the judge who is to award the prize to the best of them. We have a vivid glimpse of the leisured and rather self-centred life of the man of letters, typical of the age and the culture. The essay is again evidence of the practice of comparison (*sunkrisis*), which perhaps is responsible for the survival of some of the plays we have: *Choephori* and the two *Electras*; *Seven against Thebes* and *Phoenissae*. Dio's stereotype of the three tragedians is not very different from that of Aristophanes in the *Frogs*: a grandiloquent Aeschylus, a smart Euripides, and a Sophocles between the two, sharing the virtues of both, the charm (*hēdonē*) as well as the magnificence (*megaloprepeia*). The triad corresponds to the triad of styles (grand, simple, and 'middle') in the commonest form of the theory of *kharactēres*. There are, however, some additional points. Aeschylus' portrayal of the heroic character is appropriate to 'the ancient ways of heroes', and even his Odysseus is old-fashioned 'compared with people who nowadays claim to be simple or magnanimous' (52.5). Euripides' ingenuity in excusing the chorus for their failure over many years to visit the wounded Philoctetes is judged unpraiseworthy because tragedy inevitably involves implausibilities, and there is therefore not much point in going out of one's way to avoid this one.

The most influential and suggestive of Dio's works, so far as his aesthetic views are concerned, is one which is not specifically concerned with literature but with theology and the visual arts. This is the speech (*Or.* 12) he delivered at the festival at Olympia, most probably in AD 101. Its main point is a defence of anthropomorphic images of the gods, Pheidias' statue of Zeus being the obvious occasion of the discussion. The artist, the lawyer, and the poet, Dio argues, all offer mankind an additional power, over and above our natural instinct, or envisaging and comprehending the divine. Pheidias, the story goes, drew inspiration from the lines of Homer (*Il.* 1.525–30) in which Zeus

> with his dark eyebrows nodded
> and hair immortal on his deathless head
> stirred, and he made great Olympus shake.

So, when Pheidias, in Dio's rhetorical fiction, defends himself (12.55ff.) against the charge that his workmanship and his representation of a human form may not be a worthy way of setting forth the majesty of the god, it is to the precedent of Homer that he appeals (12.62). Homer gave Zeus the anthropomorphic features of hair and chin and made him talk and take counsel, sleep and drink and go to bed with Hera. Indeed, in one place (*Il.* 2.478), Homer actually compares Agamemnon's eyes and head to Zeus's. Pheidias never did that; he could claim to be a wiser craftsman than the poet, though inhibited by the difficulty of his material. Poets have a much easier life. Words, which present things vividly to our minds – including things which cannot be depicted visually – are to be had in abundance and with ease. They came particularly readily to Homer, who used all dialects and coined words freely, especially onomatopoeic ones, for his particular needs. Poets, again, know no restrictions of movement or place; the sculptor, by contrast, works in stone and in a limited and determined space. His work can neither move nor speak. Yet he uses the best materials that man can handle. It is Zeus himself who is the greatest craftsman, welding the elements in the universe. There is probably little that is original in these observations. They belong to a tradition of reflection on mimesis and on the likenesses and differences between the visual and verbal arts, which goes back beyond Plato at least to Ion of Chios and to the often quoted dictum attributed to Simonides that 'painting is silent poetry, and poetry painting that talks'. Dio gives it all a warm, impressive tone; he is a good witness to the educated piety of his time, the Platonist and Stoic 'cosmic religion' that satisfied and moved the hearts of many. But of course he is also a rhetorician. All this was said at Olympia, in a moment vulnerable to excitement and fervour. It is the rhetorical context that, as in other works, is decisive for the content.

2 Plutarch

Plutarch was Dio's close contemporary, and there is reason to think that their paths crossed: the 'Catalogue of Lamprias', an ancient list of Plutarch's works, contains the titles *To Dio, spoken at Olympia* and *Address to Dio*. But he was a writer of a different stamp, less concerned to mimic the Classics and himself no orator. His works usually have individual addressees; they are thus presented as letters, not as speeches. They display a wide range of learning, philosophical as well as historical and literary. Among them are several devoted to literary topics. There were more once: notably a Hesiod commentary of which we have substantial fragments.

Pride of place belongs to *How a Young Man Should Hear the Poets* – that is to say 'read' or 'understand' them, the verb 'to hear' being common for all kinds of literary encounter, even in a culture where writing has come to be at least as important as speaking. Plutarch writes to a friend about the education of their sons; as a nineteenth-century French critic elegantly put it, 'la prévoyance du père de famille se mêle aux subtilités du philosophe érudit'.[2] Poetry, the staple of early education, has its dangers, and the young need an antidote. It is easy to see that Plutarch is here providing a practical answer, on the level of common sense, to Plato's condemnation of mimetic poetry. Many of his examples overlap with those in the *Republic*. At the same time, his title is close to that of a lost book by the Hellenistic Stoic philosopher Chrysippus, and no doubt he owes concepts and approaches to this. Plutarch however was himself a Platonist, not a Stoic, and one of his main concerns is to reconcile Plato with the prevailing educational tradition. We shall see the antithesis to this in the Stoic Heraclitus and elaboration of the theme in the neo-Platonists.

One of Plutarch's first moves is to distinguish the lies – *pseudē*, also

[2] Egger, *Histoire de la critique*, p. 267.

translatable as 'fictions' – that poets commit deliberately from those that are involuntary. The cause of deliberate 'lying' is that it is essential to the pleasure of poetry: 'we know no poetry without fable or fiction'. It is easily recognised and easily guarded against. 'Involuntary' falsehood is a more serious matter. There are many false statements which poets make because they believe them true. For example (17b), the fearsome stories of the underworld, burning rivers and savage punishments, do not represent the beliefs of Homer or Pindar or Sophocles, in whose poems we find them depicted; but the pathos and fear of death expressed in lines such as

> but his soul had flown from his limbs and gone to the house of Hades
> mourning its fate, leaving manhood and youth behind it   (*Il.* 6.856, 22.362)

represent the genuine belief and illusion of the poet. Homer really does think death is frightening. Yet this is untrue, at least to the philosopher. Plutarch does not tell us on what criterion we are to judge intention and belief; but his assumption seems to be that poets are reasonable and sensible people like himself, not likely to be led astray by wild superstition or childish terrors, but unphilosophical and possessing the prejudices and errors of common humanity. Our problem is then to read them in such a way as to get the benefit without acquiring the false ideas that can so easily rub off on us. Of course, the criterion of success in mimesis is realistic resemblance to the object imitated; but our moral approval, which we are free to grant or withhold, must not extend to imitations of bad actions, characters, or emotions. We must always consider context and propriety. The tyrant Eteocles or the old moneylender in comedy can properly be made to say things a decent man would not say. Homer is often scrupulous in warning us beforehand of the tone of a speech (19c). Before making Achilles utter the much-criticised words, 'You drunken sot, with your dog's eyes and deer's courage' (*Il.* 1.225), he introduces the speech by saying:

> Once more the son of Peleus addressed Agamemnon
> with bitter words, for his anger was not yet done.

Plutarch is particularly interesting where he shows the usefulness of a historical knowledge of changes of meaning. Thus (24d) he recognises that *aretē* in Classical poetry does not always mean 'the best and most divine condition in us, which we conceive as rightness of reason, perfection of reasonable nature, and a harmonious disposition of the soul', but rather 'honour, power, good fortune, or something like this'. This is to anticipate an historical point of view which modern scholarship has made familiar and sometimes exaggerated. Plutarch's motive for the observation is, once again, moral; but this recognition that words do change their connotations and that one should not read later beliefs into Homer is an important application of grammatical scholarship.

It is then not very surprising that, despite his anxiety to make Homer acceptable, Plutarch is not attracted by the use of allegory to explain away the 'discreditable fables'. Indeed (19e), he regards 'what were once called *huponoiai* and are now called allegories'[3] as, in some instances at least, forced and unnecessary. He therefore rejects the opinion that Hera's adornment of herself in readiness for Zeus represents a purification of the air,[4] on the ground that Homer makes it clear (*Il.* 14.32) that such self-adornment and deceit gives only short-lived pleasure and may quickly turn to disgust and anger. In other words, the context itself gives a moral explanation which renders the scientific one beside the point. We shall see later how the neo-Platonists understood this most famous of 'improper tales'. And though Plutarch is cautious or even negative towards allegory here, that attitude is not maintained throughout his work: in *Isis and Osiris*, in particular, he is very ready to use all kinds of allegorical explanations to justify and clarify the symbolism of the cult. .

Finally, an example which shows Plutarch's methods and preoccupations in *How a Young Man Should Hear the Poets* particularly clearly. It concerns a passage where there is, he thinks, genuine obscurity (27b). Nausicaa in the *Odyssey* (6.244) is made to say to her maidservants, with reference to Odysseus:

> If only I had a husband like that,
> living here, and he wanted to stay here!

Now if, like Calypso, says Plutarch, she felt flirtatious and eager to marry, we ought to criticise her forwardness and boldness; but if she has perceived in Odysseus, from his speech, the sort of man he is and wishes to have a husband like that, rather than some Phaeacian sailor and dancer, then she is to be commended. This balanced view alludes to a considerable controversy. A medieval Greek commentary on this passage, probably derived from ancient sources, reports that 'the solution depends on consideration of character', that is to say on the character of the Phaeacians, and this is obviously Plutarch's view.

Throughout this book, Plutarch is concerned with the 'moral reader': the one who 'fastens on to what is said that is morally valuable' (30d). This is not always the case in his other works. As with Dio, context and purpose determine the choice of argument and allusion. An example is one of his few speeches, the highly rhetorical piece on the question 'Whether the Athenians are more distinguished for war or for wisdom'. The theme requires that deeds shall always appear more important than words. Hence literary renown must be shown to be derivative from the real renown of which it is the reflection (345f.). Hence the fussy wordcraft of Isocrates is contrasted with the real

---

[3] Plato, *Rep.* 378d: 'the young man is not able to judge what is *huponoia* and what is not, and what he acquires among his opinions at that age tends to be indelible and irremovable'.

[4] Hera (HRA) is an anagram of AHR, 'air'.

battles that could be won in the time he took to write a speech (350d). Hence the importance attached to the anecdote about the poet Menander, who thought he could claim to have finished his play when he had thought out the plot, and only had to add the words: 'even poets think actions are more indispensable and important than words' (347e; cf. 16b). The speech is a source for some other famous literary anecdotes too: Simonides on 'talking painting', Corinna counselling Pindar to 'sow with the hand and not with the sack', and the suggestive epigram of Gorgias about the deceit (*apatē*) of drama, in which 'the deceiver is more just than the non-deceiver, and the deceived wiser than the undeceived' (346f–d).

Plutarch's *Table Talk* (*Symposiaca*) is another quarry for literary ideas. The participants in the various dinner conversations that he records or invents often raise questions of this nature, but in ways specially appropriate to the setting. What entertainments are appropriate after dinner? We hear of riddles, number-games, mimes, and scenes from Menander (5. Preface = 672–3). Why Menander? The reasons emerge from another dinner conversation (7.8 = 711–13) and from a separate 'Comparison of Aristophanes and Menander' (853–4), of which an epitome survives.[5] Old Comedy has too much vulgarity, too much political seriousness, and too many obscure allusions. The dinner party would turn into a schoolroom while all this was explained. Menander, on the other hand, is easy and urbane, free from homosexual or other obscene jokes, and brings his plays to a happy ending in stable marriages and fortunate recognitions. But there is nothing to prevent dinner guests enjoying serious conversation, or at least learned lightness.

On one occasion (1.5 = 622c) we find the party discussing the real meaning of Euripides' saying that 'love makes a man a poet, though he were none before'. We hear of Theophrastus' theory that musical rhythm and melody have three psychological sources: pain, pleasure, and possession (*enthousiasmos*), love coming easily under this last head. On another evening (5.1 = 673c) the company includes some Epicureans. The question is raised why we enjoy imitations of anger and grief but do not enjoy watching others experience these emotions in real life. The Epicurean answer is that the actor is superior to the sufferer because he is not suffering; we understand this, and we take pleasure in admiring his *apatheia*. Plutarch himself advances an alternative view. It is, he thinks, the rational activity of art that, as rational beings, we naturally admire, just as we enjoy games that involve some intellectual effort. Cocks and crows make an unpleasant noise, but we find pleasure in those who have the skill to mimic them. It is distressing to see consumptives wasting away; but statues and paintings of them give pleasure. The conversation ends (674c) with the story of 'Parmeno's pig'. This Parmeno (see also 18c; cf. Plato, *Rep.* 397a) could imitate a pig to perfection. One of his rivals one day

---

[5] Tr. in Russell and Winterbottom, *Ancient Literary Criticism*, pp. 531–2.

brought a real pig under his arm and made it squeal. Those present said, as they usually did, 'It doesn't compare with Parmeno's pig'; whereupon the man released the real one, showing, says Plutarch, 'that the same sense experience does not have the same effect upon the mind when there is no sense that the phenomenon is due to the activity of reason or effort.'

From these scattered evidences of concern for the psychological bases of literary experience, we may turn in conclusion to another specialist work, the rather puzzling essay on *Herodotus' Malice* (*Moralia* 854ff.). The thesis is that Herodotus' admittedly charming and beguiling style conceals a malicious spirit, especially towards the Boeotians, Plutarch's own countrymen, and the Corinthians, with regard to the part they played in the Persian War. Plutarch is moved to defend 'both his ancestors and the truth'. He prefaces his detailed critique with a passage which is of considerable interest for historiography. It is a list of the diagnostic signs by which one can tell a 'malicious' historian. Such a man will use hard words where moderate ones would do, inject a discreditable story where it is not relevant, leave out the good points of a character, choose the less creditable version of events, make the more damaging conjecture about motives, deny moral value to good actions by attributing them to luck, and mix praise and blame in such a way that the praise loses its force. These criteria derive from rhetorical thinking. A prosecutor concerned to denigrate his opponent's character has just this range of options. Plutarch himself, of course, wrote history, or at least *Lives*. The moral seriousness – some would say blandness – that he consistently shows there reflects his concern to practise what he preaches.

Plutarch's work is varied, and as we have seen, the views expressed are often conditioned by the needs of the moment. Nevertheless, he clearly has a certain consistency of attitude. Generally remote from the burgeoning rhetorical tradition of his time, and professing to be very much the philosopher rather than the rhetorician, he confronts the literature of the past with an eye always to its moral value and useful content. And like the neo-Platonists after him, his natural successors, he found the ancient conflict between Plato and Homer an embarrassment and a stimulus to inquiry.

3 Longinus on sublimity

Plato is important also in *On Sublimity*, the most famous and influential book that falls within our purview, though here it is his literary excellence, not his quarrel with the poets, that is at issue. The single manuscript on which the survival of *On Sublimity* depends is unclear about the authorship, and the situation encourages us to believe that the work was ascribed in Byzantine times either to 'Dionysius' or to 'Longinus'.[6] If 'Dionysius' is Dionysius of

---

[6] *Parisinus graecus* 2036, the ms. in question, has 'of Dionysius Longinus' with the title of the book, 'of Dionysius or Longinus' in its table of contents.

Halicarnassus, the idea is absurd, given the style and content of his genuine works discussed earlier in this volume. If 'Longinus' is the famous teacher of the neo-Platonist Porphyry, a third-century scholar and statesman whom some called 'a living library and walking Museum' (Eunapius, p. 352 Wright), and who probably discussed similar subjects,[7] this sets the book in a later and ill-documented period. Moreover, there is late evidence that this Longinus, who certainly wrote on rhetoric, found fault with Plato's mixture of styles and with the excessively poetical grandeur of his prose. This is in clear contradiction to *On Sublimity*. The reasons for believing the book to belong to the first or early second century are strong. Indeed, though objections are raised from time to time, there is a very general view that the reasons are convincing. For one thing, there are powerful arguments from silence. There is nothing in the book bearing on the great sophists of the second century, though later theorists such as Hermogenes tend to mention some of these. Again, there is nothing about Plato's philosophy, but only the passionate apologia for his style. Such philosophical background as there is seems to be predominantly Stoic. Finally, there is the closing chapter, with its discussion not only of literary decline but of political 'slavery'. To that we must return.

At first sight, the treatise seems orderly and well planned. This is however something of an illusion. Our difficulties do not all arise from the misfortune that about a third of the whole is lost, as a result of the absence of pages from the manuscript at several places. They are also a result of the nature and plan of the whole. The first eight chapters form an extended preface, in which the characteristic prefatory topics appear. The author professes to be answering, or complementing, the unsatisfactory account of 'sublimity' (*hupsos*) given by Caecilius of Calacte, a contemporary of Dionysius who seems to have shared that writer's classicising attitudes and distaste for much of Plato. The subject is defined: *hupsos*, we are told, is the excellence which most of all gives great writers their eternal renown; it is a quality which amazes and astonishes rather than persuades in ordinary, gentle ways; and it can be found in a single phrase, for it does not need a whole context for its display. Next, the possibility of a *tekhnē* of this excellence has to be demonstrated against those who think that such a thing comes solely by nature (*phusis*) and not by a combination of nature and art. Further definition is given by describing the false sublime, the kinds of bombast and frigidity which results from misguided or inadequate efforts at grandeur. True sublimity will stand the test of time and of repeated study by intelligent readers of any conceivable background, age, or education (7.3–4).

It is already clear from this preface – indeed from the opening sentences – that the writer sees his task as helping would-be orators to 'think big', not merely to use grand words and grand composition. When he comes (8) to

---

[7] Proclus, *In Timaeum* 1.66 Diehl.

propose the headings under which he will discuss the matter, he assigns the greatest importance to what he calls the first two of five 'sources' of sublimity and defines these as grandeur of thought and powerful emotion (*pathos*). These are 'for the most part' spontaneous. 'Art' is more closely involved in the other three 'sources': figures, diction, and composition (*sunthesis*). Caecilius' principal failing is now said to be his neglect of emotion, which is distinct from sublimity, but a uniquely effective contributor to it. Serious problems arise when we seek to accommodate the rest of the book to this scheme, even if we disregard the two references elsewhere (3.5, 44.12) to a separate treatment of *pathos* and assume that this is something quite outside the present treatise. The first 'source' clearly begins at the beginning of chapter 9; then at the end of chapter 15 there is a sentence of summary which apparently refers solely to the first source, but it is followed immediately by the discussion of figures, which (we are told) came third on the list, after 'emotion'. Many explanations of this have been given.[8]

From this point on, the headings of the scheme are followed one by one, though unevenly and sometimes perfunctorily. There is a model discussion of Demosthenes' famous 'Marathon oath' (*De corona* 208), much ingenious and amusing exemplification of rhetorical questions (18), anaphora (20), hyperbaton (22), and other figures; metaphor (32) and synthesis (39) are handled in some detail, but other things passed over rather quickly. The most striking part of all this latter half of the book is however the famous digression (33–6), in which the writer reaches new heights of eloquence himself and seems to be stating his literary *credo*. It arises out of Caecilius' expressed preference for Lysias over Plato, which our author, one of whose aims is surely the rehabilitation of Plato as a literary artist,[9] regards as absurd. We should not count faults, but successes. Writers without a blemish – Bacchylides, Ion of Chios, Apollonius and other Alexandrians – are not to be compared with the truly great – Homer, Pindar, Sophocles – even though captious critics can find faults in the latter. It is with authors as with the works of nature: we admire the mighty rivers, not the tiny, pellucid spring. The secret of the great writers is their vision of the universe and its divine control. Their *hupsos* 'lifts them up near the great mind of god'. It will endure forever, and it testifies to the co-operation of art and nature. There are two important points to be made about this passage. First, it is no digression, since it clearly presents the author's central position. It is indeed the nature of this book that the discursive parts are more vital to its message than the development of the scheme of five sources. Secondly, it is a manifesto directed against what we may call the Callimachean ideal, much preached in the Roman poets, of the perfect small-scale masterpiece. Longinus' choice of metaphor brings this home: it

---

[8] Most recently, Bompaire, 'Le pathos', pp. 323–43.
[9] Russell, 'Longinus revisited', pp. 72–86.

was Callimachus (*Hymn* 2.105–12) who drew the contrast between the river of Assyria, carrying its filth down to the sea, and the little trickle of pure water from a holy spring, whence the Bees bring water to Deo, and made this a literary analogy.

The second major interpretative problem of *On Sublimity* arises out of the concluding chapter (44), in which the author sets up a debate between a 'philosopher' and himself. This too, unexpected as it appears, is closely connected with the main theme of the book, since it defines more precisely the kind of moral improvement needed if the present age is to rival the 'sublime' productions of the past.[10] The 'philosopher' maintains that the dearth of contemporary writers with the natural ability to achieve 'sublimity' is due to the lack of freedom. Any form of 'slavery', however just, inhibits the mind as cages are said to inhibit the growth of dwarfs. Longinus counters by attributing the phenomenon not to 'the present world peace', which he tacitly equates with the loss of liberty accused by his opponent, but to our moral servitude to greed and luxury. This exchange of views naturally raises questions about the social and political context in which the book was written. The reference to 'world peace' has commonly, and with justification, been thought to argue against a third-century date, for the world was then torn by wars, external as well as civil; only a very sheltered and scholastic writer could use such a phrase of such circumstances. But it leaves open the whole of the early principate, from Augustus anyway to the end of the second century. Can we narrow the date down further? Parallels have often been drawn with other first-century discussions of literary decline: the two Senecas, Quintilian, and especially the speech of Maternus in Tacitus' *Dialogue on Orators* (40ff.). These parallels are conclusive in setting the work somewhere in the period between Augustus and Hadrian, but not in demonstrating that it has to be later than Tacitus (perhaps AD 100), for we have no proof that the ideas put forward in the *Dialogue* were new.[11] It has often been held that *On Sublimity* belongs to the beginning of the likely period, even to the reign of Augustus. The main reason given for this is the polemic against Caecilius, unlikely (it is said) except near his own time. Against this it may be said that ancient polemic in rhetorical and philosophical schools knows no such time limits: witness, for example, the heated polemic of Plutarch against the works of the Epicurean Colotes, 400 years old. Yet convincing arguments against an Augustan date are difficult to find. The best is probably the attribution to the 'philosopher' of the complaint against 'slavery' and the firm association of oratory with *dēmokratia*, which must here mean the *libera res publica* which the principate destroyed. Now it is true that even Cicero reacted somewhat in these terms to the dictatorship of Caesar (*De officiis* 2.67; *Brutus* 46); but

---

[10] For an ingenious theory that ch. 44 has been displaced from the end of ch. 15, see R. Brandt, *Vom Erhabenen* (Darmstadt, 1966), pp. 125–6.

[11] But see Heldmann, *Entwicklung und Verfall*, pp. 286–93.

the tone suggests much more the 'Stoic republicanism' of the time of Claudius and Nero, and there are no doubt various circles of first-century Roman society in which this attitude could be heard.

What complicates the question further is the amalgam of Greek and Roman topics in this first speech. The basic idea, that rhetoric is the child of freedom, has a Greek origin and a Greek setting in the tradition that the early teachers of rhetoric were Sicilians who met the needs of the democracy established after the expulsion of the fifth-century tyrants of Syracuse by providing hints and models for people who had to plead in the courts for property or life or seek political influence in the popular assemblies. It was easy to reverse this hypothesis to fit the transition to *unius dominatio*. The other speech, too, has strong Classical overtones, echoes of Plato's analysis of 'decline' in physical culture and military training (*Laws* 831 – 2) and of his link between musical 'decline' and excessive attention to the 'pleasure' of an audience rather than to the 'correctness' of the art (*Laws* 700 – 1). Such ideas were widespread. There are quite close verbal parallels to Longinus also in Philo (*Quod omnis probus* 62 – 74; *De ebrietate Noe* 198), nearer in time to *On Sublimity* and outside the mainstream of Roman thought. All this uncertainty would be over if the addressee of the book – Postumius Florentianus according to the manuscript, Postumius Terentianus according to Manutius' conjecture, generally accepted – could be securely identified. A little factual knowledge would blow away the speculative cobwebs.

Neither the problem of the structure, however, nor the doubts about the date have seriously diminished the importance and influence of the book. Neither issue diminishes the pleasure and enlightenment that its peculiar eloquence often provides. Much of it is close discussion of examples, but wider themes often appear. Here, as an instance, is the famous passage in which it is argued that the *Odyssey* – called (9.15) a 'comedy of manners' (*kōmōdia ēthologoumenē*) – must be the work of Homer's old age:

In the *Odyssey*, on the other hand – and there are many reasons for adding this to our inquiry – he demonstrates that when a great mind begins to decline, a love of story-telling characterises its old age. We can tell that the *Odyssey* was his second work from various considerations, in particular from his insertion of the residue of the Trojan troubles in the poem in the form of episodes, and from the way in which he pays tribute of lamentation and pity to the heroes, treating them as persons long known. The *Odyssey* is simply an epilogue to the *Iliad* ... For the same reason, I maintain, he made the whole body of the *Iliad*, which was written at the height of his powers, dramatic and exciting, whereas most of the *Odyssey* consists of narrative, which is a characteristic of old age. Homer in the *Odyssey* may be compared to the setting sun: the size remains without the force. He no longer sustains the tension as it was in the tale of Troy, nor that consistent level of elevation which never admitted any falling off. The outpouring of passions crowding one on another has gone; so has the versatility, the realism, the abundance of imagery taken from the life. We see greatness on the ebb. It is as though the Ocean were withdrawing into itself and flowing quietly in its own bed. Homer is lost in the realm of the fabulous and incredible. In saying this, I have not forgotten the storms in the *Odyssey*, the story of Cyclops, and a few other episodes; I am speaking of old age – but it is the old age of a Homer.[12]

The central message is particularly clear in the apparent digression. It is that the spirit and moral grandeur of the writer are decisive in success in this, the highest kind of writing, and that unevenness and technical inadequacy can sometimes be forgiven. None of this is particularly new. A comparison can be made with Horace's *Ars poetica*, which also stresses the combination of art and nature and forgives errors in the truly great. But the warmth of Longinus and his catholic range of examples are beyond the reach of other rhetors. It is fascinating to see how he exploits the delicate lyric techniques of Sappho (10.1 – 3) in the interests of grand passion. We may feel unsure about his precise intentions. What did he think his addressee, as 'man of affairs' (*politikos anēr*), really wanted to do? Compose declamations? Panegyrics? Ambassadorial addresses? Perhaps all these; the smell of the declamation school is certainly strong (e.g., 15.8 – 11). But we cannot avoid the feeling that the author's view was not limited to this sort of thing. He had an ideal of great literature which was going to endure, and he thought it was still possible to produce work which would stand the test of time as the great classics do. Not much read, it seems, in ancient or Byzantine times, *On Sublimity* had its great period in the Renaissance, especially in the late seventeenth century and in the eighteenth. Boileau's translation (1674) marks an epoch. The story of this is, as Longinus himself might say, 'set aside for another place' (cf. 3.5); suffice it to say here that *On Sublimity*, Aristotle's *Poetics*, and Horace's *Ars poetica*, are the three Classical works with the greatest influence on the course of European criticism.[13]

4 Lucian and Philostratus

We turn next to the splendours of the Second Sophistic, of which Longinus was, it seems, unconscious. The great orators themselves have little to contribute. Aelius Aristides' vast defences of rhetoric against Plato resume earlier stages in the educational quarrel of philosophy and rhetoric, but offer hardly anything for the present theme. His remarks (*Or.* 45) on the superior licence of poets and his claim to be the originator of the prose 'hymn' to the gods recall Dio Chrysostom.[14] He spent his life performing and abusing his competitors; he wrote for posterity, and posterity preserved his works; but he is not a literary critic. We have to look instead at Lucian (born about AD 120), a

---

[12] *On Sublimity* 9.11 – 14, quoted from Russell and Winterbottom, *Ancient Literary Criticism*, pp. 470 – 1.

[13] See works of Abrams, Brody, and Martano in the bibliography; Alain Michel, 'La théorie du sublime', pp. 378 – 407.

[14] Boulanger, *Aristide*, pp. 303 – 7; Russell and Winterbottom, *Ancient Literary Criticism*, p. 558.

sophist but on the fringe of the movement, and at Philostratus (born about
AD 170), its tendentious historian.

The work of Lucian that has most claim on our attention is *On Writing
History*, a satirical and humorous essay (like all Lucian), but yet containing
a kernel of serious doctrine. The absurdity that occasions the satire is that
of pedantic mimics of Thucydides who, it seems, are writing contemporary
history. Whether the names and quotations that Lucian gives us are real or
(as is more likely) fictitious is debated. The parody is masterly; but Lucian
includes with it an apparently serious statement of the qualifications and
methods of a good historian, which makes a pendant to Plutarch's characterisation of a malicious one. The historian, according to Lucian, is employed
on work quite different from that of the poet or encomiast. It is his duty to
collect his facts honestly and make a preliminary digest of them (*hupomnēma*)
before attempting his real work. To do this properly he needs to have had
practical experience in politics and war, like Thucydides, and he must make
independence and incorruptibility his first care. When he comes to the actual
writing, he must remember above all that history is mainly narrative and
needs the virtues of rapidity and clarity that that part of oratory particularly
requires. All this recalls the prefatory professions of the historians.

Lucian's sense of the absurdity of his 'Thucydideans' is parallel to his
satirical treatment of the rhetors and grammarians. Himself a natural mimic
of Attic style (perhaps it came all the easier because Greek was his second
language, Aramaic his first), he loves to make fun of people who claim to
impart the secret of success by recommending short cuts. In *The Speakers'
Teacher* (*Rhetorum praeceptor* 2, p. 317 Macleod), he presents a young man who
asks how he can become a sophist. The teacher advises him to develop
ignorance, audacity, a loud voice, an effeminate walk, and a taste for striking
clothes. Then he should learn a few Attic words and be prepared to put them
in anywhere. Fluency in extemporisation is all-important; orderliness of
arrangement does not matter. If in doubt about your reception, hire *claqueurs*.
In *Lexiphanes*, a similar work, the target is more specifically the pedantic
Atticists, and especially perhaps the grammarian Pollux. Their absurdities
are also material for the charming declamation *The Case of the Consonants*,[15]
in which Sigma accuses Tau, before a jury of the Vowels, of stealing from
him a large number of words in which he had his rightful place. What we have
in these works, as in many other parts of Lucian, is criticism by caricature,
directed at types of pretentiousness and charlatanism rather than at named
individuals. Of poetry, Lucian has little to say, though Hesiod should perhaps
be mentioned. This little discourse is based on the prologue of the *Theogony*.
The thought, like that of Plato's *Ion*, is that the poet has no knowledge but
only inspiration, and that of no very secure kind.

---

[15] Misleadingly called *Iudicium vocalium*, I, pp. 139–43 Macleod.

While Lucian was involved in the sophistic world as a practitioner, Philostratus became its historian and biographer. One would expect *Lives of the Sophists* to be a rich quarry for critical judgements and opinions. The expectation is disappointed. It is true that Philostratus advances a thesis of literary history, namely that the sophists of his own day are in a line of descent from Hippias and Prodicus and their Classical contemporaries. This view is hinted at also in Longinus (3.2–5), and it clearly has some truth in it. Epideictic themes and Gorgianic figures form natural links between the two groups, and historical continuity could also be seen in the opposition of both to the rival educational tradition of the philosophers. Philostratus' view of Dio Chrysostom is interesting. He reckoned him among philosophers who were also sophists, and thereby drew upon himself the criticism of Synesius of Cyrene, in the late fourth century, who found reasons for supposing that Dio began his career as a sophist and subsequently became a philosopher. This 'conversion' has been much discussed, and Synesius shown to be wrong,[16] but it is of interest to observe a historical controversy of this kind arising. Apart from this, Philostratus' descriptions of styles and performances are banal and vague. Where we can check him against better evidence he comes off badly; his account of the first-century sophist Isaeus, for example, contradicts Pliny, who heard the man (*Epistles* 2.3).

Philostratus' importance in the history of criticism derives rather from those passages in the *Life of Apollonius of Tyana* which contain hints or fragments of aesthetic theory. For example (2.20): Apollonius is at Taxila in India, waiting to see the king. On the walls of the temple are tablets of bronze, varied with metals of other colours, in which are depicted the battles of Porus and Alexander. The sight leads Apollonius to discuss the nature of painting and to argue that there must be a mimetic faculty in the spectator, as well as a mimetic art in the painter, in order for a work to achieve its end. We have to possess a notion of the subject of the picture before we can admire and appreciate it. The effect of art is thus a co-operation between artist and public, both of whom have to possess the 'mimetic' faculty. A more famous episode (6.19) takes another line.[17] Apollonius is discussing the representations of the gods with the Egyptian wise man Thespesion. He criticises the animal images he sees everywhere. Thespesion then asks whether Pheidias and Praxiteles 'went up to heaven and took a mould of the shape of the gods', or had some other directing power to guide them. Apollonius asserts that there was indeed such a power. Over and above Imitation, there is Imagination (*phantasia*) which 'fashions what it has not seen', and is undismayed by any object. Though there is nothing here about poetry, it is clear that we are dealing with concepts and problems which Dio's *Olympicus* had also treated; and Longinus

[16] J. L. Moles, 'The career and conversion of Dio Chrysostom', *JHS*, 98 (1978), 79–100.
[17] Trimpi, *Muses of One Mind*, p. 103; Birmelin, 'Kunsttheoretische Gedanken'.

too knows a *phantasia* that can go beyond what any eye can see (*On Sublimity* 15). Philostratus and his contemporaries lived in a world in which sculpture and painting, exhibited in public places, made a constant assault on the sensibilities of the educated. A witness to this is the collection of *Eikones*, ecphrases of mythological paintings, by his son-in-law, Philostratus Lemnius. These were much imitated by later sophists and influential in the eighteenth-century revival of understanding of Greek art.

5 Hermogenes and other rhetoricians

The individual authors and books we have been considering all have some rhetorical concerns and some philosophical concerns. Plutarch, the Platonist moral teacher, seeks to use the tools of *grammatikē* to justify a literary education. Dio has the stance of Socrates and the practice of a rhetorician. Lucian takes both professions as his butt. Longinus, writing a book that fits squarely into the rhetor's curriculum, demands of his pupil moral improvement and high thinking. Philostratus interests himself both in the personalities and performances of orators and in religious and even mystical speculation. This dual approach to literature is especially conspicuous in the academic world of the late Empire; but before we come to its final stages, we must look more generally at the rhetoricians.

Lucian's helpful suggestion that fifteen or twenty Attic words, scattered at random through a speech, will ensure success, offers a reminder that the frontier between *grammatikos* and *rhētor* is a fluid one. It was vital for the rhetor to speak correct Attic. He was also accustomed to use poets as teaching material. So here were two ways in which he trespassed on the province of his colleague. His attitude to literature, however, was specific to his own art. The aim was to expose how the process of persuasion worked, so that the pupil and imitator could copy. The rhetor tries to let his pupil into the secret of how, let us say, Demosthenes planned a campaign and carried it out, what devices he used to entrap and manipulate his audience, and so on. Literary history and literary theory do not much interest him. His art is timeless, based (he believes) on the perennial weaknesses of human nature; and his interest in its theoretical basis is limited to establishing, against his opponents, that it has a claim to be a *tekhnē*, and is not just an inexplicable knack. He does not, therefore, reflect on the principles of fiction, but leaves this to the philosophers, though his work is very largely declamation, that is to say, the treatment of fictitious cases in an unreal or vaguely historical setting, and this is itself a species of fiction, with its own kind of deceit and intellectual stimulus.

The textbooks that survive fall, for the most part, into a few, easily defined categories. We have, first, precepts and models for *progymnasmata* (elementary exercises including fable, narrative, chria, etc.); second, treatises on 'invention', mainly concerned with *stasis*; third, recipes for various stylistic tones or effects (*ideai*); fourth, treatises on figures; fifth, treatises on epideictic oratory, containing a large amount of model material; sixth, collections of model declamations. We should add, though these are mostly of Byzantine date, 'prolegomena', general introductions explaining the history and scope of the art, and finally, commentaries, often very voluminous, on the standard textbooks on *progymnasmata* and *staseis*. Only incidentally is literary criticism found in all this material, but there are some places where it may profitably be sought.

The most important Greek writers on style in the second century are 'Aristides' and Hermogenes. 'Aristides', so-called because the anonymous treatise is preserved with the works of the sophist Aelius Aristides, sets out a simpler system, but the concept of *idea* is the same in both. *Ideai* are qualities like dignity, vehemence, force, sweetness, clarity, and many others, produced by appropriate thought, diction, word arrangement, figures, and rhythm. They differ from the *genera dicendi* of the three-style theory, and also from Demetrius' four *kharaktēres*, in being indeterminate in number, for it was not difficult to discern a new nuance and give it a name. Some *ideai* were mutually compatible, others not. Some authors excel in one or another, Demosthenes (at least in Hermogenes' system) is the model for all; indeed, Hermogenes claims that what he is really doing is analysing Demosthenes' universal excellence.

He does, however, extend his range far beyond Demosthenes. This is very clear in the discussion of *semnotēs*, 'solemnity' or 'dignity', a quality which resembles Longinian *hupsos* (pp. 242 – 54 Rabe). Like Longinus, Hermogenes regularly begins with 'thoughts' (the *ideai* are not simply verbal), and here he enumerates the 'thoughts' most appropriate to 'solemnity'. These are, first, 'things said about gods *qua* gods' and about natural phenomena that are due to divine action, which can sometimes be mentioned in such a way as to advance the rhetorical force of a speech; his example (pp. 244 – 5 Rabe) is a description of a storm which heightens the effect of a speech based on the battle of Arginusae (406 BC) and the generals' failure to pick up the dead. Next we have solemn statements about great moral or religious issues, and after that allusions to major historical events, especially the battles of the Persian Wars. Next to 'thoughts' come what he calls 'methods', which are something like figures of thought. For the purposes of 'solemnity' it is well to avoid expressions of doubt or hesitation, though there may be a place for allegory and for suggestiveness; instances are cited from Plato's *Phaedrus* and *Timaeus*. Under diction (pp. 247 – 50 Rabe), Hermogenes, like Demetrius and Dionysius before him, attaches great importance to euphony and to the special effects of particular sounds. In 'solemnity' long A and long O are desirable, recurrent I is to be avoided, because it makes one contract the mouth and bare the gums. Metaphor, naturally, is a good thing, though it must be used with moderation: 'professing good hope' is a legitimate way of saying 'hoping for good', but bolder metaphors, like 'the cities were sick', are more characteristic of 'asperity' than of the solemn tone. Indeed, extremes of metaphorical boldness are not suitable for any respectable kind of speech: the Gorgianic extravagance of 'vultures, living tombs', condemned by Longinus also (3.2), illustrates the sort of thing one can find in 'bogus sophists', certainly not in Demosthenes. Finally under diction we are recommended to use nouns rather than verbs, keeping the number of finite verbs down as much as possible. This is no new precept, and it owes its force to observation of Thucydides.[18] Hermogenes then (p. 250 Rabe) proceeds to figures, recommending rather simple ones (*epikrisis*[19] and dogmatic statements of your own opinion) and the avoidance of anything that breaks up the steady movement of the dignified pronouncement. So no apostrophe, no parenthesis. *Cola* should be short; rhythm dactylic, epitrite, or spondaic; hiatus should not be avoided, because that is fussy; and sentences should end in a resounding clausula with a preponderance of long syllables. This is a typical example of Hermogenes' method. The precepts are mostly conventional, the organisation clear and firm, the idea kept steadily in mind by concentration on a few well-known passages, in this case from Plato, Thucydides, and the orators.

The last part of the second book of *Peri ideōn* is something different, for here Hermogenes turns to consider the character of individual authors. He begins with the traditional division of political oratory into deliberative, judicial, and panegyric species. He then, however, subdivides panegyric into one class concerned with political questions and one which is not so restricted, but goes beyond the limits of *politikos logos* altogether. His example (p. 388 Rabe) of the first kind is revealing: it is nothing Classical, but the declamation theme of the *propompeia*, that is to say the question whether Athens or Sparta should have ceremonial precedence after the Persian War. Of the more general kind of panegyric in prose, the model is Plato, whom Hermogenes elevates to the same pre-eminence in this area as Demosthenes has in the *politikos logos*. There remains poetry, 'for this is also a panegyric matter, indeed the most panegyrical of any kind of discourse', and the model of this is Homer. It is interesting to contrast the passage which follows with the rhetorical recommendations of Homer that we find, for example, in Quintilian (10.1.40 – 51). Hermogenes has no such practical goal:

> Homer's is the best kind of poetry and Homer the best poet. I could just as well say he is the best orator or the best prose writer, but perhaps it comes to the same thing; for, as poetry is an imitation of all things, and the writer who (quite apart from his verbal artifice) best imitates orators, speakers, and musicians performing, like Phemius and Demodocus, as well as all the other characters and actions, is the best poet, and that being so, in calling him the best poet one is also calling him the best orator and

---

[18] On Thucydides 'nominal' style, cf. Dion. Hal., *Thucydides* 24.

[19] *Epikrisis* = 'confirmation and validation of what has been said', e.g., by adding 'and very right too' to a statement; cf. *Rhetores Graeci*, ed. Walz, III, p. 707.

prose writer. He may well not be the best of generals or carpenters or whatever, though he imitates these excellently too, but their art is not words nor dependant on words... Homer is the best of poets, orators, and prose writers in every type of speech: more than any other he achieves grandeur, charm, polish [*epimeleia*[20]], force, and, what is most important in poetry, imitation that is clear and appropriate to the subject both in language and in the introduction of characters, not to speak of vividness in plot and variety in the division of lines, from which metre acquires a measure of variation, all at the proper time and in due degree; and in addition to all this, he chose what is by nature the best metre of all and contrived best of all to form a varied unity of all elements.

(p. 389 Rabe)

There is much here to suggest that a rhetorical education, in Hermogenes' hands, was also an education in literature generally. This is borne out by what he says in the sequel about Xenophon and the historians – not only Herodotus, the 'most panegyrical', but Thucydides and Hecataeus; he even spares a few words (p. 412 Rabe) for Theopompus, Ephorus, Hellanicus, and Philistus, 'though the Greeks have never thought their writing worthy of rivalry and imitation [*zēlos*; *mimēsis*[21]], so far as I am aware.'

The study of figures also naturally goes far beyond the bounds of practical rhetoric. The doctrine had been developed in Hellenistic times; there is no reason to think that grammarians and rhetors of the imperial age made much advance on what they found in Caecilius or his contemporary Gorgias. The standard definition (e.g., Tiberius 1; Longinus 16) involves the inevitably obscure concept of 'natural' language: 'a figure [*skhēma*] is that which expresses the meaning not naturally or straightforwardly, but by deviating from the norm for the sake of ornament or effectiveness'. Distinctions were made between tropes and figures, figures of speech and figures of thought. These are suggestive and important. The application of the doctrine also led to subtle and sometimes illuminating analyses of Classical writing. It is not for nothing that Longinus' dissection of Demosthenes' 'Marathon oath' (16) is so celebrated. At the same time, it led to a good deal of confusion and much misguided ingenuity.

The standard work on figures in later Greek times was that of Alexander, son of Numenius, of the second century. An epitome survives, the preface to which contains interesting theoretical considerations. The author seeks to answer those who say that there is nothing special about figures of thought because every *logos* has a *skhēma*, in as much as it depends on mental attitudes and the mind always possesses an attitude of some particular kind or other, which constitutes a *skhēma*. His answer is threefold. First, if all discourse were figured, the trained speaker would have no advantage over the ordinary person. Secondly, even if it is true that our mental processes always involve movement of some kind or other, these movements are not always 'natural'.

---

[20] But see Hagedorn, *Zur Ideenlehre*, p. 53.

[21] On the difference, or lack of it, between *zēlos* and *mimēsis*, see Longinus, ed. Russell, p. 10.

It follows that discourse which reproduces these also sometimes possesses a configuration which is 'not according to nature'. Thirdly, even if all discourse is figured, the discourse we find in oratory and other kinds of literature is an artificial version of this, contrived to give an impression rather than to express a real attitude. If I say 'Where shall I go?' in real life there is no figure. If an orator makes a show of not knowing what word to use or how to express something, though he really does know, that is the figure of *diaporēsis*. These arguments are clearly alternatives. The first is an appeal to fact, or at least self-advantage, since no rhetor on either side of the controversy could acknowledge that his profession was altogether useless. The second assumes a distinction between 'natural' and 'artificial' both in behaviour and in words. The third makes a distinction between discourse in general and the formalised discourse of oratory and literature. Neither of these last two is explained further, either here or later on (13.11ff.) when similar arguments are adduced to demonstrate the existence of the figures of speech. Rhetorical style (*plasis*), we are then told, is different from that of the layman; words have natural, and thus presumably less natural, orders and arrangements, and rhetors imitate these. Some figures of speech are easier than others to reduce to their 'natural' configuration. We have here at least fragments of a theory, the origins of which, it seems, go back to Hellenistic, and particularly Stoic, grammatical theories.[22]

Schēma in another sense is the subject of two short treatises preserved with some others in a collection wrongly attributed to Dionysius and known as his 'Art of Rhetoric' (VI, pp. 295–374 Radermacher). The questions raised here are of some interest for literary theory. The subject is speeches, or other works, which are intended for a purpose other than that which they overtly profess. Three cases are distinguished. One is that in which the writer wraps up his meaning out of caution, because of the standing of his addressee or the feelings of his audience. The second is when he works toward a different end from that which he professes; and the third is when he aims at a directly opposite effect. Literary judgements naturally follow. Plato's *Apology* is seen to have four functions: as a defence (the professed aim); as a condemnation of the Athenians for what they are doing; as an encomium of Socrates; and as advice on how to live the life of a philosopher. Demosthenes, we are told, imitates this in *De corona*. Here too there is a defence, an accusation, an encomium, and a demonstration of what a democratic politician should be like. Further lessons of the same kind are based on Homer and Xenophon. In the ninth book of the *Iliad* (434–523) Phoenix promises to follow Achilles anywhere, but by giving the reasons for doing so he incidentally gives the reasons that should dissuade Achilles from abandoning the army. Xenophon, we are told, puts Clearchus in exactly the same situation (*Anabasis* 1.3.3–6):

[22] Barwick, 'Stoische Sprachlehre', pp. 97–111.

he will go anywhere with his soldiers, but they must not desert Cyrus' cause. There follows (pp. 316–22) an elaborate exposition of the Iliadic Embassy, an excellent example of the rhetors' way of interpreting and using a poetical text.

Two other short treatises in the same collection also have significance for criticism. They deal with the standards to be applied to declamation. The author first (p. 375) lays down four main headings under which any work can be judged: these are *ēthos*, *gnōmē*, *tekhnē*, and *lexis*: 'character', 'meaning', 'technique', and 'language'. No one could claim that these concepts are at all clearly envisaged or worked out. The kernel of the matter, and any originality the author may possess, lies in the notion of ethos and the way in which it is applied. There are, we are told, two kinds of ethos: a general or philosophical one, which proves to be the overall moral tendency of the work, which has to be acceptable by ordinary standards, and a particular or rhetorical one, which involves suiting the words to the nationality, age, race, moral character, fortune, and profession of the speaker. It appears (VI, p. 349 Radermacher) that there is a relationship between these two. The 'one great ethos', that is to say the moral one, is the basis of the whole structure; lack of commitment to a proper moral ideal is incompatible with producing a work of value. This is a little like Longinus, except that it is not the whole character of the author that is here called into play but his acceptance of a coherent and adequate standpoint for the purpose of the declamation. The individual 'characters' are to be subordinated to this, as the sophists and craftsmen in Plato's dialogues contribute in their way to the effect of the whole. When 'bad' views are necessary, they should be assigned to appropriately discredited characters, as Homer used Thersites to discredit Achilles' cause. This reminds us of Plutarch. Together with the use made of Plato, and the interest shown in the dramatic structure of his dialogues, it is a salutary reminder that the rhetorical tradition at its most scholastic is not uninfluenced by the attitudes and pretensions of the philosophers.

Greek rhetorical treatises of the imperial period had little impact on the teaching of rhetoric in Latin; the *ideai*, for example were largely unknown or ignored in the West, which stuck with the older concept of three *genera dicendi*. The *ideai* were, however, well known to Byzantine scholars, for whom Hermogenes' works were the major authority on rhetoric. George of Trebizond introduced the concept, as well as other features of Greek rhetoric, into Italy in the fifteenth century and it subsequently played a role in both the theory of style and in literary composition.[23]

---

[23] John Monfasani, *George of Trebizond* (Leiden, 1976), pp. 286–8; Patterson, *Hermogenes*, pp. 3–40.

6 *Allegorical interpretation*

Nor for their part were the philosophers untouched by the rhetoricians. It would be a mistake to think of these two groups of teachers as having sharply opposed attitudes to literature, the one seeking moral value and mystical interpretation, the other positivist and rationalist. There is a reminder of this in the third-century treatise on music by Aristides Quintilianus, replete with Platonist and Pythagorean ideas, but also using the whole apparatus of styles and figures.[24] The two sides come together also in the anonymous *Life and Poetry of Homer*, preserved among the works of Plutarch.[25]

Nevertheless, the philosophical approach to literature deserves to be looked at on its own. It is of course largely a Platonist tradition, for it was Plato who dominated the scene from the second century onwards and whose own literary mastery helped, as it were, to conquer the rhetoricians. It can hardly be without some glance at Plato that Hermogenes used the Platonic word *ideai*, rather than *kharaktēres*, for the types of style, emphasising thereby their abstractness and absoluteness. The older, allegorical tradition was, however, Stoic, and we must begin by going back a little to consider some of this. The two books we have first to consider are works of the first century of our era, and their style and tone are characteristic of the period before the great Atticist revival in Greek. One, if it is rightly attributed to Cornutus, the teacher of the poet Persius, belongs to the middle of the century. Entitled *A Summary of the Traditions of Greek Theology*, it consists of a systematic account of the names and genealogies of the gods, represented as an ancient tradition that reveals many of the secrets of the universe. Cornutus is not primarily concerned with the poets, but his attitude towards them is interesting and sharply different from that of the defenders of Homer. He believes that Homer and especially Hesiod, for all their preservation of much valuable wisdom, are nevertheless to be used with caution. They add to the tradition out of their own invention, and 'this is how most of the old theology was destroyed'. 'The ancients', to whom the myths were due, 'were no ordinary men but capable of comprehending the nature of the universe and well qualified to teach of it philosophically by means of symbols or riddles' (p. 76, 2–5 Lang).

This position marks Cornutus out as quite different from 'Heraclitus', the author of a book of *Homeric Problems* which gives us our clearest view of the practice of allegorical interpretation as applied to Homer before the development of neo-Platonism. The work is entirely defensive in purpose. 'Everything in Homer is impious unless everything is allegorical,' say Homer's accusers. How then is it, asks Heraclitus, that he is read by pious men all the

---

[24] A.-J. Festugière, 'L'âme et la musique, d'après Aristide Quintilien', *TAPA*, 85 (1954), 55–78.

[25] This compilation contains discussion of many of the issues found in other works under discussion; see Ziegler, 'Plutarchos', coll. 805–7.

days of their life? In fact, Homer often expresses pious sentiments directly, and when he does not, it is for us 'initiates' to track down the truth. To explain 'allegory' Heraclitus adopts a standard grammarian's definition: it is the trope that 'says one thing and signifies another'. The early lyric poets illustrate it, especially Alcaeus, who 'compares most of the troubles due to tyrants with storms at sea' (5.5). This is an obvious allegory, and there are similar examples in Homer: the personification of Strife (*Il.* 4.442) and the famous saying about war (19.222 – 4) 'in which the bronze spills much straw upon the ground, but there is little harvest, when Zeus tilts the balance'. If this is so, why should we hesitate to use allegory as a defence in cases where Homer seems to be speaking unworthily of the gods? The inference is that, as there are some cases where Homer clearly intends allegory, the other allegories which are to be revealed are also intentional. He is 'the great hierophant of heaven and the gods, who opened to human minds roads to heaven that were untrodden and closed to them' (76). In this spirit, Heraclitus goes through *Iliad* and *Odyssey* book by book, episode by episode. He is deeply indebted to predecessors, and we see the same ideas frequently echoed in later Greek commentaries on Homer. An example from Heraclitus' treatment of the first book of the *Iliad* may serve to illustrate the style:

They find fault with Homer for the throwing down of Hephaestus, first because he makes him lame, thereby disfiguring the divine nature, and secondly because he came near to mortal danger ... Even here Homer conceals a philosophical truth. He does not give us the story of the lame Hephaestus to delight readers with poetical fables ... There are two kinds of fire: one ethereal ... in the highest elevation of the universe, second to nothing in perfection; the other the fire we know, whose matter is terrestrial, corruptible, kindled every time by its nourishment. This is why he calls the most subtle fire Helios or Zeus, and the fire on earth Hephaestus, being readily kindled and extinguished; by comparison with the perfect fire it is plausibly thought of as 'lame', especially as any crippled foot needs a stick. Our fire could not survive without wood, and so is symbolically called 'lame'. (26)

This is pure Stoicism, and the polemical thrust of Heraclitus is against the other schools, not only the Epicureans but Plato. There are many points made against both. Plato owes his psychological theory to plagiarism from Homer (17) and has no right to find fault with him, seeing that he himself recommends homosexual love and wife-sharing (78). Epicurus, a true pleasure-loving 'Phaeacian', has stolen from Homer the hedonistic philosophy that Odysseus deceptively expounded when he had to curry favour with the Phaeacians:

'Nothing seems to me better than
when joy possesses the whole people
and feasters are listening to the singer in the house ...'

These were the words not of the hero of Troy ... but of the poor relic of Poseidon's anger, whom fierce storms cast up for the Phaeacians to pity. (79)

Heraclitus' allegorical *therapeia* of Homer is mainly moral, but it also involves Stoic physics and a certain amount of rationalistic explanation of the sort current even in the fifth and fourth centuries BC. He argues, for example, that the plague is caused by Apollo, that is by the sun, because Homer's story required the long days of summer for the battles that ensue. Heraclitus exemplifies two features typical of the responses to poetry prevalent in this period: he promises initiation into a secret interpretation, and he presses hard on every word of his text. For him, as for many others, knowledge of the books brought something like salvation. It is worth noticing also that in common with other interpreters of the period, he does not hesitate to identify the meaning he sees in the text with the conscious intent of the poet, however unhistorical this may be.

7. Neo-Platonic interpretation

From the third to the sixth century the dominance of neo-Platonism gave a new spirit to these attempts to justify and interpret Classical literature. Neo-Platonist metaphysics made it easier than it had been for Plato to find a place of value in the universe for the products of art. 'If anyone dishonours the arts', writes Plotinus (5.8.1) 'because their productivity comes by imitation of nature, we must reply that natural objects also imitate something else; that we must understand that they do not simply imitate what is seen but go back to the principles [*logoi*] from which nature comes; that they do much also on their own account, since they possess beauty and can add to it where it is lacking: Pheidias fashioned his Zeus on no perceptible model, but grasping the sort of being Zeus would be if he chose to appear to our eyes.'

Two main literary problems confronted the neo-Platonists. Why did Plato write dialogues? And how is he to be reconciled with Homer? A discussion of the first problem, albeit late in date, comes from the 'Prolegomena' to Plato ascribed to the sixth-century Alexandrian Platonist, Olympiodorus.[26] The argument begins (13, p. 207 Hermann) by asking why Plato, who denounced writing in the *Phaedrus*, nevertheless decided to write, as well as to instruct pupils. The answer given is that he was imitating God, who made not only the things we cannot see – Angels and Souls and Intellects – but also things which are open to our senses, the heavenly bodies and the world of living and dying creatures. Plato's private discussions, on which Aristotle was believed to have written,[27] correspond to the invisible, his dialogues to the visible world. But why dialogues rather than simple expositions of doctrine? In particular, why, when Plato elsewhere criticises variety and inequality, as in

---

[26] The author of the Prolegomena may be another sixth-century Platonist named Elias; Westerink, *Prolegomena*, pp. xlix–l.

[27] For belief in Plato's 'unwritten doctrine', see Merlan in *Cambridge History of Later Greek and Early Medieval Philosophy*, p. 15.

flute-playing, should he select a literary form which requires 'question and answer by various persons with the delineation of their appropriate characteristics?' Why is drama so bad and dialogue so good? The suggested answer is that in Plato bad characters are reformed or corrected, 'purified and withdrawn from their material life' before the end of the dialogue, whereas in drama they retain their original qualities to the end. The dialogue, moreover, is an imitation of the *kosmos*; one might even say that the *kosmos* is itself a dialogue, because, just as there are superior and inferior natures in the world, and the soul dwells now with one class and now with another, so in the dialogue, the soul is judge and agrees now with the person under examination and now with the examiner. Again, Plato himself makes an analogy between logos and a living animal (*Ph.* 264c), and as the *kosmos* is the most beautiful of all living things, the dialogue is the most beautiful form of discourse. A fourth reason for Plato's choice is an Aristotelian one: we like *mimēsis*, as our childhood love of fable reveals. Yet again, to present friendship or ambition not as abstracts but in individual exemplifications is a more effective way of securing our approval or disapproval; we are put in the position of the souls in Hades who see the punishments of others. A sixth reason (one would think it the most obvious of all) is that the dialogue imitates the actual process of dialectic; a seventh that it holds our attention better than a straightforward exposition.

The analogy between *kosmos* and dialogue may be pursued further, and Olympiodorus expounds one way of doing so at length. In the *kosmos*, he says (16, p. 210), we find Matter, Form, and Nature, which imposes Form on Matter, Soul, Mind, and Divinity. In the dialogue, character, time, and place correspond to Matter. But here is a difficulty. Some Platonic dialogues have no defined setting. The explanation of this is that the characters alone are essential to dialogue, and necessarily appear in its definition, whereas time and place are ancillary. These characters possess varying degrees of knowledge, opinion, or ignorance. They are not necessarily historical. It would have been impossible for Plato to find out all the details, such as when Socrates 'bent his leg' (*Phaedo* 60b). On the other hand, the details are not wholly fictitious either, for they would not then have had any truth. They are rather the features which are relevant to the exposition of a single theme; Plato is like a painter who selects the colours he needs for a particular subject. Choice of place also is not accidental; festivals are favoured because that is the time for hymns to be sung to the gods. Olympiodorus regards style in writing as corresponding to Form in metaphysics (17, p. 211). He does not use the Hermagorean *ideai*, but adopts the old tripartite division into three *kharaktēres*. The grand style is for theology, the plain, or 'slight' (*ischnos*) style for everyday themes; the middle or mixed style may be achieved either by combination or juxtaposition, the latter seen in the *Gorgias*, where myth and argument are distinct, the former in the 'moral dialogues', where it is especially appropriate because virtues are 'means'. Except for this last, characteristically forced, symbolic appropriateness, there is nothing in the rest of the discussion of style which a modern scholar might not take as a basis for a study of Plato. It certainly represents a different and more fruitful attitude from that of the strict classicists, like Dionysius, who admired only the simple Socratic manner and condemned the elaborate and mythical manner as 'dithyrambic'.

Further pursuit of the analogy between dialogue and neo-Platonic *kosmos* leads Olympiodorus into much artificiality and implausibility (17, p. 212 Hermann). Nature corresponds to 'type of discussion'; that is to say, whether the dialogue is dogma, inquiry, or a mixture of the two. Soul is analogous to the demonstrative arguments; Intellect, the highest element, to the problem around which the demonstrations revolve. It is in this, therefore, that the true unity and coherence lie. This is not a unique discussion, but fairly typical of the schools' approach to the reading of Plato. The metaphysical system is made out to be the key to the literary problem of the dialogues. The same key was supposed also to unlock the problem of the acceptability of the poets, by offering a new and impressive secret meaning, in virtue of which Plato and his old enemies could be wholly reconciled.

Of the major neo-Platonist writers who advanced this cause, the first we should consider is Porphyry of Tyre, the pupil, biographer, and editor of Plotinus. His Homeric studies were famous. The surviving essay *On the Cave of the Nymphs* was perhaps written before he became a member of Plotinus' school about AD 252; he was then already a scholar of wide culture, profoundly interested in religious philosophy. The subject is the description of the Cave of the Nymphs on Ithaca, where Odysseus conceals the gifts the Phaeacians had given him (*Od.* 13.102–12). It is a strange place, with its bowls and jars of stone, where bees have their hives, and its stone looms on which the nymphs weave sea-purple garments. It has a perpetual flow of water and two entrances, one to the north by which men can descend and one to the south, where only the immortals go. An earlier philosopher named Cronius[28] (a second-century Platonist or Pythagorean) had alleged that this description could not be factual, for there was no other record of it, and yet could not be a fiction of 'poetic licence' either, because it was implausible to suggest that either man or nature would have constructed it thus. 'The world is full of men and of gods, and the Ithacan cave is far from convincing us that in it there is a way down for men and a way up for gods' (2). The implication is that 'poetic licence' produces stories which have a plausibility (*pithanon*); where this is absent, we must be dealing with something else. Cronius concluded that the Cave was an allegory, intended 'not only for the wise but for ordinary people', and it is incumbent upon us to explore the significance of every detail; the oddness of the detail is an indication of the presence of allegory.

[28] On Cronius, see Merlan in *Cambridge History of Later Greek and Early Medieval Philosophy*, p. 104, n. 5.

Porphyry, however, has reservations. He points out that Artemidorus of Ephesus, a reliable geographer, said that there was a beach on Ithaca with a cave sacred to the nymphs where Odysseus is said to have landed. So, says Porphyry (4), it cannot all be Homer's *plasma*. It does not seem to have occurred to him that the inhabitants of Ithaca would be sure to have a cave which they could point out to tourists as the place immortalised in the poem. Its actual existence, he continues, does not exempt us from the duty of inter-pretation. Indeed, if the cave was holy before Homer wrote about it, it is all the more deserving of having its symbolic meaning unravelled, for it must be 'full of ancient wisdom'. So the cave represents the *kosmos*, the Nymphs the souls who descend to be born, the stone looms are bones and the sea-purple is flesh and blood, and so on. At least, this is one way of looking at it. From another, the cave may be said to represent the intelligible essence, for its darkness, rockiness, and dampness suggest the world we live in, while its obscurity to the sense, solidity, and permanence suggest the Intelligible. It may indeed be true that Homer added some details of his own, out of his profound wisdom; he did not, however, invent the whole theme, but found it ready for him.

Porphyry's attitude is clearly different from that of Cornutus, for whom the poets corrupted the 'ancient wisdom' rather than transmitting it. It also seems to allow that the allegory can be revealed to ordinary people and need not be kept as a mystery for the few. It is significant that it is an explanation not of a narrative but of an ecphrasis, or description, and so of objects rather than events; this brings it close to the many symbolic features of cults of all kinds. And finally, alternative explanations are legitimate. The cave has no single one-to-one interpretation, but a plurality of possible meanings. This tolerance of polysemy, unusual in classical critics, may recommend Porphyry to modern literary theorists. It is perhaps typical of the neo-Platonic world view, where religion and philosophy are dominated by the notion that every-thing stands for something else, or indeed for several different things, in the various stages and levels of the hierarchy of the universe.

All this forms the background to the work of Proclus, the fifth-century systematiser of neo-Platonism, whose commentaries on the *Republic* offer the fullest and most sophisticated discussion of the place of poetry in intellectual life that any ancient author has left us. Proclus had studied in Alexandria and was known in his youth as a notable rhetorician. He moved to Athens about AD 430, at the age of nineteen. Both philosophy and rhetoric were then flourishing there. The sophists tempted him, but he clung to philosophy. When he was only twenty-eight he wrote one of his most astonishing works, the commentary on the *Timaeus*. A learned and exact scholastic, he was also much involved, as was typical of his age, in less rational activities. He is said to have had success as a rainmaker and was deeply interested in the magical art of theurgy. Indeed, both he and his teachers treated the theurgic *Chaldaean*

Oracles,[29] which originated in the late second century, and the Orphic poems, which were of very various dates and provenance, as objects of detailed study and commentary in the same way as they treated Plato and Homer.

Proclus' first discussion of poetry known to us is in the *Timaeus* commentary (1, pp. 63 – 6 Diehl). It is cast in the form of a note on a passage (19d – e) in which Socrates is made to say that no past or present poet could praise the people and city of Atlantis adequately, because the 'imitative race' can only imitate things with which it has become familiar. Proclus tells us how the passage had been a stumbling-block to his predecessors. Longinus and the neo-Platonist Origen had raised the question whether Plato meant to include Homer among the poets who would be inadequate to the task. On Porphyry's authority, he relates (p. 64,29 Diehl) how the neo-Platonist Origen 'shouted, turned red, and was covered in sweat' for three days on end in an effort to show that Homer, who had the mimetic skill successfully to portray the gods fighting one another, must be perfectly capable of imitating virtuous deeds. Porphyry's view had been that Homer's capacity for elevation and grandeur is incontrovertible, but he has not the power to display 'intellectual freedom from emotion and the philosophic life'; the 'life of the best state' is a theme too high for poets, or for anyone who has not lived the life of virtue himself (p. 66,14f. Diehl). Proclus is not content. He would rather believe, and adduces Platonic texts to bear witness, that Plato distinguishes inspired poetry from that of 'human art'. It is only the latter that is unequal to the praise of 'the valour of this city' and the great deeds of its citizens. Inspired sublimity (*hupsos*) is due to the gods: witness the grand style of oracles. (He is thinking no doubt of the *Chaldaean Oracles* rather than Classical examples from Delphi.) 'Sublimity due to art involves much that is contrived and puffed out, making much use of metaphor, like the poetry of Antimachus' (p. 64,20). The terminology recalls *On Sublimity* (3.1), and its appearance in these circles lends some colour to those who would see that work as part of the literary scene of the third or fourth century rather than the first. Antimachus is an interesting example to choose; he was a poet of whom Plato was thought to have approved (Proclus, *In Timaeum* 1.90 Diehl).

It is naturally in the *Republic* commentary that Proclus offers his demonstration that 'Homer is exempt from Plato's condemnation of the poets'. He devotes the fifth and sixth 'essays' to the question, but propounds rather different theories in each. We will confine ourselves here to the sixth essay, which seems to be later. There are, we are told (1.69, p. 205 Kroll), three lives or conditions of the soul. The best and most perfect is the life united with the gods, linking like with like, the light of the soul with the light beyond, the most unitary element of its being and life with the One that is beyond all being and life. The second is the life in which the soul turns from this divine existence

[29] Ed. Edouard des Places (Paris, 1971).

back to itself, uses intellect and knowledge to unravel the multitude of principles, contemplates all changes of forms, unites the Thinking with the Thought, and makes an image of the intelligible being by comprehending in one the nature of intelligible things. The third condition is that in which soul mingles and co-operates with lower powers, employing 'fantasies' and irrational perceptions, and becoming 'full of the inferior'. This grandiose scheme is based on the idea that the soul has three possible activities, one akin to the One, one akin to the Intellect, and the third irrational.

Plato, distinguishing rational and irrational parts of the soul, had sought to show that poetry appealed only to the lowest part; Proclus will show that some sort of poetry appeals to all. To the first condition of soul corresponds the highest sort of poetry, a 'madness better than sanity', capable of 'setting the soul amid the causes of reality, bringing Filled and Filler together in an ineffable unity' (1, pp. 177ff.). This is to assign to the highest poetry the highest kind of union with the One which the neo-Platonist philosopher could hope to attain, an extraordinary claim. To the second kind of psychical life belongs a poetry that 'understands the essence of things and enjoys the vision of beautiful and good deeds, expressing them all in a metrical and rhythmical style'. There are many works of good poets that fill this prescription, full of wisdom and good advice, and offering recollection of the cycles of the soul's incarnations and of the eternal principles and powers involved therein. Third is the poetry of imitation (*mimētikē*). Proclus divides this into two parts. One sort of mimetic poetry uses *eikasia*, 'likeness', and is directed to realism of imitation. The other deals in apparent likenesses, displaying things only 'as they appear'. This is mere 'shadow drawing' (*skiagraphia*), not exact knowledge, and its object is *psuchagōgia*, directed in particular at the emotional part of the mind, that part in which pleasure and pain are experienced.

The next stage (1, pp. 180ff.) is to show that Plato recognised these three types of poetry. The first is found in *Phaedrus* 245a, a favourite text, also discussed by Syrianus and Hermias. But Proclus sees it also in the inspired poetry discussed in Plato's *Ion*, apparently oblivious of the conclusion of that dialogue, where it is made clear that inspiration is very far from providing knowledge. Better texts are *Laws* (682a) and *Timaeus* (40d). With their help, Proclus can show that Plato 'does not dishonour' poetry, even though he may think it dangerous fare for the young, who cannot unravel its hidden meanings. Plato also, we are told, knows the second type: witness *Laws* (630a), where Theognis is a teacher of all virtue, and more especially *Alcibiades II* (142e), where Plato acknowledges Theognis as *phronimos*, meaning thereby, according to Proclus, that he has indeed true knowledge of right and wrong, not due to 'enthusiasm' or 'right opinion'. Finally (1, pp. 189–92), a series of passages is adduced to justify the subdivision of mimetic poetry into 'eikastic' and 'phantastic' (*Sophist* 235d; *Laws* 667c; *Rep.* 597e).

Plato is thus established as an authority for the theory; unless chapter and verse could be given, the theory, it seems, would be as naught. Homer too must be proved to know it. He not only operates in all three modes, he recognises their existence. He is inspired when he reveals mystic truths about the gods; he displays knowledge when he writes of the life of the soul and moral duty; he is eikastic when he assigns appropriate forms to characters and actions; and he is phantastic when he charms us by appealing to 'what seems to the many'. Proclus gives examples, in ascending order, from lowest to highest (1, p. 192). When Homer says (*Od.* 3.1) that the sun rises out of a 'lake', this is mere appearance, not what really happens. When he shows heroes acting with courage or wisdom or ambitions, this is what heroes are really like; we have *eikasia*. His 'knowledge' is shown in his separation of the different parts of the soul (as when Odysseus says 'Bear up, my heart') or when he enumerates the four elements of which the world is composed. Finally, when Homer teaches us of the division of creation into its three realms, or the bonds of Hephaestus or the union of Zeus and Hera, he is inspired and possessed by the muses. Moreover, he sees the differences himself, as his portrayal of other poets shows. Demodocus (*Od.* 6.448–90) is the inspired bard, Phemius (1.33) the poet of knowledge, like the nameless bard whom Agamemnon left to watch over Clytemnestra (3.267), and Thamyris (*Il.* 2.599) clearly belongs to the third class, since the muses were angry with him and made him blind (1, pp. 193–5).

But what kind of interpretation are we now to put upon, for example, the union of Zeus and Hera? It is here that we see most clearly the difference between a neo-Platonist like Proclus and earlier allegorists. The 'discreditable' episode of Hera's deception and tempting of Zeus had been interpreted in many ways, as an allegory of the coming spring or as the union of air and ethereal fire, assuring life and fecundity throughout the world. For Syrianus and Proclus it is quite different (1, pp. 132ff.). Zeus is the Demiurge, or creative principle, and also *Nous* (Mind), or to be more precise the *Nous* that acts on the world. Hera is the creative fecundity of the Demiurge. The myth separates what is really one. Zeus represents the Monad, Hera the Dyad. All the details have inner significance in these terms. For example, they come together in the open, not in the chamber that Hephaestus built for them; that means their union takes place in the intelligible world, not in the world open to our senses. The poem is thus entirely subservient to the metaphysics.

The long story from Dio to Proclus has been viewed here as a combination of two interpretative traditions, the rhetorical and the philosophical, educationally opposed to each other, but none the less interdependent and often in practice allied. Almost everything we have discussed comes from an educational context. It is all 'within the academy'. The needs of the young student, or at best the adult making a political début, are constantly to the fore. The critics themselves, if that is what we should call Hermogenes and

Proclus, often made their mark at an early age. These kinds of literary expertise come to the young. Maturity of judgement does not seem to be highly rated. The wisdom comes not from the experienced reader, but from the ancients themselves. Everything is concentrated on them. We can hardly find any comment on the contemporary literary scene which is constructive or appreciative. Here is a contrast with the Alexandrians and Augustans, not so much with Plato or even Aristotle, for whom, after all, tragedy had already reached its full development. What we do find is a strong strain of polemic, usually directed against novelty (*kainospoudon*, Longinus 5.1) and marked by both the recurrence of a vocabulary of invective – 'effeminate', 'corrupt', 'sophistic' – and a persistent inclination to sense decay. Yet this was an age in which new literary forms did appear: the novel, for example, or the 'essay' as Plutarch wrote it. No criticism of these exists. Oratory, epic, drama, and the philosophical dialogue are the only genres discussed. The ways in which the rhetorical and philosophical techniques of interpretation were applied in the emerging Christian literature will be discussed in the next chapter. The skills displayed by the Greek critics of the Empire were propagated in the Byzantine world, in the Latin West, and among the Arabs.

11

CHRISTIANITY AND CRITICISM

This chapter will survey a variety of intellectual movements in the time of the Roman Empire which are related to criticism, complementing what has been said in the previous chapter about neo-Platonism and extending the range into the writings of Fathers of the Church before Augustine and Jerome and the Latin grammarians and rhetoricians of late antiquity. Some of this material provides background for Medieval criticism, to be discussed in volume II; some developments are also of interest in that they seem to foreshadow critical issues of the twentieth century.

1 The search for meaning through interpretation

Greek intellectuals of the Roman Empire discussed epistemology and adumbrated semiotic and hermeneutic theories of interpretation. There was, however, wide difference of opinion among them. At one extreme lies the tradition of Pyrrhonian scepticism, which had begun at the end of the fourth century BC and influenced the Academic school of the Hellenistic period in its controversy with Stoic belief that certainty could be obtained from sense perception. Among surviving works of the Classical period, scepticism is best represented in Cicero's *Academics*. The fullest exposition of a radical scepticism is, however, found in the writings of Sextus Empiricus in the late second century of the Christian era. Sextus rejected sense perception as a basis of knowledge, and with it all claims for certainty in logic, physics, and ethics. The sceptical principles set forth in Sextus' *Outlines of Pyrrhonism* are applied in detail in *Against the Dogmatists* to undermine the validity of teaching in grammar, rhetoric, mathematics, astronomy, and music. In extreme form, scepticism implies that we can never know an author's intent, never make a valid interpretation of a text, and must always end in a 'suspension of judgement' (*epokhē*), though this epistemological position need not prevent the sceptic from enjoying experience, including the reading of poetry, and from living imperturbably in the real world. Though Sextus often quotes Homer and speaks of the poet's 'brilliance' (*Against the Grammarians* 203), he claims the grammarians have nothing to contribute to understanding texts:

'neither in the case of the best poem, since being clear it has no need of exegesis, nor in the case of the bad poem, since it is bad in itself' (319).

In the course of his refutation of the Stoic theory of knowledge Sextus states and criticises Stoic semiotic theory.[1] The Stoics held, he says (*Against the Logicians* 2.11 – 12), that the thing existing (e.g., the man Dion) and the thing signifying (the sound 'Dion'), both regarded as material, are linked by the *lekton* (the name 'Dion'), an incorporeal signified located in language itself which allows sound to be related to objects. In their semiotic theory the Stoics did not use the term 'sign' (*sēmeion*), but reserved that for a feature of their propositional logic where it refers to an antecedent judgement in a valid hypothetical syllogism: if a woman has milk it is a 'sign' that she has conceived (*Outlines* 2.104 – 6). It is here thought of as an event rather than a substance and is non-linguistic. Sextus assumes that a sign is operative in both cases, but treats linguistic signs as directly evoking a signified, whereas a logical sign, such as an antecedent event, both has its own meaning and indirectly evokes its consequent as well (*Outlines* 2.117 – 18; *Logicians* 2.264 – 71). Although he does not point it out, it was the indirect meaning of signs that was exploited by the Stoics and neo-Platonists in allegorical interpretation. He does note, however, (*Outlines* 2.99 – 101) that the Stoics distinguished between 'hypomnestic', or 'suggestive', signs, which by their clarity at the time of perception suggest to us something associated, as smoke suggests fire, and 'endeictic', or 'indicative' signs, not clearly associated with the thing signified, but still signs by their own particular nature, 'as bodily motions are signs of the existence of soul'. Sextus assents 'undogmatically' to the utility of suggestive signs in living experience; he rejects the interpretation of indicative signs, for he thinks there is no necessary link between bodily movement and the existence of soul. This would seem to undermine much of what goes on in allegorical interpretation.

In the period between his involvement with Manichaeism and his conversion to Christianity, Saint Augustine was attracted to scepticism, as represented by Cicero's *Academics*, but in the months immediately following his experience of conversion wrote the dialogue *Against the Academics* in which the possibility of knowledge is asserted. Though the dialogue discusses the problem within the traditions of the rationalising philosophical schools, true knowledge, Augustine eventually came to believe, must come ultimately from God's grace and supernatural revelation through the scriptures. An interesting detail in the dialogue is that during the intervals in the conversation Augustine was reading Virgil's *Aeneid* with the young men present.

In marked contrast to the sceptical tradition is the dogmatism of the neo-Platonic and Christian writers, the latter often imbued with some form of

---

[1] Todorov, *Theories of the Symbol*, pp. 18 – 27, but the subject is more complex than he allows; see Graeser, 'Stoic theory of meaning', pp. 77 – 100.

Platonism. What the scriptures were to the Christians, the Platonic dialogues were to the neo-Platonists: divinely inspired texts which provided a fully adequate basis of all knowledge. Stoic allegorical interpretation provided both with a model, but they took an additional step, anticipated by Philo as noted in chapter 6, section 1 above, in their privileging of certain texts as *a priori* true. The interpretation of the inspired texts was, however, fraught with difficulty. Neo-Platonists often turned to mysticism and magic in their search for truth, and Christians to fasting, the mortification of the body, and prayerful meditation, and both were driven to develop their own hermeneutics. Though for both groups reason was a tool of knowledge, internal inconsistencies in their sacred texts and certain cultural assumptions forced a resort to allegory. Among the neo-Platonists this is seen in the impulse to rescue the Homeric poems from the apparent strictures of Plato, as discussed in the last chapter; among the Christians in the need to reconcile the Old with the New Testament. In addition, neo-Platonists wished to reconcile the teachings of Aristotle with those of Plato, and some learned Christians sought to show that Christian truth had been dimly perceived by Greek philosophers. Both movements followed the lead of Alexandrian scholarship in the writing of commentaries. In both cases, a feature of such commentaries is that every word is significant as part of some greater whole. The neo-Platonists are much concerned in introductions to their commentaries with identification of the *skopos* of a dialogue, its over-all theme to which every word must contribute, and in bringing out the unity of the thought.[2] Although their interest in unity might seem to anticipate something like the New Criticism of the 1930s, they proceeded with considerably less disciplined control and in a belief that all meaning represents the conscious intent of the author. For the Christians, the author is God; it need not be assumed that the human authors of the scriptures were fully aware of what they were writing, for they were vessels into which divine revelation, too great for any human mind, had been poured (Exodus 4:12; Matthew 10:19; Mark 13:11).

Christian allegorical interpretation begins with St Paul. Writing against Judaising Christians in Galatians (4:21–31), he does not deny the historicity of the story of Abraham, Hagar, and Sarah in Genesis, but regards it as told for a spiritual meaning, symbolising the Old and New Covenants. Major stages in the development of Christian exegesis between Paul and Augustine are represented by the writings of Clement of Alexandria at the end of the second century and his student Origen in the early third, both well-trained in literature and philosophy, both criticised for heretical views by the later Greek church. Only one of Clement's works was known directly in the Latin West, Cassiodorus' translations of his *Adumbrationes*, or *Scriptural Outlines*;

---

[2] Coulter, *Literary Microcosm*, pp. 77–94.

several of Origen's writings were translated, by Rufinus and by Jerome, and read by Augustine and his successors.

In his best known work, *Protrepticus*, Clement addresses the Greeks and seeks to show (esp. chapters 5 – 6) that their philosophers had caught a glimpse of the true nature of God, but that fuller light was to be found in the Hebrew prophets. Some truth can be found in the Greek poets as well, especially in passages where Homer, Sophocles, and Euripides seem to reveal the false-hood of the pagan gods (7). The *Stromata* ('bags containing bed linen' = 'Miscellanies') sets out Clement's thoughts on Christian gnosticism (esoteric knowledge) in contrast to what is seen in heretical gnostic writings, known from the criticism of many of the Fathers and now from texts discovered at Nag Hammadi in upper Egypt.[3] Philosophy is 'a divine gift to the Greeks'; it does not 'drag us away from the faith, as if we were bewitched by some delusive art, but rather, so to speak, by the use of an ampler circuit, obtains a common exercise demonstrative of the faith' (1.2.20). Philosophy was a *propaideia* to bring the Greeks to Christ, as the law was intended to bring the Hebrews (1.5.28). Human knowledge and reason are necessary for inter-pretation of the scriptures (1.9). Homer, Plato, and other Greek philosophers had been in Egypt and learned there something of the books of Moses (1.15.66, 1.25.165) – a common claim by the Christian apologists.

The *Stromata* is littered with quotations from Greek poets and references to Plato and other philosophers. It also contains a number of interesting passages on interpretation, of which the most famous is probably the discussion of the forms of Egyptian writing (5.4.20 – 1). The most elementary form is called epistolographic; second is hieratic, used by sacred scribes; third is the sacred writing, hieroglyphic. In hieroglyphic writing there are two elements combined in each written word. One is literal, *kuriologikē*, represent-ing the sound of the word; the other is symbolic, *sumbolikē*, but this latter may be either imitative (e.g., a circle for the sun) or figurative, using conventional characters which have originated in imitation but have lost representational character, or finally symbolic 'by enigma', for example the sun represented as a beetle 'because having made a round figure of ox-dung, it rolls it before its face'. The opposition between the kyriologic and the symbolic genus may be regarded as the opposition between unmotivated and motivated signs, whereas the opposition between the imitative and other species of symbolic writing is between the direct and the indirect.[4]

In chapters 8 and 9 of Book V Clement discusses the uses of symbols, both direct and indirect, among the barbarians, by Greeks and Romans, and in the scriptures. 'The species of symbolic interpretation',[5] he says (5.8.46), 'is most useful for many things, contributing to right theology, piety, the

---

[3] Discussion by Elaine Pagels, *The Gnostic Gospels* (New York, 1979).
[4] Todorov, *Theories of the Symbol*, p. 35.
[5] τὸ τῆς συμβολικῆς ἑρμηνείας εἶδος.

demonstration of knowledge, brevity of expression, and exposition of the truth; as the grammarian Didymus says, "it is characteristic of the wiseman to use symbolic language rightly and to understand what is revealed through it".' 'All things glimpsed through some covering reveal a truth that is greater and more holy; like fruits glistening through water, their forms are seen through the veils that provide them gratifying secondary meanings [*sunemphaseis*]. Their illuminations prevent us from understanding even clear things in a single way [*monotropōs*]. Since it is possible to regard most things by synecdoche, we do so, on the basis of what is spoken covertly' (5.9.56). In the course of these chapters Clement touches on several reasons why the truth is often veiled in symbols, but in the case of philosophical and religious truth the fundamental reasons seem the need to protect it from vulgar misunderstanding and to require that it be apprehended through mental effort which increases its value when once grasped. Augustine will come to similar conclusions.

Clement did not write commentaries, but his pupil Origen did, on a vast scale, in which he developed and applied his master's theories of interpretation. In his treatise *On First Principles*, known in the West from Rufinus' translation, he also formulated a system of levels of interpretation of scripture which was to have important influence, through Ambrose and Augustine, on the future history of exegesis. Origen regarded the Bible as in every respect inspired. Just as man consists of body, soul, and spirit, so God has intentionally arranged the scriptures in three levels for man's salvation (4.2.4–9). The corporeal level is that of the letter, the literal meaning, addressed to those who are still children and do not yet recognise God. The level of soul is the moral level, where a passage has a specific, but non-literal interpretation to an audience (as did the passage from Paul to which Augustine opened the Bible in the moment of his conversion, *Confessions* 8.29). The spiritual level is theological and reveals the essential truths of Christianity. Origen thought that many passages in the Bible were incomprehensible unless regarded as *tupoi*, or figures, to be interpreted allegorically. 'Divine wisdom', he says (4.2.9)

has arranged certain stumbling blocks and offences against historical sense by introducing impossibilities and inconveniences in their midst, so that the very interruption of the narrative stands as a barrier against the reader; it denies him the easy path of common understanding, and recalls us, excluded and debarred from that, to the beginning of another way, so that it opens up the immense extent of divine knowledge through the entrance of a narrow path to a higher and loftier road.

That many different meanings can be found in the text is not a problem, since the inspiration of the scriptures contains for more meaning than we can ever fathom (4.3.14). The spiritual meaning, the universal message of Christianity, provides a check against misinterpretation – what is to become the rule of love to Augustine (*On Christian Doctrine* 1.40). Many things cannot be conveyed by human language; truth is apprehended by the soul, but strengthened and explored by study of the words of scripture, where there are one or more parallel and higher meanings which the Christian can hope to perceive.

Christian scholars ordinarily accepted the traditional authorships of their sacred texts, but there were some problems and they occasionally applied techniques of secular learning to the determination of authorship. The best example is probably the argument of Origen's student Dionysius of Alexandria (died AD 265), that the author of the Fourth Gospel was not the author of the Apocalypse. His reasoning is excerpted by Eusebius (*Church History* 7.25): the evangelist John does not identify himself in the text, the John of Revelations does so; the two writers employ different concepts and terms; they differ in grammatical usages.[6]

Study of interpretative theory leads in many directions. For hermeneutics gone wild, a sobering study are the revelations of the so-called Hermes Trismegistus in the corpus of *Hermetica*. Examination of the interpretative methods of medical writers, for example Galen, or legal writers, for example Gaius, would take us in the opposite direction from magic to the real world. One other work of interpretation is so remarkable that it requires at least a brief mention, and will link up with our discussion of Macrobius below. This is the *Oneirocritica*, or *Interpretation of Dreams*, by the second century 'philosopher' Artemidorus. He distinguishes first between *enhupnia*, or the manifestation of present conditions of body or mind in sleep, induced by a need or excess of something, by fear or hope, and *oneiroi*, dreams which call the sleeper's attention to a prediction of future events and which, after sleep, awaken and excite the soul by inducing active undertakings as the result of the dream. *Oneiroi* are the subject of his study. Some dreams, he says (1.2), are 'theorematic' or direct, others allegorical or indirect, through which the soul is conveying something obscurely by physical means. Earlier writers had divided allegorical dreams into five classes: involving the self; involving others; involving both self and others; public; and cosmic. Dreams may indicate many things through many images, a few things through a few, many through few, or few through many (1.4). The images seen in dreams are then classified by types, beginning with images of birth and the body, growing up, sexual activity, and moving on to social, political, and religious activities, ending with visions of the gods and death (1.10).

All of this might easily be recast to provide a detailed system of allegorical interpretation of symbols in literature. Artemidorus' advice to the dream interpreter (1.11) could also be taken as advice to the literary interpreter: some dreams are best interpreted by reading them from beginning to end; in others the beginning can only be understood by reading from the end.

[6] Colson, 'Two examples', pp. 365–74.

As in the case of much of Classical literature, dreams are often mutilated, fragmentary, or corrupt; the interpreter then must reconstruct the text by supplementing it, transposing it, or emending it. In so doing, he should not rely on manuals, but use his native intelligence: 'a man who thinks he will be perfect by theory without any natural talents will remain imperfect and incomplete, and all the more, the more set he is in this habit' (1.12). Dreams interpreted by Artemidorus include both those found in literature and those he collected from real life. His work is systematic, practical, and rational, avoiding superstition and mysticism and also avoiding the question whether dreams are sent by the gods or motivated by something within the dreamer. 'Although his prognostics sometimes rely upon elaborate puns, forced anagrammatical transpositions, and obscure principles involving the equal numerical value of the names of dream objects, he usually handles his material in a logical, seemingly scientific way.'[7] All in all, his work would not be a bad paradigm for the literary interpretation of future centuries. It is preserved in one manuscript of the eleventh century, but was of increased interest in the humanistic period, from which we have at least six manuscripts and the 1518 printed edition of Aldus.

2 The synthesis of Classical and Christian culture

Virtually every possible attitude toward secular literature can be found among early Christians, though they are consistently at pains to put distance between themselves and the paganism inherent in Classical poetry. One extreme could be represented by St Antony, living in the desert and rejecting every aspect of human society and culture, or from among those who deigned to live in the world and write treatises, by Epiphanius of Ephesus (died AD 403), whose *Panarion*, or *Breadbasket*, opposes any compromise with Classical culture. The toleration of Christianity resulting from Constantine's Edict of Milan (313) contributed to some relaxation of tensions. It became possible not only for a good Christian to have a good education, but even to become a teacher of rhetoric, as Prohaeresius did in fourth-century Athens (Eunapius, p. 513 Wright). The Cappadocian Fathers in particular – Gregory of Nazianzus, Gregory of Nyssa, and Basil the Great – were men of learning who sought a synthesis of the best of the two cultures, Classical and Christian.[8] Basil's treatise *To the Young, on How They Should Profit from Greek Writings*, though it warns against pagan mythology, atheism, and immorality, finds edifying content in Homer, Hesiod, and Plato.[9]

Of the great Latin Fathers, five – Tertullian, Cyprian, Arnobius, Lactantius, and Augustine – had taught rhetoric at some time, while others –

---

[7] White, *Artemidorus*, p. 7.
[8] Kennedy, *Greek Rhetoric*, pp. 215–41.
[9] N. G. Wilson, *Saint Basil*.

Minucius Felix, Ambrose, Hilary, and Jerome – were at least thoroughly trained in Classical literature. Of those within the purview of this volume, Lactantius most admits to an interest in secular literature, though Minucius Felix's one surviving work, the *Octavius*, reflects literary appreciation in its successful imitation of a Ciceronian dialogue. Tertullian, the earliest (*c.* AD 160–225) of the Latin Fathers and the most powerful stylist in his own right, was long regarded as a radical opponent of all Classical culture, a view epitomised in two phrases: 'What has Athens to do with Jerusalem?' and 'Credo quia absurdum'. The first is a genuine quotation,[10] but is specifically directed against gnostics led into heresy by Greek philosophy. Taking Tertullian's works as a whole, with their many references to Greek philosophy, the answer is 'Quite a lot'. In common with other Christian writers he takes the line that the truths in Greek philosophy were derived from some knowledge of the earlier books of the Old Testament (*Apology* 21). Tertullian's writings do not include the words 'I believe because it is absurd', and the origin is unknown.[11] The closest to the sentiment in his works is the statement: 'The son of God was crucified; there is no shame because it is shameful. And the son of God died; it is believable because it is foolish. And buried, he rose again; it is certain because it is impossible' (*De carne Christi* 5.4).[12] This is as good a short example as could be found of Tertullian's pointed style.

The older view, that Tertullian was a spokesman for complete separation of Christianity and Classical culture,[13] has in recent years given way to increased recognition in his writings of a synthesis of Christian doctrine with philosophical traditions (largely Platonic and Stoic and with special emphasis on logic and dialectic) and with rhetoric, Roman law, history, and the satiric techniques of Juvenal and Tacitus. Classical literature was there to use for Christian purposes and was a rich source of examples.[14] A knowledge of letters is necessary, he says (*De corona* 8.2), for the business of life. Some study of literature cannot be avoided by a Christian, but he must not teach it (*De idolatria* 10). Demosthenes and Cicero were eloquent men (*Apology* 11.15–16); Plato has dignity, Aristotle equanimity (*De anima* 3.2); but Aristotelian dialectic is the mother of heresy (*De praescriptione haereticorum* 7). With characteristic irony, Tertullian recommends the reading of the scriptures for those who would seek entertainment:

If the study of the stage delights you, we have enough writings, enough verses, enough aphorisms, enough songs, enough voices; ours are not fables, but verities,

---

[10] Quid ergo Athenis et Hierosolymis? Quid Academiae et Ecclesiae? Quid haereticis and Christianis? (*De praescriptione haereticorum* 7.9).

[11] Barnes, *Tertullian*, p. 223.

[12] Crucifixus est dei filius; non pudet, quia pudendum est. Et mortuus est dei filius; credibile est, quia ineptum est. Et sepultus resurrexit; certum est, quia impossibile. (*De carne Christi* 5.4)

[13] Cf., e.g., Cochrane, *Christianity and Classical Culture*, p. 227.

[14] Hélène Petrie, *L'exemplum chez Tertullien* (Neuilly-sur-Seine, 1940).

not artifices, but simplicities. Are you looking for fighting and wrestling? Here they are – things of no small account and lots of them. Look at impurity thrown down by chastity, perfidy slain by faith, cruelty crushed by pity, impudence overshadowed by modesty, and such are the contests among us in which we ourselves are crowned. Do you want some blood too? You have the blood of Christ.   (*De spectaculis* 29)

Tertullian's denunciation of the theatre on moral and religious grounds is bitter (*De spectaculis* 10), but in a different context, attacking the gnosticism of Simon Magus, he can write an apostrophe to Helen of Troy, whom in common with others of the time he regarded as an historical figure: 'Poor Helen! You have had a hard time of it between the poets and the heretics who have branded you an adulteress and a prostitute' (*De anima* 34.5). The mention of Helen, who figured in the gnostic cult of Simon Magus as the third member of the Trinity, providing a source for her later appearance in the Faust legend, is only one of the more bizarre examples of how some Christian sects incorporated figures of Greek mythology into their thinking. Another is the case of Odysseus, sometimes treated by Christian writers as a symbol of Christ on the Cross.[15]

Tertullian is a brilliant allegorist; his best allegorical passages are perhaps to be found in *De patientia*. But he did not write commentaries, and he was well aware of the dangers of allegory when practised by heretics. Thus he attacks those who claimed that the resurrection of the dead was an 'image' or 'figure' for the moral change to a new life:

Now if this were the case, the images themselves could not have been recognisable, unless the verities had been declared, from which the images were sketched. And, indeed, if all things are figures, what can that be of which they are figures? How can you hold up a mirror for your face if there is no face? But in truth all are not figures, but there are also verities [literal statements].   (*De resurrectione mortuorum* 20.1–2)

Here and elsewhere Tertullian shows familiarity with Stoic semiotic theory.[16]

Cyprian, writing a generation later, was equally well educated and writes a more Ciceronian Latin than Tertullian, but with his paganism he put off all interest in literature and never quotes a Classical writer. In contrast, Arnobius, at the beginning of the fourth century, avoids scriptural quotation and seeks to refute paganism by quoting Classical authors, especially the Epicurean Lucretius.[17] That Arnobius' student Lactantius could be regarded as 'the Christian Cicero' was already recognized by Saint Jerome (*Ep.* 58.10) and taken up in the Renaissance by Pico della Mirandola (*De studio philosophiae* 1.7) and other humanists. Lactantius, writing in the first quarter of the fourth century, can be said to be Ciceronian in several senses: he wrote the finest

[15] W. B. Stanford, *The Ulysses Theme* (1963; reprinted Ann Arbor, Michigan, 1968), pp. 156–7.
[16] Ayers, *Language, Logic, and Reason*, pp. 7–15.
[17] Hagendahl, *Latin Fathers*, pp. 12–47.

Ciceronian prose of late antiquity; he admired and praises Cicero the man, the orator, and the philosopher (e.g., *Divine Institutes* 1.15), and quotes him frequently, more frequently than he quotes scripture;[18] his version of Christian humanism (6.10 – 12) is derived from Cicero; and finally, his treatise *On the Workmanship of God* describes itself (chapter 1) as a supplement to the fourth book of Cicero's *De republica*. Cicero is often cited in the *Divine Institutes* as an authority whose insights are true, occasionally only as the neutral source of an example, sometimes as misguided, in which case Lactantius argues against him. He is fond of using what Cicero says in one context as a basis for refuting him in another (2.8.13). The result, as here, is a kind of 'deconstruction' in which the text is opened up by finding inconsistencies with other texts, and Cicero's basically sound assumptions are used to undermine his assumed Academic scepticism (cf. 3.14.7 – 21). The dramatic nature of the Ciceronian dialogue may be overlooked in this process, at other times (e.g., 3.16.9) it is recognised.

The poets, though they too are quoted as authorities, do not engage Lactantius' attention to the same degree as Cicero. He discusses them as a group near the beginning of the *Divine Institutes* (1.5). Nothing can be learned from Homer, who described human things rather than divine. Hesiod could have told us something, but made the mistake of beginning with Chaos rather than Creation. He was not inspired, as he wished to be, but meditated and prepared his work. Virgil is greater, 'not far from the truth' (1.5.11), but the most exceptional of the poets, rather surprisingly, is Ovid, who acknowledged (*Met.* 1.57 – 79) that the world was fashioned by God. Though its authenticity has been doubted, Lactantius is the traditional author of a mythological poem, with a combination of pagan and Christian references, *On the Bird Phoenix*. One sign of the widening acceptance of Classical culture by Christians is the willingness of persons who regarded themselves as Christians to write mythological poetry, sometimes quite devoid of Christian reference, as in the case of Ausonius, sometimes with Christian moralising, as later in the case of Dracontius; and the willingness of the Christian court to sponsor poets who celebrated the imperial family in mythological terms, as in the case of Honorius' patronage of Claudian at the end of the fourth century. Whether Claudian could have regarded himself as a Christian is uncertain, but by that time public worship of the pagan gods was prohibited.

Taken as a whole, the ante-Nicene Fathers (that is, those writing before the Council of Nicaea in AD 325) may be said to show a movement toward agreement on certain principles relating to literature and criticism. First, literacy is necessary for the Christian and will involve some reading of Classical literature. Euhemerism is often adopted in treatment of the gods: some, at least, were once men regarded as deified by their followers. This process had

[18] Ogilvie, *Library*, pp. 58 – 72.

continued in the deification and cult of Roman emperors. But many of the
gods are devils, fallen angels, and they are dangerous and powerful forces in
the world. Second, historical and even mythological stories from Classical
writers can be cited as examples in Christian writing and speaking. They may
be given an allegorical interpretation in accord with orthodox Christian
doctrine. Third, truths can be found in the philosophers, both Greeks like
Pythagoras, Plato, and Aristotle, and Romans like Cicero and Seneca. The
truths of early Greek philosophy were originally derived from Hebraic ideas,
learned in Egypt. Similarly, truth can be found in some poetry, which St Paul
seemed to acknowledge in Acts (17:28): among Latin poets in Lucretius, who
attacked the traditional notion of the gods, in Virgil, who prophesied the birth
of Christ in the fourth *Eclogue*,[19] in Ovid, and in the satirists. The Bible is
divinely inspired and the only sure guide for men. It is true at the literal level,
but has a moral and theological level of meaning as well. At the latter two
levels it is necessary to make use of allegorical interpretation, especially in
the exegesis of the Old Testament, but allegory is a slippery tool, often used
by heretics. The literary qualities of the Bible are rarely noted, but biblical
imagery had become a part of Christian rhetoric as early as the apostolic
period and is widely employed by patristic writers.

3 Late Latin secular criticism

Latin poetry, historiography, and oratory were moribund from the middle
of the second to the middle of the fourth century; though there was important
philosophical writing in Greek, it was slow to find a counterpart in Latin. The
important Latin writers of the times are the Christians discussed above. What
secular literary criticism existed was found in the schools of grammar and
rhetoric. A literary revival took place in the middle of the fourth century and
lasted into the fifth. It produced criticism, chiefly in the form of learned
commentaries on major Classical Latin authors: Terence, Cicero, Virgil,
Horace, Statius, and Juvenal. Important practical aids to criticism were the
gradual replacement, between the second and the fourth century, of the scroll
by the codex as the common form of the book, facilitating consultation of
specific passages and providing space for marginal scholia, and the increasing
use of parchment rather than papyrus, including the use of a parchment
binding, making a book far more durable.[20]

The pagan and secular tradition in poetry in this late Latin renaissance
is represented at its best by Claudian, the development of Christian poetry
by Prudentius. In between lies Ausonius, the first French poet, though writing
in Latin. His life spanned most of the fourth century, and he wrote both

---

[19] Authoritatively so proclaimed by the Emperor Constantine, *Oratio ad coelum sanctorum* 19–21.
[20] Reynolds and Wilson, *Scribes and Scholars*, pp. 30–2.

pagan and Christian poetry with technical versatility. He is of interest here as perhaps the best example of a view that poetry is the rhetorical amplification of any subject in verse. He had taught rhetoric at Bordeaux for thirty years before going to Rome as the tutor of Gratian and then as a public official, rising to the consulship in AD 379. Ausonius' best poem is usually thought to be the *Mosella*, an ecphrasis in 483 hexameters of the river Moselle and its valley, which achieves some descriptive charm and demonstrates ingenuity in cataloguing the different kinds of fish that can be found in the river. The *Parentalia* consists of epigrams in honour of members of Ausonius' family; the *Professors of Bordeaux*, in a variety of metres, celebrates grammarians and rhetorians he had known there. These are all rather conventional works. Greater rhetorical challenges were presented by more intractable subjects: the *Technopaegnion*, or 'Game of Skill', is a series of poems based on monosyllables; each line ends with a monosyllable, and in one poem (3), the monosyllable at the end of a line also begins the next line. Ausonius' objective is revealed in a prose preface, addressed to the proconsul Pacatus: 'I have woven a playful little work in my usual way of setting out something a little greater; but "though slight the task, not slight the glory" (Virgil, *Geo*. 4.6). You will bring it about that they have some value.' Another *tour de force* is the *Griphus*, or 'Riddle' on the number three, about which Ausonius is apologetic in his preface to Symmachus: 'When you are doing nothing you should read this and, to find something to do, defend it.' A third is the *Cento nuptialis*, made up entirely of quotations from Virgil, woven together to describe a wedding, including a detailed, if metaphorical, description of the deflowering of the bride. *Cento* means 'patchwork' in Greek, or 'quilt' in Latin, but beginning in the fourth century designates a minor verse form in which the beauty of the original context, familiar to educated readers, is transmuted by the poet's ingenuity into new thought. Falconia Proba dedicated to the Emperor Honorius a Virgilian cento retelling stories of the Bible.

Late Latin commentaries demonstrate learning, respect for Classical texts, and varying degrees of literary insight. The best may be Aelius Donatus' commentary on Terence, but the most important is Servius' commentary on Virgil (*c.* AD 400), heavily dependent on an earlier commentary by Donatus, who was Servius' teacher and is best known as author of the standard grammar of late antiquity and the Middle Ages. Servius' Virgilian commentary survives in two versions, one an amplification of the other. The fuller version, known as Servius Danielis from its seventeenth-century editor, Pierre Daniel, apparently incorporates extensive material from Donatus not used by Servius in his published edition.[21]

In reading Servius' commentaries it is important to remember that his primary function was to teach the proper use of Latin to adolescents; they

---

[21] E. K. Rand, 'Is Donatus' Servius commentary lost?' *CQ* 11 (1916), 158–64.

are often cautioned in the notes against actually using words or constructions employed by Virgil and against figurative language. The thrust of the commentary is thus prescriptive and reflects the view that there is a 'natural' use of language, formalised by rule and expressed in the 'art' of grammar, from which poets diverge in the process of versification and to secure ornamentation.[22] At the same time, the student can expect to learn much from the text about Roman history, mythology, and religion, and all these subjects are commented upon. In the preface to the commentary on the first book of the *Aeneid* an approach is outlined which follows the practice of Roman grammarians and came later to be known as the *accessus*: 'The following must be considered in explicating authors: the poet's life, the title of the work, the quality of the song, the intent of the writer, the number of books, the order of the books, and explanation.' There follows a brief life of Virgil, derived through Donatus from Suetonius (commentary is a cumulative process, building on but rarely acknowledging the work of previous scholars). 'The quality of the song', we are told, 'is clear: for it is heroic metre and mixed action, where the poet both speaks and introduces other speakers. It is heroic because it includes divine and human characters, containing the true with the fictive ... The style is grandiloquent, made up of elevated diction and noble thoughts ... (We know that there are three kinds of style: *humile, medium, grandiloquum*.) The intent of Virgil is this: to imitate Homer and to praise Augustus through his ancestors ...' As to the number of books, there is no question, though that problem arises in the case of other works. The order is consistent with the advice of Horace (*AP* 43) to begin epic 'from the midst'.

'Explanation' is the task of the running commentary which follows and which includes matters of grammar, rhetoric, and prosody (usages are not infrequently explained as the result of 'metrical necessity'). Although Servius employs the term 'allegory' only to designate a figure of speech, he often employs allegorical interpretation to bring out the meaning of different levels of the text, treating the poem at times as an allegory of Roman history, and often explaining passages (especially in *Aeneid* VI) as philosophical, religious, or moral allegory. The gods are sometimes interpreted as physical forces, sometimes as originally human beings (euhemerism). A result was probably to make Virgil's poetry more acceptable to Christian readers, though there is no reference to Christianity in the commentary (not even on *Eclogue* IV). Of the prefaces other than that to *Aeneid* I, the most interesting is probably that to Book IV, telling of Aeneas' adventures with Dido. We are here told that 'the whole book is taken over' (*translatus est*) from the third book of Apollonius' *Argonautica*. 'It is almost entirely concerned with "affection", though it has pathos at the end when the departure of Aeneas produces grief. The whole is certainly made up of plans and subtleties [intrigues?], for [*sic*]

[22] Kaster, 'A grammarian's authority', p. 223.

it has an almost comic style; no wonder, since the subject is love.' By 'comic style' is apparently meant the simple and light style which Donatus had identified in his commentary on Terence as appropriate to comedy (cf., e.g., on *Phormio* 5).[23] The voice of the grammarian is here heard authoritatively lecturing his students on the approved relationship of style to content.

Servius is a character in Macrobius' dialogue *Saturnalia*, but is there dramatically changed into a defender of archaic usage, rather than an admonitory preceptor of good contemporary prose as he appears in his own writings.[24] Other speakers include the antiquarian Praetextatus, the orator Symmachus, the rhetorician Eusebius, the philosopher Eustathius, the physician Disarius, an Avienus who may be the fabulist, and several others, making up a representative group of the leading intellectuals in fourth-century Rome. They and others like them were the centre of pagan resistance to Christianity and active in the Classical renascence of the time,[25] but their cultural interests are somewhat idealised by Macrobius.[26] Neither Christianity nor contemporary politics are discussed in the dialogue, the main topic of which is the erudition of Virgil in such matters as religious cult, philosophy, and rhetoric. Since the *Saturnalia* was well known in the Middle Ages, it made a significant contribution to the belief in the omniscience of Virgil. Its literary antecedents are the symposiac literature of the Greeks, including Athenaeus, and the Romans, including Aulus Gellius. The dramatic date is apparently 384, the same year in which Augustine was reading the *Aeneid* at Cassiacum; the date of publication is, however, probably as late as the 430s.[27]

The *Saturnalia* gives a picture of how the liberal education imparted to the young by teachers like Servius continued to be a source of conversation and speculation among adults in their leisure hours. Macrobius' purpose, however, as announced in his preface, is just as educational as that of Servius. He writes to provide his son Eustachius with a knowledge of nature, which he does by organising topically the knowledge that might otherwise be scattered through commentaries. We see here, as often, the very pragmatic approach of the Romans to literature. Virgil remains the central educational text: he was acquainted with all knowledge (1.1.12); a poet whose aim was to combine learning with elegant diction (3.11.9). Literary criticism is mostly concentrated in Books IV (fragmentary) through VI. As noted above, Servius had said that Virgil's first intention was to imitate Homer, and some of the most valuable parts of the *Saturnalia* are the discussions of Virgil's relationship to Homer. The *Aeneid* is called a mirrored reflection of the *Iliad* and

[23] S. Anderson, 'Servius and the "Comic spirit" of *Aeneid* IV', *Arethusa*, 14 (1981), 115–25.
[24] Kaster, 'A grammarian's authority', pp. 218–21.
[25] Herbert Bloch, 'The pagan revival in the West at the end of the fourth century', in Momigliano (ed.), *Paganism and Christianity*, pp. 193–218.
[26] Kaster, 'Macrobius and Servius', pp. 222–3.
[27] Alan Cameron, 'The date and identity of Macrobius', *JRS*, 56 (1966), 25–38.

Odyssey, describing first Aeneas' wanderings, then his wars (5.2.13). Virgil
sometimes improves on his model (5.11), sometimes equals it (5.12), sometimes falls short (5.13). At his best, Virgil was a more careful observer of
nature, gives greater detail, and is closer to reality. The sixth book of the
Saturnalia examines Virgil's debt to earlier Roman writers; their words often
sound better in his new contexts (6.1.2–6). The critical assumptions of the
Saturnalia are that art is imitation of nature, that poets work within literary
traditions, seeking originality by recasting and improving upon the art of their
predecessors, that great poets are characterised by genius, acute power of
observation, and learning; and that the function of literature is to provide
instruction with the greatest pleasure. The philosophy seen in the *Saturnalia*
is a popularised synthesis of Stoicism and neo-Platonism. Allegorical interpretation is a common tool.

Macrobius' commentary on the *Dream of Scipio* from the last book of
Cicero's *De republica* is a far more serious application of neo-Platonism to an
earlier text and was a major source for knowledge of neo-Platonism in the
medieval West. Macrobius may have used Porphyry's commentary on Plato's
Timaeus, a dialogue often cited in the discussion. Like the *Saturnalia*, the
commentary is dedicated to Eustachius and intended as part of his education.
The practical goal is understanding of justice, but justice is regarded as
dependent on the immortality of the soul (1.1.5). Macrobius invents the term
figmentum, 'fictitious creation' to describe what was earlier called *muthos* or
fabula, and he distinguishes two purposes in such creation: entertainment
and moral improvement, the latter having religious and philosophical uses
(1.2).[28] Since the text recounts a dream, some observations on the interpretation of dreams are made (1.3), reminiscent of what we have met in
Artemidorus. Consistent with neo-Platonic method, Macrobius defines the
skopos (Latin *propositum*) of the text, which is that the souls of those who have
deserved well of the republic, after their bodily lives, return to the sky and
there enjoy perpetual happiness (1.4.1).

Although Donatus, Servius, and later Priscian are the best known and
became the most influential of the late Latin grammarians, the work of
Diomedes (late fourth century) is of interest in that it contains a full account
of grammatical tropes, many of which are important features of allegorical
interpretation,[29] and the most systematic surviving account of poetic genres
(I, pp. 482–92 Keil). The three general classes of poetry are said to be
dramatic, narrative, and mixed. The dramatic species are tragic, comic,
satyric, and the mime; the narrative are *angeltice*, or gnomic poetry, for
example that of Theognis, *historice*, such as the genealogical poetry attributed
to Hesiod, and *didascalice*, or didactic poetry such as Virgil's *Georgics*. The

[28] Rollinson, *Allegory*, pp. 11–14.
[29] *Ibid.*, pp. 87, 98.

mixed, or 'common' species are heroic and lyric. There follows a definition and brief description of epic, elegy, and iambic poetry, of epode, satire, bucolic poetry, tragedy, and various comic forms. The rest of the work is devoted to discussion of metres, including a lengthy section on those of Horace.

What Virgil was in poetry, the basic text of the school of the grammarian, occasionally complemented by Terence, Horace, or other writers, Cicero was in the school of rhetoric, source both of theory and practice. Other prose writers seem to have been read chiefly for their contents: Livy for Roman history; Varro for antiquities; but Ammianus Marcellinus, writing in the fourth century, continued the history of Tacitus and was somewhat influenced by his style. Both in poetry and in prose, the canon was narrowing, leading to the neglect and eventual loss of many works. Even in the case of Cicero, the canon retracts. Augustine drew on *De oratore* and *Orator*, but Cicero's early handbook *De inventione* was already becoming the authoritative treatment of rhetoric it remained throughout the Middle Ages. The commentary on it by Victorinus dates from the fourth century (he also made translations of Plato, Aristotle, and Porphyry and wrote commentaries on the Pauline epistles), that of Grillius from the fifth century. Except for Grillius, the writings on rhetoric from late Latin times make up the *Rhetores Latini minores*, as edited by Halm in 1863. These include some short works on figures of speech and handbooks treating the whole system of rhetoric by Consultus Fortunatianus,[30] Sulpitius Victor, Julius Severianus, and Julius Victor. It is interesting to note how much emphasis continued to be put on invention, and especially on the theory of the *constitutio* or *status* of a question. The logical side of rhetoric continued to be emphasised and had application to argumentation not only in lawcourts, but increasingly in ecclesiastical controversy. There is very little new development of rhetorical theory, and the rhetoricians do not seem to have been much influenced by contemporary Greek theory as set out in the corpus of Hermogenes.[31] The two cultures, Greek and Roman, were drawing apart as the political and religious separation of East and West continued. Few Romans of late antiquity could read Greek with ease, and those few who could turned to philosophers, not poets.

The minor Latin rhetoricians of late antiquity had some readership in the Middle Ages, but much better known were the encyclopedias or compendia of the liberal arts, of which that by Martianus Capella was written in the early fifth century, those by Cassiodorus and Isidore in periods beyond the limit of this volume. We should not think of the teaching of the liberal arts as yet organised into the system of trivium and quadrivium, as was done later, but there was some recognition of a cycle of studies for which systematic instruction in grammar and rhetoric was provided in schools, and the other subjects – dialectic, arithmetic, geometry, astronomy, and music, occasionally other

---

[30] Consultus, not Chirius; see *Ars rhetorica*, ed. Calboli-Montefusco, pp. 13–20.
[31] But see Leff, 'Topics', p. 35, and Fortunatianus, ed. Calboli-Montefusco, pp. 521–2.

disciplines as well – could be studied by the more serious from textbooks or with private teachers. The knowledge, once acquired, could then provide the basis for the interpretation of texts. Martianus' account of grammar and rhetoric and the other arts is a very dry summary of traditional theory. The first book of his work, however, describes in perversely complex Latin – what passed for erudition in this mannered age – the allegorical marriage of Mercury (Greek Hermes, and thus the father of hermeneutics) with Philology, and the appearance of the liberal arts as handmaidens attending them. The latter are thus given allegorical forms which continue in Medieval literature and art.

4　The heritage of Classical criticism

The greatest bequest of Classical criticism to later centuries has doubtless been its three seminal texts: *Poetics*, *Ars poetica*, *On Sublimity*. Of these three, Horace's work has been the most continuously, though not always widely, known and appreciated; Aristotle's work, surely the greatest critical treatise of all time, was known to a few through Latin translation in the later Middle Ages, made a major impact on the literature and criticism of the Renaissance, and has had an important role in twentieth-century critical thought; Longinus' work, if it is his, burst on the scene in the seventeenth century and inspired a cult of the sublime which lasted well into the nineteenth. More consistently pervasive than any of these works has been the system of Classical rhetoric, known to the Middle Ages through Cicero's *De inventione* and *Rhetorica ad Herennium*, long also attributed to him, and summarised in the compendia of Martianus, Cassiodorus, and Isidore. The fuller rhetorical tradition re-emerges in the fifteenth century with the rediscovery of complete versions of Cicero's other rhetorical works and of Quintilian's *Institutio*, and later with a growing appreciation of Aristotle's *Rhetoric*.

The Classical critics – grammarians, rhetoricians, and philosophers – created the basic critical vocabulary and terminology which has been used ever since, and they anticipated many of the critical issues and stances of modern times. Not the least among these has been the concept of Classicism, the definition of genre, the theory of imitation, and, under the influence of rhetoric, the assumption that the intent of the author is the basis of validity in interpretation. Another important heritage of antiquity has been the quarrel between the philosophers and poets, or more specifically between Plato and his followers and Aristotle and his, and the associated quarrel between philosophy and rhetoric. Finally, the tradition of literary scholarship or philology in textual, historical, biographical, and contextual criticism, enriched or corrupted, as the case may be, by the allegorical interpretations of philosophers and extended by Christian writers into exegesis of the Bible, traces its history back to the Alexandrian library and before and forward to the monasteries, cathedral schools, and universities of the West.

BIBLIOGRAPHY

Primary sources

Collections

Arnim, Hans von (ed.), *Stoicorum veterum fragmenta* (4 vols., Leipzig, 1903–24; rpt. Dubuque, Iowa, 1964–5).

Diels, Hermann, and Kranz, Walther (eds.), *Die Fragmente der Vorsokratiker* (6th ed., 3 vols., Zurich, 1951–2; rpt. 1966).

Dorsch, T. S. (tr.), *Classical Literary Criticism* (Aristotle, *On the Art of Poetry*; Horace, *On the Art of Poetry*; Longinus, *On the Sublime*) (Penguin, 1965).

Fyfe, W. H., and Roberts, W. R. (trs.), Aristotle, *The Poetics*; Longinus, *On the Sublime*; Demetrius, *On Style* (*LCL*) (London, 1932).

Halm, Carolus (ed.), *Rhetores Latini minores* (Leipzig, 1863; rpt. Frankfurt, 1964).

Jacoby, Felix *et al.* (eds.), *Die Fragmente der griechischen Historiker* (in progress, 4 vols. so far, Leiden, 1923–77).

Jan, Karl von (ed.), *Musici scriptores Graeci* (Leipzig, 1895).

Keil, Henricus (ed.), *Grammatici Latini* (7 vols., Leipzig, 1855–1923).

Kirk, G. S., Raven, J. E., and Schofield, Malcolm, *The Presocratic Philosophers* (2nd ed., Cambridge, 1983).

Kock, Theodore (ed.), *Comicorum Atticorum fragmenta* (3 vols., Leipzig, 1880–8).

Lanata, Giuliana (ed.), *Poetica pre-Platonica, testimonianze e frammenti* (Florence, 1963).

Morel, Willy (ed.), *Fragmenta poetarum Latinorum epicorum et lyricorum* (Leipzig, 1927).

Page, D. L. (ed.), *Epigrammata Graeca* (Oxford, 1975).

; *Poetae melici Graeci* (Oxford, 1962).

Radermacher, Ludwig (ed.), 'Artium scriptores (Reste der voraristotelischen Rhetorik)', Oesterreichische Akademie der Wissenschaften, Philosophisch-historische Klasse, *Sitzungsberichte* 227, 3 (Vienna, 1951).

Russell, D. A., and Winterbottom, Michael (eds.), *Ancient Literary Criticism: The Principal Texts in New Translations* (Oxford, 1972).

Spengel, Leonard (ed.), *Rhetores Graeci* (3 vols., Leipzig, 1853–6; rpt. Frankfurt, 1966).

Sprague, R. K. (ed.), *The Older Sophists: A Complete Translation by Several Hands* (Columbia, South Carolina, 1972).

Walz, Christian (ed.), *Rhetores Graeci* (9 vols., London, 1832–6; rpt. Osnabruck, 1968).

Warmington, E. H. (ed. and tr.), *The Remains of Old Latin* (*LCL*) (3 vols., London, 1938–56).

Wehrli, F. E. (ed.), *Die Schule des Aristoteles* (fr. of the Peripatetic philosophers) (10 vols., Basel, 1944 – 59).

West, M. L. (ed.), *Iambi et elegi Graeci* (2 vols., Oxford, 1971 – 2).

Authors and Works

Alcaeus, Greek lyric poet, *fl. c.* 600 BC:
  Fr., ed. E.-M. Voigt (Amsterdam, 1971).

Alcman, Greek lyric poet, *fl. c.* 630 BC:
  Fr., ed. D. L. Page, in *Poetae melici Graeci* (see above, Collections), pp. 1 – 91.

Alexander Numenii, Greek rhetorician, 2nd cent. AD:
  Peri schēmatōn (*On Figures*), ed. Leonard Spengel, *Rhetores Graeci* (see above, Collections), III, pp. 11 – 40.

Andronicus, Livius, Latin epic and dramatic poet, 3rd cent. BC:
  Fr., ed. and tr. E. H. Warmington, *The Remains of Old Latin* (see above, Collections), II, pp. 2 – 43.

Archilochus, Greek iambic and elegiac poet, *fl. c.* 648 BC:
  Fr., ed. Giovanni Tarditi (Rome, 1968); ed. M. L. West, *Iambi* (see above, Collections), I, pp. 1 – 108.

Aristarchus of Samothrace, Greek grammarian, *c.* 215 – 143 BC:
  Fr., ed. Karl Lehrs, *De Aristarchi studiis Homericis* (Leipzig, 1882).

Aristides, Aelius, Greek sophist, AD 117 – *c.* 187:
  Orationes, ed. and tr. C. A. Behr (*LCL*) (4 vols., in progress, London, 1973 –);
  Or. 2 – 4, ed. F. W. Lenz and C. A. Behr (2 vols.; Leiden, 1976 – 8); *Or.* 45, ed. Bruno Keil (Berlin, 1898).

Aristophanes, Greek comic poet, *c.* 450 – *c.* 385 BC:
  Clouds, ed. with commentary A. H. Sommerstein (Warminster, 1982);
  Frogs, ed. with commentary W. B. Stanford (London, 1963).

Aristophanes of Byzantium, Greek grammarian, *c.* 257 – 180 BC:
  Fr., ed. W. J. Slater (Berlin, 1986).

Aristotle, Greek philosopher, 384 – 322 BC:
  Works in English, ed. J. A. Smith and W. D. Ross (12 vols., Oxford, 1908 – 52); ed. Jonathan Barnes (2 vols., Princeton, 1984);
  Categories, On Interpretation, Prior Analytics, ed. and tr. H. P. Cooke and Hugh Tredennick (*LCL*) (London, 1938);
  Fragmenta, ed. Valentin Rose (3rd ed., Leipzig, 1886);
  Poetics, ed. and tr. W. H. Fyfe (*LCL*) (London, 1932); ed. Rudolf Kassel (Oxford, 1968); ed. with commentary D. W. Lucas (Oxford, 1968); ed. and tr. Roselyn Dupont-Roc and Jean Lallot, with pr. by Tzvetan Todorov (Paris, 1980); tr. Ingram Bywater (Oxford, 1920); tr. with commentary Leon Golden and O. B. Hardison (Englewood Cliffs, New Jersey, 1968; rpt. Tallahassee, Florida, 1981); tr. James Hutton (New York, 1982); tr. with commentary Stephen Halliwell (London, 1987); tr. Richard Janko (Indianapolis, 1987); tr. M. W. Hubbard, in D. A. Russell and Michael Winterbottom (eds.), *Ancient Literary Criticism* (see above, Collections), pp. 85 – 132;
  Rhetoric, ed. with commentary E. M. Cope and J. E. Sandys (3 vols., Cambridge, 1877); ed. and tr. J. H. Freese (*LCL*) (London, 1926); ed. W. D. Ross (Oxford,

1959); ed. Rudolf Kassel (Berlin, 1976); Commentary on Book I, W. A. M. Grimaldi (New York, 1980);

Lexica: André Wartelle, *Lexique de la Rhétorique d'Aristote*; *Lexique de la Poétique d'Aristote* (Paris, 1981; 1985).

Artemidorus of Daldis, Greek philosopher, 2nd cent. AD:

Onirocriticon, ed. R. A. Pack (Leipzig, 1963); tr. R. J. White (Park Ridge, New Jersey, 1975).

Ausonius, Decimus Magnus, Latin poet, d. AD *c.* 395:

Works, ed. and tr. H. G. Evelyn-White (*LCL*) (2 vols., London, 1919 – 21).

Bacchylides, Greek lyric poet, 5th cent. BC:

Fr., ed. Bruno Snell and Herweg Maehler (Leipzig, 1971).

Basil the Great, Greek theologian, AD *c.* 330 – 379:

To the Young on How They Should Read Greek Writings, ed. and tr. Fernand Boulanger (Paris, 1935; rpt. 1965); ed. N. G. Wilson (London, 1975).

Callimachus, Greek poet, *c.* 305 – *c.* 240 BC:

Fr., ed. Rudolf Pfeiffer (2 vols., Oxford, 1949 – 53);

Aetia and other poems, ed. and tr. C. A. Trypanis (*LCL*) (London, 1958);

Hymns and Epigrams, ed. and tr. A. W. Mair (*LCL*) (London, 1955).

Cicero, Marcus Tulius, Roman orator and philosopher, 106 – 43 BC:

Rhetorica, ed. A. S. Wilkins (2 vols., Oxford, 1902 – 3);

Brutus, Orator, ed. and tr. G. L. Hendrickson (*LCL*) (London, 1939);

Brutus, ed. with commentary A. E. Douglas (Oxford, 1966);

Orator, ed. with commentary J. E. Sandys (Cambridge, 1885);

De inventione, De optimo genere oratorum, Topica, ed. and tr. H. M. Hubbell (*LCL*) (London, 1949);

De natura deorum, Academica, ed. and tr. Harris Rackham (*LCL*) (London, 1933);

De oratore, ed. with commentary A. S. Wilkins (3 vols., Oxford, 1888 – 92; rpt. Hildesheim, 1965); ed. with commentary A. D. Leeman and Harm Pinkster (in progress, Heidelberg, 1981 –); ed. and tr. E. W. Sutton and Harris Rackham (*LCL*) (2 vols., London, 1948).

Clement of Alexandria, Greek theologian, AD *c.* 150 – *c.* 215:

Protrepticus, ed. and tr. G. W. Butterworth (*LCL*) (London, 1960);

Stromata, ed. Otto Stählin and Ludwig Früchtel (Berlin, 1960); tr. William Wilson, *Ante-Nicene Christian Library* (4 vols. published as 2 vols., Edinburgh, 1867), IV.

Cornutus, Lucius Annaeus, Greek philosopher, 1st cent. AD:

Ars rhetorica, ed. Casper Hammer, in *Rhetores Graeci* (Leipzig, 1894), pp. 352 – 98;

Theologiae, ed. C. Lang (Leipzig, 1881).

Demetrius (?), Greek rhetorician, 1st cent. BC (?):

Peri hermēneias (*On Style*), ed. Ludwig Radermarcher (Leipzig, 1901; rpt. Stuttgart, 1967); ed. with tr. and notes W. R. Roberts (Cambridge, 1902) (tr. also in Aristotle, *Poetics*, etc. *LCL*, London 1932); tr. with notes G. M. A. Grube (Toronto, 1961); tr. D. C. Innes, in D. A. Russell and Michael Winterbottom (eds.), *Ancient Literary Criticism* (see above, Collections), pp. 171 – 215.

Dio of Prusa (Dio Chrysostom), Greek orator, AD *c.* 40 – 120:

Orationes, ed. Hans von Arnim (2 vols., Berlin, 1893 – 6); ed. G. de Budé (2 vols., Leipzig, 1916 – 19); ed. and tr. J. W. Cohoon and H. L. Crosby (*LCL*) (5 vols., London, 1932 – 51).

Diogenes Laertius, Greek historian of philosophy, 3rd cent. AD(?):
   Lives of the Philosophers, ed. and tr. R. D. Hicks (*LCL*) (2 vols., London, 1938).
Diomedes, Latin grammarian, 4th cent. AD:
   Ars grammatica, ed. Henricus Keil, in *Grammatici Latini* (see above, Collections), I,
   pp. 299–529.
Dionysius of Halicarnassus, Greek historian and rhetorician, *fl.* 30 BC:
   Critical works, including the spurious *Ars rhetorica*, ed. Hermann Usener and
   Ludwig Radermacher (2 vols., Leipzig, 1899–1929); tr. Stephen Usener (*LCL*)
   (in progress, 2 vols. so far, London, 1974–   ); ed. and tr. Germaine Aujac (in
   progress, 2 vols. so far, Paris, 1978–   );
   De Dinarcho, ed. with commentary Gerardo Marenghi (Florence, 1970);
   De Thucydide, ed. with commentary Giuseppe Pavano (Palermo, 1958); tr. with
   commentary W. K. Pritchett (Berkeley, 1975);
   Three Literary Letters, ed. and tr. W. R. Roberts (Cambridge, 1901);
   On Literary Composition, ed. and tr. W. R. Roberts (Cambridge, 1910).
Ennius, Quintus, Latin epic and dramatic poet, 239–169 BC:
   Fr., ed. and tr. E. H. Warmington, *The Remains of Old Latin* (see above, Collections),
   I (whole vol.).
   Annales, ed. with commentary Otto Skutsch (Oxford, 1985).
Eratosthenes of Cyrene, Greek philologist and scientist, *c.* 275–194 BC:
   Geographia, fr. ed. Hugo Berger (Leipzig, 1880; rpt. Amsterdam, 1964).
Eunapius of Sardis, Greek sophist, AD *c.* 346–414:
   Lives of the Philosophers, ed. Giuseppe Giangrande (Rome, 1956); ed. and tr.
   W. C. Wright (*LCL*) (London, 1922).
Fortunatianus, Consultus, Latin rhetorician, 4th cent. AD:
   Ars rhetorica, ed. and tr. with commentary, Lucia Calboli-Montefusco (Bologna,
   1979).
Fronto, Marcus Cornelius, Roman orator, AD *c.* 100–166:
   Epistles, ed. and tr. C. R. Haines (*LCL*) (2 vols., London, 1928).
Gellius, Aulus, Latin grammarian, AD *c.* 130–180:
   Noctes Atticae, ed. P. K. Marshall (2 vols., Oxford, 1968); ed. and tr. J. C. Rolfe
   (*LCL*) (3 vols., London, 1946).
Gorgias of Leontini, Greek sophist, *c.* 480–*c.* 380 BC:
   Encomium of Helen and fr., ed. Hermann Diels and Walther Kranz (see above,
   Collections), III, pp. 271–307; ed. Ludwig Radermacher (see above, Collec-
   tions), pp. 42–66; tr. Larue Van Hook, in *Isocrates* (*LCL*) (London, 1945), III,
   pp. 55–7; tr. G. A. Kennedy, in R. K. Sprague (ed.) (see above, Collections),
   pp. 30–67.
Heraclitus of Ephesus, Greek philosopher, *fl. c.* 480 BC:
   Fr., ed. Hermann Diels and Walther Kranz (see above, Collections), I, pp.
   139–90.
Heraclitus, Greek philosopher, 1st cent. AD:
   Allegoriae Homericae, ed. Félix Buffière (Paris, 1962).
Hermagoras of Temnos, Greek rhetorician, 2nd cent. BC:
   Fr., ed. Dieter Matthes, *Lustrum*, 3 (1958), 58–214.
Hermetica, gnostic treatises on astrology, magic, and alchemy, 2nd to 4th cent.
   AD (?):

Corpus, ed. Walter Scott (4 vols., Oxford, 1924–6).

Hermogenes of Tarsus, Greek rhetorician, *fl.* AD 176:

Peri ideōn (*On Ideas of Style*), ed. Hugo Rabe (Leipzig, 1913); tr. C.W. Wooten (Chapel Hill, 1987).

Hesiod, Greek poet, *fl. c.* 700 BC (?):

Theogonia, Opera et dies, Scutum, Fragmenta selecta, ed. Friedrich Solmsen, Reinhold Merkelbach, and M.L. West (2nd ed., Oxford, 1983);

Theogony, ed. with commentary M.L. West (Oxford, 1966);

Works and Days, ed. with commentary M.L. West (Oxford, 1978);

Fr., ed. Reinhold Merkelbach and M.L. West (Oxford, 1967).

Homer, Greek poet, *fl. c.* 700 BC (?):

Works, ed. D.B. Monroe and T.W. Allen (5 vols., Oxford, 1902–12).

Homeric Hymns, fr. of the Cyclic Epics, etc., 7–6th cent. BC:

ed. T.W. Allen in Homeri *Opera* (Oxford, 1912), V, pp. 1–92; ed. and tr. H.G. Evelyn-White in *Hesiod* (*LCL*) (London, 1936), pp. 286–597.

Horatius Flaccus, Quintus, Latin poet, 65–8 BC:

Works, ed. with commentary E.C. Wickham (3rd ed., 2 vols., Oxford, 1891–6); ed. Friedrich Klingner (3rd ed., Leipzig, 1959);

(*Ars poetica* = *Epistles* 2.3)

Epistles, ed. with commentary A.S. Wilkins (London, 1896); ed. with commentary C.O. Brink (2 vols., Cambridge, 1971–82);

Odes, ed. with commentary, Kenneth Quinn (London, 1980); Books 1–2, ed. with commentary R.G.M. Nisbet and Margaret Hubbard (2 vols., Oxford, 1970–8);

Satires, ed. with commentary Arthur Palmer (London, 1891);

Satires and *Epistles*, tr. Niall Rudd (Penguin, 1979); tr. of *Epistles* 2.1, 2.3 (*Ars poetica*) and *Satires* 1.4, 1.10, in Russell and Winterbottom (eds.), *Ancient Literary Criticism* (see above, Collections), pp. 266–91.

Isocrates, Greek orator, 436–338 BC:

Orationes, ed. and tr. G.B. Norlin and LaRue Van Hook (*LCL*) (3 vols., London, 1928–45); ed. and tr. Georges Mathieu and Emile Brémond (4 vols., Paris, 1956–62).

Juvenalis, Decimus Junius, Latin satirist, AD *c.* 65–*c.* 120:

Satires, ed. W.V. Classen (Oxford, 1959); tr. Peter Green (Penguin, 1967).

Lactantius, Lucius Caelius Firmianus, Latin theologian, AD *c.* 250–*c.* 325:

Divinae institutiones, ed. Samuel Brandt (*Corpus scriptorum ecclesiasticorum Latinorum*, 19) (Vienna, 1890); tr. M.F. McDonald (Washington, 1964).

Longinus, Greek rhetorician, 1st or 2nd cent. AD:

Peri hupseōs (*On Sublimity*), ed. and tr. with commentary W.R. Roberts (Cambridge, 1907); ed. with commentary D.A. Russell (Oxford, 1964); tr. A.D. Russell (Oxford, 1965), rev. in Russell and Winterbottom (eds.), *Ancient Literary Criticism* (see above, Collections), pp. 462–503; Boileau's tr. (1674), ed. C.H. Boudhors (Paris, 1942).

Lucian of Samosata, Greek satirist, AD *c.* 120–180:

Works, ed. and tr. A.M. Harmon *et al.* (*LCL*) (8 vols., London, 1913–67); ed. M.D. Macleod (in progress, 4 vols. so far, Oxford, 1972–); tr. H.W. and F.G. Fowler (4 vols., Oxford, 1905);

How to Write History, ed. with commentary Helene Homeyer (Munich, 1965).

Lucilius, Gaius, Latin satirist, *c.* 170 – 102 BC:
Fr., ed. and tr. E. H. Warmington, *The Remains of Old Latin* (see above,
Collections), III, pp. 2 – 423; ed. Werner Krenkel (2 vols., Leiden, 1970).

Macrobius, Ambrosius Theodosius, Latin grammarian, *fl.* AD 400:
Commentarii in somnium Scipionis, ed. J. A. Willis (Leipzig, 1963); tr. W. H. Stahl
(New York, 1952);
Saturnalia, ed. J. A. Willis (Leipzig, 1970).

Martianus Capella, Latin encyclopaedist, early 5th cent. AD:
De nuptiis Mercurii et Philologiae, ed. J. A. Willis (Leipzig, 1983); tr. W. H. Stahl,
Richard Johnson, and E. L. Burge (2 vols., New York, 1971 – 7); commentary
by Danuta Shanzer (Berkeley, 1987).

Menander, Greek rhetorician, *fl.* AD 300 (?):
Treatises on Epideictic, ed. and tr. D. A. Russell and N. G. Wilson (Oxford, 1981).

Naevius, Gnaeus, Latin epic and dramatic poet, *c.* 270 – 202 BC:
Fr., ed. and tr. E. H. Warmington, *The Remains of Old Latin* (see above, Collections),
II, pp. 46 – 156.

Olympiodorus of Alexandria, Greek philosopher, 6th cent. AD:
Prolegomena (to Platonic philosophy), ed. K. F. Hermann, in *Platonis dialogi* (6 vols.,
Leipzig, 1877 – 99), VI (1884), pp. 196 – 222; ed. and tr. L. G. Westerink
(Amsterdam, 1962); (to Aristotelian logic), ed. Adolf Busse, *Commentaria in
Aristotelem Graeca* (Berlin, 1902), XII, 1, pp. 1 – 25.

Origenes Adamantus, Greek theologian, AD *c.* 185 – *c.* 255:
De principiis, ed. Henri Crouzel and Manlio Simonetti (5 vols., Paris, 1978);
tr. G. W. Butterworth (London, 1936).

Parmenides of Elea, Greek philosopher, *fl. c.* 480 BC:
Fr., ed. Hermann Diels and Walther Kranz (see above, Collections), I, pp. 217 – 46.

Parthenius, Greek poet, 1st cent. BC:
Love Romances and fr., ed. and tr. S. Gaselee, in *Longus, Daphnis and Chloe* (*LCL*)
(London, 1916), pp. 256 – 379.

Petronius Arbiter, Latin satirist, d. AD 66:
Satiricon, ed. and tr. Alfred Ernout (Paris, 1958); tr. William Arrowsmith (New York,
1959).

Philo of Alexandria (Philo Judaeus), Greek theologian, *c.* 20 BC – AD *c.* 40:
Works, ed. and tr. F. H. Colson and G. H. Whitaker (*LCL*) (12 vols., London,
1929 – 53).

Philodemus of Gadara, Greek philosopher, *c.* 110 – 35 BC:
Peri poiēmatōn (*On Poems*), ed. and tr. Francisca Sbordone, *Ricerche sui papiri ercolanesi*,
1 – 2 (1969 – 71); Book 5, ed. and tr. Christian Jensen (Berlin, 1923; rpt. Zurich,
1973);
Rhetorica, ed. Siegfried Sudhaus (2 vols., Leipzig, 1892); tr. H. M. Hubbell, *Trans-
actions of the Connecticut Academy of Arts and Sciences*, 23 (1920), 243 – 382; Books 1 – 2,
ed. and tr. F. Longo Auricchio, *Ricerche sui papiri ercolanesi*, 3 (1977); Book 5,
ed. and tr. M. Ferrario, *Cronica ercolanesia*, 10 (1980), 55 – 124;
Hypomnematikon, in Sudhaus (ed.) (see above), II, pp. 196 – 303;
On the Good King According to Homer, ed. Alessandro Olivieri (Leipzig, 1909); ed. and
tr. Tiziano Dorandi (Naples, 1982).

Philostratus, Flavius, Greek sophist, *fl.* AD 200:

Life of Apollonius of Tyana, ed. C. L. Layser (Leipzig, 1870; rpt. Hildesheim, 1964); tr. C. P. Jones (Penguin, 1970);

Lives of the Sophists, ed. C. L. Kayser (Leipzig, 1871); rpt. Hildesheim, 1964); ed. and tr. W. C. Wright (*LCL*) (London, 1922).

Philostratus Lemnius, Greek sophist, *fl.* AD *c.* 220:

Imagines, ed. C. L. Kayser (Leipzig, 1871; rpt. Hildesheim, 1964); tr. Arthur Fairbanks (*LCL*) (London, 1931).

Pindar, Greek lyric poet, *c.* 520 – *c.* 438 BC:

Epinician Odes and fr., ed. C. M. Bowra (2nd ed., Oxford, 1947);

Fr., ed. Bruno Snell and Herweg Maehler (Leipzig, 1975);

Scholia, ed. A. B. Drachman (3 vols., Leipzig, 1903 – 27).

Plato, Greek philosopher, *c.* 429 – 347 BC:

Works, ed. John Burnet (5 vols., Oxford, 1903 – 15); ed. and tr. Maurice Croiset *et al.* (14 vols., Paris, 1925 – 56); tr. Benjamin Jowett (4 vols., Oxford, 1871; rev. D. J. Allen and H. E. Dale, 1953); tr. R. E. Allen (in progress, 1 vol. so far, New Haven, 1984 –);

Cratylus, ed. and tr. H. N. Fowler (*LCL*) (London, 1937); commentary by J. C. Rijlaarsdam, *Platon über die Sprache* (Utrecht, 1978);

Gorgias, ed. with commentary E. R. Dodds (Oxford, 1959); tr. W. C. Helmbold (Indianapolis, 1952; rpt. 1981);

Ion, ed. with notes J. M. MacGregor (Cambridge, 1912; rpt. 1956); tr. D. A. Russell in Russell and Winterbottom (eds.), *Ancient Literary Criticism* (see above, Collections), pp. 39 – 50;

Laws, ed. with commentary E. B. England (2 vols., Manchester, 1921; rpt. New York, 1975); tr. with notes T. L. Pangle (New York, 1980);

Republic, ed. with commentary James Adam (2 vols., Cambridge, 1902; 2nd ed. rev. D. A. Rees, 1963); tr. Allan Bloom (New York, 1968); tr. G. M. A. Grube (Indianapolis, 1974);

Phaedrus, tr. with commentary Reginald Hackforth (Cambridge, 1952); commentary by G. J. de Vries (Amsterdam, 1969);

Protagoras, tr. with notes C. C. W. Taylor (Oxford, 1976); commentary by B. A. F. Hubbard and E. S. Karnofsky (Chicago, 1982);

Bibliography: Harold Cherniss (1950 – 57) in *Lustrum*, 4 (1959); 5 (1960), esp. 520 – 54; Luc Brisson (1958 – 75) in *Lustrum*, 20 (1977), 5 – 304; Marcel Deschoux, *Comprendre Platon: Un siècle de bibliographie platonicienne de la langue française, 1880 – 1980* (Paris, 1981).

Plautus, Titus Maccius, Latin comic poet, *c.* 254 – 184 BC:

Plays, ed. and tr. Paul Nixon (*LCL*) (5 vols., London, 1916 – 38).

Plinius Caecilius Secundus, Gaius, Latin orator and epistolographer, AD 61 – 112:

Epistulae, ed. R. A. B. Mynors (Oxford, 1963); tr. Betty Radice (*LCL*) (2 vols., London, 1975); commentary by A. N. Sherwin-White (Oxford, 1966).

Plutarch, Greek biographer and philosopher, AD *c.* 50 – 125:

Essays, genuine and spurious, known collectively as *Moralia*, ed. and tr. F. C. Babbitt *et al.* (*LCL*) (15 vols., London, 1927 – 69); ed. and tr. Robert Klaerr *et al.* (in progress, 4 vols. so far, Paris, 1974 –);

Spurious works discussed in the text: *Life and Poetry of Homer*, ed. G. N. Bernardakis, in *Plutarchi moralia*, (7 vols., Leipzig, 1888–96), VII (1896); ed. T. W. Allen, Homeri *Opera* (Oxford, 1912), V, pp. 238–44;

On Music, ed. Klaus Ziegler, in *Plutarchi moralia*, VI, 3 (3rd ed., Leipzig, 1966), pp. 1–37.

Porphyry of Tyre, Greek philosopher, AD 234–*c*. 304:

On the Cave of the Nymphs, ed. and tr. Classics Seminar 609, *Arethusa*, Monograph 1 (Buffalo, 1969); ed. with commentary L. Simonini (Milan, 1986); tr. Robert Lamberton (Barrytown, New York, 1983).

Proclus, Greek philosopher, AD 412–485:

Commentaries on Plato's Republic, ed. Wilhelm Kroll (Leipzig, 1899); tr. A.-J. Festugière (Paris, 1970); on Plato's *Timaeus*, ed. Ernst Diehl (Leipzig, 1903); tr. A.-J. Festugière (4 vols., Paris, 1966–8).

Quintilianus, Marcus Fabius, Latin rhetorician, AD *c*. 35–*c*. 95:

Institutio oratoria, ed. Michael Winterbottom (2 vols., Oxford, 1970); ed. and tr. Jean Cousin (7 vols., Paris, 1975–80); tr. H. E. Butler (*LCL*) (4 vols., London, 1921–2).

Rhetorica ad Alexandrum, Greek treatise preserved with the works of Aristotle, attributed to Anaximenes of Lampsacus, late 4th cent. BC:

ed. Manfred Fuhrmann (Leipzig, 1966); tr. Harris Rackham, in Aristotle, *Problems* (*LCL*) (London, 1957), II, pp. 258–449.

Rhetorica ad Herennium, Latin treatise preserved with the works of Cicero, sometimes attributed to Cornificius, written about 84 BC:

ed. and tr. with notes Harry Caplan (*LCL*) (London, 1954); ed. with commentary Gualtiero Calboli (Bologna, 1969).

Seneca, Lucius Annaeus (the Elder), Latin historian, *c*. 55 BC–AD *c*. 40:

Controversiae and *Suasoriae*, ed. and tr. Michael Winterbottom (*LCL*) (2 vols., London, 1974).

Seneca, Lucius Annaeus (the Younger), Latin philosopher, *c*. 1 BC–AD 65:

Epistulae morales, ed. and tr. R. M. Gummere (*LCL*) (3 vols., London, 1917–25).

Servius, Latin grammarian, *fl*. AD 400:

Commentarii in Vergilii carmina, ed. Georg Thilo and Hermann Hagen (3 vols., Leipzig, 1881–1901); ed. E. K. Rand *et al*. (in progress, 3 vols. so far, American Philological Association, 1946–).

Sextus Empiricus, Greek philosopher, *fl*. AD 180:

Works, ed. and tr. R. G. Bury (*LCL*) (4 vols., London, 1933–49).

Suetonius Tranquillus, Gaius, Latin biographer and grammarian, AD *c*. 69–140:

De grammaticis et rhetoribus, ed. with commentary Francesco della Corte (3rd ed., Turin, 1968); ed. and tr. J. C. Rolfe, *Suetonius* (*LCL*) (London, 1914), II, pp. 394–449; *De poetis*, ed. with commentary, Augusto Rostagni (Turin, 1944); ed. and tr. Rolfe, *Suetonius* (see above), pp. 450–507.

Syrianus, Greek philosopher and rhetorician, 5th cent. AD:

Commentarii in Hermogenem, ed. Hugo Rabe (2 vols., Leipzig, 1893).

Tacitus, Cornelius, Latin historian, AD 65–*c*. 115:

Dialogus de oratoribus, ed. with commentary Alfred Gudeman (2nd ed., Berlin, 1914); ed. Henry Furneaux (Oxford, 1939); tr. H. W. Benario (Indianapolis, 1967); tr. Michael Winterbottom, in Russell and Winterbottom (eds.), *Ancient Literary Criticism* (see above, Collections), pp. 432–59.

Terentius Afer, Publius, Latin comic poet, 185–159 BC:
Plays, ed. with commentary, S. G. Ashmore (2nd ed., New York, 1908); ed. and
tr. John Sargeaunt (*LCL*) (2 vols., London, 1912).
Tertullianus, Quintus Septimius Florens, Latin theologian, AD *c.* 160–*c.* 225:
Works, ed. E. Dekkers, *Corpus Christianorum*, series Latina, 1–2 (Turnhout, 1954);
Apology, On Spectacles, ed. and tr. T. R. Glover (*LCL*) (London, 1977).
Theophrastus, Greek philosopher, *c.* 370–*c.* 284 BC:
Peri lexeōs (*On Style*), ed. Augustus Meyer (Leipzig, 1910).
Varro, Marcus Terentius, Latin encyclopaedist, 116–27 BC:
De lingua Latina, ed. and tr. R. G. Kent (*LCL*) (2 vols., London, 1951);
Fr., ed. Hyginus Funaioli, *Grammaticae Romanae fragmenta* (Leipzig, 1907).
Velleius Paterculus, Gaius, Latin historian, *c.* 19 BC–AD *c.* 35:
Roman Histories, ed. and tr. F. W. Shipley (*LCL*) (London, 1924).
Xenophanes of Colophon, Greek philosopher, 6th cent. BC:
Fr., ed. Hermann Diels and Walther Kranz (see above, Collections), I, pp. 113–39.
Zenodotus of Ephesus, Greek grammarian, *fl. c.* 284 BC:
Fr., ed. Adolf Römer, *Abhandlungen der königlichen bayerischen Akademie der Wissenschaften*, Philosophisch-philologische Klasse, 17 (1886).

Secondary Sources

General works on classical criticism

Atkins, J. W. H., *Literary Criticism in Antiquity: A Sketch of its Development* (2 vols., Cambridge, 1934; rpt. London, 1952).
Baldwin, C. S., *Ancient Rhetoric and Poetic* (New York, 1924; rpt. 1959).
Bundy, M. W., 'The theory of imagination in classical and medieval thought', *University of Illinois Studies in Language and Literature*, 12, 2–3 (1927), 7–289.
The Cambridge History of Classical Literature; I: Greek Literature, ed. P. E. Easterling and B. M. W. Knox (Cambridge, 1985); *II: Latin Literature*, ed. E. J. Kenney and W. V. Clausen (Cambridge, 1982).
Clark, D. L., *Rhetoric in Greco-Roman Education* (New York, 1957).
Crane, R. S. (ed.), *Critics and Criticism: Ancient and Modern* (Chicago, 1952).
Drijepondt, H. L. F., *Die Antike Theorie der Varietas: Dynamik und Wechsel in auf und ab als Charakteristikum vom Stil und Structur* (*Spudasmata*, 37) (Hildesheim, 1979).
Eden, Kathy, *Poetic and Legal Fiction in the Aristotelian Tradition* (Princeton, 1986).
Egger, Emile, *Essai sur l'histoire de la critique chez les grecs* (Paris, 1849).
Fuhrmann, Manfred, *Einführung in die antike Dichtungstheorie* (Darmstadt, 1973).
Grube, G. M. A., *The Greek and Roman Critics* (London, 1965).
Hadot, Ilsetraut, *Arts libéraux et philosophie dans la pensée antique* (Paris, 1984).
Havelock, E. A., and Hershebell, Jackson (eds.), *Communication Arts in the Ancient World* (New York, 1978).
Heldmann, Konrad, *Antike Theorien über Entwicklung und Verfall der Redekunst* (*Zetemata*, 77) (Munich, 1982).
Jaeger, Werner, *Paideia: The Ideals of Greek Culture*, tr. Gilbert Highet (2nd ed., 3 vols., New York, 1945).

Kennedy, G. A., *Classical Rhetoric and its Christian and Secular Tradition from Ancient to Modern Times* (Chapel Hill, 1980).

Lausberg, Heinrich, *Elemente der literarischen Rhetorik* (2nd ed., Munich, 1963). *Handbuch der literarischen Rhetorik* (2 vols., Munich, 1960).

Lesky, Albin, *A History of Greek Literature*, tr. James Willis and Cornelis de Heer (London, 1966).

Marrou, H.-I., *A History of Education in Antiquity*, tr. George Lamb (London, 1956).

Martin, Josef, *Antike Rhetorik: Technik und Method (Handbuch der Altertumswissenschaft*, II, 3) (Munich, 1974).

McCall, M. H., *Ancient Rhetorical Theories of Simile and Comparison* (Cambridge, Mass., 1969).

Michel, Alain, *La parole et la beauté: Rhétorique et esthétique dans la tradition occidentale* (Paris, 1982).

Norden, Eduard, *Die Antike Kunstprosa* (5th ed., Stuttgart, 1958).

Pfeiffer, Rudolf, *History of Classical Scholarship from the Beginnings to the End of the Hellenistic Age* (Oxford, 1968).

Roberts, W. R., *Greek Rhetoric and Literary Criticism* (New York, 1928; rpt. 1963).

Rollinson, Philip, *Classical Theories of Allegory and Christian Culture* (Pittsburgh, 1981).

Russell, D. A., *Criticism in Antiquity* (London, 1981).

Ruthven, K. K., *Critical Assumptions* (Cambridge, 1979).

Saintsbury, G. E. B., *A History of Criticism and Literary Taste in Europe* (3 vols., Edinburgh, 1900–4).

Scaglione, Aldo, *The Classical Theory of Composition from its Origins to the Present: A Historical Survey* (Chapel Hill, 1972).

Todorov, Tzvetan, *Theories of the Symbol*, tr. Catherine Porter (Ithaca, 1982).

Trimpi, Wesley, *Muses of One Mind: The Literary Analysis of Experience and its Continuity* (Princeton, 1983).

Van Hook, LaRue, *The Metaphorical Terminology of Greek Rhetoric and Literary Criticism* (Chicago, 1905).

Verdennius, W. J., 'The principles of Greek literary criticism', *Mnemosyne*, new series 4, 36 (1983), 14–59.

Whitman, John, *Allegory: The Dynamics of an Ancient and Medieval Technique* (Cambridge, Mass., 1987).

Chapters 1–4

Alexiou, Margaret, *The Ritual Lament in Greek Tradition* (Cambridge, 1974).

Allen, T. W., *Homer: The Origins and the Transmission* (Oxford, 1924).

Allen, W. S., *Accent and Rhythm: Prosodic Features of Latin and Greek: A Study in Theory and Reconstruction* (Cambridge, 1973).

Anderson, W. D., *Ethos and Education in Greek Music: The Evidence of Poetry and Philosophy* (Cambridge, Mass., 1966).

Annas, Julia, *An Introduction to Plato's Republic* (Oxford, 1981). 'Plato on the triviality of literature', in Moravcsik and Temko (eds.), *Plato on Beauty* (see below), pp. 1–28.

Arnhart, Larry, *Aristotle on Political Reasoning: A Commentary on the Rhetoric* (DeKalb, Illinois, 1981).

Bareis, K. H., *Comoedia: Die Entwicklung der Komodiendiskussion von Aristotles bis Ben Jonson* (Frankfurt, 1982).

Barker, Andrew, *Greek Musical Writings; I: The Musician and his Art* (Cambridge, 1984).

Barnes, Jonathan *et al.* (eds.), *Articles on Aristotle; 4: Psychology and Aesthetics* (London, 1979).

Bausinger, Hermann, *Formen der 'Volkespoesie'* (2nd ed., Berlin, 1980).

Belfiore, Elizabeth, 'Aristotle's concept of praxis in the *Poetics*', *Classical Journal*, 79 (1983), 110–24.

'"Lies unlike the truth": Plato on Hesiod, *Theogony* 27', *TAPA* 115 (1985), 47–57.

'Plato's greatest accusation against poetry', *Canadian Journal of Philosophy*, Suppl. vol. 9 (1983), 39–62.

'A theory of imitation in Plato's *Republic*', *TAPA*, 114 (1984), 121–46.

Ben-Amos, Dan, 'Analytical categories and ethnic genres', in Dan Ben-Amos (ed.), *Folklore Genres* (Austin, 1976), pp. 215–42.

Benveniste, Emile, *Le vocabulaire des institutions indo-européennes; I: Economie, parenté, société; II: Pouvoir, droit, religion* (Paris, 1969); *Indo-European Language and Society* tr. E. Palmer (London, 1973).

Brelich, Angelo, *Guerre, agoni e culti nella Grecia arcaica* (Bonn, 1961).

Bremer, J. M., *Hamartia: Tragic Error in the Poetics of Aristotle and in Greek Tragedy* (Amsterdam, 1969).

Brisson, Luc, *Platon: Les mots et les mythes* (Paris, 1982).

Bundy, E. L., *Studia Pindarica* (Berkeley, 1986).

Burger, Ronna, *Plato's Phaedrus: A Defense of a Philosophic Art of Writing* (University, Alabama, 1980).

Burkert, Walter, *Greek Religion*, tr. J. Raffan (Cambridge, Mass., 1985).

Homo Necans: The Anthropology of Ancient Greek Sacrificial Ritual and Myth, tr. P. Bing (Berkeley, 1983).

'Mythische Denken', in H. Poser (ed.), *Philosophie und Mythos* (Berlin, 1979), pp. 16–39.

Burnett, A. P., *The Art of Bacchylides* (Cambridge, Mass., 1985).

Butcher, S. H., *Aristotle's Theory of Poetry and Fine Art* (4th ed., London, 1907).

Calame, Claude, *Les choeurs de jeunes filles en Grèce archaïque; I: Morphologie, fonction religieuse et sociale; II: Alcman* (Rome, 1977).

Cameron, Alistair, *Plato's Affair with Tragedy* (Cincinnati, 1978).

Campbell, D. A., 'Flutes and elegiac couplets', *JHS*, 84 (1964), 63–8.

Cassirer, Ernst, 'Eidos und eidolon: Das Problem des Schönen und der Kunst in Platons Dialogen', *Vorträge der Bibliothek Warburg* (1922–3), 1–27.

Chantraine, Pierre, *Dictionnaire étymologique de la langue grecque* (4 vols., continuously paginated, Paris, 1968–80).

Cole, Thomas, 'Archaic truth', *Quaderni Urbinati*, 13 (1983), 7–28.

Collingwood, R. G., 'Plato's philosophy of art', *Mind*, 34 (1925), 154–72.

Comotti, Giovanni, *La musica nella cultura greca e romana* (Turin, 1979).

Conley, T. M., 'The Greekless reader and Aristotle's *Rhetoric*', *Quarterly Journal of Speech*, 65 (1979), 74–9.

Cooper, Lane, *The Poetics of Aristotle: Its Meaning and Influence* (Boston, 1923; rpt. New York, 1963).

Cross, R.C., and Woozley, A.D., *Plato's Republic: A Philosophical Commentary* (London, 1964).

Derbolav, Josef, *Platons Sprachphilosophie im Kratylos und in den späteren Schriften* (Darmstadt, 1972).

Derrida, Jacques, 'La pharmacie de Plato', in *La dissemination* (Paris, 1972), pp. 71–197; *Dissemination*, tr. Barbara Johnson (Chicago, 1981), pp. 61–171.

Descat, Raymond, 'Idéologie et communication dans la poésie grecque archaïque', *Quaderni Urbinati*, new series 9 (1981), 7–27.

Detienne, Marcel, *Les maîtres de vérité dans la Grèce archaïque* (2nd ed., Paris, 1973).

Diller, Hans, 'Probleme des Platonischen *Ion*', *Hermes*, 83 (1955), 171–87.

Dorter, Kenneth, 'The *Ion*. Plato's characterisation of art', *Journal of Aesthetics and Art Criticism*, 32 (1973), 65–78.

Ducrot, Oswald, and Todorov, Tzvetan, *Dictionnaire encyclopédique des sciences du langage* (Paris, 1972); *Encyclopedic Dictionary of the Sciences of Language*, tr. C. Porter (Baltimore, 1979).

Düring, Ingmar, *Aristoteles: Darstellung und Interpretationen seines Denken* (Heidelberg, 1966).

Edmunds, Lowell, 'The genre of Theognidean poetry', in T.J. Figueira and Gregory Nagy (eds.), *Theognis of Megara: Poetry and the Polis* (Baltimore, 1985), pp. 96–111.

Elias, J.A., *Plato's Defence of Poetry* (London, 1984).

Else, G.F., *Aristotle's Poetics: The Argument* (Cambridge, Mass., 1957).

'"Imitation" in the fifth century', *CP*, 53 (1958), 73–90.

Plato and Aristotle on Poetry, ed. Peter Burian (Chapel Hill, 1986).

'The structure and date of book 10 of Plato's *Republic*', *Abhandlungen der Heidelberger Akademie der Wissenschaften*, Philosophisch-historische Klasse (1972), Abhandlung 3.

Ferrari, G.R.F., *Listening to the Cicadas: A Study of Plato's Phaedrus* (Cambridge, 1987).

Figueira, T.J., 'The Theognidea and Megarian society', in T.J. Figueira and Gregory Nagy (eds.), *Theognis of Megara: Poetry and the Polis* (Baltimore, 1985), pp. 112–58.

Finnegan, R.H., *Oral Poetry: Its Nature, Significance, and Social Context* (Cambridge, 1977).

Flasher, Hellmut, *Der Dialog Ion als Zeugnis Platonischer Philosophie* (Berlin, 1958).

Foley, H.P., *Ritual Irony: Poetry and Sacrifice in Euripides* (Ithaca, 1985).

Fontenrose, Joseph, *The Delphic Oracle: Its Responses and Operations, with a Catalogue of Responses* (Berkeley, 1978).

Ford, A.L., 'Early Greek terms for poetry: *Aoidē, Epos, Poiēsis*', Ph.D. dissertation, Yale University, 1981.

'The seal of Theognis', in T.J. Figueira and Gregory Nagy (eds.), *Theognis of Megara: Poetry and the Polis* (Baltimore, 1985), pp. 82–95.

Forderer, Manfred, *Zum Homerischen Margites* (Amsterdam, 1960).

Fortenbaugh, W.W., *Aristotle on Emotion: A Contribution to Philosophical Psychology, Rhetoric, Poetics, Politics, and Ethics* (New York, 1975).

Fowler, R.L., 'Aristotle on the period (*Rhet.* 3.9)', *CQ*, 32 (1982), 89–99.

Fränkel, Hermann, *Early Greek Poetry and Philosophy*, tr. Moses Hadas and James Willis (New York, 1975).

Frede, Dorothea, 'The impossibility of perfection: Socrates' criticism of Simonides' poem in the *Protagoras*', *Review of Metaphysics*, 39 (1986), 729–53.

Gadamer, Hans-Georg, 'Plato and the poets', in *Dialogue and Dialectic: Eight Hermeneutical Studies in Plato*, tr. P.C. Smith (New Haven, 1980), pp. 39–72.

Gaiser, Konrad, *Name und Sache in Platons Kratylos* (Heidelberg, 1974).

Gernet, Louis, *Anthropologie de la Grèce antique* (Paris, 1968); *The Anthropology of Ancient Greece*, tr. John Hamilton and Blaise Nagy (Baltimore, 1981).

Gill, Christopher, 'The ethos/pathos distinction in rhetorical and literary criticism', *CQ*, 34 (1984), 149–66.

Golden, Leon, 'Plato's concept of *mimesis*', *British Journal of Aesthetics*, 15, 2 (1975), 118–31.

Goldschmidt, V., 'Le problème de la tragédie', *REG*, 61 (1948), 19–63.

Gomme, A. W., *The Greek Attitude to Poetry and History* (Berkeley, 1954).

Goody, Jack, 'The consequences of literacy', in Jack Goody (ed.), *Literacy in Traditional Societies* (Cambridge, 1969), pp. 27–68.

Gould, Thomas, 'Plato's hostility to art', *Arion*, 3 (1964), 70–91.

Greene, W. C., 'Plato's view of poetry', *HSCP*, 29 (1918), 1–75.

Grey, D. R., 'Art in the *Republic*', *Philosophy*, 27 (1952), 291–310.

Griffin, Jasper, 'The epic cycle and the uniqueness of Homer', *JHS*, 97 (1977), 39–53.

Griswold, Charles, 'The ideas and criticism of poetry in Plato's *Republic*, book 10', *Journal of the History of Philosophy*, 19, 2 (1981), 135–50.

Self-Knowledge in Plato's Phaedrus (New Haven, 1986).

Guillén, Claudio, *Entre lo uno y lo diverso: Introducción a la literatura comparanda* (Barcelona, 1985).

Gundert, Hermann, 'Enthousiasmos und logos bei Platon', *Lexis*, 2 (1949), 25–46; rpt. in *Platonstudien* (Amsterdam, 1977), pp. 1–22.

'Die Simonides-Interpretation in Platons *Protagoras*', in *Hermeneia: Festschrift Otto Regenbogen* (Heidelberg, 1952), pp. 71–93; rpt. in *Platonstudien* (Amsterdam, 1977), pp. 23–45.

'Zum Spiel bei Platon', in *Beispiele. Festschrift für Eugen Fink* (Heidelberg, 1954), pp. 188–221; rpt. in *Platonstudien* (Amsterdam, 1977), pp. 65–98.

Guthrie, W. K. C., *A History of Greek Philosophy* (6 vols., Cambridge, 1962–81).

Halliwell, Stephen, *Aristotle's Poetics* (London, 1986).

Harriott, Rosemary, *Poetry and Criticism before Plato* (London, 1969).

Hartog, F., *Le miroir d'Herodote: Essai sur la représentation de l'autre* (Paris, 1980).

Harvey, A. E., 'The classification of Greek lyric poetry', *CQ*, 5 (1955), 157–75.

Havelock, E. A., *The Literate Revolution and its Consequences* (Princeton, 1981).

Preface to Plato (Cambridge, Mass., 1963).

Henderson, M. I., 'Ancient Greek music', in Egon Wellesz (ed.), *New Oxford History of Music; I: Ancient and Oriental Music* (London, 1957), pp. 336–403.

Herington, C. J., *Poetry into Drama: Early Tragedy and the Greek Poetic Tradition* (Berkeley, 1985).

Herrick, M. T., *The Poetics of Aristotle in England* (New Haven, 1930).

House, Humphry, *Aristotle's Poetics*, rev. by Colin Hardie (London, 1956).

Hubbard, T. K., *The Pindaric Mind: A Study of Logical Structure in Early Greek Poetry* (Leiden, 1985).

Huxley, G. L., 'Historical criticism in Aristotle's *Homeric Questions*', *Proceedings of the Royal Irish Academy*, 79 (1979), 73–81.

Irigoin, Jean, *Histoire du texte de Pindare* (Paris, 1952).

Jakobson, Roman, 'Linguistics and poetics', in Thomas Sebeok (ed.), *Style in Language* (Cambridge, Mass., 1960), pp. 350–77.

'Signe zéro', in *Selected Writings* (The Hague, 1971), II, pp. 211–19.

Janko, Richard, *Aristotle on Comedy* (London, 1984).

Johnstone, C. L., 'An Aristotelian trilogy: Ethics, rhetoric, politics, and the search for truth', *Philosophy and Rhetoric*, 13 (1980), 1–24.

Joly, Henri, *Le renversement Platonicien: Logos, episteme, polis* (2nd. ed., Paris, 1980).

Jones, John, *On Aristotle and Greek Tragedy* (London, 1962).

Kannicht, Richard, 'Der alte Streit zwischen Philosophie und Dichtung', *Altsprachliche Unterricht*, 23, 6 (1980), 6–36.

Kerford, G. B., *The Sophistic Movement* (Cambridge, 1981).

Kerford, G. B. (ed.), *The Sophists and their Legacy (Hermes Einzelschriften*, 44) (Wiesbaden, 1981).

Keuls, Eva, *Plato and Greek Painting* (Leiden, 1918).

Kirkwood, G. M., *Early Greek Monody: The History of a Poetic Type* (Ithaca, 1974).

Koller, Hermann, 'Das kitharodischen Prooimion: Eine formgeschtliche Untersuchung', *Philologus*, 100 (1956), 159–206.

Die Mimesis in der Antike (Bern, 1954).

Krischer, Tilman, 'Herodots Prooimion', *Hermes*, 93 (1965), 159–67.

Kuhn, Helmut, 'The true tragedy: On the relationship between Greek tragedy and Plato', *HSCP,* 52 (1941), 1–40; 53 (1942), 37–88.

Kurke, Leslie, 'Pindar's Oikonomia: the house as organizing metaphor in the odes of Pindar', Ph.D. dissertation, Princeton University, 1987.

Lanza, Diego, *Il tiranno e suo pubblico* (Turin, 1977).

Lefkowitz, Mary, '*Tō kai egō*: The first person in Pindar', *HSCP*, 67 (1963), 177–253.

Lodge, R. O., *Plato's Theory of Art* (London, 1953).

Lord, A. B., *The Singer of Tales* (Cambridge, Mass., 1960).

Lord, Carnes, *Education and Culture in the Political Thought of Aristotle* (New York, 1982).

'The intention of Aristotle's *Rhetoric*', *Hermes*, 109 (1981), 326–39.

Lucas, F. L., *Tragedy: Serious Drama in Relation to Aristotle's Poetics* (2nd ed., London, 1957).

Mackenzie, M. M., 'Paradox in Plato's *Phaedrus*', *Proceedings of the Cambridge Philological Society*, 27 (1982), 62–76.

Maehler, Herwig, *Die Auffassung des Dichterberufs im frühen Griechentum bis zur Zeit Pindars* (Göttingen, 1963).

Martin, R. P., 'Hesiod, Odysseus, and the instruction of princes', *TAPA*, 114 (1984), 29–48.

Marzullo, Benedetto, 'Die visuelle Dimension des Teathers bei Aristoteles', *Philologus*, 124 (1980), 189–200.

McKirahan, R. D. Jr., *Plato and Socrates: A Comprehensive Bibliography, 1958–1973* (New York, 1978).

Merriam, A. P., *The Anthropology of Music* (Evanston, Illinois, 1964).

Miller, A. M., '*Phthonos* and *paraphasis*: *Nemean* 8. 19–34', *GRBS*, 23 (1982), 111–20.

Moravscik, Julius, and Tempo, Philip (eds.) *Plato on Beauty, Wisdom, and the Arts* (Totowa, New Jersey, 1982).

Most, G. W., 'Greek lyric poets', in T. J. Luce (ed.), *Ancient Writers, Greece and Rome* (2 vols., New York, 1982), I, pp. 75–98.

The Measures of Praise: Structure and Function in Pindar's Second and Seventh Nemean Odes (Göttingen, 1985).

Mullen, William, *Choreia: Pindar and Dance* (Princeton, 1982).

Murdoch, Iris, *The Fire and the Sun: Why Plato Banished the Artists* (Oxford, 1977).

Murphy, N. R., *The Interpretation of Plato's Republic* (Oxford, 1951).

Nagy, Gregory, 'Ancient Greek praise and epic poetry', in J. M. Foley (ed.), *Tradition in Literature: Interpretation in Context* (Columbia, Missouri, 1986), pp. 89–102.

The Best of the Achaeans: Concepts of the Hero in Archaic Greek Poetry (Baltimore, 1979).

Comparative Studies in Greek and Indic Meter (Cambridge, Mass., 1974).

'Herodotus the *logios*', *Arethusa*, 20 (1987), 175–84, 209–10.

'Hesiod', in T. J. Luce (ed.), *Ancient Writers, Greece and Rome* (2 vols., New York, 1982), I, pp. 43–72.

'On the origins of the Greek hexameter', in Bela Brogyanyi (ed.), *Festschrift Oswald Szemerényi* (Amsterdam, 1979), pp. 611–31.

'*Sēma* and *noēsis*: Some illustrations', *Arethusa*, 16 (1983), 35–55.

'Theognis of Megara: A poet's vision of his city', in T. J. Figueira and Gregory Nagy (eds.), *Theognis of Megara: Poetry and the Polis* (Baltimore, 1985), pp. 22–81.

Nehamas, Alexander, 'Plato on imitation and poetry in *Republic* 10', in Moravscik and Temko (eds.), *Plato on Beauty* (see above), pp. 47–78.

Neschke, A. B., *Die Poetik des Aristoteles. Textstruktur und Textbedeutung; I: Interpretationen; II: Analysen* (Frankfurt, 1980).

Nettl, Bruno, *Music in Primitive Culture* (Cambridge, Mass., 1956).

Theory and Method in Ethnomusicology (New York, 1964).

Nettleship, R. L., *Lectures on the Republic of Plato* (London, 1925).

Nilsson, M. P., *Griechische Feste* (Leipzig, 1906).

Nussbaum, M. C., *The Fragility of Goodness: Luck and Ethics in Greek Tragedy and Philosophy* (Cambridge, 1986).

Oates, W. J., *Plato's View of Art* (New York, 1972).

Olson, Elder (ed.), *Aristotle's Poetics and English Literature* (Chicago, 1965).

Ong, W. J., *Orality and Literacy. The Technologizing of the Word* (London, 1982).

Parry, Milman, *The Making of Homeric Verse: The Collected Papers of Milman Parry*, ed. Adam Parry (Oxford, 1971).

Partee, M. H., 'Plato's banishment of poetry', *Journal of Aesthetics and Art Criticism*, 28 (1970), 209–22.

Plato's Poetics: The Authority of Beauty (Salt Lake City, 1981).

Pfeiffer, Rudolf, *Classical Scholarship*. See above, General works on classical criticism.

Pfister, Friedrich, *Der Reliquienkult im Altertum* (2 vols., Giessen, 1909).

Pickard-Cambridge, A. W., *Dithyramb, Tragedy and Comedy* (2nd ed., rev. by T. B. L. Webster, Oxford, 1962).

Pucci, Pietro, *Odysseus Polytropos: Intertextual Readings in the Odyssey and the Iliad* (Ithaca, 1987).

Race, W. H., *Pindar* (Boston, 1986).

Reitzenstein, Richard, *Epigramm und Skolien: Ein Beitrag zur Geschichte der alexandrinischen Dichtung* (Giessen, 1893).

Rijk, L. M., 'On ancient and medieval semantics and metaphysics: Plato's semantics in his critical period', *Vivarium*, 19 (1981), 81–125; 20 (1982), 97–127.

Ritter, Constantin, *Platos Gesetze* (Leipzig, 1986).

Robb, Kevin (ed.), *Language and Thought in Early Greek Philosophy* (LaSalle, Illinois, 1983).

Rohde, Erwin, *Psyche: Seelencult und Umsterblichkeitsglaube der Griechen* (2 vols., Freiburg, 1898); *Psyche*, tr. W. B. Hillis (New York, 1925; rpt. 1966).

Rösler, Wolfgang, *Dichter und Gruppe: Eine Untersuchung zu den Bedingung und zur historischen Funktion frührer Lyrik am Beispiel Alkaios* (Munich, 1980).

'Die Entdeckung der Fiktionsalität in der Antike', *Poetica* (Munich), 12 (1980), 283–319.

Rosen, S. H., 'Collingwood and Greek aesthetics', *Phronesis*, 4 (1959), 135–48.

Rosenmeyer, T. G., 'Elegiac and elegos', *California Studies in Classical Antiquity*, 1 (1968), 217–31.

Rossi, L. E., 'I generi letterari e le loro leggi scrite e non scritte nelle letterature classiche', *Bulletin of the Institute of Classical Studies*, 18 (London, 1971), 69–94.

Ryan, E. E., 'Plato's *Gorgias* and *Phaedrus* and Aristotle's theory of rhetoric: A speculative account', *Athenaeum*, 57 (1979), 452–61.

Ryle, Gilbert, *Plato's Progress* (Cambridge, 1966).

Saunders, T. J., *Notes on the Laws of Plato* (London, 1972).

Schaerer, René, *La question platonicienne: Etude sur les rapports de la pensée et de l'expression dans les dialogues* (2nd ed., Neuchâtel, 1969).

Schaper, Eva, *Prelude to Aesthetics* (London, 1968).

Scheinberg, Susan, 'The bee maidens of the Homeric *Hymn to Hermes*', HSCP, 83 (1979), 1–28.

Schmitt, Rüdiger, *Dichtung und Dichtersprache in indogermanischer Zeit* (Weisbaden, 1967).

Schofield, Malcolm and Nussbaum, M. C. (eds.), *Language and Logos* (Cambridge, 1982).

Schul, Pierre- Maxim, *Platon et l'art de son temps* (Paris, 1952).

Schwyzer, Eduard, *Griechische Grammatik*, vol. 1 (Munich, 1939).

Seaford, Richard, 'The *hyporchēma* of Pratinas', *Maia*, 29 (1977–8), 81–94.

'On the origins of satyric drama', *Maia*, 28 (1976), 209–21.

Segal, C. P., 'Gorgias and the psychology of the *logos*', HSCP, 66 (1962), 99–155.

Slater, W. J., 'Lyric narrative: Structure and principle', in T. D'Evelyn *et al.* (eds.), *Studies in Classical Lyric: A Hommage to Elroy Bundy* (*Classical Antiquity*, 2) (Berkeley, 1983), pp. 117–32.

Smithson, Isaiah, 'The moral view of Aristotle's *Poetics*', *Journal of the History of Ideas*, 44 (1983), 3–17.

Snodgrass, A. M., *The Dark Age of Greece: An Archaeological Survey of the Eleventh to the Eighth Centuries* (Edinburgh, 1971).

Sörbom, Göran, *Mimesis and Art* (Uppsala, 1966).

Stalley, R. F., *An Introduction to Plato's Laws* (Indianapolis, 1983).

Steven, R. G., 'Plato and the art of his time', *CQ*, 27 (1933), 149–55.

Stinton, T. C. W., '*Hamartia* in Aristotle and Greek tragedy', *CQ*, 25 (1975), 221–54.

Svenbro, Jesper, 'La découpe du poème: Notes sur les origines sacrifielles de la poétique grecque', *Poétique*, 58 (1984), 215–32.

La parole et le marbre: Aux origines de la poétique grecque (Lund, 1976; rev. Italian ed., Turin, 1984).

Swiggers, Pierre, 'Cognitive aspects of Aristotle's theory of metaphor', *Glotta*, 62 (1984), 40–5.

Szlezák, T. A., *Plato und die Schriftlichkeit der Philosophie* (Berlin, 1985).

Tambiah, S. J., 'A performative approach to ritual', *Proceedings of the British Academy*, 65 (1981), 113–69.

Tate, J. '"Imitation" in Plato's *Republic*', *CQ*, 22 (1928), 16–23.

'Plato and allegorical interpretation', *CQ*, 23 (1929), 142–54; 24 (1930), 1–10.

'Plato and "imitation"', *CQ*, 26 (1932), 161–9.

'Plato, art, and Mr Maritain', *The New Scholasticism*, 22 (1938), 107–42.

Tigerstedt, E. N., *Plato's Idea of Poetical Inspiration* (Helsinki, 1969).

Untersteiner, Mario, *The Sophists*, tr. Kathleen Freeman (Oxford, 1953).

Verdennius, W. J., *Mimesis: Plato's Doctrine of Artistic Imitation and its Meaning to Us* (Leiden, 1949).

Vernant, Jean-Pierre, 'Image et apparence dans la théorie platonicienne de la "mimêsis"', *Journal de Psychologie*, 2 (1975), 133–60; rpt. as 'Naissance d'images', in *Religions, Histoires, Raison* (Paris, 1979), pp. 105–37.

Vicaire, Paul, *Platon: Critique littéraire* (Paris, 1960).

Wagner, Christian, 'Katharsis in der aristotelischen Tragödiendefinition', *Grazer Beiträge*, 11 (1984), 67–87.

Walsh, G. B., *The Varieties of Enchantment: Early Greek Views of the Nature and Function of Poetry* (Chapel Hill, 1984).

Waugh, L. R., 'Marked and unmarked: A choice between unequals in semiotic structure', *Semiotica*, 38 (1982), 299–318.

West, M. L., *Greek Metre* (Oxford, 1982).

'The singing of Homer', *JHS*, 101 (1981), 113–29.

White, J. B., *When Words Lose their Meaning: Constitutions and Reconstitutions of Language, Character, and Community* (Chicago, 1984).

Whitman, C. H., *Homer and the Heroic Tradition* (Cambridge, Mass., 1958).

Wieland, Wolfgang, *Platon und die Formen des Wissens* (Göttingen, 1982).

Will, Edouard, 'Notes sur *misthos*', in Jean Bingen *et al.* (eds.), *Le monde grecque: Hommage à Claire Préaux* (Brussels, 1975), pp. 426–38.

Woodbury, Leonard, 'Pindar and the mercenary muse: *Isthmian* 2.1–13', *TAPA*, 99 (1968), 527–42.

Young, D. C., 'Pindar', in T. J. Luce (ed.), *Ancient Writers, Greece and Rome* (New York, 1982), pp. 157–77.

'Pindar, Aristotle, and Homer: A study in ancient criticism', in T. D'Evelyn *et al.* (eds.), *Studies in Classical Lyric: A Hommage to Elroy Bundy* (*Classical Antiquity*, 2) (Berkeley, 1983), pp. 156–70.

Zetzel, J. E. G., 'Re-creating the canon', see below, bibliography to chapters 5–9.

Zumthor, Paul, *Introduction à la poésie orale* (Paris, 1983).

Chapters 5–9

Ahl, Frederick, 'The art of safe criticism in Greece and Rome', *AJP*, 105 (1984), 174–208.

Baldwin, Barry, *Studies in Aulus Gellius* (Lawrence, Kansas, 1975).

Barwick, Karl, 'Probleme der Stoischen Sprachlehre und Rhetorik', *Abhandlungen der Sächsischen Akademie der Wissenschaften zu Leipzig*, Philologisch-historische Klasse, 49, 3 (Berlin, 1957).

Becker, Carl, *Das Spätwork des Horaz* (Göttingen, 1963).

Bonner, S. F., *Dionysius of Halicarnassus: A Study in the Development of Critical Method* (Cambridge, 1939).
Education in Ancient Rome (London, 1977).
Roman Declamation in the Late Republic and Early Empire (Liverpool, 1949).
Bowersock, Glen, *Augustus and the Greek World* (Oxford, 1965).
Brink, C. O., 'Philodemus, *Peri poiēmatōn*, Book IV', *Maia*, 24 (1972), 342–4.
   Horace on Poetry; I: Prolegomena to the Literary Epistles (Cambridge, 1963); *II: Ars poetica* (1971); *III: Epistles, Book II* (1982).
Brink, C. O. et al., *Varron; six exposés* (*Entretien Hardt*, 9) (Geneva, 1963).
Bulloch, A. W. 'Hellenistic poetry', in *Cambridge History of Classical Literature* (see above, General works), I, pp. 541–621.
Cairns, Francis, *Generic Composition in Greek and Roman Poetry* (Edinburgh, 1972).
Caplan, Harry, 'The decay of eloquence at Rome in the first century', in *Of Eloquence: Studies in Ancient and Medieval Rhetoric* (Ithaca, 1970), pp. 160–95.
Cavazza, Franco, *Studio su Varrone etimologo e grammatico* (Florence, 1981).
Champlin, E. J., *Fronto and Antonine Rome* (Cambridge, Mass., 1980).
Coffey, Michael, *Roman Satire* (London, 1976).
Cope, E. M., *An Introduction to Aristotle's Rhetoric with Analysis, Notes, and Appendices* (London, 1867; rpt. New York, 1970).
Dahlmann, Hellfried, *Varro und die hellenistische Sprachtheorie* (Berlin, 1932).
   'Varroniana', *ANRW*, 1, 3 (1973), 3–25.
D'Alton, J. F., *Roman Literary Theory and Criticism* (London, 1931; rpt. New York, 1962).
DeLacy, Phillip, 'The Epicurean analysis of language', *AJP*, 60 (1939), 85–92.
   'Stoic views of poetry', *AJP*, 69 (1948), 241–71.
Dingel, Joachim, *Seneca und die Dichtung* (Heidelberg, 1974).
Dougals, A. E., 'A Ciceronian contribution to rhetorical theory', *Eranos*, 55 (1957), 17–24.
   'The intellectual background of Cicero's *Rhetorica*', *ANRW*, 1, 3 (1973), 95–138.
Duret, Luc, 'Dans l'ombre des plus grands: poètes et prosateurs mal connus de l'époque augustienne', *ANRW*, II, 30, 3 (1983), 1,447–60.
Erickson, K. V., *Aristotle's Rhetoric: Five Centuries of Philological Research* (Metuchen, New Jersey, 1975).
Erickson, K. V. (ed.), *Aristotle: The Classical Heritage of Rhetoric* (Metuchen, New Jersey, 1974).
Fairweather, Janet, *Seneca the Elder* (Cambridge, 1981).
Fantham, Elaine, 'Imitation and decline: Rhetorical theory and practice in the first century after Christ', *CP*, 73 (1978), 102–16.
   'Imitation and evolution: The discussion of rhetorical imitation in Cicero, *De oratore* II, 87–97, and some related problems of Ciceronian theory', *CP*, 73 (1978), 1–16.
   'On the use of *genus*-terminology in Cicero's rhetorical works', *Hermes*, 107 (1979), 441–58.
Flashar, Hellmut (ed.), *Le classicisme à Rome aux premiers siècles avant et après J. C.* (*Entretiens Hardt*, 25) (Geneva, 1979).
Fortenbaugh, W. W., 'Theophrastus on delivery', *Rutgers University Studies*, 2 (1985), 269–88.

Friedlander, Paul, 'The pattern of sound and atomistic theory in Lucretius' *De rerum natura*', *AJP*, 62 (1941), 16–34.

Gaines, R. N., 'Qualities of rhetorical expression in Philodemus', *TAPA*, 112 (1982), 71–81.

Goldberg, S. M., *Understanding Terence* (Princeton, 1986).

Graeser, Andreas, 'The Stoic theory of meaning', in J. M. Rist (ed.), *The Stoics* (Berkeley, 1978), pp. 77–100.

Greenberg, N. A., 'Metathesis as an instrument in the criticism of poetry', *TAPA*, 89 (1958), 262–70.

'The use of *poiēma* and *poiēsis*', *HSCP*, 65 (1961), 263–89.

Grimal, Pierre, *Horace: Art poètique* (Paris, 1966).

Grimaldi, W. M. A., *Studies in the Philosophy of Aristotle's Rhetoric (Hermes Einzelschriften, 25)* (Wiesbaden, 1972).

Grube, G. M. A., 'Theodorus of Gadara', *AJP*, 80 (1959), 337–65.

'Thrasymachus, Theophrastus, and Dionysius of Halicarnassus', *AJP*, 73 (1952), 251–67.

Guillemin, A. M., *Pline et la vie littéraire de son temps* (Paris, 1929).

Hellwig, Antje, *Untersuchungen zur Theorie der Rhetorik bei Platon und Aristoteles (Hypomnemata, 38)* (Göttingen, 1973).

Holford-Strevens, Leofranc, *Aulus Gellius* (London, 1987).

Horsfall, N. M., 'The *collegium poetarum*', *Bulletin of the Institute of Classical Studies of the University of London*, 23 (1976), 79–95.

Hurst, A., 'Un critique grec dans la Rome d'Auguste', *ANRW*, 30, 1 (1982), 839–65.

Imbert, Claude, 'Stoic logic and Alexandrian poetics', in Malcolm Schofield *et al.* (eds.), *Doubt and Dogmatism* (Oxford, 1980), pp. 182–216.

Innes, D. C., 'Theophrastus and the theory of style', *Rutgers University Studies*, 2 (1985), 251–67.

Jordan, W. J., 'Aristotle's concept of metaphor in rhetoric', in Erickson (ed.), *Aristotle* (see above), pp. 235–50.

Kennedy, G. A., *The Art of Persuasion in Greece* (Princeton, 1963).

The Art of Rhetoric in the Roman World (Princeton, 1972).

'Encoplius and Agamemnon in Petronius', *AJP*, 99 (1978), 171–8.

Quintilian (New York, 1969).

Klingner, Friedrich, 'Horazens Brief an die Pisonem', *Berichte der Sächsische Akademie der Wissenschaften*, Philosophisch-historische Klasse, 88 (1936), 3–31.

Latte, Kurt, 'Reste frühellenistischer Poetik im Pisonembrief des Horaz, *Hermes*, 60 (1925), 1–13.

Leeman, A. D., *Orationis Ratio: The Stylistic Theories and Practice of the Roman Orators, Historians, and Philosophers* (2 vols., Amsterdam, 1963).

Longo Auricchio, F., 'Filodemo: La *Rhetorica* e la *Musica*', in *Syzetesis: Studi offerti a Marcello Gigante* (Naples, 1983), pp. 553–62.

Macleod, C. W., 'The poet, the critic, and the moralist: Horace, *Epistles* 1.19', *CQ*, 27 (1977), 359–76.

'The poetry of ethics in Horace, *Epistles* 1.19', *JRS*, 69 (1979), 16–27.

Marache, Rene, *La critique littéraire de langue latine et le développement du gout archaïsant au IIe siècle de notre ère* (Rennes, 1952).

Michel, Alain, *Le dialogue des orateurs de Tacite et la philosophie de Cicéron* (Paris, 1962).

Rhétorique et philosophie chez Cicéron: Essai sur les fondements philosophiques de l'art de persuader (Paris, 1960).

Momigliano, Arnaldo, *Greek Biography* (Cambridge, 1971).

Norden, Eduard, 'Die Composition und Litteraturgattung der Horazischen *Epistula ad Pisones*', *Hermes*, 40 (1905), 481–528.

Pfeiffer, Rudolf, *Classical Scholarship*. See above, General works.

Podlecki, A.J., 'The Peripatetics as literary critics', *Phoenix*, 23 (1969), 114–37.

Pohl, Karin, *Die Lehre von den drei Wortfügungsarten: Untersuchungen zu Dionysius von Halicarnassus, De compositione verborum* (Tübingen, 1968).

Quadlbauer, Franz, 'Die *genera dicendi* bis Plinius d.J.', *Wiener Studien*, 51 (1958), 55–111.

Quinn, Kenneth, 'The poet and his audience in the Augustan age', *ANRW*, II, 30, 1 (1982), 76–180.

Rawson, Elizabeth, *Cicero: A Portrait* (London, 1975; rev. ed., Ithaca, 1983).

Intellectual Life in the Late Roman Republic (London, 1985).

Rollinson, Philip, *Allegory*. See above, General works.

de Romilly, Jacqueline, *Magic and Rhetoric in Ancient Greece* (Cambridge, Mass., 1975).

Rostagni, Arnaldo, 'Filodemo contro l'estetica classica', *Scritti minori* (Turin, 1965), 356–446.

Rudd, Niall, *The Satires of Horace* (Cambridge, 1966).

Russell, D.A., '*Ars poetica*', in C.D.N. Costa (ed.), *Horace* (London, 1973), pp. 113–34.

'*De imitatione*', in D. West and A. Woodman (eds.), *Creative Imitation and Latin Literature* (Cambridge, 1979), pp. 1–16.

Sbordone, Francesca, *Sui papiri della Poetica di Filodemo* (Naples, 1983).

Schenkeveld, D.M., '*Hoi kritikoi* in Philodemus', *Mnemosyne*, 21 (1968), 176–214.

'Strabo on Homer', *Mnemosyne*, 29 (1976), 50–64.

Studies in Demetrius (Amsterdam, 1964).

Shorey, Paul, '*Phusis, Meletē, Epistēmē*', *TAPA*, 40 (1909), 185–201.

Skutsch, Otto (ed.), *Ennius: sept exposés* (*Entretien Hardt*, 17) (Geneva, 1972).

Slater, W.J., 'Aristophanes of Byzantium on the *Pinakes* of Callimachus', *Phoenix*, 30 (1976), 234–41.

Smith, R.W., *The Art of Rhetoric in Alexandria* (The Hague, 1974).

Snyder, J.M., *Puns and Poetry in Lucretius' De Rerum Natura* (Amsterdam, 1980).

Solmsen, Friedrich, 'The Aristotelian tradition in ancient rhetoric', *AJP*, 62 (1941), 35–50, 169–90; rpt. in Erickson (ed.), *Classical Heritage*, (see above), pp. 278–309.

Steidle, Wolf, *Studien zur Ars poetica des Horaz; Interpretation des auf Dichtkunst und Gedicht bezüglichen Hauptteiles, Verse 1–294* (Würzburg, 1939).

Stroux, Johannes, *De Theophrasti Virtutibus Dicendi* (Leipzig, 1912).

Sullivan, J.P., 'Petronius, Seneca, and Lucan: A literary feud', *TAPA*, 99 (1968), 453–67.

The Satyricon of Petronius: A Literary Study (Bloomington, Indiana, 1968).

Sussman, L.A., *The Elder Seneca* (Leiden, 1978).

Syme, Ronald, *Tacitus* (2 vols., Oxford, 1958).

Williams, G.W., *Change and Decline: Roman Literature in the Early Empire* (Berkeley, 1978).

Tradition and Originality in Roman Poetry (Oxford, 1968).

Winterbottom, Michael, 'Cicero and the silver age', in Walther Ludwig (ed.), *Eloquence et rhétorique chez Cicéron (Entretiens Hardt*, 27) (Geneva, 1982), pp. 237–66.

Wooten, C.W., *Cicero's Philippics and their Demosthenic Model* (Chapel Hill, 1983).

'Le développement du style asiatique pendant l'époque hellénistique', *REG*, 88 (1975), 217–22.

Zanker, G., '*Enargeia* in the ancient criticism of poetry', *Rheinische Museum*, 124 (1981), 297–311.

Zetzel, J.E.G., 'Re-creating the canon: Augustan poetry and the Alexandrian poet', *Critical Inquiry*, 10 (1983), 83–105.

Chapters 10–11

Abrams, M.H., *The Mirror and the Lamp: Romantic Theory and the Critical Tradition* (Oxford, 1953).

Anderson, Graham, *Lucian: Theme and Variation in the Second Sophistic* (Leiden, 1976). *Philostratus* (London, 1986).

Arnim, Hans von, *Leben und Werke des Dio von Prusa* (Berlin, 1898).

Ayers, R.H., *Language, Logic, and Reason in the Church Fathers* (Hildesheim, 1979).

Babut, Daniel, *Plutarque et le Stoïcisme* (Paris, 1969).

Barnes, T.D., *Tertullian: A Historical and Literary Study* (Oxford, 1985).

Bidez, Joseph, *Vie de Porphyre* (Ghent, 1913).

Birmelin, Ella, 'Die kunsttheoretischen Gedanken in Philostrats *Apollonios*', *Philologus*, 88 (1933), 149–80, 392–414.

Bompaire, Jacques, 'Le pathos dans le Traité du Sublime', *REG*, 86 (1973), 323–43.

Boulanger, André, *Aelius Aristide et la sophistique dans la province d'Asie au IIe siècle de notre ère* (Paris, 1923).

Brody, Jules, *Boileau and Longinus* (Geneva, 1958).

Buffière, Félix, *Les mythes d'Homère et la pensée grecque* (Paris, 1956).

The Cambridge History of Later Greek and Early Medieval Philosophy, ed. A.H. Armstrong (Cambridge, 1967).

Cochrane, N.C., *Christianity and Classical Culture: A Study of Thought and Action from Augustus to Augustine* (London, 1944).

Colson, F.H., 'Two examples of literary and rhetorical criticism in the Fathers', *Journal of Theological Studies*, 25 (1924), 364–77.

Coulter, J.A., *The Literary Microcosm: Theories of Interpretation of the Later Neoplatonists* (Leiden, 1976).

Ellspermann, G.L., *The Attitude of the Early Christian Latin Writers toward Pagan Literature and Learning (Catholic University of America Patristic Studies*, 82) (Washington, 1949).

Fredouille, J.-C., *Tertullien et la conversion de la culture antique* (Paris, 1972).

Goodspeed, E.J., *A History of Early Christian Literature*, rev. and enlarged by Robert M. Grant (Chicago, 1966).

Grese, W.C., *Corpus Hermeticum XIII and Early Christian Literature* (Leiden, 1979).

Hagedorn, Dieter, *Zur Ideenlehre des Hermogenes (Hypomnemata*, 8) (Göttingen, 1964).

Hagendahl, Harald, *Latin Fathers and the Classics: A Study on the Apologists, Jerome, and Other Christian Writers (Acta Universitatis Gothoburgensis*, 64, 2) (Göteborg, 1958).

Jaeger, Werner, *Early Christianity and Greek Paideia* (Cambridge, Mass., 1961).

Jones, C. P., *The Roman World of Dio Chrysostom* (Cambridge, Mass., 1978).

Kaster, R. A., 'The grammarian's authority', *CP*, 75 (1980), 216–41.
'Macrobius and Servius: *Verecundia* and the grammarian's function', *HSCP*, 84 (1981), 219–62.
'Servius and *idonei auctores*', *AJP*, 99 (1978), 181–209.

Kennedy, G. A., *Greek Rhetoric under Christian Emperors* (Princeton, 1983).

Kindstrand, J. F., *Homer in der zweiten Sophistik (Studia Graeca Upsaliensia*, 7) (Uppsala, 1973).

Lamberton, Robert, *Homer the Theologian: Neoplatonist Allegorical Reading and the Growth of the Epic Tradition* (Berkeley, 1986).

Leff, M. C., 'The topics of argumentative invention in Latin rhetorical theory from Cicero to Boethius', *Rhetorica*, 1 (1983), 23–44.

Luzzatto, M. T., *Tragedia greca e cultura ellenistica: l'orazione LII di Dione di Prusa* (Bologna, 1983).

Martano, Giuseppe, 'Il Saggio sul Sublime: Una interessante pagina di retorice e di estetica dell'antichita', *ANRW*, 32, 1 (1984), 364–403.

Michel, Alain, 'Rhétorique et poétique: La théorie du sublime de Platon aux modernes', *Revue des Etudes Latines*, 54 (1976), 278–307.

Memoli, A. F., *Studi sulla prosa d'arte negli scrittori Cristiani* (Naples, 1979).

Momigliano, Arnaldo (ed.), *The Conflict between Paganism and Christianity in the Fourth Century: Essays* (Oxford, 1963).

Moore, J. L., 'Servius on the tropes and figures of Vergil', *AJP*, 12 (1981), 157–92, 267–92.

Ogilvie, R. M., *The Library of Lactantius* (Oxford, 1978).

Patterson, A. M., *Hermogenes in the Renaissance* (Princeton, 1970).

Pepin, Jean, 'Porphyre, exégète d'Homère', in Heinrich Dörrie (ed.), *Porphyre: huit exposés (Entretiens Hardt*, 12) (Geneva, 1966), 231–66.

Reardon, B. P., *Les courants littéraires des IIᵉ et IIIᵉ siècles après J.-C.* (Paris, 1971).

Reynolds, L. D., and Wilson, N. G., *Scribes and Scholars: A Guide to the Transmission of Greek and Latin Literature* (2nd ed., Oxford, 1978).

Richardson, N. J., 'Literary criticism in the exegetical scholia to the *Iliad*', *CQ*, 30 (1980), 265–87.

Rollinson, Philip, *Allegory*. See above, General works.

Russell, D. A., *Greek Declamation* (Cambridge, 1983).

Schenkeveld, D. M., 'The structure of Plutarch's *De audiendis poetis*', *Mnemosyne*, 35 (1982), 60–71.

Schwab, Theodor, *Alexandros Numeniu Peri schēmatōn in seiner Verhältnis zu Kaikilios, Tiberios, und seiner späterer Benutzern* (Paderborn, 1916).

Sheppard, A. D. R., *Studies on the Fifth and Sixth Essays of Proclus' Commentary on the Republic (Hypomnemata*, 61) (Göttingen, 1980).

Sider, R. D., *Ancient Rhetoric and the Art of Tertullian* (London, 1971).

Svoboda, K., 'Les idées esthétiques de Plutarque', *Annuaire de l'Institut de Philologie et d'Histoire Orientales*, 2 (Brussels, 1934) (*Mélanges Bidez*), 917–46.

Tagliasacchi, A. M., 'Le teorie estetiche e la critica letteraria in Plutarco', *Acme*, 14 (1961), 71–117.

Valgiglio, Ernesto, 'Il tema della poesia nell pensiero di Plutarco', *Maia*, 19 (1967), 319–35.

Valgimigli, Manara, *Contributi alla storia della critica letteraria in Graecia; I: La critica letteraria di Dione Crisistomo* (Bologna, 1912).

Wallace, E. O., *The Notes on Philosophy in the Commentary of Servius on the Eclogues, the Georgics, and the Aeneid of Virgil* (New York, 1938).

Westerink, L. G., *Anonymous Prolegomena to Platonist Philosophy* (Leiden, 1962).

Wilson, N. G., *Saint Basil on the Value of Greek Literature* (London, 1975).

Wojtczak, Georgius, *De Lactantio Ciceronis aemulo et sectatore* (Warsaw, 1969).

Ziegler, Konrat, 'Plutarchos', *Paulys Realencyclopädie der classischen Altertumswissenschaft*, 21, 1 (Stuttgart, 1951), coll. 636–962.

INDEX